MAGILL'S
LITERARY ANNUAL
1992

MAGILL'S LITERARY ANNUAL 1992

*Essay-Reviews of 200 Outstanding Books
Published in the United States during 1991*

With an Annotated Categories List

Volume One

A-Mao

Edited by
FRANK N. MAGILL

SALEM PRESS
Pasadena, California   Englewood Cliffs, New Jersey

LIBRARY OF CONGRESS CATALOG CARD NO. 77-99209
ISBN 0-89356-292-0

FIRST PRINTING

PRINTED IN THE UNITED STATES OF AMERICA

PUBLISHER'S NOTE

Magill's Literary Annual, 1992, is the thirty-seventh publication in a series that began in 1954. The philosophy behind the annual has been to evaluate critically each year a given number of major examples of serious literature published during the previous year. Our continuous effort is to provide coverage for works that are likely to be of more than passing general interest and that will stand up to the test of time. Individual critical articles for the first twenty-two years were collected and published in *Survey of Contemporary Literature* in 1977.

For the reader new to the Magill reference format, the following brief explanation should serve to facilitate the research process. The two hundred works represented in this year's annual are drawn from the following categories: fiction; poetry; literary criticism, literary history, and literary theory; essays; literary biography; autobiography, memoirs, diaries, and letters; biography; history; current affairs; science, history of science, and technology; travel; education; fine arts; nature, natural history, and the environment; psychology; and philosophy. The articles are arranged alphabetically by book title in the two volume set. A complete list of the titles included can be found at the beginning of volume 1. Following a list of titles are the titles arranged by category in an annotated listing. This list provides the reader with the title, author, page number, and a brief one-sentence description of the particular work. The names of all contributing reviewers for the literary annual are listed alphabetically in the front of the book as well as at the end of their reviews. At the end of volume 2, there are two indexes: an index of Biographical Works by Subject and the Cumulative Author Index. The index of biographical works covers the years 1977 to 1992, and it is arranged by subject rather than by author or title. Thus, readers will be able to locate easily a review of any biographical work published in the Magill annuals since 1977 (including memoirs, diaries, and letters—as well as biographies and autobiographies) by looking up the name of the person. Following the index of Biographical Works by Subject is the Cumulative Author Index. Beneath each author's name appear the titles of all of his or her works reviewed in the Magill annuals since 1977. Next to each title, in parentheses, is the year of the annual in which the review appeared, followed by the page number.

Each article begins with a block of top matter that indicates the title, author, publisher, and price of the work. When possible, the year of the author's birth is also provided. The top matter also includes the number of pages of the book, the type of work, and, when appropriate, the time period and locale represented in the text. Next, there is the same capsulized description of the work that appears in the annotated list of titles. When pertinent, a list of principal characters or of personages introduces the review.

The articles themselves are approximately two thousand words in length. They are original essay-reviews that analyze and present the focus, intent, and relative success of the author, as well as the makeup and point of view of the work under discussion. To assist the reader further, the articles are supplemented by a list of additional reviews for further study in a bibliographic format.

LIST OF TITLES

LIST OF TITLES

TITLES BY CATEGORY

ANNOTATED

page

FICTION

page

TITLES BY CATEGORY

TITLES BY CATEGORY

POETRY

page

page

LITERARY CRITICISM
LITERARY HISTORY
LITERARY THEORY

page

TITLES BY CATEGORY

page

LITERARY BIOGRAPHY

TITLES BY CATEGORY

page

TITLES BY CATEGORY

page

HISTORY

page

page

CURRENT AFFAIRS

page

page

FINE ARTS

NATURE
NATURAL HISTORY
THE ENVIRONMENT

page

CONTRIBUTING REVIEWERS FOR 1992 ANNUAL

Michael Adams
Fairleigh Dickinson University

Andrew J. Angyal
Elon College

Stanley Archer
Texas A&M University

Edwin T. Arnold
Appalachian State University

Jean Ashton
New York Historical Society

Bryan Aubrey
Maharishi International University

Dean Baldwin
Behrend College, Pennsylvania State University

Dan Barnett
California State University, Chico
Butte College

Robert A. Bascom
United Bible Societies

Carolyn Wilkerson Bell
Randolph-Macon Woman's College

Mary G. Berg
Wheaton College

Gordon N. Bergquist
Creighton University

David Warren Bowen
Livingston University

Harold Branam
Temple University

Gerhard Brand
California State University, Los Angeles

Peter Brier
California State University, Los Angeles

Jean R. Brink
Arizona State University

Thomas J. Campbell
Pacific Lutheran University

John Carpenter
University of Michigan

C. L. Chua
California State University, Fresno

Norman S. Cohen
Occidental College

Peter Crawford
Independent Scholar

Bill Delaney
Independent Scholar

Leon Driskell
University of Louisville

William U. Eiland
University of Georgia

Robert P. Ellis
Worcester State College

Thomas L. Erskine
Salisbury State University

Robert Faggen
Claremont McKenna College

Bruce E. Fleming
United States Naval Academy

Robert J. Forman
St. John's University, New York

Leslie E. Gerber
Appalachian State University

Dana Gerhardt
Independent Scholar

Richard Glatzer
Independent Scholar

Sidney Gottlieb
Sacred Heart University

Daniel L. Guillory
Millikin University

Donald E. Hall
California State University, Northridge

Terry Heller
Coe College

Ronald William Howard
Mississippi College

Theodore C. Humphrey
California State Polytechnic University, Pomona

Philip K. Jason
United States Naval Academy

Shakuntala Jayaswal
University of New Haven

Jane Anderson Jones
Manatee Community College

Steven G. Kellman
University of Texas at San Antonio

Karen A. Kildahl
South Dakota State University

Vera M. Kutzinski
Yale University

James B. Lane
Indiana University Northwest

Eugene S. Larson
Los Angeles Pierce College

Leon Lewis
Appalachian State University

Janet Lorenz
Independent Scholar

R. C. Lutz
University of the Pacific

Janet McCann
Texas A&M University

Mark McCloskey
Glendale College
Occidental College

Margaret McFadden
Appalachian State University

Paul D. Mageli
Independent Scholar

Lois A. Marchino
University of Texas at El Paso

Liz Marshall
University of Pittsburgh

Charles E. May
California State University, Long Beach

Laurence W. Mazzeno
Mesa State College

Kenneth Meadwell
University of Winnipeg, Manitoba, Canada

Gordon L. Miller
Independent Scholar

Leslie B. Mittleman
California State University, Long Beach

Robert A. Morace
Daemen College

Gregory L. Morris
Behrend College, Pennsylvania State University

Robert E. Morsberger
California State Polytechnic University, Pomona

Edwin Moses
Bloomsburg University

Daniel P. Murphy
Hanover College

John M. Muste
Ohio State University

Stella Nesanovich
McNeese State University

George O'Brien
Georgetown University

Robert J. Paradowski
Rochester Institute of Technology

Thomas R. Peake
King College

David Peck
California State University, Long Beach

John Powell
Hannibal-LaGrange College

John D. Raymer
Holy Cross College

Rosemary M. Canfield Reisman
Troy State University

Claire J. Robinson
Maharishi International University

Bernard F. Rodgers, Jr.
Simon's Rock of Bard College

Judith Rollins
Simmons College

Carl Rollyson
*Baruch College of the City University of
New York*

Joseph Rosenblum
University of North Carolina at Greensboro

CONTRIBUTING REVIEWERS FOR 1992 ANNUAL

John K. Roth
Claremont McKenna College

Marc Rothenberg
Smithsonian Institution

Francis Michael Sharp
University of the Pacific

R. Baird Shuman
University of Illinois at Urbana-Champaign

Thomas J. Sienkewicz
Monmouth College

Marjorie Smelstor
University of Wisconsin-Eau Claire

Harold L. Smith
University of Houston, Victoria

Ira Smolensky
Monmouth College

Michael Sprinker
State University of New York at Stony Brook
University of California, Irvine

Bradley E. Starr
California State University, Fullerton

James Sullivan
California State University, Los Angeles

Ronald G. Walker
Western Illinois University

Harry M. Ward
University of Richmond

Bruce Wiebe
Independent Scholar

John Wilson
Independent Scholar

James A. Winders
Appalachian State University

Michael Witkoski
Independent Scholar

Cynthia F. Wong
Western Illinois University

Harry Zohn
Brandeis University

MAGILL'S
LITERARY ANNUAL
1992

ABRAHAM LINCOLN AND
THE SECOND AMERICAN REVOLUTION

Author: James M. McPherson (1935-   )
Publisher: Oxford University Press (New York). 173 pp. $17.95
Type of work: History
Time: 1850-1876
Locale: The United States

A collection of seven essays analyzing the American Civil War and the contribution of Abraham Lincoln as president

> *Principal personage:*
> ABRAHAM LINCOLN, the sixteenth president of the United States

No other part of the American past has inspired as many written words as the Civil War. Each year, hundreds of new volumes join the thousands that clog shelves in libraries all over the world. With millions of pages already devoted to the subject, some might argue that there is nothing left to write about the war. When an event transcends the normal pattern of history to become a turning point in the life of a particular society, however, the very best historical interpretation often becomes much more than a simple narrative; it becomes a metaphorical evocation of the meaning of that particular culture. James M. McPherson's *Abraham Lincoln and the Second American Revolution* is just such a work.

McPherson, Edwards Professor of American History at Princeton University, established himself as a leading authority on the Civil War with his Pulitzer Prize-winning *Battle Cry of Freedom: The Civil War Era* (1988). In his new collection of essays, whose title is taken from the second essay, "Lincoln and the Second American Revolution," McPherson ties together seven separate arguments with one central theme, the revolutionary nature of the Civil War experience. While each essay could stand alone and has appeared in other versions, placing them in the same volume strengthens each and provides a more coherent overall image.

The opening and closing essays deal with the central theme directly by addressing the question of what the war actually accomplished. The five other essays deal with the leadership of Abraham Lincoln. Connecting leadership with the war's outcome is crucial to McPherson's interpretation. For him, history is not the operation of powerful forces on passive human beings. Such broad themes as the evolution of economic systems are important for any understanding of events, but McPherson believes that in the final analysis, history develops as it does because people make decisions. The "Second American Revolution" would not have occurred as it did, and perhaps might not have been a revolution at all, without the gentle hand of Abraham Lincoln.

The first argument comes to grips with a question of semantics. Should the Civil War be called a "revolution"? Obviously, the answer would depend on how one defines the term, but after treating a number of the possible variations and the resulting interpretations, McPherson argues convincingly that in order to understand the meaning of the Civil War within the context of American history the term "revolution" is indeed appropriate. While it is true that many of the gains of the former slaves were lost in a counterrevolution during the Reconstruction and the economic transformation from an agricultural to an industrial society would have occurred without war, the changes were still revolutionary. After all, slavery was abolished, and the lot of postwar blacks, while hardly ideal, was certainly better than that of chattel slaves. Most important, even with the growth of the Jim Crow system after Reconstruction, a foundation was laid for future change, and the nation was committed, at least symbolically, to the idea of equality. Moreover, the new political dominance of the Republican Party changed the nature of the American system. With the South weakened economically and politically, the Republican commitment to free-labor capitalism was allowed to develop unchecked and become almost synonymous with the American way of life.

Even if one accepts McPherson's position, it is not necessary to assume that the revolutionary outcome was the product of conscious decisions on the part of the war's participants. Here the focus of the second essay, Lincoln's moral and political leadership, is crucial. Such respected historians as James G. Randall, T. Harry Williams, and Norman Graebner have argued that the president was essentially a conservative, which makes the depiction of Lincoln as a "revolutionary" somewhat incongruous. Admittedly, their argument is a strong one. There is little in Lincoln's career or actions as president to suggest that he was a revolutionary ideologue. In fact, McPherson himself agrees with Graebner's statement that Lincoln "accepted the need of dealing with things as they were, not as he would have wished them to be." Where Graebner believes that Lincoln's pragmatism made him a conservative, however, McPherson concludes that his realistic appraisal of what could actually be achieved produced a unique and very successful kind of revolutionary, "a pragmatic revolutionary." Rather than attempting to force events into a particular, preconceived mold, Lincoln guided events carefully, like a jockey controlling an unruly horse. It was the president's hand on the reins that ended slavery and brought, in his own words, "a new birth of freedom."

In the next two essays, "Lincoln and Liberty" and "Lincoln and the Strategy of Unconditional Surrender," McPherson goes more deeply into his analysis of Lincoln. The first of these essays deals with ideology and the second with the concept of nationalism embodied in the evolving goal of preserving the Union. In a speech in Baltimore, Lincoln himself admitted that "the world has never had a good definition of the word liberty, and the American people, just now, are much in want of one." The problem was that both sides in the Civil War claimed to be fighting for liberty. It was Lincoln's idea of liberty, according to McPherson, that was revolutionary. The South had taken one aspect of liberty as understood by the nation's founders, the liberty to own property without government interference, and exaggerated its significance. The North, on the other hand, looked to the maintenance of popular government through the Union as the protection of liberty for all men. In fact, the position of Lincoln and his party was evolving toward what the British philosopher Isaiah Berlin called "Positive Liberty" in contrast to "Negative Liberty." The former meant that government had an obligation to create liberty, while the latter simply called on government to stay out of private lives. The Northern victory meant that the central government of the United States was to become a much more active, although sometimes reluctant, agent in the lives of all Americans.

Initially, the goal of preserving the Union did not require a significant change in the concept of government. In fact, Lincoln went out of his way to make clear that his election did not give him the authority to interfere with slavery where it already existed. The government, in Lincoln's estimation, was forced to go to war in order to preserve democracy, something that Americans in both the North and South professed to revere. The continued intransigence of the South, however, required a total Northern victory and the complete destruction of the Southern system based on slavery. The gradual evolution of Lincoln's strategy to that of a "total war," with unconditional surrender the only acceptable outcome, meant, ironically, that Lincoln's personal ideological preference would prevail over the constitutional weakness of the federal government. Emancipation and the national adoption of the Republicans' free-labor ideology were necessary for victory.

The next two essays, "How Lincoln Won the War with Metaphors" and "The Hedgehog and the Foxes," deal with Lincoln's style of leadership and its contribution to the revolutionary nature of the Civil War. Most historians agree that Lincoln had an unusual ability to communicate with the Northern masses, but McPherson focuses directly on the nature of his rhetoric. Perhaps the clearest illustration of this argument is the contrast with Jefferson Davis. Davis was much better educated than Lincoln and, in a formal sense, much better equipped to use the English language. When Davis produced a state paper or a political speech, however, his formally correct style was cold and had little lasting impact on his audience. As befits a revolutionary, Lincoln spoke and wrote in the language of the people. His penchant for stories and parables meant that his message was often disguised in metaphor, generally metaphor easily understood if not simplistic. His metaphors range from the poetic, such as the justly famous Gettysburg Address, to stories about killing skunks. This skill in communication, McPherson believes, has been underestimated by historians as a factor in the ultimate Northern victory. The Southerners had the psychological advantage of fighting for their homes and way of life, but the North had Lincoln to articulate its cause in a way that gave the struggle meaning.

The meaning of the war for Abraham Lincoln is crucial to McPherson's own metaphor, which compares the president to a hedgehog. The seemingly strange combination is based on a line from the Greek poet Archilochus: "The fox knows many things, but the hedgehog knows one big thing." Once again using the philosophical insight of Isaiah Berlin as a model, McPherson argues that the president's ability to relate every decision to one central vision, the "preservation of the United States and its constitutional government," was a crucial element in his leadership. While such other Republican leaders as William H. Seward and Horace Greeley were foxes who often seemed more clever than the plodding Lincoln, their failure to develop a consistent vision of the meaning of the war would have led to disaster had they been in charge. Instead, the president's conduct during the war provides one of the finest examples in history of democratic leadership. With his vision of America always before him, Lincoln was able to lead the people, not follow them, to his "new birth of freedom."

What this new freedom meant for the future is explained in McPherson's concluding essay, "Liberty and Power in the Second American Revolution." Here McPherson recapitulates themes from his earlier essays and confronts directly the position of many "postrevisionist" historians who maintain that the Civil War actually changed very little. What produces such views is simply a distortion of perspective. Of course, the Civil War did not bring instant freedom and equality for America's most oppressed minority. In fact, no revolution has brought immediate and lasting justice for the oppressed. After the Civil War, however, the nation was committed to a course that would bear fruit a century later during the Civil Rights movement. It is also true that an industrial society would have replaced the agricultural society of the country's first decades without the terrible bloodshed of war; however, the commitment to "positive government" required to win the war gave the nation a new perspective on the role of government in the lives of citizens. Again, the real impact of these changes would not become apparent until the twentieth century. If the term "revolution" is to mean anything, it must refer to events that alter significantly the course of a particular human society. Certainly, twentieth century America would have been a very different place without the country's "Second Revolution" in the nineteenth century.

David Warren Bowen

Sources for Further Study

America. CLXIV, March 2, 1991, p. 244.
American Heritage. XLII, May, 1991, p. 12.
Booklist. LXXXVII, December 1, 1990, p. 715.
Chicago Tribune. February 3, 1991, XIV, p. 6.
Forbes. CXLVII, March 4, 1991, p. 24.
Kirkus Reviews. LVIII, November 1, 1990, p. 1516.
Los Angeles Times Book Review. February 3, 1991, p. 6.
New York Times Book Review. XCVI, January 20, 1991, p. 13.
Publishers Weekly. CCXXXVIII, January 18, 1991, p. 40.
The Washington Post Book World. XXI, February 3, 1991, p. 6.

THE ACCIDENT

Author: David Plante (1940-   )
Publisher: Ticknor & Fields (New York). 151 pp. $18.95
Type of work: Novel
Time: 1959
Locale: Louvain, Belgium, and surroundings

During his junior year abroad at a Catholic university, the unnamed narrator—an atheist jealous of his life-loving friends—finds himself sliding toward a total spiritual and physical crisis; the accident suffered by a fellow American, Tom, finally enables the narrator to overcome his despair and begin to appreciate life

> *Principal characters:*
> THE NARRATOR, a lean, nineteen-year-old French-American
> TOM DONLON, a rotund Irish-American student of Latin
> KAREN LARVENS, a blonde, blunt, rebellious student
> VINCENT VOSAC, a gaunt and dark-haired Polish-American member of the in-crowd at Louvain
> PAULINE FLANAGAN, a thin graduate student with frameless glasses
> JACQUES, a bearded Belgian student
> MR. LARVENS, Karen's rich industrialist father

David Plante's *The Accident* is an intense character study of its unnamed protagonist, whom the novel follows in and out of a grave spiritual crisis and whose American friends and acquaintances all represent different answers to the twin challenges of how he should lead his life and in what he should believe. Because of this focus on the central character, which his creator further strengthens by making him a highly subjective and at times very unreliable narrator, the novel's success depends entirely on the reader's accepting the idea that the protagonist's crisis represents an authentic and important inner conflict.

After the problematic, almost overwritten first few pages, *The Accident* moves on to an intimate portrayal of its protagonist's relationships with several young Americans who, in addition to serving as foils, are marked by their own personal struggles at a European Catholic university in 1959.

The task of re-creating this time and recapturing its mood, together with its particular tearing conflicts, without appearing merely to dig up past issues is a formidable challenge. Aided by his own experience—Plante himself spent the academic year 1959-1960 in Louvain—the author moves carefully through a territory in which the philosophical questions raised by the (French) existentialists were fresh and pressing and where taking the Lord's name in vain was a serious profanity. At the same time, however, the problems besetting young Americans trying to find acceptance at college and among their circles of friends retain a topical relevance, and it is between these two poles of timeboundness and timelessness that the narrative of *The Accident* tries to strike a precarious balance.

Like Holden Caulfield in J. D. Salinger's *The Catcher in the Rye* (1951), perhaps the most widely recognized original voice of young America on the verge of the widespread upheavals of the 1960's, Plante's protagonist begins his journey into the threatening abyss of self with a train ride, during which he reveals an uncanny knack for the merciless analysis of others' frailties as well as his own. Traveling to Belgium at the end of his summer vacation in Spain, where he had gone in desperate pursuit of a total spiritual experience, the narrator meets the first of his American fellow students, Pauline Flanagan. He takes a strong dislike to Pauline because, as he reveals later in one of the frequent moments of self-criticism that counter-balance his superior attitude, he subconsciously envies her ability to shift easily between the roles of "regular guy" and postgraduate Christian student-teacher of theology.

Throughout *The Accident*, Plante uses such subordinate characters as Pauline economically, for they also provide his protagonist with an important piece in the developing puzzle of his crisis. In Pauline's case, this happens as she leads him to a small park opposite the tower in which the Renaissance scholar Cornelis Jansen "lived and thought up" the religion of the narrator's French-American ancestors, which by now has been assimilated into orthodox Catholicism—a faith he cannot accept. Like Pauline, the park will recur in the narrative at critical moments in the narrator's inner development.

It is through the narrator's friendship with Tom Donlon, however, that his inner troubles are most comprehensively revealed. With his typical arrogance, which carries just a whiff of despair, the narrator argues that he befriends Tom merely because he was the only American "who had the patience to listen to me talk about Spain" once school had started. Yet Tom proves to be much more. A joyful believer in Catholicism, in the all-permeating nature of God's grace, and in a deity who has allowed humanity to make its own decisions where the acceptance or rejection of faith is concerned, Tom not only represents the spiritual alternative of Christianity but also embodies the very principle of choice: Unlike the narrator, who wants "experience" to force him into belief, Tom decides to force himself to accept faith and to act compassionately—an attitude toward the challenges of life that stands in stark contrast to that of the protagonist.

In keeping with Plante's overall authorial economy, every one of his characters is assigned a clearly defined yet thoroughly scrutinized function in his or her relationship with the narrator. Consequently, the self-important poser Vincent Vosac doubles as a darker, more shallow, pathetic version of the narrator; all his elaborate schemes to show his superiority leave him the only person of whom the narrator is not jealous. In contrast, Karen Larvens' interest in Tom infuriates him, and her forceful bluntness explodes both Vincent's and the narrator's pretensions. While Vincent, with a silent nod of acceptance from the narrator, orders a special drink to show his sophisticated familiarity with local customs, Karen points out that warm wine is in fact out of season and taunts the two with her concern for Tom. In this relationship, however, Karen's own complexity is also revealed, as she cannot help herself teasing Tom incessantly about his firm Catholic belief and his gentle nature.

After a detailed exposition, events in *The Accident* quickly deteriorate as the narrator, jealous of the developing closeness between Karen and Tom and even of the intellectual camaraderie between Pauline and Tom, starts mentally to torture the latter. This leads to a strange trip to Brussels, during which Tom, who has been there with Karen and her father, fails to find a place to eat and is left behind by the narrator—an event strangely foretold, or doubled, by Vincent's earlier account of Tom's once having been abandoned by a female date in Manhattan after a similar failure to lead. Still hungry, the narrator seeks out Tom. As his hunger brings on an unstoppable series of violent spasms, his inner crisis culminates in an utter despair of finding a man with "experience" enough to still his ever-present, vaguely defined longings. Before leaving abruptly, he suddenly and repeatedly kisses Tom, in a frenzy. This act, together with sparsely sprinkled hints elsewhere in the text, may remind a reader of Plante's earlier protagonist Daniel Francoeur, who, in Plante's *The Woods* (1982), had to come to terms with his homosexual yearnings.

Tom's unquestioning compassion dictates finally the notion of alleviating the narrator's crisis by taking him to Spain along with Karen and Vincent. As the four embark on the journey in a small car rented by Karen, Plante lays the foundations for the climactic event by having Tom selflessly allow Vincent to assign him the seat behind his, which alone will prove to be fatal. Racing through the rain and despite the warning signal of a spin on the wet road after a close passing maneuver, Vincent's reckless driving causes the accident that kills no one but Tom.

Recovering more quickly from their injuries than Vincent, who, in obvious accordance with strict poetic justice, has to remain in the symbolic purgatory of the hospital, tormented by tubes from the stomach and penis, the narrator and Karen return to Louvain. There, at a memorial mass for Tom, the narrator finally has a spiritual revelation in which he sees his friend living and himself dying in his stead. Inverting the vision, the narrator wakes up to the beauty of his surroundings, his life, and his friends. As he begins, still half-sneeringly, to form a close relationship with Karen, the narrator discovers that she, too, is struck by a similar mood of fellowship. Together, they begin to tour the pastoral countryside and even return to Brussels just in time for the local carnival, where they pick up an orange that they will eat later, in the park opposite Jansen's tower, the site of the narrator's agonized discussions with Tom. With the two characters so clearly developing into disciples of the unjustly killed Tom, it becomes hard to ignore the parallels and not perceive Tom as a Christ figure; Plante even supplies, through Karen, a bottle of wine from which she and the narrator drink with Tom just minutes before their fatal crash, while Vincent remains abstemious but hell-bent on speed.

Despite its deceptively naturalist, almost minimalist prose, which generally eschews metaphors and pretends to the starkly realistic, *The Accident* is a highly symbolic novel in which even the most minute elements eventually prove important. Plante's care in assigning meaning and elaborate function to almost all of the elements of his novel reveals an artistic mastery reminiscent of the work of Vladimir Nabokov. This enormous authorial control, cleverly hidden behind the self-obsessed narrator, is also well served by Plante's choice of a narrative structure that, with its closely circumscribed European setting populated by a strictly limited number of key American characters, consciously follows the tradition of Henry James, whose legacy the author explored at length in his first published novel, aptly entitled *The Ghost of Henry James* (1970).

Ultimately, it remains a question how attractive, and interesting, the protagonist manages to become. Like Salinger's Caulfield, Plante's protagonist has his full share of aversion toward the "phonies" of his world and is highly subjective; he dreams not of a field of rye but of an island in his ancestral North America that he desires, he states, "to return . . . to the state I imagined it had been in before any humans had stepped onto it." Yet his narrative is also burdened by a deeply earnest tone—so very absent in Salinger—that is typical of Plante's work but that makes his characters appear to be old and weary beyond their brief years. All in all, *The Accident* is a well-crafted work, but for a full appreciation of it as a novel, a reader has to be willing to engage the characters on their own terms and to submit to a world where humor comes at best in the guise of gentle irony and the shadows of despair stretch long all day.

R. C. Lutz

Sources for Further Study

America. CLXV, July 20, 1991, p. 49.
Atlanta Journal Constitution. June 23, 1991, p. N9.
Booklist. LXXXVII, February 1, 1991, p. 1099.
Kirkus Reviews. LIX, February 15, 1991, p. 207.
Library Journal. CXVI, March 15, 1991, p. 117.
Los Angeles Times. August 9, 1991, p. E10.
The New York Times Book Review. XCVI, June 23, 1991, p. 10.
Publishers Weekly. CCXXXVIII, March 8, 1991, p. 67.
The Washington Post Book World. XXI, May 19, 1991, p. 4.

ALL-BRIGHT COURT

Author: Connie Porter (1959-   )
Publisher: Houghton Mifflin (Boston). 224 pp. $19.95
Type of work: Novel
Time: The 1960's and the 1970's
Locale: Lackawanna, New York

A novel that explores the dreams, the disappointments, and the hard-won victories of black families in a Northern steel town

> *Principal characters:*
> SAMUEL TAYLOR, a steelworker
> MARY KATE PARKER TAYLOR, his wife
> MICHAEL "MIKEY" TAYLOR, their oldest son
> VENITA, a childless friend of Mary Kate
> MOSES, Venita's husband

Connie Porter's first novel, *All-Bright Court*, is a story of disillusionments and defeated dreams, but it is also a revelation of human endurance, which, along with humor, a sense of magic, compassion, and love, enables at least some of its characters to transcend their desperate lives. The book is written in a series of chapters, each of which tells a separate story. These incidents are unified by the fact that they all occur in a single community, by their recurring characters, and by the reiteration of pattern and theme.

The setting of the novel is All-Bright Court, an optimistically named tenement in the steel town of Lackawanna, located in upstate New York. All-Bright Court is made up of cinder block houses built during World War I as temporary quarters for white workers in the steel mills. In the 1950's, when the steel company at last built prefabricated houses for the white workers to buy, they painted the deteriorating concrete block houses in a rainbow of colors, named the area All-Bright Court, and moved in black workers from the South, who naïvely took the appearance for the reality. There Porter's characters live, learning to take shelter from the iron dust that falls upon them daily, but unable to shield themselves from the exploitation and the economic oppression that destroys the lives of blacks and whites alike.

Many of the people in All-Bright Court are like Samuel Taylor, a young black man from Mississippi, whose dreams of a bright future are based on his being able to sit at the same counter with whites and having a modern kitchen and indoor plumbing in his rented house. The reality Samuel must face every day, however, is the steel mill, where men are sacrificed to profit. If they are not killed in accidents resulting from outdated equipment, they die from lung diseases. If they strike, they and their families go hungry, and even the victories they occasionally win are too often mere compromises with their exploiters that leave the workers little better off than they were before.

In this environment, dreams die and lives are tragically wasted. For example, the "old man's son," Isaac, is obviously bright. Before he is two years old, he is talking in complete sentences. That display of intelligence alone is enough to cause him to be branded as "crazy" by the neighborhood. Then, because he is high-strung and easily frustrated, Isaac is put in a vocational school, where he is desperately bored, instead of in a school where his writing talent could be developed. Before long, Isaac turns to drugs and crime, and when last mentioned, he has been arrested for robbery.

The brief life of the "hungry boy," Dennis, is as tragic as that of Isaac. Porter first describes Dennis lying in a field, stuffing stolen bologna into his mouth. Earlier, the Taylors had tried to help him. When Dennis became a playmate of the Taylors' oldest child, Michael, or "Mikey," Mary Kate Taylor would take in the child and feed him. She had learned that Dennis' mother was an alcoholic and that Dennis dreaded going home to their empty house, where there was no food and often no electricity. One night, Mary Kate took Dennis in, bathed him, washed his urine-scented clothes, and put him to bed. His mother took offense at anyone's cleaning up her son, however, and, understandably angry, Sam ordered his family to leave Dennis alone. Dennis subsequently steals food and lives in a field, totally alone. Eventually, he is killed by a stray bullet during the riots that follow Martin Luther King, Jr.'s death.

Unlike Dennis' mother, Samuel and Mary Kate Taylor have not given up. Both of them work hard. Mary Kate keeps her house and her children spotless. The Taylors have strict rules for their children, but they surround them with love. In every way they can, Sam and Mary Kate are preparing them to take advantage of new opportunities, which they believe will come to blacks as a result of the Civil Rights movement. As it happens, Mikey does indeed benefit from changing times. As part of a new program for especially intelligent young blacks, he is sent on a scholarship to a white private school. Certainly, Mikey benefits from the superior education he receives there. It is difficult to be a token black, however, and although Mikey does manage the difficult task of moving between the two worlds, even speaking two languages, as a result of his good fortune he loses his sense of purpose and his sense of identity. Where Sam had encouraged his children to have dreams and fulfill them, Mikey wishes only to run away from his life at All-Bright Court, not to move toward the fulfillment of a goal. At the end of the book, Mikey will not even consider going to a black college. He is bound for the Ivy League and, as his father realizes, for what will be a white man's kind of life in a white man's world. Ironically, though Mikey—unlike Isaac and Dennis—will be considered successful, he, too, will, in a sense, be lost, because he will be alienated from his real self and from his traditions.

There is a fine balance in Porter's book between the public world and the private world. On one hand, she writes about the effect of historical events on the people of All-Bright Court. For example, one of the recurring discussions in the book is the question of strikes. The steelworkers remember with nostalgia their triumphs in earlier days, when their industry was healthy and there was room to bargain. Now, however, they have become vulnerable, because the industry itself is suffering. Events thousands of miles away such as the rebuilding of industrial Germany and its steel

industry threaten the jobs of workers in Lackawanna. As a result, a great many of
them are laid off, and those who still have jobs are afraid to strike. When they do,
they lose, and in order to work again, they are forced into a no-strike agreement,
which, as Sam says, makes the men little more than slaves.

Another historical reality that affects All-Bright Court is the Vietnam War. A
number of the young men are sent to Vietnam. Some do not come home. Some, like
Henry, come home maimed. The war also invades the living rooms of All-Bright
Court; Porter dramatizes the effect of television coverage on little Dorene Taylor,
who has no idea where Vietnam is and therefore becomes terrified whenever the
news is on, thinking that the bombs will begin to drop on All-Bright Court, that
napalm will begin to shower from the sky, doing to her what it has done to the
children she sees on the television screen.

It is not an invasion, though, but a civil war that comes to Lackawanna, the erup-
tion of rage that empties All-Bright Court after the assassination of Martin Luther
King, Jr., and sends the people of the court to attack the white-owned stores where
they usually trade. What begins out of anger and grief turns into an orgy of looting,
into what Isaac delightedly announces is Christmas, when the residents can take
whatever they want from the stores that have been smashed open. Sam and Mary
Kate are horrified; they think the looting is a betrayal of everything for which King
stood. Furthermore, it is the people of All-Bright Court who suffer most, who, like
Dennis, are killed by the bullets, and who, in any case, will have to cross town to
shop, since the stores they have destroyed will never be reopened.

Although history seems to betray the people of All-Bright Court, they find strength
in their traditions, in themselves, and in their relationships that enable them to transcend their own bleak world. From their past, for example, they have retained rich
folk traditions, which add a dimension of excitement to their lives. It is wonderful to
speculate about the doings of the mysterious woman named Greene, who suddenly
turns up with a mouthful of gold teeth, six children, and no visible means of support. When her house is almost immediately invaded by bats, it is obvious that she
is a conjure woman. This knowledge gives a kind of magic, if also fear, to everyone's
associations with her.

Other, if less dramatic, relationships between people make life interesting. One
example is the friendship between Henry and Skip, who has poor judgment but
superior powers of persuasion. Whatever Skip projects, Henry will do. In the hilarious chapter appropriately entitled "Fire," Skip gives Henry a hair treatment, and
even when he is suffering excruciating pain, Henry cannot believe that Skip could
make a mistake. At the end of the novel, Skip has written to Henry to extol the
virtues of life in Watts. It is obvious that Henry will go to join him, getting into
heaven knows what kind of trouble.

Friendship is a source of strength for Venita and Mary Kate. Venita is childless
and lonely; Mary Kate is so burdened with her large family that she has no time for
herself. Venita's visits to Mary Kate become the most treasured moments of their
days. Moreover, out of this friendship grows an unlikely friendship between the ac-

tivist Sam and Venita's more passive husband, Moses, whom Sam had always contemptuously referred to as an "Uncle Tom." With Mary Kate's encouragement, Venita finally takes in a deserted child, whom she needs as much as the child needs her.

The theme of reconciliation is stressed in the development of a tolerant friendship between Sam and Moses and also, in the final chapter, in Mikey's reconciliation with his father. Throughout the novel, various characters have been referred to as "lost." Unlike Isaac or Dennis, however, Mikey is making a success of his life. He is realizing the dreams his father has had for him; in fact, in the preceding chapter, he has been discussing his college plans. It is only in his distancing himself from his background and thus, almost inevitably, from his family that Mikey can be considered to have lost something, to have lost a part of himself. With her usual deftness, Porter quite realistically permits Mikey to become lost in a blizzard when he is on his way home from school. Dropping his books, which now cannot help him, he falls in the snow. Then, in the triumphant conclusion of the incident and of the novel, Mikey sees his father coming to his rescue, as he has always done. Though Mikey cannot hear Sam's words, which indeed may never again mean much to him, he will never forget what Sam is, a real hero in the darkness.

All-Bright Court is an admirable novel, skillfully constructed and beautifully written, with a simplicity of style that many writers take decades to develop. Above all, the characters Porter develops and the lives she dramatizes reveal her sympathetic understanding of people who, even in loss, manage to endure and often, by mere strength of character, to transcend the limitations of their world.

Rosemary M. Canfield Reisman

Sources for Further Study

Booklist. LXXXVII, July, 1991, p. 2030.
Chicago Tribune. August 25, 1991, XIV, p. 4.
Essence. XXII, September, 1991, p. 50.
Kirkus Reviews. LIX, July 1, 1991, p. 819.
Library Journal. CXVI, June 15, 1991, p. 106.
Los Angeles Times Book Review. October 13, 1991, p. 9.
The New York Times Book Review. XCVI, October 27, 1991, p. 12.
The New Yorker. LXVII, September 9, 1991, p. 96.
Publishers Weekly. CCXXXVIII, June 14, 1991, p. 46.
The Washington Post Book World. XXI, August 11, 1991, p. 3.

ALMANAC OF THE DEAD

Author: Leslie Marmon Silko (1948-   )
Publisher: Simon & Schuster (New York). 763 pp. $25.00
Type of work: Novel
Time: From 1500 to the near future, but mainly in some vague contemporary present
Locale: The American Southwest, particularly around Tucson, Arizona, and San Diego, California; northern Mexico

This immense novel is a dramatic history of the American Southwest, particularly of its native populations, what has happened to them since the invasion of whites, and what may happen in the near future when they begin to reclaim their lands

> *Principal characters:*
> LECHA CAZADOR, a Yaqui Indian and psychic, who foretells the future and helps to bring it about
> ZETA, her twin sister, who is involved in drug and arms shipments
> SEESE, a young woman who has had her baby kidnapped and who comes to work for Lecha in order to find the child
> STERLING, a Laguna Pueblo Indian who works on the Cazador ranch as a gardener
> MENARDO PANSON, a Mexican mestizo who has made millions in dealing drugs, weapons, and security
> ANGELITA, a Mexican revolutionary who is helping to raise an army to march north to reclaim tribal lands
> EL FEO, her lover and another leader of this revolution
> TACHO, his twin brother and Menardo's chauffeur, a man guided by the spirit world

Almanac of the Dead is a novel that is larger than life, larger almost than history. Spanning the five hundred years of European rule in Mexico and America's Southwest, this epic charts the exploitation of the land and its peoples by Europeans and their descendants until the book's final, apocalyptic scenes, when, in some near and violent future, the forces of the dispossessed, guided by the spirits of the dead, gather together to take back their lands.

Part Native American history, part mythic prophecy, part contemporary cultural analysis, *Almanac of the Dead* is more and less than all of these. Its focus is on the recent present and on what has happened to people—European American, Mexican, and Native American—who have been corrupted by the greed and violence of the contemporary world. The book, however, hops back and forth between the present and the past to trace the history of this world and the roots of the characters' failures.

If the novel seems a disparate mix of elements, it is. The map on the inside and back covers of the book lists dozens of major characters in stories that take place in Tucson, San Diego, and points south. Yet this "Five Hundred Year Map," as Leslie Marmon Silko writes, also "foretells the future of all the Americas" and the violent prophecy that is yet to be: "the disappearance of all things European."

The novel is divided into six parts, each part consisting of from one to eight books and each book containing from four to twenty chapters. There are at least half a dozen sets of characters who dominate the different parts of the novel, often for hundreds of pages at a time, and readers may lose touch with certain characters in some sections. By the end, however, most of the major characters have touched the others' lives (often sexually, usually violently), and many gather in the apocalyptic ending. It is a gripping and frightening fictional vision.

The center of the novel is Tucson. In the present, Lecha and Zeta Cazador are living on a remote ranch left to them years before by their father after his suicide. They are Yaqui (Pima) Indians born in Mexico who years before emigrated north from their Sonoran childhood home. Now they are surrounded by security systems and vicious dogs and are involved—as nearly everyone is here—in drugs and gun-running.

Lecha has returned to the ranch after a stint as a television psychic, but she is also suffering from cancer. Before she dies, she wants to decipher the "almanac of the dead," the ancient notebooks that she and her sister have inherited from their maternal grandmother, Yoeme, notebooks that give the history of their people and foretell the future. (The story of how the books were smuggled north by children years before is one of the fascinating fictional nuggets in this rich lode.)

Seese has moved from San Diego and sought Lecha out after seeing her on television; she hopes that Lecha, as a psychic, can help to find her kidnapped baby. By the end, however, Seese realizes the child is dead, and she has instead become Lecha's assistant, administering drugs to slow her illness and deciphering the notebooks. Seese has herself withdrawn from a cocaine habit, but her attempts to sell the drugs she has saved help to propel the dramatic and violent events at the end of the novel.

Seese's story of her escape from San Diego is one of two that opens the novel; the other is Sterling's, whose story frames the novel. A Laguna Pueblo who has been banished from his reservation because he let outsiders violate their sacred stone idols, at the end of the novel he will return to see the reservation's giant stone snake again. These are only a few of the major characters in Tucson; others include Ferro (Lecha's son), Paulie (his former lover), Jamey (his current lover), Root (Lecha's old lover), Mosca, Calabazas, and many more.

The second center of the novel is some hundreds of miles south on another stop in the drug trade, in Tuxtla Gutierrez, Mexico, and in the person of Menardo, a mestizo who has become rich and powerful and has built a lavish house. Menardo spends his days and nights in fear of assassination; ironically, he dies when Tacho, his chauffeur, fires a gun at him to test a bullet-proof vest.

If the novel has a thematic focus, it is the corruption of the present. Few characters are free of the criminal drug use and trafficking that goes on. Whole sets of major characters are actively involved in smuggling and selling drugs and using the money to sell arms to various shadowy groups. The fringe art world in San Diego from which Seese fled is defined by its drug use but involves a number of perverse sexual businesses (torture, the sexual abuse of children, and pornography). It is not a pretty picture that Silko paints, but it is a highly believable one.

On the flip side of this world of drugs and corruption is the world of Native

American life and spirits, people and forces that are helping to change this world. The best parts of *Almanac of the Dead* concern Native American history, both in Mexico and in the southwestern United States. Out of this history, a number of symbols and prophecies have emerged: The almanac is one; so, too, is the giant stone snake that has made a mysterious appearance in the Laguna Pueblo reservation near Albuquerque. In the south, the forces are the twin brothers, El Feo and Tacho, who are guided by twin macaw spirit beings. Underlying the divided political geography are related myths: The ancient Mexican serpent god Quetzalcoatl emerges as the giant stone snake of the Native American north. There is considerable mystery and mysticism in this novel, most of it based in actual American history and myth. At the center is a prophecy:

> The dispossessed people of the earth would rise up and take back lands that had been their birthright, and these lands would never again be held as private property, but as lands belonging to the people forever to protect.

Almanac of the Dead, in short, is three or four novels in one, and not all of them come together by the end. There are some individual stories of real power—of Geronimo in the nineteenth century, for example, or of Lecha in Alaska, or of the corrupt Judge Arne and his basset hounds in Tucson—but there are also eddies in which these and other characters get lost for long periods of time. The novel heats up in its last 150 pages and builds to an apocalyptic conclusion by drawing many of the characters to a holistic healers' convention in Tucson, where several mystics give their prophecies of the future. There is real power in this ending, but Silko cannot maintain that pace throughout this large novel, and many of the stories and not a few of the characters in the center of the novel get lost along the way.

As just one example, much of part 3 involves "the army of the homeless," a force of the dispossessed being raised on Tucson's fringes by several driven, crazed characters. At the end of the novel, the army is destroyed by the police in a paragraph or two. The ending cannot pull together all the stories; Silko may have attempted too large a canvas here.

It is not easy to find the literary equivalents for what Silko is attempting; it is easier, perhaps, to speak of the world of painting, of Pieter Brueghel and Hieronymus Bosch, for example, with their numerous detailed characters, or—perhaps more pointedly—of the paintings of Diego Rivera and Frieda Kahlo (particularly for his sweep and her mysticism). There are, of course, literary parallels as well. Like Marge Piercy or Howard Fast, Silko is attempting a radical American epic, a portrait of American life that gives insights into American history at the same time that it allows one to see the full panorama. Similarly, she may remind readers of such Latin American writers as Gabriel García Márquez who work in the contemporary magical realism mode Silko is clearly tapping. Her work may also remind readers of John Nichols' *The Milagro Beanfield War* (1974), Rudolfo Anaya's *Bless Me, Ultima* (1972), and the works of other writers of the Southwest who have attempted to tell the same story of the mix of white, Mexican, and Indian roots and lives. Finally, Silko resembles Russell Hoban, the British Peter Ackroyd, and other chroniclers of the dysto-pian vision. Here is the future, and it is sick and frightening.

Silko has also given a painting of contemporary America that perhaps resembles Pablo Picasso's *Guernica* as much as anything: It is violent and twisted and frag-mented, but it carries an important message. Silko knows what drugs and injustice are doing to the world. She also knows her Native American history and the stories and prophecies that are just beneath its surface. She has written a mammoth chroni-cle of what happens when one world takes over another and of when the myths will live again. This is hardly a political tract; the energy for the violent changes that are about to take place in the novel come out of the mythic past and out of the corrupt present, not out of some political handbook. (As one of the characters notes, Karl Marx got his ideas from native communes in North America; like their members, he understood that "the earth belongs to no one.") If this is a radical novel, it is a native, indigenous radicalism that demands that readers listen to the voices of proph-ecy and rebellion that have been ringing loudly in America for hundreds of years.

David Peck

Sources for Further Study

Booklist. LXXXVIII, December 15, 1991, p. 751.
Chicago Tribune. December 1, 1991, XIV, p. 3.
Interview. XXI, December, 1991, p. 58.
Library Journal. CXVI, October 15, 1991, p. 124.
The New Republic. CCV, November 4, 1991, p. 39.
The New York Times Book Review. XCVI, December 22, 1991, p. 6.
Newsweek. CXVIII, November 18, 1991, p. 84.
Publishers Weekly. CCXXXVIII, September 6, 1991, p. 94.
Time. CXXXVIII, December 9, 1991, p. 86.
The Washington Post. November 26, 1991, p. B3.

THE AMERICAN KALEIDOSCOPE
Race, Ethnicity, and the Civic Culture

Author: Lawrence H. Fuchs
Publisher: Wesleyan University Press/University Press of New England (Hanover, New Hampshire). 618 pp. $45.00; paperback $24.95
Type of work: History and current affairs
Time: The seventeenth century to the 1990's
Locale: The United States

An invaluable aid to understanding America's multicultural society, this study places current issues of racial, ethnic, and civic identity in historical context—issues that will become increasingly significant in an era of global migration

The collapse of Communism in the Eastern Bloc and the break-up of the Soviet Union, the emergence of the European Community, the growing economic dominance of Japan—these and other developments have prompted considerable speculation about the prospects for a "new world order." Yet such analyses, whether optimistic or pessimistic, have for the most part consigned to the periphery or ignored altogether a factor that will become increasingly significant in the near future: worldwide migration of people on an unprecedented scale.

All over the world, nations which in the past have had relatively homogeneous populations are experiencing an influx of immigrants. Many of these immigrants are sojourners; they are seeking employment to support their families back home, not permanent residence. Such, for example, were the nearly twenty thousand Vietnamese workers in Kuwait who were displaced by the Gulf War. Others, however, do end up staying in their adopted country. In France and Germany, the growing number of immigrants—who are bearing children at a much higher rate than the national average—has resulted in severe racial tensions and intense political controversy. In Italy and Spain, immigrants from Africa have provoked similar reactions. Scenarios such as these are being played out around the world—in Scandinavia, where long-established social policies are being put to a new test by immigrants and migrant workers; in ethnically homogeneous Japan, where the number of foreign workers is steadily increasing.

Sporadic press coverage of these stories has focused almost exclusively on the moral issues involved, with the presumption that any opposition to immigration is evidence of racism and xenophobia. Indeed, in France and Germany, anti-immigrant groups have employed rhetoric that echoes Nazi slogans. What is absent from most of these articles is acknowledgment that concern over the consequences of immigration might have a legitimate basis. In contrast, a special report on international migration in the Los Angeles Times (October 1, 1991) noted that, "By century's end, migration will not only color political decisions but may also seriously jeopardize national stability of both sending and receiving nations."

This global situation provides a context for current issues of racial, ethnic, and civic identity in the United States. Immigration to the United States in the 1980's was at its highest point since the great wave of immigration in the first decades of the twentieth century, and legislation passed by Congress in 1990 will permit an even greater increase. As a result, the United States, always known as a nation of immigrants, has become even more diverse. In Los Angeles, almost 30 percent of the population is foreign-born; in Miami, more than 50 percent. Ethnic enclaves are to be found throughout the country: Colombians in New York City's Jackson Heights, Hmong refugees in Minneapolis-Saint Paul, Vietnamese fishermen in Louisiana.

Coinciding with this "new immigration"—triggered by a major shift in U.S. immigration policy in 1965—there has been a marked increase in racial and ethnic consciousness among African Americans, Hispanic Americans, Native Americans, and Asian Americans. Calls for recognition of America's multicultural diversity have raised questions about how Americans define themselves: as participants in a shared civic culture, or first and foremost as members of a particular racial or ethnic group?

These questions have been debated in almost every forum in the land, but much of the debate has been unproductive. In *The American Kaleidoscope: Race, Ethnicity, and the Civic Culture*, Lawrence H. Fuchs has written a book which could contribute to substantive discussion of multiculturalism. The story he tells is familiar enough in its broad outlines: It is a celebration of America's uniquely inclusive political culture, tempered by an uncompromising account of the ongoing struggle of racial and ethnic minorities to overcome disenfranchisement and discrimination. (Fuchs particularly emphasizes the African-American experience.)

Yet if the story is familiar, much in the telling is fresh and compelling. Fuchs has mastered an enormous quantity of material, which he integrates seamlessly into his narrative. Rarely does one encounter a work of history in which evidence (ranging from statistics to personal anecdotes) is linked so persuasively with interpretation. No other book so clearly illuminates the fascinating and troubling "contemporary American ethnic landscape" in the light of "historical patterns of ethnicity."

While he acknowledges that "no metaphor can capture completely the complexity of ethnic dynamics in the U.S.," Fuchs's title rejects the old metaphor of America as a melting pot. Fuchs concedes that "the concepts associated with the melting pot"—notions of assimilation and absorption into the mainstream—represent a fundamental truth about the immigrant experience, yet he insists that this metaphor is not and never has been adequate "to describe the dynamics of ethnic diversity and acculturation, certainly not for Indians or blacks, not even for immigrants and their children." As an alternative, Fuchs proposes the metaphor of a kaleidoscope (for which he credits John Higham's book *Send These to Me: Immigrants in Urban America*, 1974). From the beginning, Fuchs argues, American ethnicity has been kaleidoscopic, characterized by complexity and rapidly changing patterns.

True enough—and Fuchs could have made his point even more effectively if he had stated explicitly what is implicit in his narrative: that the retrospective attribution of monolithic solidarity to "whites" or "Anglos" or "Euro-Americans"—a staple of current polemics—distorts history beyond recognition. For in part 1, "The Civic Culture and Voluntary Pluralism," Fuchs shows how immigrant groups as diverse as Irish Catholics, Slovenians, Italians, and Jews, despite resistance by nativists, were able to describe themselves as Americans: "free to maintain affection for and loyalty to their ancestral regions and cultures while at the same time proclaiming an American identity by embracing the founding myths and participating in the political life of the republic."

In contrast to this voluntary pluralism, the four chapters that make up part 2 center on what Fuchs terms "coercive pluralisms." Native Americans were the victims of "predatory pluralism," a term that keeps Fuchs's schema intact at the cost of precision. It means simply that whites coveted the Indians' land and stopped at nothing to take possession of it. African Americans were the victims of "caste pluralism," a system designed to furnish a permanent subservient class whose members would be excluded from participation in the civic culture. Noting that, on a rational economic basis, poor whites in the post-Civil War South might have made common cause with blacks, Fuchs draws attention to the widespread acceptance of the "sacredness" of the caste system. Finally, Fuchs shows how Asians and Mexicans were exploited by "sojourner pluralism," a system "intended to meet the labor needs of an expanding American economy without having to admit nonwhite immigrant laborers to the civic culture."

Part 3, "The Outsiders Move In: The Triumph of the Civic Culture," tells how these excluded groups began to gain equal treatment under the law and access to the political process. World War II was a turning point, as those who had been victims of the coercive pluralisms nevertheless participated fully and often heroically in the war effort. Even more significant was the black Civil Rights movement, which aroused the conscience of the nation and inspired other groups to assert their rights and take a new pride in their racial or ethnic identity.

Part 4, "The American Kaleidoscope: The Ethnic Landscape, 1970-1989," is the most original section of the book, offering one of the best available profiles of a changing America in the period of the new immigration. With a wealth of pertinent statistics and illustrative examples, Fuchs vividly conveys the "quickening pace of ethnic interaction." Enormous diversity is not limited to New York, Los Angeles, and Chicago; by 1980, for example, "Nashville, Tennessee, while only .8 percent Hispanic and .5 percent Asian, had become home for sixty-three ethnic groups, including Kurds and Laotians."

Finally, in part 5, "Pluralism, Public Policy, and the Civic Culture, 1970-1989," Fuchs discusses the ways in which public policy, subject to sharp debate, sought to ensure equal opportunity for all. Here he treats affirmative action, bilingual education, and other controversial public policy issues. He gives special attention to the long-term consequences of racism, tracing the grim realities of today's black urban underclass to "generations of segregation and isolation from mainstream American institutions, breeding a deep sense of psychological isolation from well-to-do whites and African-Americans, whose values, attitudes, and life-styles sometimes seemed almost foreign to many in the underclass." And he concludes his fundamentally optimistic survey with the observation that, "By 1990, the biggest domestic challenge to those who believed in equal rights lay in enhancing opportunity for children born into the underclass."

Many universities are now requiring first-year students to take a course relating to issues of race and ethnicity. Serious questions have been raised about the validity of such courses and the manner in which they are conducted. Setting aside these questions for the moment, it would be hard to find a better book for such a course than *The American Kaleidoscope.*

To a degree that is unfortunately unusual in current debates, Fuchs combines a strong appreciation of the founding vision of America with a realistic acknowledgment of failures to live up to that vision. His sympathy for the oppressed sometimes leads him into wishful thinking, as in his discussion of the Black Panthers. Students who note Fuchs's regret that Martin Luther King, Jr., "did not live to see the transformation of the Black Panthers"—their transformation, that is, into benign organizers of free breakfast programs and free medical clinics—should be referred to David Horowitz and Peter Collier's *Destructive Generation: Second Thoughts About the Sixties* (1989), where the sordid career of Huey Newton and the gangsterism of the Panthers are documented in chilling detail. Moreover, Fuchs's commitments place him among those for whom diversity is an absolute good. While he briefly considers outbreaks of hostility against recent immigrants under the heading "Xenophobia, Racism, and Bigotry: Conflict in the Kaleidoscope," he never begins to consider reasoned, principled objections to current immigration policies. Between the liberal consensus represented by Fuchs and the nativist slurs given currency by Pat Buchanan there should be a middle ground where debate can be carried on without immediate recourse to name-calling.

John Wilson

Sources for Further Study

America. CLXIV, March 2, 1991, p. 245.
Booklist. LXXXVII, January 15, 1991, p. 985.
Choice. XXVIII, June, 1991, p. 1698.
The Christian Century. CVIII, May 29, 1991, p. 602.
Library Journal. CXV, October 1, 1990, p. 106.
Los Angeles Times Book Review. February 10, 1991, p. 11.
The New Republic. CCIII, December 31, 1990, p. 27.
The New York Review of Books. XXXVII, November 22, 1990, p. 19.
Publishers Weekly. CCXXXVII, December 7, 1990, p. 63.
The Washington Post Book World. XXI, January 13, 1991, p. 3.

ANNE SEXTON
A Biography

Author: Diane Wood Middlebrook
Publisher: Houghton Mifflin (Boston). Illustrated. 488 pp. $24.95
Type of work: Literary biography
Time: 1928-1975
Locale: Massachusetts

This first full-scale biography of poet Anne Sexton explores the relationship between Sexton's life and her prolific outpouring of poetry, drama, and other creative works

> *Principal personages:*
> ANNE SEXTON, a noted poet
> ALFRED "KAYO" MULLER SEXTON II, Anne's husband
> LINDA GRAY SEXTON, Anne's elder daughter
> JOY SEXTON, Anne's younger daughter
> MARY GRAY STAPLES HARVEY, Anne's mother
> RALPH HARVEY, Anne's father
> MAXINE KUMIN, a poet, Anne's friend

Anne Sexton's life and death tend to overshadow her poetry. A flamboyant performer of her own works, a woman whose life was characterized by frequent suicide attempts and love affairs, a poet whose words about taking her own life were prophetically realized in her suicide—these are some of the sensational details that suggest Anne Sexton was the principal character in a soap opera. Diane Wood Middlebrook does not view Sexton as a melodramatic victim, however; instead, she offers a biography that probes the complex relationship between Sexton's art and her illness.

Invited to write this first full-length biography of Sexton by the poet's daughter, Linda Gray Sexton, Middlebrook spent ten years researching and writing *Anne Sexton: A Biography.* During this decade, she spoke with ninety of Sexton's colleagues, examined Sexton's personal papers and unpublished poetry, and was given access to taped psychiatric sessions between Sexton and her first psychiatrist, Dr. Martin T. Orne, who has written the foreword to the biography. The controversial release and use of these tapes will likely continue to be a point of discussion regarding this book. What is not controversial, however, is the engaging style, attention to detail, and narrative strength of this portrait. Dividing the book into four parts, Middlebrook carefully sketches Sexton's life and, with equal care, analyzes her art and the relationship between the two.

The first section, "Becoming Anne Sexton," centers on Sexton's unhappy childhood with an alcoholic father who perhaps sexually abused her (Middlebrook is careful not to conclude that this actually occurred, but she strongly suggests its possibility) and a mother who was weak and abusive in her own right. Marrying businessman Alfred "Kayo" Muller Sexton II was an extension of these abusive relationships, for Kayo's frustrations with Anne resulted in his physically attacking her on numerous occasions. After the birth of her two daughters, Sexton became increasingly disturbed. During this period, she received help from Orne, a psychiatrist barely a year older than Sexton who was completing his Ph.D. in psychology at Harvard while working as a resident in psychiatry at Massachusetts Mental Health Center. During the course of his treatment of Sexton, Orne encouraged her to write poetry as a part of her therapy. These early attempts to use poetry in a therapeutic fashion were the beginnings of both her personal and poetic life, as Sexton once noted in an interview about an attempted suicide during this period: "The surface cracked when I was about twenty-eight. I had a psychotic break and tried to kill myself. . . . It was a kind of rebirth at twenty-nine." She announced this rebirth in 1957 by signing her poetry, for the first time, "Anne Sexton," no longer "Mrs. A. M. Sexton."

This new signature was indicative of Sexton's transformation from "Housewife Into Poet," the title of the second section of the biography. Sexton immersed herself in both the production and the world of poetry. That world included some of the most significant American poets: Maxine Kumin—a woman whose friendship would sustain Sexton until the day of her death—Robert Lowell, W. D. Snodgrass, John Holmes, James Wright, Ted Hughes, Sylvia Plath, and many others. Collectively, these poets became mentors and family for Sexton, helping her find her own voice and develop a craft that was unique for its blunt, often offensive, language and ideas. Challenged by emerging questions about feminism as it related to female writers and increasingly experimental in her reliance upon the unconscious in producing her poetry, Sexton published her first two books in the opening years of the decade now associated with unbridled freedom and experimentation, the 1960's. *To Bedlam and Part Way Back*, published in 1960, was followed by *All My Pretty Ones* (1962), the collection many poets think is Sexton's best book. By the time of her death, eighteen thousand copies of *All My Pretty Ones* had been sold, a remarkable number. Despite setbacks in her therapy and frequent, often unhappy, love affairs, Sexton met the 1960's as a poet recognized for her distinctive, if at times jarring, creative voice.

She also emerged as "The Prizewinner," the appropriate title of the third section of this biography. By 1967, she had produced a sufficient quantity and quality of poetry to be the worthy recipient of two major awards: the Shelley Memorial Prize, awarded annually by the Poetry Society of America, and the Pulitzer Prize for poetry. Despite these recognitions and numerous others, Sexton's psychological state continued to deteriorate. She was, in her own view, an Icarus figure, not a Daedalus. These images had been offered to Sexton as types of poets. Daedalus, the father of Icarus, with his son had fled from Crete by fastening on wings of wax and feather; Daedalus escaped, while his son flew too near the sun, which melted the wax and sent Icarus falling to his death in the sea. Daedalus thus became, for Sexton, the model of the practical, plodding artist; Icarus, by contrast, was the poet whose craziness carried him high. Anne Sexton was clearly following Icarus' example.

As "The Performer"—the title of the fourth section of the book—this Icarus figure was a charismatic reader who was in demand throughout the country. Wherever she appeared to read her poetry, she mesmerized audiences with readings that were dramatic and memorable. The poetry she read continued to reveal the trademarks that Middlebrook identifies as fourfold: frequent use of simile, repetitious structure, a "pool of metaphors," and "the knock and jangle of assonance." These trademarks are powerful when the poetry is read on paper; they were even more powerful when Sexton, wearing a long red dress that looked as dramatic as her voice sounded, read her poems aloud. Unknown to most of her mesmerized audiences, however, was the increasing displacement of the poet by this performer. Just as the housewife had been transformed into the poet, so the poet was becoming the performer, having switched into a public mode that belied the disintegration of the personal, poetic self. Anne Sexton the charismatic reader was also Anne Sexton the lonely alcoholic and drug-dependent woman who had divorced her husband, estranged herself from her daughters, and distanced herself from many friends. Isolated and afraid, she believed she could never become healthy. Rather than accept that state of permanent pathology, she chose another option in 1974, at the age of forty-five: suicide. With dignity and deliberation, she made her farewells to the important people in her life—without ever implying to them that these were the last farewells—and then she donned her mother's old fur coat. As Middlebrook notes, "The worn satin lining must have warmed quickly against her flesh; death was going to feel something like an embrace, like falling asleep in familiar arms." With a glass of vodka in her hands, she went into her garage, stepped into her car, turned on the ignition and then the radio, and awaited the end of her life.

Diane Wood Middlebrook's biography of this gifted poet is written like a novel that is also literary criticism and social history. The characters, the plot, and the setting are inherently interesting, but Middlebrook's storytelling makes this narrative a powerful one indeed. Similarly, the careful analyses of specific poems and particular poetic strategies illuminate both Sexton's artistic process and the relationship between her poems and her illness. Thus, for example, Middlebrook details the production of *The Death Notebooks*, the last book published in Sexton's lifetime, and, specifically "O Ye Tongues," the last poem in it. Through a careful analysis of this poem, which is really a sequence of ten psalms, Middlebrook shows not only the influence of the eighteenth century poet Christopher Smart but also the way in which this sequence was a culmination of Sexton's entire career. Finally, this biography is also a useful foray into social history, particularly the development of the women's movement as it relates to the literary world. Though Sexton was bothered by the question of whether she was a feminist—possibly, Middlebrook suggests, because of the word's associations with anger—Sexton spent her life dealing with issues related to her identity as a woman. This biography ably chronicles the issue and shows how Sexton's struggles were and are a reflection of larger social and cultural issues facing human beings in the twentieth century. Erica Jong, a friend of Sexton and author of *Fear of Flying* (1973), remarked, "If Anne had stuck around another ten years, the world might have caught up with her." Anne Sexton was both a woman of her time and a woman ahead of her time. This biography documents both Anne Sextons.

Marjorie Smelstor

Sources for Further Study

Chicago Tribune. August 18, 1991, XIV, p. 6.
The Chronicle of Higher Education. September 18, 1991, p. A8.
London Review of Books. XIII, November 7, 1991, p. 17.
Los Angeles Times Book Review. August 25, 1991, p. 4.
The Nation. CCLIII, September 23, 1991, p. 342.
The New England Journal of Medicine. CCCXXV, November 14, 1991, p. 1450.
The New Republic. CCV, November 4, 1991, p. 32.
The New York Times Book Review. XCVI, August 18, 1991, p. 1.
Publishers Weekly. CCXXXVIII, July 5, 1991, p. 50.
The Times Literary Supplement. November 1, 1991, p. 8.
The Washington Post Book World. XXI, August 11, 1991, p. 1.

AN ATLAS OF THE DIFFICULT WORLD
Poems 1988-1991

Author: Adrienne Rich (1929-   )
Publisher: W. W. Norton (New York). 57 pp. $17.95; paperback $7.95
Type of work: Poetry

In her fifteenth book of poetry, Adrienne Rich continues to awaken the social consciences of her readers through a series of insightful poems

Adrienne Rich published her first book of poetry in 1951, when W. H. Auden selected *A Change of World* for the Yale Younger Poets Award. Since that first publication, Rich has published fourteen volumes of poetry and a number of prose volumes, including the ground-breaking feminist work *Of Woman Born: Motherhood as Experience and Institution* (1976). Over her forty-year career, Rich's critical theories have continued to evolve and her poetry to deepen and amaze by its passion and political insight. Rejecting formalism and the obscurity of much modernist poetry, Rich has emerged as America's preeminent feminist poet and critic, the champion of "a common language" that speaks to or unites all people, regardless of cultural origin. It is fitting that *An Atlas of the Difficult World* broadens her themes and concerns from solely women's issues to the larger topics of America's moral and spiritual state and the suffering of Jews, the artist, and the lover. Women are still very present in *An Atlas of the Difficult World*, for much of the text is written from a clearly female perspective. Rich, however, has moved beyond the purely feminist to depict themes that awaken the social consciences of her readers to the injustices and violence that stalk America and the world.

Visionary in content, elegiac in tone, and Whitmanesque in scope, the book divides into two principal sections, offering a total of twenty-five poems written between 1988 and 1991. The first section consists solely of the thirteen-part title poem, which maps the social and spiritual landscape of the United States, crisscrossing the country from California to New England and back in order to capture divergent elements and to forge a link between the author's consciousness and experience and the country's moral state. The second section consists of twelve poems, several in multiple parts. The title poem is, however, the central offering and the most dynamic and stirring piece in the collection. Much of its material focuses on the death of innocence, the disintegration of the American dream, and the struggle for what Rich calls "the soul of her country." Viewing the violence that has come to mark America she recounts in the opening section the story of a man beating a woman, destroying her writing, and throwing "the kerosene/ lantern into her face." Yet it is not such personal violence that draws Rich, nor is it the environmental disasters that mark the landscape: the aftermath of a California earthquake and the chemical pollution in "THE SALAD BOWL OF THE WORLD" that poisons migrant workers with Malathion. Rather, as the poet writes, she would prefer not

                                    to know
        wreckage, dreck and waste, but these are the materials
        and so are the slow life of the moon's belly
        over wreckage, dreck, and waste, wild treefrogs calling in
        another season, light and music still pouring over
        our fissured, cracked terrain.

As the above passage indicates, it is the diverse, multiple elements of America that Adrienne Rich seeks to map in her *Atlas of the Difficult World*: America's pain, but also its underlying natural beauty, the gifts of "light and music" and the treefrog's song.

From the outset, moreover, Rich presents the role of the writer as essential in bringing this unity of pain and beauty to the readers' awareness. Writing is meant to be salvific, as is clear when Rich tells of her students in writing workshops who seek answers to the meaninglessness of their lives and turn to poems "hoping they have redemption stored/ in their lines." Indeed, Rich announces in her opening poem that she is deliberately taking a new path, a spiritual search. Addressing her readers directly, she says,

                                    If you had known me
        once, you'd still know me now though in a different
        light and life. This is no place you ever knew me.
        . . . .

                                    These are not the roads
        you knew me by. But the woman driving, walking, watching
        for life and death, is the same.

In her essay "Notes Toward a Politics of Location" (1984), Rich emphasized the centrality of location to her art. It was necessary, she wrote, to understand how location at one point on a map was also a place in history. This necessity is perhaps no place clearer than in the title poem of *An Atlas of the Difficult World*, which uses the metaphors of maps and roads to measure and trace American culture's social and spiritual health. In part 2, for example, looking at "a map of our country" held out to the reader, the poet finds a landscape painted by innumerable ills: The "Sea of Indifference" has a spot on the map, as do "the breadbasket of foreclosed farms," "the suburbs of acquiescence," and

        the capital of money and dolor whose spires
        flare up through air inversions whose bridges are crumbling
        whose children are drifting blind alleys pent
        between coiled rolls of razor wire. . . .

The powerful images of this passage suggest Rich's strong sense of political responsibility and complicity in the social injustice done the poor and working-class people of the United States. Searching for something that unifies the country, she turns to Vermont in autumn. Reminiscent of Walt Whitman's "A Noiseless Patient Spider," a poem alluded to by Rich's patient watching of a spider weaving a web in her study, this section of *An Atlas of the Difficult World* acknowledges Rich's own complicity, her privileged girlhood spent reading and dreaming of a literary life without consideration of the lives of "the rural working poor" around her at that moment, lives of girls her own age whose dreams were "extinguished in the remote back-country I had come to love." In the context of the poem, the experience of revisiting New England is not merely a way of indicting herself; rather, it forges a tie between the poet and those people she did not notice but of whom she is now aware. It is a journey involving a loss of innocence, which the poet expresses as a change in the wind's velocity and direction, another image of location.

Part 4 is Rich's call for a new vision, her search for "something that binds/ the map of this country together." Curiously, she finds her symbol in the lowly girasol, with its black eyes, lining the "roadsides from Vermont to California." It is here also that the poet calls for an end to the waste of nature and human talents created through artificial and arbitrary divisions. What the country needs are teachers, advisers, those who do "the work of perception/ work of the poet." These have been wasted, just as the resources of nature have been. In one of the strongest sections of her long title poem, the poet calls for a beginning to the "never-to-be-finished, still unbegun work of repair."

Other poems in *An Atlas of the Difficult World* replicate these themes of destruction, loss of innocence, and the search for unity. Throughout, the poet's vision is broad, epic, moving. One section borrows a line from Hart Crane's *The Bridge*; another borrows lines from the American poet Muriel Rukeyser. Ghosts of pioneers and immigrants appear—all those who were isolated from their original culture, who lost their heritage and perhaps their poetry and art to become drudges in the New World. "The Dream Site" for these people is New York, a decaying city "where once . . . sacks of garbage rose/ like barricades." Always concrete and particular, Rich moves across the sweep of American history and landscape by calling to mind the stories of individuals: a mother who buried her daughter, then went on alone to cook in Western mining camps; a German-Jewish refugee who killed herself; two women brutally attacked on the Appalachian Trail because of their sexual preference; Annie Sullivan and the other Irish immigrants who fled the potato famine in the nineteenth century. Rich's poems in this collection are a feast of details that find life feeding on violence, hardship, and death, the dream of America disappointing yet constant, always renewable. Otherwise, why would the poet search for meaning in this vast country of citizens "like and unlike so many"? Her answer comes in part 11.

Drawing on the Persian Gulf arms buildup in late 1990 and the ensuing Gulf War in early 1991, Rich writes passionately of how she is "bent on fathoming what it means to love my country." Disturbed by repeated references to the United States Patriot missiles the poet cries out:

A patriot is not a weapon. A patriot is one who wrestles for the
soul of her country
as she wrestles for her own being. . . .

Rich's language is evocative and powerful, her images drawn from the six o'clock news or morning headline. Repeatedly, she eschews abstraction and idealism in order to bring the reader to consciousness. By the end of the title poem, she directly addresses a multitude of readers in the poem "Dedications." Using the epic catalog and repetition Whitman adapted for *Leaves of Grass* (1855), Rich speaks to her readers across the country, in all places and situations, of all ages and both sexes. Where several times in earlier sections of *An Atlas of the Difficult World* the poet has asked what moors or binds the citizens of the country, here she suggests that it is their very number and diversity that unify, just as surely as it is their reading of the poet's words.

The second half of *An Atlas of the Difficult World* opens with five poems portraying women in various manifestations. The first poem, "She," suggests H. Rider Haggard's novel of that title (1887) by amassing images of decay and suggesting the illusiveness of the mysterious woman of the title. "That Mouth" calls attention to the limitations placed on a girl by both her father and her mother, while it is the whole world, not pieces, to which she holds title. "Marghanita" offers a portrait of the woman as artist and rebel who is, ironically, the only one to return home to clean up after the death of her twin. One of the best short lyrics in section 2, it explores the love-hate relationship with one's other self and the necessity of destruction in the creative process. "Olivia," the last of the short poems depicting women, addresses the subject of woman as political and ideological chameleon.

The ten-part poem "Eastern War Time" powerfully evokes the experiences of Jews in America and in Europe during World War II. Actually ten separate short poems, it contrasts Rich's own protected girlhood, filled with the certitudes of studying classical Latin in school, with the cold uncertainties of life for her counterparts in Europe. To drive home the horror of the Holocaust, Rich uses the text of a telegram sent through the American legation in Bern, Switzerland, August 11, 1942, to the U.S. State Department in Washington as part of the second poem. Outlining Adolf Hitler's "final solution" to the Jewish question in Europe, the telegram and the poem that replicates it suggest the complicity of the American government in the extermination and exportation of millions. "Eastern War Time" captures the shocking intrusions of hatred into the lives of European and American Jews alike, for in one poem Rich recounts the story of Leo Frank, an American Jew accused of murdering a factory girl and later hanged by vigilantes. Perhaps the most powerful in this series is the last section, where memory speaks as the voice of all those lost in World War II, especially women and children. It is a stirring evocation of history through the catalog of personal pain and individual losses.

The second half of *An Atlas of the Difficult World* concludes with poems on friendship, art, and transformation. "Tattered Kaddish" is Rich's song of praise to life that simultaneously, as is the Jewish custom, mourns a death—here a young suicide. "Through Corralitos Under Rolls of Cloud" is a five-part poem that offers a notable exception to Rich's usual free-form verse style. Each of the five parts is twelve lines that often employ interlocking end rhymes reminiscent of the formalism of Rich's poetry prior to *Snapshots of a Daughter-in-Law: Poems 1954-1962* (1963). "For a Friend in Travail" records the poet's efforts to identify with the suffering of a friend, while "1948: Jews" offers an ironic statement about the burden of Jewishness following the death of six million in Europe. "Two Arts," the one poem that is seemingly unconnected with the others in this collection, contrasts the creative process with the finished product that is judged by a grant committee. The second part of the poem also describes the pain of the artistic process. Both "Darklight" and "Final Notations," the last two poems in *An Atlas of the Difficult World*, suggest a movement toward the end of life or toward a new view, a transformation through art that involves the whole person.

Drawing her images from domestic life, the countryside and landscape of California and New England, from personal memory and history, Rich has created a highly accessible work in *An Atlas of the Difficult World*, A nominee for the 1991 National Book Award in poetry, it is a collection fully deserving of the highest praise.

Stella Nesanovich

Sources for Further Study

Booklist. LXXXVIII, October 1, 1991, p. 235.
Boston Globe. December 1, 1991, p. 17.
Library Journal. CXVI, October 15, 1991, p. 85.
The New York Review of Books. XXXVIII, November 21, 1991, p. 50.
The New York Times Book Review. XCVI, December 8, 1991, p. 7.
Publishers Weekly. CCXXXVIII, August 30, 1991, p. 73.
San Francisco Chronicle. October 27, 1991, p. REV11.

AZTECS
An Interpretation

Author: Inga Clendinnen
Publisher: Cambridge University Press (New York). Illustrated. 398 pp. $24.95
Type of work: Historical anthropology
Time: The fifteenth and sixteenth centuries
Locale: The Aztec empire in pre-Conquest Mexico

Clendinnen is faced with a problem of translation not only of Spanish and Nahuatl texts such as the Florentine Codex (her major resource) into English but of a traditional and radically foreign culture into the medium of modern scientific discourse; that she does not always succeed probably has more to do with problems of untranslatability than anything else

Dee Brown records the following tale about a Native American from a Northwest tribe in an encounter with a pioneer woman: "He and a small band visited a tent camp, and seeing bright-colored quilts and shiny utensils all about and no one near but a few 'white squaws,' he decided to help himself. One of the 'white squaws,' however, began defending her possessions with a heavy tent pole. 'She laid it about, right and left, over heads, shoulders, and backs until she put them to flight.' Next day the warrior returned, apologized for his conduct, and offered the woman's husband five hundred dollars for her. He was quite disappointed to learn she was not for sale." This vignette is a powerful reminder of the cultural gap which exists between all cultures, but especially between "traditional" and "technological" societies. Understanding others is supremely difficult. Fortunately for the reader, understanding this book is only moderately so. Inga Clendinnen has set about to explore this gap at its most difficult point: where it touches what has come to be thought of as core human values. The question she seeks to answer in her book could be put this way: How is it that high Mexica culture (that is, the people who with others ruled the Aztec empire) could appropriate human sacrifice as a regular, systemic, fully integrated part of their society and its workings? Her answer is chillingly straightforward. At certain key points their view of reality was fundamentally different from that of the modern reader (or for that matter from that of many contemporary traditional societies). In political discourse, commitment to a certain view of reality goes by the name of ideology, in the social sphere it is called ethos or mores, and in religion it is sometimes called theology. For a fully integrated traditional society all of these names mean too much and too little. Too much because they imply cultural development and distribution of labor not always present in Mexica society, too little because, as is so often the case, the whole is greater than the sum of its parts.

First Clendinnen must defend her premise that human sacrifice was in fact a functional, organic part of the cultural self-understanding of the Mexica, not only their priest and warriors but also the rest of their society—or at least of enough of the rest to make the whole thing work for several centuries prior to the Spanish conquest. She does this by piling up so much data (extracted in the main from the Florentine Codex, a compilation of recollections of Mexica men a generation after the conquest) that it is hard to resist her contention that human sacrifice was indeed an integral part of the working of Mexica society.

Ideas put forward by others, that this practice was imposed from above in a hierarchical society, or was a relatively infrequent occurrence, blown out of proportion by the Spanish conquerors, are not so much dismissed as buried in the evidence Clendinnen amasses. Mexica culture was indeed hierarchical, perhaps more so than many had previously imagined, but Clendinnen's data show involvement of all layers of society in the sacrificial system, and to the extent that social mobility did exist, it was also integrated into the warrior-captive-sacrifice matrix. The theory that such sacrifices were only occasional is simply destroyed by examples on virtually every page of the book. Indeed, the second point is made so well that even the author realizes that the sheer number of victims strains credulity. She asks, and rightly so, how did the Mexica dispose of twenty thousand bodies over the course of several days of feasting and sacrifice? The answer may lie in the first point: Many people were involved at all levels to make this system work.

Clendinnen divides her book into four major parts, the first three of which build the case (the fourth functioning as a historical closure): part 1, "The City"; part 2, "Roles", part 3, "The Sacred"; and part 4, "The City Destroyed." Her conclusion is this: that the Mexica believed they had to sustain their sacred (natural) forces, or gods, with human flesh (hearts) and blood in order to pay for having been sustained by them and to assure the continuance of this sustenance. This is not entirely new, but the way Clendinnen explains it tries to make sense of it from a Mexica perspective. It is this aspect of the book most readers will find disquieting. It is hard to find analogies, but perhaps one or two will help. Hearing a good defense lawyer ask probing, graphic, yet technical and precise questions of an alleged rape victim on the witness stand, one is moved both to disgust and to admiration. The lawyer tries to get "inside" the experience in order to expose a meaning different from the one attached to the event by the witness. If anthropology has any value, it must try to explain, if not sympathetically then at least empathetically, those practices which even the investigator finds abhorrent in the extreme. Eventually, ethnohistorians will have to try to explain how the gas ovens "worked" in German society during that brief and terrible period in their history, and how the gulag functioned as a part of Stalinist society in the former Soviet Union.

This does not mean Clendinnen approves of the sacrifices, or that she really does not care one way or another. She in fact pauses from time to time to remind her modern reader that she is as horrified as she expects the reader to be at much of what she is describing so coldly and vividly. But moral comment is not her goal. Clendinnen tries instead to present the "interior architecture" of the Mexica social system as a whole, from as close to a Mexica perspective as someone radically divorced in time and space from the events in question can reasonably be expected to achieve. She does this well, but the result is distinctly unnerving, even nauseating. It is not unlike reading graphic news accounts of a serial killer's methods or detailed descriptions of child abuse. What is lacking is an explanation of what motivated the

Mexica while participating in these events. This in spite of the fact that Clendinnen *describes* the affective quite well, injecting statements about what the participants must have been feeling at nearly every opportunity in the discussion. In the end, it may not be entirely Clendinnen's fault. The complex and contradictory feelings of another are finally a private affair, whether on a personal or social level.

Clendinnen has been criticized for drawing the bulk of her analogies for understanding Mexica values and attitudes from other less "developed" (usually North American) Amerindian cultures. The idea here is that the Aztec culture was "high" culture (with a highly developed material culture, art, and even an impressive science when compared with contemporary cultures), and in that way more closely resembled the "high" cultures of the ancient Near East (for example, Egypt, Assyria) than those more genetically, geographically, and temporally proximate.

One thing is certain: Analogies are hard to resist. For whatever reasons, certain (some have said archetypal) conceptual frameworks, motifs, and attitudes are fairly widespread and enduring throughout world cultures, succumbing, it seems, only to that complex of changes commonly subsumed under the title "modern (Western) society." Whether one can blame the Enlightenment, or the Industrial Revolution, or a combination of these and other forces, the gap is there, and it is wide. Certain ancient Greek philosophers may sound modern indeed, but the society in which they lived was not. Clendinnen maps some of the most distinctive areas of Mexica social life and self-understanding, if ultimately failing to explain entirely their most distinctive practice of human sacrifice.

One complex of ideas and attitudes has to do with things considered clean and unclean, and the overlapping of these sets with the sets of things sacred or profane. Modern remnants of these views do not do them justice. While in modern Western societies moral faults are considered "dirty," for example, one does not include in that category physical defects, as would the Mexica and most of the rest of the world's cultures until this century. Still less would this dirtiness be understood as contamination of the regular world from the world of the sacred, a transgressing of boundaries which must be expunged in order to reestablish the proper balance of the cosmos. Thus the ancient Jewish concept that holy scripture "defiled the hands," the Samoan preoccupation with limiting contact with pregnant women, and the Mexica practice of not bathing or cutting one's hair when fasting in preparation for some sacred ceremony, all have at bottom the same concern: to keep the proper relationship between the sacred and the normal spheres. The lines are not moral, they are metaphorical and religious.

Another fundament of Mexica identity is the use of pathos to influence others, and especially the gods. This seems strange in view of the capricious natures these gods or forces were considered to exhibit, but nonetheless there is good evidence in Mexica and other sources that many cultures consider their gods reachable by the dramatic display of emotion and suffering. Clendinnen describes it poignantly, once again using one of her analogies from the Mexica's North American cousins: "The Winnebago protagonist in Paul Radin's *Autobiography of a Winnebago Indian,* deliberately left behind by his parents as they embarked on a fishing trip, pursued them along the shore, running, weeping—until his display of desperation reached a sufficient level of intensity to cause them to turn the canoe in to land, and to take him along. This was not a single episode, but a known strategy; if his passion of longing was sufficiently strong, his parents would yield. Desperate need if sufficiently dramatically expressed worked coercively on the unwilling giver." The biblical account of Elijah and the frantic prophets of Baal comes to mind. For the Mexica, it was the Lord of the Close and Near, Tezcatlipoca, who embodied the capricious but reachable forces they most wished to influence in their favor.

The idea of valuing honor above life is fairly widespread, but the degree of institutionalized forms available for expressing this value in societies such as the Mexica are shocking to anyone not a part of such a culture. The interesting thing about this value, as with so many values, is its contradictory nature. While Amerindian vows of bravery on the battlefield were universally admired, there was also an understanding that the daredevil making such a vow would be protected as much as possible from the most obvious dangers to which he had so rashly subjected himself. To this day in many parts of rural Mexico an offended kinsman is expected to seek out blood vengeance, even for the accidental killing of his relative, and he would be forever shamed if he did not do everything in his power to achieve his end. Yet the very community which would despise him for cowardice for not attempting to gain his revenge is also obligated to try to stop him from carrying it out, perhaps from a deep-seated understanding of the cyclical nature of such a system of violence.

Clendinnen's book is a study in contradictions, from the internal tensions of the Mexica culture to the inherent contradiction of trying to explain from Mexica perspective what it meant to be a part of that society, but doing so in the language of modern ethnohistory, writing of such horrible acts with such studied, glib dispassion. It is amazing that she succeeds at all; in fact, she not only gives readers glimpses into the daily life of the Mexica but also helps them to understand themselves.

Robert A. Bascom

Sources for Further Study

Library Journal. CXVI, October 1, 1991, p. 120.
London Review of Books. XIV, January 9, 1992, p. 15.
Science News. CXL, October 12, 1991, p. 236.

BERNARD SHAW
Volume III: 1918-1950, The Lure of Fantasy

Author: Michael Holroyd (1935-   )
Publisher: Random House (New York). Illustrated. 544 pp. $30.00
Type of work: Literary Biography
Time: 1918-1950
Locale: Principally England

This is the third and final volume of what is certain to be the standard biography of Bernard Shaw, covering the last thirty-two years of his life, in which he became a grand old man of letters while remaining as feisty and controversial as ever

> *Principal personages:*
> GEORGE BERNARD SHAW, the socialist, playwright, critic, pundit, and
>   showman
> CHARLOTTE PAYNE-TOWNSHEND SHAW, his wife
> BLANCHE PATCH, his secretary

On September 5, 1939, at the beginning of Great Britain's involvement in World War II, Bernard Shaw wrote to *The Times* arguing that all actors, variety artists, musicians, and entertainers should be exempted from national service and continue to perform their important professional services. There were probably few at the time who thought that this was a reasonable way to contribute to the war effort, but there were also probably few who were much surprised to see such assertions from Bernard Shaw at a great moment of national crisis. Many people, in fact, likely expected something outrageous from Shaw, even if they were not sure of the form it would take, for Bernard Shaw had become a name. The coverage of any important event in national or international affairs (and many an unimportant one) was never complete without a sparkling quote from the sage of Ayot St. Lawrence. Shaw was always quotable, usually controversial, and frequently challenging.

These years of a secure spot in the national and international consciousness are the subject of this final volume on the long and controversial career of George Bernard Shaw. The first volume, *Bernard Shaw, 1856-1898: The Search for Love* (1988), chronicled his rise from poverty and isolation in Dublin to a measure of dramatic success and involvement with social reform in London. The second volume, *Bernard Shaw, 1898-1918: The Pursuit of Power* (1989), covered the growing reputation of Shaw as dramatist and stalwart of the Fabian Society up to the tarnishing of his public image by his apparently perverse pronouncements on World War I. The final thirty-two years of his life, however, saw him as an established figure of British national life; his position was secure as a grand old man of letters and a prolific commentator on all aspects of national life. The third volume concludes the story (though a further volume of references is scheduled to follow). The subtitle of volume 3 is intended to evoke a dramatic quality found in most of the plays of these years, in which Shaw resorts to visionary pronouncements and scenes and to a number of nonnaturalistic characters and settings. The reader, however, should not take from the subtitle any idea that Holroyd is suggesting that Shaw lived in some sort of dream world.

Holroyd has clearly mastered his subject; more than fifteen years of research have enabled him to present more facts and details of Shaw than any previous biographer has and probably more than any future work will collect. The three volumes are, in some sense, an "official" biography, Holroyd having been chosen by the legatees of the Shaw estate to provide an assessment of Shaw's life and work for a new generation of readers. The life has probably been definitively assessed, but anything like a final assessment of Shaw's work remains to be done. This is not intended as a criticism of Holroyd's work, but rather as an acknowledgment that relatively little literary or dramatic criticism can be combined with the life of one who lived so long and produced so much. Holroyd does deal with the background and circumstances of Shaw's works, particularly the plays, as well as touch on the reception of those works. He does attempt to summarize the ideas that Shaw embodies in particular works, which after a time becomes a bit repetitious, because Shaw's basic ideas changed hardly at all after the late nineteenth century. Holroyd takes some pains to identify sources for characters from the plays with friends and acquaintances of Shaw—especially women. One may quarrel with pronouncements such as that Prola in *The Simpleton of the Unexpected Isles* (1935) was inspired by a vision of Stella Campbell's beauty recollected in tranquility, or that the prime minister's wife in *On The Rocks* (1933) derives from Shaw's mother's indifference to him. While it is certainly true that Shaw often used his friends as partial models for many characters—as the opposed soldiers in *Arms and the Man* (1894) were based on R. B. Cunninghame Graham and Sidney Webb, or Private Meek in *Too True To Be Good* (1932) was based on T. E. Lawrence—Holroyd perhaps a bit too often makes definite ascriptions based on rather thin psychologizing; at the very least, this is one of the places in the book (there are many) where the lack of ready references does leave even the general reader a bit wondering.

As he had in the first two volumes, Holroyd devotes much time and space to Shaw's relations with women. The interpretation of Shaw as an emotionally frustrated man from his earliest days who expressed his needs indirectly through his voluminous outpouring of prose remains a constant in this work. Notable among those with whom Shaw dallied and sparred (mostly on paper) in this portion of his life are Ellen Terry, Nancy Astor, Blanche Patch, his wife Charlotte, Mrs. Patrick Campbell, Molly Tompkins, the Benedictine nun Dame Laurentia McLachlan, and many others.

One of the new and most fascinating elements of this volume is Shaw's involvement with the cinema. Shaw was much taken with the new medium and quickly realized its possibilities. He was reluctant to have his plays filmed for the silent screen (though he had many offers), but when sound came to film he was eager to participate. He was personally involved (sometimes too much so, some of the film people thought) in the filming of five of his plays. Other plays of the canon were discussed for the films, and sometimes scenarios were written, but nothing came of the attempts. Shaw understood well that a stage play was a different sort of thing from a film and undertook to supply proper "cinematic" scenes to make his plays more understandable and effective on the screen. Alas, he was always to be disappointed in the final product. The producers, directors, or distributors had their own ideas of what would work; often Shaw's scenarios were abandoned or altered; the Shavian themes of plays were muddled by farce or sentiment. Yet Shaw kept his faith in the possibilities of the new medium.

Through the whole of this third volume, the dominant note in Shaw's life emerges: he worked! The reader cannot but be impressed by the sheer quantity of material Shaw produced after the age of sixty. He completed at least ten major plays and a number of slighter dramatic efforts; he wrote at least three major prose works; and he conducted a vast correspondence that ran to hundreds of thousands of letters. He could not bear to be idle; when he was ill or truly needed a rest, his wife, his secretary, his housekeepers, and Nancy Astor would conspire to keep visitors and written work away from him—often unsuccessfully. He was always busy and even on vacations and trips would be writing plays or finishing proofs. Shaw is certainly one of the great letter writers of the past one hundred years; he is witty, fertile, and full of good advice combined with trenchant observations on politics, art, the theater, and life. It is not simply that Shaw did a lot of work, but that he was always working. He enjoyed it and certainly saw what he did or planned to do as a commitment he had made to life. In his own life, he was clearly the best walking recommendation for the Life Force.

Alongside this record of work, one must be impressed with the number of friends Shaw had. These were not only the great and the near-great, but often complete unknowns who would write to Shaw for advice and often receive it, perhaps beginning a lengthy correspondence in which the parties never met face to face. It is no wonder that, with friends and acquaintances such as Nancy Astor, Winston Churchill, the heavyweight boxer Gene Tunney, Sidney and Beatrice Webb, Lady Augusta Gregory, hundreds of theatrical folk from producers to actors, Lawrence of Arabia, biographers such as Hesketh Pearson and Archibald Henderson, H. G. Wells, and William Butler Yeats, Shaw came to bestride the first half of the twentieth century. When he traveled, as he frequently did before 1936 (twice going around the world), he acquired more friends and correspondents. He became an international name as well as a British institution. An intriguing facet of Shaw's intercourse with all these thousands of people was, whatever the tenor of the correspondence, the constant urging for them to do and to achieve. Shaw's friendships emphasized those who were doers, who created, who led. It is certainly true that Shaw was often not far from considering what certain people, especially politicians and public personages, could do to advance the various causes of social reform that had occupied Shaw since the nineteenth century. The index of this volume pays tribute to this part of the Shaw record; the great majority of index entries is composed of the names of people. The text itself is full of names, many still recognizable and many pretty well forgotten. This great load of names has two effects upon the book. First, it tends to clog the narrative a bit; the necessity of explaining and introducing many of these people sometimes clogs the main story. Second, the necessary concern for all these people and their relations with Shaw tends to veil and hide the real Shaw a bit; the real, private man who lurked behind the public persona of GBS is not always on view. Certainly, part of the reason for this is to be found in Shaw himself, who was sparing of intimate personal revelations and who was almost always aware that he was on public display.

This great accumulation and cultivation of so many friends resulted in a wide variety of opinions about Shaw the man. Many found him hard-hearted and cold-blooded; this was especially true when Shaw was dealing with or commenting on groups or people in some sort of aggregate. On the other hand, many commented on Shaw's constant concern, his personal charm, his excellent manners, no matter with whom he was dealing. While Shaw could seem unfeeling to many, Holroyd records numerous instances of Shaw's personal benevolence to individuals, the loaning or outright granting of money for education or a needed operation, often given anonymously, behind the recipient's back, and always with absolute lack of publicity. Shaw was certainly one who shielded his personal charities, a fact that should be remembered by those who dismiss him as nothing more than a showman and public clown.

In addition to the great roster of friends and the record of productive work, there is a note of sadness in this final volume. Not only does Shaw grow older and more subject to the infirmities of age, but also there is through these years a note of disillusion. Shaw's faith, essentially a late nineteenth century faith, that his generation could change the world was fading. Shaw has, as the years pass, less and less belief that the Fabian socialism to which he had devoted so much would become the system of the day. In short, people were not listening to the serious messages Shaw used his comic genius to present. As essentially a Victorian, Shaw shared with such as Thomas Carlyle, John Ruskin, and Matthew Arnold a positive genius for acute analysis of the prevailing ills of society and humankind, but those Victorians were less successful at providing practical solutions for those ills. Shaw was probably not much different. Shaw's ideas changed little over the years. While his vehicles were often amusing and insightful, their tenor was the same from play to play and from one prose work to the next. As a result, Shaw came to seem to the newer generations more and more irrelevant; there was a feeling that time had passed him by. To this may be added the common plight of those who are essentially serious comic writers: The audience is so taken with the comedy or the unconventionality or the wit that the serious messages get ignored. It was as if no one was listening any longer, and Shaw had spent a whole very calculated career getting people to listen.

The result in the plays of the period is a darkening vision, a turning from democracy. More and more, Shaw turns away from his traditional short-term solution for humankind—socialism—and toward his long-term solution—Creative Evolution. It is this great admiration for the strength of will that leads Shaw into what many considered to be excessive admiration for the totalitarian leaders of the day, Mussolini, Hitler, and Stalin. In the plays, this vision results in an emphasis on those characters who have the will and the energy to act, to accomplish. The plays represent a kind of search by Shaw for leaders; since democracy fails to throw up leaders, then leaders must come forth on their own and take charge—whether the leader be King Magnus or Private Meek. Shaw's more "fascist" views in this period can certainly be explained and accounted for, but perhaps not so easily excused. It is because of some of these views that Shaw is seen as cold-hearted. Shaw, while never uncontroversial, continued to preach the same message as he had from his earliest public appearances: humankind has fallen in love with ideals, with patriotism, romance, parenthood, and even democracy, and shall never straighten out itself or its society until it comes to a proper understanding of its true natural history. Shaw's constant concern was to provide this true natural history.

Holroyd's three volumes are certain to be the standard work on Shaw's life; they are as long and fascinating as was the career of their subject. Holroyd's biography, with its emphasis on Shaw's work and energy, captures the spirit of the man. The book interests and even intrigues, both in its overall accomplishment and in many of its individual parts.

Gordon N. Bergquist

Sources for Further Study

Boston Globe. October 20, 1991, p. 16.
Chicago Tribune. October 27, 1991, XIV, p. 1.
The Economist. CCCXXI, October 26, 1991, p. 113.
Library Journal. CXVI, October 1, 1991, p. 112.
Los Angeles Times. October 10, 1991, p. E12.
New Statesman and Society. IV, September 6, 1991, p. 37.
The New York Times Book Review. XCVI, October 20, 1991, p. 3.
The Spectator. CCLXVII, August 31, 1991, p. 21.
The Times Literary Supplement. September 6, 1991, p. 6.
The Washington Post Book World. XXI, October 6, 1991, p. 1.

BET THEY'LL MISS US WHEN WE'RE GONE

Author: Marianne Wiggins (1947-   )
Publisher: HarperCollins (New York). 180 pp. $19.98
Type of work: Short stories

A dramatization of the causes and effects of vulnerability

Like her most recent works, the novel *John Dollar* (1989) and the story collection *Herself in Love* (1987), Marianne Wiggins' *Bet They'll Miss Us When We're Gone* is concerned with vulnerable characters.

Angel, the eleven-year-old protagonist of "Angel," has been abandoned by her parents. Her maternal grandmother, Fanny, takes care of her. If they are close, it is not through words at first, for Fanny does not speak Angel's English nor Angel Fanny's Greek, though they do share a small vocabulary in both languages.

Fanny's husband, Papou, has died, and her sons' marriages are tragic. Her son George is put in jail for murdering his wife Brenda's lover, and Brenda leaves him. Jeanette, the wife of Fanny's son Archie, is killed in a car accident. Cat, the wife of her son Nick, dies of a stomach ailment. None of these women, whom Fanny collectively calls "the Dots" after her son Mike's wife Dot, has children, which is a further, and even more basic, disappointment to her.

That something good can come from death itself Ray Gould, the undertaker who lives next door, shows Angel in his deft use of makeup on cadavers and in his bringing flowers left over from funerals to the house. He functions as an image pointing out that the living need lovely memories of the dead.

Angel translates this into the bits and pieces she collects from departure and death—Brenda's old lipstick, for example, which this "Dot" gives her when murder drives her from her marriage, and Cat's "Miss Conviviality" trophy, which she won when she was young. These objects help Angel to keep her missing parents in her memory.

Fanny and Angel need each other for two reasons. The first is practical: Angel needs a mother, and Fanny needs a helper. Angel gives Fanny (who is a diabetic) her injections, helps her clean the rugs each week, and acts as a translator for her when she visits George in jail.

The second and more important reason is emotional. This need is made plain at the story's end, when Angel and Fanny, alone in the house, share their mementoes with each other. Words do not have to be understood to be felt in this scene. By holding Fanny's wedding shawl while Fanny speaks of her marriage, Angel understands what the past means to her grandmother. By holding Angel's treasures while Angel tells stories about them, Fanny understands what they mean to her granddaughter. These objects, memories, and words fuse to reveal a vulnerable love and to counteract loss.

"Zelf-Portret," "Croeso I Gymru," "Shibboletboo," and "Grocer's Daughter" present characters whose identities are vulnerable. In these stories, language itself assumes the task of rescuing identity.

"Zelf-Portret" is drenched in a frustration that would be despair if it were not for the story's wordplay. The narrator says, "What breaks the heart in the end are the facts, not the fiction." She seems to mean that what happens in life, including the act of writing, has no true identity outside itself.

Art tries to overcome this fact. It uses analogy to do so, but it fails, for analogy is "lies . . . beginning from that line . . . where it touches at another zelf." This "zelf" (identity) can be the writer's own, which, in this story, is both the woman who rides a train in The Netherlands and visits Anne Frank's hiding place there and the woman who needs to write about this and about writing about it.

If the second "zelf" is closer to the reader than the first because it happens in the writer's tussle with words on the page, it is still only an illusion, for the writer's experience of this frustrating project is no longer going on; it is the past. Even when it was going on, it was self-contained, partly because the past instantly claimed it.

This is true of Anne Frank and Hieronymous Bosch, too, for Frank's attic room, her pictures, and her diary are not the feelings she had nor the death that came to her, and Bosch's paintings are not the visions that disturbed him into making them.

No wonder the narrator dotes on death, for which her allusions and puns let one see but cannot let one feel her feeling. She spends much of the story's time on Anne Frank's absence and annihilation, words such as the "nether" in Netherlands and the "low" in Low Country, and especially on the letter "z," as in last (the last letter of the alphabet), going nowhere (the Dutch *z.o.z.*, meaning "continue"), slipperiness (the Dutch word *zee*, meaning "sea"), and experience (self, damned to ending where it begins, as the narrator shows by substituting "z" for "s" in the word).

Marianne Wiggins was once married to Salman Rushdie, an experience that forms the background of "Croeso I Gymru." "The president of a bankrupt desert nation," an "aged psychopath," as the narrator calls him, has demanded her husband's death for writing a book that he (the Ayatollah Khomeini, of course) finds blasphemous, and to save themselves, the couple goes into hiding in Wales. To the narrator, this exile means an identity cancelled by a fear of words and an identity regained by a love of words.

The narrator says, alluding to Julius Caesar's commentary on the Celts' view of the power of writing, "those who could write of . . . rite and of worship . . . must be feared." She imputes this fear to her husband's enemy, and it makes her wonder, *"What are words made of?"*

All she knows is that learning, at least in her case, depends on words, and that without learning, and writing down what she wants to and does learn, she is the no one that her husband's would-be assassin has forced her to pretend to be.

Thus she learns as much as she can about Wales, especially its language. *Dafad* means "sheep," *dyfodol* "future," *marw* "dead," she finds out, and in her hunger to know as much as she can about where she is, she roams the hills, visits the towns, broods on the pictures and legends on coins, and searches out the minutiae in the local newspaper such as the doings of women's clubs—their charming competitions, for example, like the one "for an unusual pebble." In this way, the narrator tries to find in words a form of saying "yes" and "I," not "no" and "no one"; to find, in short, herself.

An identity denied is at the heart of "Shibboletboo." To the town that the narrator, speaking in patois, seems to represent, Boo, the main character in the story, has a silent identity, for she is dead when the story opens, and during her life she was mute.

Her real name was Nancy, and the reason she was called "Boo" was that her older brother and sister, Jimmy Junior ("Major") and Lorelei ("The Spinster"), spoke a private language as children that Nancy could not learn, since they would not help her. (This language was based on substituting "boo" for the last letters or syllables of words.)

This suffix became Nancy's nickname (in fact, her only name); it also is the word for why she did not speak. She had, in the town's mind, no identity other than "Boo." Her siblings are at fault for this, for they failed to love her. Without love, there is silence. Without speech, the real self vanishes from view.

This is not entirely true, however, in Boo's case. While those who were at her funeral are at her brother's house afterward, a revelation about her arrives when her friend Ray announces that her last words were, "Ray? *Why* is men behabe so nast?"

So she could speak, and though her use of the word "nasty" pays tribute to the childhood language by dropping the last letter, it does not put "boo" in its place. Boo's question thus shows the cause of her trouble (the suffix "boo") and her refusal to be, in her self, defined by it.

"Grocer's Daughter" is mostly a character sketch of the narrator's father, John Wiggins, and it means to make up in written words—which are natural to the narrator but were not to her father—for the "unfinished business" she has with him.

She means that she never fully told him of her love for him. As a child, all she could do was absorb what he was and did, and what he taught her. For example, he taught her "how to pitch softball . . . how to spot a plant called preacher-in-the-pulpit . . . how to drive a car . . . to ride a bike." He also gave her maxims, such as, "Keep your feet off other people's furniture," "Go nowhere in a hurry," "Sing," and especially, "Don't waste."

What was he that she now understands was part of their distance from each other? His "life was landlocked. . . . Water was not an element he knew, except as rain on crops." Also, he had never, as far as she knew, seen an island. She, in contrast, is writing her memorial of him on an island (England) "where all roads lead to water."

What does she do, besides writing, to close this distance? As a farmer's son and a grocer, her father gave her advice about vegetables, which she follows now by planting "only what my family guarantees to eat." When she cooks, she wears "grocer's aprons."

Describing what her father was as a person is the main task of love to which the narrator sets her words. By using words to express how much she misses him, how morally solid he was, how he liked to play jokes, laugh, and sing, even how he always "wore pleated pants in dark colors," she recovers his identity from death, which is only proper, since, as she says, his only motive was life.

Vulnerability and memory often go together in *Bet They'll Miss Us When We're Gone.* Old age makes Harry in "A Cup of Jo" and Nina in "Rex" vulnerable. Both characters have trouble communicating what they remember—Harry to his niece and Nina to her daughter, Pat. For them, life is a feeling embedded in recollections that senility, in Harry's case, and being lost, in Nina's (a storm has interrupted her flight to see two of her daughters), bring to the fore in them.

Harry recalls a fishing trip he once went on to the Snake River with his now-dead friend Joey; the sensations of that event, triggered by the smell of hot coffee, are as strong as they were in the past, and seem to summarize what life at its best meant to Harry.

Nina recalls the questions her daughter Pat asked when she was a child; the difficulty of answering them, triggered by Pat's abrupt questions about Nina's accidental companion Ed in the airport (perhaps in a dream Nina may be having there), seems to reveal to Nina how hard it is to make sense out of life, let alone to communicate the feeling it comes down to in her.

The death of his wife, Marlene, makes Carl Tanner vulnerable in "Balloons 'N' Tunes." To deal with this, he talks to her as though she were still alive; to support the illusion that she is, he hangs her bra on a window, gets drunk, and dismisses the sane interruption of a neighbor, Dolores. His excuse for opposing his vulnerability by denying death is that he could not fulfill Marlene's last wish, which was for her ashes to be spread on the Appomattox River. As Carl was doing this, a truck with "Balloons 'N' Tunes" lettered on the side rushed by, creating a wind that scattered the ashes away from the river. The occurrence, random and mysterious, gives Carl's grief an exit, as it were, from acceptance into fantasy. The unforeseen intervention of the truck is crazy, and this allows him to be crazy, too, to make what is remembered what is actually going on.

In "Counting," Mildred, a retired chemistry teacher, is vulnerable because she is old and alone. She defends herself by counting up the violent deaths reported in newspapers and by spending a lot of her time in supermarkets.

In "Evolution," Vy, an amateur actress, is vulnerable because she fears the future— generally the end of the world, and particularly the corruption of her daughter Cicely through "mutagens" in her food. She is comforted by turning off dripping faucets and, in the end, by making "A Real Loud Noise" to Cicely so that she'll take her mother seriously.

In "Eso Es," Modesto is "a shy man who loves birds." He is afraid of women and especially of strangers. In fact, it seems he is, unknown to himself, an angel. This fact makes him vulnerable to the weight and noise of the world, dramatized by the fireworks that frighten the birds of Zaragoza, Spain, and by Modesto's uncle, a loud-mouthed and gluttonous "eye doctor." Modesto thinks he himself is trying to stop the fireworks to save the birds, but he is really signaling heaven to rescue him; that happens when an angel kills Modesto's pet birds and Modesto himself.

Whether trapped or solaced by memory or language, or both, or by personal quirks, the characters in *Bet They'll Miss Us When We're Gone* cannot escape vulnerability itself. This makes it easy to feel akin to them and easy to like them. In turn, that helps to make up for the fact that plot often goes nowhere in these stories, which sometimes seem more concerned with the writer herself than with the tale she is telling.

Mark McCloskey

Sources for Further Study

Boston Globe. July 4, 1991, p. 49.
Kirkus Reviews. LIX, April 15, 1991, p. 505.
Library Journal. CXVI, June 1, 1991, p. 198.
Los Angeles Times. May 30, 1991, p. E8.
The New York Times Book Review XCVI, June 30, 1991, p. 9.
Publishers Weekly. CCXXXVIII, May 3, 1991, p. 61.
San Francisco Chronicle. June 30, 1991, p. REV4.
Vogue. CLXXXI, July, 1991, p. 85.
The Wall Street Journal. July 19, 1991, p. A9.
The Washington Post Book World. XXI, June 9, 1991, p. 10.

BETWEEN THE CHAINS

Author: Turner Cassity (1929-   )
Publisher: University of Chicago Press (Chicago). 84 pp. $22.00; paperback $8.95
Type of work: Poetry

An ironic view of deterministic factors in human behavior

In *Between the Chains*, Turner Cassity continues to display the taste for ideas, irony, meter, and rhyme shown in *Hurricane Lamp* (1986) and his six other volumes of poetry. In the title poem, the "chains" are those once used to block off a street in Johannesburg. To Cassity, these chains are various habits, one might say, by which humans are bound.

Memory, since it is a theme that begins and ends the book, invites one to see it as chains between which the ironically juxtaposed urges to let go and to hold back take place. "Persistence of Memory," the first poem in the book, says that "the chains of masochism prompt" us to remember what we would rather forget: "Trash, payments, locks," as well as sickness and death. In "Hedy Lamarr and a Chocolate Bar," the narrator speaks of the control the unreachable female had over him when he was a boy watching Hedy Lamarr in a movie—and still has, he suggests, because memory keeps this event alive in him.

"Links," "Invitations," and "Laying It on the Line," at the end of the book, return the poet to his memory. "Links" refers both to the smoke rings that the poet's grandfather blew and to poetry. The smoke rings are an image for how the poet is bound to an urge to perform like his grandfather. He says, "I . . . Redeem my breath from utter shapelessness." The irony here is the ephemeral nature of what he is bound by.

Such tenuous but binding phenomena appear elsewhere in the book. In "Invitations," the poet remembers the neighborhood in which he grew up; he finds "ambition" and the "willingness to learn and try" gone from those who stayed there. If he himself has escaped such failure, he cannot escape the memory of it, nor, in "Laying It on the Line," the memory of a failed love. He says, "I was in love with you/ a long time;/ I am still," and he assures this lover (and the reader) that "just for you,/ just once, I broke my meter."

"Ruth Keelikolani (1883)" and "On Several Photographs of Nikola Tesla" show characters who are prisoners. In the first poem, a Hawaiian princess is a prisoner of tradition ("the old Hawaiian ways") and commits suicide in honor of it. In the second poem, the inventor of alternating current is a prisoner of the future in that he dreams ahead of his time. He is also obsessed with "feeding pigeons." For both reasons, his inventions are stolen, and he backs out of a marriage to "J. P. Morgan's daughter"; he is, that is to say, a prisoner of the impractical—ironically, of his own genius.

Economic power is a chain that binds humans. The mansions of the rich may fall apart, but the capitalists whom they symbolize continue to enslave others in "Power

Failure." "Bank Notes," in saying, "in its simplicity of greed/ The Banque de l'Indo-Chine . . . looks increasingly to be,/ Of their and our more recent wars, a clear first cause," seems to mean that those who control the means of survival (money) cause desolation. "Parlor Song" is about a racism so binding that those who tell stories about it see themselves in the stories as its victims when they are not: "The anecdotes of slights/ And beatings are laid now on their own flesh."

The irony implicit in capitalism and racism takes other forms in human life as well. "Acid Rain on Sherwood Forest," for example, insists that it is as natural for humans to invent weapons as to create pension plans for the workers who make the weapons. In "Inducted," the young men who are the promise of life are the perennial prisoners of armies that are the promise of death. In a lighter vein, "Campion in Uniform" juxtaposes Thomas Campion's cherries, an image of sexual desire, against misordered army food, an image of tedium, while "For the Scrapbook of Mrs. Charles Black" puts side by side a soldier's need for release from routine and an army camp town's refusal to give him anything stronger to drink than a "champagne cocktail."

Army life is also the subject of "Mainstreaming." This poem features several ironies. A company in Fort Jackson is full of "borderline retardees," for example, some of whom manage to get blown up in a grenade accident. One of the members of this company is Connor Kennington, the narrator's friend, who has rebelled against his family by joining "the ranks" of the army; that is, he has traded a world of privilege for one of idiocy. The good luck that his background suggests, however, sees to it that he is assigned to Hawaii after basic training, while the idiots in his company are doomed to Korea.

In some of Cassity's poems, vice is a target for irony. "The Incorruptible" shows a high school band on its way to a competition in Kansas City. The chaperon-narrator muses on the sin for which this city is famous and on the naïveté that insulates the teenagers in his charge from it. He also imagines the irony of these innocents, on an outing to temptation in their youth, turning "into Pillars of Society" after they are old enough to have experienced vice. "Publicans and Sinners," on the other hand, locates irony in social distinction, making fun of the latter by pointing out that the only difference between the upper and lower class is the glamour of the vice they both practice: "Bright green casino felt or grubby dice,/ The difference, at last, is imprecise," says the poet. Cassity presents another social irony in "Texarkana," where the "cowboys" in the Texas half of this city "carouse," while the people in the Arkansas half "Have quiet vices, or have none." Alluding to the Berlin Wall, the poet does not find opposites side by side in human nature surprising.

Cassity brings up the mind in his book. The mind is another ironic chain in that knowing too little, and wanting to know too much, can make people fools—namely, prisoners.

That the character addressed in "An Attempt to Explain Anorexia Nervosa to Lillian Russell" responds in punctuation and a dollar sign to what the narrator tells her shows her to be a prisoner of ignorance. Plump, rich, and in love with fancy cuisine, she knows nothing about a disease inimical to what she is and wants, and in this way she is an image of how pleasure and good fortune can determine the extent of our thinking.

Sometimes, though, ignorance, ironically pretending to be knowledge, binds us to charlatans. "Knowledge Is Power, But Only If You Misuse It" says that as long as we think we can know the future or read one another's minds, there will be those who will oblige by tricking us.

If so many things rule who we are, what we want, and how we behave, then choice does not mean much. "Other Directed" (a parody of Robert Frost's "The Road Not Taken") and "One of the Boys" (a parody of Thom Gunn's "My Sad Captains") make fun of choice. The first poem says that, since the world is awful, one should choose an easy path in it; the second poem says that those who choose romantic role models are silly, since they will have to become practical, whether they like it or not, as they get older.

Many poems in *Between the Chains* are in blank verse, and a good many in a kind of hexameter version of blank verse. When Cassity writes in stanzas, they are regular in that they are repeated, and they are frequently rhymed. "Links," "Between the Chains," "Texarkana," "Mathematics Is Never Any Help," and "One of the Boys" are in rhymed couplets—the first in iambic pentameter/tetrameter, the second in iambic tetrameter, the third in iambic tetrameter/trimeter, the fourth in heroic couplets, and the fifth in iambic hexameter. "Persistence of Memory" and "Power Failure" are in unrhymed triplets; longer stanzas structure "Fin de Siècle" (quatrains), "Publicans and Sinners" (five-line stanzas), "Invitations" and "The Incorruptible" (six-line stanzas), and "Campion in Uniform" (seven-line stanzas). All these poems are rhymed, though the last rhymes only the first and last lines of its two stanzas.

The prosodic strictures of Cassity's poems are, one suspects, one of the "chains" he alludes to in the title of the book. To judge from the satirical glee of his tone in general and the frequently pedagogical stance he takes, Cassity is happily bound to this prosody. On the one occasion he abandons it, in "Laying It on the Line," the last poem in the book, in which he admits to using free verse as a ruse to conceal a disappointed love, he cannot help but return to meter at the end—iambic pentameter, in fact. He refers to a lack of meter as the "equivalent of opening my veins," then says, "But as you see, the beat keeps coming back."

Though Turner Cassity's poems do more to distance than shake the reader, they are refreshing insofar as they say things ingenious at least and incisive at most about a world larger than the poet himself, and do so in rhythms skillfully lifted above the level of prose.

If, finally, a little of the prissy and self-satisfied belittles the tone of Cassity's poetry, such poems in the book as "The Incorruptible," "An Attempt to Explain Anorexia Nervosa to Lillian Russell," and "Links" outflank this tone, for their humor is more indigenous to their themes than pressed upon them.

Mark McCloskey

Sources for Further Study

Lambda Book Report. II, September, 1991, p. 37.
The New York Times Book Review. XCVI, December 8, 1991, p. 7.
Publishers Weekly. CCXXXVIII, May 3, 1991, p. 68.

BIOGRAPHY

Author: Celia Gitelson
Publisher: Alfred A. Knopf (New York). 260 pp. $19.00
Type of work: Novel
Time: The 1990's
Locale: New York City and Bennington, Vermont

A comic yet sad story of a biographer's involvement with his subject, superbly balanced between two lives that turn out to be doubles of each other

> *Principal characters:*
> RAPHAEL ALTER, a seasoned biographer, known for his sensitive portraits of American poets, now at work on a biography of Maxwell Leibert
> ANGEL MUÑOZ, the dedicated superintendent of Alter's Manhattan apartment building
> CHLOE, Maxwell Leibert's young mistress
> ULYSSES (LEE) LEIBERT, the dead poet's son and executor of his literary estate
> SAM PINTCHIK, Maxwell Leibert's editor
> DR. ERICH SALLINGER, Maxwell Leibert's psychiatrist
> TRUMAN SWANBERG, a retired professor of eschatology and one of Maxwell Leibert's drinking buddies
> SIMON LEIPZIG, one of Raphael Alter's tenants and the survivor of a concentration camp, who becomes Alter's responsibility after a heart attack
> MARTIN ASWITH, one of Raphael Alter's tenants, whose sick daughter Alter briefly tends

Raphael Alter has chosen a way of life (so he thinks) that insulates him from the attentions of others. After acquiring a Ph.D. and working briefly for a Manhattan advertising agency, he settles comfortably into a career as a biographer, living off the rents of a Manhattan apartment building inherited from his father and shipping off his mother to a retirement home in Florida. Alter devotes most of his time to research, maintaining as much distance from his renters as possible, ignoring their complaints about the dilapidated building and making only cosmetic repairs. He senses that the building is crumbling about him, but he cannot summon the energy or the interest to rehabilitate either it or his increasingly inadequate life, which he begins to realize is almost utterly devoid of any true human contact.

Alter's interest in biography stems from his family background. He remembers listening behind doors to his parents, trying to figure out their lives. This was an especially difficult task because his father was a gambler who rarely revealed his real life, which included several mistresses, some of whom lived in the apartment building he had won during a week-long poker game. Accustomed to his father's secrecy and apparently enjoying the task of ferreting out lives, Alter has made a life of biography and not much else. He leaves his telephone number unlisted—an odd thing for a biographer to do—because he does not want to be harassed by late-night telephone calls from friends of his biographical subjects who may have a grievance.

Things begin to change when Alter is contacted by Chloe (she is given no last name in the novel), who reluctantly offers herself as a source of information on Maxwell Leibert. She agrees to meet Alter but does not, at their first meeting, tell him what it is she knows about the poet. Accustomed to coaxing information out of his interviewees, Alter proceeds slowly, trying to win Chloe's trust while also combing through Leibert's journals and correspondence looking for clues to Chloe's significance.

Chloe is not like Alter's other sources, for she does not seem self-serving. Unlike Leibert's son Ulysses, for example, she does not try to manipulate what the biographer has to say about his subject. Ulysses specializes in inviting Alter to his apartment, offering documents that he wants to share with Alter, and complaining when the biographer does not want to treat the biography as a joint effort. Dr. Erich Sallinger, Leibert's psychiatrist, not only withholds information from Alter (invoking confidentiality) but misleads the biographer about Leibert's desperate state of mind. Sallinger even charges the biographer for interviews as though he were a patient. Others write Alter asking for money for letters, treating the biographer as though he were in charge of Leibert's estate.

Used to these various ploys, Alter has developed a noncommittal attitude, never rejecting these advances from his sources or their bids for attention but slowly working himself into their lives, ingratiating himself until the price he finally has to pay is quite moderate, in both emotional and financial terms. He takes the same tack with his tenants who pester him about repairs. Feigning sympathy, promising improvements, he does almost nothing, relying on his dutiful superintendent, Angel Muñoz, to keep the building functioning, if only at the most minimal level.

None of this squalor matters much to Alter until he begins to realize that something is missing from both his sense of himself and of Leibert. Many loose ends dog Alter. What has happened to Leibert's second wife? She has disappeared and no one can locate her. What has happened to Leibert's last manuscript, a cycle of poems inspired by the work of the poet's friend, the noted scholar of eschatology Truman Swanberg, a favorite drinking buddy of Leibert's who insists that Leibert did not merely talk about this new work but had a substantial portion of it written before he was run over by a car.

Alter begins to put the loose ends together when Chloe decides she will reveal a secret about Leibert that will fundamentally change the biographer's view of his subject. When she proposes to meet Leibert in his apartment, he is disconcerted, realizing that she will have the opportunity to judge him and to make up her mind about what she will tell him. Yet Alter has no choice, since to refuse her is to risk losing her information. There is also some indication that Alter had become interested in Chloe and is trying to gauge what it is about her that might have attracted Leibert. Later, Dr. Sallinger will suggest that Alter is, in fact, living through Leibert, imagining what he does not have the talent or the energy to accomplish for himself. Significantly, Alter does not protest this analysis of his character.

For the first time in years, Alter cleans his apartment, scraping away years of grime, throwing out the detritus of his minimal existence, creating a space, so to speak, for another person. It is at Alter's apartment that Chloe proposes a trip to Vermont, still refusing to say what they will find there and insisting it is the only way that she can reveal to Alter (and make him understand) what it is about Leibert that cannot be merely put into words for the biographer's convenience. In total control, Chloe informs Alter that she will contact him when the arrangements for the trip are settled.

In the meantime, Alter begins to undergo a transformation. He actually listens to his tenants and takes an interest in their lives. He is amazed when one of them, Martin Aswith, comments on his biographies, for Alter has not imagined that anyone in the building has read them. For the first time, Aswith tells him, Alter has a look in his face that invites confidences, and so the tenant expresses his pleasure in Alter's books.

In some sense, all biographies bring the dead back to life. The irony, in Alter's case, is that he has been dead inside for a long time. In his own life, he has withdrawn into what he admits is a "self-imposed autism." He is the biographer as bystander. He yearns for more of an involvement with others, but it is only with Chloe—a source he has had to woo constantly—that he begins to see that his life can change only if he is willing to resuscitate himself. To do so will require the messiness of involvement in the lives of others and the abandonment of the biographical distance that safely sequesters him in documents and in the conventional routines of his interviews.

Alter stays with Aswith, who has a sick child, remaining in the room when the tenant falls asleep and cradling the child in his arms while her father rests. Far more dramatic is the collapse of one of his older tenants, Simon Leipzig, whom Alter literally brings back to life with mouth-to-mouth resuscitation, a stimulating experience for Alter once he gets past his initial repugnance.

Yet Alter almost balks when he finds that Chloe has brought him to Vermont to stay the night in the house Leibert occupied while teaching at Bennington College. Not knowing what to expect, Alter instinctively shies away from entering the house, realizing that he has become too close to his subject and may find out more than he is willing to write about. Chloe, however, is thinking as much about herself as she is about Leibert. There is something about Leibert that can be explained only by visiting the house and making Alter a witness to the past.

What Alter finds cannot be revealed without destroying the shock value of the novel's final pages. It does radically change his view of Leibert, making it impossible for him to finish the biography—not because of any lack of sympathy for the poet, although what Alter finds is gruesome, but because he has learned too much about his subject. He has become a part of Leibert's biography in a way that destroys his objectivity and his ability to tell a life as a story. Leibert's life becomes something that has happened to Alter and changes Alter's view of himself.

Rather than finishing the biography, Alter decides to repair his building, setting about purchasing materials that he can ill afford given the meager revenue from his rent-controlled apartments. Before he can renovate, however, the building next door crashes into Alter's, and he and his superintendent have just enough time to evacuate the tenants, with Alter promising a new building financed by the damages he expects to collect.

It may seem like a lighthearted ending, but it is true to the deft tragicomic touch Celia Gitelson employs throughout the novel. There are many comic scenes in which Alter's tenants recount their tales of woe, but such scenes are true to the way stories of misfortune are often presented to a biographer who is used to listening to the unfortunate and finding a way to manage their stories in prose. Gitelson has a good ear for dialogue and uses the superintendent as a kind of chorus. Angel Muñoz is a hardworking, sensitive, and moral man, but he is also a realist, telling the reformed Alter that his tenants will not thank him for renovating the building.

Gitelson, who lives in Manhattan, has an unfailing grasp of the way its people talk and of the harried quality of urban existence. She does not sentimentalize the older people in the apartment house, nor does she make it easy for Alter to change his ways. The tension between the biographer and his world, in other words, is finely tuned; it is easy to see why Alter stays away from trouble, from entanglements with both his tenants and his interviewees, but it is also credible that his wariness wears him down, making him seem to himself a man without vital connections to his own world hoping to lose himself in the past and to live through his subjects. Alter's realization that he is Leibert's double, that the only pattern he has given his life is that of his subject, ratifies his sense of emptiness. Thus he cannot complete his biography of Leibert without risking perhaps the extinction of himself.

In a final clever stroke, Gitelson shows what Alter's future will be like by including a bibliography of his books. It is by the work Alter chooses to complete that his story is truly known. One of the books is *Maxwell Leibert: Journals, 1945-1974*, edited by Raphael and Chloe Alter, with an afterword by Ulysses Leibert. This novel is a rare case in which the subject, not the biographer, has the last word.

Carl Rollyson

Sources for Further Study

Booklist. LXXXVII, August, 1991, p. 2099.
Boston Globe. August 24, 1991, p. 10.
Chicago Tribune. September 1, 1991, XIV, p. 5.
Kirkus Reviews. LIX, July 1, 1991, p. 809.
Library Journal. CXVI, August, 1991, p. 144.
The New York Times Book Review. XCVI, September 8, 1991, p. 24.
Publishers Weekly. CCXXXVIII, July 5, 1991, p. 55.
The Village Voice. November 19, 1991, p. 72.
The Wall Street Journal. October 15, 1991, p. A20.
The Washington Post Book World. XXI, September 15, 1991, p. 3.

THE BIRTH OF THE MODERN
World Society 1815-1830

Author: Paul Johnson (1928-   )
Publisher: HarperCollins (New York). 1095 pp. $35.00
Type of work: History
Time: 1815-1830
Locale: Worldwide

The author provides a sweeping assessment of the changes in world society that helped shape the modern consciousness and modern political and social systems

Reading *The Birth of the Modern: World Society 1815-1830* is like going for a visit to the British Museum; the reader, like the museum-goer, is almost immediately overwhelmed with the equivalent of curios and artifacts that give visitors an idea of life in an exciting past. In the twelve lengthy chapters of his study of world society from 1815 to 1830, historian Paul Johnson surveys the development of the special relationship between the United States and Great Britain; the completion of the Congress of Vienna, which provided a framework for modern nation-states to establish world hegemony through their colonial activities; the emergence of Great Britain as the world's policeman; the decline of the wilderness in America and elsewhere as advances in transportation, communications, and science allowed people to shrink the globe; the changing relationships between the sexes; the growth of independence movements in places such as South and Central America; the development of new political and social philosophies; the emergence of the artist as a champion of political causes; the impact of irrational monetary policies in America and Western Europe; and the final triumph of democracy as an idea for government that captured near-universal attention and widespread acceptance.

The sweep of this study is broad, but it is counterbalanced by the author's decision to limit his investigation to the fifteen years that immediately followed two events that he sees as having been decisive in ushering in the modern era: the defeat of Napoleon at Waterloo and the American victory over the British invasion force at New Orleans. Naturally, there are inherent difficulties in trying to limit one's investigations by any set of beginning and ending dates, no matter how convenient the bracketing seems on the surface. What one soon discovers is that events of a year or a decade earlier play too significant a role to ignore, and the impact of events within the "window" are so important that they cannot be left without mention. Within these artificial time limits, the author has expanded his study beyond horizons normally fixed by historians, choosing to look not at a single country or region of the globe but at the entire world as it changed during what Johnson sees as crucial years of development. Hence, though Johnson's study is more narrowly focused, it recalls Daniel Boorstin's *The Discoverers* (1983) in its sweeping look at the way an idea can take hold of an age and transform peoples throughout the world. In Boorstin's book, such ideas are manifold and are rooted in technology. In *The Birth of the Modern*, a single political idea is seen emerging from myriad technological and sociological changes occurring simultaneously around the globe during these fifteen years: the idea of democracy.

What readers may find surprising are the many innovations and "firsts" that emerge from these fifteen years. Naturally, Johnson is quick to catalog them for his readers: the first modern police state, created by Napoleon (actually established before 1815, of course); the first use by a Western power of superior technology to subdue a nonwhite population; the first instance of gunboat diplomacy, employed by the British to help abolish slavery; the first time in history that people saw science as providing a way out of "the suffering and degradation" that had seemed "inherent in the human condition." The period also saw the birth of modern electioneering, the first truly popular election (the 1828 United States presidential contest), the growth of public opinion and the press in determining affairs of state, and the rise of ministerial government, in which ministers supplanted sovereigns as the real powers in the management of political affairs.

Johnson is particularly good at sketching characters—great and small—in a few brief paragraphs. In the first pages of the book, he treats readers to a portrait of the American general Andrew Jackson, hero of the Battle of New Orleans, which ushered in the era about which Johnson writes (Jackson returns much later as the central figure in the first truly democratic presidential election in his country). There are, among hundreds, sketches of British traveler and novelist Frances Trollope; the painter Francisco de Goya; Henry, the third Earl Bathurst, an important but not always remembered political figure who helped shape the British Empire from his post in the colonial office; British prime ministers George Canning, Robert Stewart, Viscount Castlereagh, and Frederick Robinson; the Duke of Wellington, the Empire's hero and symbol of Toryism during the period; philosopher Georg Wilhelm Friedrich Hegel; novelist George Sand (one of several women portrayed); entrepreneur Thomas Stamford Raffles; and composers Ludwig van Beethoven ("one of the central pillars of the modern"), Gioacchino Rossini, and Felix Mendelssohn. It is as if Johnson has expanded the doctrine that history is merely the record of the lives of great men to include great women and some not-so-great men and women as well.

Throughout the study, Johnson uses certain figures as touchstones for grounding his thesis that the world during this period was on an inevitable path toward democratization and the liberation of the human spirit from the intellectual bonds that had enslaved it for centuries. Not surprisingly, the English Romantic poets reappear in virtually every chapter. While John Keats plays only a minor role (he did not live long enough to contribute significantly to contemporary society), Lord Byron, Percy Bysshe Shelley, Samuel Taylor Coleridge, and especially William Wordsworth are seen preaching their gospels of liberation and singing their paeans to the individual, whose triumph over society is their fondest hope. Johnson seems to favor the intellectual revolutionary, but he is considerably less inclined to like those who attempted to bring about drastic social change through more violent means. He is especially critical of South American activists; his portrait of Simón Bolívar is particularly harsh.

Johnson is at times biographer, at times military or political analyst, and at yet other times demographer, statistician, and sociologist. He uses numbers, carefully juxtaposed and integrated in graceful, analytic prose, to dispel some of the myths about these turbulent times. Though Johnson is not given to making categorical judgments about the impact of specific events (he tends to let the evidence accumulate to suggest the general trend toward modernization), on occasion he does, as when he concludes his discussion of the Greek war of 1821-1824 with the observation that the "cult of pallikaria gave rise to a corresponding capacity for national self-deception, a tendency to blame the failings of Greece on outside forces conspiring against Hellas and its people, and this tendency has also endured."

In his own way, Johnson is a revisionist—or perhaps more appropriately neotraditionalist—searching out the evidence that proves recent liberal revisionists wrong. Johnson's basic conservatism comes across in a variety of ways. He is sympathetic to politicians such as Castlereagh who worked for gradual rather than revolutionary changes. He takes contemporary historians to task for pleading the case against imperialist governments noting for example that in the clash between peoples that resulted from population shifts, "no race had a monopoly of virtue or evil." He defends the notorious Six Acts passed by the British parliament after the Peterloo Massacre. He argues that, despite recent feminist claims to the contrary, society in 1815-1830 was considerably less paternalistic than modern critics would claim. He is hard on trade unions, and he criticizes historians who have praised radical groups such as the Turkish klephts and Indian Thugees for being social revolutionaries; in Johnson's view, they were simply brigands whose actions threatened the order of society. Finally, he praises the Tory party for its willingness to accept among its leadership members of the middle class, Jews, and—in the twentieth century—women.

Like the best historians, Johnson finds the right example to illustrate his thesis. For example, to highlight the involvement of artists in political matters, he focuses on the efforts of the poet William Wordsworth in preserving the Parliament seat from his home district for his patron, the Earl of Lonsdale. Like any good historian, Johnson displays a healthy eclecticism in his interest; within a dozen pages one reads about the backstage maneuvering over an international treaty and the development of slang expressions. Further, his prodigious scholarship allows him to draw illustrations from all over the world to illustrate how the modern spirit was being born during these tumultuous years after the fall of Napoleon, the last real emperor in the traditional sense of the word. Further, Johnson is a competent stylist who on occasion writes vividly, as when he describes changes in the French government: "Never before or since have so many journalists and academics got their snouts in the trough at the same time."

As any book of this scope does, *The Birth of the Modern* runs the risk of being criticized by scholars for explaining too little and for summarizing (glibly) too much. Yet Johnson seems to rely on sound sources and to provide enough detail to make his conclusions plausible. There are unfortunate lapses, of course. For example, in writing of art and social critic John Ruskin's childhood, he copies E. T. Cook's conclusion (actually taken from Ruskin's autobiography) that the man of letters was deprived of a normal childhood and had to make do with "a box of bricks and a bunch of keys" for toys. Ruskin scholars will know that this myth has already been debunked by John D. Hunt in *Wider Sea: A Life of John Ruskin* (1982), but the general reader will be misled. This example may not be the most important in the book, but if one can be wrong in little things, one may be wrong about bigger ones.

Though the book is heavily footnoted and has a detailed index, it contains no bibliography—an unfortunate omission, since it is commonplace to turn to the back to find a particular source only to discover that the note contains a cryptic subsequent reference. One must hunt forward to find the full citation. This is indeed a caviling criticism, however, much like shooting gnats off a charging rhinoceros.

The Birth of the Modern is a big book—physically and intellectually. To comprehend fully the magnitude of Johnson's achievement one need only survey the book's notes to see how widely he has searched to assemble the materials from which he constructs his argument. Readers may find that it takes considerable time and concentration to follow along with Johnson through this complex examination of the world in transition, but the effort should prove remarkably rewarding.

Laurence W. Mazzeno

Sources for Further Study

The Christian Science Monitor. July 23, 1991, p. 13.
Los Angeles Times Book Review. June 2, 1991, p. 9.
National Review. XLIII, June 24, 1991, p. 42.
The New Republic. CCV, August 12, 1991, p. 36.
New Statesman and Society. IV, September 20, 1991, p. 44.
The New York Times Book Review. XCVI, June 23, 1991, p. 3.
The New Yorker. LXVII, June 10, 1991, p. 112.
Publishers Weekly. CCXXXVIII, May 3, 1991, p. 56.
The Times Literary Supplement. September 6, 1991, p. 12.
The Wall Street Journal. June 11, 1991, p. A12.
The Washington Post Book World. XXI, June 9, 1991, p. 1.

BOLEROS

Author: Jay Wright (1935?-   )
Publisher: Princeton University Press (Princeton, New Jersey). 95 pp. $9.95
Type of work: Poetry

A long poem that explores the cross-cultural resources of African-American creativity at the intersections of poetry and music

Jay Wright's poetry is a compelling invitation to take up residence in uncertain multiplicities. *Boleros,* his seventh book of poetry, is no exception in this regard. That this poet, a native of Albuquerque, New Mexico, who is sure neither of his birth date nor of his family name, should have a passion for pursuing the hidden logic of origins both personal and collective is hardly surprising. What may come as a surprise, however, to those unaccustomed to Wright's densely textured writing is his erudite familiarity and challenging engagement with a wide variety of literary and cultural traditions, ranging from the pre-Columbian Americas to medieval and Renaissance Europe, West Africa, Egypt, and India. Throughout all of his poetry, Wright's autobiographical personae embark on ambitious journeys across the uncharted territories of his uncompromisingly cross-cultural imagination. Fragments from many different historical and cultural settings come together in an intricate weave of historical and mythological allusions that seeks to articulate the spiritual and intellectual resources available to the twentieth century African-American artist. "Confident,/ cocky,/ still uncomforted," Wright insists that cultural boundaries need not separate peoples; they are in fact places where communication and communities become possible.

That there is nothing simple about Wright's poetic procedure, which he elucidates in his essay "Desire's Design, Vision's Resonance: Black Poetry's Ritual and Historical Voice" (1987), is evident even from the dedication page in *Boleros.* Part of the dedication to his wife, Lois, is a phonetic representation of one of the 266 Great Signs that organize Dogon/Bambara cosmology. These signs or ideograms are of central importance to Wright's earlier writings, especially to *The Double Invention of Komo* (1980). "*Dyee*—la connaissance de l'étoile" appropriately signifies union, wholeness, and harmony achieved through knowledge, through a sense of order. In addition to signaling Wright's abiding interest in traditional African societies and their theologies, this translated "sign" also calls attention to the overall project that organizes and energizes *Boleros'* forty-two poems: to reconstruct or reinvent obscured ties between the "West" and its "others." Wright's focus on names and naming is well suited to that gargantuan task. In the volume's fifth poem (known simply as "5"), he writes:

> All names are invocations, or curses.
> One must imagine the fictive event that leads to
> He-Who-Shoots-Porcupines-By-Night,
> or Andrew Golightly, or Theodore, or Sally.

In the case of *Boleros*, these fictive events not only point to the tales of his own ancestry Wright was accustomed to hearing from his father, George Murphy, also known as Mercer Murphy Wright, who claimed Cherokee, African, and Irish descent; they also encompass and probe the entire history of so-called Western civilization: "All these silences, all these intimations/ of something still to be constructed" ("14").

What, for example, were the events that led to the names of the nine Greek muses Wright recalls in the first part of *Boleros*? What "invocations" or "curses" inspired the names of the twelve "Saint's Days" adorned with "graces and the seasons" in the poem's second part? What stories lie buried in the names of the various places scattered throughout the book, places such as California's San Pedro, Florida's St. Augustine, New Mexico's Santa Fe, Mexico's Oaxaca and Xalapa?

Wright's poetic parade of Greek muses—Erato, Calliope, Euterpe, Thalia, Melpomene, Polyhymnia, Clio, Terpsichore, and Urania—is particularly striking given the usually all-male composition of his imaginary communities and especially the emphasis on male initiation rituals in *The Double Invention of Komo*. Though women are never entirely absent from Wright's poetry, which frequently identifies creativity as a female principle, it is not until *Elaine's Book* (1988) that female voices assume historical rather than purely mythic stature in his poetry. While the construction of female muses is a worn convention among male poets, Wright's invocations are perplexing. Following his premise that "All names are false," he worries the presumably stable Greek identities of these muses by correlating each with a concept taken from one of his favorite cultural archives, the Egyptian *Book of the Dead*: for example, "(ERATO←→KHAT)." It is important to note that the relation between these two terms or "names" is not one of equation. Rather than simply replacing Western identities with African ones, Wright creates a situation of transculturation. Each of these poems acknowledges and pays tribute to the cross-cultural possibilities opened up by Herodotus' claim that the names of almost all the Greek gods came from Egypt, and hence from Africa It is not surprising, then, to find that the Akan deity Odomankoma "guides Urania's hand" ("21"), or that Clio communes with both the Dogon god Nommo and the African-American pianist Art Tatum in the "cloth of the Word" ("19").

Like Martin Bernal's compelling philological research in *Black Athena: The Afro-Asiatic Roots of Classical Civilization* (1987), no doubt one of Wright's inspirations, these syncretic constructs are designed to challenge Romantic scholarship's systematic discrediting of the probable existence of Egyptian/African and Semitic influences on Greek culture. As Bernal points out, with the rise of the transatlantic slave trade and "scientific" racism, the very idea of such cultural "impurities" at the heart of Western civilization became increasingly intolerable to late-eighteenth and early-nineteenth century Europe's academic establishment and its fiercely nationalist ideology. Those inclined to dismiss Wright's reconstructions as the fanciful labor of a nonexpert challenging established scholarly paradigms may do well to remember his extensive research in world literatures, philosophy, music, anthropology, the history of religions, and the history of science.

In "Saints' Days," twelve poems that progress from January to December, other presences and voices enter as the poet moves from his "ancient theater" to "a new world." "Santa Bárbara (December 4th)," for example, brings together Greek Hera, Akan Oyạ, and former slave Jarena Lee. The latter's religious autobiographies, from which Wright quotes liberally in this poem, are now part of Oxford University Press's voluminous collection of writing by nineteenth century black women. Two lines from "Santa Bárbara" provide a succinct summary of Wright's poetic ruminations: "My gift is in the ceaseless journey from moment to moment,/ from place to place, places given in dreams and clothed by the Spirit." Perhaps the most powerful poem in this sequence, however, is "Nuestra Señora de los Remedios (September 24th)," a dramatic meditation on racial violence and redemption that turns on the word *remedios*: "Time now to reconstruct salvation." Poems such as this one bring to mind another important ancestral figure, the Robert Hayden of "Middle Passage," one of the finest pieces of writing in African-American literature.

Boleros moves rapidly between both historical and geographic locations. Many of these places, redolent with personal memories, are familiar from Wright's earlier poems, most notably San Pedro, California, where he grew up in the 1950's; Jalapa, where he stayed from 1969 to 1971 before moving to the Scotland of Hugh MacDiarmid, the old poet "whose gift is the mist of tongues" ("7"); and New Hampshire, where he and his wife settled in 1973. The poet also takes up a number of new imaginary residences, most significant among them St. Augustine, Florida, the first city the Spanish founded on the North American continent, and Benares, or Banāres, in Uttar Pradesh, known as the "City of the Sun" and one of the intellectual and cultural centers of traditional India. The persistent, sudden shifts from Guadalajara to Glasgow, from eastern Canada to Santa Fe, from Salt Lake City to Piermont, New Hampshire, to Egypt, and to West Africa are at times disorienting and almost dizzying. It is as if one were caught in an intricate ritualistic dance that transforms ordinary landscapes into an elaborate symbolic geography where temporal and spatial divides become increasingly tenuous and ultimately fluid. Appropriately, the crossroads at which the poet-traveler intermittently comes to rest are figured as rivers such as the Rio Grande and the Ganges: "Black spirits such as mine will always come/ to a crossroads such as this, where the water moves/ with enabling force" ("17"). Langston Hughes's famous "I have known rivers . . ." resonates in these lines.

Wright's poetic language is as rich as his symbolic geography is varied and expansive. As always, the poet's travels become explorations of poetic form. Most striking in this regard are the two trios of poems that follow the hushed "New England Days" and make up *Boleros'* fourth and fifth sections. As it turns out, "Sources and Roots" and "Coda" are the title's most concrete reference points. These relatively brief poems, most of which open with lines from popular Latin American tunes (such as "Un siglo de ausencia"), are daring in their use of Spanish lyric conventions in an English-language environment. The results of such unexpected contacts are marvelously slung and rounded couplets that mischievously wreak havoc with English patterns of accentuation.

Dime en donde encontrar-
te, disposable heart, red star
by which I set my course and flow,
a vessel marked by the dim glow
of pride. I am a song that cleaves
to its Guinea way, stops, deceives
itself, falls through a lowered tone
and returns, enhanced by its own
failure, to the key it sustains. ("39")

Such a virtuoso Afro-Latin performance, that "[picks] the composer's pocket" in
the spirit of Art Tatum and other great jazz musicians, places Wright's work squarely
at the crossroads of poetry and music and shows him at his very best.

Much has been said and written about modern and contemporary African-American
poetry's distinctive musical idiom. The most frequently cited examples in this regard
are the blues poems of Langston Hughes and Sterling Brown and the jazz poetry of
Michael S. Harper and Amiri Baraka. Yet the question of what improvisation, the
core of both jazz and the blues, might really mean to poetic practice has rarely been
considered. What Wright's poems show quite clearly is that improvisation as a creative principle is neither a form of imitation nor spontaneous composition. To Wright,
an accomplished bass player and poet, successful, innovative improvisation presup-
poses knowledge of and respect for sets of formal rules, even as those rules are
stretched, bent, and even broken. In other words, it requires a rigorous sense of
limits and of order. It is from such intellectual discipline that new possibilities begin
to emerge, in music as well as in poetry. Wright's poems are carefully crafted im-
provisations that respect "original" procedures, that is, prior performances, by systematically pushing them beyond their limits and enhancing them. One difficulty is
knowing what those "sources" are, and in his case there are many, since *Boleros*,
like Wright's other work, assimilates a vast body of cultural knowledge. More important, perhaps, is a willingness to relinquish consumerist attitudes toward literature and listen attentively to the "healing music of my head,/ my soul's improvisation" ("19"). After reading *Boleros*, one ought seriously to reconsider the notion
that the musical feats of Charlie Parker and John Coltrane have no equivalent in
African-American poetry. They do now.

Vera M. Kutzinski

Source for Further Study

Library Journal. CXVI, May 15, 1991, p. 86.

BRIEF LIVES

Author: Anita Brookner (1938-   )
First published: 1990, in Great Britain
Publisher: Random House (New York). 260 pp. $20.00
Type of work: Novel
Time: The 1940's through the 1980's
Locale: London

This novel explores the relationships and loneliness in the lives of the aging heroine and her friends

> *Principal characters:*
> FAY LANGDON, the narrator and heroine, a widow and a former singer
> MARGARET "JULIA" WILBERFORCE, a retired actress, also a widow
> CHARLIE MORTON, Julia's husband, deceased
> OWEN LANGDON, Fay's husband and the partner of Charlie, also deceased
> LAVINIA LANGDON, Fay's mother-in-law
> PEARL CHESNEY, Julia's former dresser and attendant
> MILLIE SAVAGE, Fay's longtime friend and former roommate
> ALAN CARTER, a physician and friend of Fay

After two novels with male protagonists, *Latecomers* (1988) and *Lewis Percy* (1989), Anita Brookner has in *Brief Lives* returned to familiar ground: the lives of women. Indeed, the title refers not only to life's disappointments and brevity, but also, ironically, to the short periods a woman has with a man, whether husband or lover, despite her lifelong quest for true love. The lasting relationships in a woman's life, the ones she returns to, the narrator Fay Langdon makes clear, are those with other women. Spurred by an obituary of an old acquaintance, Julia Wilberforce, Fay recollects her friendship with Julia as well as her own romantic history. Not only does the news of Julia's death launch the narrative, but *Brief Lives* also closes with Julia's voice as Fay imagines it from beyond the grave.

The women of Anita Brookner's novels are almost always disappointed in love and marriage, for what they seek, as Fay recalls from her own girlhood, is a cinematic version of love, a Hollywood ideal of balanced female need and loving male attentiveness. The cost of this girlish dream is clear from Fay's life story, particularly her lingering emptiness and despair as she approaches old age alone. Writing in the tradition of several centuries of women novelists adept at combining realism with romance, Brookner presents Fay's story retrospectively, carefully structuring the narrative to reveal the causes for the central conflict between romantic aspiration and the reality of male-female relationships. Yet Fay is not the only female character in *Brief Lives* who suffers loneliness and disappointment. Julia's marriage to Charlie was also a compromise, his devotion unable to meet the expectations her love for her brother fostered. So compromised was her marriage, despite Charlie's apparent devotion, that she never openly knew of an adulterous affair between her husband and Fay, her friend and the wife of Charlie's legal partner. Pearl Chesney, aging and alone, also illustrates the emptiness of women's lives without love and companionship, as do the lives of Lavinia Langdon, Fay's mother-in-law, and Maureen, a factotum for Julia. Recognizing the common fate of women, Fay expresses a generalized grief and "an unwilling solidarity with all female destinies," their common need to "rely on alliances forged long ago."

Typical of Brookner heroines, Fay is passive and scrupulous. Julia, by contrast, is narcissistic, demanding, and tormenting—a parallel to many such self-centered female characters in Brookner's earlier novels. Despite their opposing attributes, however, Fay and Julia remain important presences for each other. Julia needs someone to care for her, and, after her husband's death, though she has Pearl and Maureen, she demands Fay's attention, enlisting her help in returning and garnering library books and, unconsciously, exploiting Fay's unexpiated guilt over her affair with Charlie. Even long after Charlie's death, which ends her affair, as death also ends her marriage, Fay obligingly abandons her preparations for dinner with a male friend in order to aid Julia.

So poignant is Brookner's wisdom and irony in capturing the begrudging ties of these women that she has Fay's and Julia's friendship outlast their husbands, the sources of their original acquaintance, and Fay persists in attending to Julia even after acknowledging that the latter has been her downfall. Because of Julia, Fay has shown Dr. Alan Carter, her hope for a future companion, "an unpleasant side," "a hapless deranged side" of herself, causing the flight of "that fastidious and so-successful unmarried man." Yet she reconciles with Julia, and with Pearl in tow, they spend an agreeable evening together over food and drink. They form a moving tableau, these three aging women without men "One returns to the company of women when any blow falls," Fay comments near the end of the novel, for in many situations "only one's own kind will do." Having faced what life has in store for them as elderly widows, the three give in. Fay observes: "We drank wine like old lags and ate ice cream like girls. Assuaged, eyes bright, lipstick smudged, we sat back and nodded at each other in recognition." It is the young around them who are "self-conscious," the objects of sympathy yet satire to their aging observers.

Besides her poignant rendering of the lives of lonely women, Anita Brookner demonstrates in *Brief Lives* striking stylistic similarities to Henry James and Edith Wharton, whose works she admires. Like them, she explores the daily social intercourse and thoughts of her characters in order to focus on their increasing awareness and the refinement of feeling. The reader observes Fay's daily efforts to please her husband, the subtle adjustments and compromises she makes, her willing passivity until, after several years, she awakens fully to how her marriage, with all its unfulfilled longing, is a misalliance. Even then, there is no anger, simply gradual recognition and pity. "I faced the fact," she comments,

> that he would rarely if ever make love to me in the years ahead, and that all I could hope for was his hand, in an unguarded moment, catching hold of mine, or his arm laid about my shoulders. The strange thing was that this realization did not frighten me or even make me indignant, for what was coming into being was a sort of pity.

Yet a page later, Fay describes "a coldness" that descends on her spirit, "the coldness which marks the recognition that equality in love will never be attained," and "for a moment or two," she recounts, "I sat in horror, knowing that love had gone and would never return." It is this type of refinement of feeling and Jamesian recognition scene that marks Brookner's novels and gives them appeal for discerning, mature readers.

Brookner is also, as the above sentences illustrate, an accomplished stylist. Fay's voice, her sentences, are at once halting yet poised—a parallel to her character. She speaks with balance and painfully acquired wisdom. "Now I realize that it is marriage which is the great temptation for a woman, and that one can, and perhaps should, resist it," she comments. Elsewhere, she says, "Respectability is as much as can be hoped for; there is no woman so respectable as the one who has rediscovered virtue." There are wisdom and rue as well as stylistic refinement in such sentences, and many similar ones fill the pages of *Brief Lives*.

With their sophisticated style and sentiment, Anita Brookner's novels are not for the fainthearted, nor are they for the worldly adventurous. *Brief Lives* is no exception. Set in such prosaically named places as Onslow Square and Gertrude Street— one suspects a hidden allusion to Hamlet's mother—her characters inhabit a closed domestic world. Attention to food and living arrangements is paramount. Settling matters of leases and house sales, planning a cold chicken curry and rice salad to serve Dr. Carter for dinner—such constitute Fay Langdon's world. More than delineating the limitations of her characters, however, Brookner's attention to such concerns also defines the sphere of their freedom. In these domestic matters, at least, women of Fay's generation—those born before World War II—have choices.

Conscious images of light and dark play consistently throughout *Brief Lives*, reinforcing Fay's emotional states. She recalls nostalgically her girlhood as a time of happiness and light, a magical interval before dark. Her home in Gertrude Street with Owen, significantly, is darkly decorated. With Owen frequently away on business trips, the sun becomes for Fay a "symbol of all that has been lost. . . ." The years after Owen's death, which coincide with Fay's affair with Charlie, she remembers as "mainly dark," autumnal. Death as well as darkness emerges near the end of the novel. Fay acknowledges "the symbolism of the end of the day" as a parallel to "a sort of anguish, an anguish which is not entirely temporal." The solitude that encases her is both frightening and inevitable, and Fay's awareness of it is mirrored in the growing images of darkness that pervade the novel.

Brief Lives is ultimately a novel about loss, but the acquisition of freedom and the struggle for dignity in the face of this diminution of life are perhaps its strongest themes. Fay's longing for happiness and true love fit the novel to the romance genre, but in many ways it is a moral tale focused on the consequences that dovetail with the themes of loss, freedom, and dignity. Fay's pilgrimage to freedom leads to loneliness, just as her search for love has led to disappointment. Her taking Charlie as a lover begins "a long training in duplicity, in calculation, in almost continuous discomfort. . . ." She pays, ultimately, "too dearly for love." As a mistress to Charlie, she finds "there is no appropriate attitude" for her when he dies. She is at once "spared Job's comforters who attend the wife," but she is also alone and must comfort herself. In the course of the novel, moreover, Fay not only loses Owen and Charlie; she also loses her mother, her youth, her beauty, her singing voice, and even Julia, who moves to Spain to live with her brother. These departures all have the effect of freeing Fay of encumbrances and the desire to please others. Yet there is pain and struggle in these losses, a struggle particularly to overcome melancholy and self-pity. "I was a pretty girl," she tells the reader at the outset. "I married well. . . . It all seems a long time ago. But what most women want I once had. I try to remember that." A more significant loss, however, may be the potential for love itself. In the last recognition scene, Fay sees that with Pearl and Julia gone, she is "free now, free of encumbrances, free of hope, that greatest of all encumbrances."

Brief Lives is another brilliant tile in the mosaic of human relationships that Anita Brookner has made with her fiction. Its stylistic refinement, its moving portrait of aging women, its insight into female friendships and the disappointments of love speak to the mature reader, the discerner of life's meaning.

Stella Nesanovich

Sources for Further Study

The Atlantic. CCLXVIII, September, 1991, p. 124.
Chicago Tribune. July 14, 1991, XIV, p. 6.
The Christian Science Monitor. August 5, 1991, p. 13.
Los Angeles Times Book Review. July 7, 1991, p. 3.
The Nation. CCLIII, September 9, 1991, p. 274.
New Statesman and Society. III, August 31, 1990, p. 35.
The New York Times Book Review. XCVI, July 21, 1991, p. 14.
Publishers Weekly. CCXXXVIII, April 12, 1991, p. 44.
Time. CXXXVII, June 24, 1991, p. 65.
The Times Literary Supplement. August 24, 1990, p. 889.
The Washington Post Book World. XXI, July 28, 1991, p. 12.

BROTHERLY LOVE

Author: Pete Dexter (1943-   )
Publisher: Random House (New York). 274 pp. $22.00
Type of work: Novel
Time: 1961-1986
Locale: Philadelphia

   This powerful novel of violence and madness, guilt and redemption among Philadelphia union officials is tragic in the classic sense

> *Principal characters:*
> PETER FLOOD, the protagonist, a roofer and union official
> MICHAEL FLOOD, Peter's cousin, a union boss
> CHARLEY FLOOD, Peter's father, a union official
> PHILLIP FLOOD, Michael's father, a union boss
> NICK DIMAGGIO, a prizefighter and mechanic
> HARRY DIMAGGIO, Nick's son, a prizefighter

Brotherly Love is a not-quite-typical example of the fictional mode, common and perhaps even dominant in the 1980's and into the 1990's, that might be called black realism. Spiritually, emotionally, intellectually, the characters in such fiction are adrift. Their work is never a true vocation; it serves no important social function and exists only to fulfill desires that are often extravagantly greedy. Similarly, relationships are rarely serious, rarely last, exist primarily to gratify the senses and the ego. Often the pace and the prose of such fiction are languorous; in this novel, refreshingly, they are energetic. In one vital respect, moreover, *Brotherly Love* differs from and is superior to ordinary black realism: It contains a moral center. This alone, apart from the commoner virtue of gritty verisimilitude, makes it worth reading and pondering.

   By beginning with a newspaper story recounting the violent death of the central characters, Pete Dexter imbues his story with a sense of dark inevitability: "Southeastern Pennsylvania Trade Union Council President Michael Flood and his brother, Peter, were found shot to death yesterday in what police sources have described as a 'mob hit.'" The story goes on to mention that Michael's father "was killed 16 years ago when a bomb rigged to his front door went off as he entered his South Philadelphia home." This is taut exposition, with an incisive narrative hook, and, in retrospect, introduction of a central theme: In the world of this novel, shoddy and dishonest work is endemic. The reporter did not bother to get his facts straight: Michael's father was murdered twelve years earlier, not sixteen; Michael and Peter were cousins, not brothers. The police, corrupt and lazy, never solved the earlier crime; they will write this one off, incorrectly, as mob violence as well.

   In this novel, more clearly than in most, there is a single, straightforward precipitating event. During the winter of 1961, Peter, then aged eight, had been charged with watching his baby sister. In this careless and casually vicious world, the accident or some terrible accident seems almost inevitable: A car, coming too fast, skids on the ice; a dangerous dog prevents the boy from getting to his sister as she bolts into the street; an innocent child dies. As a direct result, Peter and his cousin

Michael die twenty-five years later. The chain of causality remains unbroken for all those years, however, because of comprehensive and widespread human failure. A careless driver kills Peter's sister; greed, narcissism, a destructive code of honor, the inability to love do the rest.

Peter's family lacks the resources to weather the tragedy. They seem almost entirely unable or unwilling to communicate, particularly to express feeling. The father and mother are married in no sense other than legal, the biological parents of Peter but nothing more. His mother withdraws into silence, into mental illness, and ultimately leaves the family. His father is obsessed with avenging himself on the driver, a police lieutenant who lives next door, who killed his child. According to his primitive code, nothing but a death for a death can make it right; and finally he does kill the man, which of course makes things more wrong. He himself is killed in retribution, not because murder is a capital crime, but because he rocked the boat: He acted against the prudent counsel of his superior in the mob. Peter is thus left feeling responsible not only for the death of his sister but also for the destruction of his family. Meanwhile, Peter's uncle, Phillip Flood, moves his own family into Peter's house and works to consolidate and advance his position in the union. Human loss translates in this world into nothing more than a power vacuum, to be filled as quickly and smoothly as possible.

Part 2 of *Brotherly Love*, set in 1966 when Peter is thirteen, introduces the moral center of the book. It is surely no coincidence that Nick DiMaggio—retired prize fighter and owner of a small training gym, honest and competent mechanic, devoted father to his nine-year old son—shares the name of a famous and much-honored athlete. The Floods's neighbor in South Philadelphia, he has been careful to distance himself from that tragically violent, mob-shadowed clan. To come to the attention of Phillip Flood is dangerous, he senses, and indeed has near-fatal consequences for him in the end.

Nevertheless, when Peter and Michael are confronted by four older black boys intent on stealing everything they have, including their shoes, he decides to intervene—but only on condition that the boys attempt to stand up for themselves. Michael breaks away and runs, leaving his shoes; Peter throws a soft, scared punch, the best he can do, and Nick, with his boxer's power and craft, rescues him. This scene reveals much about the novel's values and its sense of reality. For it is Michael, the physical coward, who ultimately becomes the corrupt, pathologically violent union boss. Competence as a fighter, competence as a roofer in this blue-collar union, counts for less than nothing: It is the ability to make and manipulate connections, above all to twist the truth, that yields power. At twelve, Michael is a budding politician; Peter, not despite but because of his superior courage and straightforwardness, an outsider. Nick himself is the ultimate outsider, with values incomprehensible to the other characters. Essentially, he believes that integrity and familial relationships are more important than influence and money. Thus he trains his son to be a skilled fighter because the discipline is good for him, because independence and self-esteem honestly earned are valuable; but he will not exploit the boy's talent for cash by letting him turn professional.

When Phillip brings his son and nephew to Nick's gym to learn the manly art of self-defense, it is Peter who takes to it: though doggedly, with no natural flair, absorbing punishment until it occurs to Nick that perhaps he likes to get hit. If he does, it is because of unabsolved guilt over the death of his sister; he has already exhibited self-destructive recklessness, making painful leaps off rooftops. Phillip also arranges for Peter's sexual initiation, with a prostitute in the back seat of a car. This sets the tone for all his relationships with women in the future; in this novel, men and women do not connect honestly and emotionally but bargain for money and power. Peter, for all his sporadic longing for love, has been twisted by his inner traumas and by the violent cynicism around him; sex in the back seat is all he can manage. In its portrayal of the failure of love (Nick's relationship with his wife, apparently an exception, occurs offstage), *Brotherly Love* is typical black realism.

By 1972, part 3, Phillip Flood is president of the union; Peter, at nineteen, is working as a roofer, having dropped out of school several years earlier; Michael has gone into "the business end of the business." Peter is happy on the rooftops, but, endlessly haunted by his guilt, he "cannot stay where he is comfortable forever." So he returns to the gym to spar with Harry DiMaggio, who, sensing the danger to his father in any contact with the Flood family, fights without restraint and breaks Peter's nose twice in five days. "Maybe he don't want to be in that family," Nick says to his son, and the insight is crucial: Peter is trapped by his fate, by the mere accident of his birth. Lacking the intellect and perhaps the courage to break away entirely, too ethically aware to belong, he has no place of his own. He is lost, dispossessed: a restless wanderer at the edges of an alien world.

Part 4, also set in 1972, consists of only two pages. Yet it is at this point, as the author suggests by jumping fourteen years to the long final section, that the final element, leading inevitably to the bloody tragedy recounted at the beginning, falls into place. Michael calls Peter with the news that his father has been murdered by a rival mob and demands his help; without someone he can trust to help him consolidate power, he will be "as dead as Phil." Peter, unable to escape the tie of blood, agrees. His decision, however, is only superficially like Nick DiMaggio's to help two boys in trouble years earlier—for ultimately it is impossible to be half a member of the mob, half one's own man.

By 1986, Michael has been so corrupted by power that by any reasonable definition he is crazy. His worldview resembles that of one of the later, madder Roman emperors: He is a god; the humans around him exist only to serve him; the slightest affront to his dignity is punishable by death. Everyone in his circle is inevitably corrupted as well; so that, for example, because Michael desires the beautiful wife of a naïve nightclub owner, Peter serves as pimp by taking the man on jaunts to Atlantic City. To be close to Michael means to lose one's soul or one's life: The nightclub owner, disastrously in debt to Michael and in despair when his wife leaves him, kills himself.

Michael, who can no longer tolerate the existence of anyone who does not worship him, at length turns his attention to Nick and his son. He first attempts to humiliate them by insisting on a fight between Harry and one of his bodyguards, a hulking weightlifter. He has no idea, however, what years of disciplined training can do against mere raw power: Harry destroys the weightlifter in less than a minute. Michael retaliates by having an old man whom Nick had befriended killed, then brings to the gym a dangerous professional fighter to spar with Harry. Nick, protecting his son, slaps Michael across the face, and Michael decrees his death.

He decides that Peter, about whose abject loyalty he has understandable doubts, will be the one to commit the murder, but he has failed to realize just how appalled and thus morally distanced Peter has become. When the shotgun is put into his hands, it is his cousin, the insane emperor, whom he kills; he then goes to the house his mother left him in New Jersey to wait for the killers to come for him. His guilt, at last, is expiated.

In its plot and its vision, *Brotherly Love* is tragic in the classical sense. Typically, as in *Hamlet* (c. 1601), the hero is caught between a destructive societal code—the revenge code, in William Shakespeare's play—and his own moral doubts and human frailties. From the moment he undertakes to avenge his father, Hamlet is doomed, yet his actions have large salutary consequences: At the end, the life of Denmark has been renewed. Similarly, Peter Flood, by declaring his loyalty to the corrupt system personified by his cousin, has doomed himself. Peter is no prince; the system will remain intact. Yet at the end he has committed himself definitely to good, whatever his motives, and has accomplished a great good thing: Nick and Harry have been saved, and, with the removal of a man even his fellow mobsters have come to regard as a mad dog, will be able to live in peace.

With its heavy reliance on short, punchy sentences, *Brotherly Love* at times reads like a parody of the fiction of Ernest Hemingway, a trap into which all too much American fiction of the tough-guy school unfortunately falls. Yet in the uncompromising seriousness of its moral vision, this novel partakes of the best of Hemingway as well. Peter Flood, in his struggle for a place in a world that finally he cannot accept, seems on the whole more interesting than the footloose Jake Barnes, perpetually at loose ends in *The Sun Also Rises* (1926). Hemingway would surely have admired Nick DiMaggio for his courage, competence, and integrity, and the reader of *Brotherly Love* can as well, without reservation. Nick is that rarest of literary creations, a wholly believable, wholly sympathetic character. For having had not only the skill but, more significantly, the vision and courage to create him, Pete Dexter should be honored and his book read.

Edwin Moses

Sources for Further Study

Booklist. LXXXVIII, September 1, 1991, p. 4.
Chicago Tribune. October 13, 1991, XIV, p. 1.

The Christian Science Monitor. October 28, 1991, p. 13.
Library Journal. CXVI, October 1, 1991, p. 139.
Los Angeles Times Book Review. October 6, 1991, p. 3.
The New York Times Book Review. XCVI, October 13, 1991, p. 3.
Philadelphia Inquirer. October 13, 1991, p. H1.
Publishers Weekly. CCXXXVIII, October 4, 1991, p. 70.
Time. CXXXVIII, November 4, 1991, p. 93.
The Wall Street Journal. October 7, 1991, p. A12.

BULLY FOR BRONTOSAURUS
Reflections in Natural History

Author: Stephen Jay Gould (1941-   )
Publisher: W. W. Norton (New York). Illustrated. 540 pp. $22.95
Type of work: Scientific essays

Ranging over such disparate topics as the platypus, male nipples, and Joe Dimaggio's fifty-six-game hitting streak, this collection of essays has as its unifying theme the impact of Darwinian evolutionary change on geological, biological, and human phenomena

> Principal personages:
> CHARLES DARWIN (1809-1882), the British naturalist and principal architect of the theory of evolution by means of natural selection
> LOUIS AGASSIZ (1807-1873), a Swiss-American geologist and zoologist who opposed Darwin's ideas on evolution
> WILLIAM JENNINGS BRYAN (1860-1925), an American politician who was hostile to Darwinian evolution
> ST GEORGE JACKSON MIVART (1827-1900), Roman Catholic English evolutionist who maintained that God's action was necessary to account for the development of the human mind

In one of the clinical stories discussed in *The Man Who Mistook His Wife for a Hat and Other Clinical Tales* (1986), the neurologist Oliver Sacks states that every human being has an inner narrative the meaning of which constitutes his or her identity. In the course of many centuries, scientists have discovered that our planet and the life that evolved on it have a continuous history (although punctuated by periods of dramatic, discontinuous change), and the universal laws undergirding this history constitute its meaning. In *Bully for Brontosaurus: Reflections in Natural History*, Stephen Jay Gould is concerned with both these internal and external stories as well as the interactions between them. In many of his essays he focuses both on the story of curious forms of life and on the personal stories of those involved in the study of these forms. In all this he is fascinated by the wondrous ability of the human brain to bring to light enthralling things about nature and to think even more enthralling things about what they mean.

Gould, who has taught biology, geology, and the history of science at Harvard University, has become, through his many articles and books, one of the most skillful and successful popularizers of science in the twentieth century. Phi Beta Kappa honored his previous work, *Wonderful Life: The Burgess Shale and the Nature of History* (1989), as the most outstanding book in science for 1990. For many years, Gould has written "This View of Life," a monthly column for *Natural History* magazine, and he has selected the best of his essays to appear in four earlier books. He believes that this fifth volume, *Bully for Brontosaurus*, is his best because he has matured as a scientist and as a writer and because he has become more discriminating about what to include (he culled thirty-five essays from more than sixty). Some critics have found his popularizations to be oversimplifications of very complex issues, but Gould, unlike the scholars who disparage the "vulgarization" of science, sees himself in the same tradition as Galileo Galilei, a scientist who enjoyed making his ideas and discoveries, as well as those of others, accessible to a wide audience.

The thirty-five chapters of *Bully for Brontosaurus* are organized into ten parts. At first glance, both the parts and the chapters appear to be dismayingly diverse. The parts range from "History in Evolution" to "Planets as Persons," and the chapter titles range from "George Canning's Left Buttock and the Origin of the Species" through "Male Nipples and Clitoral Ripples" to "The Horn of Triton" (Triton is one of Neptune's moons). Although certain themes help to interrelate many of these essays, the book suffers from the faults peculiar to this genre of collected magazine articles: repetitions, jarring differences in approach, tone, and content, and lack of narrative thrust from essay to essay and from part to part. It is certainly easier for a writer to reprint published articles than to mold a heterogeneous mass of material into a unified work with a propulsive argument. From such past books as *Ontogeny and Phylogeny* (1985), which is thematically organized and insightfully argued, it is clear that Gould is capable of such an integration of different facts and ideas, even though that book, too, had a haphazard origin. On the other hand, the kaleidoscope of essays in *Bully for Brontosaurus* has its advantages; for example, the essays can be read in any order with little loss of meaning.

Underlying the diversity of topics is a common approach for many of the essays. Gould generally begins with something to arouse the interest of the reader—some oddity of nature, the juxtaposition of widely dissimilar things that he promises he will connect, or a traditional interpretation of some idea or event that he states he will explain in a new way. He then works from this provocative starting point, usually via digressions, to some new perspective or fresh understanding. Surprises confront the reader at every turn of his analysis, and oddities are made to seem even odder before all is explained. Gould's tone of intellectual confidence informs every level of his discussions. He has great faith in the power of the scientific method to solve the puzzles of nature.

A good example of Gould's technique is found in the first essay of *Bully for Brontosaurus*, in which he promises to reveal a connection between Darwin's *On the Origin of Species by Means of Natural Selection* (1859) and a bullet in the left buttock of the statesman George Canning. Robert Stewart, Viscount Castlereagh, shot Canning in this unlikely place during a duel (Castlereagh was a dove during the War of 1812, whereas Canning was a hawk). The captain of HMS *Beagle*, the ship that took Darwin around the world, was Robert Fitzroy, whose mother was Castlereagh's sister. Castlereagh, a manic depressive, eventually committed suicide, and Fitzroy feared that his family had a predisposition to self-destruction that was hereditary, hence his desire for a congenial companion—Darwin—on his long voyage. Darwin became an adept naturalist on the trip, and without this experience he never would have written *On the Origin of Species*. Gould recognizes that this type of analysis has serious limitations, and the role of chance in history is even more complex than he indicates. The causation of suicide, with its psychological, social, cultural, and hereditary factors, is dauntingly mysterious, and no connections among such factors are certain because they are often modified by new discoveries.

For Gould, the quirks of history have similarities to the accidents of evolution, and the theme of evolution is a leitmotif throughout his book. He views evolution as the constant interplay between necessary scientific laws and the random happenings to which living and nonliving matter are subject. Some critics have claimed that he exaggerates the accidental in his interpretation of evolution and that his analysis is, at its root, simply a conventional treatment of how plants and animals adapt to their surroundings. Gould, for his part, insists that evolution is driven by chance and that traditional evolutionary thinking is mistaken in being insufficiently concerned with random events. When something appears to be odd or out of place, scientists must study it to deepen their understanding of evolution. Gould has called this criterion of imperfection the "panda principle" for his favorite example, the panda's "thumb" (which is actually an enlarged wrist bone, a makeshift replacement for a real thumb in a distant forebear).

Gould has become well known for his theory of evolution as punctuated equilibrium; that is, he sees evolution as a continuous process interspersed with discontinuities. In one of the essays in *Bully for Brontosaurus*, Gould expresses admiration for some of the views of William Whiston, Isaac Newton's successor as Lucasian professor of mathematics at the University of Cambridge. Whiston, like Newton, deeply believed that the events depicted in the Bible were historically true, but, like Newton, he also believed that the universe was a great machine. Whiston therefore theorized that miraculous biblical events had mechanical explanations—for example, that a comet caused Noah's flood. For Gould, the difference between Whiston's views and the modern theory of mass extinctions through extraterrestrial impact is not as great as most would think.

One of Gould's *bêtes noires* is the ladder of evolution. The ladder is linear and hierarchical; it points, as in Robert Frost's poem "After Apple-Picking," toward heaven, and, in the image "ladder of evolution," toward humankind. Yet evolution is not a process moving toward the destination of humanity. For Gould, *Homo sapiens* is simply the consequence of a long series of ancient accidents. A better image for evolution, he suggests, is a bush in which no twigs are preferentially situated. The ladder is an anthropocentric image, the bush a biocentric one. In Gould's vision of evolution, as in Darwin's, all talk of "higher" and "lower" must be avoided, and all schemes of progress, be they the development of the horse to a "more perfect" form or the human being as the crown and completion of evolution, are deceptive and erroneous. For the true state of affairs, Gould suggests going to nature and actually observing how things are done. For example, the tiny kiwi birds of New Zealand lay enormous eggs. Producing these large eggs certainly stresses the kiwi's biological systems, but the large eggs are very nutritious and confer survival advantages on the kiwi chicks. The kiwi egg did not become big because of these advantages, however. Kiwis evolved from much bigger birds, and as the kiwi body became smaller, their eggs maintained their former size. Does this process sound like orthogenesis?

Just as the evolution of life in all of its fascinating forms intrigues Gould, so too does the history of man. Indeed, biologists are similar to historians in many ways, and the biologists' narratives of the evolution of life forms share a dependence on chance occurrences with the historians' accounts of the life of a people, country, institution, or doctrine. In several of his historical essays, Gould is concerned with the context and development of the doctrine of Darwinism. Although he is a staunch defender of Darwin's theory, he is no "bulldog" à la Thomas Henry Huxley. Gould's defense is always informed by a great sensitivity to the scientific and human values that many of Darwin's opponents were trying to preserve. St. George Mivart, for example, brought an objection against natural selection that troubled Darwin himself. Mivart pointed out the uselessness of Darwin's mechanism in explaining the incipient stages of useful structures. For example, with two percent of a wing, the precursor to the bird could not fly, so why develop this useless structure any further? Both Darwin and Gould point out, however, that an incipient wing, while disadvantageous in terms of flight, might possess other advantages; for example, incipient wings might assist in thermoregulation. Then, as these wing structures became larger in the course of evolution, a conversion from one function (thermoregulation) to another (flight) could occur.

Human values have been a very important part of the debate over Darwinism in the nineteenth and twentieth centuries. The great novelist Leo Tolstoy told his son that Darwinism was unable to give life meaning, since it undermined morality by teaching that violence triumphed over love. Similarly, the American politician William Jennings Bryan battled against evolutionism because he believed that Darwinism preached that might made right. Bryan has often been a figure of ridicule, particularly in depictions of his behavior during the trial of John T. Scopes in Tennessee, but Gould is sensitive to Bryan's virtues. He obviously sympathizes with many of the progressive political positions that Bryan held; for example, Bryan was for women's suffrage, against American imperialism in the Philippines, and against the might-makes-right principle in relations among nations. Neither Tolstoy nor Bryan was a scientist, however, and Gould believes that their charges against Darwinism are unfair and based on misunderstandings. Tolstoy and Bryan exaggerated the metaphor of struggle in Darwin's analysis of nature, and they neglected his studies on cooperation among various living things. Gould is attracted to the anarchist Pyotr Kropotkin's argument that mutual aid rather than struggle is the criterion for evolutionary success, particularly when interactions between groups of organisms and the environment are involved.

Tolstoy and Bryan certainly made their mistakes, but, according to Gould, scientists also erred by extending their biological discoveries into the realm of morality. Science, he emphasizes, cannot answer moral questions and therefore cannot shape social and political policies. Since scientists live in a world dominated by nonscientists, they must learn to respect other ways of knowing, and these religious, philosophical, and artistic ways of knowing have validity in their own domains. Implied in Gould's analysis seems to be a belief that the universe has levels of reality, and he believes that it is dangerous to mix levels cavalierly. An interesting instance of this mixing occurs in a postscript to one of the essays. President Jimmy Carter, who had read Gould's *Wonderful Life*, wrote Gould that the evolution of the human being was so improbable that this "ascent of man" must indicate divine intent. Gould disagrees, believing that all one can say from the scientific evidence is that the human species resulted from a series of unlikely accidents. In the nineteenth century, a discussion similar to the one between Gould and Carter occurred between Louis Agassiz and the psychologist and philosopher William James, who pointed out that the evolution of human beings was not an argument for God's benevolence, as Agassiz held, but an account of how opportunism rules natural events, and since the end result—humanity—is the only available example, it is impossible to compute the probability of this event.

Evolution, with its scientific, historical, and moral implications, does not exhaust the ways in which Gould makes use of this theme. One of the essays in *Bully for Brontosaurus* that provoked a great response when it was first published concerned how the QWERTY keyboard arrangement came to dominate typewriter design. This arrangement, still widely used despite the presence of superior systems, developed in the early years of the typewriter when inventors selected the positions of the letters to minimize jamming. Since this meant that often-used letters were in awkward places, the QWERTY arrangement was, logically considered, neither the fastest nor the most efficient, but it survived because it was the luckiest, and in that sense it resembles various plants and animals that have squeaked through to survive into the present.

Finally, Gould's personal interests and his life itself are mined for several essay topics. For example, his interest in baseball is the subject of an essay on creation myths (baseball was not started by Abner Doubleday in Cooperstown, New York; it came from a variety of English stick-and-ball games). He also manages to compare Joe Dimaggio's fifty-six-game hitting streak in 1941, which he calls "the greatest accomplishment in the history of the sport," with the combination of skill and luck that led to the survival of unlikely species. His own life is the source of a moving essay about his battle against mesothelioma, a deadly cancer. Upon his discovery of this illness in 1982, he went to the Harvard library and found that mesothelioma was incurable, with a median mortality of eight months after discovery. Most people would have interpreted this information pessimistically—that death would most likely occur in eight months—but Gould, with his deep belief that variation is the basic reality of life, interpreted the statistics optimistically—that half the people with this diagnosis lived longer than eight months. A long tail in the statistics also gave him hope, as did the excellent medical treatment and care he received. He lived to complete the book under review and continued to write his column for *Natural History*. In all of his work he has been animated by a sense of wonder that he effectively communicates to others. In the title essay of this collection, Gould supports the popular name of a dinosaur, Brontosaurus, over its scientific name, Apatosaurus—

hence "Bully for Brontosaurus." After having been instructed, enlightened, edified, and inspired by his essays, one might well exclaim, "Bully for Gould!"

Robert J. Paradowski

Sources for Further Study

Booklist. LXXXVII, March 15, 1991, p. 1433.
Commonweal. CXVIII, September 27, 1991, p. 553.
Library Journal. CXVI, May 15, 1991, p. 105.
Los Angeles Times. May 14, 1991, p. E2.
Nature. CCCLII, July 11, 1991, p. 117.
New Scientist. CXXX, June 22, 1991, p. 47.
New Statesman and Society. IV, May 3, 1991, p. 33.
The New York Times Book Review. XCVI, May 12, 1991, p. 11.
Publishers Weekly. CCXXXVIII, March 22, 1991, p. 65.
The Washington Post Book World. XXI, May 19, 1991, p. 1.

THE BURNT PAGES

Author: John Ash (1948-   )
Publisher: Random House (New York). 101 pp. $19.00
Type of work: Poetry

A series of reflections on culture and history by an English poet deeply influenced by contemporary American poetry

Questions of influence, tradition, heritage, and their relevance to the theory and practice of literature, and particularly their significance in the establishment of individual poets' intelligences and fields of concentration, have been of primary interest among writers for most of the twentieth century. In academic circles, these questions have been placed on a more systematic, theoretical level since the 1970's, thanks in large part, though not exclusively, to the work of the critic Harold Bloom. John Ash's poetry in *The Burnt Pages* is, among other things, a fascinating instance of what Professor Bloom has called "the anxiety of influence." Since the poems that exemplify this anxiety are both complex and, to some extent, derivative, though in a manner that is resourceful and imaginative rather than contrived and obvious, it is appropriate to establish something of the larger cultural context by which some of the effects that Ash creates in his work can be appreciated.

As an English poet living and working and drawing much of his imaginative sustenance from the United States, and from New York City in particular, John Ash represents an instance of influence that may be superficially considered unique. Historically speaking, the tide of influence has been considered to flow from east to west. European culture in all its phases was regarded as a model upon which American artists were well advised to draw, just as in Europe the classical world of Greece and Rome was thought not merely aesthetically and artistically inspirational but also, in practical terms, a source of models and forms that would discipline the imagination and assist in rendering objective a given artist's vision. Works by Henry James in fiction, and by T. S. Eliot and Ezra Pound in poetry, addressed by theme and example some of the issues raised by the artistic power of Europe, a power that was expressed both in terms of tradition and also in terms of the force of tradition in the conduct and management of civilized society.

The example of Pound and Eliot with regard to matters of tradition and influence, evident in their various theoretical writings no less than in their poetic practice, is generally acknowledged for its landmark status in literary history. One reason that it has been given such a status, however, is a result of the various reactions that occurred against their European preoccupations. The generation of American writers who came after Eliot and Pound found their example impossible to follow. In England, also, it became necessary to discover artistic approaches that would be departures from what had become somewhat dogmatic cultural orthodoxies. The most important example of the English reaction to Pound's and Eliot's assertion, in different forms, of a homogenized tradition of English and European culture is the work of W. H. Auden. Although Auden's decision to emigrate to the United States in 1939 was not made necessarily for exclusively artistic reasons, both his presence there and his poetic practice proved immensely influential.

Auden's example is not the only, or even the major, instance of a shift of emphasis in English poetic concerns resulting from the impact of Pound and Eliot. Their example also produced what might be termed an American strain in English poetry, originating in the work of the Pound-influenced Basil Bunting and continuing, under rather different auspices, in the poetry of Tom Raworth, Charles Tomlinson, and Lee Harwood, among others. Equally important is the rejection of this strain by many English poets, most notably Philip Larkin. In the light of these developments, the impact of Auden's American departure has been felt less emphatically in his native country than in his adopted one. Nevertheless, Auden's American career has continued to act as an important prototype for a number of different English poets— Thom Gunn provides a case in point—and its relevance and significance to the international dimension of poetry in English since 1945 cannot be overlooked.

In *The Burnt Pages*, there is a strong sense of the complex burden of poetic and other, more commonplace, and even more enervating, history. The book is the author's sixth collection of verse; a number of his earlier works were published by the influential English poetry press Carcanet, and this is his first volume to have its initial publication in the United States. As evidence of the poet's awareness of even literary history's complex heritage, *The Burnt Pages* contains a number of echoes from Auden. For example, in "Misconception of Richness," the figure in the poem is introduced "standing on the wrong side of the world,/ at the wrong end of the year," words that echo Auden's "right song for the wrong time of year." In "World's Floor," there is an elaborate restatement of Auden's dictum that "poetry makes nothing happen." A number of the poems invoke obliquely, by their tone and their implicit interrogation of art, Auden's "Musée des Beaux Arts." More generally, the poems that deal with New York refer to the unusual imaginative conditions that Auden's experience inaugurated for English poets. These conditions present exile and estrangement, dislocation and revitalization, and psychological environments providing virtually equal measures of vulnerability and liberation.

As a result, a considerable number of the poems in *The Burnt Pages* deal with traveling, arriving, welcoming, looking back, absence. Allusions to Auden, however, even if they provide a context for the trajectory of Ash's career and some of its cultural implications, are merely one somewhat esoteric instance of the dialogue with history that goes on throughout the book. Many poems strike a similar note in that they consist of rehearsals of alternatives that then cannot be adopted. There is a persistent sense of bridges and boats being burned, from which perhaps the book derives its title. In "Smoke," it is the sky that is likened to "a burnt page." This startling image of emptiness and indifference invites the reader to imagine the page as having been written on, since that is the way in which the sense of the irretrievable may most easily be imagined. Considered in this way, the use of the title phrase in "Smoke" goes beyond its limited, localized usage. The status of such a page is similar to that of the artists mentioned in one of the most satisfying works in *The*

Burnt Pages, the prose poem "Fifth Spring, Sixth Autumn." These artists' work is to be found in the mosaics of Greek churches. It is possible only to speculate about their actual existences and historical reality. Yet their work endures. In the absence of factual information, the work is transmitted freely and uncontaminated by irrelevance. "This," the poem says, "is a lesson in lost causes."

The poet's burnt pages have a similar relevance, conjuring up associations of detritus, immolation, waste, mortality. In an uncharacteristic and perhaps unnecessarily cruel pun, what burnt pages remind the reader of is ash. At the same time, however, the fact of the pages' having been burned is also a reminder that they might have contained something. Like the Byzantine mosaic artists, the pages become a hieroglyph of possibility by virtue of what is inaccessible about them. Such a gloss on the title of *The Burnt Pages*, together with an awareness of the associations of the title of the poem in which the phrase occurs, brings into focus some of this poet's larger thematic concerns. In particular, his emphasis on the reality of the transitory emerges less as a matter of regret than as a matter of fact. This emphasis enables the poet to address his imaginative encounters with history in a manner that enhances rather than dulls their problematic character. The sense that history may make in its irrational and unpredictable, but nevertheless inevitable, progress is reflected in Ash's poems.

This reflection occurs not merely in what the poet wants to say about history but also in the way he says it. There are so few passages of straightforward utterance in *The Burnt Pages* that the reader is likely to be skeptical of those that are encountered. Nevertheless, even if there are good reasons for not quite believing the following statement, acceptance of it even on a provisional basis is a help in reading poetry that is erratic and surprising in the speed with which it moves from one phase of its subject to another, poetry with an enameled and glistening surface that can seem somewhat off-putting. The statement in question is made in the second poem in the book, "Forgetting": "I know I mix the present with the past,/ but that's how I like it:/ there is no other way to go on." This strategy of mixing is to be found from line to line, stanza to stanza, and poem to poem in *The Burnt Pages*. Yet there are at least two reasons why it should not be regarded merely as a method or mannerism.

One reason is that it admits, and makes legitimate, the book's heterogenous contents. What the poems reflect of history pertains to history of various kinds, personal, social, contemporary, and ancient. The method of mixing, therefore, admits juxtapositions of presence and loss (as in "Forgetting"), of fragments and forms (as in the witty "New and Selected Poems"), of ancient and modern. The juxtaposition between the last pair of conditions is perhaps the one that functions most resonantly throughout *The Burnt Pages*. The ancient entity in question is Byzantium, of which the poet has considerable, though not particularly off-putting, scholarly knowledge. Its civilization is paralleled, rather than explicitly compared and contrasted, with that of the twentieth century's great imperial power, the United States.

By virtue of that equation, New York City is the new Constantinople. In particular, since John Ash also writes reviews of exhibitions of contemporary painting, the sense of color, light, and space that he brings not merely to the structure of what might be called the neo-Byzantine poems but also to their language makes the juxtaposition particularly effective. Through concentrating for the most part on the aesthetic and expressive character of experience, he is able to raise questions about what most concerns any civilization at any time, questions concerning the true and the good and the means by which either of these two categories may be sustained. In that sense, a major emphasis of *The Burnt Pages* falls on the poet's meditations on the relevance of art and whether its relevance becomes clear only in the face of barbarism. In a period when cultural activity is being encouraged at the expense of political engagement, these meditations have a suggestive, symptomatic expressiveness.

The second reason that the poet must be allowed to "mix" his effects is that it reveals his relationship with some of the more adventurous of contemporary American poets. John Ash's poetry has often been compared to that of John Ashbery. To some extent, this comparison is illuminating and appropriate. A large number of the poems in *The Burnt Pages* resemble Ashbery's by being at the same time abortive and incessant narratives, full of possibilities but lacking in conclusiveness. On the other hand, Ash's sense of poetic language is essentially iconic and lacks the fluidity of his virtual namesake's. Sometimes, too, Ash's approach to his material is disarmingly obvious, as in the *fin de siècle* coloration that suffuses one of the collection's most ambitious poems, "Twentieth Century." In keeping with the overall interests and motifs of *The Burnt Pages*, it seems that Ash is most helpfully regarded as a poet in transition, or perhaps a poet committed to transition. Thus, while his work is undoubtedly indebted to Ashbery, it also has elements of so-called language poets such as Leslie Scalapino. More noteworthy, however, than Ash's historical or contemporary status is his work's rendering of the restlessness and menace that besets the contemporary imagination. In addressing such forces, and in his efforts, largely exemplified by his interests in Byzantium, to find a framework sufficiently resonant and plausible to contain the fretfulness, ardor, and dismay of life at the end of the century, John Ash's verse is both worthwhile and challenging.

George O'Brien

Sources for Further Study

Chicago Tribune. January 12, 1992, XIV, p. 5.
The Washington Post Book World. XXII, January 19, 1992, p. 8.

THE CAMPAIGN

Author: Carlos Fuentes (1928-   )
First published: La Campaña, 1990
Translated from the Spanish by Alfred Mac Adam
Publisher: Farrar, Straus & Giroux (New York). 246 pp. $22.95
Type of work: Historical novel
Time: 1810-1821
Locale: Argentina, Peru, Bolivia, Chile, Venezuela, and Mexico

The saga of a young man from Buenos Aires whose quest for love is interwoven with his participation in the struggle for independence from Spain during a decade of revolution

> *Principal characters:*
> BALTASAR BUSTOS, the idealistic son of an Argentine landowner
> OFELIA SALAMANCA, the aristocratic woman Bustos loves and seeks
> MANUEL VARELA, a printer, Bustos' friend, and the narrator of the story
> XAVIER DORREGO, Bustos' and Varela's friend
> JULIAN RIOS, Bustos' Jesuit mentor
> ANSELMO QUINTANA, a Mexican revolutionary leader and priest

Set during the exciting and tumultuous revolutionary years between 1810 and the early 1820's, when Spanish America fought for its independence from Spain, *The Campaign* interweaves many connected stories and themes into an ingeniously complex novel. *The Campaign* is the first volume of a trilogy about the era from 1810 to the Mexican Revolution of 1910, and it is about the beginnings of Spanish America's quest for modern identity and self-definition. The novel is both a vigorous tale of action and a series of commentaries about the purpose of this action, about the implications of freedom and equality, and about the role of language itself. The story begins and ends in Buenos Aires, but the intermediate chapters describe the travels of the main character, Baltasar Bustos, as he journeys to the interior of Argentina, to Upper Peru, to Lima and Santiago, Maracaibo and Veracruz in pursuit of both a revolutionary ideal and the great erotic passion of his life. *The Campaign* is an account of the education of this young man, who symbolizes his times, who participates in the major events of the foundational decade that began in 1810, and who reflects at length upon the ramifications of this experience.

The story begins with melodrama: On the night of May 24, 1810, the very eve of the declaration of independence, Baltasar Bustos, then a young law clerk, kidnaps the newborn son of Ofelia Salamanca, wife of Marquis de Cabra, president of the superior court for the viceroyalty of the Río de la Plata. In the baby's place, he leaves a black infant, son of a prostitute who has just been publicly flogged. For Baltasar, this is a revolutionary act of justice: an insistence upon racial equality. The results of this impulsive, idealistic action are played out through the book, against a backdrop of a continent aflame with revolutionary fervor. Unexpected and chance occurrences determine subsequent events. Baltasar intends to put into practice the theories of Jean-Jacques Rousseau, Voltaire, and Denis Diderot, whose books he and his close friends, Varela (the book's narrator) and Dorrego, have been discussing, but an accidental fire erases the traces of his baby substitution, and Baltasar's life is transformed by his glimpse of the white baby's mother, the beautiful Ofelia Salamanca. Ofelia becomes for him not only an irresistible sexual attraction but also "what he most desired: an unattainable ideal, the pure bride of pure desire, untouched." *The Campaign* is the story of Bustos' double quest for the love of Ofelia and for the success of the American rebellion against the forces of Spain, crucially weakened at home by defeat by Napoleon Bonaparte's army.

The story eventually provides resolution of Bustos' dual passions as well as a reconnection with the misplaced white baby, who comes to symbolize the revolutionary rebirth and hopeful future of the American republics. Within this unifying framework of Bustos' multiple quests, a series of adventures and insights along the way are arranged in loosely associated order. Carlos Fuentes' narrative technique is kaleidoscopic: Each new chapter (set in a new geographic location) recombines and reiterates already familiar elements but rearranges these elements into a new pattern. Time spins forward and backward, including extensive historical background for the independence movement and circling ahead in prophecies and commentaries to comprehend present retrospective knowledge of the years that followed the idealism of 1810.

Baltasar Bustos' educational journey takes him from his circle of friends in Buenos Aires on a tour of the centers of revolutionary ferment. The continuity of a Buenos Aires perspective is maintained by the narrator, Bustos' printer friend Manuel Varela, who tells the story based on Bustos' letters to him. Attention is frequently drawn to the artifact of the written or printed word. Society is measured against the words of Rousseau, Voltaire, and Diderot. Bustos' letters try to describe the realities of revolution, but language often fails, just as it does in Upper Peru when Bustos makes an emotional speech about freedom to an Indian audience that does not understand his Spanish. The relationship of legal declarations and documents to social realities is often debated. Sets of words may represent or change perceptions, but they may also falsify them. Lawyers fight for independence with words, writing up declarations and "a splendid series of laws that abolished slavery, that restored lands to communities, and that guaranteed individual rights." Bustos, the law clerk from Buenos Aires, sees that both direct action and the written word are crucial. The lawyers also die in defense of what they believe. "Thus, the circle of the written closed over its authors, capturing them in the noble fiction of their own inventive powers: the written is the real and we are its authors." Fuentes repeatedly includes his own book in the sets of words about Spanish-American realities and expands his text to include other familiar contemporary sets of words as well. Varela, the narrator-printer, speaks of having in his hands "a life of the Liberator Simón Bolívar, a manuscript stained with rain and tied with tricolor ribbons, which the author, who called himself Aureliano García, had sent to me, as best he could, from Barranquilla." This reference to Gabriel García Márquez' book about Bolívar, *El general en su laberinto* (1989; *The General in His Labyrinth*, 1990), with a nod to Aureliano Buendía, a central character in García Márquez' novel *Cien años de soledad* (1967; *One Hundred Years of Solitude*, 1970), is one of many literary jokes, but also makes the serious point that our reality (and our perception of history) includes all the many interpretations of it, and is, in fact, composed of and by these interpretations. Historical reality can be represented only by words. Fuentes speaks of Baltasar Bustos as very aware "that he had written a chronicle of those years—the one I'm holding in my hands right now, which one day you, reader, will also hold in yours—in the stream of letters" he had sent to his friends.

Each chapter, each geographical destination, represents a step in the education of Baltasar Bustos and a set of choices the young man must make. He encounters a series of mentors who explain or show him their perspectives on truth, and he must decide in each case whether to follow this guidance. In the chapter on "The Pampa," Bustos comes to terms with his authoritarian landowner father, who lives among untamed gauchos in a primitive freedom that is doomed, ironically, by the revolution. In "El Dorado," Bustos is introduced to the world of Indian tradition. He is initiated into sexuality by Indian women and led by an ancient seer, Simón Rodríguez, down into the bowels of the earth into a surreal vision of a city of pure light, a golden, glowing city that may be a vision of either the past or the future. In Simón Rodríguez' words, "today we witnessed only one brief moment of that unending ribbon where truth is inscribed, and we do not know if what we saw is part of our imagination today, of an imagination that precedes us, or if it proclaims an imagination to come." The revelations of this ambiguous vision, terrible to Baltasar Bustos because they cause him to doubt his rational convictions, are counterbalanced by Bustos' plunge into physical action in battle on the side of guerrilla fighters who harass and decimate the Spanish forces. Bustos learns about ideological complexity and kills his first man, and Indian, his "real enemy brother," with whom he exchanges clothing. Mirror images and doubles abound throughout *The Campaign*, beginning with the two babies (one black, one white) and continuing as Bustos meets versions of aspects of himself at every turn: a gaucho brother who looks just like him, the Indian brother (also named Baltasar) whose death he avenges by killing another Indian brother, and a series of other men who represent facets of himself. Bustos himself becomes two quite separate men: the plump, myopic city gentleman and the lean, tough guerrilla fighter. He alternates between these two selves as he makes his way through the snares of Peruvian and Chilean society, telling and retelling the stories of his dreams, obsessions, and exploits in a gradual process of self-understanding.

Bustos' involvement with national struggles for political enlightenment becomes more fused with his obsessive search for Ofelia Salamanca as Bustos serves with San Martín's Army of the Andes and fights in the battle of Chacabuco. The fighting trio of friends (Echagüe, Arias, and Bustos) on the battlefield mirrors the Buenos Aires trio of peacetime theorists. Independence is won, but San Martín utters prophetic words about the difficulties of sustaining freedom and equality and the need for institutions that will promulgate national unity.

When Bustos' quest for his love takes him on to Venezuela, he is haunted by the popular ballads about his obsession with Ofelia that follow him everywhere. As he travels through the hills where Simón Bolívar's battles were fought, he believes that "all that was left to him was to bounce from war to war, from south to north and from north to south, to carry out his legendary destiny, which had already been mapped out in popular song." The Venezuelan backwoods are as surreal as the vision of El Dorado, and as disorienting. It is necessary for Bustos to reconnect with compassion and a sense of shared humanity, achieved only when he accompanies a dying Spanish officer, for him to be able to be rewarded with the final message from Ofelia Salamanca summoning him to join her in Veracruz. In Mexico, in "the final phase of his campaign of love and war," Bustos meets the last powerful mentor and brother figure, General Anselmo Quintana, the rebel priest who summarizes and symbolizes the progress of the wars for independence in Mexico, the last of the major struggles for freedom from Spain. With Quintana's lessons, Bustos' panoramic survey of the Americas in turmoil is complete, and his dual passion for Ofelia and for political renewal reaches the end of line, appropriately fused together. Bustos' return to Buenos Aires with Ofelia's son is both a homecoming and a new beginning. Bustos and his beloved have been joined all along, but only at the end does he understand this. In the boy, Bustos has found his true younger brother, and through his experiences, he has connected his theories with his practices and his ideas with his ideals.

In *The Campaign*, Carlos Fuentes has combined the suspense of a mystery with a dense panorama of historical detail. Bustos' pilgrimage through the major centers of revolutionary Spanish America creates the opportunity for a historical travelogue that serves as a backbone for clusters of commentaries, prophecies, and vivid images in surreal descriptions of battles, visions, and dreams. It is an epic full of optimism and exhilarating energy, the enthusiasm of political beginnings and the joy of language.

Mary G. Berg

Sources for Further Study

Booklist. LXXXVII, July, 1991, p. 2011.
Chicago Tribune. October 13, 1991, XIV, p. 7.
The Economist. CCCXXI, November 16, 1991, p. 112.
Kirkus Reviews. LIX, July 1, 1991, p. 808.
Library Journal. CXVI, September, 1991, p. 230.
Los Angeles Times Book Review. October 20, 1991, p. 2.
The New York Times Book Review. XCVI, October 6, 1991, p. 3.
Publishers Weekly. CCXXXVIII, August 2, 1991, p. 63.
The Times Literary Supplement. November 15, 1991, p. 6.
The Washington Post. October 31, 1991, p. C1.

CHARLES DARWIN
A New Life

Author: John Bowlby (1907-1990)
First published: 1990, in Great Britain
Publisher: W. W. Norton (New York). Illustrated. 466 pp. $24.95
Type of work: Biography
Time: 1809-1882
Locale: Primarily England

Bowlby offers a carefully researched and richly detailed account of the life of England's greatest biologist

Principal personages:
CHARLES DARWIN, the English biologist who formulated the theory of evolution
EMMA WEDGWOOD DARWIN, his wife
ROBERT FITZROY, the captain of HMS *Beagle*, later an opponent of Darwin's theory
CHARLES LYELL, an English geologist and supporter of Darwin
JOSEPH HOOKER, an eminent botanist and early friend and supporter of Darwin
ROBERT DARWIN, Charles's father, a physician
THOMAS HENRY HUXLEY, a zoologist and essayist, outspoken advocate of evolution
ALFRED RUSSEL WALLACE, a naturalist and evolutionary theorist
JOSIAH WEDGWOOD, a partner in the Wedgwood Pottery and Darwin's father-in-law

The biographer of Charles Darwin confronts a major challenge: to narrate his seemingly simple domestic life in the English countryside and, at the same time, to clarify and place in their contexts his complex, revolutionary, and far-reaching intellectual achievements, for few scientists or intellectuals in history have had greater influence on their period and subsequent ones than Darwin. In his journals, correspondence, and autobiography, he recorded numerous details and anecdotes as sources for a biographer. His lengthy narrative of the five-year expedition aboard the *Beagle* (1831-1836), for example, accounted for his activities during the most important formative period of his life. As the ship's naturalist, he made scientific observations and collected specimens worldwide, especially along the South American coast, for later study and analysis.

Following his return to England, Darwin married his cousin Emma Wedgwood in 1839 and settled into life as a scientist living quietly on a country estate. Through his physician father's wealth and generosity, he was able to live independently in Downs, Surrey, only a few miles south of London. There he and Emma reared their large family, seven of the ten children surviving to adulthood.

As John Bowlby explains, Darwin set a careful daily schedule and followed it seven days a week, except when family affairs or medical problems took him away from home. Remarkably, Darwin's schedule allowed for only three hours of work daily, and it has been ruefully observed that on this limited work schedule he managed to revolutionize the field of biology. Yet, as Bowlby points out, this conclusion is misleading. "Work" meant only time spent on the specific paper or book he was engaged in writing at the time. It did not include such activities as observation, reading, correspondence, and reflection, which occupied several additional hours daily.

While Bowlby keeps the reader informed of Darwin's interactions with family and friends and of his related activities, the more challenging and more significant task is to account for his scientific career and place him within the milieu of nineteenth century science so as to demonstrate his original contributions. Everyone knows that Darwin formulated the theory of evolution; few people know of his long years of systematic study of such subjects as earthworms, barnacles, coral reefs, the Venus's-flytrap, and animal psychology.

Although Darwin became something of a collector during his student years at Christ's College, Cambridge, the major stimulus to his scientific career was his time as a ship's naturalist aboard the *Beagle* on its long journey around the world. Commanded by a dour Scots captain, Robert FitzRoy, the ship had as its primary mission the charting of the South American coast below the equator. Bowlby has ascertained that FitzRoy's charts were so accurate that some are still in use. Darwin was expected to advance a number of scientific fields during the voyage, though at the outset he concentrated on geology. Among the books he selected for the voyage was a copy of Charles Lyell's *Principles of Geology* (1830-1833), a revolutionary work that adduced evidence for concluding the earth to be much older than previously thought. Yet Darwin had time to study botany, zoology, paleontology, and what is now called anthropology. On one trip over the Andes, he observed fossils of sea creatures embedded in limestone above the ten-thousand-foot level, and his reflections on the length of time required for the complex processes that had thrust up the deposits from the sea bottom supported Lyell's view of the earth's antiquity.

Yet Darwin achieved few significant theoretical insights during the voyage itself. When the governor of the Galápagos told him that the giant tortoises were slightly different on each island, the fact made no particular impression at the time. Later it became an obvious example of isolated populations of a species undergoing diverse development. Darwin did, however, note that the finches on the islands seemed related to those on the continent, though slightly different, and he made similar observations about sea iguanas on different islands. Experience with the natives of Tierra del Fuego impressed upon him both the distance between their level of civilization and that of Europeans and the difficulties involved in attempting to change them. The voyage left him with ample evidence that species were mutable, a revolutionary though not entirely new idea. By 1839, after studying his notes and continuing his observations of living organisms, he had become convinced that all life was related and that human beings were no exception.

Bowlby places Darwin clearly within the tradition of evolutionary thought in order to reveal his original contributions. Darwin was by no means the first writer to believe in evolution of life on the planet; so far as is known, his grandfather was the first Englishman to ascribe to the view, in well-known and eloquent verses. Erasmus Darwin (1731-1802) accepted the radical view that species were variable and incorporated it into his poetry, celebrating a progressivist view of life. Somewhat later, in 1809, the French scientist Jean-Baptiste-Pierre de Lamarck outlined evolutionary theory with a highly speculative view of the way it took place. Evolution became more plausible but hardly more widely accepted after Lyell's *Principles of Geology* offered evidence for geologic time that extended back millions of years. Another Englishman, Robert Chambers, argued for evolution in his *Vestiges of the Natural History of Creation* (1844) and found himself ridiculed for his views of the processes that brought it about. After lengthy study of the matter, Darwin outlined the evidence for the view in *On the Origin of Species by Means of Natural Selection* (1859). Darwin's fellow scientist A. R. Wallace reached similar conclusions independently at about the same time, though he always credited Darwin with the discovery.

Darwin had indeed made the fullest and most systematic account of the evidence in support of the theory; evidence that at the time rested upon distribution of plants and animals over the continents, on the successful alteration of domestic species through selective breeding, on observations about extinction as revealed through paleontology, on comparative anatomy, and on the presence of vestigial organs. Darwin had accumulated his evidence from observations and studies during the *Beagle* expedition and from additional studies following his return.

Yet Darwin did not limit his study to presentation of evidence; he also attempted to show how evolution had occurred, to clarify the mechanism that drove the process of change. He termed this "natural selection," as opposed to the artificial selection employed by breeders of domestic animals. Highly influenced by Thomas Malthus' *An Essay on the Principle of Population* (1798), he observed that in nature many more individuals are born than can survive. Those that do survive pass on their traits to their offspring; thus a natural winnowing contributes to the improvement of the species. The explanation proved to Darwin and others the most unsatisfactory part of the theory, and following the publication he continued to explore other possibilities of mutation and development of species. Unaware of Gregor Mendel's work on genetics, he put forth the incorrect view that pangenesis accounted for inherited characteristics.

While he followed the controversy that ensued after the publication of his most theoretical book, Darwin chose usually not to involve himself in it, in part because of his chronic ill health and in part because of his retiring temperament. He left his defense in the hands of supporters such as Charles Lyell, Thomas Henry Huxley, and the eminent botanist Joseph Hooker. Sometimes even his followers did not agree with him on every point. Lyell, for example, considered humans to be an exception to the theory long after Darwin had abandoned that idea and had begun serious study of emotions and other "human" qualities of other mammals.

Meanwhile, he continued to produce a steady stream of scientific articles and monographs, many having little theoretical content. He lived to see his reputation and acclaim steadily increase, though often more rapidly abroad than in England. While controversy swirled in England, the eminent naturalist Asa Gray of Harvard became his advocate in America, and the Prussian government awarded him its highest honor, the medal Pour le Mérite.

The richly illustrated text offers more than the usual scholarly apparatus and illustrations. In addition to its thorough documentation, the book includes explanatory notes at the bottoms of pages in order to give additional perspective on the contents. Useful extra compilations include a chronology of Darwin's life and an appended "Who's Who" identifying 172 individuals who played some part in Darwin's life. Among the many illustrations are genealogical charts of Darwin's ancestors and descendants. The chapters on the voyage of the *Beagle* provide maps that detail the journey clearly, showing its course along the South American coast and through the Galápagos Islands. A cross-section diagram of the ship depicts its below-deck arrangement and lading. Numerous black-and-white reproductions of photographs and portraits of Darwin, members of his family, his friends and supporters, and his opponents are provided.

A psychiatrist by training and experience, Bowlby devotes extended attention to the recurring illnesses that plagued Darwin for most of his life. These involved palpitations of the heart, gastrointestinal distress (including vomiting and pain), occasional depression, and a variety of skin problems. These afflictions did not interfere significantly with his work schedule, though they may in some measure account for his aversion to travel and his uneasiness in company. Earlier biographers have suggested a variety of explanations, both physical and psychological, to account for Darwin's symptoms. A popular diagnosis has been that he suffered from Chagra's disease, a chronic illness that produces similar symptoms. It was known that Darwin was bitten by the insect that carries the disease while he was in South America. Bowlby, on the other hand, believes that childhood trauma resulting from the early death of his mother may account for the symptoms. The family ignored the grief, and the two older sisters who cared for the young Darwin never mentioned their mother, thus depriving him of a period of grief. Like the diagnosis of disease, Bowlby's hypothesis is plausible, yet it does not explain similar symptoms in the earlier generation of Darwin's family, nor those in his children. Evidence of these symptoms is rife in the extensive family correspondence that Bowlby cites frequently. Bowlby supports his conclusion with a considerable amount of psychological explanation but does not definitely settle the long-standing question.

With his thorough understanding of family relationships and interaction, Bowlby creates a memorable and poignant account of the Darwins' family life during the nineteenth century. As he observes, the afflictions that they endured were by no means unique. Large families, the norm for the period, meant more physical suffering from infectious diseases and more bereavements through early deaths. These sufferings took a heavy psychological toll upon the women of the age, often contributing to mental breakdowns that brought further family stress and anguish. Darwin and his immediate family were spared the worst consequences of suffering but had to endure their portion of premature deaths of children. Bowlby's portrait of Darwin amply clarifies his towering scientific achievements and his warm, sympathetic, and vulnerable personal character.

Stanley Archer

Sources for Further Study

Contemporary Review. CCLVIII, February, 1991, p. 107.
Lancet. CCCXXXVI, July 21, 1990, p. 146.
Los Angeles Times Book Review. June 9, 1991, p. 12.
Nature. CCCXLVII, September 6, 1990, p. 27.
New Scientist. CXXVII, August 11, 1990, p. 57.
The New York Times. XCVI, July 14, 1991, p. 12.
The New Yorker. LXVII, August 12, 1991, p. 79.
Publishers Weekly. CCXXXVIII, February 8, 1991, p. 47.
Science. CCLII, May 17, 1991, p. 992.
The Times Literary Supplement. July 6, 1990, p. 719.

CHARLES OLSON
The Allegory of a Poet's Life

Author: Tom Clark (1941-   )
Publisher: W. W. Norton (New York). 403 pp. $27.95
Type of work: Literary biography
Time: 1910-1970
Locale: Gloucester, Massachusetts; New York, New York; Washington, D.C.; Black Mountain, North Carolina; Buffalo, New York

The first biography of Charles Olson, postmodern poet and influential cultural visionary, whose wide-ranging public life was an outward expression of a complex and mysterious private one

Principal personages:
> CHARLES OLSON, the poet, revolutionary thinker, inspirational teacher, and troubled genius
> CONSTANCE WILCOX, Olson's first common-law wife, mother of Katherine
> BETTY KAISER, Olson's second common-law wife, mother of Charles Peter
> FRANCES BOLDEREFF, a longtime friend of the poet, avid correspondent, and psychic supporter
> ROBERT CREELEY, Olson's poetic brother and "running mate"
> ROBERT DUNCAN, Olson's fellow poet and intellectual ally and friend
> EDWARD DAHLBERG, an idiosyncratic writer, Olson's semimentor, sometime rival and sometime friend
> ALLEN GINSBERG, the most prominent of the counterculture poets Olson inspired and challenged
> ALAN CRANSTON, a promising young politician Olson worked with in Washington, later senator from California

The most interesting subjects for biographical projects are often the most difficult to write about. Psychological complexity enriches the landscape while making it harder to navigate. If the life brought under scrutiny has been the source of some artistic achievement, the difficulty is compounded by the necessity for linking the subject's work and his days. In the case of an artist whose work is elusive and unconventional, interpretation and clarification enter the equation as well. For Tom Clark, an accomplished poet, a former poetry editor of *The Paris Review*, and the author of volumes on the lives of Louis-Ferdinand Céline, Damon Runyon, Jack Kerouac, and Ted Berrigan, all these factors contributed to a challenge of unusual dimensions when he undertook a biography of Charles Olson.

The appeal of the project for Clark is obvious. He interviewed Olson during the mid-1960's and, like many others, was left with an impression of an exceptional figure, a source of energy and fascination. He knew that Olson's life was unusually diverse, his contacts with people in American social and artistic circles uniquely various. Many of these people were still alive and willing to discuss their encounters, while others had written accounts of their meetings, friendships, or confrontations with Olson. He knew that Olson kept a detailed, candid journal from his earliest years, and he recognized that the relationship between Olson's life and his writing would shed light on both if he could find a method to draw all the letters, essays, and poetry into a suitable frame of meaning.

Clark realized that a conventional treatment would be unsatisfactory. The mass-of-facts approach was pointless; fragments of factual material were already responsible for the contradictory claims of Olson's supporters and revilers that clouded his life and work. In addition, Olson's writing similarly captivated or repelled students and critics, while his personal intensity made his every relationship a study in tension, even torment, as well as inspiration akin to awe and love. Once swept into his magnetic presence, a person seemed either charmed or dismayed—sometimes alternately (or simultaneously) being driven to both polarities.

Clark decided that his study would be an act of "creative criticism" (as Ezra Pound put it) in which the interpenetration of mind and art would be revealed by what John Keats called "continual allegory." Acknowledging that the mystery of any life can never be totally explained, Clark believed that the strands of the linkage between "inner and outer myth" might be presented so as to produce "a magic resonance" that clarified and reanimated both realms. In this fashion, all the material he had gathered could be shaped so as to provide a direction toward (if not a definitive reading of) the poet's major work.

Realizing how esoteric such an approach might become, Clark applies his skills as a storyteller to the events of Olson's life. To balance the demands on the reader and on himself as he ranges through the processes of poetic composition, Clark organizes the circumstances of Olson's life into a brisk, lively, and engaging narration, using the propelling power of action and incident to maintain a level of fascination with his subject. Intending to reach the literate reader who is not a literary professional, Clark effectively highlights crucial information, overcoming the obstacle of huge blocks of facts that congeal into brain numbing clumps of data in many biographies. Beginning with a quick history of the New England coast, which sustained the fishing trade that dominated Olson's dreams in the poet's youth, Clark establishes the motif of paternal influence that became a primary element in Olson's development as a man and a writer. From the start, Clark is unafraid to offer psychoanalytic interpretation, realizing that any other approach would betray his allegorical system. Without resorting to the jargon of the psychologist, Clark depends on the lucidity and logic of his argument to establish his authority. To support his speculation, he introduces relevant excerpts from Olson's poems as well as recollections of important events as they appear in the journals, scrupulously citing his sources in extensive notes.

Following a succinct accounting of Olson's early years, Clark shows how the complex processes of Olson's mind initiated in a series of educational experiences, including his brief but tarnished glory as a champion orator at Worcester Classical School, where his already impressive stature combined with a voice he could use as an instrument or weapon enabled him to overcome (temporarily) a permanent fear of performance. The contrasting qualities of an imposing physical presence (Olson eventually stood six feet eight inches tall, was proportionally broad of chest and shoulder, and moved, as the dancer Merce Cunningham said, like a "light walrus") and a desire to "show 'em" were mixed with a deep sense of reserve and an inclination toward inward reflection; this is the first of several central paradoxes that Clark uses to build his thematic formulation of Olson's life as allegory—the meaning of everything doubled and coded beyond its immediate appearance. Olson demonstrated his gifts for literature and language from the start of his collegiate career, earning Phi Beta Kappa honors at Wesleyan University and then planning an M.A. thesis on Herman Melville at Wesleyan's Graduate School. Olson intended to reach an original conclusion by avoiding all prior Melville criticism. This characteristic push toward the original often left him so far outside familiar parameters that observers were either intrigued enough to follow his brilliant leaps or so put off by his lack of conventional patterns of thought that they tended to disparage everything he said.

Even if he had not become a major figure in mid-twentieth century American literature, Olson's course during the next decades would have been worth charting, as he moved through some of the most interesting quarters of modernist culture in the United States. Continuing his passionate pursuit of what he believed was the true Melville through the 1930's, Olson took a teaching position at Clarke University in 1934, where he began to shape an extraordinary classroom presence. He began a Ph.D. project on Melville at Harvard in 1936 with the noted scholar F. O. Matthiessen, spent some time at sea with New England whaling men personally investigating his coastal heritage, and launched into a friendship and rivalry with the idiosyncratic genius Edward Dahlberg. In this segment of the book, Clark contrasts Olson's active intellectual and social life with his sometimes tormented, often lonely sense of himself as permanently isolated and draws together the elements that were accumulating in the formation of Olson's nascent visionary theory of human intelligence and consciousness, laying the groundwork for a detailed examination of these theories in the latter pages of the volume.

As exciting as the 1930's seemed, they were essentially a prologue for what was to follow. Shaped by his father's (a postman's) proletarian perspective, Olson always had a strong sense of social justice. He worked for the American Civil Liberties Union (ACLU) in the late 1930's and for the progressive journal *The Common Ground* in 1942, and then a meeting with Alan Cranston directed him to a job in the Office of War Information (OWI), where Olson found he could combine his writing skills with a specific contribution to the war against fascism. His secret work in the attempt to psychoanalyze and destabilize Hitler (which Clark does not cover) was eventually to become another component of his historical synthesis, but while he found life in World War II Washington exciting and satisfying, the increasing bureaucratic regimentation of the OWI and its slide into more reactionary policies led to his resignation. Although he continued to pursue a political vocation through the Democratic National Convention of 1944, where he served on the Central Committee, the reelection of President Franklin Roosevelt later that year marked a turning point in

Olson's life. Acting on instinct as much as analysis, he rejected politics for poetry, concluding a successful venture into the public sphere and beginning an uncertain and financially difficult course he would follow for the remainder of his life. Clark makes it clear that Olson never regretted his choice, that he regarded it in retrospect as inevitable. Its consequences for his family were severe, but at the time he did not realize the toll it would take. From then on, his wife Connie had to supply both psychic and organizational support as Olson subordinated everything else to his work.

Clark then moves deeper into Olson's mind, shifting the focus of the narrative from the matrix of social and intellectual ideas that engaged Olson to the new patterns of poetic consciousness in Olson's emerging sense of his own language, voice, and style. In a kind of transitional action, Olson met Ezra Pound in St. Elizabeths Hospital, where Pound was being held as "insane" to avoid a trial for treason. Pound was a significant influence on Olson before their first meeting, and both his politics and poetic theories interested Olson, but after some respectful conversations, the two moved toward a serious dispute. Olson believed that he was confronting another ominous, powerful paternal figure who had to be overthrown, while Pound believed that Olson was "fundamentally" wrong about poetry and history. The frustration Olson felt was increased when his study of Melville was finally published to poor reviews, but at the same time, Olson began to meet supportive fellow artists such as Robert Duncan, who became a lifelong friend and helper, William Carlos Williams (a more benevolent paternal figure), who encouraged Olson's new theories of poetic composition, and, when he took a position as a temporary lecturer at the near-legendary Black Mountain College in North Carolina, an entire group of artists of the avant-garde. In what he labeled "a strange spot, a holy place," Olson's teaching flowered into the charismatic performance that would touch everyone who saw it, if not always in a positive manner. In another crucial encounter, Olson met Frances Boldereff, an intelligent, attractive woman who became a sort of shadow-anima for him for the rest of his life, and whose presence Clark alleges contributed significantly to the double-level of the developing allegory of Olson's poetic life. Their relationship, kept secret from even Olson's closest friends, drew the intimately personal into the subreaches of his poetry, so that theories of history became intertwined with the profound concerns of his being.

Completing the company of Olson's closest allies, Robert Creeley, to whom Olson first spoke through letters in 1950, offered him a kind of wary friendship, support from someone in the new generation of American poets, access to a network of outlaw publications, and a shared interest in modes of language that Clark describes as "uniquely intense, compulsive, and idiosyncratic." Olson's correspondence with Creeley and Boldereff continued for the rest of his life, and Clark uses the materials of these letters to illustrate the gradual but steady shift from the public to the private in Olson's life. He describes this hermetic ingathering of forces by calling Olson "an intuitive dogmatist of private vision" and bases his interpretation of many poems on this process. After overseeing the liquidation of Black Mountain College's assets in 1957, Olson retreated to Gloucester, surrounding himself with masses of books and notes and creating a sanctuary of sorts where he could map the coordinates of his encompassing projection of a new revolutionary view of artistic consciousness, "the human universe."

In spite of his solitary existence, Olson still teemed with energy, and when he emerged from "the republic of the soul," as on the occasion of the Vancouver Poetry Conference of 1963, the Berkeley Poetry Conference of 1965, or his brief but dynamic sojourn as a teacher at the State University of New York at Buffalo in between, the force he had accumulated in introspective thinking was thrust out with chaotic energy. Clark records the reactions of the students, fellow poets, and assorted cultural explorers (many now famous) who were present on these occasions, and their accounts are testimony to the manner in which their lives were affected through contact with a unique presence.

As he is covering the last decade of Olson's life, Clark presents many of the poems that were composed during that time, clarifying obscure references, explaining intention clearly, placing the work in the frame of Olson's theoretical thinking, and to some extent unraveling the threads of Olson's logic. Without offering extensive analysis, Clark provides a solid ground for understanding, going considerably beyond the artificial boundaries of many factual biographies to connect the artist to his work in an incisive series of interpretive excursions. When Clark attempts to convey the full dimensions of Olson's personal myth, his discussion of a method that is "elliptical and hyperbolic" for mapping "spaces of topology and congruence" illustrates the difficulties that drove many more traditional thinkers away, but the appeal of an original and powerful mind is there as well. As Carol Bergé put it, Olson's discourse was like the collision of "hip modern lingo, Hittite, lightning and the oracle of Delphi."

Clark's presentation of Olson's final years is painfully honest. Despite his faults— his self-concern, his disregard of the needs of his family—Olson becomes extremely sympathetic as Clark depicts his pain from cancer and his death in 1970. Even in the last stages of his life Olson was capable of a final flourish, as in his appearance at the Beloit Lectures in Modern Poetry in 1968, where he moved through a "cloud of awe and enigma" to project a "majestic, even compelling beauty." At the conclusion of the book, the mood of sadness and the sense of loss Clark evokes is a measure of his success at capturing the spirit of his subject, and while no book can completely cover a life, this volume suggests how rich, complex, and singular—though not easily known—a human being can be. Initial biographies are never conclusive, but even considering the limits of Clark's efforts, this volume will remain an essential document for students of modern American literature, as well as for anyone interested in "the vulnerable passage of a classic American genius," as Creeley epitomizes his old friend.

Leon Lewis

Sources for Further Study

Booklist. LXXXVII, April 15, 1991, p. 1614.
Choice. XXIX, September, 1991, p. 90.
Kirkus Reviews. LIX, March 15, 1991, p. 370.
Library Journal. CXVI, March 15, 1991, p. 89.
Los Angeles Times Book Review. April 28, 1991, p. 4.
Publishers Weekly. CCXXXVIII, February 15, 1991, p. 82.
The Review of Contemporary Fiction. XI, Fall, 1991, p. 296.
San Francisco Chronicle. April 14, 1991, p. REV9.
The Washington Post Book World. XXI, April 14, 1991, p. 4.

CLOSING ARGUMENTS

Author: Frederick Busch (1941-   )
Publisher: Ticknor & Fields (New York). 288 pp. $19.95
Type of work: Novel
Time: The 1990's
Locale: Randall, a small town in upstate New York

Combining suspense and narrative complexity, Busch has written a dazzling and powerful novel which disturbs both in its subject matter and its implications

>   *Principal characters:*
>   MARCUS "MARK" BRENNAN, the narrator, an attorney
>   ROCHELLE, his wife
>   JACK and MICKEY, their son and daughter
>   ESTELLA PRITCHETT, a client of Brennan, on trial for murder
>   ADINA "DEE" TILLIM, assistant district attorney
>   SIDNEY BIRNBAUM, a journalist
>   PHAN TUY, a Vietnamese interrogator

Closing Arguments, Frederick Busch's fifteenth book of fiction and seventeenth overall, takes its title from a screenplay that Busch wrote with Scott Millar for Home Box Office in 1987. Subtitled "The Life and Death of Roy Cohn," that *Closing Arguments* deals with the man who served as Senator Joseph McCarthy's assistant in the early 1950's and who went on to become a high-priced New York lawyer, a noted celebrity, and finally an AIDS victim. As Busch explained to Donald Greiner, Cohn "is a very complex phenomenon, and he's a darker side of the great Gatsby: an American crook who gave birth to himself in the great tradition of American self-inventing characters." *Closing Arguments*, the novel, also deals with a lawyer—not a national figure such as Cohn but a country lawyer in his early forties who is also a local hero in the kind of small upstate New York town common in Busch's fiction. It is a place where, as Busch has said, "a lot of the people are sad, undernourished and full of hate," an appropriate setting for this updating of Theodore Dreiser's *An American Tragedy* (1925).

A lesser figure than Cohn but better off (financially anyway) than most of his rural neighbors, Marcus (Mark) Brennan is the means by which Busch continues his exploration of the underbelly of the American dream, F. Scott Fitzgerald's "romantic possibilities" gone awry. Former Marine Phantom pilot (nickname Goblin), escaped POW, war hero but also victim of the post-traumatic stress disorder that afflicts so many Vietnam veterans, Mark knows just who and what he is: knows that he does real estate closing for a livelihood, knows that his wife Rochelle, a nurse turned hospital administrator, is having affairs, knows that he has failed as a father, and knows too that he would prefer that Rochelle not complete her "reconciliation project," the monument that is her way of healing the social and psychological wounds of war and, not incidentally, restoring Mark to his rightful place as husband, hero, father. Fond of quoting Sun Tzu on the art of war but otherwise given to expressing himself in a terse, often cynically knowing, even blackly humorous way, Mark is not only the novel's hero; he is its self-conscious and strangely detached narrator. His story, which is Busch's novel, takes an appropriately judicial form, a courtroom drama beginning, naturally enough, with an "Opening Argument":

> Let's say I'm telling you the story of the upstate lawyer, the post-traumatic combat stress, the splendid wife, their solitudes and infidelities, their children, his client with her awkward affinities, the sense of impending recognition by which he is haunted.
>
> You can see me, can't you? You can see me in my office after hours, after dark, after dawn. The bottle of ink, the sharp-nibbed pen, the pad of yellow sheets with their line after line.

The reader, placed here in the position of judge and juror, cannot, of course, actually see Mark except through and in the revelations (and concealments) of his seemingly honest yet nonetheless subjective and ultimately horrific account. Mark's narrative unfolds in multiple directions: his relations with Rochelle, his son Jack, and his daughter Mickey, with his past (particularly his flashbacks to his abusive parents and his internment in a POW camp after he was shot down), and above all with the client whose case he takes on a *pro bono* basis, because it is his turn. The client is Estella Pritchett, a Social Services caseworker noted for her efforts to protect children but now accused of murdering Larry Ziegler, another Vietnam veteran, a respected local businessman who died of asphyxiation during one of his and Estella's regular once-a-week bouts of "rough sex" in a seedy motel called The Stone's Throw. Mark's interest in her and the hold she soon comes to have over him give the story much of its drive and focus. As sexy as she is dangerous but only as dangerous as she is vulnerable, Estella cannot distinguish between love and death, guilt and innocence. Forced to play well above his normal professional and emotional levels, Mark seeks to penetrate the mystery she represents in a double sense: sexually (though here she, not Mark, takes the aggressive "male" part) and cognitively (learning that she has been abused not only by her mother, as she admits, but sexually by her father, as she repeatedly denies).

At the time he was completing the first draft of the other *Closing Arguments*, the screenplay about Roy Cohn, Busch began work on a second script, "a sweet thriller" about children. *Closing Arguments* is also a "sweet thriller" about children—about, more specifically, abused children, and, more generally, about the dynamics of power, love, violence, frustration, desire, and dreams. Power—or more often, powerlessness—is the key. When Estella shows up on the last day of her trial wearing a "suicidal" red dress, Mark notes, "women in a jury would have disapproved, and men would have resented her power to stimulate them." There is, however, no jury in *Closing Arguments*; on Mark's advice, Estella has waived her right to a jury trial. She acquiesces to his power legally as he does to hers sexually. In doing so, she puts herself at the mercy of Judge John Backus, one of the novel's many father figures. (Mark often seems to be playing to the judge both to win his approval for the legal skills Mark does not in fact possess and to gain the upper hand by either persuasion or deception; simultaneously Mark appears to be playing to and for Jack, trying to prove himself in his son's eyes.) One of the most interesting of the novel's various fathers is Phan Tuy, the Vietnamese interrogator who forces Mark to write and re-write the autobiography which is also to serve as his confession and who metes out what he terms "just punishment" for Mark's alleged offenses. Strangely but signifi-cantly, Phan Tuy reminds Mark of "many of the rural poor in New York State," many of whom Mark, as a small-town lawyer, knows stand accused of abusing their children. Abused by his own parents, Mark chooses to distance himself from his own children, in this way substituting emotional neglect for physical abuse. When Jack twice gets into trouble, it is Lee Barton Palmer, a local vice officer, who steps in to play the father's role, not out of any love for Jack but because of Mark, who, unlike Palmer's younger brother, came home a hero, not in a body bag.

In *Closing Arguments*, child abuse and Vietnam are often narratively linked. To escape from the POW camp (and from the abusing Phan Tuy/father), Mark must kill a young guard, probably no more than thirteen years old. The killing is described with all the detail of a Marine manual on hand-to-hand combat, or of Stanley Ku-brick's film *Full Metal Jacket* (1987). The Vietnam connection shows up again in Mark's choosing to explain Estella's behavior in terms of the post-traumatic stress disorder suffered by abused children like Estella as well as Vietnam veterans. Child abuse and post-traumatic stress disorder are but two of the wide range of topical references in *Closing Arguments*, everything from the well-publicized Preppy Mur-der Case and the film *Fatal Attraction* (1987) to the case of the parents who wanted to "return" the child they had adopted but no longer wanted, the testimony of "ex-pert witnesses," and the growing realization in the late 1980's of Freud's unwilling-ness to accept what his own clinical experience indicated: that many of his adult clients had not simply fantasized about having been sexually abused as children but had in fact experienced such abuse. Diverse as the novel may be, fragmented into a succession of short sections (most just three or four pages long), *Closing Arguments* is relentless to a point beyond fascination, somewhere nearer to intimidation, a tautly written postmodern thriller in which every scene, indeed every line resonates with echoes of and parallels to other scenes, other plots. The sexual, social, legal, family, and military spheres do not so much overlap as overlay one another: interrogator and interrogated, parent and child, husband and wife, cop and criminal, prosecutor and defending attorney, judge and judged appear locked in similar adversarial relations of power and powerlessness. Courts of law become fields of battle, homes become POW camps, love becomes hate.

"It all depends on how you see it," Mark claims. "It all depends on what you say." He might have added that "it" also depends on what you (the narrator) with-hold and what you (the narratee) are willing to believe or privilege. Attracted to the narrative of Mark's unethical relationship with Estella, a relationship which seems to parallel or repeat Larry Ziegler's, the reader may forget or marginalize the nov-el's other mystery, "the sense of impending recognition" which has haunted Mark since the opening page. It is this mystery which the freelance journalist Sidney Birn-baum—in town to cover the story of Randall's unveiling of its Vietnam war memo-rial—uncovers near the close of *Closing Arguments*. As Mark finally admits near the novel's and his own end, "Vietnam, Schelle, and now you know that I made it up." Mark's disclosure, which is made not to his wife directly but instead on the legal-size yellow pads on which he writes the narrative that is also his confession (and suicide note) as well as Busch's novel, hardly constitutes an unambiguous clarification, a tidy summation. His multiply referenced "it" raises as many questions as it answers. It casts a Hawthorne-like "lurid gleam" on Mark's Conradian heart of darkness. For Mark does more than raise a doubt about his status as hero (and pilot, prisoner of war, Vietnam veteran). He raises a doubt concerning his narrative and the act of narrating itself. How much if any of his story parallels other stories, other lives? How much draws its substance from those stories and lives? Was Mark ever in Vietnam in any capacity? Was he ever abused (or, for that matter, was Estella)? How much of his narrative of his life and times is drawn from the popular culture (as handily as the allusion to, say, *Fatal Attraction*)? "The best defense," Mark likes to say, "is a good story."

Mark will put Estella on the stand and then ask her under oath to acknowledge in public to a courtroom of her accusers, judges, and peers what she has steadfastly refused to acknowledge in private: that her father abused her sexually. Shamed and enraged, she will kill Mark, thus completing the plot Mark himself set in motion, orchestrating this last bit of rough sex, for like a good Marine, Mark chooses death before dishonor (or at least before disclosure). Before meeting Estella for this last time, he completes the narrative, telling his reader, Rochelle, that he would have saved her, protected her, had he been able. The reader may well wonder whether Mark may have another purpose in mind as well: a fine and final revenge against an unfaithful wife. Then again, perhaps (or also) Mark is only following Sun Tzu's advice: "The ultimate maneuver: cut and run."

As suspenseful as the most slickly written courtroom thriller, *Closing Arguments* is much more than just a good read, closer in its self-questioning style and spirit to two other fictions of the early 1990's, Thomas Berger's *Orrie's Story* and Tim O'Brien's *The Things They Carried* (both 1990). Like them, *Closing Arguments* raises a doubt in the reader's mind about the nature of narrative and the narrating act itself. It is a doubt that the novel's ambitious assistant district attorney would be quick to discredit: "Judge, do we deal in our courts with the law? Or must we tell our nightmares to each other? Laws are not to be broken. Anything else, outside of the law, is just words, just stories." Mark holds to a very different view. "When we figure out what truth we're telling," he explains to Estella early in the novel, "then we'll work on how to tell somebody that particular truth." Having no particular truth to tell, willing to probe all the possibilities, *Closing Arguments* proves both a moral as well as a narrative labyrinth. Transgressing the limits which the assistant district attorney wishes to impose on truth as well as on fiction without, however, endorsing the manipulative cynicism to which Mark subscribes, Busch's novel is consummate in its artistry, complex in its vision, disturbing in its implications, above all dizzying in its permutational possibilities.

Robert A. Morace

Sources for Further Study

Booklist. LXXXVII, June 1, 1991, p. 1842.
Boston Globe. August 11, 1991, p. 93.
Chicago Tribune. August 28, 1991, V, p. 3.
Kirkus Reviews. LIX, June 1, 1991, p. 683.
Library Journal. CXVI, July, 1991, p. 131.
Los Angeles Times. August 15, 1991, p. E6.
The New York Times Book Review. XCVI, August 18, 1991, p. 6.
Publishers Weekly. CCXXXVIII, June 7, 1991, p. 55.
USA Today. August 8, 1991, p. D4.
The Washington Post Book World. XXI, August 4, 1991, p. 1.

COLETTE
A Life

Author: Herbert Lottman (1927-   )
Publisher: Little, Brown (Boston). Illustrated. 344 pp. $24.95
Type of work: Literary biography
Time: 1873-1954
Locale: Saint-Sauveur-en-Puisaye, France; the South of France and Monte Carlo; Paris and Brussels

A biography of the most famous woman writer of twentieth century Europe, whose uninhibited personal life and flamboyant theatrical performances, like her prose, illustrated her desire to explore the possibilities of female sexuality

> Principal personages:
> SIDONIE-GABRIELLE COLETTE, a writer and performer
> HENRI ("WILLY") GAUTHIER-VILLARS, her first husband and literary collaborator
> MATHILDE ("MISSY") DE MORNY, MARCHIONESS DE BELBOEUF, Colette's lesbian lover
> HENRI ("SIDI") DE JOUVENEL, her second husband, a baron and a journalist
> COLETTE DE JOUVENEL, Colette's daughter
> BERTRAND DE JOUVENEL, Henri de Jouvenel's son by an earlier marriage, Colette's lover
> MAURICE GOUDEKET, Colette's third husband, a Jewish pearl dealer

Herbert Lottman's *Colette: A Life* begins with an interesting question: To what extent was Colette the writer identical to Claudine, the character she created in her notorious early books? As a fifteen-year-old schoolgirl in a small, rural French town, Claudine takes great interest in her own sexual impulses and in the sexual activities of others. She notices the growing attachment between the headmistress and her assistant, with whom Claudine herself is passionately in love; the infatuation of the assistant's young sister for Claudine; and the approaches the medical inspector makes to schoolgirls like Claudine, when he is not, according to rumor, in bed with the headmistress. According to this biography, when she was at school, Sidonie-Gabrielle Colette, who was to be the writer called simply "Colette," appeared to be more interested in pranks than in sexual titillation. Moreover, the real Colette seems merely to have imagined the schoolroom scandals in her book. The character of the medical inspector, for example, was based on a political enemy of her father, a respectable doctor who in real life was never accused of making attempts on the virtue of schoolgirls.

Lottman makes it clear that differentiating between Claudine the fictitious character and Colette the young writer is even more difficult because there are so many versions as to the kind of collaboration that produced the four books about Claudine. When she was twenty, Colette married Henri Gauthier-Villars, an editor and critic fourteen years older than she, who was in the habit of assigning books to other writers, amending their manuscripts to include insulting portraits of his enemies, and then publishing the books under his own name. Evidently Henri ("Willy") saw possibilities in his new bride's humorous anecdotes about her school days. Whether he wrote *Claudine à l'école* (1900; *Claudine at School*, 1956) from her notes or whether he simply published under his own name a book that his wife had actually written, Willy took the credit for this work. His domination over his young wife, however, was to be short-lived. Once she got to Paris and into Willy's sophisticated circle, Colette matured rapidly. Even though Paris adored Colette, who was assumed to be the true Claudine, even though everyone wanted to read the next three titillating Claudine novels as they emerged from Willy's book factory, one a year, and to see the Claudine play when it was produced, Colette moved closer and closer to rebellion. As Lottman points out, she took no pride in works that were only partly hers. Indeed, three decades later, Colette expressed profound dislike for the Claudine books. She was destined for artistic, as well as personal, independence.

In 1904, Colette published the first work in which Willy had no hand. By 1905, she and Willy had separated, Willy to become the protector of another young woman, Colette to begin the explorations into art and into sensuality that would occupy her life.

In his carefully documented biography, Lottman makes it clear that Colette's creativity functioned on two levels at once, one being publication or performance, the other her actual life experiences, which were reported in the press, discussed, and revised by Colette herself until they, too, became a kind of fiction. For example, both Colette and Willy were fascinated with lesbianism, which was a major activity at the school they invented for the first book on which they collaborated. At Colette's own school, however, it seems likely that such love affairs were no more than schoolgirl crushes, imaginary, not actual, encounters. Nevertheless, Colette soon progressed from literature to life. During her marriage, there were some tentative relationships with women, encouraged by Willy, who was curious as to her and his own reactions. After her separation from Willy, she had a passionate affair with Mathilde de Morny, the Marchioness de Belboeuf, or "Missy." The relationship became the sensation of Paris. In the kind of publicity-seeking that was characteristic of her, Colette proclaimed their liaison in print, posed with Missy for magazine illustrations showing them as a loving couple, and performed love scenes in pantomimes at the Moulin Rouge. After near-riots, these performances were finally banned by the police. Ironically, as a result of his association with the now-notorious Colette, Willy lost his job on a conservative newspaper, even though he and his wife were separated at the time of the Moulin Rouge episodes.

Lottman seems uncertain as to whether Colette ever loved anyone with whom she was sexually involved. He suggests that her real interest was not in her partners but in the sensations that they aroused. Sometimes she re-created these episodes and described the accompanying sensations in her novels; sometimes she reversed the order, checking the validity of her own imagination by imitating her own fiction in real life. An example of the second pattern involved Bertrand de Jouvenel, the son of her second husband, Henri ("Sidi") de Jouvenel, by his earlier marriage to Claire

Boas. Colette promised Claire that she would look after Bertrand; she did, even to
the extent of personally initiating the twenty-year-old into the sexual mysteries with
which she was so familiar, just as an older woman had done in the book that Colette
had just published, *Chéri* (1920).

Although, as critics have noted, Lottman never does succeed in explaining the
reasons for Colette's actions—probably because in many cases there were no reasons, just whims or reactions—he does re-create the musical-comedy atmosphere in
which she lived. Colette seems to be always in motion, living at one place or another, performing here and there, touring interesting localities in order to produce
articles about them, or just restlessly changing her location. As she moves about,
she is constantly abandoning and reclaiming old lovers and acquiring new ones. The
comic pattern of Colette's life is illustrated by a series of events in the late spring
and early summer of 1911, shortly before her marriage to Henri de Jouvenel. After
Henri had told his previous mistress, Isabelle de Comminges, that he was in love
with someone else, she threatened to kill her rival. Unwisely, Colette went to Paris
to talk to Isabelle, who was nicknamed "the Panther," and the two women seemed
to establish a friendship. After thinking it over, however, the Panther went to Colette's apartment to kill her rival, and Colette had to escape through a window. She
fled to her home in the country, where she was carefully guarded, and then, hearing
that the Panther was on her trail, raced back to Paris. Fortunately, during her pursuit
of Colette, the spurned mistress had come across one of Colette's discarded male
lovers, and those two went off to Morocco together. There they broke up, and the
Panther decamped with an officer in the Foreign Legion. Such episodes are not
significant except as they illustrate the kind of life Colette lived. Lottman's detailed
description of these threats, flights, confrontations, and reversals makes his point; no
further comment is necessary.

While escapades such as these delighted Colette's friends and readers, there were
areas in her life with which a biographer must deal more seriously. One of these is
the relationship between Colette and her daughter by Henri de Jouvenel, Colette de
Jouvenel (or Colette II, as Lottman refers to her). It has been noted that Colette
actually spent very little time with her child but depended upon a nurse to rear her,
and that when her daughter was still young, Colette sent her away to boarding school.
Lottman, however, does not see these facts as any indication that Colette lacked
maternal instincts. Actually, he points out, most parents of the time who were frequently absent would make arrangements for their children like those made for Colette II. Furthermore, the biographer has collected a considerable amount of narrative evidence to prove that when she was with her daughter, Colette displayed the
sincerest affection and obviously took her duties as guide and disciplinarian very
seriously. When Colette II grew up, her mother worried about her seeming lack of
direction, which Lottman indicates resulted from feelings of inferiority not uncom-
mon in the offspring of geniuses. Even though Colette II did not get along with her
mother's third husband, Maurice Goudeket, there was a close relationship between
mother and daughter until the end of Colette's life.

A second matter that Lottman considers at length is Colette's collaboration with the Nazis. Unlike her daughter, who wrote antifascist articles and crusaded for the punishment of collaborators, Colette seems not to have been particularly interested in politics. It is hard to believe, however, that she could have ignored the atrocities the Nazis committed in Occupied France, that she could have been on socially friendly terms with high-ranking Germans, and that she could have agreed to write for the Nazi-run newspapers—even such innocuous columns as hints for homemakers in times of scarcity. In this biography, Colette's motivations for her actions are explained, if not, perhaps, completely justified. According to Lottman, she was fearful for her husband, Goudeket, who was well known and Jewish. At first, she hoped to keep him safe simply by keeping him at home, out of the public eye. When the Nazis decided to arrest a number of prominent Jewish residents of Paris, however, Maurice was included on the list. In order to secure his release from prison, Colette determined to approach everyone who might be able to help her, including collaborators and high officials of the German government of France, and to do whatever they wished her to do. Eventually, she won Maurice's freedom. During the rest of the Occupation, however, always conscious that he might once again be arrested, Colette continued to cultivate the people whose influence she might some day need. Finally, she and Maurice agreed that his presence in Paris was too dangerous, and he fled to Saint-Tropez, where he lived as invisibly as possible until the end of the war. One would certainly not consider her actions heroic; however, she betrayed no one, and she undoubtedly did save her Jewish husband's life.

Others have provided the necessary critical assessment of Colette's work, pointing out that her style is superb, that her plots are unhackneyed, that her grasp of psychology is impressive, and that by looking, as a woman, into the sexual nature of women, she has had an important influence on later women writers. Although his discussions of individual works are valuable, particularly because he includes all the biographical details that bear upon their creation, Lottman offers few new critical insights in this biography. He does, however, fulfill his intention: to trace Colette's development as a person and as a writer by proceeding in chronological order from event to event, from letter to letter, from publication to publication, and from fact to fact, so that his readers can see all the elements of her life, personal and literary, at every point in it.

Certainly, a work so inclusive cannot be as exciting as one of the novels Colette wrote or as the life that she herself was inventing and dramatizing even while she lived it. Furthermore, one does not feel that Lottman is as certain of Colette's identity as he was of his subjects in his earlier biographies of Albert Camus and Gustave Flaubert, probably because Colette herself was so protean a creature. Nevertheless, this sensible, exhaustive, and reliable study is a very useful addition to the body of scholarship about one of the most important and influential writers of her generation.

Rosemary M. Canfield Reisman

Sources for Further Study

Booklist. LXXXVII, December 15, 1990, p. 798.
Chicago Tribune. February 20, 1991, V, p. 3.
Kirkus Reviews. LVIII, December 15, 1990, p. 1725.
Library Journal. CXV, November 1, 1990, p. 91.
The New Republic. CCV, November 18, 1991, p. 45.
New Statesman and Society. IV, March 8, 1991, p. 33.
The New York Times Book Review. XCVI, February 24, 1991, p. 28.
The Observer. March 10, 1991, p. 60.
Publishers Weekly. CCLVII, December 14, 1990, p. 59.
The Times Literary Supplement. March 8, 1991, p. 10.

THE COLLECTED POEMS
1952-1990

Author: Yevgeny Yevtushenko
Publisher: Henry Holt (New York). 659 pp. $29.95
Type of work: Poetry

In this, the forty-seventh published edition of his poetry and the third volume of his collected verse, the Soviet Union's greatest and best-known living poet records a four-decade-long pursuit of truth about himself, those he loves, his nation, the world, and God

Since his reputation in global literary circles was established in the 1960's, Yevgeny Yevtushenko has attempted to explain his country not only to others but to himself as well, hoping to uncover what lies at the heart of the place Winston Churchill termed "a mystery inside an enigma." With cool precision and a passionate heart, he examines his Siberian childhood at remote Zima Junction, his adolescent visions, his maturity as a well-known, world-traveling poet, and his later years as a combination legislator-versifier.

The poet's Spartan childhood on the tundra is a wonderfully evoked distillation of sadness caused by Stalinist cruelties visited upon Zima and exuberant youthful joys and fantasies. Through dry-humored and sometimes caustic turns of phrase, he captures how it felt and feels to be Yevtushenko, Soviet national, a man caught up in his huge nation's beauty, cruelty, menace, and promise—its great promise contrasting with a present degradation of spirit. It is Yevtushenko's genius to be able to make poetic sense of his infinitely complex homeland, acting as its spiritual interpreter to the nations.

So too, in his view, it is the poet's role to speak for humanity as a whole: He brings the essentially voiceless a voice; his poetry speaks of their discontents and dreams. Moreover, he sees himself as fortunate, a man to whom God inexplicably has given the chance to champion the mute and downtrodden, for he has lived longer than many of the Soviet Union's great writers and has seen far more of the world than any of them.

Certainly, it was his great poem "Babii Yar," composed in 1961, that spoke for the greatest number of voiceless people—the silenced victims of Nazi terror lying in mass graves at Babii Yar in the Ukraine. Amid unmarked graves of thousands of slaughtered Jews, Yevtushenko finds the opportunity to speak not only of man's mad cruelty but also of the love that tied together the victims. Then, too, the poem, like so many purporting to be about other places and other times, is really an indictment of Stalinist horrors, as many astute Soviet readers would have readily perceived. With its heady, spellbinding reflections on a terrible place, "Babii Yar" enhanced Yevtushenko's international reputation: No finer lines about twentieth century mass murder had ever been written.

His themes are many—some having to do with the Soviet scene and others with his personal life and place in the world. The chief theme of those dealing with the Soviet Union is that of a sensitive man struggling with the deadening weight of bureaucracy and the systematic destruction of his individual liberty. He shows, however, that some way—whether by pride, stealth, wit, or luck—he will sustain his inner self, nurture his individuality despite the effort of the totalitarian state to crush them.

In his most confessional poems, Yevtushenko marvels at the fabulous differences among people he encounters on the street and wishes to know them in order to discover how they survive their oppressive world. He admires those who appear alive to their world and loathes those who have become gray functionaries (university professors, government officials, and rich, presumptuous foreigners who treat the poet as a kind of pet). He worries not only about Soviet absolutism but also about the Western cult of the celebrity that might transform him from artist to cultural icon. While he dearly desires to be freed from the tyranny of fame, the sole escape route is immersion in his art. Yet total immersion is impossible, and he must venture forth in the world in order to find his connection with the world and the artistic visions that connection supplies.

Another theme of Yevtushenko's is that, despite horrors wrought by evil forces at work in the world, life adds up to something—it has inherent meaning. Insights come to him in small ways as well as large: through the peace brought him by the sight of snow sifting through the Moscow night, the pungent smell of raspberries in summer, a new flower glimpsed on a fig tree, a half-blade of grass taken from a field. Many small things remind him of the larger mystery surrounding all humans and of the seeming joy and peace found there. The Russian earth has great power: It endures winter hardships and pushes forth grass and flowers when the sun returns in spring. Winter snows bite into his soul, and they bring to mind the soul of his homeland and the people who have formed him. Yet the city also contains numerous sights—everyday vistas—that focus his mind elsewhere and speak to him of the unity of humankind. Moscow streets, with their long lines of people waiting to buy goods, their strolling lovers, and their introspective workers, are delightful, despite their grayness. Like the hardy flowers of the rural Soviet Union, the young people of Moscow manage somehow to delight in life, their joy an emblem of the joy at the heart of all things.

Yevtushenko also addresses his country's future, which he believes could be far different from its present if only Russians would shake off their spiritual torpor. Much of his poetry speaks either directly or indirectly about Russia, its place in the world, and its future, his message ranging from the veiled lines "I'm afraid for everyone./ I've no desire to dance,/ but you can't/ not dance" from his 1955 poem "Weddings," to the restrained anger of his celebrated 1964 poem "The City of Yes and the City of No," with its anguished lines about being caught between Eastern tyranny and Western moral flaccidity, "My nerves are strained/ like wires/ between the city of No/ and the city of Yes," to the furious shout of the people in the 1978 poem "The Unexpressed," "We are/ like stifled sobs./ We long so/ for our liberation:/ express us!/ express us!"

Working against the tide of Communism is the eventually conquering tide of individuality—the desire of people to be important entities in their own right ratherthan cogs in a Soviet machine. As he says in his near-epic poem "Fuku: A Poem (Excerpts)" written between 1963 and 1985, "In every border post/ there's something insecure./ Each one of them/ is longing for leaves and for flowers." Yevtushenko's forthright stand against all systems that oppress people is evident in poems throughout this volume, and yet the notion still circulates that he gave in to Communist masters and betrayed the freedom movement.

Even though Yevtushenko's career began after the death of dictator Joseph Stalin, it took considerable courage to write lines such as the following, which form a kind of prayer to Christ for a reopened Russian Church: "Do not permit that for the simple souls/ all should begin in a mirage of miracles,/ and end with bolted doors" (from "The Easter Procession," 1975) or these from his 1977 ode to freedom, "Tomorrow's Wind": "And the wind,/ making a gift of itself/ to the universe,/ is born,/ sprawling/ in a burst,/ and structures/ built on sand/ rightfully will crumble." Here was no passive poet avoiding political commentary but rather a man speaking as openly as he could in defense of personal and artistic liberty and against intellectual sloth and enslavement.

This yearning for freedom does not always take the form of reaction to the totalitarian state, however; Yevtushenko often writes about the frustration he feels in his private life. As an artist, he resents not having enough time to think and write; he is tossed from interview to social gathering, where mindless chatter destroys his inner train of thought. He would rather be seen as someone dangerous to be around than as someone's pet monkey, a creature performing tricks to please the jaded bourgeoisie. In his 1955 poem "Fury," Yevtushenko announces his intention to be taken seriously: "After all—/ life is interesting/ when you're furious!" So he is determined to write powerfully—not to mince words—and yet to do so involves a painful effort, an unrelenting daily struggle that sometimes seems directionless.

In "Nice People" (1977), he bemoans having to meet "nice" rich Westerners who emasculate him with their smothering attentions. In a sense, their condescending arrogance is more of a threat to the poet than is the hostility of the state, for at least the state takes him seriously and sees his work as important and as a present danger. Better to write in the East than in the West, for at least in Russia poets have long been thought to have the power to bring about change, while in the West—the United States especially—poets are thought impractical and powerless.

This desire to be taken seriously also is found in his love poetry. In order to love and be loved, he must be given attention and respect, and yet he is often denied these sustaining things.

Love of parents, love of single women, a spouse, a friend, a child: All are important to the poet, and he frequently writes about these personal attachments, perhaps never more passionately than in his monumental "Zima Junction: A Poem" (1955), which helped him be widely recognized. Nostalgia for persons and a special place fuels "Zima Junction," a paean to the kind and stubborn peasants, the laboring draft horses, lumbering wagons and carts, and cozy wooden homes of the far North. Most important to Yevtushenko are the spiritual leaders of his youth, ranging from old, unpredictable Uncle Andrei and his carpenter Uncle Volodia to his fellow adventurer Vovka, all of whom make him laugh with their tales and exploits, their lives a testimony to humankind's endurance in the face of life's hostility. In the village, the individual is important: He or she gives life color and shape, meaning and fulfillment. Given the harsh Russian winters, places as remote as Zima must provide their own homespun entertainments, and it is the entertainers he lovingly recalls.

With the publication of his collected works, Yevtushenko's position as one of the world's preeminent poetic voices is solidified. Here, evident to anyone who reads the volume in its entirety, is the distinctive voice of a true people's poet, a poet who does not descend into sentimentality, morbidity, or clichéd rhetoric. His images are powerful and often sustained, drawing their power from nature and Russian literary and cultural tradition. Yevtushenko, using Siberian folklore and Russian stories, both ancient and modern, speaks not to the detested academician or socialite but to common people everywhere, whether they be of the city, the town, or the rural district. His locales, with some notable exceptions, are ones well-known to him, and he learns from them what he needs to know about life: Siberia teaches him a love of simple things; Moscow, a sense of the weight of history and the future shape of the Soviet Union; the West, an impression of frivolity and decadence tempered by friendships made there.

Often referred to as the "new Pushkin" or "the best poet since Pushkin," Yevtushenko is as complex and sophisticated a poet as Russia has ever produced, a master of nuance, language, and imagery. A courageous man but no martyr, he has walked a narrow bridge between speaking out against the evils he has found in Soviet society and displeasing the government to the extent that it stop him from writing. Carefully he criticizes the deadening bureaucracy he sees, often placing his messages between the lines, where Russian readers know they will be located. He has long known that in order for him to give his readers the magic of his verse, he must not write political diatribes.

Yevtushenko combines the strengths of a number of poets: Carl Sandburg, Walt Whitman, T. S. Eliot, and Pablo Neruda. He possesses Sandburg's sense of the poet as entertainer and enlightener; Whitman's love of place and common folk as well as his ability to describe varied terrain in an expansive way; Eliot's quiet reflectiveness; and Neruda's astonishing, nubile imagery. Yet, in another sense, he is his own man too—a seasoned fighter of a poet, ready to take on a new poetic challenge and astound his readers with yet another poem of power and beauty.

John D. Raymer

Sources for Further Study

Booklist. LXXXVII, November 15, 1990, p. 596.
The Economist. CCCXIX, April 20, 1991, p. 91.

The Hudson Review. XLIV, Summer, 1991, p. 343.
Library Journal. CXV, December, 1990, p. 129.
The New Republic. CCIV, May 6, 1991, p. 33.
New Statesman and Society. IV, March 15, 1991, p. 37.
The New York Times. January 23, 1991, p. C16.
Publishers Weekly. CCXXXVII, December 7, 1990, p. 62.
The Times Literary Supplement. June 14, 1991, p. 3.
The Virginia Quarterly Review. LXVII, Summer, 1991, p. 102.

COMPLETE COLLECTED STORIES

Author: V. S. Pritchett (1900-   )
Publisher: Random House (New York). 1220 pp. $35.00
Type of work: Short stories

Eighty-two stories spanning nearly the whole of Pritchett's illustrious career

Is it possible that, at age ninety, V. S. Pritchett will finally get his due as one of England's greatest short-story writers? Certainly reviewers have done their part: commentators as various and distinguished as Margaret Drabble, Frank Kermode, Irving Howe, and Paul Theroux have exhausted their collective store of superlatives in praising his stories. Both *The New York Times Book Review* and *The New York Review of Books* devoted long, thoughtful encomiums to his latest volume. Even Pritchett's publishers have ignored the conventional wisdom about volumes of short stories and essays and have actively promoted Pritchett's work. Such attention for a writer whose forte is the short story and not the novel is almost unprecedented in publishing history.

Complete Collected Stories brings together the contents of all of Pritchett's previous volumes except *The Spanish Virgin and Other Stories* (1930). Sir Victor (he was knighted in 1975) has consistently repudiated this first child of his imagination as unworthy of standing beside his later offspring. Understandable as his attitude may be, he thereby does a disservice to those readers who relish the opportunity this volume provides to follow the writer's career in the short story as it has developed over more than sixty years. The stylistic uncertainties of those early stories have charms of their own, and there is a dramatic intensity in some of them that Pritchett rarely duplicated in his mature work.

Nevertheless, Pritchett is memorable for the variety and vitality of his characters. Plot in the loose sense may underlie his stories, but characters dominate. Frank O'Connor's dictum that the short story deals with those on the margins of society applies perfectly to Pritchett's creations, for even if by social standing and occupation they are part of the mainstream, there is always something quirky and individual about them, something that puts them on the fringe.

Theorists of the short-story genre have sometimes claimed that story writers do not develop and mature as novelists do. Certainly there are accomplished writers of the short story—Rudyard Kipling, Saki, Sir Arthur Conan Doyle, and Ring Lardner come to mind—of whom this may be fairly said. Yet it may be that the brevity of the form and the accompanying economies of narration and style do not preclude growth and development so much as make it more subtle and hard to detect. Moreover, like any author, the short-story writer deals in only a handful of themes, and since these focus almost exclusively on people rather than social institutions, there is bound to be an underlying sameness to an author's collected work. Nevertheless, *Complete Collected Stories* offers careful readers the opportunity to monitor the development of Pritchett's art.

The first four stories in this collection demonstrate Pritchett's early experiments, successful and unsuccessful. "Sense of Humour" is his first fully characteristic and entirely successful story. On one level, it is a simple boy-meets-girl affair, the tale of a courtship between a traveling salesman and a hotel clerk who describes herself as having a sense of humor. Not surprisingly, there is a rival for Muriel's affections, the tenacious Colin, who dogs the couple's courtship by following their every move on his motorcycle. Except for the scrupulous economy of Pritchett's style and the almost abrasive ordinariness of the dialogue, this is the stuff of women's magazine fiction—until Colin is killed and Muriel's undertaker father is entrusted with funeral arrangements. Colin's untimely death leads Muriel prematurely into the narrator's bed: grief, guilt, sympathy, and sex are inextricably muddled, just as the resulting arrangements for Colin's funeral are a mixture of convenience, economy, and a decent respect for the dead. This is pure Pritchett comedy, at once searching and sympathetic, tender and ironic.

The other three stories are less characteristic and successful. "A Spring Morning" depicts two teenagers in exuberant horseplay, with barely submerged sexual undertones, atypically Freudian in its psychology. "Main Road" is a 1930's-style proletarian piece about two starving drifters looking for work but finding crime instead. It prefigures Pritchett's novel *Dead Man Leading* (1937) both in its motif of the starving wanderers and in its desperate emotional intensity, but it represents more a blind alley than a harbinger of things to come. Finally, "The Evils of Spain" is a sketch in every sense of the word, as its characters are barely realized and its theme elusive at best. What it does show, however, is Pritchett experimenting with the sort of chaotic, everyone-talking-at-once dialogue that he would later use to such happy effect in a story such as "Noisy Flushes the Birds."

The main line of Pritchett's development, then, leads from "Sense of Humour" to "Handsome Is as Handsome Does," and through acknowledged masterpieces such as "The Sailor," "The Saint," "The Fly in the Ointment," "The Wheelbarrow," and "When My Girl Comes Home," to more recent successes such as "Blind Love," "The Skeleton," "The Camberwell Beauty," "The Lady from Guatemala," and "The Accompanist." This list, of course, is an outline, not a complete catalog of Pritchett's finest stories. The "main line" Pritchett story, as nearly every commentator has remarked, concerns the British lower-middle class, the class from which Pritchett himself sprang and to which he has remained remarkably faithful over the years, even though he must surely move in more exalted circles nowadays. They are people seldom dealt with in fiction, people whom most writers would regard as comic in their bad taste, conformity, and religious fanaticism. Pritchett sees these failings clearly and uncompromisingly, but he finds much of substance behind the comic and even pathetic façade—dignity in disillusionment, resilience of character, the transforming power of love and sex, and reservoirs of deep emotion beneath placid exteriors.

In what senses, then, can it be said that Pritchett has developed within the framework of his typical subject matter and themes? One answer lies in his increasingly subtle analysis of character. "The Saint" (1945), for example, for all of its rich comedy and unobtrusive symbolism, deals in a rather easy target for satire—the religious fanatic. Mr. Hubert Timberlake of the Church of the Last Purification, of Toronto, Canada, is not ridiculed, however, so much as absurdly humiliated by his own humorlessness. Pritchett cannot be accused of savaging his hapless victim; indeed, the story would not be so wonderfully effective if he had. Nevertheless, Mr. Timberlake's demeanor is wooden, and his slapstick dunking as a result of a punting accident is a piece of low comedy. The financial jibes aimed at Mr. Timberlake's income from preaching are gratuitous. The reader laughs at Mr. Timberlake, not with him. Similarly, by telling the story through the eyes of his young protagonist, Pritchett has gained a certain deadpan naïveté at the expense of stylistic subtlety, while the overt moralizing at the end indicates a certain mistrust of the reader's acumen.

Pritchett's growing mastery can be seen in "The Wheelbarrow" (1961), another story about religious fanaticism and hypocrisy, combined with a subtler form of sexual teasing than was found in "A Spring Morning." In fact, everything about this story is more subtle than "The Saint": Robert Evans does not wear his faith on his sleeve as Mr. Timberlake does, and only as the story progresses does the reader see by degrees that his sins are cupidity and lechery. Much of the conflict is between him and the woman called simply "Miss Freshwater's niece," who has hired laypreacher Evans to help her clear out her late aunt's home. As they work their way through the contents of the house, both characters are revealed as complex. Her mockery of his faith gradually gives way to a kind of skeptical respect, while his desire for material things (focused on a wheelbarrow) is seen less as hypocrisy than as a simple human urging. The omniscient point of view permits Pritchett to make use of his precise, suggestive style. Not all readers would agree that "The Wheelbarrow" is a better story than "The Saint." They are, obviously, different, each excellent in its way; but there has been at the same time an unmistakable growth in technique, control, and subtlety.

To follow Pritchett's progress through this volume is to be continually impressed by the range and depth of his virtuosity. A number of reviewers were especially struck by the complexity and control of "When My Girl Comes Home," a story that reveals, among other things, the moral bankruptcy left in the wake of World War II. This is Pritchett at his most novelistic, distilling a novel's worth of material into a taut story of fifty pages. Among its themes is the pervasive power of self-delusion at both the personal and societal levels. Yet it is also a story of sheer survival and resilience, by means both foul and fair. "The Camberwell Beauty" demonstrates Pritchett's absolute mastery of the first-person narrator—a technique he first learned to control in "A Sense of Humour." "The Camberwell Beauty" is a tour de force of Pritchettian themes and techniques—a story that takes preposterous risks with the reader's credulity and succeeds in making the fantastic believable. "The Accompanist" weaves some of the same materials—a love triangle, a passion for collecting, thwarted sex—into a new form narrated by a different voice.

If there is a broad main river of Pritchett's art, however, there are also numerous

tributaries and backwaters. Chief among these is a lifelong series of autobiographical stories based on Pritchett's impossible father. This stream runs through "The
Lion's Den," "It May Never Happen," "Aunt Gertrude," "The Clerk's Tale," "The
Collection," "Just a Little More," and "The Spree." Pritchett's father even makes an
appearance in "Blind Love." The chronological arrangement of *Complete Collected
Stories* enables readers to follow Pritchett's attitude toward his father as it changes
from satire in the early stories to sympathy in the late ones. (Unfortunately, the
undoubtedly early "The Collection" is placed in the middle because it was not collected until 1956. Anomalies like this constitute a good argument for arranging the
stories by date of composition or first publication, rather than by first book publication.)

Another tributary is made up of stories about particularly eccentric individuals,
beginning with the early "Miss Baker" and progressing onward to "The Oedipus
Complex," "The Landlord," "Passing the Ball," and "The Satisfactory," through
"The Skeleton" to "The Spanish Bed." Here one can see Pritchett mellowing, from
his almost savage treatment of "Miss Baker" to his subtler and more sympathetic
depictions of those whose eccentricities are almost always disguises to hide some
vulnerable spot, some emotional wound they feel compelled to cover at all costs.
There are also stories of absurd humor, love stories involving unlikely matches, and
stories of children and adolescents.

The point to be emphasized is not simply the variety of subjects or Pritchett's
increasingly humane vision; rather, it is the continual experimenting and restless energy of his invention. If it is the peculiar vice of aging novelists to pontificate, it is
the vice of short-story writers to repeat themselves. Pritchett has avoided this trap to
a remarkable degree, for even when there are similarities of situation, theme, or
character, there are compensating originalities.

Perhaps most original of all is his style—crystal clear, incisive, quirky, refreshing
in its invention of metaphor. In the early stories there is a tendency to overwriting,
to patches verging on the purple. By stern discipline, Pritchett has pared his sentences to essentials. Where once a paragraph would describe a sunset, now a word
suffices: "The sun had floundered down into the clouds." People can be captured in
a sentence. Of a dead woman he has written, "she looked like a white leaf that has
been found after a lifetime pressed between the pages of a book and as delicate as a
saint"; of an overweight businessman, "Below the neck the body rests like three
balloons at bursting point."

The vitality and inventiveness of his prose, the variety of his characters, the breadth
and depth of his vision, and the sheer individuality of his achievement should assure
Pritchett of a permanent place in the annals of the short story. Yet while he is universally praised in reviews and briefly written about by chroniclers of the short story, he
has scant place in that ultimate repository of literary fame, the college literature
anthology. Of the twenty or so most widely used short-story anthologies currently in
print, only two reprint a story of Pritchett's. Meanwhile, the academicians are busily
promoting the fiction of minorities past and present. This is a laudable activity, but

in our haste to be inclusive and representative, let us hope that a writer of Pritchett's caliber is not overlooked because he deals not in the plight of the socially oppressed but in the telltale beatings of the lonely human heart.

Dean Baldwin

Sources for Further Study

Chicago Tribune. March 24, 1991, XIV, p. 1.
Library Journal. CXVI, April 1, 1991, p. 155.
London Review of Books. XII, December 20, 1990, p. 17.
The New Republic. CCIV, May 27, 1991, p. 38.
New Statesman and Society. III, November 23, 1990, p. 38.
The New York Review of Books. XXXVIII, June 13, 1991, p. 8.
The New York Times Book Review. XCVI, March 24, 1991, p 1
Publishers Weekly. CCXXXVIII, February 22, 1991, p. 208.
The Times Literary Supplement. November 23, 1990, p. 1255.
The Washington Post Book World. XXI, April 7, 1991, p 5.

COMPLETE SHORT POETRY

Author: Louis Zukofsky (1904-1978)
Foreword by Robert Creeley
Publisher: The Johns Hopkins University Press (Baltimore). 365 pp. $34.95
Type of work: Poetry

The first publication in one volume of the shorter works of one of America's challenging twentieth century experimental poets

Despite being admired and encouraged while still in his twenties by such poetic luminaries as Ezra Pound and T. S. Eliot, and being friends with such illustrious contemporaries as William Carlos Williams, in addition to being the principal exponent of the Objectivist theory of poetry, Louis Zukofsky has become the most overlooked major American poet of the twentieth century. In part, this neglect may be explained by the reaction against experimentation among poets and critics in Zukofsky's closing years, when he might have expected greater recognition for the fruits of his imaginative labors. In addition, the concentration of so much of his poetic energies in the massive opus *"A"* (1978) perhaps deprived him of an audience weaned on lyrics. At the same time, however, as is amply demonstrated by his *Complete Short Poetry*, there is no denying the essential difficulty of Zukofsky's work and the inevitable conclusion that much of its appeal is to minority tastes.

Despite problems relating to his significance in the history of twentieth century American poetry, to his challenging prosody and restless experimentation, and to the ideology of taste to which such problems ultimately pertain, Zukofsky is by no means a poet to be written off. The publication of this handsome edition of his *Complete Short Poetry* is important in a number of ways. It facilitates the availability of the complete Zukofsky canon, thereby potentially prompting renewed critical interest in the poet. And, as the choice of Robert Creeley as author of the volume's foreword reminds us, Zukofsky was an important influence on those American poets of the 1950's and 1960's whose work continues to bear an uneasy and illuminating relationship to the canon of postwar American verse. Creeley himself is an obvious case in point, as are—to name the most prominent—Robert Duncan, Jack Spicer, and Denise Levertov. In view of this volume's intrinsic interest as well as its historical value, therefore, it is to be regretted that it does not include bibliographical or other editorial material.

By collecting for the first time all of Zukofsky's shorter verse, this book supplants the earlier *All: The Collected Short Poems, 1923-1964* (1971). To the contents of that volume has now been added the remarkable versions of the Latin poet Catullus, which Zukofsky made with his wife, the composer Celia Zukofsky. Also reprinted in *Complete Short Poetry* is the late work *80 Flowers* (1978), hitherto available only in a limited edition. Other individual items, culled from the small magazines to which Zukofsky contributed, are also included, though their provenance is not given.

Complete Short Poetry gives an indelible impression of the poet's range. There are few poets for whom the arbitrary separation of form from content is less justifiable than it is for Zukofsky. In all cases, and as a matter of artistic integrity as well as prosodic principle, form is content for Zukofsky, and it is the peculiarly subtle resourcefulness that he brought to this principle which places him on the same level of literary significance as Pound and Williams. Given the challenge of his prosody, however, and the ostensibly obscure theory which underlies and governs it, a separation of content from form will prove useful.

The son of Russian emigrants who did not speak English, Zukofsky proved himself in the first instance to be academically brilliant. It is illuminating to consider many of the themes which recur throughout *Complete Short Poetry* as the result of the interplay between the poet's origins and his attainments. His attachment to the life of New York, which assumes various related expressions throughout his poetic career, is filtered through a sensibility that is at once extraordinarily refined and intellectually sophisticated. The life of the city in some of the early work contained in the section entitled "29 Poems" evokes echoes of William Carlos Williams and also of such New York painters of the 1920's as John Sloan. Though perceived through an inimitably oblique perspective, the scenes are loving testaments to the city and its inhabitants. The poem "Ferry" ("Gleams, a green lamp/ In the fog") and the rhythm of one of the untitled poems' opening lines—"Cars once steel and green, now old,/ Find their grave at Cedar Manor"—not only effectively conjure certain moods and atmospheres but also release the poet's pleasure and engagement with his material.

In addition to, and much more important than, these early poems' affection for the poet's native place and their Whitmanesque embrace of even its less prepossessing features is their clear attachment to the people. This attachment is expressed in such asides to his family as this, to his mother, from the early "Poem beginning 'The'": "Now I kiss you who could never sing Bach, never read Shakespeare." Yet in these presumed limitations, she implicitly remains as much a subject for poetry as some more conventionalized theme. While, as this section of the same poem goes on to claim, "Assimilation is not hard," it is not clear that Zukofsky was ever entirely seduced by its blandishments, preferring to express himself in poetic realities which are not readily assimilable, to create poems which are realities by virtue of that very daunting yet undoubtedly human characteristic.

Zukofsky's fidelity to his New York should not be considered a simplistic honoring of roots. A major facet of Zukofsky's overall significance is the manner in which his work accomplishes a sustained critique of a facile humanism. One of the achievements of these poems of the 1920's and 1930's is the manner in which their original commitments are translated in a plausible political poetry. This transformation is clearly announced in such poems as "Aubade, 1925," " 'The Immediate Aim,' " and the biting "During the Passaic Strike of 1926." The nature of Zukofsky's transformative practice, even in an explicitly political context, may be studied by comparing his early "Memory of V. I. Ulianov" and the "Hymns to Lenin" of the Scottish radical poet, Hugh MacDiarmid. Zukofsky is unwilling to make his poem a vehicle for an excoriating commentary on things as they are. By comparison, MacDiarmid offers a speech from a soapbox. In Zukofsky's hands, even subjects rich in historical reverberations are permitted to outlive their strictly empirical integument.

The transformative interplay between the world of conditions and commitment on the one hand, and the poetry which may be made from it on the other, is present just as appealingly in poems of greater delicacy of tone and subtlety of movement. Such poems express the poet's fascination with the family of man, as well as his capacity for regarding such an entity with tenderness and joy. Zukofsky's regard should not, however, be thought of as generalized to the point of attaining nothing more than sophomoric intensity. The increasing emphasis on, or orientation around, his own family life which the survey of his career offered by *Complete Short Poetry* offers, should not be considered a diminution either of his aesthetic commitments or his moral interests. The poems for his son Paul and for his wife, for all the simplicity of their vocabulary, are sophisticated emotional testaments: unabashed, playful, exuberant, decorous, charming, the very kind of verse which, by virtue of its glancing evanescence, becomes memorable by being so transient, becomes a permanent monument to atmosphere rather than to content.

It is difficult, for example, to think of a twentieth century poet to whom Valentine's Day was as frequent a source of inspiration as it was to Zukofsky. The airy inscriptions with which he records the day, however, are far from being complacent emotings. On the contrary, they impress by the grace and tact with which they articulate good faith. Among the poems featuring his son, "So That Even a Lover" readily comes to mind as an equally affecting expression of a delighted consciousness. The value of these qualities may be perceived in the rather more complex pieces in *80 Flowers*, which, while conceived in the domestic spirit of the poet's Long Island garden, are emblematic of Zukofsky's career-long engrossment with the livingness of the world, and with his benign rage to capture this in words. The language of flowers, in other words, is not invited to speak symbolically for something other than the natural phenomena themselves. The seventeenth century English lyricist Robert Herrick was a favorite of Zukofsky, and it is easy to hear afresh Herrick's geniality and relish of the experience of the moment.

His perspective makes of delicacy and tenderness an ethos rather than a repertoire. "The simple truth is/ That men love the good," as he unselfconsciously and persuasively attests in "Reading and Talking." And the expression of that ethos is as much the form of its poetic occasion as that occasion's content. Like many poets, Zukofsky hymns transformation, as distinct from recapitulation. What makes his imaginative practice significant and influential, however, is not the fact of transformation. His verse is not that of the idle, facile purveyor of metaphors. On the contrary, many of the poems here enact their transformative energies while stopping short of metaphor. At one level, Zukofsky is clearly interested in identifying with the prevailing outlook of his most powerful contemporaries, and intends to "make it new." This commitment is achieved in terms made familiar by the modernist poets, notably Eliot and Pound, through the prosody of free verse and in a relativized sense of poetic form. At the same time, however, Zukofsky is equally clearly interested in mapping out his own theory of poetry. His theorizing culminated in the doctrine of

Objectivism, the principles of which were developed largely by Zukofsky though also with the support and example of, among others, two important contemporaries, George Oppen and Charles Reznikoff.

The most original aspect of this aesthetic strategy is its preoccupation with process. An Objectivist poem articulates its subject's potential for poetic representation. The deferral of metaphor, together with the condensed syntax and formal idiosyncracies, of Zukofsky's verse are all enlisted to reveal that potential. By his act of revelation, the poet makes his poetic object. And it is to fashioning of such objects that the Objectivist poet devotes himself, rather than to, for example, expressing himself. This change in emphasis regarding the poet's aesthetic quest is perhaps the most important contribution to twentieth century poetics which the Objectivists— and notably Zukofsky—made. The new emphasis identifies the dynamics of social, historical, and interpersonal relations as being poetic and the poet's responsibility to chart what of poetry is in them, thereby enabling them "to speak," as Zukofsky intended, "to all men."

It is debatable, however, if Zukofsky would have successfully developed Objectivist theories in practice were it not for his passionate interest in music. A helpful way of thinking of his poetry is in musical terms. This approach will not only alert the reader to Zukofsky's extremely keen ear for verbal texture and for his extraordinarily vivid sense of tempo but also help explain the numerous musical allusions with which the *Complete Short Poetry* is suffused, and in particular the volume's recurring overtures to song. More important, what Zukofsky desires poetry to be is something analogous to what music is, an experience rather than a product. The difference between how Zukofsky thought of poetry and how poetry was—and indeed continues to be—regarded conventionally is the difference between what a musician is heard to play and the printed score upon which his playing is based. The art's significance resides in its modes of transmission and reception, in its analogical rather than its reproductive properties, in the distinctiveness of its amalgamation of idioms, rhythms, and sounds, and, above all, in its being unmistakably faithful to its own nature. The reader with a keen appreciation of the rhetorical and aesthetic resources of counterpoint will find Zukofsky's verse intriguing and rewarding. Arguably the most ambitious attempt in *Complete Short Poetry* to assemble a musical language, as such, is in the versions of Catullus, where the aim is not to translate in the literal sense but to find an English which would convey the tone values of the original.

Zukofsky's musical inclinations provide a ready set of reasons for appreciating his significant contribution to the growth and development of the prosody of a distinctively American poetics. Perhaps the most noteworthy reason is the sense of integrity which both adorns and illuminates his career, an integrity which possesses a particularly exemplary force not only from an artistic standpoint but also, as perhaps Zukofsky himself would not have been surprised to discover, in a political sense, in view of the increasing cooption of literary artists to serve institutional objectives often far removed from literary concerns. Despite the difficulties, or rather the intellectual sophistication, of his aesthetic theories and the challenge presented by his syntactical and formal spontaneity, Zukofsky's work will continue to be prized precisely for the success with which "The lines of this new song are nothing/ But a tune making the nothing full."

George O'Brien

Sources for Further Study

Choice. XXVIII, July, 1991, p. 1784.
Library Journal. CXVI, April 15, 1991, p. 97.
The Times Literary Supplement. November 1, 1991, p. 10.
University Press Book News. III, June, 1991, p. 37.
The Village Voice. December 10, 1991, p. S17.
The Virginia Quarterly Review. LXVII, Fall, 1991, p. 135.
World Literature Today. LXV, Autumn, 1991, p. 711.

CONSCIOUSNESS EXPLAINED

Author: Daniel C. Dennett (1942-   )
Publisher: Little, Brown (Boston). Illustrated. 511 pp. $27.95
Type of work: Science and philosophy

A functionalist account of consciousness that attempts to bridge the gap between subjective experience and the computer-like operations of the brain with a model of the mind similar to that of a word processor

Philosopher Daniel Dennett takes as his purpose in *Consciousness Explained* the task of characterizing consciousness in terms of physical events in the brain that are not conscious. This, Dennett admits, is counterintuitive, for though consciousness may well be "supported by" or "connected to" the brain, consciousness itself seems fundamentally distinct from (mere) physical processes. How those processes actually can be one's sensation of intense grief or one's experience of a too-sour orange is the burden of his exposition. Part of the difficulty Dennett faces is in overcoming the heritage of René Descartes (1596-1650), whose *Meditations* (1641) helped establish in popular sentiment the notion of the dualism of mind and body. For Descartes, mind was a kind of "stuff" altogether different from physical matter but every bit as real. The brain could be studied empirically because it was subject to physical laws, but mind by definition was outside the reach of the physical sciences. The difference between the content of one's conscious experience, the sense of what it is like to be oneself, and the firing of synapses in the brain seemed absolute. Dennett rejects Cartesian dualism in part because of its difficulty of explaining coherently how a nonphysical mind could affect, and in turn be affected by, a physical body, but also because dualism is resistant to empirical investigation.

Such investigation must be from the "third-person" point of view, he says, and so the "data" of one's inner experience must be made publicly available in a way that does not already presume a particular theory of the mind. In the first part of *Consciousness Explained* Dennett develops a method (he dubs it heterophenomenology) by which a subject's description of the phenomena of his or her "inner life" (the intentionality or "aboutness" of conscious experience) becomes a text which in effect constitutes a kind of fictional world—fictional because the subject can only report what it seems like, say to make an important decision, not what is actually going on inside the person: That actuality is unavailable to introspection but is the proper study of the empirical theorist. This distinction is crucial to Dennett's own theory, which he develops in the second section of the book.

Dennett calls his model of consciousness the Multiple Drafts theory, arguing that "all varieties of perception—indeed, all varieties of thought or mental activity— are accomplished in the brain by parallel, multitrack processes of interpretation and elaboration of sensory inputs. Information entering the nervous system is under continuous 'editorial revision.'" There is no single spot in the brain where consciousness "happens"; once one part of the brain has made a certain discrimination (of movement, say, or color), that information is an available part of the eventual pastiche that is conscious experience.

Dennett is not content with banishing dualism; he is also determined to root out from prevailing materialist theories of the brain any notion of a "Cartesian Theater," a central location where the brain must re-present each of its discriminations. That is false, says Dennett, for such a notion would require a further explanation of how the "audience" in the Theater—called a "homunculus" or "little person" by philosophers—was itself conscious of the events on display. If the "explanation" involved positing another "theater" in the brain of the homunculus, and so on, clearly the question of the nature of consciousness would simply be forever deferred. According to Dennett, this brand of materialism is no better than Cartesian dualism; and though few if any cognitive scientists and philosophers would call themselves Cartesian materialists, the author is convinced the influence of Descartes continues to muddy the theoretical waters.

Perhaps the most appropriate metaphor for Dennett's Multiple Drafts theory is that of a word processor. Any computer hardware running a particular word processing program in effect becomes a "virtual machine" for that program, responding as if the hardware had been designed just for running that program. Diverse computers—even large parallel processing units—that run the same program become the same virtual machine. The word processing program may seem relatively straightforward, with one event happening after another in serial order, but "in reality" many calculations are coming from various subsystems of the computer to be integrated into the program's handling of the data. Dennett suggests that since the brain is a parallel processing unit, its so-called "stream of consciousness" might well be reproducible on any other such computer system. But beware: "the Multiple Drafts model avoids the tempting mistake of supposing that there must be a single narrative (the 'final' or 'published' draft, you might say) that is canonical—that is the *actual* stream of consciousness of the subject, whether or not the experimenter (or even the subject) can gain access to it." Just as many calculations all over the computer are required to make a word processing program show the contents of the open file, so deep in the brain a kind of pandemonium reigns:

> In our brains there is a cobbled-together collection of specialist brain circuits, which, thanks to a family of habits inculcated partly by culture and partly by individual self-exploration, conspire together to produce a more or less orderly, more or less effective, more or less well-designed virtual machine. . . . Who's in charge? First one coalition and then another, shifting in ways that are not chaotic thanks to good meta-habits that tend to entrain coherent, purposeful sequences rather than an interminable helter-skelter power grab.

The specialist brain circuits, says Dennett, are the products of Darwinian evolution; that process works slowly in the medium of genetic variation, he says, but when genetic variation produced organisms capable of wide-ranging adaptation, this "phenotypic plasticity" produced greater variations. With the development of human society there came a new and even more rapid kind of variation—cultural evolution. Borrowing a term from contemporary evolutionist Richard Dawkins, Dennett traces the functioning of what Dawkins calls "memes" in the development of human culture. Memes are defined as complex ideas (such as the idea of revolution or the idea of clothing or the ideas of truth and beauty) which take up residence in the brain, duplicating themselves by language and ensuring their survival through the establishment of particular cultural expressions; as Dennett puts it, "A scholar is just a library's way of making another library." The infestation of human brains with memes is central to Dennett's view of the nature of consciousness:

> Human consciousness is *itself* a huge complex of memes (or more exactly, meme-effects in brains) that can best be understood as the operation of a . . . virtual machine *implemented* in the *parallel architecture* of a brain that was not designed for any such activities. The powers of this *virtual machine* vastly enhance the underlying powers of the organic *hardware* on which it runs, but at the same time many of its most curious features, and especially its limitations, can be explained as the byproducts of the *kludges* . . . the computer hacker's term for the *ad hoc* jury-rigs that are usually patched onto software in the course of debugging to get the stuff actually to work.

Consciousness is not a seamless fabric; it has deficiencies and gaps that the organism learns to work around. For example, human beings talk to themselves because one specialized discriminator in the brain needs to communicate with another; language creates a "virtual wire." In another example, Dennett describes a person walking into a room who sees on the wallpaper hundreds of identical designs. The person almost instantly recognizes that all the designs are the same but that does not mean each instance of the design is stored as an image in the brain; it would be physically impossible for the eye to take in all of the instances, and (since there is no Cartesian Theater) no "place" where all the images are interpreted. What happens, says Dennett, is that the brain makes the assumption that the images are the same and represents that fact. The result is *as if* the person had "seen" all of the designs, but that is not the case. To take another example, the brain can represent a certain time sequence in a different order from that of a given set of inputs. One might get in one's car and put on a hat; but later, as the multiple drafts of "the experience" are vying for attention, one's brain may represent a different temporal order: one remembers putting on a hat and then entering one's car. A person "feels" that the latter is the "way it happened."

The self, says Dennett, is an abstraction analogous to the mathematical "center of gravity." The stories humans tell about themselves (and to themselves) constitute the abstraction Dennett calls the "center of narrative gravity." These stories constitute an "as if" unity of the self, just as the word processing program seems unified even though many calculations seemingly unrelated to the processing of words are occurring at each moment. Consciousness is a virtual machine, a program running on a complex parallel processing system; the representations of the various subsystem discriminators just are the conscious "feel" of the color yellow or sense of regret over a road not taken.

Dennett, director of the Center for Cognitive Studies at Tufts University, is a teleological functionalist, one who strives to take seriously the "aboutness" (the intentionality) of consciousness and one who recognizes the interests and purposes of organisms (or the memes inhabiting them), but one who believes that there is nothing unique to consciousness "over and above" the functioning of the brain's subsystems. His theory asks the reader to agree that the brain can produce a "representation of presence" without there being a "presence of representation" (that is, images in the head) and that that is what one experiences when one consciously experiences the presence of another.

Dennett's critics have charged him with explaining away the "specialness" of consciousness and with using images such as "the editing of multiple drafts" that are simply too vague or that mask the ways consciousness functions that are not computer-like. In the third section of his book (and in its two appendices for philosophers and scientists) he attempts to respond to some of the difficulties of his theory. He uses what he calls the "systems reply" in suggesting that while admittedly no subsection of the brain is conscious, taken as a complex system consciousness is what "seems" heterophenomenologically to occur. His picture of the decentered self constituted by language bears a remarkable resemblance to the view of the self put forth by certain literary theories, most notably Deconstruction, and a theory of the mind that draws too heavily on contemporary metaphors may soon find itself irrelevant. Yet Dennett's overview of the literature of cognitive science and philosophy provides a rich introduction to some of the most creative responses to the ancient question of "who (or what) am I?"

Dan Barnett

Sources for Further Study

Booklist. LXXXVIII, October 1, 1991, p. 222.
Boston Globe. November 3, 1991, p. 94.
Kirkus Reviews. LIX, September 15, 1991, p. 1194.
London Review of Books. XIII, November 21, 1991, p. 3.
Los Angeles Times Book Review. November 24, 1991, p. 6.
The New Republic. CCV, December 23, 1991, p. 40.
The New York Times Book Review. XCVI, November 10, 1991, p. 1.
Publishers Weekly. CCXXXVIII, August 16, 1991, p. 41.
Science News. CXL, December 14, 1991, p. 395.
The Wall Street Journal. November 7, 1991, p. A12.

COUNSEL TO THE PRESIDENT
A Memoir

Author: Clark Clifford (1906-   ), with Richard Holbrooke (1941-   )
Publisher: Random House (New York). Illustrated. 709 pp. $25.00
Type of work: Autobiography
Time: 1906-the 1990's
Locale: Primarily St. Louis, Missouri, and Washington, D.C.

An absorbing memoir by a former adviser to three presidents

> *Principal personages:*
> CLARK CLIFFORD, a statesman and adviser to three Democratic presidents
> HARRY S. TRUMAN, the president of the United States 1945-1953
> JOHN F. KENNEDY, the president of the United States 1961-1963
> LYNDON JOHNSON, the president of the United States 1963-1969

Clark Clifford made himself a legend. Coming to Washington at the end of World War II, Clifford became a trusted adviser to a succession of Democratic presidents and built a law firm that prospered on the strength of his influence. Clifford became the consummate Washington insider, the very model of a Beltway sage. *Counsel to the President: A Memoir*, written with Richard Holbrooke, was apparently intended to formalize Clifford's conception of himself as a wise statesman. Unfortunately for Clifford, the publication of his autobiography coincided with the Bank of Credit and Commerce International (BCCI) banking scandal and the revelation that he had been a business associate of the errant Arab bankers. Clifford dismisses the scandal in an extended footnote in which he denies any wrongdoing. Nevertheless, *Counsel to the President* may end up a monument to an image discredited by history. Whatever the ultimate verdict of time on the character of Clark Clifford, however, he did play an important role in the public life of his day. His memoirs shed much light, both intended and inadvertent, on the history of Cold War America.

Clark Clifford was born on Christmas Day, 1906, in Fort Scott, Kansas, where his father worked as an auditor for the Missouri Pacific Railroad. After a family move, Clifford grew up in St. Louis, Missouri, and for the first half of his life that city was the bound of his ambitions. Clifford enjoyed a happy and secure middle-class childhood. When he came of age, he attended Washington University in St. Louis. There, in what proved to be a fateful decision, Clifford chose to pursue the law as a profession.

In his memoirs, Clifford proudly remarks that, starting in 1928, his legal career spanned more than sixty years. Clifford's conception of his public service is rooted in his identity as a lawyer. Clifford, in his own eyes, has been from first to last an advocate, fighting for causes in which he believed. From humble beginnings as a trial lawyer, defending with little success down-and-out clients, Clifford gradually built himself a thriving practice. More important, the discipline of mastering the myriad details of court cases developed in Clifford the ability to work logically through complicated issues, while practice in appealing to juries sharpened his skill in the art of persuasion. Though he did not know it at the time, Clifford's years before the bar in St. Louis had prepared him well for unexpected challenges in the nation's capital.

American entry into World War II changed the direction of Clark Clifford's life. In the wake of Pearl Harbor, Clifford joined the Missouri State Guard and served as its judge advocate general. As time passed, Clifford grew restive with this sedentary duty. In the spring of 1944, Clifford obtained a commission as a lieutenant, junior grade in the United States Naval Reserve. His wartime service in the Navy consisted of a number of staff jobs that never took him out of the United States. Clifford was helping assemble supplies for the projected invasion of Japan in June, 1945, when he was contacted by J. K. Vardaman, an old friend from St. Louis who had recently been appointed Naval Aide to President Harry S. Truman. Vardaman wanted an assistant he could trust in the hothouse atmosphere of Washington and offered the job to Clifford. The prospect of working in the White House and witnessing the making of history proved irresistible to Clifford. He accepted the position as Vardaman's assistant, and in July, 1945, reported for duty.

Soon after Clifford arrived at the White House, the president, with Vardaman, left for the Potsdam Conference. With the president away, Clifford had little to do. The only task he had been assigned was to supervise the redesign of the presidential seal and flag, so he busied himself learning the White House routine and introducing himself to members of President Truman's staff. Clifford's most important contact at this time was Judge Samuel I. Rosenman, special counsel to the president. Rosenman was winding up a distinguished career during which he had acted as a close political adviser and speechwriter for Franklin D. Roosevelt and then Truman. Clifford impressed the older man, and as he made himself useful around the White House, he became known as Rosenman's protégé. Soon Clifford was engaged in a variety of tasks having little to do with naval matters. Under Rosenman's watchful eye, he began assisting in the drafting of speeches for the president and attending Oval Office discussions of policy. In April, 1946, Clifford succeeded Vardaman as naval aide to the president. Nine weeks later, Harry Truman named him his special counsel.

Clark Clifford rose rapidly to a position of influence in the Truman Administration because of his intelligence, a flair for speechwriting, and almost instinctive political skills. Though he had never before been intimately involved in politics, Clifford quickly became one of Truman's most trusted and powerful advisers. Clifford consolidated his position by perfecting the attributes of the modern American courtier. From his mentor, Judge Rosenman, Clifford learned that presidential assistants existed only to serve the president. If presidential assistants became controversial or cultivated public personae distinctive from the president, they had outlived their usefulness. Clifford became a master at accomplishing his goals behind the scenes, guiding presidents with confidential memoranda or a few words dropped in a private conversation. Amiability is as important as discretion in a courtier, and Clifford labored diligently to tailor his approach and advice to the man he served.

During the Truman Administration, Clifford became the impresario of the president's famous poker parties, at which the most powerful men in Washington relaxed and talked politics. Clifford, who had never been a card-playing man, took to studying manuals on poker so he could take part in Truman's games. So devoted was Clifford to his chosen role as adviser to presidents that he became one of the first paladins of what would be called the "imperial presidency." Throughout his memoir, Clifford repeatedly expresses his reverence for the presidency, while giving little evidence of a similar regard for the other branches of government. As a man who wielded power through his personal relationships with chief executives, Clifford exaggerated the role of the president, forgetting that American governance is driven by more than the will of a man in the White House.

Clark Clifford experienced no ideological difficulties in committing himself to the service of Harry Truman. Clifford was by family tradition a Democrat and by inclination a liberal. Though always a pragmatist with a keen sense of what was politically possible, Clifford consistently advocated the liberal position in internecine battles with conservatives in the Truman Administration. To help advance his ideas, he surreptitiously organized some liberal young officials into a Monday Night Group that met to discuss ideas about governmental initiatives and political strategies. The Monday Night Group helped shape Clifford's advice to the president on such momentous issues as the desegregation of the armed forces, the special session of Congress in 1948, and the veto of the Taft-Hartley Act. The decisive Republican victory in the congressional elections of 1946 assisted Clifford in his quest for a liberal ascendancy in the administration by convincing Truman that he had to revive the spirit of the New Deal if he was to survive politically.

Clifford also played a part in the development of the great foreign policy initiatives of the Truman Administration. Though he disliked the excesses of the second red scare that erupted during the Truman years, Clifford was nevertheless a dedicated cold warrior who shared the administration's growing conviction that the United States had to resist Soviet aggression. In 1946, in the wake of George Kennan's famous Long Telegram, President Truman asked Clifford and his assistant George Elsey to prepare a record of the agreements the Soviet Union had broken. On his own initiative, Clifford had his mandate broadened to canvas the opinions of the government officials most concerned with relations with the Soviet Union. The resultant Clifford-Elsey Report urged the creation of a coherent strategy to restrain the Soviet threat. So vigorous were the report's recommendations for military and economic aid for nations resisting Soviet encroachment that President Truman, still hoping for better relations with the Soviet Union, had all copies of the report gathered up and removed from circulation. Time and events hardened the president's attitude toward the Soviets, and Clifford had the satisfaction of supervising the drafting of the speech embodying the Truman Doctrine. Clifford also helped write the National Security Act of 1947, which created both the modern Department of Defense and the Central Intelligence Agency. Motivated by both idealism and political calculation, Clifford strongly supported Truman's decision to disregard the advice of the State Department and his military chiefs by recognizing the newborn State of Israel.

Clark Clifford's most vital contribution to Truman's presidency came in 1948, when he developed what proved to be a winning strategy for that year's presidential election. Beset by a resurgent Republican Party and Democratic defections on both the right and left, Truman's candidacy seemed doomed. Clifford, however, encouraged the president to return resolutely to his liberal roots and remind the people what years of Democratic social policies had done for them. Clifford participated in Truman's famous whistle-stop campaign across the country, at times even condescending to mix with the crowd and start the applause at crucial moments in the president's speeches. When Truman won his dramatic electoral victory in November, Clifford wanted to resign as special counsel to pursue his neglected personal affairs. The president persuaded him to stay on for another year. This enabled Clifford to be present at the creation of the Fair Deal and to play a major role in launching Truman's Point Four program of technical assistance to developing nations.

In 1950, Clifford left the administration and began building his powerful law firm, though he continued to make himself available to President Truman as an adviser. Among the clients Clifford acquired during the 1950's was Senator John F. Kennedy of Massachusetts. Clifford acted as Kennedy's legal troubleshooter, handling a number of delicate tasks for the senator, some of which he still declines to divulge. Clifford's most spectacular achievement as Kennedy's lawyer was to browbeat the ABC television network into retracting a report that the senator had not in fact written his prizewinning book *Profiles in Courage* (1956). When Kennedy was elected president in 1960, Clifford headed his transition team. Though the new president offered Clifford a number of posts in his administration, he refused them all, preferring to continue his unofficial role. Eventually, the only position Clifford accepted from Kennedy was a seat on the president's Foreign Intelligence Advisory Board, which was organized in the wake of the disastrous Bay of Pigs invasion of Cuba to advise the president on intelligence matters.

Clifford had known Lyndon Johnson since his days in the Truman Administration, and had a great respect for his political abilities and his ambition to better the condition of the underprivileged in America. When Johnson succeeded Kennedy as president, Clifford easily transferred his loyalties to the new administration and maintained his position as a confidential adviser to the chief executive. As such, Clifford was privy to important policy debates about American involvement in Vietnam. President Johnson had inherited a growing debacle in Southeast Asia and had to decide whether to retrieve the situation by committing American military forces to the war in Vietnam. From the outset, Clifford opposed further American intervention, believing Vietnam to be out of the sphere of the United States' vital interests. When Johnson sent troops into battle in Vietnam, however, Clifford fell into step behind the president and even argued for more intensive bombing of the enemy, hoping that this might force a resolution to the problem. Vietnam, though, proved a morass for the administration. As the years passed, Clifford grew more convinced that the United States had to leave Vietnam. His opportunity to help speed this withdrawal came in March, 1968, when he accepted an appointment as secretary of defense. President Johnson thought he was placing into office a hawk who would support his policies in Vietnam. In fact, Clifford, appalled by the strength demonstrated by the Communists in Vietnam during the Tet Offensive, was determined to negotiate with the enemy and end the war. Utilizing all of his skills as a courtier, Clifford worked assiduously to encourage Johnson to halt the bombing of North Vietnam and open peace talks with the Communist Vietnamese. He deserves much of the credit for Johnson's diplomatic initiatives in 1968. Yet success in ending the bombing and starting peace talks in Paris gave way to frustration, as one hurdle after another prevented a cessation of hostilities. Clifford watched helplessly as the year became one of successive disasters for the Democrats, culminating in the election of Richard Nixon as president.

A Republican era ensued in the wake of Nixon's election, leaving Clifford cut off from the center of power. He performed a few diplomatic missions for President Jimmy Carter but never became one of the Georgian's intimate advisers. During these years, Clifford concentrated on his business affairs, including the ill fated DCCI venture. Despite his disappointment with the course of politics in recent decades, Clifford ends his book with a hopeful prediction that a new era of liberalism is in the offing. *Counsel to the President*, for all its understandable partisanship and lacunae, is an engaging and absorbing survey of post-World War II American politics. Clark Clifford may never receive the accolades he desires, but he sat near to power in an important and vibrant period, and his memoirs provide insight into a lost world.

Daniel P. Murphy

Sources for Further Study

Library Journal. CXVI, May 15, 1991, p. 88.
The New Republic. CCV, July 8, 1991, p. 32.
Newsweek. CXVII, May 20, 1991, p. 52.
The New York Review of Books. July 18, 1991, p. 19.
The New York Times Book Review. May 19, 1991, p. 1.
The Progressive. LV, August, 1991, p. 39.
Publishers Weekly. CCXXXVIII, May 3, 1991, p. 58.
Time. CXXXVII, May 27, 1991, p. 66.
The Washington Monthly. XXIII, June, 1991, p. 48.

THE CRISIS YEARS
Kennedy and Khrushchev, 1960-1963

Author: Michael R. Beschloss (1955-   )
Publisher: HarperCollins (New York). Illustrated. 816 pp. $29.95
Type of work: History
Time: 1960-1963
Locale: Washington, D.C.

A detailed narrative of the relationship between John F. Kennedy and Nikita Khrushchev during a critical period in the Cold War

> *Principal personages:*
> JOHN F. KENNEDY, the president of the United States from 1961 to 1963
> NIKITA S. KHRUSHCHEV, the premier of the Soviet Union from 1958 to 1964
> ROBERT KENNEDY, the U.S. attorney general and brother of President Kennedy
> McGEORGE BUNDY, President Kennedy's special assistant for national security affairs
> ROBERT McNAMARA, the U.S. secretary of defense under President Kennedy
> DEAN RUSK, the U.S. secretary of state under President Kennedy

Michael Beschloss is a television journalist and the author of an important study of Dwight Eisenhower's Soviet policy entitled *Mayday: Eisenhower, Khrushchev, and the U-2 Affair* (1986). In writing *The Crisis Years: Kennedy and Khrushchev, 1960-1963*, Beschloss has made extensive use of newly declassified material, including tapes of White House conversations, records from Soviet archives, and interviews with key figures such as Richard Helms, the former Central Intelligence Agency (CIA) director.

This volume examines U.S.-Soviet relations from 1960 to 1963, a period that Beschloss appropriately labels the "crisis years" because it was a period in which the two great powers came closer to nuclear war than at any other time in history. Although President John F. Kennedy became a capable crisis manager, Beschloss suggests that, in part because of his inexperience, Kennedy bore substantial responsibility for creating many of the crises that dominated his presidency. Beschloss claims that Nikita Khrushchev wished for rapprochement with the United States so that he could cut Soviet military spending and use the funds for consumer goods. Kennedy, however, consistently misjudged Khrushchev and pursued policies toward the Soviet Union that unnecessarily brought the United States and the Soviet Union to the brink of war.

During the 1960 election campaign, Richard Nixon pressed President Eisenhower to proceed with the invasion of Cuba before the election occurred, in the belief that the successful overthrow of Fidel Castro's communist government would help Nixon's election prospects. When Kennedy took office, he was immediately faced with making a decision as to whether to proceed with the invasion of Cuba that had been planned by the Eisenhower Administration. Beschloss indicates that Kennedy opposed an invasion by American troops for two reasons: He wished to align the United States with the emerging Third World nations and anticipated that an American invasion would be perceived as similar to the Soviet Union's invasion of Hungary in 1956, and he feared that if American troops invaded Cuba, Khrushchev would retaliate by sending Soviet troops into West Berlin and forcing Kennedy to choose between war with the Soviets or abandoning Berlin.

Although initially reluctant to approve the CIA-planned invasion using Cuban exiles, early in April, 1961, Kennedy changed his mind and told his aides to proceed with it. Beschloss notes that Kennedy had met with his father, Joseph Kennedy, over the weekend before making his decision and that the latter was strongly in favor of invading Cuba; Beschloss concludes that it was probably Joseph Kennedy who persuaded President Kennedy to take what proved to be an unwise step. Yet President Kennedy agreed to the plan only on the condition that no U.S. troops would be involved. As the invasion unfolded and it became clear that it would fail unless American forces were used, Kennedy refused to allow direct American intervention, because he believed it would trigger a Soviet attack on Berlin. Beschloss attributes the failure of the invasion to Kennedy's basic ambivalence about it; his attempt to conceal American involvement led him to insist on the operation's being too small to succeed.

Kennedy's first meeting with Khrushchev following his election occurred in Vienna at the 1961 summit conference. Kennedy hoped a face-to-face meeting would enable them to establish a personal relationship that might ease tensions between the two countries. Instead, Beschloss suggests that the meeting was a disaster for Kennedy. Inexperienced in foreign policy, he inadvertently antagonized Khrushchev. The latter left the meeting insisting that the Soviet Union would sign a peace treaty with East Germany and that it would then be up to the United States to decide whether there would be war or peace. Kennedy was shaken by Khrushchev's attempt to bully him and admitted it had been the roughest experience in his life. He drew the conclusion that he would have to do something to demonstrate his toughness or Khrushchev would likely make further attempts to take advantage of his youth and inexperience.

Beschloss' claim that Kennedy did not oppose the establishment of the Berlin Wall—indeed he privately welcomed it—is one of the more striking revelations presented in this volume. With thousands of East Germans fleeing to the West by crossing into West Berlin during 1961, Khrushchev was under great pressure to take some action. In a public statement in July, Senator James Fulbright had acknowledged that East Germany had a right to close its border if it wished and expressed surprise it had not done so. When Kennedy did not repudiate this suggestion and did not warn Khrushchev against closing the East German border, Kennedy signaled the Soviets that this step would be acceptable to the United States. According to Beschloss, Kennedy viewed the wall as a solution to the Berlin crisis rather than as a new source of friction, because it reduced the pressure on Khrushchev to take action against West Berlin.

On October 27, 1961, U.S. and Soviet tanks faced each other across the Berlin Wall in a confrontation that could easily have led to war. This military standoff developed after East Germany attempted to restrict U.S. access to East Berlin. Kennedy's personal representative in Berlin, General Lucius Clay, favored a show of military force to maintain Allied access rights, but both Kennedy and Soviet leaders feared that an accidental discharge of weapons might set off a war. Without informing Clay, Kennedy asked the Soviet government to remove its tanks and promised to withdraw the U.S. tanks if this were done. When the Soviets acceded to this request, it gave the impression to Clay and the American public that the Soviets had backed down when confronted with a show of force; Beschloss suggests Kennedy's secret diplomacy was the real reason.

During the 1960 election campaign, Kennedy criticized the Republican administration for allowing the Soviet Union to surge ahead of the United States in the deployment of intercontinental ballistic missiles. In fact, the United States had the advantage, but Eisenhower had shrewdly avoided stating this publicly, as he knew the result would be increased spending by the Soviets on their missile program and thus an arms race. Kennedy, however, was under great domestic pressure from the political right to increase defense spending to catch up with the Soviets. He also feared that if Khrushchev underestimated U.S. missile strength it might encourage him to initiate aggressive action against Berlin. Kennedy therefore authorized a Department of Defense official to state publicly that the United States had a vast superiority in nuclear weapons over the Soviet Union. This shocked Khrushchev and exposed him to criticism from the Soviet military and from Chinese leaders. Beschloss suggests that Khrushchev's reckless attempt to place offensive missiles in Cuba in 1962 was an attempt to close the Soviet missile gap in response to this public exposure of Soviet military weakness.

Although Kennedy was on the verge of ordering an air strike against the Cuban missile sites when he first became aware of them, Beschloss gives Kennedy credit for handling the 1962 Cuban missile crisis much better than the 1961 invasion of Cuba. He resisted advice for precipitate action that might have unleashed war with the Soviet Union, choosing instead to use American naval vessels to "quarantine" Cuba, thereby giving Khrushchev time to order the ships carrying missiles to return home. Beschloss notes that both Kennedy and Robert McNamara, the secretary of defense, believed the missiles in Cuba made no difference to the nuclear balance of power, and that the majority of the executive committee of the National Security Council shared this view. They recognized, though, that the missiles were important because they appeared to change the balance of power, and a failure to act against them would be suicidal in domestic politics.

At a crucial point in the crisis, a U-2 spy plane was shot down over Cuba. Under the impression that the antiaircraft missiles in Cuba were under Soviet control, Kennedy at first assumed this was a deliberate escalation of the crisis by Khrushchev. Fortunately, Kennedy resisted the advice to launch an air strike in retaliation, as it is now known that Khrushchev was not responsible for the act. Two local military commanders acting on their own initiative fired the missile. Beschloss notes that Khrushchev was upset and alarmed when he learned what had happened, as he feared that the negotiations underway might be sabotaged by the incident.

Kennedy's attempt to resolve the crisis without war brought him into conflict with the Joint Chiefs of Staff, who had consistently urged an air strike followed by an invasion. While the negotiations were underway, the pressure for military action increased, as it was believed each day's delay meant the missiles were closer to being ready to fire. When Khrushchev ended the crisis by agreeing to withdraw the missiles, an elated Kennedy met with the Joint Chiefs to inform them that the situation had been successfully resolved. He was stunned by their furious reaction; the Air Force chief of staff, General Curtis LeMay, pounded the table and announced that it was the greatest defeat in the nation's history.

Despite his youth and athletic image, Kennedy was in poor health when he became president and was only able to fulfill his presidential duties by relying upon strong medication that could have impaired his judgment. Kennedy suffered from Addison's disease, for which he took regular doses of cortisone, a medication that could inflate the user's libido and affect his decisionmaking ability by causing wide fluctuations in mood. He also experienced chronic back pain, which had become so severe that he had agreed to a life-threatening spinal fusion operation in 1954. Instead of using exercise and physical therapy to strengthen his back, Kennedy relied upon injections of procaine to reduce the pain. When he met with Khrushchev at the Vienna summit conference, Kennedy was also receiving amphetamine injections from a physician of questionable reputation. As Beschloss points out, Kennedy did not allow an individual doctor to supervise his various medical treatments to ensure that the interaction of the various drugs he was taking did not affect his judgment.

Kennedy's relations with women have attracted considerable attention, and Beschloss carefully spells out the political importance of this issue. A married politician who has sexual relations with women other than his wife risks being blackmailed; a single man who has a sexual relationship with a woman considered a security risk is also risking his political career. Kennedy did both. In 1942, while he was a naval intelligence officer and single, Kennedy had an affair with a Swedish woman, Ingra Arvad Fejos, who was under Federal Bureau of Investigation (FBI) surveillance as a suspected Nazi spy; Kennedy proceeded with the relationship even though he knew Fejos was being investigated by the government. Beschloss suggests Kennedy's father intervened with the Franklin D. Roosevelt Administration to have Kennedy transferred to a PT boat in the Pacific in order to bring an end to the relationship before it ruined any chance Kennedy might have for a political career. The FBI had proof of this relationship, and it gave J. Edgar Hoover a powerful weapon over Kennedy.

Kennedy continued to have numerous affairs after he was married and after he became president. This exposed him to blackmail from various groups within the United States as well as from foreign interests. In 1963, Kennedy had a sexual relationship with Ellen Feimmel Rometsch, an East German woman whose parents and relatives were in East Germany and who was known to be a friend of at least one member of the Soviet embassy. Fearing a scandal, Robert Kennedy had the woman deported and the matter hushed up, but the FBI had knowledge of the affair, thus placing Kennedy's political future in Hoover's hands. Kennedy also had an affair with Judith Campbell, who was the mistress of a Mafia boss, Sam Giancana. Campbell later claimed that she had served as a liaison between Kennedy and Giancana and that Kennedy had asked the latter for assistance during the 1960 election campaign. While the exact nature of the relationship between Kennedy and Giancana remains uncertain, Beschloss correctly states that it exposed Kennedy to possible blackmail from the Mafia.

Kennedy's reputation among historians has declined dramatically in recent years. Although Beschloss attempts to be fair to Kennedy and does recognize his successes, *The Crisis Years* will reinforce this historiographical trend. By drawing upon previously unused sources, Beschloss demonstrates that Kennedy's ineptitude in dealing with Khrushchev unnecessarily increased Cold War tensions and contributed to the recurring crises that marked Kennedy's presidency. This is an excellent study of an important period in U.S. and world history.

Harold L. Smith

Sources for Further Study

Chicago Tribune. June 2, 1991, XIV, p. 1.
Foreign Affairs. LXX, Fall, 1991, p. 174.
London Review of Books. XIII, October 10, 1991, p. 8.
Los Angeles Times Book Review. June 23, 1991, p. 1.
New Statesman and Society. IV, August 30, 1991, p. 46.
The New York Times Book Review. XCVI, June 16, 1991, p. 3.
The New Yorker. LXVII, August 26, 1991, p. 77.
Publishers Weekly. CCXXXVIII, April 19, 1991, p. 50.
Time. CXXXVII, May 6, 1991, p. 17.
The Wall Street Journal. August 1, 1991, p. A10.
The Washington Post Book World. XXI, June 9, 1991, p. 1.

THE CROOKED TIMBER OF HUMANITY
Chapters in the History of Ideas

Author: Isaiah Berlin (1909-   )
Edited by Henry Hardy
Publisher: Alfred A. Knopf (New York). 277 pp. $22.00
Type of work: History of ideas

Eight essays that pursue the quest for Utopia and the origins of fascism and nationalism

In the late 1970's and early 1980's, Henry Hardy carefully edited four volumes of Sir Isaiah Berlin's essays, collectively entitling them *Selected Writings. Russian Thinkers* (1978) examined the ideas of Ivan Turgenev, Leo Tolstoy, Vissarion Belinsky, Aleksandr Herzen, and other nineteenth century giants. *Concepts and Categories* (1979) consisted of sometimes difficult but always rewarding technical philosophical essays. *Against the Current: Essays in the History of Ideas* (1980) analyzed both the intellectual program of the Enlightenment and contradictory, antirational reactions to it. *Personal Impressions* (1981) was a collection of memoirs concerning statesmen, academicians, and writers.

Hardy wryly calls *The Crooked Timber of Humanity* "the fifth of four volumes," since half of its essays had been excluded from *Against the Current*, another was essentially written by 1960 but then set aside, and only three were written during the 1980's. The title of the present volume is derived from the German philosopher Immanuel Kant's declaration, in a 1784 essay, that "out of the crooked timber of humanity no straight thing was ever made"—an admonition, as Berlin interprets it, against dogmatism and perfectionism.

Isaiah Berlin's credentials as a philosopher and historian of ideas are daunting. He is a polymathic thinker who taught social and political theory at Oxford from 1938 to 1967, became president of its Wolfson College until 1975, was president of the British Academy from 1974 to 1978, and holds honorary degrees and fellowships from the most distinguished universities of the United States, England, Scotland, Wales, and Israel. As an erudite historian of ideas, Berlin has no equal in the English-speaking world, and he expresses himself in prose of exceptional clarity and elegance, even though he was born in Riga, Latvia, and had to master English when a schoolboy.

Berlin's style is remarkably distinctive among contemporary writers of nonfiction. His syntax is intricate, compound-complex, a rush of clauses and propositions that combines formal precision with intellectual passion, achieving rhetorical sonorities and nobility while usually avoiding bombast or preciosity. The nineteenth century prose of Thomas Macaulay and John Ruskin might be among Berlin's models; assuredly not the plain, succinct modes of E. M. Forster or George Orwell. The effect is to render the process as well as results of a brilliant scholar's pursuit of ideas.

In *The Crooked Timber of Humanity's* first essay, "The Pursuit of the Ideal," Berlin threads strands of his intellectual autobiography. In reading Tolstoy and other writers of the mid-nineteenth century, he found a common belief that the world's central problems had solutions and that these could be discovered and implemented by humankind. At Oxford, when a student, he read the writings of many philosophers, particularly rationalists and empiricists, who were convinced that society could be reorganized so that prejudices, unexamined dogmas, and all political cruelties and stupidities could be eliminated. All these views shared the tenets of Platonic idealism, that "all genuine questions must have one true answer . . . that there must be a dependable path towards the discovery of these truths . . . [and] that the true answers, when found, must necessarily be compatible with one another and form a single whole."

The first thinker who shook Berlin's faith in this theory of progress was Niccolo Machiavelli, who regarded the Christian virtues of humility, acceptance of suffering, unworldliness, and hope for an afterlife as impractical for governing a state. Machiavelli argued that ruling instead requires such pagan virtues as courage, vitality, self-assertion, and a capacity for ruthlessness and cruelty. Machiavelli profoundly disturbed Berlin's confidence in the cosmic harmony of values.

Machiavelli's skepticism was sharply reinforced by the work of Giambattista Vico, who founded the modern doctrine of cultural pluralism. According to Vico, every society has its own sense of itself, its own vision of reality. These visions differ with each successive social whole, so that the values of, for example, the Homeric Greeks differed sharply from those of Renaissance Florence or seventeenth century France.

Further challenging the universalism of Platonism was the German eighteenth century philosopher Johann Gottfried von Herder, who compared national cultures in many lands and periods, insisting that every society has its own center of moral gravity, or life-style. People may seek many differing goals, yet they are capable of understanding and learning from one another. Still, concludes Berlin, persuaded by Vico and Herder, "the notion of the perfect whole, the ultimate solution, in which all good things coexist, seems to me to be not merely unattainable . . . but conceptually incoherent. . . . We are doomed to choose, and every choice may entail an irreparable loss."

Moreover, the concept of a perfect society may well be highly dangerous: If heads of state are convinced that theirs is the one and only true path toward solving society's problems, they may end up becoming Adolf Hitler, Joseph Stalin, Mao Tsetung, or Pol Pot, smashing all who resist or question their journey. Concluding this somewhat confessional chapter, Berlin opts for a utilitarian, pluralistic equilibrium that attempts to avoid desperate dilemmas or intolerable choices, aware that absolutism leads to inhumanism but also aware that his pragmatic middle course will strike some readers as flat, dull, and rather unheroic.

The second essay, "The Decline of Utopian Ideas in the West," probes more deeply some of the themes of the first. Of particular interest is Berlin's contrast between the rationalism and scientism of the French-dominated Enlightenment, which sought to liberate humanity from cruelty, superstition, injustice, and obscurantism, and the countermovement of the German-speaking peoples, whose devout inward visions were first voiced by Herder. Herder identified cultural differences and developments quite differently from the interpretations expressed by Voltaire, for example. The latter posited a single Western order of human excellence, with France, of course, at its pinnacle. Herder instead insisted on the incommensurability of German, French, and other cultures' values, qualities of character, and activities. He defined *das Volk*, the people, as the only natural unit of communal identity, thus preparing the way for German unification and the ideal of a greater Germany.

Herder became the forerunner of such militantly *völkisch* and Romantic writers as Johann Fichte, Friedrich von Schlegel, Ludwig Tieck, and Novalis. They stressed the primacy of one's will over one's reason, the self-assertion and self-realization of the individual against classical canons of restraint, decorum, harmony, and uniformity. Thus the dream of Utopian perfection, based on eternal and binding values and virtues, was dispelled by a Romantic insistence on variety and diversity in societies with open textures and many conflicts. Unwilling to commit himself fully to either Utopianism or irrationalism, Berlin repeats his plea for equilibrium, tolerance, sympathy, and understanding.

"Giambattista Vico and Cultural History" hails Vico as the father of "cultural pluralism, according to which each authentic culture has its own unique vision, its own scale of values, which . . . is superseded by other visions and values, but never wholly so." Berlin emphasizes Vico's enlightened belief that no epoch or culture is a windowless box without connections to other societies and periods, that "what men have made, other men can understand." Rather, Vico is the founder of historical anthropology, assigning a crucial role to the quality he calls *fantasia*, or imaginative insight, which could revivify the past and enable the historian to establish vital bridges of understanding across cultures. Vico, however, disbelieves in the religion of progress: While each culture creates its own masterpieces, these cannot be transplanted elsewhere; it is idle to compare Sophocles to Vergil or Vergil to Jean Racine. There are no timeless or universal standards, nor is there a timeless and universal human nature.

In "Alleged Relativism in Eighteenth-Century European Thought," Berlin takes pains to distinguish pluralism from relativism, which denies even the possibility of any objective knowledge or truth, holding that beliefs are wholly conditioned by social systems and groups. He defends Vico and Herder from some historians' classification as relativists. Rather, relativism in its modern form stems from the metaphysics of Arthur Schopenhauer and Friedrich Nietzsche and the influence of thinkers who were not themselves relativists, such as Karl Marx and Sigmund Freud. Pluralism, on the other hand, while denying that there can be only one true morality or aesthetics or religion, does allow for equally objective alternative values. Without explicitly declaring himself, Berlin strongly implies that pluralism best expresses his own view of the world.

The central, by far longest, and most impressively sustained commentary in this book is "Joseph de Maistre and the Origins of Fascism." Maistre has generally been regarded as the French Enlightenment's and French Revolution's most eloquent and powerful enemy, a fiercely right-wing absolutist who espoused a Roman Catholic theocracy and expounded views of the hardest, narrowest, and most obscurantist dogmatism. While not disagreeing with this assessment, Berlin finds it largely inadequate, and regards Maistre as having been born before rather than after his proper time.

Maistre was, to be sure, an ultramontane legitimist who opposed rationalism, individualism, liberal compromise, and secular enlightenment. "He dwelt on the incurably bad and corrupt nature of man, and consequently the unavoidable need for authority, hierarchy, obedience and subjection." Consequently he preached the inevitability "of conflict and suffering, sin and retribution, bloodshed and war." Berlin sees Maistre as essentially a totalitarian who can be classified as a protofascist. Blood, pain, and punishment are the notions that haunt Maistre's dire world; corrupt and feeble mankind must be harshly disciplined by perpetually vigilant and coercive guardians, headed by the pope, with the executioner the keystone of the authoritarian arch. Maistre's catalog of enemies prefigures fascism's: atheists, Freemasons, Jews, Jacobins, scientists, democrats, idealists, intellectuals of every stripe, and more.

What disturbs Berlin most is the violent tone of Maistre's dark discourses: He proclaims an Augustinian religion of blood, terror, and self-immolation, the necessity of chains to curb humanity's urge toward self-destruction, and an occult worship of despotism. Against the Enlightenment's extolment of reason, freedom, harmony, goodness, progress, and the pursuit of happiness, he delights in describing people's wish to sacrifice, serve, and suffer, to crawl before authority or, contrarily, to pursue utmost power for its exhilaration. Maistre's vision of society as largely weak, sinful, self-contradictory, and irrational derives both from Christian sources and from Plato. It anticipates the opinions of Fyodor Dostoevski, Nietzsche, and such twentieth century authoritarian apologists as Charles Maurras, Knut Hamsun, T. S. Eliot, and Vilfredo Pareto. Maistre, Berlin concludes, reveals desolating truths about human nature rejected in his own time but all too frequently embraced in the twentieth century.

The richest essay among the remaining three is "The Apotheosis of the Romantic Will," which relates Romanticism to Utopianism and fascism. More fully than in "The Pursuit of the Ideal," Berlin pursues the rational core of the West's intellectual tradition from Pythagoras and Plato to the Enlightenment's Utopians and thence to Immanuel Kant, who insisted on free will and feasible commitment to chosen goals. Opposing this rationalism were Jean-Jacques Rousseau and such German Romantic writers as Johann Schiller, Herder, and Fichte, whom Berlin labels the true father of German romanticism. Fichte believed in an eternal, divine spirit outside time and space to which one will was subject. He and his followers stressed lonely individualism, with persons of moral integrity warring against a society governed by greed, corruption, and stupidity. Fichte and fellow Romantics "celebrated the power of the will to freedom, to creative self-expression, with fateful consequences for the history and outlook of the years that followed." Will was all that mattered; its actions determined thoughts and values, not vice versa.

German Romantic writers led the attack on the concept of a world of harmonious and objective principles, regarding it as a baseless, utilitarian fabrication. E. T. A. Hoffmann and others sought to expose the terrifying chaos beneath bourgeois norms, preparing the way for Schopenhauer's cosmos subject to a blind, aimless, fragmented will, for Dostoevski's antirational undergroundling, and for Franz Kafka's surreal victims. Thus modern literature and philosophy, influenced by Romanticism, have rejected the validity of any golden age, any perfect society that could provide correct solutions to humanity's central problems. Too many writers, however, have also followed the dangerous fallacy that life can be shaped like a work of art, and that a political leader can be a sublime artist. This, states Berlin, has led to the savage brutality of authoritarian politics.

Isaiah Berlin's own liberalism is cautiously moderate, no longer fired by the idealism of the Enlightenment. He affirms his faith in individualism, in liberty, in tolerance, in imaginative understanding, in intelligence, and in learning; above all, in a mind open to all ideas and closed only to totalitarianism.

Gerhard Brand

Sources for Further Study

Chicago Tribune. April 27, 1991, V, p. 3.
The Christian Science Monitor. August 26, 1991, p. 13.
London Review of Books. XII, December 20, 1990, p. 3.
Los Angeles Times. April 10, 1991, p. E2.
The New Republic. CCIV, April 29, 1991, p. 31.
The New York Review of Books. XXXVIII, April 25, 1991, p. 52.
The New York Times Book Review. XCVI, March 24, 1991, p. 1.
Publishers Weekly. CCXXXVIII, January 25, 1991, p. 41.
The Times Literary Supplement. October 5, 1990, p. 1053.
The Washington Post Book World. XXI, March 31, 1991, p. 4.

A DANGEROUS WOMAN

Author: Mary McGarry Morris (1943-   )
Publisher: Viking Press (New York). 358 pp. $19.95
Type of work: Novel
Time: The early 1990's
Locale: A town in New York

In a cheerless portrait of social dysfunction, misfit Martha Horgan becomes dangerous to others and to herself

> *Principal characters:*
> MARTHA HORGAN, a thirty-two-year-old woman unable to act like the people around her
> FRANCES BEECHAM, Martha's aunt and guardian, who considers Martha an embarrassing burden
> COLIN "MACK" MACKEY, an indigent handyman and would-be writer, whose curiosity about Martha she considers love
> STEVE BELL, Frances' lawyer and longtime lover, who refuses to leave his alcoholic wife
> BIRDY DUSSER, a manager of the dry-cleaning shop where Martha has worked briefly
> GETSO, an employee at the dry cleaner's and Birdy's boyfriend
> JULIA PRINE, a townswoman whose prurient interest in Martha's actions mirrors the hostile judgments that keep Martha an outcast
> WESLEY MOUNT, a local mortician with an interest in Martha

Mary McGarry Morris' *A Dangerous Woman* focuses on the emotionally disabled Martha Horgan and the people around her who feed her inadequacies until disaster is inevitable. It is a cheerless and disturbing novel that offers little comfort or hope.

The novel begins: "The murder is seldom discussed without someone recalling that warm autumn night years before when Martha Horgan was only seventeen," but it is not until nearly the end of the novel that "the murder" is revealed. Instead, the opening chapter details the gang rape of the adolescent Martha. The townspeople find it convenient to blame the victim, saying she is crazy and oversexed. Literally myopic, Martha stares through her thick glasses, trying in vain to see how to act like others. Her failures to do so confirm the worst expectations of the people around her and perpetuate an endless cycle of inappropriate actions and reactions.

Martha's mother died when Martha was a baby, and her father, who reared her, seldom spoke to her. She had no siblings or friends. Martha was so isolated as a child that a single afternoon with another girl is transfigured into a dominating fantasy that the girl is Martha's best friend, and for long afterward Martha repeats the girl's comments as if they were her own. This pattern continues, especially since the townspeople decide that Martha is a permanently defenseless object of scorn. Even a second generation of children have learned to point at her and taunt her with cries of "Marthorgan," as though she is a ridiculous oddity. It is little wonder that when she encounters anything less than cruelty she is likely to overrate it as love and undying friendship.

Martha's fixation with Birdy Dusser, manager of the local dry-cleaning shop, is a prime example of Martha's inability to adapt to the society around her and is a major cause of the tragedies that unfold in the novel. Birdy shows some friendliness toward Martha when Martha comes to work at the shop, and for the first time Martha feels some sense of self-worth and acceptance. One day, though, an important customer comes to pick up his jacket, which through an oversight of the owner is not ready. The owner tells him it is the fault of his incompetent employees and that he is making one of the workers press it a second time. Martha, whose understanding of truth is rigid, runs after the customer shouting that he has been overcharged, that the jacket was not really cleaned but merely spot-cleaned at the last minute, that her boss is cheating him. Birdy supports the boss's claim that of course the jacket was properly cleaned, and the boss shrugs at the customer, saying that nothing else could be expected from Martha Horgan. He then fires her.

Because Martha has seen another employee, Getso, take money from the cash register, she decides that she must have been fired because the boss thinks she stole it. Cut off from her only source of happiness at work, she begins haunting Birdy, phoning endlessly at both the shop and Birdy's home, writing at least one long letter every day to Birdy, and following her around to try to convince her that the accusations are false and to warn her against the real thief, Getso. Birdy wants nothing to do with such obsessions and refuses to talk to her. The situation is complicated when Birdy starts dating Getso and Martha sees Getso with another woman. She rants even more at Birdy, thinking that she should warn her against such a cheat, and she tries to enlist others to mail letters or phone Birdy on her behalf.

It is this compulsive behavior toward Birdy that eventually leads to Martha's unpremeditated stabbing attack on Getso and the horrors that conclude the novel. It is also representative of the cycles of sick action and reaction between Martha and those around her. Indeed, Martha is socially and mentally retarded, but she is made much more so by the way others treat her. Martha's aunt and guardian, Frances Beecham, strips away Martha's precarious self-esteem by telling her that she, Frances, had arranged for the job at the cleaners and not only had paid Martha's entire salary but also had paid the owner extra to hire her. Thus Birdy's initial welcome to Martha was not merely from kindness, as Martha thought. In the incident with the improperly cleaned jacket, Birdy willingly lies to protect the boss at Martha's expense, and later she does not want Martha telling people that her boyfriend Getso is dating another woman. She refuses to talk with Martha, and she tells others that Martha's behavior is increasingly insane.

The novel is filled with such betrayals. Martha's father had agreed with the townspeople not to bring charges against the boys who raped her. Frances betrays the spirit of being a guardian. She considers Martha an embarrassing burden and always expects the worst of her. Mack, a young, indigent handyman, likes to think that he is kinder to Martha than the others are, but he seduces her, denies her, and takes up with Frances instead. Julia Prine, representative of the townspeople, shows an occasional interest in Martha simply so she can thrill to potential scandal, and she tries repeatedly to arrange things for Martha without Martha's knowledge or consent. The other townspeople readily participate in stereotyping and scapegoating Martha and typically treat her with contempt.

Perhaps the biggest betrayal of all is the insistent assumption that nothing can be done to help Martha. No one, Martha included, seems to believe that there is any therapy or medical or psychological assistance possible for her. Frances, as Martha's guardian, addresses that issue specifically, saying that dragging Martha from doctor to doctor would not help her. Martha's condition, Frances thinks, is a result of "that immutability people call bad luck or fate. . . . Martha would always be Martha, immured in her own oddness and pain."

Martha has accepted this version of herself as well. One of the things Julia tries to arrange is to have Martha sent to Harmony House, a home for retarded adults. Given everyone's inability and general unwillingness to help Martha, Harmony House might be a slightly more hopeful alternative. Although Martha has always felt herself to be different from others, however, she believes that she is not as retarded as those who must go there. She has seen Hock, one of the residents, come in to the cleaners when the attendants allow him to pick up laundry. Martha does not want to categorize herself with him.

Wesley Mount, the local funeral director, perhaps suggests a point of transition in the townspeople's hierarchy of sane and insane. He is judged as less crazy than Hock or Martha, but as a strange and pitiable fellow. More than one person snickers that he should get together with Martha. Wesley indeed takes some interest in her, and he tries not to make the same mistake he has before with other women of overwhelming her with sudden and unwanted attention. Martha rejects the implication that Wesley would be a likely suitor, but it is to him that she turns when she kills Getso.

Although the focus of the novel is on Martha Horgan and her limitations and problems, the other characters—regarded as sane—are essentially weak and flawed losers. Frances' pretense of strength is only superficial. She had married a much older man for his money and social position, yet in all the years as his widow she can never quite believe that the estate is really hers. She drives off needed workers with her parsimony and her critical temper. For many years she has had a sexual relationship with lawyer Steve Bell. He is constantly manipulated by his alcoholic wife, and in turn he manipulates Frances emotionally. When Steve abandons her, Frances turns to Mack and alternately bribes and blackmails him into complying with her wishes. Mack is too spineless to leave her or to be honest about his sexual encounter with Martha. There are, in fact, no well-adjusted and likable characters in the book.

The conclusion of the novel brings no resolution or comfort. When Martha tells Mack that she is pregnant, he denies paternity and indicates that he will say Getso is the child's father. It is really only another in a string of unfortunate events and co-incidences that leads Martha to Birdy's house, where she finds not Birdy but Getso, and again later, when she winds up holding a little boy hostage.

In the courtroom, Martha realizes that Steve, the lawyer, along with Frances and Mack, all want her to say that Getso raped her. She suddenly understands that "the truth did not matter." Later, when she tells Frances and Steve that Mack is her baby's father, Mack acknowledges that he took advantage of her but adds that Martha thought it was love. Martha is determined to believe that it was indeed love, though she knows that is not the truth. The novel thus ends with the quality of never-ending nightmare that has pervaded it, not only for Martha but in the portrayals of the other characters as well. They are all victims, both of their own limitations and of the perverted social attitudes and lies they have developed. They are all, ultimately, dangerous people in this cynical version of existential alienation that offers no hope.

Lois A. Marchino

Sources for Further Study

The Antioch Review. XLIX, Spring, 1991, p. 308.
Chicago Tribune. January 27, 1991, XIV, p. 5.
Los Angeles Times Book Review. January 20, 1991, p. 3.
The New York Times Book Review. XCVI, January 13, 1991, p. 9.
The New Yorker. LXVI, February 11, 1991, p. 95.
Newsweek. CXVII, April 8, 1991, p. 61.
Publishers Weekly. CCXXXVII, October 5, 1990, p. 91.
Time. CXXXVII, January 28, 1991, p. 89.
The Times Literary Supplement. June 14, 1991, p. 26.
Women's Review of Books. VIII, April, 1991, p. 7.

DAUGHTERS

Author: Paule Marshall (1929-   )
Publisher: Macmillan (New York). 408 pp. $19.95
Type of work: Novel
Time: The 1930's-the 1980's
Locale: New York City and "Triunion" in the West Indies

Ursa Mackenzie struggles to free herself not only from the domineering influence of her father but also from the lingering consequences of colonialism and slavery

Principal characters:
URSA BEATRICE MACKENZIE, a powerful, intelligent, troubled woman
ESTELLE BEATRICE HARRISON MACKENZIE, Ursa's mother
PRIMUS MACKENZIE, Ursa's father, a member of Triunion's house of parliament
ASTRAL DELORES FORDE, Primus' mistress
MALVERN, a friend of Astral
URSA LOUISE WILKERSON MACKENZIE (MIS-MACK), a shopkeeper and mother of Primus Mackenzie
CELESTINE MARIE-CLAIRE BELLEGARDE, the Mackenzie family retainer, who reared Primus and who serves as chorus
VINCERETA "VINEY" DANIELS, a New York City friend of Ursa
BOOKER HARRISON, Estelle's father
BEATRICE HARRISON, Estelle's mother
LOWELL CARRUTHERS, a sometime friend and lover of Ursa
JUSTIN BEAUFILS, a youthful Triunion politician who unseats Primus Mackenzie
SANDY LAWSON, a black New Jersey politician who sells out
MAE RYLAND, a black political activist

Daughters is a rich and powerful novel, carefully conceived and craftily constructed around a set of tensions that connect the worlds of Triunion, a fictional Caribbean island-nation, and New York City in the person of Ursa Beatrice Mackenzie. In the opening pages, Ursa Mackenzie leaves a New York City clinic feeling guilty about having had an abortion. Her abortion becomes a metaphor for a host of failed dreams and ruined lives, a legacy of slavery, colonialism, and racism in the Americas. *Daughters*, Paule Marshall's fourth novel, examines the role in the New World of black women, who must, because of the pernicious and lasting effects of slavery, racism, and sexism, find the courage and resourcefulness to act alone. Whether West Indian or New York African American, black women must lead the struggle to be free and whole.

Ursa is the daughter of Estelle Harrison of Hartford, Connecticut, herself the daughter of Tennessee parents who had fled north. Ursa's father is Primus Mackenzie, born into an ascendant class of West Indian blacks and destined to lead his people. Sent away from his village home to attend school at age eight, Primus learns European ways, English ways, as the road to power. Later, as a rising young lawyer in Triunion, he is brought by the Carnegie Endowment on International Relations to the United States to "see how it was done." He falls in love with Estelle, a grade-school teacher and a member of a hospitality committee.

From her first exposure to Triunion, Estelle is fascinated by Congo Jane and her consort Will Cudjoe, who are immortalized in a heroic group sculpture called the National Monument. After Ursa's birth, Estelle often takes Ursa to the monument, puts the child on her shoulders, and lifts her up toward the two "warrior-lovers." Marshall connects the leadership of the black woman, the necessity of struggle, and the figures of Ursa and Estelle. Later, when Ursa's professor at "Mt. H." college rejects her senior thesis proposal to study the forces of connection and community between black men and women as represented by Congo Jane and Will Cudjoe, it becomes clear that the struggle continues. When Ursa returns to Triunion for the climax of the novel, she takes a flying tumble off "Little Gran' Morne," a twelve-foot-high rockpile that the children had always called "the Monument," an echo of the name of the National Monument to Congo Jane and Will Cudjoe. Ursa's fall that morning suggests a loss of innocence about her father and her obligation as an adult to do what is necessary to preserve the Government Lands, a publicly owned area, for the people of Triunion and not to let the land be perverted into a monument of another kind, one to North American and colonial greed and exploitation.

Nearly forty years earlier, in 1943, Estelle spends her honeymoon with Primus on the campaign trail as he seeks a seat in the Triunion parliament. On their way back home, their car breaks down after dark; Estelle looks for a flashlight, hoping the problem is "something we can fix." Primus laughs, claims that "I don't even know how to open the bonnet on this thing," and sends a small boy running down the mountain in the dark to fetch help. At dawn, Primus has the boy's mother bring coffee to them. Estelle has a flash of insight into Primus' character but postpones pursuing it. It will be, it turns out, her daughter who will confront him.

Primus Mackenzie's early dream was to make a "model village for all these people you see scattered about on these hills or into a cooperative farm, or both" or to establish a cannery in Government Lands; his plans, however, are transformed by time and disillusion into a scheme—in which he himself invests—to create a resort in which rich North Americans may play, thus destroying access to and use of the lands and beaches by the people in the process. Primus has sold out to the "hang-men who run the government" and allowed his better dreams to be deflected and defeated. Although Ursa, Primus' only child, reveals the resort scheme to his constituents and causes his defeat, Marshall suggests that Ursa's violation of the values of family loyalty is justified by the higher calling of loyalty to the community. Part of Primus' problem, Marshall suggests, is that he has no real vision of his own but instead aspires to remake Triunion after the U.S. pattern; the seductive visions of colonialism obscure the power and potential of his own culture. This problem is shared by other black men, whether executives such as Lowell Carruthers, with whom Ursa has a lengthy affair, or Sandy Lawson, who had shown promise as a New Jersey political leader. Although angry at neocolonial domination and seeing themselves as "always running after white folk with the long hand out," they lack the power to fight off that domination.

The women, however, do not. In different ways, each of the memorable women who act in important supporting roles develops and wields the power to battle against such oppression. Celestine Marie-Claire Bellegarde, a French Creole, is one of "Mis-Mack's" "doormouth" children, whom she takes in and who, because of her intelligence and loyalty, becomes housekeeper and family retainer, continuing to wait on Primus even after he is married, her loyalty to him unbending. Astral Forde, an ambitious country woman, becomes Primus' long-term mistress; loyal and intelligent, she and Ursa bond in a powerful scene after Mackenzie's defeat. Viney, Ursa's New York City friend, is a determined single mother, and Mae Ryland is a community organizer and political force in New Jersey. Each of these women, powerful in her suffering and determination, is connected in Ursa's mind with the heroic figure of Congo Jane.

Marshall argues that the African sense of culture, ecology, and community, nearly destroyed by the disruptive transplantation into the New World through slavery, is, nevertheless, better than the colonial values of Christianity, property, and development. Black men, even those who, like Primus Mackenzie, Lowell Carruthers, and Sandy Lawson, are well educated and have positions of power and influence, are unable to implement the true vision. They continue to be defeated by colonial forces. Only Ursa and the other daughters can and must discover the true values and restore and reinvigorate them, despite the futility and ineptitude of black men. Black women have the will to throw off the shackles of slavery and colonial oppression and create a better, stronger, new world, a world of vision and power, even if, ironically, they must apparently betray family values—or perhaps, to put it more positively, must painfully rethink family values, subordinating them to the higher values of community and nature.

The defeat of hopes for strong, free, and productive post-liberation societies in the West Indies is a fact of history. Whether through coup of left or right, "free elections" influenced by a Pax Americana, or support from other post-World War II powers, the promise of an orderly, humane, and democratic society seems always to be denied. In *Daughters*, however, Marshall locates the causes for such failures within the hearts and minds of individuals as they react to larger forces. These include not only the powerful oppositions between conservative and revolutionary elements within Triunion society but also those more elemental tensions between love and hate, dependence and independence, father and daughter, husband and wife. This novel has them all.

Marshall also commands language and symbol, character and plotting, to create a fully realized art evocative of the human heart in conflict with itself. The language of the novel represents the richness of African-American New York street talk, West Indian English Creole, Barbadian and Antilles Creole, Standard English, and Standard West Indian; at one point, Primus writes to Estelle about the "people up Gran' Morne behaving like they're still maroons fighting the French, refusing even to speak the official language; and the rest of us still with this colonial thinking, acting more British than the British." Thus, Marshall illuminates a major topic—colonialism in all its guises and its destructive consequences. In addition, Marshall weaves folklore deftly into the fabric of the novel to reveal character and motivation, establish theme, and create atmosphere. Adding to the general texture of the novel are such facial and vocal folk gestures as "cut-eye" and "suck teeth," common Caribbean expressions of disgust, annoyance, and denigration. A traditional and powerful oath, "I kiss my right hand to God," reveals Ursa to be a child of Triunion as well as of the United States. Folk phrases such as "Miss Murry in a hurry," used to describe a busy woman, or "standing there like a foolie-the-fifth," used to describe a country bumpkin, create texture and character. The description of eating mangos in the surf and other traditional food customs contribute to an evocation of place and time and their impact on scene and character. Perhaps the most extraordinary example of folklore in the novel is Marshall's metaphoric use of a traditional child's game, "Statues," when, at a reception held by the Triunion planning and development board, Estelle's anger at such events and their values breaks out. Turning to one of the visiting U.S. businessmen, she asks whether he recalls the game. Without waiting for a reply, she assumes the pose of the Statue of Liberty—and holds the pose until the entire reception is silent; "all sixty or more guests . . . turning into statues of themselves." Estelle's game is a stunning criticism not only of the visiting dignitaries but also of Primus and the entire "game" of development and power. In another example of folklore's functioning to reveal theme, Astral Forde, after a terrible abortion, the consequence of being raped by a soccer player, throws dirt behind her: "Throw down little dirt when you leave the place so the child won't come back to hag your spirit," her friend Malvern had instructed her. Ironically, this is Astral's only pregnancy; her ability to have children, indeed, to have a successful, sustainable relationship, is blighted by the experience. Its thematic significance is even larger, a contribution to the larger political themes of the novel, a significance underscored by Ursa and Astral's reconciliation at the end. Thus, it is in the intimate gestures of mothers and daughters, of woman to woman, not in the large political schemes of male politicians, that Marshall ultimately situates salvation, the hope of community, the anodyne for loneliness and despair.

Theodore C. Humphrey

Sources for Further Study

Booklist. LXXXVIII, October 15, 1991, p. 410.
Chicago Tribune. October 6, 1991, XIV, p. 3.
Essence. XXII, October, 1991, p. 48.
Library Journal. CXVI, November 1, 1991, p. 132.
Los Angeles Times Book Review. October 6, 1991, p. 1.

New Woman. XXI, November, 1991, p. 26.
The New York Times Book Review. XCVI, October 27, 1991, p. 3.
Publishers Weekly. CCXXXVIII, July 19, 1991, p. 48.
The Washington Post Book World. XXI, September 22, 1991, p. 1.
Women's Review of New Books. VIII, July, 1991, p. 24.

DAVID HUMPHREYS' "LIFE OF GENERAL WASHINGTON"
With George Washington's "Remarks"

Authors: David Humphreys (1752-1818) and George Washington (1732-1799)
Edited, with an introduction, by Rosemarie Zagarri
Publisher: University of Georgia Press (Athens). Illustrated. 129 pp. $24.95
Type of work: Biography
Time: 1732-1789
Locale: Virginia, Maryland, Pennsylvania, New Jersey, and New York

A short biography of George Washington by an intimate acquaintance, along with Washington's comments made to the author

> *Principal personages:*
> GEORGE WASHINGTON, the commander-in-chief of the American Revolutionary Army and first president of the United States
> DAVID HUMPHREYS, an author and soldier; aide de camp and secretary to Washington

David Humphreys' life of Washington, interspersed with Washington's own comments and reflections, has little value as a biography, but it is important for the light it sheds on the relationship between Humphreys and Washington and for Washington's own self-evaluation. To Humphreys, Washington is always godlike and the exemplary gentleman and soldier. Washington's "Remarks," bracketed with the narrative, offer clues to Washington's mentality and personal attributes. The editor includes Humphreys' outlines for the biography, "non-biographical material" from Humphreys' notebooks, where fragments of the "Life" were found, and notes that are expository and collate the three manuscript segments.

For the "Life" itself, the editor has pieced together sections found in three archives: the Rosenbach Museum and Library in Philadelphia, the Yale University Library, and the *Forbes Magazine* Collection in New York. Only a five-page excerpt of the "Life" has been previously published, uncredited, in Jedediah Morse's *The American Geography* (1789) and subsequently in various magazines and pamphlets. Washington's "Remarks" were first printed in *Scribner's Magazine* in 1893 and then in several historical journals. In this edition, the "Life" and the "Remarks" together total only fifty pages.

It is evident that Humphreys, who solicited and obtained Washington's permission to write the biography, gave up soon after he started. Undoubtedly, he found himself with an almost insurmountable task, considering the enormous quantity of Washington's papers and correspondence. Washington himself was transcribing his letters and papers at the time that Humphreys was residing at Mount Vernon; moreover, Washington probably preferred a later assessment of his place in history, and was, therefore, reluctantly cooperative. As it is, Humphreys' "Life" is no more than a biography based on conversations (oral interviews) over the dinner table and the like. Washington did not want the information he gave Humphreys published as such but only to be used for writing a biography; he requested that the "Remarks" either be returned to him or burned, which instructions were not followed by Humphreys.

Humphreys was one of the many young men who served on Washington's personal staff during the revolutionary war. While these young men were kept occupied with myriad orders and communications, they formed a lasting attachment with their commander-in-chief. All were careful not to cast any aspersion on Washington's judgment or personal traits; one who did, Alexander Hamilton, requested a transfer, though the differences between the two men were eventually patched up. Humphreys, in the "Life," only questions Washington on two points, both of which actually underscore Washington's virtues. In one instance, he mentions that officers during the war thought Washington exposed himself too much in battle; in the other, when Washington was deciding whether he should accept the presidency, Humphreys has himself saying: "You ought, at sometimes, Sir, to look upon the bright side of the picture; and not always to be pondering the objects you find on the Reverse."

It is known that Washington liked witty conversation and storytelling, and, as Humphreys notes, reserved an hour after dinner for "convivial hilarity." Humphreys fitted right in. One of the four "Connecticut Wits"—John Trumbull, Timothy Dwight, and Lemuel Hopkins were the other three—he wrote satiric poetry and also epics, as did others, on the "rising glory" of America. Humphreys' first poem, "An Address to the Armies," was published in 1780. In all, he wrote thirty poems, mostly in the 1780's. His common theme was the glorification of the struggle for American independence and the promising prospects of the nation's future. Once he digressed and wrote a play, *The Widow of Malabar* (1790), a tragedy concerning sutteeism in India. Humphreys did diplomatic duty in Europe from 1784 to 1786, and upon his return resided at Mount Vernon for six weeks. He then served a term in the Connecticut legislature. From November, 1787, to April, 1789, Humphreys lived at Mount Vernon as one of Washington's family of eight, which included Tobias Lear (Washington's private secretary), George Augustine Washington and his wife, Frances Bassett Washington (Washington's nephew and Martha Washington's nephew and niece, respectively), and two grandchildren of Mrs. Washington. Interestingly, Humphreys mentions Martha Washington only twice: "His health was gradually restored; he married Mrs Custis, a handsome & amiable young widow, possessed of an ample jointure"; and notice of Martha accompanying Washington on a visit to his mother. After the idyllic life at Mount Vernon, Humphreys served as Washington's secretary during the first year of Washington's presidency; thereafter, he was minister to Portugal and then retired to Connecticut, where he established a profitable woolen manufactory. Humphreys remained a bachelor until 1797.

Exuding from the pages of Humphreys' laudation is a Washington who is perfect in every way and who is attentive to duty and reputation and to attending his plantations. Washington at Mount Vernon had a strict routine that he followed, rising at dawn and spending most of the day inspecting the farmwork. Humphreys affords a rare view of Washington at home. Rather startlingly, he mentions that during the late afternoon dinner, Washington regularly consumed a pint of rum, punch, and a "draught" of beer.

The "Life" opens with Washington's family background and his youth and closes on the eve of Washington's assumption of the presidency. Significantly, much space is given to the French and Indian War. Nothing at all is said about the campaigns of the revolution as such or any specifics of Washington's generalship. Considering the well-known mistakes and miscalculations by Washington, Humphreys obviously did not want to create any dispute and incur Washington's wrath. Humphreys' own aristocratic bent and Yankee point of view betray themselves in discussion of Washington's family and the Virginia gentry. He credits all the Washingtons as having the ability to acquire wealth. Rather amusingly, he points out that the gentry believed that they had to send their sons to England for their education; if they were "brought up at home," they would be "in danger of becoming indolent & helpless from the usual indulgence giving a horse & a servant to attend them . . . if not imperious & dissipated from the habit of commanding slaves & living in a measure without controul." Humphreys, however, knowing that Washington had only limited formal schooling, quickly adds that Virginians "educated in a domestic manner, who had fortitude enough to resist the temptations to which they were exposed in their youth, have commonly been distinguished by success in their various professions."

Knowing that Washington would not object, Humphreys mentioned that Washington was "reserved" as a youth, but, of course had "something uncommonly noble in his manners." Washington had a "genteel [sic] deportment" and was "remarkably robust & athletic." Readers will enjoy Washington's own version of a famous tall tale. Notes Humphreys: "I have several times heard him say, he never met any man who could throw a stone to so great a distance as himself; and, that when standing in the valley beneath the natural bridge of Virginia, he has thrown one up to that stupendous arch."

Humphreys goes on at length emphasizing the hardships that Washington endured during the French and Indian War. In actuality, Washington was seldom with his troops, instead staying in Winchester or Alexandria while letting his second-in-command, Lieutenant Colonel Adam Stephen, and others conduct the day-to-day training and army administration. Even while his men were engaged in road and fort building on the Pennsylvania frontier during 1758, Washington was back at Fort Cumberland (on the Potomac). Yet 1754 and 1755 did find Washington in the field in one capacity or another. It seems from Washington's account in the biography and from his correspondence that the dark times of Virginia's entry into the French and Indian War were more embedded in his mind than almost any other experiences. Washington obliged Humphreys with a third-person account, though pleading "badness of his memory," which in some respects seems to have been the case. Washington avoids controversial topics, particularly that of his Indians scalping Frenchmen and the charge that was leveled against Washington that he had "assassinated" the French officer who headed a forward party at Little Meadows. Despite his somewhat hazy memory, Washington's description of his participation in the war lasts twelve pages, about one-fourth of Humphreys' biography. Humphreys contrasts Washington and his predecessor in command of the Virginia regiment; Colonel Joshua Fry (who was killed by a fall from a horse) was "an aged and inactive man," while Washington had much better qualities of leadership. The defeat of Edward Braddock's forces by the French is told in regard to Washington's willingness to assume leadership during the debacle. Washington mentions that he had one horse killed and two wounded under him and that musket balls had passed through his hat and clothes. Of interest, too, is Washington's telling how he was almost ambushed and killed by Indians in 1756 while on a fort-building tour on Virginia's frontier; the Indians had even given Washington a name, "Caunotaucarius," meaning "the towntaker." Humphreys, as does Washington, avoids any mention of Washington's running dispute with General John Forbes in the final campaign against the French in western Pennsylvania over which military road to use. Nor does Humphreys mention Washington's activities as a land speculator and member of several western land companies, most notably the Ohio Company, and in searching out bounty lands provided for service against the French.

Both Humphreys and Washington see fit to skip over the years 1763-1775. Humphreys mentions only that during this time Washington "cultivated the arts of peace" and served in local office. It would not have served Humphreys' purpose to cite Washington's being knocked down in a quarrel or to note that he was rather solicitous of votes for a seat in the House of Burgesses.

When the revolutionary war came, Washington was "designated by Heaven for their leader"; Humphreys remarks, "it is hoped Posterity will be taught, in what manner he transformed an undisciplined body of Peasantry into a regular army of Soldiers. Commentaries on his Campaigns would be at once highly interesting & instructive to them." Humphreys credits Washington with curtailing sectionalism in the military and with promoting "cordiality" in "the American Camp." In fact, Humphreys and Washington both knew of the intense rivalry and animosity within the officer corps. As to the politics of the war, an astounding observation is the acknowledgment of the so-called Conway Cabal, which many historians have discounted as having no real basis in fact. It seems that Washington and Humphreys actually did think that there was a conspiracy in and out of Congress to displace Washington as commander-in-chief.

After bestowing plaudits upon Washington as the great hero of the revolution, Humphreys moves to ground more safe and familiar to him—Washington as Cincinnatus. The simple life was constantly interrupted by a stream of visitors, from military officers to "every foreigner, of distinction, who visits America." As soon as one guest departed, another arrived. Humphreys gives a description of Mount Vernon and comments on Washington's agricultural pursuits.

Humphreys takes note of the Constitutional Convention, which took Washington to Philadelphia and left Humphreys at Mount Vernon. Humphreys names himself, undoubtedly with exaggeration, as the person having the greatest influence upon Washington's decision to accept the presidency. Washington believed that he would appear too contradictory in his principles if he accepted—having declared for domesticity, he did not want to seem ambitious; furthermore, he thought that setting an example of disinterestedness would bode well for the future of a virtuous republic. Humphreys says that he persuaded Washington to become president by pointing out that he was the one indispensable person needed in establishing the government and that Washington as president would enhance the United States' image abroad. Washington did accept, and Humphreys discusses some concerns of the new president: the problem of dispensing patronage; the fear of the vice president and the Senate, in collusion, becoming too powerful; and a curious suggestion of creating a "Cabinet," which would be mainly an information-processing agency.

The nonbiographical material from Humphreys' notebooks has some value; contained among the items are speech drafts for Washington and phrases and subjects of interest to Humphreys. Otherwise, the material has little relevance to the biography. The casualty list of Braddock's defeat in 1755, which is included, has often been published.

Though extremely laudatory and uncritical and also self-serving for Humphreys, the biography offers a better understanding of Washington and his own assessment of himself. It is as much autobiography as biography, and one can imagine, so to speak, Washington leaning over Humphreys' shoulder to make sure that nothing that was said was derogatory.

While Humphreys seeks both to mythologize and to humanize Washington, at least he did not invent anecdotes such as Parson Weems's cherry tree; Washington would have been infuriated at such fiction. Yet, as defective as Humphreys' tribute to Washington is as biography, the reader will find that as oral history it is revealing and entertaining.

Harry M. Ward

Sources for Further Study

Chronicle of Higher Education. XXXVII, July 10, 1991, p. A5.
Library Journal. CXVI, August, 1991, p. 118.
National Review. XLIII, April 29, 1991, p. 52.
University Press Book News. III, September, 1991, p. 11.

DEAD CERTAINTIES
(Unwarranted Speculations)

Author: Simon Schama (1945-   )
Publisher: Alfred A. Knopf (New York). Illustrated. 333 pp. $21.00
Type of work: History
Time: The eighteenth and nineteenth centuries
Locale: Quebec, Canada; London; Boston

An intriguing experiment in historical narration involving two famous deaths

> *Principal personages:*
> JAMES WOLFE, the British general responsible for the capture of Quebec in
>   1759
> BENJAMIN WEST, the American painter in eighteenth century London
> FRANCIS PARKMAN, the distinguished American historian
> GEORGE PARKMAN, a physician, businessman, and victim in a celebrated
>   murder
> JOHN WEBSTER, a professor of chemistry at Harvard convicted of murder-
>   ing George Parkman
> LEMUEL SHAW, the chief justice of the Supreme Court of Massachusetts

Simon Schama's *Dead Certainties* is an essay on the limitations of history. Such a work from this author demands attention, for Schama is a distinguished historian who has written best-selling histories of The Netherlands of the seventeenth century (*The Embarrassment of Riches: An Interpretation of Dutch Culture in the Golden Age,* 1987) and the French Revolution (*Citizens: A Chronicle of the French Revolution,* 1989). In *Dead Certainties,* though he deals with historical subjects, Schama eschews the traditional scholarly apparatus and tells his stories from a variety of viewpoints, some invented for his purposes, and without regard for the niceties of chronology. Instead of striving for clarity in his narrative and a magisterial interpretation to guide his readers, Schama deliberately weaves a tapestry of cross-purposes and loose ends and forbears from drawing conclusions. Schama has artfully created a monument to epistemological uncertainty in his aptly titled book. His message is that certitude is a quality that will never be achieved in investigating the past. Because of the evanescent nature of the past, with the images of collective memory always slipping just beyond the grasp, history is, of necessity, an exercise in storytelling. Without the imaginative effort of the historian in imposing order on the elements of his narrative, history would exist simply as the dry and dusty record of discrete facts. In making this point, Schama boils down and makes accessible to the general reader the gist of several decades of theorizing about the nature of history. Though Schama drops no names and cites no tomes, his work reflects the influence of the postmodern criticism of authority in literature. *Dead Certainties,* designed as it is for popular consumption, not only represents a significant assault on the nineteenth century notion of history as a science but also questions the more modest proposition that objective knowledge about the past is possible.

Structurally, *Dead Certainties* is two books in one. In a relatively brief section, Schama explores the symbolic ramifications of the death of General James Wolfe at his victory on the Plains of Abraham outside Quebec in 1759. This victory broke the power of France in Canada and ensured British supremacy in North America. The bulk of *Dead Certainties* is devoted to the grisly murder of Dr. George Parkman of Boston in 1849 and the subsequent trial of John Webster, a professor of chemistry at Harvard. The only direct link between these two stories is the figure of Francis Parkman, the great American historian who memorably depicted Wolfe and his victory in his history of the struggle between France and Britain for control of the New World and who was the nephew of the victim in the celebrated murder case. Yet Schama takes no pains to draw connections between the two parts of his book. Though Francis Parkman glorified James Wolfe, he played no role in uncovering or avenging his uncle's death. What really unifies the disparate ends of James Wolfe and George Parkman is the way in which people later used these deaths for their own purposes. The gap between the bloody violence of these men's deaths and the meanings imposed on them illustrates Schama's message about the ultimately arbitrary nature of history and its intrinsic relation to the art of storytelling.

Schama spins his stories out of a masterful mix of fact and fiction. *Dead Certainties* is a triumph of technique over traditional historical values. The first part of Schama's book reveals the strengths and weaknesses of such an approach. Schama opens with an invention — the supposed memoirs of a British soldier who struggled up the cliffs of Quebec and stood on the Plains of Abraham with James Wolfe. This imaginative device vividly re-creates the events of September 13, 1759, and effectively sets the scene for what is to follow. Schama jumps from the mind of his hypothetical private soldier into that of James Wolfe himself, and travels back in time in a pithy recapitulation of the general's career and the events leading up to his last battle. In his thirties at the time of his death, Wolfe had been born into a soldier's life. His officer father saw to it that he left home for the military at the age of fourteen, and he saw his first battle at the age of sixteen. Courage and skill, as well as good connections, fostered rapid promotions. Only Wolfe's delicate health, of which he was morbidly conscious, threatened the potential brilliance of his career. The mission to capture the city of Quebec, the hub of French power in North America, offered Wolfe the military apotheosis he craved. Soon, however, things began to go wrong. The French skillfully defended their city, frustrating Wolfe's plans for months, until the Saint Lawrence River threatened to freeze over, trapping his army. An assault on the French lines at the Montmorency Falls ended as a bloody failure. Wolfe's frail constitution began to break down. He suffered from a variety of maladies and believed himself to be dying. It was against this background of defeat and expected dissolution that Wolfe devised his bold scheme to take Quebec. He proposed to scale cliffs supposedly too steep to climb which the French guarded lightly because of their inaccessibility. This would leave Wolfe's force on the Plains of Abraham, just outside the city, and give him the chance to fight the battle that, won or lost, would restore his honor. Thus Wolfe's successful strategy was a product of desperation as well as military genius.

Schama then turns from the anxious meditations of James Wolfe in the North American wilderness to London in 1771 and the exhibition of Benjamin West's masterpiece *The Death of Wolfe* (1771). West was a young American artist hoping to establish a reputation for himself in the British metropolis. Defying the convention that heroic figures be painted in classical rather than contemporary dress, West depicted Wolfe in his bloodied uniform. The stricken commander lies in the arms of his officers, his eyes fixed on heaven, as word is brought of the rout of the French. In the background of this dramatic scene, West painted a compressed recapitulation of the events surrounding the death of Wolfe—ships disembarking troops, the climb up the cliffs to the Plains of Abraham, and the final, triumphant volley that broke the resistance of the army defending Quebec. Even as Wolfe expires beneath a folded British flag and the smoke of battle, the light of approaching morning breaks over the city of Quebec, heralding that an empire had been born. At once shocking and gratifying, West's painting became a sensation. It had the desired effect on West's career, leading to his appointment as court painter to George III. It also broke down the conventions of historical painting and led to a new naturalism in historical art. The rhetorical power of West's painting enshrined for generations the image of James Wolfe as an almost saintly martyr to Britain's greatness.

Schama shifts next to Boston in 1893 and the reading at the Massachusetts Historical Society of an autobiographical memoir by the recently deceased historian Francis Parkman. The gentlemen of the society, expecting familiar, well-bred words from beyond the grave, were startled by an astonishingly candid memoir, in which the seemingly self-contained and stoic Parkman detailed the suffering his great work had cost him. Schama then moves back in time to 1880 and enters both Parkman's house and mind as he labors on his history series *France and England in North America* (1865-1892). Parkman's work was rooted in his childhood. As a remedy for his physical frailty, he was sent to live on a farm, and there developed a lifelong love for the American wilderness. At Harvard, Parkman received his inspiration to write a history celebrating the men who had explored and fought to control that wilderness. At every vacation, he punished his fragile body with excursions tracing the paths of long-dead explorers. In 1846, Parkman traveled the famed Oregon Trail in search of experience in the wild and contacts with Indians. He found both, but the experience nearly killed him and completed the destruction of his health. Parkman settled down to writing history, grappling with illness and eyesight so poor he could not read more than ten minutes at a time. A maid had to read aloud most of the documents he consulted. Work under such conditions was literally painstaking. Because of his own infirmities, and his own frustrating struggle, Parkman came to empathize with James Wolfe, the hero of his climactic volume. Indeed, Schama argues that, as Parkman wrote, in some sense he became Wolfe, bridging time and distance with a shared identity of suffering and achievement. From this apotheosis of the historical imagination, Schama returns to his invented British soldier and describes the decisive battle outside Quebec and Wolfe's tortured death. He concludes the piece with a letter from Wolfe's fiancée to his mother asking for some token by which to remember her lost lover.

Schama's exploration of the many deaths of James Wolfe is a brilliant literary experiment. He crosses the dimensions with a novelist's ease and skill and creates a memorable entertainment. Yet for all the virtuosity of his presentation, Schama provides no startling new insights into his material. Historians have long known of the self-doubts of James Wolfe, the opportunism of Benjamin West, and the grim determination of Francis Parkman. Jumbling these stories together does nothing to illuminate them severally. Even Schama's observation that there exist many versions of, and uses for, historical events boils down to a well-worn banality. Only the implication that there is no definitive version of the death of General Wolfe gives the work some intellectual force. In the end, moreover, this tacit assertion proves to be more shadow than substance, a fact borne out by Schama's account of the death of George Parkman, in which the techniques he used in treating James Wolfe are reinvoked, only on a greater scale and with a more lurid subject.

George Parkman was a physician whose great dream had been the establishment of a humane asylum for the insane in Boston. A variety of factors conspired to foil Parkman's philanthropic project. Disappointed in this ambition, Parkman channeled his energies elsewhere. Turning to real estate, he bought up large tracts of land in Boston. One of the most prominent landlords in the city, Parkman gained a reputation for eccentricity because he walked about town collecting his rents himself. On the afternoon of November 23, 1849, George Parkman disappeared. He was last seen walking in the direction of the Harvard Medical College. A week later, body parts identified as those of George Parkman were discovered in the medical college building. Professor John Webster was arrested for the crime. Webster's undoing was the enmity of Ephraim Littlefield, the janitor at the medical college. A former grave robber who had served the needs of Harvard medical students, Littlefield had never enjoyed friendly relations with Professor Webster. His suspicions were aroused when, soon after Parkman's disappearance, Webster gave him a Thanksgiving turkey. On his own initiative, Littlefield tunneled into Webster's privy vault at the medical college and found human remains. A male torso was later discovered in a chest in the professor's laboratory.

The trial of John Webster became a nineteenth century media event. So shocking a crime among Boston's elite seemed to imply incipient corruption in respectable circles. The widespread support for Webster on the part of his colleagues and other leading citizens tended to polarize opinion on the trial along class lines. Newspapers from around the country followed the proceedings; tens of thousands of people filed through the courtroom at ten-minute intervals. Though Webster maintained his innocence, the prosecution easily demonstrated that the professor habitually lived beyond his means. He had borrowed a large sum of money from George Parkman, who at the time of the murder had been dunning him for repayment. This, the physical evidence, and an important statement on circumstantial evidence from the presiding judge, Massachusetts chief justice Lemuel Shaw, served to convict the professor.

Webster later confessed to the crime in a vain attempt at getting his death sentence commuted.

Schama's account of the Parkman murder case enthralls the reader as he masterfully moves from one viewpoint to the next, backward and forward in time. Yet as with Schama's narrative of the death of James Wolfe, there is less here than meets the eye. To further his thesis about the indeterminacy of knowledge about the past, Schama works hard to raise doubts about the official explanation of George Parkman's murder. The facts of the case are so clear, however, that Schama's ingenious twists and turns seem more like deliberate mystification than illumination. Thus Schama's fascination with indeterminacy ultimately leads nowhere. The facts, which Schama himself never questions, speak for themselves. Because Schama questions only interpretations and not facts, he fails to threaten seriously the foundations of the historical discipline. *Dead Certainties* deserves to be widely read for Schama's storytelling skill. As a history, though, Schama's work is a game, enjoyable but frivolous.

Daniel P. Murphy

Sources for Further Study

Chicago Tribune. May 19, 1991, XIV, p. 1.
Commonweal. CXVIII, September 13, 1991, p. 519.
National Review. XLIII, August 26, 1991, p. 42.
New Statesman and Society. IV, June 7, 1991, p. 42.
The New York Review of Books. XXXVIII, June 27, 1991, p. 12.
The New York Times Book Review. XCVI, May 12, 1991, p. 3.
The New Yorker. LXVII, July 22, 1991, p. 83.
Publishers Weekly. CCXXXVIII, May 17, 1991, p. 46.
The Times Literary Supplement. June 14, 1991, p. 5.
The Washington Post Book World. XXI, May 5, 1991, p. 8.

DEAD ELVIS
A Chronicle of a Cultural Obsession

Author: Greil Marcus (1946-   )
Publisher: Doubleday (New York). 233 pp. $25.00
Type of work: Essays and cultural criticism

A profusely illustrated collection of brief accounts of incidents and episodes that reveal a widespread cultural obsession with "Dead Elvis" Presley (1935-1977)

Not so many years ago, the idea that rock and roll or related aspects of American pop culture could provide suitable material for serious writing would have been laughable. Greil Marcus was one of the writers who changed all that. Through his writing in *Rolling Stone* and through the significant books he both authored and edited, he demonstrated myriad ways to connect what was vital in American pop music to the deepest currents in American culture in general, wedding, one might say, pop music criticism to "American Studies" in its more ambitious academic manifestations.

Lipstick Traces: A Secret History of the Twentieth Century (1989) stands as his major work, one that suggested startling parallels between punk rock and the modernist avant-garde. His earlier *Mystery Train: Images of America in Rock 'n' Roll Music* (1975) was a tour de force that explored liminal, subterranean aspects of culture brought to the fore through the music of Elvis Presley, The Band, Randy Newman, Sly and the Family Stone, and others. Marcus' edited books as well have been distinctive contributions to often overlooked aspects of recent pop culture. The collection *Rock and Roll Will Stand* (1969) captures the spirit of that brief cultural moment of the late 1960's when Martha and the Vandellas' "Dancing in the Streets" segued into The Rolling Stones's "Street Fighting Man," and somehow, each seemed equally central to the concept of revolution. Two additional edited collections of essential rock music criticism are among Marcus' accomplishments.

Dead Elvis: A Chronicle of a Cultural Obsession defies categorization; it is an eccentric and unprecedented book. The first observation to be made is that it is an exceedingly attractive book, with arresting typography, fine-quality paper, and impressive overall design. It abounds with striking illustrations and art reproductions, many of them in full color. Marcus explains the genesis of the book by way of a personal account of his learning of Elvis Presley's death. He describes his resolve, formulated soon afterward, to collect what turned out to be a never-ending stream of "Elvis sightings," defined by Marcus broadly as any cultural appropriation of Elvis and his legend (not simply screaming tabloid claims of Elvis' continued existence).

Marcus presents his book as a kind of biography of Elvis Presley's life since his death. By "life" he appears to mean the obsessive fascination with Presley's image, his sound, and what could only be described as his charisma or mystique. Any of or all these aspects of "Elvisness" surface in the wide variety of cultural manifestations Marcus cites. These include tabloid articles, comic strips, and the use of Elvis references by comedians, musicians, filmmakers, writers, and artists. The handsome reproductions of paintings include many so-called alternative music album covers, such as the laser art of Chila Kumari Burman, whose *Portrait of Elvis Presley in the Style of Jackson Pollock* adorned a 1989 release by The Mekons, a critically acclaimed (by Marcus and others) British band.

While such features enhance the book's appeal, it is, more or less admittedly, the disgorged contents of whatever file cabinet Marcus used to store his post-1977 Presley tidbits. As an established music critic attuned to each new stirring and swelling of the pop-culture current, Marcus was well positioned to amass the curious materials that would eventually occasion *Dead Elvis.* The book's organizing principle is also its greatest limitation, however, since even such a thorough student of contemporary media cannot help but overlook significant items and details to be gleaned from an ongoing cultural process the very scale of which defies one author's attempts to chart its course.

Greil Marcus knows progressive pop music thoroughly, and he enlivens his text with quotes from song lyrics that, more often than not, approach the subject of Elvis with far more irreverence and satire than the keepers of the Graceland flame could possibly stomach. Examples include the obscure early-1980's New York band Cool It Reba, wise-guy Los Angeles songwriter Warren Zevon, and the early 1990's cult band Dread Zeppelin, who manage to send up Led Zeppelin and reggae along with "The King." There are bands as well who somehow affirm the Presley legend even as they seek to express their rejection of it. Living Colour, one of the most important and innovative bands of recent years, expressed their scorn in "Elvis Is Dead." Despite their contempt for the Elvis cult, this band takes their place alongside Elvis impersonators and every other example that serves the author's purpose in cataloging the "dead Elvis" phenomena. One of 1991's most impressive pop albums was *Never Loved Elvis* by a band called The Wonder Stuff. Where Living Colour developed a single song from their 1990 album *Time's Up* to a slap at Elvisness, The Wonder Stuff chose to designate an entire collection of songs through this gesture of cultural negation. *Never Loved Elvis* appeared too late in 1991 to receive mention in *Dead Elvis*, and this points to an inescapable problem with Marcus' book: Many more Elvis references and "sightings" will likely accumulate, so the book will rapidly become dated. There may be no way around this problem, and perhaps it is beside the point. By making *Dead Elvis* the kind of book it is, Marcus displays his prowess at a game virtually anybody can play, given the right amount of energy and degree of obsession. It may be that Marcus will update his book in subsequent editions, unless he has abandoned his "Elvis watch." More likely, others will imitate his approach.

Of course, not just anybody can match Marcus' knowledge of popular music. As his book demonstrates, the entire popular music industry remains permeated with the influence and (more negative than positive) example of the career of Elvis Presley. Marcus uses his knowledge of punk music effectively to show how the career moves of even such symbols of defiance as Johnny Rotten of The Sex Pistols could not help but be made with reference to "The King." One of the most important punk-period albums, *London Calling* by The Clash, appeared with a cover that emulated the cover of the first Presley album. The examples Marcus uses show the curious mixture of admiration and contempt with which later rock and roll performers have approached "The King's" legend.

That legend has been accompanied by more than its share of sordid, tacky details and gossip. Marcus can barely contain his anger at the selective, distorted use made by sensationalist biographers of the detailed testimony provided by many music-industry insiders about the life and the music of this influential performer. No single writer comes under stronger attack than Albert Goldman, whose 1981 biography *Elvis* presented its subject as a paranoid, narcoticized, kinky sexual freak tormented by his inner spiritual demons and a towering inferiority complex about his rural white Southern ancestry. For all its distortions, Marcus sadly admits, this is the biography that will continue to circulate most widely. He lambastes Goldman for his tastelessness, but occasionally, he sinks to the same level in his vengeful desire to draw blood yet again. A true nadir is reached when, having explained that Goldman's sneers at the alleged Presley ethnic inferiority complex went to the extreme point of suggesting that Elvis was ashamed of his uncircumcised penis, Marcus cannot resist retaliating by implying that the real story was Goldman's insecurity about his own circumcised organ. This gives new meaning to the phrase "hitting below the belt."

As vicious as this may seem, even Marcus, whose earlier writings on Elvis in *Mystery Train* show how much he admired the man, cannot resist getting in his occasional digs at Elvis, especially in his late, dissolute phase. There are several gratuitous comments about the singer's legendary obesity, as well as the usual sophisticated put-downs of the tackiness of Graceland and the other trappings with which Elvis surrounded himself. Such digressions, however, are less in evidence than the other extreme in Marcus' book, which is his need to place Elvis as archetype on the pedestal of myth. Marcus, succumbing to the familiar tendency once endemic in the field of American Studies, avoids Elvis the man in favor of the image of Elvis that lends itself to cultural mythmaking.

The mythic Elvis that suits Marcus' purposes heroically fuses the liberating erotic energy of black music with white working-class Southern populism, culminating in a joyously defiant, exhilarating gesture that proclaims the right of the seemingly least-promising member of American culture to reach the pinnacle of celebrity status within it. There is no more quintessentially American theme. In his earlier book *Mystery Train*, Marcus was able to indulge his appetite for meditating on archetypal essences without excluding the populist, democratic cultural context thus celebrated. The Elvis of that book served to guarantee the egalitarian promise and hostility to cultural elitism his success seemed to be about. Unfortunately, in *Dead Elvis*, Marcus increasingly abandons open-ended cultural process for the dictates of symbol and myth. He appears to introduce his readers to a broad range of cultural uses and appropriations of Elvis-related phenomena, but he does so only to retreat into the mythology he seeks to reinforce. As a result, no matter how inventive or creative reworkings of Elvis imagery or references may be (Howard Finster's art, the cinema of Jim Jarmusch, performances by Dread Zeppelin), to Marcus they all reaffirm a single, unchanging mythic essence. He will not risk the unity or stability of what for him is an enduring cultural symbol by envisioning the ability of present or future uses to redefine its essence. The game is rigged: Myth must win out over history in every instance.

It is not so much that Marcus is hopelessly misguided by wishing to emphasize myth, but that he insists too forcefully on the uniqueness of the mythic role he ascribes to Elvis. Recent American literature, relatively neglected by Marcus in favor of cinema, television, music, and the pulp press, provides an example of the use of the Elvis myth and the legendary status of Adolf Hitler in mutually illuminating ways. This occurs in Don DeLillo's 1985 novel *White Noise*, which contains hilarious but hauntingly thoughtful episodes recounting conversations between two academic specialists on, respectively, Adolf Hitler and Elvis Presley. Although Marcus includes a reference to the underground band "Elvis Hitler," he is surprisingly silent about such a significant intervention into the very cultural territory he himself charts.

Lester Bangs, whose writings Marcus edited in a collection published in 1987, was a talented writer of rock music criticism who emphasized aspects of Elvis similar to the ones that interest Marcus. Bangs credited Elvis with introducing, however derivatively, a subversive eroticism into American popular music. From that point on, previous popular music would seem hopelessly antiseptic and wholesome. Having given that nod to Elvis, though, Bangs was much more willing than Marcus to turn his attention to later developments without referring back to the "King" Marcus seems to need to maintain on the throne of rock and roll. There is greater warmth and energy in his writings on topics similar to those Marcus addresses. Yet even Bangs's relatively more democratic impulses were marred by moments of extreme condescension and aristocratic disdain for audience taste.

This points to a problem in rock music criticism generally, and one that may distinguish it somewhat from literary or film criticism. Owing perhaps to the greater immediate emotional impact of music (imagine a literary critic tapping his feet while writing), writers seem to reach greater extremes of subjectivity. There is a shrillness of tone that exceeds what one tends to find in other types of criticism. People are exceedingly passionate about their musical preferences, music critics no less so. Ultimately, then, readers learn more about the obsessions and prejudices of the critic than they do about the cultural significance of the music. That, finally, is the dilemma one faces with *Dead Elvis*: One gets glimpses of the varied and eccentric uses being made of "Elvis" throughout recent American (even global) culture, but all too often Marcus, armed with his own uncompromising vision, obstructs the view.

James A. Winders

Sources for Further Study

Atlanta Journal Constitution. December 22, 1991, p. K10.
Booklist. LXXXVIII, October 1, 1991, p. 202.
Cosmopolitan. CCXI, November, 1991, p. 36.
Kirkus Reviews. LIX, September 1, 1991, p. 1142.
Los Angeles Times Book Review. November 24, 1991, p. 1.
The New York Times Book Review. XCVI, November 3, 1991, p. 11.
Publishers Weekly. CCXXXVIII, November 15, 1991, p. 53.
San Francisco Chronicle. December 1, 1991, p. REV4.
The Village Voice. December 10, 1991, p. S5.
The Washington Post Book World. XXI, December 1, 1991, p. 16.

DEN OF THIEVES
The Untold Story of the Men Who Plundered Wall Street
and the Chase That Brought Them Down

Author: James B. Stewart
Publisher: Simon & Schuster (New York). Illustrated. 493 pp. $35.00
Type of work: Current affairs
Time: The 1970's to 1990
Locale: New York and Los Angeles

An account of the insider trading that centered on the brokerage firm Drexel Burnham Lambert during the 1980's

> *Principal personages:*
> MICHAEL R. MILKEN, the head of high-yield securities at Drexel Burnham Lambert
> IVAN F. BOESKY, an arbitrageur
> MARTIN SIEGEL, an investment banker for Kidder, Peabody & Co. and later head of Mergers and Acquisitions for Drexel Burnham Lambert
> DENNIS B. LEVINE, an investment banker for Drexel Burnham Lambert

Between 1980 and 1990, two major revolutions began. One—actually a series of revolutions in Central Europe—spelled the end of state socialism. Encompassing the downfall of a long-maligned and readily identifiable enemy and replete with easily recognized acts of heroism, this revolution was the perfect media story. The media capitalized upon it accordingly, and many came away believing that justice had been done and that all was right with the world. The other revolution, which began with the advent of the 1980's, was not so easily understood, and though the media named it "The Reagan Revolution," it went largely unnoticed by the mass of people. This is understandable; the battles—and they were large ones, the largest of their kind in history—were fought in boardrooms and men's clubs inaccessible to most Americans. The usurped were the masses of middle-class Americans who did not and perhaps never will understand the depth and magnitude of the aggressions directed against them.

In *Den of Thieves*, James B. Stewart documents the tip of the iceberg of this revolution. As the tip, it is easily recognizable, featuring names such as Michael Milken and Ivan Boesky, which during the end of the 1980's were heard with some frequency. To expose any more of the iceberg is perhaps an impossible task, given the secrecy shared between members of the corporate elite. Yet the documentation presented in such books as *Den of Thieves*, Roy C. Smith's *The Money Wars* (1990), and Connie Bruck's *The Predators' Ball* (1988), however modest, is crucial insofar as it gives an idea of just how huge the rest of the iceberg must be.

Den of Thieves is split into two sections. The first, entitled "Above the Law," is an account of how the crimes the book describes were committed; the second and less interesting section, "The Chase," details how the criminals were brought to justice. Stewart focuses on four principal conspirators: Michael R. Milken, Ivan F. Boesky,

Martin Siegel, and Dennis B. Levine. Of the four, Levine receives the harshest treatment by Stewart. Portrayed as a braggart, a compulsive big spender, and a fool who
liked to throw his self-aggrandized weight around, he wanted a piece of what he
perceived to be the real action happening on Wall Street—the insider trading. Overly
confident that he would never be caught, he was the first to be imprisoned for his
part in the growing scandal. He began his activities on a small scale by enlisting
three friends—Robert Wilkis and Ira Sokolow, investment bankers, and Ilan Reich,
a partner with a New York law firm—who agreed to share information regarding
clients of their firms who were engaged in takeover battles.

During the 1980's, because of the Reagan Administration's undermining of anti-
trust laws, companies began taking over other companies with greater frequency.
During a takeover, one company will offer the shareholders of the targeted company
a price above the market value for their stocks. The resulting negotiations necessitate
the hiring of brokerage firms and a small army of lawyers. Knowing ahead of time
that a particular company is the target of a takeover can be extremely valuable information and can lead to market manipulation to the detriment of the average stock-
holder; consequently, the Securities and Exchange Commission (SEC) attempts to
ensure that such information is not acted upon by prohibiting brokers from trading
in their clients' stocks. Monitoring such activity is a fairly simple matter. On the
other hand, ensuring that such information is not surreptitiously shared among brokers and lawyers and then acted upon is not so easy, especially since illegal earnings
from such dealings can be hidden in overseas bank accounts.

Dennis Levine began trading on inside information during the first week of his
being hired by Smith Barney, Harris Upham & Co., an investment bank. In his thirst
for inside tips, he would make copies at night of documents found on other brokers'
desks. He badgered his friends Reich and Wilkis for information until both nearly
had nervous breakdowns. During the summer of 1984, based on tips from Reich,
Levine's profits topped $2 million. On one tip from Sokolow, he made $2.7 million.
Levine, however, had far bigger plans. After years of trying, he made contact with
Ivan Boesky, one of the biggest arbitrageurs on Wall Street.

Traditionally, arbitrage has been a quiet, conservative business, consisting of the
buying and selling of stocks based on incremental differences in their prices in different markets. Thus, arbitrage serves a leveling function, keeping the price spread
of a stock small and in general decreasing the volatility of the market. With the
arrival of flamboyant figures such as Boesky—who began with a few thousand dollars that he turned, illegally, into $3 billion of leveraged capital—arbitrageurs began
investing more heavily in takeover gambits. Because arbitrageurs buy and sell a large
and varied number of stocks on a daily basis, determining that an arbitrageur is
trading particular stocks based on inside information is all but impossible. Boesky
took full advantage of this lack of regulation and welcomed the information that
Levine volunteered. Naturally, he also sought out new sources. One of these sources
was Martin Siegel.

Siegel had come to Wall Street from Harvard during the 1970's. He quickly became a minor star of the investment world when he invented the "golden para-chute"—the generous payoff executives receive in case their company is the target of a takeover. This is supposed to deflate the aggressions of companies initiating take-overs, but instead merely tends to enrich executives. As a major figure in the world of mergers and acquisitions, Siegel was bound to meet Boesky sooner or later. It so happened, according to Stewart, that when Siegel finally did meet with Boesky, he was beset with financial worries. The new house and land in Connecticut, the full-time nanny, the need for an appropriate Manhattan apartment in the low millions—all this was putting a terrible strain on his $600,000-a-year salary. Apparently, he was ripe for Boesky's overtures: the promise of a generous "consulting" bonus in return for any fruitful tips. There was a price to pay; he eventually was turned in by Boesky, and he was also besieged by a continually upset stomach.

The tens of millions of dollars Boesky made through his contacts with Levine and Siegel pale in comparison to the incredible sums reaped from his relationship with Michael Milken. Though Milken has been hailed as the inventor of "junk bonds," he could better be considered their dedicated evangelist. Junk bonds—bonds paying high interest that are issued by companies rated as being potentially unstable—have long existed. Milken's discovery was that he could play off investors' greed and ignorance, selling the bonds in a pyramid scheme that at some point was bound to fail. As long as investors' confidence was up, they bought junk bonds, forcing the price up correspondingly. When confidence failed, as it did a few months after Mil-ken was indicted, those investors left holding the bonds lost heavily.

Junk bonds and takeovers went hand in hand. In order to raise the huge sums needed to finance takeovers, companies issued junk bonds. Because both Boesky and Milken were fueled with the same ambition—to become the most powerful force not only on Wall Street but also in corporate America, "to tee-up GM, Ford, and IBM and make them cringe," as Milken put it—the two were naturally drawn together. At first, Milken was indebted to Boesky, both for the tips Boesky was able to gather from his wide circle of informants and also for the huge amount of capital Boesky was able to throw around in order to accomplish particular goals. In one instance, a client of Milken, Golden Nugget, had begun secretly accumulating the stock of MCA in preparation for a takeover. To trained observers, the heavy buying in MCA indicated a possible takeover. Golden Nugget, however, got cold feet. If Golden Nugget had suddenly begun selling the stock it had accumulated, the price of the stock would have plunged, and Golden Nugget might have been ruined. Mil-ken therefore asked Boesky to step in and buy shares of MCA at the inflated price on the condition that Drexel would pay for any of Boesky's losses. When the bill from Boesky came, Milken secretly skimmed money from the portfolios of his clients to pay back Boesky.

It was with scams such as this that Milken earned $550 million in 1985 alone, and Boesky became a billionaire. Eventually, however, the game failed. An anonymous tip alerted the SEC that two brokers in Caracas were trading on inside information. The trades were small—a few hundred dollars at a time—but suspicious in that they preceded the public announcements of various takeovers. Officials traced the source of the information to a broker at Merrill Lynch named Brian Campbell. Campbell's trading records were suspicious as well, and each of his trades was matchable to a previous trade made by Campbell's biggest client, the Bahamas branch of a Swiss bank, Bank Leu International. This meant that someone at Bank Leu was providing Campbell with inside information. The source turned out to be a bank official, Bernhard Meier, who appeared to be receiving his information from one of his clients, a "Mr. Diamond." Under considerable pressure, Meier revealed the identity of Mr. Diamond, who turned out to be Dennis Levine.

Levine, as part of a plea bargain, implicated Boesky. Boesky, also as part of a plea bargain, implicated both Siegel and Milken. Siegel immediately broke down, providing the SEC with enough evidence to implicate all the friends with whom he had shared information over the years. Milken, on the other hand, fought back, throwing tens of millions of dollars into lawyers' fees and public-relations efforts. Eventually all received sentences: Levine, two years, Boesky, three years, Siegel, two months (for having so fully cooperated), and Milken, ten years. All paid fines, Milken's by far the largest at $600 million. How many millions —and in Milken's case, hundreds of millions —the four retained is unknown.

Den of Thieves turns out to be a story of how the super greedy get their hands slapped. The normally greedy —a bank robber, a counterfeiter —steal a few thousand dollars and get the stiffest sentence possible. On the other hand, Milken and his minions, whose greed caused the near-collapse of the savings and loan industry and cost taxpayers billions of dollars, got away with a vacation in a minimum-security prison. Meanwhile, business goes on around the world, as usual.

Peter Crawford

Sources for Further Study

Business Week. October 28, 1991, p. 16.
The Christian Science Monitor. January 14, 1992, p. 13.
The Economist. CCCXXI, November 2, 1991, p. 85.
Financial World. CLX, November 12, 1991, p. 104.
Fortune. CXXIV, October 21, 1991, p. 195.
Library Journal. CXVI, October 1, 1991, p. 118.
Los Angeles Times Book Review. October 20, 1991, p. 4.
The Nation. CCLIII, December 16, 1991, p. 783.
The New York Times Book Review. XCVI, October 13, 1991, p. 1.
Newsweek. CXVIII, October 14, 1991, p. 48.
The Washington Post Book World. XXI, October 20, 1991, p. 5.

D. H. LAWRENCE
The Early Years, 1885-1912

Author: John Worthen (1943-   )
Publisher: Cambridge University Press (New York). Illustrated. 626 pp. $35.00
Type of work: Literary biography
Time: 1885-1912
Locale: Eastwood, Nottinghamshire; London, England

This biography of D. H. Lawrence's life in Nottinghamshire (the coal-mining district of his birth) and of his years as teacher in a London suburb offers new insights into his relationships with his mother Lydia, Jessie Chambers, Louie Burrows, Frieda Weekley, and other individuals who influenced his formative years

> Principal personages:
> DAVID HERBERT RICHARDS LAWRENCE, the British poet and novelist
> LYDIA BEARDSALL LAWRENCE, his mother, the most important influence on his early life
> ARTHUR JOHN LAWRENCE, his father, a collier whose stormy marriage to Lydia inspired Lawrence's first major novel
> JESSIE CHAMBERS, Lawrence's first love, confidante, and earliest literary adviser
> LOUISA ("LOUIE") BURROWS, Lawrence's fiancée (though never his wife)
> FRIEDA VON RICHTHOFEN WEEKLEY, the daughter of Friedrich von Richthofen, wife of Professor Ernest Weekley and subsequently of Lawrence

Many will approach John Worthen's massive study of D. H. Lawrence's early life believing that they already know much about its subject. After all, *Sons and Lovers* (1913) is the Lawrence novel one probably reads first, and everybody realizes that its fictive location, Bestwood, is Lawrence's Eastwood and that the Morel family is Lawrence's own. Like his contemporary Thomas Mann, Lawrence used his life to create his art; yet *Sons and Lovers* resembles Mann's *Buddenbrooks* (1901) only insofar as they are both autobiographical novels. Though both novels represent the same chronological period, Mann surveys his early life from the relatively comfortable vantage point of the German burgher middle class; Lawrence, on the other hand, has a solidly working-class perspective. Judged by its original point of view alone, as a novel about a coal miner's family by the son of a collier, *Sons and Lovers* emerges as distinctively more original, though considerably more uneven and less learned, than its German counterpart.

This comparison made, it is important to note that Worthen does not indulge in similar speculations. He is concerned, however, with Lawrence's formation as an artist, and he perceives that Lawrence's background is essential to that formation. Learning to find the nonintellectual stance that characterizes all Lawrence's best-known works was a major obstacle Lawrence had to overcome, and Worthen succeeds in demonstrating that the aesthetic distance between Lawrence's first novel, *The White Peacock* (1910), and third, *Sons and Lovers*, lay primarily in the decision to drop the middle-class veneer that had characterized virtually all Edwardian fiction published before it. The American expatriate Ford Madox Ford, author of the similarly pioneering novel *The Good Soldier* (1915), counseled Lawrence to approach fiction in this way and in so doing hastened Lawrence's development as a recognized author.

It is likely, too, that Ford's bohemian relationship with Viola Hunt hastened development of the Lawrence persona as high priest of love. Unlike Mann, who also had read Arthur Schopenhauer and Friedrich Nietzsche but who never had abandoned his class or its standards, Lawrence was virtually forced into his credo that humanity was all of a piece and by nature nonintellectual. He felt that he could never marry Jessie Chambers, a woman of his own social class and his intellectual equal; that he could marry Louisa ("Louie") Burrows, who was of his own class but his intellectual inferior; but that he had to marry Frieda von Richthofen Weekley, of German nobility and already married with three children. What made the situation even less socially acceptable was the fact that Frieda's husband, Professor Ernest Weekley, had been Lawrence's languages tutor at Nottingham University and had become Lawrence's trusted friend.

Leaving one's children for a man six years her junior, following him through France, Switzerland, and Italy, and living the life of exiles from Edwardian England would be daring and socially unacceptable even by the standards of the late twentieth century; in 1912, it was virtually inconceivable for a wife and mother to have done such things. This bold action forced Lawrence even more deeply into his mythic persona. In his painting, an avocation he had begun in childhood but continued throughout his life, he portrays himself as Pan crucified, combining the ascetic associations of Christ with the sensuality of the Greek goat-man deity. His most famous poem of his years in Italy, "Snake" (1923), similarly indicates his preference for the sensual and his simultaneous awareness of what the civilized world demands. Mann used myth as a metaphor for his aesthetics; fifteen years after Lawrence's death, the American playwright Tennessee Williams would use it as a vehicle to obscure family history and personal details he was reluctant to reveal explicitly. All three authors represent an important matrix of modernism, but for Lawrence myth and man became inseparable.

One of Worthen's most difficult tasks is, therefore, to cut away the definite preconceptions of Lawrence's personality that nearly every academic reader has. Worthen does this by using Lawrence's awareness of class distinctions as the exponential motif of his study. He is, no doubt, on firm ground in doing this; Edwardian England was class-ridden, and Lawrence, born fifteen years before Queen Victoria's death, experienced the full effect of a society that taught people to know their place. A collier's son of the time should have become a collier, and Lawrence might have had to do so were it not for the determination of his mother, Lydia Beardsall Lawrence.

Lydia's marriage to Arthur John Lawrence was every bit as unhappy as that of Gertrude Coppard and Walter Morel in *Sons and Lovers* and for much the same reasons. The Beardsalls, as moderately prosperous lace manufacturers, had lived on the fringe of the middle class. Reverses in business had degraded them socially as well, and the charm of Arthur, though enticing before marriage, came to underscore the entrapment Lydia felt when she discovered that she had married into a family of coal miners. She combatted these feelings in several ways: through pretensions to style in dress and house furnishings, by a series of moves to more comfortable houses, through long periods of silent argument with her husband, but most especially by attempting to spare her children the life of the coal pit.

(William) Ernest Lawrence, the Lawrences' second son, almost succeeded in leaving the coal pit behind, and it was upon him that Lydia had pinned her hopes. Ernest's counterpart in *Sons and Lovers* is named William (Ernest's unused first name), and their lives and unexpected deaths in London and even their engagements to women nicknamed "Gipsy" run parallel. Paul Morel, who becomes central to the novel, is, of course, Lawrence, and the possessive love Gertrude has for Paul after her son William's death resembles that of Lydia for Lawrence after the death of Ernest.

Lawrence, unlike Paul, finds a way out of his class by becoming a certificated elementary school teacher. Paradoxically, however, the school in which he acquires his first full-time teaching experience is in Croyden, a London working-class suburb, and one-third of his class consists of orphaned boys. Thus, although he had nominally escaped his background, his profession effectively thrust Lawrence back among the working-class poor every day. He was also geographically removed in Croyden from Jessie Chambers, the young woman of the Haggs Farm, Eastwood, who had perceptively read and criticized his work.

Jessie emerges as the most wronged figure of Lawrence's early years. She clearly loved Lawrence on an intellectual as well as a physical level, yet Lawrence abandoned her—to a large extent, it would appear, at his mother's urging. Lydia had repeatedly said that Jessie would leave her no room, that she would fill her place on both the sensual and the intellectual plane. One of the ironies that fill Lawrence's life is that Jessie's having forwarded a selection of Lawrence's early poems to Ford provided his first publication, in the prestigious *English Review* that Ford then edited; it also provided entry into a circle of influential people that included William Butler Yeats and Ezra Pound.

It must have been a simultaneously heady, exhausting, and bewildering experience for the son of a Nottinghamshire collier to teach poor and working-class boys during the day, write in the evening, and socialize with the London literati on weekends. It is clear that these literary acquaintanceships also introduced him to women far more sophisticated than he, among them Helen Corke and Blanche Jennings. Though these never were serious love relationships, they certainly did not provide the right atmosphere for Lawrence's engagement to Louie Burrows, an Eastwood woman, intelligent and a teacher but definitely nonintellectual, of whom his mother approved.

Worthen traces the development of Lawrence's first masterwork, *Sons and Lovers*, against these increasingly complex early relationships with women. He discerns a clear pattern: All the women important in Lawrence's life were unconventional, prepossessed, and essentially independent. None, including Lawrence's mother, was typical of the period in which she was reared. It seems extraordinary that the essentially timid Lawrence would find the boldness to marry a woman who was already a married mother and six years his senior but noteworthy that he did so only after his mother's death. Lydia, despite her pretensions to education, remained a fundamentally unsophisticated woman throughout her life. She was strongly puritanical about many things and disliked the direction in which her son's writing was heading. It was as if after her death Lawrence considered that he was free to carry out the literary and sexual experiments of which she would certainly have disapproved.

D. H. Lawrence: The Early Years, 1885-1912 is the first of three volumes that will form the complete Cambridge biography. Volume 2, by Mark Kinkead-Weekes, will treat the years 1912-1922 and is scheduled for publication in late 1992. Volume 3, by David Ellis, will consider Lawrence's final years in Australia and the American Southwest; it is scheduled for early 1994 publication. The three biographers have developed a uniform thesis on Lawrence's life and work that, if Worthen's volume is any indication, will likely prove definitive.

Robert J. Forman

Sources for Further Study

Booklist. LXXXVIII, September 15, 1991, p. 113.
Kirkus Reviews. LIX, June 15, 1991, p. 781.
Library Journal. CXVI, July, 1991, p. 98.
New Statesman and Society. IV, August 30, 1991, p. 46.
The New York Times Book Review. XCVI, September 22, 1991, p. 26.
The Observer. August 11, 1991, p. 51.
Publishers Weekly. CCXXXVIII, August 2, 1991, p. 56.
The Spectator. CCLXVII, September 7, 1991, p. 29.
The Times Literary Supplement. September 13, 1991, p. 12.

DICKENS

Author: Peter Ackroyd (1949-   )
Publisher: HarperCollins (New York). Illustrated. 1195 pp. $35.00
Type of work: Literary biography
Time: 1812-1870
Locale: England and the European continent

A detailed and informative life study of the greatest English novelist of the nineteenth century

Principal personages:
> CHARLES DICKENS, the novelist, journalist, and entertainer who achieved fame as his country's premier writer of fiction during the middle decades of the nineteenth century
> CATHERINE DICKENS, his wife of more than twenty years, from whom he was separated during middle age
> JOHN FORSTER, his lifelong friend and first biographer
> GEORGINA HOGARTH, Catherine Dickens' sister and the Dickenses' household companion for years
> ELLEN TERNAN, a young actress with whom Dickens became infatuated in the late 1850's

Had Joanna Richardson not used the phrase as the title for her life of Tennyson some thirty years earlier, Peter Ackroyd might have chosen to call his study of Dickens *The Preeminent Victorian.* Certainly even more than Tennyson, Dickens captured in his life and writings that which was most decidedly characteristic of the period in which he lived and worked. The novelist upheld conventional virtues (and sinned against them, as many of his contemporaries did) and was strident in his pronouncements in favor of social change. He was a product of the new technologies as much as he was a harbinger of their dangers: Trains took him across the country at hitherto unheard-of speeds, announcements of his dramatic performances were heralded by telegraph and in daily papers, and those performances were illuminated by the new gaslight systems installed in auditoriums everywhere. The increasing rate of literacy among the middle classes and even among some of the lower classes, coupled with a growing interest in the novel as a popular form of entertainment, assured him of an audience unheard of a century earlier—and lost a century later when electronic media superseded the printed word as the media of choice for entertainment.

Ackroyd's biography is something like a Dickens novel itself: almost eleven hundred pages of text followed by more than a hundred pages of notes. It is massive, detailed, and filled with suspenseful writing, including chapters that leave readers anxious to learn what is to come next. Like Dickens, Ackroyd focuses on character, displaying repeatedly how the force of Dickens' personality shaped events, determined the destiny of his fictional heroes, and influenced those around the author himself.

Dickens led an incredibly active life, even by the standards of the nineteenth century, when prodigious activity seemed commonplace among the giants of politics, literature, and social reform. He produced more than a dozen major novels, edited periodicals for almost thirty years, and spent considerable time organizing theatricals in which he took roles on stage and behind the scenes. During the last two decades of his life, he traversed the country and traveled to America to deliver a series of dramatic readings, offering a one-man show that brought to life the most sentimental and gruesome scenes from his novels.

Ackroyd tries to capture the energy of his subject, relying heavily on anecdotes to dramatize the tremendous variety of activities in which Dickens was engaged and displaying the wide range of interests and friendships he developed over his lifetime. Ackroyd argues that, beneath the comic spirit that characterized Dickens' life and works "there is a sorrowfulness . . . almost a coldness, about aspects of Dickens' life on earth." Ackroyd points out that images of imprisonment run throughout Dickens' writings; the novelist seems haunted by the notion that life itself is a prison from which death gives the only guaranteed escape. At the same time, Dickens was intent on living life to its fullest, thriving when the stress of his competing interests weighed most heavily upon him. In fact, though other biographers have emphasized the toll that the reading tours took on Dickens, Ackroyd is not so sure that these dramatic performances were directly and largely responsible for the novelist's relatively early demise. He believes the tours gave Dickens an opportunity to release some of the anxiety he was feeling about his life, especially after he was separated from his wife and began his clandestine relationship with Ellen Ternan.

Ackroyd spends considerable time describing Dickens' childhood in Rochester and London because he believes that those early years, during which Dickens came to despise his parents' treatment of him, were critical in shaping all of his fiction. The overriding theme of Ackroyd's study is that the events of Dickens' childhood were stamped on the novelist's memory—and on his subconscious—and everything done by the man was simply an attempt to resurrect the child whose life had been made miserable by a spendthrift father and a callous mother. Ackroyd sees in virtually every work of fiction an attempt by the novelist to get back at parents whom he considered unfit. In a sense, Dickens is for Ackroyd a Peter Pan figure, a boy who does not want to grow up. His behavior even in his later years was calculated to let him live out the childhood that had been denied him when his parents refused him an education and made him work to support the family. Like most scholars who have written about Dickens, Ackroyd sees the writer's experience in Warren's blacking factory as the pivotal event of his life. Reduced at a young age to working among the lower classes and then seeing his father imprisoned for debt, Dickens spent the rest of his life securing his financial fortune and his reputation in society; no one was permitted to snub him, and no one was ever to learn during his lifetime of the horrors he had suffered (at least in his own mind) as a result of parental improvidence.

Choosing to focus on the man rather than the works, Ackroyd treads lightly in the realm of literary criticism. One might assume that he does so because he is by profession a novelist rather than a scholar, but the reasons go deeper than that. On occasion, Ackroyd makes offhand remarks about the pedantry exhibited by many scholars, dismissing many of their idle speculations as immaterial to an understanding of the power of Dickens' novels. His criticism of the novels is uneven. Some, especially the early works, are passed over almost without critical comment; Ackroyd spends more time talking about their composition than about their substance. On the other hand, there is substantial commentary on several of the novels, especially *David Copperfield* (1850). Both *Little Dorrit* (1857) and *Our Mutual Friend* (1865) are dealt with in some detail, and *The Mystery of Edwin Drood* (1870) gets its fair share of attention. The common thread running through all Ackroyd's literary analysis is that Dickens drew substantially from the contemporary scene for materials in his fiction, working from recent observation as well as from the reservoir of childhood memories that seemed to provide an eternal wellspring of ideas for his imagination.

Ackroyd proves himself a thorough scholar, poring through Dickens' letters, hundreds of monographs and articles written in the past century and a half, and the novels themselves for clues to understanding his subject. Like most literary biographers, Ackroyd works backward from the fiction and the nonfiction, offering assessments of Dickens' character from comments he puts in the mouths of his literary creations. Such an approach may be dangerous with some writers, but when Dickens is the subject the process may be warranted, for it is clear that the characters of his imagination were just as real to Dickens as the people with whom he lived and worked.

Though Ackroyd has done exceptional scholarly work in preparing his study of Dickens, the text is prepared for the general reader rather than the scholar. Ackroyd includes no footnotes or endnotes, opting instead to include descriptive notes for each chapter at the end of the text proper. This practice can be annoying to readers who want to find the specific source for an anecdote or a judgment about Dickens' motivations for his actions or for certain fictional creations, but the absence of annotations on the pages of Ackroyd's narrative has the advantage of making the text clean and easily readable. Ackroyd's style can best be described as "chatty," filled with rhetorical questions and asides to his readers, crisscrossed with contemporary references that help readers place the novelist and understand Dickens in the light of developments during the past hundred years that make him distant from Ackroyd's readers yet immediately accessible to them. Like his subject, Ackroyd strives for the dramatic in his presentation of evidence. The most obvious evidence of this is his repeated use of sentence fragments—often only a string of single words—to call attention to a point he wishes to stress. For example, to call attention to images Dickens stored in his memory from his days as a youngster in London, Ackroyd offers the following description: "The Adelphi arches. The coal heavers. The Strand. The flaring gas. All to be born again within his imagination." For occasional effect, such lists are useful; unfortunately, Ackroyd becomes obsessed with presenting them to his readers, and the effect can at times be tedious rather than dramatic.

Perhaps the most unusual aspect of this biography is the inclusion of seven brief vignettes that, much like the intercalary chapters in John Steinbeck's *The Grapes of Wrath* (1939), provide a contrapuntal commentary on the main narrative. In several of these, Ackroyd offers his own fictional accounts of various Dickens characters or of the novelist's meetings with other real-life figures from his own age or the present. In one inserted near the end of his study, Ackroyd cagily disarms potential critics of his biography by explaining his method of composition and dismissing criticisms before they can be leveled at him. One may detect a note of cynicism in his revelation that he believes "scholarly footnotes themselves have always been a sort of trick, an academic habit established upon the nineteenth-century illusion that scholarship can fulfil the demands of a science and based, too, upon the nineteenth century preoccupation with *origins.*" In the same digression, he explains that he has tried to integrate commentary on the novels into the biographical narrative rather than set off such criticism in separate chapters (as most literary biographers do). Most important, Ackroyd acknowledges that his work is colored by the age in which it has been written as much as it is affected by the age in which Dickens lived. What Ackroyd's "age" does for him is cause him to be repeatedly self-reflective. He appears quite frequently as an intrusive narrator who reminds his readers that they are reading a kind of "fiction" in his re-creation of Dickens' life. Thus, when he admits that he may have "made too much of the fact that . . . Dickens *saw* reality as a reflection of his own fiction," he is confessing to a method that is characteristic of twentieth century biographical studies in general, where biographers assume that their task gives them the license to become psychoanalysts.

Laurence W. Mazzeno

Sources for Further Study

Choice. XXVIII, July, 1991, p. 1777.
Commonweal. CXVIII, June 14, 1991, p. 408.
The Hudson Review. XLIV, Summer, 1991, p. 301.
Los Angeles Times Book Review. January 20, 1991, p. 1.
National Review. XLIII, April 1, 1991, p. 45.
The New Republic. CCIV, June 10, 1991, p. 35.
The New York Review of Books. XXXVIII, May 16, 1991, p. 8.
The New York Times Book Review. XCVI, January 13, 1991, p. 1.
Publishers Weekly. CCXXXVIII, January 4, 1991, p. 62.
The Washington Post Book World. XXI, February 10, 1991, p. 1.

EDGAR A. POE
Mournful and Never-ending Remembrance

Author: Kenneth Silverman (1936-   )
Publisher: HarperCollins (New York). 564 pp. $27.50
Type of work: Literary biography
Time: 1809-1849
Locale: Boston, Richmond, Philadelphia, and New York City

The first major biography of Poe in fifty years, a triumph of modern scholarship and litera-
ture, a close reading of the writer's life and work, and a significant contribution to contempo-
rary biography

> *Principal personages:*
> EDGAR ALLAN POE, the poet and short-story writer
> ELIZA POE, Edgar's beloved mother, whom he lost at an early age
> JOHN ALLAN, Poe's estranged guardian
> MARIA POE CLEMM ("MUDDY"), Edgar's aunt, whom he came to regard as
> his mother
> GEORGE REX GRAHAM, a magazine owner and editor and one of Poe's
> employers
> RUFUS GRISWOLD, the editor of a popular anthology of American poetry, a
> sometime friend of Poe and his literary executor
> THOMAS DUNN ENGLISH, a literary figure initially friendly to Poe who be-
> came one of his fiercest opponents
> FRANCES SARGENT OSGOOD, a poet and Poe confidante
> NANCY RICHMOND,
> SARAH HELEN WHITMAN, and
> ELMIRA SHELTON, women courted by Poe

There have been several stimulating reinterpretations of Edgar Allan Poe's writing
in recent years, but a full-fledged accurate, scholarly, and readable life has not been
available. Kenneth Silverman has remedied this deficiency by producing an engross-
ing life of the artist, rooted in a sensitivity to psychology and sources, and providing
succinct, perceptive readings of the entire Poe canon.

As his subtitle indicates, Silverman traces the biographical thread in Poe's poetry,
criticism, and fiction, contending that Poe never recovered from his mother's early
death and his ambiguous plight as an orphan supported but never actually adopted
by John Allan, a prosperous businessman and landowner. Silverman does a superb
job of gleaning from meager evidence a picture of Allan as a hard man who nevertheless wanted to do right by his charge, believing that Poe should have a good
education and a reasonable amount of monetary assistance. At the same time, Allan
seems to have resented supporting a child not his own, holding the view that somehow Poe should make his own fortune as Allan had made his—although Allan, in
fact, had also dealt with a grudging guardian who deprived him of the advanced
education and other refinements that befitted a man destined for success.

For his part, Poe seems to have resented his ambiguous status in the Allan home,
at once demanding that he be treated like a son and yet remaining aloof, finding it

hard to hold a place in his heart for Allan, who Poe sensed had made no room in his own for him. On the one hand, Allan made it possible for Poe to attend a year at the newly established University of Virginia. On the other hand, Allan shorted Poe in financial support, perhaps assuming that through frugality and resource (the chief distinctions of the self-made man) Poe would thrive. Poe, however, regarded himself as a gentleman; when he lacked funds, he did what the other gentlemen at Virginia did: He gambled. Then he blamed his losses on Allan's miserliness.

So it would be for the rest of Poe's youth and early manhood: constant appeals for Allan's support, elaborate explanations for his poverty. Circumstances, in Poe's view, always conspired to deprive him of his rightful place in the world. He would forsake the university after a year, then abandon a promising career at West Point, because he could not abide living with his contemporaries in a style lower than theirs. If Allan bore some responsibility in these early years for only half-outfitting Poe for success, Poe made matters worse by miring himself in self-pity and playing the beggar. Silverman reveals these aspects of Poe's character without making overt judgments, preferring to show how Poe's behavior led to wretchedness.

Feeling abandoned by the Allan family, Poe turned to Baltimore and to the remnants of his mother Eliza's family, particularly to Maria Poe Clemm, his aunt, and to Virginia Poe Clemm, his first cousin, whom he married when she was thirteen. He never seems to have expressed an interest in his father, David Poe, who abandoned the family before Eliza's death. Instead, Poe idealized women, transforming them into spiritual symbols. He was particularly attracted to ethereal creatures, who, like his mother, were doomed to die at a young age. Virginia would die in her mid-twenties, an invalid for years, and versions of her would figure in many of Poe's tales of consumptive women destined to haunt his narrators' imaginations—sometimes even returning from the grave and expressing the death-in-life, life-in-death syndrome that Silverman believes began with the death of Poe's mother, whom he would mourn never-endingly, as fixated on the loved one as was the narrator in Poe's famous poem "The Raven."

Silverman is no heavy-handed Freudian, and his biography is not thesis-ridden. On the contrary, he approaches Poe's life and work as a single story upon which Poe worked an extraordinary number of variations. In the notes, Silverman reveals the body of psychological theory on which his interpretation rests. It is too important to ignore, but he does not claim more for it than he can demonstrate in his narrative.

Poe began writing poetry in his teens, producing long poems by the age of fourteen and fixing on a definition of poetry as the production of pleasure that he was to reiterate throughout his career. Poetry should not be didactic; it should be about itself and claim an intensity of interest and unity of impression that captured the reader irrevocably, as though the work of art could itself function as a piece of eternity, complete in itself in a way that life can never be.

The extremity of Poe's views about literature may be a result of the fact that he was one of the first writers to try to make his living solely by the pen. He scorned most of the popular writers of his day, attacking Henry Wadsworth Longfellow,

Washington Irving, and many lesser writers as plagiarists wholly lacking in the originality that made him proud of himself. Angry at his inability to support his wife and aunt, disappointed by various editors, such as George Rex Graham, who failed to recognize his genius and support his plans for his own literary magazine, Poe developed a reputation for being vituperative and unethical, gradually reducing his circle of friends, isolating himself from his contemporaries and the American scene, and growing morbid at the death of his wife and the shattering of his hopes.

One of the best episodes in Silverman's biography is Poe's conflict with Thomas Dunn English, a former friend—one of many who resented Poe's sharp attacks, especially in a series on New York City's literati, in which Poe revealed many idiosyncrasies of his acquaintances and even ridiculed their personal appearances. English took his revenge in a serialized novel portraying Poe as Marmaduke Hammerhead, a hack journalist with "broad, low, receding, and deformed forehead," author of the "Black Crow." While Poe would eventually win a libel action against English, there was little sympathy expressed in the press for Poe's position.

Even in his worst periods, Poe showed remarkable resilience, regaining popularity in 1845, for example, with the publication of "The Raven," which he exploited in several lectures and drawing-room recitations. For all Poe's harsh criticism of his contemporaries, Silverman shows that he was an adept plagiarist and hypocrite, seeking the aid of the very men he despised and condemned in print.

Silverman gives full credit to Poe for his innovations in literary criticism and fiction, but he shows how it was difficult for Poe's contemporaries to accept him at his own evaluation. For one thing, he wrote copious amounts of drivel—sometimes to support himself, but sometimes to ingratiate himself with the female poets he took to courting even before his wife's death. Sometimes his reviews puzzled contemporaries, for he could offer the most fulsome praise of a writer and by the end of a review express the most vehement distaste.

The erratic quality of Poe's reviews paralleled his life, where he shifted abruptly between rationality and hysteria, sobriety and dipsomania, vowing like many alcoholics to reform and begin life anew. Yet he was dogged by a sense of doom, and in his last year alternately feared and welcomed an early death.

Did he mean to marry? He courted at least four women in his last year, proposing to one (Sarah Helen Whitman) and becoming enraged when she backed out of their engagement after having been besieged by messages warning her of Poe's instability. Yet it was also a relief for him not to go through with the marriage, and Silverman has doubts that Poe wanted anything more than companionship—even hinting in his letters to Whitman that she need not expect the marriage to be consummated. Poe always needed feminine support and wanted to enclose himself in a home where he was always tender and expected maternal affection in return. He seemed to have no interest in sexual relationships whatsoever but needed instead the steady comfort of women who believed in his genius and enjoyed caring for him—in spite of his frequent bouts of drunkenness.

Poe's last days were spent in a delirium, perhaps exacerbated initially by drinking.

Hallucinating in ways reminiscent of his more macabre short stories, he seemed to be pulling away from the world, imagining that somehow his mother was near him, and even in periods of lucidity addressing his aunt as though she were his mother— a role Muddy welcomed and fostered even after Poe's death.

Methodologically, Silverman's is one of the more important biographies in recent memory. He manages to convey both the drama of Poe's life and a sense of the evidence out of which the biography has created that drama. Silverman openly acknowledges gaps in the evidence, and where there is an abundance of data he explains (usually in the notes) why he has taken a certain tack, pointing also to previous biographers such as Marie Bonaparte who have influenced his interpretation or who still merit attention.

Silverman also solves the problem of potting the plots of Poe's work by giving summaries in several appendices. Poe aficionados can ignore these and relish the narrative, which plunges directly into interpretation that assumes basic familiarity with plot elements. Silverman tends to segregate discussion of Poe's writing in separate chapters but treats that writing in narrative form as an evolving picture of Poe's career. This involves some overlapping and circling back in time, so that one chapter devoted mostly to the events in Poe's life is followed by a chapter that backs up slightly in time to convey a sense of the writer's developing body of work. This moving backward and forward in time—usually no more than a few months in either direction—is extremely effective, allowing the biographer to pick up and return to threads of the life that are woven into the work.

Neither a Poe partisan nor a detractor, Silverman is objective without being evasive. His judgments are those of pattern, as is clear in the ending of the biography, which goes beyond Poe's death and includes Muddy's final years. For she comes to embody so many Poe family traits—in her grand estimate of Poe, in her trading on his reputation and begging for money, in her curious mixture of fidelity to his memory and destruction of his letters and the letters of others to him. Her devotion and falsification of Poe is much of a piece with his fraudulent yet honorable presentation of himself. Although Poe was contemptuous of contemporaries who claimed originality for American literature, and he explicitly called the nation's literature a copy of England's, there is no doubt that Silverman considers Poe an original, the product of a family and time that he could not evade by seeking eternity.

Carl Rollyson

Sources for Further Study

The Atlantic. CCLXVIII, December, 1991, p. 127.
Boston Globe. November 10, 1991, p. 14.
Kirkus Reviews. LIX, September 15, 1991, p. 1210.
Library Journal. CXVI, October 15, 1991, p. 82.

Los Angeles Times Book Review. November 24, 1991, p. 3.
The New York Times Book Review. XCVI, December 22, 1991, p. 1.
Publishers Weekly. CCXXXVIII, September 27, 1991, p. 50.
The Village Voice. November 19, 1991, p. 71.
The Wall Street Journal. December 27, 1991, p. A8.
The Washington Post Book World. XXI, November 24, 1991, p. 1.

ELIZABETH BISHOP
The Biography of a Poetry

Author: Lorrie Goldensohn (1935-   )
Publisher: Columbia University Press (New York). Illustrated. 306 pp. $29.95
Type of work: Literary criticism and biography
Time: 1911-1979
Locale: Nova Scotia; New England; New York; Paris; Key West, Florida; and Brazil

Goldensohn has written a literary biography of the poet Elizabeth Bishop that posits an evolution of Bishop's poetry toward autobiographical disclosure

> *Principal personages:*
> ELIZABETH BISHOP, an American poet and short-story writer
> LOTA DE MACEDO SOARES, a Brazilian park designer and city planner, friend and lover of Bishop
> MARIANNE MOORE, an American poet, friend and mentor to Bishop
> ROBERT LOWELL, an American poet, friend of Elizabeth Bishop

Since Elizabeth Bishop's death in 1979, her reputation has steadily grown to place her in the forefront of twentieth century American poets. Interest in her achievement is evidenced by the ever-increasing publication of essays, collections of essays, and full-length studies about her work. Early critical assessment tended to praise the clear, objective description and polished surfaces of Bishop's poetry while relegating her to a rather minor position in the canon as an observer of, rather than an active participant in, the poetic life struggle. Since complete editions of her poetry and prose have appeared, a critical reassessment of Bishop's supposed objectivity has been undertaken by such critics as David Kalstone, Lloyd Schwartz, and Thomas Travisano. Lorrie Goldensohn's *Elizabeth Bishop: The Biography of a Poetry* is part of this reassessment.

When Lorrie Goldensohn went to Brazil to research her study of Elizabeth Bishop, she was shown a hitherto-unknown poem that began "It is marvellous to wake up together. . . ." The poem, probably written in the early 1940's, since a draft of it was positioned between other poems of that period, was finally published in 1989. It is one of very few love poems written by Bishop, and it came to take on a central significance for Goldensohn in her conception of the evolution of Bishop's poetry and in the organization of her study of Bishop.

In her preface, Goldensohn states that she originally had in mind a chronological plan for her study, but after her experience in Brazil, her focus changed:

> This initial discovery [of the poem] steadily drew me into a rearrangement of my material, as the abrupt force of the poem delivered to me by accident made me question more closely why a later Bishop had treated love and sexuality only glancingly. I wanted to open this book with the years that brought the sharpest delineation of change in her subject matter, and to track what looked like a characteristic advance within a characteristic retreat in her self-presentation.

The study thus begins in medias res with Bishop's residency in Brazil, where she found "a place to work, a library, a society, and a semblance of family" with her

companion, Lota de Macedo Soares. Goldensohn argues that the exile in "a primitive, childlike Brazil" allowed Bishop the freedom to rediscover her lost childhood
in Nova Scotia and that "both her Brazilian present and her Nova Scotian past fused
in a triumphantly double narrative."

In tracking the advances and retreats of autobiographical disclosure in Bishop's
poems, Goldensohn slips backward and forward in time and hopscotches from one
country to another. While this approach is designed to fit Goldensohn's central argument, it may be confusing to readers confronting Bishop's work for the first time. A
brief chronological listing of the major events in Bishop's life is provided at the
beginning of the book, but it curiously omits a publication history. The best way to
read Goldensohn's book is to have on hand for reference both *Elizabeth Bishop: The
Complete Poems, 1927-1979* (1983) and *The Collected Prose* (1984). Although Goldensohn quotes copiously, especially from the poetry, it is sometimes difficult to place
the work within a chronological framework, especially in her first few chapters.

The focus of the earliest part of the book is Goldensohn's own encounter with the
places in Brazil where Bishop lived, and more importantly, with her discovery of "It
is marvellous to wake up together. . . ." She links this poem, with its imagery of
storms, cages, and birth, to the larger oeuvre. Although it is only in this unpublished
poem that Bishop linked the metaphors with an explicit eroticism, these linkages
serve to inform similar imagery in such poems as "Insomnia," "The Bight," "A
Little Exercise," and "Rain Towards Morning." Bishop never allowed "It is marvellous to wake up together. . . ." to be published, but Goldensohn points out that
she was careful to make a clean typescript copy of it and leave that copy as an
inheritance to a Brazilian friend, who read or spoke no English, to be sold at an
appropriate time after her death. Goldensohn states that Bishop's poetic expression
of erotic intimacy "seems to have halted, or been blocked, in the rooted sadness of
her childhood." Yet it seems more likely that Bishop's natural reticence coupled
with her lesbianism and the mid-century period in which she was writing closed this
avenue of public expression.

Adrienne Rich, in an article entitled "The Eye of the Outsider: The Poetry of
Elizabeth Bishop" (1983), seems to have been the first to emphasize Bishop's location in the world as outsider and to have acknowledged her conscious attempts to
explore marginality. Bishop was a child, different because parentless; a female writer
in a male literary world, whose poems were described even by Robert Lowell as
"outside of Marianne Moore, the best poems written by a woman in this century"; a
lesbian moving within the world of universally accepted heterosexuality; and a foreigner coping with an unfamiliar milieu. Goldensohn picks up on Rich's insights and
shows how Bishop forged her own individual voice and place in the clamor of twentieth century literature.

An inveterate traveler, Bishop first journeyed abroad to Northern Africa and Europe. In Paris, she was intrigued with the art and methods of the surrealists but
finally came to reject what she understood as a narcissistic disintegration of consciousness. Although she could "find" the misprint of "manmoth" for "mammoth"

in a newspaper article and transform the misprint into the strange persona of Man-Moth, she never denied an absolute objectivity to the persona. Moreover, as Goldensohn points out, "Bishop increasingly displayed a stubborn allegiance to the physical world and its inexplicable wholeness. Hers is not the poetry of a modernism drowning, or trusting to drown, in its own helpless subjectivity."

In 1938, she bought a house in Key West, Florida, and from 1938 to 1948 Bishop shuttled between New York City, Key West, and various elsewheres. While Goldensohn gives sensitive readings of such Key West poems as "Florida," "Jerónimo's House," "Roosters," and "A Little Exercise," she gives no biographical details on Bishop's life in Florida. The Key West poems are crucial in Bishop's development; Goldensohn notes that in these poems it occurs to the poet "to move outdoors and welcome her natural territory." Also, it is during this period that she creates her first female persona in "Songs for a Colored Singer." The opening of locales from enclosed spaces to outdoor vistas and "dream houses," the introduction of female voices, and the tentative steps toward self-presentation would seem to invite some biographical information and speculation. Goldensohn does detail Bishop's relationship with Marianne Moore during this period, especially the disagreement over some of the "sordid" description found in "Roosters." It was this disagreement that encouraged the younger poet to free herself from her mentor's prepublication scrutiny. It would also seem, most importantly for Goldensohn's focus, that it is during this period that "It is marvellous to wake up together. . . ." was composed. Inevitably, the question that remains for the reader of this study is, what were the important personal relationships in Bishop's life during the Key West period that perhaps encouraged the freeing of her poetic voice? As explicit as Goldensohn is about Bishop's later relationship with Lota de Macedo Soares in Brazil, the lack of information about Bishop's life in Florida is puzzling and somewhat frustrating.

The fifteen-year residency in Brazil allowed Bishop to foray into the field of historical connection. Her status as observer to the progression of Brazilian history gave her a particular vantage point from which to consider "stationing herself in the flux of time and history, as well as in mapped, geographical space." That peculiarly safe marginality coupled with the encouragement of her close friend Robert Lowell's historical involvement led to such poems as "Brazil, January 1, 1502," "Going to the Bakery," and "The Burglar of Babylon." In addition to exploring the history of an outside world, Bishop also began to tap into her own inner history. Happy in a home shared with loving companions, she began to confront the child who had been orphaned at five and traded back and forth between relatives in Nova Scotia and Boston. Again, Lowell's confessional example challenged Bishop to such self-presentation, but as always, Bishop set her own parameters.

With the death of Lota in 1967 and Bishop's subsequent settling in Boston, the final period of her life and poetry begins. At this point, Bishop comes to terms with loss in the wry villanelle "One Art" and the dramatic monologue "Crusoe in England," a curiously autobiographical poem. Bishop's greatest recognition as an important voice of American poetry came during this time. She held teaching posts at the University of Washington in Seattle, Harvard University, and New York University and was in great demand for poetry readings. In 1969, *The Complete Poems* (1969) won the National Book Award, and in 1976 Bishop was awarded the National Book Critics' Circle Award for *Geography III* (1976) and became the first American to receive the Neustadt International Prize for literature. She died of a cerebral aneurysm in 1979 at her home in Boston.

The strength of Goldensohn's study lies in her readings of the poetry, especially the poetry of Bishop's Brazilian and Boston periods. She illuminates the arcs of transfigurative energy that Bishop's poems trace, and she describes the place that Bishop carved for herself in twentieth century poetry.

> Perhaps her greatest importance to us is the positioning that kept her a sharp step back from confessional style (that is, boxed in within a too-specific personality), and several revealing technical steps outside of the formal disjunctions of high modernism. It is her odd centrality that is most compelling: her marvelous language perfectly balanced between golden and colloquial, her ear fresh and wholly American, her subject an original reading of the traditional, and her Poetical Character, a firm believer in dream, mystery, and surprise, but set in egalitarian resistance to the poet as prophetic divine.

Goldensohn's book is as she names it—a biography of a poetry—which, though it sometimes lacks crucial biographical details, opens up venues for Bishop scholarship and raises new questions. Perhaps its value lies as much in how it tantalizes the reader to want to know more as in the genuine insights it offers.

Jane Anderson Jones

Sources for Further Study

Library Journal. CXVI, September 15, 1991, p. 76.
The Miami Herald. December 22, 1991, p. 19.

THE ENCHANTED LOOM
Chapters in the History of Neuroscience

Editor: Pietro Corsi
Publisher: Oxford University Press (New York). Illustrated. 383 pp. $60.00
Type of work: History and science
Time: Antiquity to 1990

A lavishly illustrated volume on the historical development of selected aspects of brain study

> *Principal personages:*
> PAUL BROCA, a nineteenth century French physician and anthropologist who carried out clinical studies of language processes in the brain
> SANTIAGO RAMÓN Y CAJAL, a Spanish histologist who established the neuron theory of the nervous system and who, with Camillo Golgi, was awarded the Nobel Prize in medicine and physiology in 1906
> RENÉ DESCARTES, an influential seventeenth century French philosopher who proposed a mechanical model of the body and identified the brain's pineal gland as the point of interaction between mind and body
> FRANZ JOSEPH GALL, a German physician who formulated the principles and practice of phrenology during the early nineteenth century
> CAMILLO GOLGI, an Italian histologist who developed a method of staining brain tissue and who shared the 1906 Nobel Prize with Ramón y Cajal

In 1940, the English physiologist Sir Charles Sherrington likened the awakening human brain to an "enchanted loom," and he poetically proclaimed that the rising pattern of innumerable points of electrochemical light signaling our daily coming to consciousness was "as if the Milky Way entered upon some cosmic dance." Over the centuries a considerable number of investigators have similarly fallen under the spell of the brain, eager to penetrate the mysteries of mind and matter and perhaps to join the rhythm of the dance, or simply to understand its processes in order to intervene when patterns become pathology.

Perhaps of no other period in history than the period surrounding the appearance of *The Enchanted Loom* could it be truer to say that the human mind is waking up to the brain. The growing blaze of activity within the scientific community is increasingly being reflected in other segments of society. In 1989 the United States Congress enacted legislation designating the 1990's "The Decade of the Brain," and the Italian government has established an official "Decade of the Brain" committee. This book, which is number four in Oxford University Press's History of Neuroscience series, evolved as part of this awakening interest in the brain, and it represents especially the effort to convey to educated general readers some of the history and significance of research in the brain sciences.

The book emerged more directly from a series of public exhibitions, first in Florence, Italy, in 1989, and then in Paris, France, and St. Louis, Missouri, in 1990. Readers are indeed fortunate to have available in book form such a superb collection of illustrations of the history of neuroscience, together with their valuable accompanying captions and associated essays. The illustrations, by and large, follow the essays, and though in each case the text and the images bear a close topical relationship to each other, they are explicitly connected by textual references only in chapters 1, 9 (in the second essay), and 11. Both the essays and the captions contain bibliographical references to works listed in the lengthy bibliographies at the end of each part. Not all the pictorial material from the exhibitions has been included in the book (though apparently all the captions have been), but the 390 or so images presented here, which include both black-and-white and color drawings, paintings, and photographs of the research as well as the researchers, constitute a diverse and unique resource for glimpsing the changing vision of the nervous system during several periods of history.

In his preface, editor Pietro Corsi comments on the scope and intent of the volume, emphasizing the difficult but important challenge of "communicating to the general reader an idea of the connections between scientific development and the wider dimensions of cultural and social life in the Western world over the course of the last five centuries." The sixteen contributors, eight from Italy and eight from the United States, include several historians, philosophers, and other scholars, as well as numerous scientists. A number of them do indeed deal with various cultural implications of neuroscience, especially in the first two-thirds of the book, and though the chronological range extends from the ancient world to about 1990, the emphasis is on the period since the middle of the seventeenth century, and particularly on the nineteenth and twentieth centuries. The volume as a whole, and especially the illustrations, can be understood and enjoyed by most general readers, though most fully by those familiar with basic brain science.

The three main parts of the book—"The Art of Memory"; "The Discovery of the Brain: From Descartes to Gall"; and "Birth and Frontiers of Neuroscience"—are arranged in chronological order, and each has a distinctive character. Lina Bolzoni's opening chapter, "The Play of Images: The Art of Memory from Its Origins to the Seventeenth Century," which has been translated from the Italian by John Shepley, forms the entire first part. Bolzoni discusses the evolution and significance of strategies for remembering things—"mnemotechnics"—in European history from ancient Greece to the seventeenth century, commenting as well on the marginality of such techniques in the modern age of information. She describes the centrality and sacredness of memory in oral cultures and shows how writing and printing, while contributing to memory's gradual desacralization, have been used in its service. She traces the development of the art from its invention by Simonides of Ceos and its transmission to the Middle Ages through Cicero and Quintilian, to its various sixteenth and seventeenth century forms in the works of Giulio Camillo, Giordano Bruno, Petrus Ramus, and Robert Fludd. The text contains references to the excellent set of illustrations that follow it, the lengthy captions for which provide much additional information.

While the cultivation of mnemotechnics in the history of Western culture is an interesting and important topic of which to be reminded, and though the effort to understand memory's neural aspects is obviously a major focus of much modern brain research, this first part of the book contains no real indications of how the art of memory might have formed a chapter in the history of neuroscience. This is the only part of the book that deals in any detail with the centuries before the seventeenth, and it would have been helpful to have included in some way a treatment of the leading neurological and related psychological theories during this period, as is done in some of the standard histories of the subject such as Fielding Garrison's *History of Neurology* (1925) or Edwin Clarke and C. D. O'Malley's *The Human Brain and Spinal Cord* (1968). The book is thus not a true survey, and as the editor notes in the preface, it was as difficult to decide what to exclude as what to include.

The two rather long chapters in part 2 take up the main theme of the book by discussing the development of ideas on the structure and function of the brain from the mid-seventeenth century to the early nineteenth century. "Schemes and Models of the Thinking Machine (1662-1762)," written by Renato Mazzolini and translated by Henry Martin, sets the stage for the development of modern neuroscience by emphasizing the caution with which many seventeenth and eighteenth century inves tigators approached the daunting complexities of mind and brain. Mazzolini examines the emergence and influence of mechanical models of the brain, particularly René Descartes' pineal gland theory, in the work of various researchers, such as Danish anatomist Nicholas Steno, Swiss physiologist Albrecht von Haller, English anatomist Thomas Willis, and Italian physiologist and microscopist Marcello Malpighi. He also provides a brief discussion of some ancient, medieval, and Renaissance psychophysiological ideas, the book's only attempt at such an account.

Claudio Pogliano's essay, entitled "Between Form and Function: A New Science of Man," translated by Joan Sax, continues the story of efforts to tie the functions of the mind to specific structures of the brain by examining late eighteenth century attempts to correlate anatomical, especially cranial, measurements with mental and moral characteristics. More than a third of the essay is devoted to discussing this approach's most conspicuous early nineteenth century outgrowth, called "organology" by its originator Franz Joseph Gall and christened "phrenology" by his pupil Johann Caspar Spurzheim. Though this chapter includes some rather awkward phrasing and some technical anatomical terminology, it provides an interesting account of the intersection of neurological, anthropological, philosophical, religious, and political interests and ideas during this period.

Part 3 is the longest section of the book, with nine chapters, most written by scientists, that focus mainly on relatively recent twentieth century developments in the neurosciences. Historian of science Anne Harrington's excellent essay, "Beyond Phrenology: Localization Theory in the Modern Era," is the most historical chapter in this part. She examines Paul Broca's location of language functions in the left hemisphere in the 1860's, Carl Wernicke's slightly later work that, instead of drawing a cerebral blueprint based on familiar moral and psychological categories, attempted to build the mind out of neural bricks and mortar, and the late nineteenth century and twentieth century evolutionary theories of researchers such as John Hughlings

Jackson and Paul MacLean, the latter of whom developed the idea of the "triune brain," with reptilian, old mammalian, and new mammalian parts. Harrington discusses these and other developments in relation to intellectual trends in the larger social and scientific environments.

Most of the other chapters in part 3 contain summaries by practicing scientists of late twentieth century views on assorted subjects, with some historical references and discussion. The topics include the neuron, visual processes in the cortex and the retina, the action of drugs and neurotransmitters, physiological correlates of learning and memory, and the development of positron emission tomography (PET), which provides revealing pictures of biochemical processes in the brain. These essays are followed by a variety of portraits and illustrations, including some excellent and often enthralling color microscopic images of neurons (presented singly, collectively, and in culture), of synapses, of retinal cells, and of other structures, as well as some glowing PET pictures.

The two essays in chapter 9, on artificial intelligence (AI), have a more historical and philosophical flavor than the more scientific surveys that surround them. The first provides an informative brief history of AI, showing the changing relationships between neuroscience, cybernetics, and computer science from the 1940's through the 1980's (although the author incorrectly identifies the EDVAC, rather than the BINAC, as the first stored-program computer built in the United States). The second essay presents a short but lucid critique of AI that discusses some of the underlying assumptions common to much work in both artificial intelligence and neurophysiology. The author examines challenges and alternatives to traditional assumptions and approaches, particularly the possibilities opened up by David Marr's views on artificial vision, by the connectionist approach, and by Gerald Edelman's evolutionary model that provides ways of seeing brains, minds, and machines as dynamic systems that bear the shifting but distinctive stamp of the individual's perceptual and conceptual experience.

Oliver Sacks, the English-American neurologist well known for his popular books including *Awakenings* (1973) and *The Man Who Mistook His Wife for a Hat* (1985), contributed the volume's epilogue, entitled "Neurology and the Soul." He critiques the mechanistic approach, in which mental life is largely reduced to neurochemical processes, a viewpoint predominant in contemporary neuroscience and evident in several of the essays in part 3, and offers the perspective of the clinician by campaigning for the irreducible presence of the human individual in the structure and function of the nervous system. He suggests that Edelman's work has made a promising step toward a neurobiological theory of the individual.

Sacks ends by quoting Goethe: "The ancients said that animals were taught by their organs. I would say, yes, but we teach our organs in return." These considerations provide a perhaps humbling perspective on the dazzling achievements of contemporary neuroscience, presented authoritatively and confidently in part 3. They help to indicate the considerable amount, and maybe also the type, of thinking that remains to be done in order to form a picture not only of brains as merely material objects but also of brains as mental, social, and spiritual products and instruments— not only of "neurons in culture" (photographs of which can be seen in chapter 5) but also, perhaps, of "culture in neurons," which is a much more difficult picture to develop, but one which can surely be enhanced by historical awareness.

Following the epilogue is a short appendix containing a statement by Secretary of Health and Human Services Louis Sullivan and a letter from Congressman Silvio Conte concerning the establishment of "The Decade of the Brain" and the American exhibition in 1990. The book ends with an index of primarily names with some subject entries, and with information on, and a list of contributors to, the exhibitions from which the volume arose.

Gordon L. Miller

Source for Further Study

Nature. CCCLIII, September 19, 1991, p ??1

THE ENEMY'S COUNTRY
Words, Contexture, and Other Circumstances of Language

Author: Geoffrey Hill (1932-   )
Publisher: Stanford University Press (Stanford, California). 153 pp. $22.50
Type of work: Literary criticism

A richly textured defense of poetry by a major contemporary poet

Geoffrey Hill's second collection of essays is a continuation of the tapestry of meditations on the possibilities and limitations of poetry in *The Lords of Limit: Essays on Literature and Ideas* (1984). Readers of this work will find the same embattled strategies found in the earlier collection: a defense of his own poetics woven through tightly reticulated studies of lesser known works of major authors or major works of lesser known authors. Hill considers carefully ideas about language, judgment, and context in Thomas Hobbes, John Donne, John Dryden, and particularly Ezra Pound, who occupies a crucial place in Hill's aesthetic pantheon.

Reading Hill's prose poses some of the same questions one might have for Pound's poetry, particularly the later cantos: How is one to regard all of this carefully selected erudition? Is it a masquerade of ironic evasions? Is it a passion for the lost nuances of archaic circumstance and detail? Hill hurls the reader into a web of reference and learning from the first page, "A Note on the Title." Within a few sentences one is informed that prefaces and dedications by Thomas Nashe and William Davenant, works known but to the few most interested, provide the title. It is no accident that the works to which Hill refers are attacks by poets on academic pedantry. Thus begins the series of involved ironies of poetry and art which haunt not only the essays but also much of Hill's poetry. While Hill stands clearly against the anti-intellectualism and romantic love of ignorance often associated with the poet's freedom, it is also apparent that he wants to preserve the idiosyncratic love of learning which he finds in any good intellect but which he finds wanting in the vast critical apparatus of current academic opinion.

Thus, Hill's title registers his awareness that the context of public opinion about poetry comes largely from the academy. He pays tribute to erudition and scholarship, but in a way that reaffirms his own domain of oddity. And while his subject is the way various poets' language is governed and constrained by circumstances, he affirms that the poets, at their best, remain masters of these contexts and circumstances. In the light of the critical discourse in recent decades, particularly the new historicism, Hill concedes to the reality of politics in the life of a poet's mind but insists that it does not completely delimit him. And unlike the structuralists and poststructuralists, Hill rejoices in the ambiguities inherent in language but insists that they cannot be understood outside the interplay of the author's intent and the relevant historical circumstances. In this way Hill provides a defense of poetry against the debilitations of many types of modern critical judgment.

Hill's tapestry consists largely of the elaboration of a series of terms which outline the poles of his thought about poetic activity. Vergilian *labor* is contrasted with *otium* (rest or leisure) which eventually must give way in a poet to the *nec-otium* and later the *negotium*, or the way poets negotiate between indulging in their own flights of imagination and the irreducible substratum of political, social, and economic realities of the world around them. "Value" in poetry is part of the bond of language, its "obligation" to the world of its audience which is both a demand and something which the poet transcends by the act of obliging. Hill seizes joyfully on a Hobbesian coinage, "compleasance," which combines the idea of pleasure and compliance and the extra measure of satisfaction of combining the two. These terms seem to be Hill's assertion of his own jargon in response to more recent terminology—most notably the Derridean "*differance.*" The poet must become what Pound called "master of the forces which beat upon him," and to Hill "the individual poetic voice can, and must, realize its own power amid, and indeed out of, that worldly business which makes certain desires and ambitions unrealizable."

The core of Hill's argument, which unfortunately becomes at times intolerably atmospheric instead of logical, is that judgment of poetic language cannot be made outside the context of the author's intent in a particular environment. He is attacking the tendency in academic criticism to judge the merits of a poem in the abstract—as in much of the New Criticism—and the tendency of new historical and ideological critics to judge a work as complicit in a kind of ideological conspiracy of which the poet is an unwitting dupe. Hill asserts that we can and must consider the poet's intentions, and to do that we have to consider the complex interplay of language and circumstances in making judgments. Citing Hobbes, Hill asserts the primacy of intent in judging literature: "When we ask of someone 'What do you mean by it?' we are not implying that a literal translation will suffice. We are objecting to an imposition, to an intent that we suspect we discern; we are letting it be known that we wish to trace and find out the whole '*drift,* and *occasion,* and *contexture,* of the speech, as well as the *words* themselves.'" Hill's strategy for showing how this works is to select poems which are themselves carefully construed judgments of other poets and writers, poems which pose a regress of complicated problems in making literary judgment. Hill attempts then "not only the ways in which judgement is conveyed through language but also the difficulties of clearing the terms of judgement amid the mass of circumstance, the pressures of contingency."

Hill praises, for example, the balance of what Izaak Walton achieved in his writing, including *The Compleat Angler*: a love of choice and song, the religion of the service book and catechism, as well as the art of angling. *The Compleat Angler* was Walton's tribute to the life of Sir Henry Wotton, "the man," according to Hill, "who has fought his way through defeats and pyrrhic victories to achieve, at last, a felicitous mediocrity between contemplation and action, conscience and policy; a felicity for which the art of angling provides at once the mystical ideal and the practical exercise." The tension, as Hill sees it, is in the negotiation in the seventeenth century concept of art, which comprises both the skilled artlessness of angling as well as the higher art of song. Walton's tribute then is a perfect marriage, as a tribute, between the ethical and the aesthetic, awareness of context and constraint and demonstration of individual contemplation.

The major poetic examples on which Hill focuses are readings of Dryden's elegy "To the Memory of Mr. Oldham" and Pound's "Envoi (1919)," the interlude between the two major parts of "Hugh Selwyn Mauberly." Hill finds that Dryden and Pound are "comparable in their awareness of the political and economic realities of circumstance, of the ways in which the writer's judgement of word-values both affects and is affected by his understanding of, or his failure to comprehend, the current reckonings of value in the society of his day." There is some negotiation in Hill's idea of "political and economic realities," for which he preserves the more general metaphoric domain of "value," rather than the more literal subject matter of contemporary events.

Hill provides one of the most illuminating readings available of Dryden's "To the Memory of Mr. Oldham," a tribute to the poet John Oldham, who died in his early thirties. Combining subtle attention to both language and biography equal to the best work of William Empson, Hill shows that Dryden's verse is more ambiguous than notable critics such as T. S. Eliot and W. H. Auden have realized. Hill reads the poem as double-edged, praising Oldham while at the same time providing consolation for the unhappy circumstances which produced his fame. Hill shows that the patronage of Oldham by the Earl of Rochester and the Earl of Kingston and the older Dryden's falling out of favor with the same provides the drama behind the poem. Hill praises Dryden for avoiding the pitfall of an overcooked panegyric to Oldham and for combining sincere elegy with an awareness both of the younger's poet's limitations and consolation for his own neglect. Dryden admired the youthful wit in Oldham's verse but was attuned to the roughness which in part made him appealing to the more crass sensibilities of his admirers. Hill provides a fascinating reading of Dryden's Vergilian reference to the race of Nisus and Euryalus, in which the lesser runner wins in part because of accident and circumstance. Because of its restraint and balance, its subtle reworking of the tradition of elegy, and its demonstration of Dryden's acute awareness of his place among his contemporaries, "To the Memory of Mr. Oldham," is, in Hill's view, Dryden's "prize-song."

Much of Hill's aesthetic judgment builds on the spare, imagistic sensibility of Ezra Pound's *logopoeia* (defined by Pound as "the dance of the intellect among words"). Hill's own spare archaism in his poetry is a tribute to the Poundian tradition. Perhaps less like the later Pound, excepting perhaps the darker tones of *The Pisan Cantos*, Hill also admires the modernist's early poetry which gestures more to the *melopoeia*, the beautiful and the lyrical with which Pound uneasily negotiated. Hill focuses his final chapter on Pound's "Envoi (1919)" which is based upon the Renaissance lyric "Go Lovely Rose," by Edmund Waller, a poem set to perfect music by the admired composer Henry Lawes. In this poem Pound reveals his desire to create a perfect music but also the hazards of doing so in the circumstances of his own age.

The situation of "Envoi" is one which has obviously preoccupied Hill from the start. One of his first major poems, "Genesis," mimes the meter and rhythm of Christopher Smart's uncanny "A Song to David," a work aptly called by Robert Frost "the one work of splendor in an age of wit." The strong echo of the Smart poem reveals Hill's desire for the lyric perfection and religious fervor of the earlier work. But the language of Hill's "Genesis," scattered with blood sacrifice and bone, is acutely aware of the limitations of a pure and unmarred praising of man and God in the years after the Holocaust. The negotiation of desire and historical limitation gives the poem its gnarled power.

Pound's "Envoi (1919)," while it translates the song of Waller and Lawes, is itself a negotiation, standing between the better known parts of "Hugh Selwyn Mauberly." Pound's attitude toward Mauberly is ambivalent and often deeply ironic; he perhaps admires his well-wrought craftsmanship in an age of banalities but is also skeptical of that craftsmanship. If in the first sequence, Pound's object of scorn is the age, in the second sequence it is Mauberly himself. "Envoi" negotiates between the attack on the age and the attack on Mauberly by attempting the beautiful song but building into it an awareness of becoming another cliché of beauty, a giving in to the banalities of the genteel tradition of poetry. Hill's comment on the conclusion of the poem reveals his acute sense of the balance between terror and beauty, *negotium* and *otium* in self-conscious modern poetry: "The concluding words of 'Envoi (1919),' 'Til change hath broken down/ All things save Beauty alone,' maintain the idea of 'sheer perfection' though at some remove from the complacent aplomb with which that phrase is commonly uttered."

A similar kind of negotiation occurs in more condensed form in Hill's own poem "Ovid in the Third Reich," in which the poet of love ironically attempts to celebrate "the love choir" in the context of a horrific social and political travesty. Many of Hill's finest poems address the problem of writing poetry in the face of the Holocaust, of the uses of love, beauty, and elegy in the midst of what many have attempted to argue is the unspeakable. It is Hill's genius that enables him to avoid both murdering the humanity of those who suffered with insufferably grave truths and the somewhat precious dogma of maintaining silence. The "enemy's country" in Hill's own life has been twofold. It encompasses the forbidding landscape of social and political reality—a reality which Hill indicates is not unique to his own time. The "enemy's country" is also the anxiety of influence produced by the world of academic patronage, which challenges the poet's domain with multiple and often jargon-ridden theories about the necessity of maintaining silence. Hill's essays reveal how poets defend themselves in this treacherous domain while winning occasionally with well-wrought medallions of beauty.

Robert Faggen

Sources for Further Study

London Review of Books. XIII, November 7, 1991, p. 18.
The Spectator. CCLXVII, September 14, 1991, p. 33.
The Times Literary Supplement. December 27, 1991, p. 6.

FAR FROM HOME
Life and Loss in Two American Towns

Author: Ron Powers (1941-   )
Publisher: Random House (New York). 317 pp. $22.00
Type of work: Social history
Time: The late 1980's
Locale: Cairo, Illinois; Kent, Connecticut, and its environs

Far from Home: Life and Loss in Two American Towns *traces the social and economic disintegration of Cairo, Illinois, and Kent, Connecticut*

> *Principal personages:*
> RON POWERS, the author and investigator
> RICHARD "DOC" POSTON, a professor emeritus at Southern Illinois University at Carbondale
> GLENN POSHARD, an Illinois state legislator
> ALLEN E. MOSS, the mayor of Cairo, Illinois
> LARRY POTTS, a clergyman in Cairo
> BILL WOLTER, the owner of docks in Cairo
> CAROL HOFFMAN, the widow of John Hoffman, the owner of a bookstore in Kent, Connecticut
> DONALD CONNERY, a former foreign correspondent for *Time* magazine
> LESLIE CONNERY, Donald Connery's wife, a teacher
> DOROTHY GAWEL, a beloved citizen of Kent killed in an automobile accident

Cairo (pronounced "Kayrow") is located on a small wedge of land at the confluence of the Ohio and Mississippi rivers; Kentucky lies to its east, Missouri to its west. Despite Illinois' allegiance to the Union during the Civil War, Cairo is as Deep South as many small towns in Alabama or Mississippi.

Cairo was a dangerous place from the time of its birth in 1818, when virulent diseases crept out of moist lowlands around it, lands that Charles Dickens, who passed by on a trip down the Mississippi, called "a breeding place of fever, ague, and death." Typhoid and cholera claimed the lives of countless early citizens, as the older cemeteries around the town attest. Political corruption and the repression of black citizens were virulent diseases of a different sort. They also exacted a terrible toll in the town, which was socially dysfunctional almost from its inception.

Twelve hundred miles to Cairo's northeast is Kent, Connecticut, an affluent village close enough to Manhattan to be a favorite weekend haunt of city-dwellers in quest of the bucolic. Once a sleepy hamlet, Kent has become a trendy retreat for rich New Yorkers; the influx has permitted some of Kent's older citizens to sell their $20,000 houses for ten times the original purchase price, their acreage at such outrageous prices that it boggles local minds.

Kent has exchanged the simple for the sophisticated, a comfortable, natural rustication for the calculated, quietly elegant rustication of corporate executives and professionals, weekenders who flee the city as early as they can on Fridays and return there as late as they can on Sunday nights. If Cairo is economically anemic, Kent's blood is so rich it is goutish.

A common thread that unites these two disparate towns is Ron Powers, a Pulitzer Prize winner who wrote *White Town Drowsing* (1986) and a former on-air columnist for the *CBS Morning News.* Powers was born north of Cairo in Hannibal, Missouri, a Mississippi River town immortalized by Mark Twain. Moving east to launch his career, Powers became a New Yorker. When success came, he bought his chunk of heaven-on-earth, a spread in Kent, Connecticut, where he spent his weekends.

As Powers mused on the plight of Cairo, Illinois, a plight worsened by racial tensions and riots in the 1960's, he came to see the town as emblematic of something that was seriously wrong with his society. That something was pushing an ever-troubled town toward certain disaster.

At his home base, surprisingly, Powers was also witnessing (and participating in) the destruction of a relaxed way of life in rural Connecticut. People such as Powers were making inroads on a sleepy hamlet whose sleepiness had attracted him and thousands of others, people who became unwitting agents in the destruction of the very atmosphere that had drawn them to Kent in the first place.

It is out of these two forces that *Far from Home: Life and Loss in Two American Towns* grew. On a metaphoric level, the book is about the haves and the have-nots, but the opposites that these polarities suggest are not wholly antipodal. Many of the problems that afflict the towns are common to both.

The organization of the book is such that the stories of the two towns are intertwined. Powers does not devote the first half of the book to Cairo and the second half to Kent. Rather, he has a chapter or two on one town, then a chapter or two on the other, sometimes a chapter on both towns. This arrangement enhances the contrasts that are inherent in his book.

The Cairo chapters focus on Doc Poston, a retired professor of community development from Southern Illinois University (SIU) in nearby Carbondale. The tenuous field of community development is an outgrowth of funding made available half a century ago by the Rockefeller Foundation. When an ambitious new president of SIU deemed it politic to revive the field of community development, he urged Poston to come out of retirement and provide leadership. Poston agreed, with the caveat that he be permitted to work with one troubled town, nearby Cairo.

Cairo, a town in total disrepair, had never been a promising community. Blacks had been lynched there; a black prisoner as late as the 1960's had died under questionable circumstances—officially designated suicide—in his cell and was embalmed before an autopsy could be performed. The latter incident led to race riots.

When Larry Potts, the local preacher at the Cairo Baptist Church, used a baseball bat to bash the brains out of a black gardener Potts accused of attacking Mrs. Potts sexually, his barely investigated act was termed justifiable homicide. He continues to preach in the town, where his family settled generations ago.

Cairo has its rich people. Powers' investigations, which they tried to thwart, suggested that their wealth was badly tainted. His investigation of Bill Wolter's Waterfront Services shows how immune Wolter's political connections made him from the sort of scrutiny to which business people are usually subject.

The first Kent chapter of the book centers on a dinner party at the home of Carol Hoffman, a bookstore owner and an outsider around whom many of the town's official activities revolve. Other guests include such elegant exurbanites as Donald Connery, a former foreign correspondent for *Time* magazine, and his wife, Leslie, a teacher who is also a member of the volunteer fire and ambulance service.

Just as this party is ending, Leslie's beeper sounds, summoning her to a traffic accident. It turns out that the head-on accident involves a fatality: Seventy-two-year-old Dorothy Gawel, one of the town's most beloved citizens, has been killed. The country roads that account for much of Kent's charm are not up to handling the traffic that the growing population has brought to the area. Dorothy's death becomes a pervasive metaphor for what is happening to Kent as it undergoes wrenching social and economic changes.

Powers illustrates clearly how the real-estate mania that has afflicted southwestern Connecticut heated up so rapidly as to defy belief. He writes that in historic Litchfield, Connecticut, founded in 1719, a house was sold in 1985 for $110,000, the highest price ever paid for a property in Litchfield. Two years after that, two houses near the center of Litchfield sold within a six-week period for a million dollars each. By that time, the least expensive house in a town where property prices had usually been in the four- or five-digit range was listed for $127,000.

Along with the obvious, outward changes that real-estate development in the area brought with it came a weakening of the community spirit that had long characterized that part of Connecticut. Neighbors used to know neighbors, used to consult with them before they made changes that would affect them.

The "invaders" had no such sense of community. When they decided to improve their properties, they plunged right in and made the improvements, as the Henry Kissingers did, for example, when they cleared their property of blueberry bushes that had been growing there since colonial times. They did not consult with the natives, who for years had treated the blueberry bushes and their produce as community property available to anyone who wanted to pick the fruit.

The Kissingers, acting within their legal rights, sent a not-too-subtle (although unintended) message to the community when they stripped their property of foliage they no longer wanted. Their neighbors did not have public protest meetings about what the Kissingers did, but they considered it a slight that typifies what an urban invasion of a secluded rural area entails.

As different as are the two towns upon which Powers casts his penetrating gaze, they pose a broad question that touches on the ability of American towns to survive the onslaughts of modern civilization. Cairo has throughout its existence represented the fringe areas of American culture as a city of about six thousand inhabitants who have, for the most part, eked out marginal existences that often caused them to blink at law enforcement.

The dream of reconstituting this town as a showcase of America's heritage is a pipe dream. One thinks of Lanford Wilson's play *The Mound Builders* (pr. 1975; pb. 1976), set five or ten miles to the northeast of Cairo, where the old culture is simply and calculatedly inundated by a manmade lake. A new culture may grow around the lake, which could become a successful resort, but the old culture will be wiped out.

A play such as *The Mound Builders* has as much to say about Powers' Kent, Connecticut, as it has to say about Cairo and its environs. The play is about the annihilation of a culture, and that essentially is what Powers' book is about.

In viewing the two towns, however, Powers projects drastically different attitudes about each. In dealing with Kent, he seems desperately to be searching for means by which a quaint, historic town can preserve its past well enough to retain its unique identity; according to the book, it seems the battle cannot be won.

When he casts his gaze upon Cairo, Powers is calling for change more drastic than that which has afflicted Kent. For Cairo, drastic change seems to be the only hope. Cairo has lived with severe problems for nearly two centuries. If it has any chance as a community, it must bury that past, expunge all that might perpetuate it.

Kent, despite the urban invasion, will continue for some generations to be an affluent community. In fact, its affluence likely will wax rather than wane. Its country stores have already been replaced by fashionable boutiques, its family doctors by psychiatrists and plastic surgeons, its sprawling, multiacred farms by planned communities and condominiums. Its ambience will change. Its original citizens will feel displaced. Another generation of citizens, however, will soon be the natives, and the past about which they will grow nostalgic will be the very present that today's insiders decry.

With the invention of the automobile and the building of roads, the future of towns such as Kent was threatened. The urban sprawl that motor vehicles and highways allow had inevitably to stretch its tentacles deep into places such as southwestern Connecticut. It took a while for these tentacles to reach towns as remote as Kent, but more than fifty years ago such inroads could have been reliably predicted.

Powers' book provokes considerable social and economic contemplation. Well-written and thoughtfully argued, the book provides a periscope of sorts, helping readers to peer over the hill, to glimpse a future from which they may prefer to avert their glance.

R. Baird Shuman

Sources for Further Study

Library Journal. CXVI, April 15, 1991, p. 114.
The Nation. CCLIII, October 14, 1991, p. 454.
Publishers Weekly. CCLVIII, April 12, 1991, p. 50.

FATE

Author: Ai (1947-   )
Publisher: Houghton Mifflin (Boston). 77 pp. $15.95
Type of work: Poetry

Ai's fourth book of poems uses people in the public eye to provide a disconcerting view of the surface and depths of contemporary life

Each of Ai's books has a strongly distinctive character, even though they share a voice that is unique: An Ai poem is immediately recognizable. Ai's first book, *Cruelty* (1973), gave vital but frightening pictures of life among the rural poor. The shock content increased with *Killing Floor* (1979), which won the Lamont Prize offered by the Academy of American Poets for the best second book of poetry. Ai's third major collection, *Sin* (1986), added surrealistic horror to the poet's repertoire; the psychological resonances of the connections she makes in this collection bring to mind D. M. Thomas' novel *The White Hotel* (1981). *Sin* won the American Book Award. Her 1991 collection, *Fate*, displays yet a new direction, but one that unites the strands of Ai's earlier books. Many of these poems are dramatic monologues in the voices of people who are part of American myth—Alfred Hitchcock, James Dean, Elvis Presley, even Mary Jo Kopechne. These voices and the shapes of their stories define America, and the country they represent (by their silences as well as by their words) is not a place one would choose to live.

Born in Texas, Ai sketches a country of bigness—big frauds, big exploitations, big differences between rich and poor. Her poems, though, are not big, sprawling poems. The dramatic monologues of *Fate* are spare, pared-down poems with no ornament. They may be long, as the form of the dramatic monologue usually requires, but they are not wide. Each word is necessary. They characterize and analyze and they judge; they do not play with words.

Ai herself comments that her book is "about eroticism, politics, religion and show business as tragicomedy, performed by women and men banished to the bare stage of their obsessions." The reference to the stage is appropriate, as these poems could easily be read aloud by actors as a kind of contemporary eclectic *Spoon River Anthology* (1915). Instead of eulogizing lasting American values, as Edgar Lee Masters' work does, however, *Fate* explodes the myth of values barely believed in and rarely put into practice.

The opening poem, "Go," provides a sketch of Mary Jo Kopechne that makes Edward M. Kennedy a symbol of the corruption of the Kennedy idealism, the Great Society, the whole Democratic vision of the 1960's and 1970's. Kopechne herself becomes an image of the betrayed. Yet she remains a person, too, a young woman whose tragedy was not only her drowning but also the necessity of her public sacrifice to the Kennedy mystique—her fate.

Kopechne describes the accident itself: "the dark gray water/ opened its mouth/ and I slid down its throat." Yet "when it tried to swallow/ the man they call my lover *and* my killer,/ it choked and spat him back into your faces." Kopechne wonders why no revisionist rescues her from obscurity to place her at the heart of the story instead of Kennedy (which, of course, Ai does). Kopechne's lament shows she still accepts the myth: "All right, I'll say it plainly./ Jack or Bobby would have died with me." Yet from her perspective, Kopechne has participated, although unintentionally, in the diminishing of the Kennedy myth. She looks at a Ted Kennedy "grown fat and jowly/ at the table where no feast is ever served." He is bemused, confused, uncertain of his role. Thus, in accomplishing her own fate as victim, Kopechne brings about the demythologizing of others and makes her own indelible mark on history.

The fates of Ai's other speakers, too, define America as a land of big promises, big lies. "The Resurrection of Elvis Presley" is one, providing a picture in words of the bloated Elvis-figure that has superimposed itself on the image of the sinuous singer of the 1950's. More unusual, perhaps, is the voice in "James Dean," which pleads for the reality of the person in contrast to the unreality of the popular image of the actor, an image that for Dean was a role to play.

The poem begins with details of his violent death in the crash of his Porsche and his rebirth as an image. "I died,/ but the cameras kept filming/ some guy named James. . . ." The manufactured James, product of the American desire for such figures and of his willingness to play the role, continues to exist in "posters, photographs, biographies." The real James Dean comments that

> if anybody'd let me
> I'd have proved
> that I was made of nothing
> but one long, sweet kiss
> before I wasn't there.

Like the Kopechne poem, the James Dean monologue produces a person who is both a real individual and an image of social and historical significance. Here Dean becomes Hollywood and the confusion between performance and personality that Hollywood engenders. To his immortal celluloid surrogate, even Dean's death is an act.

The other dramatic monologues involving public figures both recent and remote provide the same sense of the hollowness of American values. The reader hears from James Hoffa, Alfred Hitchcock, Lyndon Johnson, Lenny Bruce, and General Custer. Other less well-recognized voices intrude: reporters and police, crime victims, children. The sense of exploitation that sails under other names—patriotism, law and order, education, business—is a constantly felt presence, but the force of this poetry comes from the people. Robert Browning comes to mind for several reasons beyond his mastery of the dramatic monologue: He, too, was portraying a corrupt society through its representatives; he, too, focused on power relations, oppressors and victims; he, too, played on the fascination with evil. David Wojahn commented in *The New York Times Book Review* that an Ai poem sounds like "a Browning monologue written in the terse manner of Sam Shepard." The uncertainties and confusions of Ai's characters reflect a time more fragmented and groping than Browning's Italian Renaissance.

In general, Ai's monologues of famous people catch the spirit of a media-dominated and spiritually impoverished era; they reveal the irony of glitz juxtaposed with gutter. There is a grotesqueness at points that recalls some of Graham Greene's short stories. In her characters, as in his, greed and exploitation are so transparent that one wonders how these people can live with themselves with no shadow of a polite fiction to hide behind.

The vintage Ai poems, however, are the portraits of unknowns, usually nameless women whose sheer guts in the bizarre situations they encounter lead them to survival. This is a return to the world of *Cruelty*, but in the earlier poems the women were sketched in a few crisp lines, their lives evoked by a handful of telling images. Here Ai allows the women to expand themselves, to explain the choices they made and those that were made for them, and to meditate upon who they are. Two outstanding examples are "The Cockfighter's Daughter" and "Eve's Story."

"The Cockfighter's Daughter" is a well-crafted short story in verse. Its nameless heroine is an abused, alienated daughter who has been living with her father and a cock named Preacher. She has come back after a failed marriage to the only home she has known and to the mixture of sensuality and violence that is her father. Now he is dead—"face down, in his homemade chili." The speaker had to "scrape the pinto beans/ and chunks of ground beef/ off his face with a knife." Her inheritance is the cock, a violent and violated creature who had clawed her father and torn a chunk out of his flesh.

> When the old man stopped the bleeding,
> the rooster was waiting on top of the pickup,
> his red eyes like Pentecostal flames.
> That's when Father named him Preacher.

The two tough orphans look at each other in mutual recognition. Then the woman goes down to the river and drives her car into it, jumping out at the last minute. She is attempting the kind of exorcism of the father that Sylvia Plath describes in "Daddy" (1963), but this woman is a survivor. She will survive, ironically, because she is not able to exorcise her father; she has too much of him in her, and his toughness will serve her well in the rough world. At poem's end she is driving off in her father's truck, fighting cock by her side, following his schedule of fights. The use of an animal to represent a lost or suppressed self is common enough in fiction, but the use of the cock in this poem is startling. He needs his violence and independence to survive, and she will need hers.

Indeed, the element of violence is never far from the surface in Ai's work, and it combines with the erotic to produce a pungent stew. Violence, sex, and religion are the three forces that determine fate in this world of exploiters and victims. A lascivious evangelist is described in "Eve's Story," a tale of the trickster tricked. The poem begins with a trivial, grotesque violence that shows nevertheless the relationship between oppressor and oppressed. The speaker's cat "gave birth to a kitten/ with no front legs." Her father twisted "the kitten's head clean off./ The body was still soft and spongy/ when I buried it." The kitten's fate illustrates the destiny of helplessness. The girl learns her lesson well and leaves home at sixteen to make her way in the world.

After being sexually exploited by the lustful preacher and then abandoned for another woman, she videotapes his acrobatics with her replacement and shows the tape to the public. He is debunked and disgraced, but she has him back and she sticks with him. They live out their lives on her savings like "any other/ retired couple in Sarasota." The speaker, reminiscing comfortably with her old rival, identifies with Eve as a sister in betrayal. The poem concludes with an image of the false promise that conditions women's lives, including Eve's, her rival's, and her own:

> . . . now the smell of apple blossoms
> hovered in the air,
> promising sweet fruit,
> promising everything we ever wanted.

These poems are described on the book jacket as "sometimes distasteful," and some of their topics, including heterosexual and homosexual rape, will disconcert some readers, especially those used to thinking of contemporary poetry as a gentle academic exercise in the obscure. It is their harsh realism, however, as well as their depth of characterization that makes Ai's poems both vital and memorable.

Janet McCann

Sources for Further Study

Belles Lettres. VI, Spring, 1991, p. 58.
Booklist. LXXXVII, January 1, 1991, p. 902.
Detroit News and Free Press. March 24, 1991, p. R7.
Library Journal. CXV, December, 1990, p. 129.
Poetry. CLIX, November, 1991, p. 108.
Publishers Weekly. CCXXXVII, December 21, 1990, p. 48.
The Virginia Quarterly Review. LXVII, Summer, 1991, p. 101.

FATHER MELANCHOLY'S DAUGHTER

Author: Gail Godwin (1937-   )
Publisher: William Morrow (New York). 404 pp. $21.95
Type of work: Novel
Time: The 1970's and 1980's
Locale: Romulus, Virginia, and Charlottesville, Virginia

A novel about the conflicts that arise when men and women attempt to balance their own needs for fulfillment against the needs of others

> *Principal characters:*
> MARGARET GOWER, the daughter of an Episcopal priest
> WALTER GOWER, her father, who is called "Father Melancholy" because of his recurring fits of depression
> RUTH BEAUCHAMP GOWER, her restless mother
> MADELYN FARLEY, Ruth's college friend, a scenic designer
> HARRIET MACGRUDER, Margaret's best friend
> BEN MACGRUDER, Margaret's friend and lover

Gail Godwin's novels all explore the basic human conflict between the needs and the demands of others and the needs and the demands of the self. In her early works, such as *The Odd Woman* (1974) and *Violet Clay* (1978), Godwin focused on a single protagonist torn between art and love, or at least the psychological and physical dependence that is often called love. In the 1980's, Godwin's works became more complex, involving more major characters and more complicated situations. For example, as the title suggests, *A Southern Family* (1987) traced the entangled lives of a number of characters, each of whom had a different interpretation of the motives of the others and of the dynamics of the family. In *Father Melancholy's Daughter*, Godwin returns to a single first-person narrator. By having that narrator seek the truth from a number of different people, however, Godwin achieves that same complexity as she did in *A Southern Family*, once again having several characters tell their stories from their own perspectives and leaving the reader to make the final interpretation.

The search for truth that is undertaken by the narrator, Margaret Gower, is the primary action of the novel. Indeed, it is clear that until she can come to an understanding of her parents' actions, she will be unable to proceed with her own life. As Margaret points out in the first chapter of the novel, her childhood ended one day when she was just six years old. That was the day she came home from school to find that her mother, Ruth Beauchamp Gower, had left without a word of explanation to her daughter. Margaret was never to see her mother again; Ruth was killed in an automobile accident nine months later.

During the next sixteen years, Margaret takes care of her father, a kind and unassuming Episcopal priest, whose periodic bouts with depression account for the reference to him as "Father Melancholy" in the title of the book. Before her mother's departure, Margaret had had a fantasy in which she penetrated the dark place where her father periodically languished, without the will to return to the world, and guided him back to the world and his daughter. Later, when she reflects on this fantasy, Margaret realizes that her replacement of Ruth in her father's life could be seen as a wish-fulfillment; however, whatever the psychological implications, on a practical level, Margaret really has no choice. It is not that Walter insists upon her devoting herself to him; he is more than willing to marry again. Unfortunately, the woman both he and Margaret have chosen forestalls his proposal by announcing her decision to enter a religious order. After that, Walter and Margaret drift into a comfortable companionship, which gives stability to both of them and enables Walter to function effectively as a priest.

What neither Walter nor Margaret realizes is that their interdependence prevents her from maturing in the normal pattern and becoming a separate person with a separate life. When Margaret goes to college in nearby Charlottesville, she is still so closely attuned to her father's moods that a telephone call from him suggesting the onset of depression will make her cancel all of her plans and hurry home. Even Margaret's relationships with men of her own generation are subordinated to her relationship with her father. She will not commit herself emotionally to her childhood friend Ben MacGruder but merely indulges herself sexually with him. When Margaret does fall in love, the object of her affections is another sensitive and wounded priest, her father's disciple, who could easily have joined their household, thus giving Margaret an added responsibility and an additional reason to avoid discovering her own identity. As it happens, the priest does not wish to marry. At any rate, it is not until after her father's sudden death that Margaret realizes she can and must decide about the direction of her own life.

Before she can move on, however, Margaret must come to understand her mother, the woman who took her freedom at the expense of a husband and young child. For sixteen years, Margaret has puzzled over accounts of mothers who abandoned their children, often for lovers, sometimes for death. Even though her father insists that there was no sexual dimension in Ruth's relationship with Madelyn Farley, Margaret has always concluded her deliberations by blaming Madelyn for Ruth's decision. Margaret remembers Madelyn's contempt for Walter, for his values and for his kind of life; she cannot help believing that somehow Madelyn seduced Ruth into sharing her vision and then reacting by taking flight. At any rate, Margaret believes that she cannot progress with her own new, independent life until she knows why her mother chose to become free by leaving those two people who loved her so much.

Ironically, it is Madelyn, seemingly her enemy, who can give Margaret the answer. Responding to a bitter message that Margaret has left on her answering machine, Madelyn arrives in Romulus with the explanations that Margaret so desperately needs. Like many women of the 1970's, Madelyn says, Ruth felt trapped and thought that she wanted to be free. Madelyn's visit simply precipitated Ruth's escape from her life. Nevertheless, Madelyn explains, again like many women of her generation, Ruth lacked the intellectual and psychological preparation for an independent life, either as an artist or simply as an individual. Therefore, after she left Walter, she simply found someone else to lean on, her strong friend Madelyn. As for Ruth's disenchantment with Walter, Madelyn explains it as another example of her habit of dependence rather than of the independence Ruth mistakenly thought she wanted. In order to feel secure, women like Ruth set up men as gods; then when the gods turn out to be merely human beings, such women reject and despise them. Indeed, Madelyn says that at the time of Ruth's death she was beginning a similar process with Madelyn herself.

This conversation with Madelyn enables Margaret to understand that real independence lies in doing one's duty, not in running away from it. For Madelyn, that duty is to art; for Walter, to religious faith. As the novel ends, Margaret has eliminated all the patterns for her life presented to her by well-intentioned friends and has made her own decision. She is applying for admission to a theological seminary.

Although *Father Melancholy's Daughter* focuses primarily on Margaret's search for understanding, the conflicts between dependence and independence, self-sacrifice and self-fulfillment, duty to others and duty to self, which are crucial in her own story, are illustrated in the lives of dozens of other characters. For example, Walter's parish includes a number of people who avoid confronting themselves by staying busy with others who are or seem to be dependent upon them. There is a sanctimonious old maid whose life consists of taking care of her mother and going to church; a doctor who is so busy with his practice that he has no time for his family; and an energetic do-gooder who depends upon the less fortunate to provide her with a purpose for existing. Love itself can lead one to an unhealthy self-denial. It is clear that Ben MacGruder's emotional well-being depends upon Margaret's attitude toward him at any given moment, and Margaret herself becomes giddy over her father's friend, the priest. The mother of one of Margaret's friends killed herself for love, thus illustrating, in what seems like an act of self-assertion, the ultimate statement of dependence upon another.

On the other hand, although Madelyn proves to be far more decent than Margaret had ever suspected, there is a ruthlessness in her total dedication to art that Margaret, at least, cannot imitate in her own search for independence and self-fulfillment. From her father, Margaret has inherited the power to nurture others. It is this capacity, along with Walter's own goodness, that makes her childhood responsibilities seem so easy; it is also this quality in her nature that drives Margaret to undertake the care of the ailing Madelyn, as well as of Madelyn's cantankerous artist father. In her need for independence, Margaret does not deny her nurturing nature; instead, she changes directions, believing that she can best fulfill herself in a more public role—specifically in the ministry, a vocation that, it should be noted, would have been almost impossible for a woman of a previous generation. Always a realist, Godwin recognizes that choices are made within the context of history.

As a Southern writer, it is not surprising that Godwin is conscious of the importance of history, of tradition, and of time. Although the actual events of the novel cover only sixteen years, the author expands her time frame in numerous ways, for example by including love letters that Ruth had written to Walter before their marriage and by reporting various stories out of the past, some factual, some exaggerations or actual fictions, that are told to Margaret by her friends and neighbors in Romulus. The point is, of course, that whether they are true or not these stories become part of Margaret's world. In fact, in one case Margaret chooses to believe one of them, even after she has learned that it is a deliberate fabrication, because somehow the account of a mother's mysterious suicide makes Margaret herself feel less exceptional.

The fact that tradition can be a source of security in this changing world is a major motif in the novel. In the early chapters, the references to liturgy and theology seem to be no more than realistic details in the lives of characters connected with the church; later, as chapters begin to have such titles as "Crosses," "Passion Week," and "A Reasonable, Holy, and Living Sacrifice," it becomes clear that the religious tradition is central to the book. The final chapter, in which Margaret announces her intention to study for the priesthood, is entitled "The Grace of Daily Obligation." Clearly, the title describes what Margaret has discovered: that self-fulfillment lies not in dependence but in selfless devotion to a higher good.

In her earlier novels, Gail Godwin created interesting, realistic characters who were faced with choices that were never simple. In *Father Melancholy's Daughter*, however, Godwin has produced a more profound book than her previous works by dealing in her characteristically honest fashion with the most difficult theme of all, the human aspiration for a spiritually significant life.

Rosemary M. Canfield Reisman

Sources for Further Study

Chicago Tribune. March 19, 1991, XIV, p. 1.
The Hudson Review. XLIV, Autumn, 1991, p. 500.
Library Journal. CXVI, February 1, 1991, p. 103.
Los Angeles Times Book Review. March 3, 1991, p. 2.
The New York Times Book Review. XCVI, March 3, 1991, p. 7.
Southern Living. XXVI, May, 1991, p. 83.
Time. CXXXVII, March 25, 1991, p. 70.
The Times Literary Supplement. May 24, 1991, p. 21.
The Times-Picayune. April 7, 1991, p. E6.
The Washington Post Book World. XXI, March 17, 1991, p. 4.

FEMINISM WITHOUT ILLUSIONS
A Critique of Individualism

Author: Elizabeth Fox-Genovese (1941-   )
Publisher: University of North Carolina Press (Chapel Hill). 347 pp. $24.95
Type of work: History and current affairs

A historical analysis of the current debates in feminism, issues such as abortion, pornography, the curricular canon, and postmodernism, with an overarching thesis that critiques individualism from a socialist-feminist perspective

Elizabeth Fox-Genovese, an early modern historian and head of the women's studies department at Emory University, has put together a book critiquing individualism from her socialist-feminist perspective, focusing on current debates in feminism and the academic community. Fox-Genovese is at her best when she is summarizing and critiquing the various positions in the debates, giving the context and historical background surrounding them; she is weakest when she attempts to propose her own program.

Fox-Genovese correctly analyzes the historical origins of feminism, tracing it to the development of individualism in Western thought in the eighteenth century. She goes on to show that, at base, feminism is caught between individualist rhetoric and social-communal needs. Individualism, argues Fox-Genovese, "actually perverts the idea of the socially obligated and personally responsible freedom" that is "the only freedom worthy of the name." Contemporary thought has perpetuated the illusion that individualism and collective life can coexist, while its rhetoric indicates that there can be no curbs on the individual will. Fox-Genovese attempts to theorize ways to protect the rights of the individual "as social, not private, rights," and (in good Marxist fashion) she wishes to ground the claims of society as prior to the rights of the individual. There are precious few specific "ways" given in the book, however.

In the first chapter, "Beyond Sisterhood," Fox-Genovese introduces her subject, focusing on the "equality versus difference" debate among women. This debate has raged for several years in the feminist community, at its most vociferous pitting minority and working-class women against mainstream, middle-class heterosexual white women. In essence, the conflict is about whether all women have certain shared concerns solely on the basis of their biological sex, or whether the different needs felt by different groups of women override these shared concerns. It is also a debate over assumptions made by the powerful larger group of women about the needs and desires of less-powerful groups.

In the following three chapters, Fox-Genovese looks at contemporary U.S. society (without saying so, she, like most Americans, generalizes from the American experience) and the issues that are most divisive among women: community versus politics (by which she means individualist, instrumentalist politics); equality versus difference (should women and men be treated the same because they are all human beings, or should women be valorized for talents and strengths that differentiate them from men?); abortion; pay equity; and pornography.

The chapter on community traces the history of the paired concepts of *Gemein-schaft* and *Gesellschaft* (community and society), enunciated in the late nineteenth century by the German sociologist Ferdinand Tönnies. Ironically, notes Fox-Genovese, the qualities he ascribed to community are those that are traditionally associated with women and the private sphere—tradition, family, emotionality, particularism, organic relations. The qualities he ascribed to society are those often associated with men and the public sphere—achievement, contract, rationality, universalism, individualism. Although feminist theory has tended, from Mary Wollstonecraft at the end of the eighteenth century to the present, to follow individualism and demand that women be treated as individual human beings, much contemporary feminism emphasizes female community and the qualities of the domestic sphere while at the same time calling for the rights of the individual. This logical bind traps feminists, according to Fox-Genovese. A few feminist theorists, notably Jean Bethke Elshtain, are agreeing with the critique of individualism made by conservative thinkers such as Alasdair MacIntyre, Michael Sandel, and Thomas Fleming. Fleming, however, while endorsing community, ends by putting a patriarchal family at the center of that community, Fox-Genovese asserts. The most creative thinkers on this problem—Robin West, Jennifer Nedelsky, and others—are approaching it from the perspective of legal theory and feminist jurisprudence. Nedelsky proposes a new model of autonomy "that will acknowledge the impossibility of separating it from the relations that make it possible and will thus build a social component into the meaning of autonomy itself." It should be noted that Fox-Genovese, in her discussion of the problems of contemporary community, does not mention either Robert Bellah's influential *Habits of the Heart* (1984) or the attendant literature surrounding that much-discussed work.

In considering the abortion issue, Fox-Genovese comes closest to advocating a program when she proposes letting go of atomistic individualism ("a woman's right to her own body") in the name of social justice for all (a society making a commitment to care for its children). She perceptively notes that both sides in the abortion debate conflate pregnancy with child rearing. Likewise, she brilliantly analyzes the comparable worth and pay equity debates by noting that comparable worth advocates assume a separate spheres model—that there are some jobs for women and different jobs for men. Setting pay equity into law does not go very far toward changing the view of a "natural" division of labor by sex.

The debate over the canon of prescribed knowledge in the U.S. educational system centers on the problem of adding materials from groups that have traditionally been absent from the educational system. It does not argue the question of whether there should be a canon at all. In other words, Fox-Genovese takes the more conservative position of expanding the prescriptive canon, not the more radical view that what is read is of less importance than the tools by which one analyzes it.

She foregrounds the importance of autobiography for any "outsider" group and continually finds useful W. E. B. DuBois' metaphor of "two-ness" in interpreting the psycho-political world of that group. "Two-ness" is the tension-ridden double consciousness that members of oppressed groups must possess and nurture, for an "acceptable" self must be presented and represented to the dominant culture, a concocted self that both hides and shields the "real" self at home in its ethnicity and history. Yet she pleads with such subcultures—African Americans, women, Hispanics, Asians, lesbians—not to throw out the dominant culture in the rush to identify and expand the study of the subordinate one. Instead, she cautions, study the relationship between the two, for the dominant has always shaped the subordinate. More telling would be an insistence on a study of how the subordinate has in fact shaped the dominant; that is much more difficult but at least as important. Fox-Genovese does not call for that, but she should have.

Double-consciousness is essential to any true historical study. It is similar to the concept of "world"-traveling that philosopher María Lugones uses in her by-now classic article "Playfulness, 'World'-Traveling, and Loving Perception," in *Hypatia* (2, no. 2, 1987), to explain the ontological status of those who live in several cultures, people who must be able—metaphorically and psychologically—to travel between worlds in order to survive.

One of the most important controversies Fox-Genovese examines is that between postmodernist historians and conservative historians on the issue of "the new history," including women's history. This argument has been raging with particular vehemence between Joan Scott and Gertrude Himmelfarb, both of whom Fox-Genovese castigates because she believes their positions are both derived from individualism. Himmelfarb's conservative ideas are based on the Enlightenment conviction that humans are "capable of rational knowledge and progress," a position implying "objective standards of excellence." Joan Scott, a self-described postmodernist, rejects this kind of history because it assumes that there is a "right way of telling the human story"; instead, "we must recognize all stories as of equal value." No person's experience should be privileged over another's; since "reality" is known only through language, "we must accept all language as equally valid." Thus, according to Fox-Genovese, Scott's supposedly more-democratic history refuses any criterion for distinguishing among personal "stories" and therefore for righting oppression and injustice. The logic of postmodernist feminism concludes that gender is "linguistic convention," ultimately denying physical difference. Worse, it does not take into account the unequal power relations in everyday life. As Fox-Genovese concludes, "A politically responsible feminist history must retain its engagement with women in the world. To accept a view of women as atomized individuals and simply to proclaim their right to tell their discrete stories obscures the structures—the specific social relations—that govern their lives."

Neither does Fox-Genovese agree with such historians of patriarchy as Gerda Lerner (*The Creation of Patriarchy*, 1986) or Dale Spender (*Women of Ideas, and What Men Have Done to Them*, 1982), who—she says—read history as a giant plot against all women and argue, ahistorically, that patriarchy has arisen from men's nature. This critique is certainly not fair to Lerner, whose thesis is that male dominance and patriarchy began at a specific point in history.

The problem with Fox-Genovese's book is that, since it is assembled from various articles written for intellectual and scholarly journals, its chapters do not flow from one to the other, and the argument often gets lost. In fact, the most cogent statement of the thesis is buried in the center of the book, at the end of the chapter on individualism and women's history. Often there is an explanation in the middle of the book that needs to have been made earlier, or, alternatively, the explanation was made earlier and has become repetitive. A related weakness is that, since some of the articles were not written for historians, Fox-Genovese makes broad generalizations unforgivable in a historical argument. Should anyone use the cliché "since time immemorial," for example, giving only one piece of evidence to support the generalization—evidence from the United States in the early nineteenth century? In another place she writes, "Such patterns of sisterhood existed in untold numbers of peasant societies," yet offers no supporting evidence whatsoever.

Throughout, the tone of distanced objectivity (Fox-Genovese repeatedly talks about "women" as if she were not a part of that group) is troublesome. Only at the end does she allow herself autobiographical disclosure—and this is revealing. She grew up privileged from the beginning. Her relatively early marriage (in graduate school) to a successful academic ensured that she would not learn the lessons of an outsider (that is, female) very quickly (except that, as the wife of a department chair, she would not be taken seriously).

In the spectrum of feminist theorists and women's studies scholars, Fox-Genovese appears to be on the conservative side. As a social historian, however, she is more liberal than many historians. She rejects the dichotomies that have rent feminism—gay/straight, radical/socialist, equalitarian/womanist—but in the end continues to advocate something like the socialist-feminist position she has always held. Given that position, it is strange that she did not bring to bear information from the social democracies of Western Europe to support her stance. Her analysis and arguments against individualism would have gained strength if she had used evidence from Sweden or (West) Germany. Still, the book is very useful—and sometimes brilliant—in its analysis of current feminist debates in the United States.

Margaret McFadden

Sources for Further Study

Booklist. LXXXVII, April 1, 1991, p. 1533.
Choice. XXIX, September, 1991, p. 150.
Commentary. XCII, September, 1991, p. 62.
Kirkus Reviews. LIX, March 1, 1991, p. 298.
Library Journal. CXVI, July, 1991, p. 118.
The New Republic. CCIV, February 18, 1991, p. 57.

The New York Times Book Review. XCVI, May 5, 1991, p. 12.
Publishers Weekly. CCXXXVIII, February 8, 1991, p. 46.
The Virginia Quarterly Review. LXVII, Summer, 1991, p. 105.
The Washington Post Book World. XXI, April 21, 1991, p. 4.

FLIGHT FROM EDEN
The Origins of Modern Literary Criticism and Theory

Author: Steven Cassedy (1952-   )
Publisher: University of California Press (Berkeley). 253 pp. $24.95
Type of work: Literary criticism

An examination of the myths and the mystical thinking that underlie modern American literary criticism and theory

Steven Cassedy's wide-ranging study is in part an intellectual history that traces the origins of modern critical consciousness to some unexpected sources. More than intellectual history, however, *Flight From Eden* is a book with a mission: to expose the varieties of mystification that characterize modern American literary criticism and theory in the structuralist and the poststructuralist era—the 1960's and the early 1970's. Cassedy identifies a number of self-deluding myths that he believes permeate the American critical establishment. Fundamentally, his purpose is to demolish the myth that there are no myths in modern American literary criticism.

A myth he attacks throughout his book is the one that claims the intellectual origins of modern literary criticism are the recent French professional critics and philosophers, principally Jacques Derrida and Roland Barthes. Cassedy argues that, in fact, its origins are to be found in some late nineteenth and early twentieth century novelists and poets in France, Germany, and Russia: Stéphane Mallarmé (1842-1898), Paul Valéry (1871-1945), Rainier Maria Rilke (1875-1926), Andrei Bely (1880-1934), and Velimir Khlebnikov (1885-1922). Although disclaiming any intention of writing an "influence" study, Cassedy shows a pattern of theorists such as Derrida engaged in "borrowings" (largely unacknowledged) from Mallarmé and others sufficient to call into question the "newness" of many supposedly "new" theoretical ideas. In an era in which literary criticism, with its forbiddingly difficult language and its philosophically obscure arguments, has declared its independence from literature, Cassedy seems to recall critics to an awareness of their secondary, derivative state. That literary criticism owes its very existence to literature would seem a fact too obvious to point out. In the 1970's, however, literary criticism itself became the important text. An example of this way of thinking is the Belgian-American literary theorist Paul de Man's definition of poetry as "the foreknowledge of criticism." Cassedy's attitude toward this development is surprising: Despite the fact that he continues to point out that "the poets were there first," in the end he seems to settle for an equality between theory and poetry, and the conclusion that "poetry and criticism are not so different," after all.

The principal focus of Cassedy's book, however, is a discussion of four major overlapping topics: language, theology, "relationalism," and ontology. In each of these areas, Cassedy attempts to show how criticism in the name of modernity has rejected an earlier, transcendent, mythic idea or absolute that he calls "Eden." In each case, he tries to demonstrate how this "flight from Eden" inevitably leads back to it again, to an unacknowledged repositing of Eden. In each case, he asserts that the revised myth and the belief that there is no myth co-exist.

In discussion of the first topic, language, Cassedy contrasts ancient and modern views. Given the woefully inadequate functioning of language today, it is easy to believe that language has somehow fallen from grace, that there was a time when language perfectly communicated in some ideal and mystical way. Cassedy argues that this mythologizing view of language has not been entirely abandoned: It survives in the tendency of some modern critics (including deconstructionists such as Derrida and Paul de Man) to privilege poetic/literary language. The modern version of the myth is that there is some intrinsic, essential quality in poetic/literary language itself that distinguishes it from, and for some makes it superior to, all other kinds of language. Cassedy believes the reality is that there are no innate and transcendent qualities of language. The effort to distinguish the difference in quality of language "between . . . a poem by Blake and a paragraph from a car repair manual" is doomed because of conceptual error. Language itself is not transcendent; it is something humans "ceaselessly create . . . for the purpose of meaningfully organizing our experience." Poetic language differs from prose "more by its function, by the way it is used, than by any intrinsic properties."

Cassedy's next topic is theology. Here, the myth is that modern literary criticism has liberated itself from theological and transcendent concerns and has become a secular, scientific, objective discipline. Cassedy has little difficulty in refuting this myth or in demonstrating that "all schools of modern criticism   turn out to be authoritarian, mystical, religious." He provides numerous examples to support his thesis. T. S. Eliot's concept of tradition in literature and the Marxist Terry Eagleton's devotion to the "socialist transformation of society" are examples of a new, unacknowledged authoritarianism. New Criticism itself became "a religious system in disguise." In discussing Russia, where the connections between literature and theology have always been strong, Cassedy reveals through an examination of the history of iconography the idealist assumptions that underlie both Orthodox theology and philosophy of language. Thus it is less surprising that the Russian-born linguist Roman Jakobson became enmeshed in mystical and religious ideas about the iconic properties of language even while he dreamed of a "science of literature." Poets such as Bely and Mallarmé either theologize aesthetics or aestheticize theology. As Cassedy demonstrates, literature itself as well as thinking about literature is permeated by theological ideas, and frequently literary theories are "a form of theology thinly disguised."

The third topic, "relationalism," refers to structuralism and its intellectual paradigm, mathematics. In the nineteenth century, mathematics shifted from an interest in the empirical and the intuitive to an interest in pure abstraction. The result is today's "formalistic mathematics . . . one that emphasizes functions and ordering operations over the empirical reality of the elements that are ordered." Following the lead of mathematicians, linguists and literary theorists began to look at literature as texts that can be "quantified, measured, diagramed, and reduced to airy structures of pluses and minuses." The essence of literature becomes the complex of relations it exhibits. Critics such as the French structuralist Claude Bremond set out to map a "logic of narrative" that will chart all possible variants of roles played by characters in fiction (such as beneficiary and victim or seducer and intimidator). Structuralists such as Bremond use charts, diagrams, and algebraic signs in their quasiscientific efforts to reduce literature to relational structures. In his discussion of Bely as "a structuralist long before Jakobson," Cassedy credits him with having shown (in "Lyric Poetry and Experiment") a correlation between a "scientific definition of rich rhythm" and the popular conception of "good" poetry. Bely took "thousands of lines of poetry and replaced them with boxes, rhombuses, baskets, roofs, crosses, and zigzags." Unfortunately, what Bely forgot is "what all the poems were about. There's nothing about the poor clerk whose fiancée has drowned in a Petersburg flood, nothing about the cheap pathos of the death of a peasant," in fact, nothing but geometric patterns.

In a provocative discussion of the Russian Futurists (who borrowed much from the Italian Futurists but concealed it, another case of unacknowledged origins), Cassedy shows how the vision of "the new as a source of human salvation in the twentieth century" is a common thread in an otherwise disparate group. The rejection of content, the rejection of nature, the blurring of boundaries between art and poetry, the effort to deprive language of its signifying function, the fascination with numbers— particularly the belief of Khlebnikov that numbers will replace words: In the future people will no longer engage in "abusive disputes, [but] will calculate"—all of these reveal a drive toward abstraction, which became the order of the day not only in Russian art but also in Western European art. To Cassedy, this abstraction is "just another form of mystical essentialism in a secularized form." Inevitably, it points to something beyond itself, "something insubstantial, invisible, or abstract, like the essence that hides in a sacred object." It is Eden, once again.

Cassedy's final and most elusive category is ontology, by which he means the ontology of works of art. What is "the peculiar manner of their existence?" he asks. Inevitably, one ontological question leads to another, which is perhaps why Cassedy's initial question nearly disappears in a kind of epistemology of ontology. After abortive excursions into the works of René Descartes, Alexander Baumgarten, Immanuel Kant, Edmund Husserl, and Waldemar Conrad, however, persevering readers are rewarded with the answer that if one is to discuss the ontology of literary artworks one must talk about the ontology of language, which brings one back to the beginning of Cassedy's book and the controversy over the nature of language.

The discussion of the ontological "myth" here is less satisfying, less clear, and less cogent than the discussions of the other myths. Yet the recurrent pattern of the flight from and return to myth and mysticism is again evident in the case of Rilke and Martin Heidegger, who both "show an essentialist vision that, though pretending to flee from the spiritual world of an earlier, Christian Europe, seems ever drawn back to it." Cassedy suspects that Heidegger's concept of "Being" is actually another term for God. He also finds significance in Rilke's choice of word to designate "the mode of being" of Rodin's sculpture: He called it *sakrosankt.*

Cassedy has written an erudite, engaging book on an important subject, a book that "will outrage some readers" according to a reviewer's comment quoted on the dust jacket. Many other readers are likely to find the book not outrageous enough. What is missing is any sense either of endorsement of or misgivings about the general directions the academic study and appreciation of literature appear to be taking. If there is anything that might provoke outrage in this book, it may be the cavalier dismissal of the case of Paul de Man and his pro-Nazi activities during World War II. If there is anything that still needs demystifying, it may be Cassedy's own unarticulated beliefs and values, as author and as professor of literature. His antipathy to socially committed criticism is clear from his comments about Jean-Paul Sartre and Terry Eagleton, but what, exactly, would Cassedy endorse? Does he believe a value-free literary criticism is possible? What is his real view of deconstructionists and their "lonely" view of language? Perhaps he would agree with Wallace Stevens: "The final belief is to believe in a fiction, which you know to be a fiction, there being nothing else." Then again, perhaps he would not. The fact that readers cannot be sure suggests that some mystification remains at the end of this demystifying book

Karen A. Kildahl

Sources for Further Study

Choice. XXIX, September, 1991, p. 85.
Journal of the History of Ideas. LII, April, 1991, p. 345.

FLOW CHART

Author: John Ashbery (1927-   )
Publisher: Alfred A. Knopf (New York). 216 pp. $20.00
Type of work: Poetry

John Ashbery's new book-length poem takes as its subject matter the self-conscious creation of the poem itself in a long stream-of-consciousness rendering of ordinary fragments of reality

Winner of the Pulitzer Prize, the National Book Critics Circle Award, and the National Book Award, a Guggenheim and MacArthur fellow, and chancellor of the Academy of American Poets, John Ashbery is one of the most honored writers of his generation. A new book by him is a literary event. It is important, however, in coming to a book by an eminent figure such as Ashbery—or a book by a poet being published for the first time—to set aside any preconceptions based on reputation or literary gossip, to read simply the words on the page—for that, as Ashbery and his followers have tirelessly insisted, is what poetry consists of: words.

In his new book-length poem, *Flow Chart*, Ashbery takes as his subject the task of writing a long, open-form poem about the process of writing that poem. His self-reflexive, opaque verse attempts both to capture its source in the deep wellsprings of consciousness and to comment on its genesis in an inchoate rush of language. The six parts of the poem alternate between text and commentary, although it is often difficult to distinguish between the two.

The poem's title reflects the dominant metaphor of the "flow chart," a contemporary image of administrative structure, hierarchy, and control or, in the definition quoted on the dust-jacket, "a schematic diagram . . . showing the progress of materials through the various stages of a manufacturing process." The title implies the author's own continual struggle to impose form and structure on his unwieldy materials. Ashbery's poem belies the implication of its title: There is no clear organizational structure here, not even the abstract lines of power and control of a corporate flow chart. Instead, his muse seems so distractable that he is unable to focus on the act of composition, so he offers random phrases—moods and impressions without a coherent context.

Cultivating a postmodern style, Ashbery refuses to concede to his readers even the most elementary structural forms or internal coherence. He rejects narrative coherence, or any attempt to impose form or order on the free play of his imagination. His voice is constantly being distracted by new impressions impinging upon his consciousness, but he refuses to impose any artistic form on these impulses. As a result, his verse seems to expend itself in tantalizing but unconnected and incoherent verbal energy.

Ashbery is often associated with the "New York School" of poets—Frank O'Hara, Kenneth Koch, and James Schuyler—and like them he shares a fascination with the Abstract Expressionist painters of the postwar New York art scene. He tries to capture in language the abstract energy and bold techniques of the canvases of Jackson Pollock, Willem de Kooning, and Franz Kline; or the nontonal sound compositions of Anton von Webern and John Cage. An art critic as well as a poet, Ashbery has consciously tried to incorporate the methods of the studio artist, using not form and color but the more inherently abstract medium of language. As a result, there is no attempt to create a shared discourse of meaning for poet and reader; instead, the reader finds an undifferentiated verbal collage of random impressions—clichés, banal phrases, trite expressions, vague and subjective generalizations about whatever comes to the poet's mind at the moment of composition. Disdaining any pretense of meaning, Ashbery's verse lapses into random verbal noise: "Alack he said what stressful sounds."

Aside from their commitment to experiment and innovation, the poets of the New York School were decidedly unprogrammatic. What they derived from avant-garde music and painting was a "concept of the poem as the chronicle of the creative act that produces it," or as O'Hara put it, the ambition "to be the work yourself." Ashbery's poems emphasize the fragmentary, tentative nature of experience, which in his view is too elusive to be captured in verse. His poetry is difficult precisely because it shuns the modernist conventions of form. His lines are dreamlike, nonsequential, solipsistic—an assemblage of personal associations, fragments of conversation, continually shifting excerpts of personal monologue. Ashbery's verse seems to aspire to a kind of automatic writing, but, without an identifiable authorial presence or center of consciousness, there can be no coherent stream-of-consciousness rendering of the speaker's experience. The poet refuses to locate the center of his poem within any identifiable context of meaning. There is no Mrs. Ramsay as in Virginia Woolf's *To the Lighthouse* (1927); no Leopold or Molly Bloom as in James Joyce's *Ulysses* (1922); no mythic protagonist as in William Carlos Williams' *Paterson* (1948-1958). It is as if, in the poet's words: "sleep itself became this chasm of repeated words,/ of shifting banks of words rising like steam/ out of someplace into something." His deliberate verbal disjunctions seem reminiscent of the dream sequences in Joyce's *Finnegans Wake* (1939). Like a vaguely remembered dream, the lines in *Flow Chart* are elusive and opaque.

Discarding linear order or formal coherence, Ashbery's poem invites arbitrary reading (or nonreading). *Flow Chart* can be read forward, backward, from the beginning, middle, or end with equal effect. Its purely hermetic verse can exasperate the most sympathetic reader. The lines tease the reader with their enigmatic sense of always being on the verge of revealing their meaning, but never quite doing so. The tedium and triviality of his verse in places invites parody.

Perhaps the reader may find a clue to interpreting *Flow Chart* in the term "participation," used by art critic Harold Rosenberg to discuss the Abstract Expressionist painters. Like the "action paintings" of Pollock or de Kooning, Ashbery's poetry demands active participation from the reader literally to create meaning from the text. His lines are deceptively reasonable and straightforward, but meaningless. For example, part 3 of *Flow Chart* begins: "That was the first time you washed your hands,/ and how monumental it seems now. Those days the wind blew only from one quarter." Now taken separately, each of these utterances has some verbal coherence, but juxtaposed, they work against each other, since there are no apparent connectives or transitions from one assertion to the next. Lacking those verbal connections, a line often seems to implode or collapse into itself. These unconnected assertions follow upon one another continuously, in a mockery of coherent discourse. The reader must take what the surface of the poem presents—since surface is all there is—and provide the verbal context, semantic connections, and transitions out of the poem's raw verbal material. There is no particular content or meaning implied, merely a sense of verbal activity. Can the poet really do with words what the Abstract Expressionist painters did with paint? Words, after all, are far more subtle, complex, and numerous than colors. Linguists have long assumed that there are an infinite number of meaningful verbal combinations possible. The reader needs some contextual clues in order to create meaning or even to sustain the reading act. The enormous psychological and aesthetic differences between viewing a painting and reading a work of literature would seem to mitigate against a purely abstract poetry. It may be possible, however, that Ashbery's intention is to frustrate the reader by undermining any possibility of shared discourse, by deconstructing contextual meaning, so that there is no real possibility of interpreting his works. His lines actively subvert the reader's expectations that the poem should mean something, that it should address itself to any sustained subject, concern, or feeling, and that it should do so in a logical and coherent manner. Logic and coherence are held up as verbal artifices imposed on inchoate experience.

Postmodernist critics may approve of Ashbery's poetics of indeterminacy of meaning, but does that not imply that he has refused the artistic responsibility of imposing shape and form on his material? Is there not a certain duplicity here: Why bother to publish anything if the world is truly as random and as chaotic as he suggests? If linguistic or epistemological meaning is impossible, then why write about it? Perhaps the poet gives his game away in his lines: "Words, however, are not the culprit. They are at worst a placebo,/ leading nowhere . . ./ to banal if agreeable note-spinning./ Covering reams of foolscap with them won't guarantee success." These lines seem to be more a confession of nihilism or futility than any poetic affirmation. As the speaker remarks toward the end of *Flow Chart*, "A lot remains to be done, doesn't it?"

One has to wonder whether Ashbery has ever put himself in the position of his readers attempting to decipher his work, or whether he feels any responsibility to his readers. Is Ashbery a poetic innovator or a master charlatan? Does he actually think this way, or does he deconstruct his thoughts as he writes? Is the poem supposed to represent snippets of overheard discourse, a collage of trivial, everyday comments made anonymously to no one in particular? Is it possible that in an Ashbery poem, as with the electronic media, "the medium is the message," to borrow Marshall McLuhan's phrase? Is *Flow Chart* the modern, electronic equivalent of Walt Whitman's "Song of Myself," the unedited rendering of images and fragments of cultural discourse? At times, Ashbery sounds like a modern Whitman, evoking the texture of ordinary life: "The baker comes out of his shop/ and smiles, rubbing his hands on his floury apron, and the wind/ picked up the veil off that woman's face and revealed her beauty/ before she hastily jammed the hat down over her forehead and trotted swiftly off." In other places, Ashbery's verse seems to echo the meaningless babble of countless radios and television sets overheard from a distance. The verbal cacophony all but overwhelms the reader: "Afternoons at the store,/ and when bluish evening, the color of television/ in a window high above the street, comes on, who has the strength to/ judge it all according to a pre-existing set of criteria and then live with it." We are awash in a sea of words and electronic images.

For all of its pretensions, *Flow Chart* represents much of what is wrong with academic poetry in this country. Ashbery's career as a poet has been nurtured by the academy; in fact, it can scarcely be said to have existed outside the academy. From Deerfield Academy to Harvard, to Columbia, to New York University, he has been steeped in academic discourse. His career has been subsidized by university appointments, fellowships, grants, and other emoluments. As a result, he has never had to write for a popular audience or cultivate a broad readership. His work has never really been tested in a broadly competitive literary marketplace in which it would have to be in some way accessible to his readers. His poetry has never had any reason to be intelligible because Ashbery has felt no responsibility to a general audience. Instead, he has largely written for a small avant-garde following of fellow poets, critics, and academicians. He has been able to scorn the normal conventions of meaning because he has largely ignored his audience.

Flow Chart represents a literary art that has utterly lost its *raison d'être*. Beneath the worn mantle of outmoded decadence, it mocks itself and its readers. Ashbery's poem represents a literary impulse that willfully and perversely denies any possibility of accessible meaning. A reader picking up *Flow Chart* for the first time might well agree with the poet's disingenuous remark, "It's the lunatic frequency this time." But perhaps Ashbery manages, in his closing lines, to mute the reader's frustrated incomprehension. In a modest disclaimer, he observes, "We are merely agents, so/ that if something wants to improve on us, that's fine."

Andrew J. Angyal

Sources for Further Study

Chicago Tribune. September 8, 1991, XIV, p. 8.
Library Journal. CXVI, May 1, 1991, p. 79.
Los Angeles Times Book Review. June 23, 1991, p. 8.
The New Republic. CCIV, June 17, 1991, p. 42.
The New York Review of Books. XXXVIII, August 15, 1991, p. 3.
The New York Times Book Review. XCVI, June 16, 1991, p. 12.
Publishers Weekly. CCXXXVIII, March 22, 1991, p. 67.
San Francisco Chronicle. July 14, 1991, p. REV3.
The Village Voice. May 14, 1991, p. 65.
The Washington Post Book World. XXI, July 14, 1991, p. 3.

FORD MADOX FORD

Author: Alan Judd (1946-)
Publisher: Harvard University Press (Cambridge, Massachusetts). 476 pp. $27.50
Type of work: Literary biography
Time: 1873-1939
Locale: Principally London and Paris

The disorderly and sometimes controversial life of the British author was the result of his dedication to his own writing and his activities in assisting other writers

> *Principal personages:*
> FORD MADOX FORD, the British novelist, editor, and essayist, subject of the biography
> JOSEPH CONRAD, the Polish-English novelist and collaborator with Ford in the writing of several books
> STEPHEN CRANE, the American novelist and friend of Ford
> EZRA POUND, the American poet and critic, friend of Ford
> ELSIE MARTINDALE, Ford's wife and the mother of two of his daughters
> VIOLET HUNT, a writer, Ford's lover
> STELLA BOWEN, an Australian artist, Ford's lover
> JANICE BIALA, an American painter, Ford's final lover
> ALAN TATE, the American poet and friend of Ford

Ford Madox Ford was an amazingly prolific writer of novels, works of criticism, and books dealing with the history and culture of his native England. Grandson of one of the eminent Pre-Raphaelite painters—Ford Madox Brown—in 1919 he changed his name from Ford Hermann Hueffer, partly in a delayed reaction to the anti-German sentiment in England occasioned by World War I, partly in homage to the memory of his grandfather. Since he was perpetually short of money, much of Ford's work was done hastily and carelessly to meet publishers' deadlines. The novelist Alan Judd in this biography, however, makes a strong case for giving Ford a far more important place in modern literature than he is usually accorded.

Critics have almost universally focused their attention on Ford's best-known novels, *The Good Soldier* (1915) and the tetralogy centered on World War I, *Parade's End* (1924-1928). Critical opinion for many years has placed both these books among the classics of modern literature. Judd sees considerable value in other works, including the nonfiction work *The Cinque Ports* (1900) and the trilogy defending one of the wives of Henry VIII, Jane Howard, entitled *The Fifth Queen* (1907-1908). In addition, Judd maintains that Ford was one of the progenitors of modern poetry, citing testimonials from poets as diverse as Ezra Pound and Robert Lowell to suggest that Ford's occasional poetry contained the seeds from which poetic modernism grew.

Earlier biographies, especially Arthur Mizener's *The Saddest Story* (1971), have emphasized Ford's many loves and his lifelong problems with money. Judd's book finds these matters unavoidable but mostly irrelevant, arguing that Ford's life is important only because of his writing and editing, and that a biographer's job is to place those literary activities foremost. He does, nevertheless, devote considerable attention to the less-literary aspects of Ford's life.

There is no question of the unconventional nature of Ford's life, especially his relations with women. It is Judd's conclusion that Ford was not much interested in sex, but that he had a compelling need to be close to women. He married Elsie Martindale in 1894, against the wishes of both their families. The marriage produced two daughters and lasted through various trials for about twelve years, until Ford's presumed affair with his wife's sister and a more protracted and public affair with the novelist Violet Hunt led to a breakdown of the marriage and separation.

He lived with Hunt for several years and went through some kind of ceremony with her that they seem to have believed was official, but Elsie, as long as they both lived, refused to give Ford a divorce. When Hunt publicly called herself "Mrs. Hueffer," Elsie sued her and won, in a much-publicized trial that gave Ford's reputation a blow from which it never really recovered. Several of his literary friends, especially Henry James, cut him off entirely, and even his closest friend and sometime collaborator, Joseph Conrad, found Ford's behavior indefensible. The two men were never as close again.

Early in World War I, Ford's enlistment as a junior officer in the British army, at the age of forty-two, was at least in part prompted by the desire to get away from Hunt, who had begun to terrify him. Judd argues that Ford's motives were also genuinely patriotic, and that he served well, despite a service record that contains strongly negative reports on his effectiveness from one of his commanding officers. There is no question that he was shell-shocked in 1916 and that his health suffered permanently from conditions at or near the front. He was sent back to England in 1917 and left the army in 1919. By that time he had begun to live with a young Australian artist, Stella Bowen, with whom he had a third daughter in 1920.

In the mid-1920's, while living in Paris and giving encouragement to younger writers of the "Lost Generation," he had an affair with another writer, Jean Rhys, but his relationship with Bowen lasted until 1928 or 1929. By 1930 he had contracted his final liaison, with the painter Janice Biala. Biala remained with him during the final decade of his life, which was spent in France and in the United States, where during his final years he was a visiting writer at Olivet College in Michigan. Biala, who gave Judd considerable help in the writing of his book, said that Ford had acknowledged affairs with twenty-eight women before settling down with her.

Despite his domestic entanglements, Ford was an incredibly prolific writer. Between 1905 and 1908, for example, he published five novels, three books about England, and two books of art criticism, as well as a number of essays and reviews. His first book, a fairy tale, was published when he was eighteen, his first novel when he was nineteen. In all he produced eighty books, including novels, collections of essays, fairy tales, travel books, literary biographies, collections of poetry, and other kinds of works. He wrote dozens of uncollected poems, essays, and stories. Despite all this activity, he never made more than a bare living from his writing.

Ford edited two of the most influential literary magazines of the century, the *En-*

glish Review (1908-1909) and, during his Paris years, the *Transatlantic Review* (1924-1925). The early magazine had among its contributors such luminaries as Joseph Conrad, H. G. Wells, Henry James, Thomas Hardy, W. H. Hudson, D. H. Lawrence, Ezra Pound, William Butler Yeats, and G. K. Chesterton. The latter journal published and gave important encouragement to a younger generation of writers including Gertrude Stein, Ernest Hemingway, E. E. Cummings, James Joyce, and William Carlos Williams. Successful as they were from an artistic point of view, both journals collapsed quickly for lack of funds.

It is highly unlikely that Ford will ever have a more sympathetic biographer than Alan Judd. The first words of the book set the tone: "There are also the rich in spirit. It overflows and is seen in everything they do. They are never mean, not even with money." Throughout this study, apparently to confirm this richness of spirit, Judd insists on the most generous interpretations of his subject's actions. In places where two or three observers have given accounts of an episode or incident that casts a bad light on Ford, Judd suggests that one can never really know the truth of what went on so long ago, as a way of suggesting that his subject probably was not as careless as others thought him.

It is clear that Ford was a generous man who felt his obligations strongly, even if he did not always meet them in conventional ways. He grew up in a family for whom the only possible careers were in the arts, and he found his niche in literature early. He assumed the attitudes of an English country gentleman: gregarious, generous, careless about money, patronizing but helpful to those less fortunate, resentful of many of the changes brought by modern life. At the same time, paradoxically, he helped usher in the modern age in literature and the other arts. His relationships with women were rarely easy and never conventional, but on the whole he was more kind to them than they were to him. Violet Hunt, in particular, went to extraordinary lengths to harass Ford after he had left her.

Judd is surely on solid ground in arguing that Ford's life, however interesting, is of less significance than his writing. Further, he uses good judgment in quoting copiously from Ford's writings, especially some of the less well-known, including his nonfiction books about England. The technique is less effective, however, when Judd prints great swatches of Ford's poetry, covering six or eight pages at a time. Since little of this poetry is known to the general reader, its presence here is helpful, but it undercuts Judd's claims for the importance of Ford as a poet. What is reprinted here is only occasionally impressive; more often it is melodramatic or simply undistinguished.

More serious problems are present in *Ford Madox Ford*. For one thing, Judd is less than fair to the academic critics who have done a creditable job of interpreting Ford's work and keeping his reputation alive; Judd is by no means the first, or even the twentieth, to argue that Ford is among the great novelists of the twentieth century. As his own limited bibliography shows, academic critics have seen to it that Ford's claims have not been ignored.

Further, Judd fails to provide any critical analysis of Ford's great works, *The*

Good Soldier and *Parade's End*. Despite his claims that they are among the major novels of this century, he declines to present any real commentary on *The Good Soldier* that would support those claims, instead saying that there has been enough criticism written about the novel. His discussion of *Parade's End* is limited to a brief discussion of the acknowledged weakness of the final volume, *The Last Post* (1928). Since his book seems intended for the general reader who is unfamiliar with Ford, his works, or the body of earlier criticism, this is a serious lapse.

It is paradoxical that *Ford Madox Ford* claims to be a book about Ford the writer but that its greatest virtue is the sense it provides of Ford the man. He comes through on these pages as generous and gregarious, a man who drank, loved to give parties, and was unfailingly kind. He was also a man who offended conventions and who inspired animosity from such disparate writers as Henry James and Ernest Hemingway. The social conservatism apparent in Ford's novels, which has troubled earlier biographers, is here presented as a natural result of Ford's heritage; the idea that the poor are better off if left to their own devices appeared cruel to Mizener, but in the age of Thatcherism it is obvious wisdom to Judd.

The true strength of *Ford Madox Ford* is its warmth in producing a portrait of a singular man and its success in making clear the connection between his life and his work. Many fact-oriented and detailed literary biographies leave the reader wondering how their writers could have done what they did. This book leaves no such questions. With his novelist's feeling for character, Judd has succeeded in conveying a strong sense of what Ford was really like, and why so many of his contemporaries were so fond of him and respected him so deeply.

John M. Muste

Sources for Further Study

The Atlantic. CCLXVII, May, 1991, p. 112.
Chicago Tribune. May 12, 1991, XIV, p. 6.
Library Journal. CXV, December, 1990, p. 127.
Los Angeles Times Book Review. March 17, 1991, p. 4.
National Review. XLIII, May 13, 1991, p. 49.
The New Republic. CCIV, April 29, 1991, p. 37.
The New York Review of Books. XXXVIII, May 30, 1991, p. 28.
The New York Times Book Review. XCVI, March 10, 1991, p. 7.
The New Yorker. LXVII, May 6, 1991, p. 108.
The Washington Post Book World. XXI, March 17, 1991, p. 1.

THE FORESEEABLE FUTURE

Author: Reynolds Price (1933-   )
Publisher: Atheneum (New York). 253 pp. $21.95
Type of work: Stories

Three long stories, set in the small-town South, share the common theme of balancing today's agonies and joys, small and large, against tomorrow's promises, real and imagined

> *Principal characters:*
> KAYES PASCHAL, a white man who leaves the black woman he loves, as well as his wife and child, for the unknowns of World War II
> WHIT WADE, a traveling insurance adjustor who returns from death to find the life he loves
> DEAN WALKER, a football coach tortured by the possibility of his wife's infidelity

Reynolds Price is wary of labels, especially the ones naming him exclusively a "Southern" writer. He would probably be just as uneasy with the description "novelist," for he is also a poet, an essayist, a playwright, a screenwriter, a professor, and a translator. He is a true man of letters for whom literature in its various guises offers the opportunity to assume the camouflage of form. For the occasion of his latest work, *The Foreseeable Future*, he assumes the mufti of a short-story writer, but, untrue to form, his stories are not "short"; nor are they long enough to be novellas. They are masterfully written odysseys that require just enough exploration to bring the characters "home," to force them to a reckoning with the future. They are also Southern in locale (all three set in North Carolina), Southern in certain eccentricities of speech and character, and Southern in sensitivity to time and place, but they are non-Southern in the universality of their concerns, in the interior peregrinations of their protagonists, and in the quiet resolution with which each pilgrim concludes his progress.

In "The Fare to the Moon," Kayes Paschal prepares to be drafted into the Army during World War II. It is an obligation he could possibly avoid by pleading that he is sole support for a wife and son. He has, however, already left his wife and son for the black woman he loves. In fact, his leaving places her in some jeopardy from the local rabble. Kayes and the other characters in this story define themselves in how they speak, in what they say. He and his brother, wife, and son all speak directly and honestly. Each, especially his mistress Leah, is dependent in some way on Kayes's decision to go for his draft physical, and each reveals in his or her own voice how this one good man's absence lessens life, makes it somehow more frightening.

Remarkably, in such a "brief" long story, Price creates whole characters, puts them in mild conflict, and resolves the situation with a lovely dream tale in which Curt, Kayes's son, can mourn his father's leaving. The language is spare, especially the lean, direct dialogue between the two brothers, both strong, rural men. It is a combination of poetic intensity and folk wisdom, especially in its more colloquial passages, as when Leah hears her mother described: "Your mama would crawl to the moon for a sound—music in her *bones.*" A young boy precedes Kayes into the induction center; he "took the lead with all the joy of a Judas goat at the slaughter pen." The meeting between Leah and Curt is for him painful but necessary, a chance to face the "clean dead-level eye-to-eye truth," a truth that also comes to Kayes from a strange source, a former schoolmate, who delivers it in a surprise "as unlikely as an angel visit." Riley Paschal tries to suggest a way for his brother to avoid the service: "You used to have your old heart murmur. What happened to that?" Kayes is ironic in his blunt reply: "My heart ain't spoke for years."

As soon as he has said it, he knows he is lying, and such is the power of Price's writing, where plot is almost incidental, that the reader knows it as well. Kayes loves all these people, even the wife he left for the more powerful, more passionate relationship that ties him solidly to the one place on earth where he can be whole and happy. Hitler and the "wide Pacific" are before him; "the people he crushed" behind. Yet in leaving them all he realizes that his desertion of them for Leah's "deep and steady" love was as necessary as breathing, the only completeness one man can find "this side of death."

In the title story, Whit Wade is a man returning from the dead. Resuscitated on a World War II battlefield, he cannot let go of the feeling that he is somehow not thoroughly alive. He sees himself as a sort of reversed revenant, returned in body but not spirit, a man who has to learn all over again how to live. Evidence that he is indeed alive greets him every morning. His wife and daughter are made of flesh and blood and with love to spare, but he is so haunted by death, his own and his companions' in battle, that he moves around them like a ghost. Symbolically, he is a claims adjustor for an insurance company and must travel for a week settling disputes, accepting or denying claims, and getting at the truth about the accidents for which men and women seek compensation. He sees himself in some ways as a victim, too, of an act of God, for which he wants to be reimbursed with understanding and a new life.

Price says that "Whit was used to God's silence," however, and he knows that he will not have two chances at dying without salvation. He believes that he has done as much as a man can by providing his family with "a stout dry house where women could face the night with no dread." Somehow, what he is expected to do is not enough. The war, his wounds, have robbed him of any reason to continue to do it.

His journey along the byways of North Carolina becomes an epic quest, an everyman's voyage to find a grail of self-knowledge, an elixir of life. The cupbearers are an eccentric, plain lot. Hungry and looking for a place to have his lunch, he stops near a trailer where lives Juanita, a medium, and her dogs. The meeting is a comic one, with Whit able to indulge his "pre-war" sense of fun to goad some wisdom out of this no-nonsense spiritualist. She asks the right questions and makes him describe his thoughts until he comes up with the right answers. She wants to know how he knew he had died.

> "I saw a vision of God as a boy or a tall young angel. I could see him talk music."
> "Had to be dead." Juanita was telling it straight to the dogs, and they consumed it with fixed

attention. For all the surprise her eyes betrayed, she might have heard such tales at least daily. Then she faced Whit again and beamed a new grin—she had what looked like fifty gold teeth and deep dimples. They took years off her, though not many pounds.

Throughout these stories, especially this one, Price infuses such humor and charges it with a generosity of spirit that is rarely mean or gratuitous. Whit embodies this spirit; his journey is no brooding, existential nightmare. His "death" is no less real for being accepted by so many people he meets as simply a matter of life. Everyone he meets contributes partially to his redemption. Whit finds that he can rely on family, friends, the goodness of children, and the careless kindnesses of strangers to show him how to live again. He is reborn through rejoining himself to humanity: "It smelled like a hint that average people—in trailers and at desks—were as ready as he for the slightest clue that a life of days, in this world here, could end up finally with a true meaning, not just the black grave."

Whit learns that living all over again means having to accept the pain, the guilt, and the joy that comes with it. Nothing can jolt him back to human feeling faster than a woman's tears: "Whit shared one trait with every other man—he'd had a mother. And whatever the cause, the sight of any woman in pain was always his own unforgivable fault." Equally upsetting is his encounter with another former soldier who cannot escape his memories of war, and Whit is forced to account for the real reason he did not go ahead and die young: He says it would have been "easy and cheap and hard on my kin." Back home, he finds himself useful to his family: Redemption means making peace with who he is, where he comes from, what he has fought for, and what he is prepared to do to meet the promises of the foreseeable future.

Dean Walker, in the final story "Back Before Day," also has a loving wife and child, Flynn and Brade. He suspects his wife not so much of infidelity but of the desire to be unfaithful with a friend who has loved her ever since high school. Dean seizes the occasion of her refusal to lie about her feelings as an excuse to escape into the dark night with his son. A jealous, possessive husband and father, a football coach who feels responsibility for his players, Dean is a relatively uncomplicated man on the outside. His anger at his wife and his inability to trust her feelings betray his own insecurity. As he tells her, his bad year in Vietnam has made him question his own worth:

> I want all grades of goodness that I don't have and won't ever get—the money to give you and Brade what you need, better sense than to sit here one more year and teach dumb boys how to crush each other. . . . I've turned out less than average, Flynn—a D-plus well-intentioned slack boy—and I never meant that, never thought it would happen. You know how fine I planned on being.

Again, Price allows Dean to show his essential goodness through the narrative; he tries to help a boy he once coached, he forgives his wife's terminally ill, would-be lover, and he returns with Brade to his home. Language is again direct, slightly quirky, and occasionally colloquial. The sex act, for example, is described in all its primal and ridiculous force: "They were close as two people manage to get, short of skinning each other, eating the choice meat and wearing the hide." Dean calms himself with his father's aphorism, "Don't ever think of your troubles in bed; you'll just want to die or burn up the world." The boy who makes a mess of his life describes how he felt when his wife left him, and he gets the saying a little twisted: "She left me last Christmas like I was some cold dog's dinner on the stoop, claimed she couldn't stand my ways."

Dean's fate is to shoulder his responsibilities with good grace, to stay decent and kind when life is most strange or hard to bear. "With that much duty on his plate for morning," each dark night promises escape only through dreams.

In these three stories, Price presents characters largely untutored in ontological or philosophical complexities. Unaided by arcane knowledge, they grapple with fate and how the small events of daily existence reverberate throughout one's life. For ultimate security, for example, Whit Wade depends on God, but He is so removed and silent that Whit must learn to rely on connections to other, essentially clueless, humans for guidance on how to get through the next day and night. Typically in Price's works, the characters look to signs that the world is an orderly place even though such calamities as war disrupt and distort life. Characters such as Kayes, Whit, and Dean try to interpret these portents, to divine the future through present mishaps, incongruities, or oddities. For ordinary men and women, such events illuminate, if only for an instant, the possibilities of happiness or despair around which they must make plans. They do not have to understand the unseen for it to become tangible, they can feel its effects.

Reynolds Price has written three stories in *The Foreseeable Future* that serve as an admirable introduction to his entire oeuvre. His general concerns and themes are all present: storytelling and interpretation of tales as a necessity of life; God's mysteries and people's need to understand them; the family, both nuclear and "of man" as the basic cohesive group for help in coping; and the delight in the language and wisdom of common men and women. One insightful critic, Lynn Veach Sadler, has referred to the "mystical grotesque" in Price's works. In these stories, life is not so much grotesque as slightly askew, and his characters struggle to set it aright.

William U. Eiland

Sources for Further Study

America. CLXV, August 31, 1991, p. 120.
Booklist. LXXXVII, March 1, 1991, p. 1283.
Chicago Tribune. June 2, 1991, XIV, p. 6.
The Christian Century. CVIII, July 10, 1991, p. 678.
Kirkus Reviews. LIX, March 1, 1991, p. 280.
Library Journal. CXVI, April 1, 1991, p. 154.

Los Angeles Times Book Review. June 16, 1991, p. 7.
The New York Times Book Review. XCVI, July 7, 1991, p. 5.
Publishers Weekly. CCXXXVIII, March 15, 1991, p. 44.
The Washington Post Book World. XXI, June 2, 1991, p. 1.

FRANZ KAFKA
Representative Man

Author: Frederick Karl (1927-   )
Publisher: Ticknor & Fields (New York). Illustrated. 810 pp. $40.00
Type of work: Literary biography
Time: 1883-1924
Locale: Primarily Czechoslovakia; briefly, Germany and Austria

A monumental biography which emphasizes the cultural and intellectual ties of one of the twentieth century's greatest prose writers

> *Principal personages:*
> FRANZ KAFKA, the noted Prague-born author of fiction and parables
> HERMANN KAFKA, his father
> JULIE KAFKA, his mother
> OTTLA KAFKA, his favorite sister
> MAX BROD, his best friend and literary executor
> FELICE BAUER, his fiancée for five years
> MILENA JESENSKA, his deepest love
> DORA DYMANT, his last love

No modern reader needs persuasion that Franz Kafka is one of the "sacred untouchables" of contemporary literature, who, along with Thomas Mann, James Joyce, Marcel Proust, and William Faulkner, ranks among the greatest prose masters of the century. His conversions of his private fantasies of guilt, shame, solitude, and dread into the materials of universally applicable art have succeeded both admirably and appallingly. The world has behaved as mindlessly and madly, cruelly and bafflingly as any image dramatized in his nightmarish fiction. Our time provides a continual exegesis of his work, which in turn has become an inner echo in our lives.

Kafka's posthumous reputation has been both enhanced and confused by a labyrinthine interpretive literature comprising more than fifteen thousand titles. As a way of justifying his addition to this massive bibliography, Frederick Karl seeks to present Kafka as the Everyman of the twentieth century's first half, epitomizing modernism, reflecting the collapse of the Austro-Hungarian Empire, depicting Central Europe's huge and rigid bureaucracy, exemplifying Sigmund Freud's leading theories, and prophesying, in such fables as *The Metamorphosis* (1915) and "The Penal Colony," the unendurable worlds of Auschwitz and the gulags. In 1924, dying, literally speechless (his vocal organs, his lungs gone), Kafka was known only to a small circle of Prague and Vienna intimates. He had published but a handful of tales, parables, and aphorisms; his novels were in fragments. Yet some forty years later, W. H. Auden could declare that Kafka's relationship to our age matched that of Dante and Shakespeare to theirs.

In an erudite, eight-hundred-page tome, Karl tries to explain the uncanny tidal waves that bore Kafka's idiosyncratic, localized, numbing vision across the planet, making it the accent and motto of our epoch, so that the term *Kafkaesque* has become what Karl calls "the representative adjective of our times." He sees Kafka as the classic outsider or victim, suffering from multiple alienations as a German-speaking Jew in a Czech-dominated milieu within a feudal and rotting Habsburg Dual Monarchy filled with anti-Semitic sentiments. Karl defines *Kafkaesque*, in its primary sense, as a perception of life in which the individual is overpowered or trapped by "the forces that wait malevolently for human endeavor to falter." Less persuasively, Karl also applies the adjective to Kafka's Sisyphean labors to do his writing, to struggle in lonely bachelorhood to fulfill himself through literature.

Unique to Karl's study is his focus on Kafka as a leading exemplar of high modernism, involving a deliberate and radical break with many of the traditional norms of Western culture and literary forms. He worked as an insurance company lawyer for an arm of the Habsburg Empire when that unwieldy government had lost all sense and meaning. He became saturated with Freud's concepts of the Oedipus complex and the role of the unconscious, even though he never declared himself a Freudian. In such early works as "Description of a Struggle," Kafka used the French philosopher Henri Bergson's notion of an intuitive stream of consciousness as more vital than conscious reasoning. Karl interprets Kafka's literary career as an effort to achieve a flow of associative memory, spirit, and intuition. Kafka envisioned his art as peeling back layers of existence, hoping to make the unconscious at least partly manifest, relying more on random reverie than objective reality, dramatizing a disordered, discontinuous, ultimately anarchic world in narratives that distort common experience.

Central to an understanding of Kafka as man and artist is an understanding of his relationship to his overbearing father, Hermann. The father, himself a butcher's son, had made his way from the Czech proletariat to respectable middle-class status as a wholesale merchant in Prague. In his hard struggle he had developed a cluster of qualities to which he probably owed his material success: self-confidence, selfishness, single-mindedness, ruthlessness, intolerance of opposition, bourgeois conformity, mistrust of most people, narrowness of interests. These were, understandably, the very qualities his son found not only alienating but awesome, not only dislikable but inaccessible. Moreover, this powerful but insensitive father expected his frail, dreamy, artistic son to succeed him in his business, since Franz's two older brothers had died in infancy, and the other three children were younger girls. Hence Franz Kafka, his father's heir-designate, bearing the brunt of expectations totally at odds with his temperament, could only prove a disappointment to his sire. No wonder Franz once considered collecting all of his writing under the single title, *The Attempt to Escape from Father.*

At the age of thirty-six, Franz wrote his father a forty-five-page letter that sought— but failed—to reduce the son's image of an omnipotent father-God and father-judge to the tangible dimensions of a flawed, capricious, often irrational human being. Franz wrote it as a plea for mutual understanding between them in their lifelong Oedipal struggle, but the purported love offering is, understandably, pervaded by his fear and envy of and rage against this man, whom he regarded as a petty yet awesome despot, grossly crude, vicious toward his employees, selfish toward his family, smugly successful in the business world but contemptuous of his son's genius.

Karl is curiously unsympathetic to Franz Kafka's battle with Hermann, pointing out that the son was not struck, manhandled, or otherwise abused, and that the Kafka household was no worse, indeed far better than most other European families. Kafka, he states, found his material in weakness, failure, defenselessness. Needing to reshape these characteristics into his writing, he could not let either of his parents escape his bitter indictment. When Franz discusses his feelings of worthlessness instilled by his father's imperialism, Karl demurs. After all, Franz had a law degree, held a responsible job with the Workers' Accident Insurance Institute which regularly promoted him, and had been publishing for seven years when he wrote his *Letter to His Father* (1952). Without his perceptions of failure, Karl argues, Kafka would have lost his most significant insights. Instead, the *Letter to His Father* validates such earlier tales as *The Judgment* (1913), reinforcing what Kafka had already composed, and perhaps indicating that he could not distinguish between fact and fiction—a disturbingly reductive judgment by Karl.

Kafka devoted most of his social energy to friendship with men, of whom Max Brod was his closest intimate. Brod was a man of extraordinary vigor, productivity, and generosity of spirit. Early in his association with Franz, he became convinced that Kafka would become Europe's most important contemporary prose writer. He therefore became Kafka's unofficial publicist and impresario; his strong will and optimistic determination contrasted dramatically with Kafka's anguished pessimism. Today, the only one of Brod's many works still available in English is his biography of Kafka.

Kafka was characteristically ambivalent about women. He despised his frail body, dreaded physical intimacy, and regarded sex as the quintessence of filth and the antithesis of love. His closest and most traumatic relationship was with Felice Bauer, a Berlin resident, whom he met August 13, 1912, in Brod's home; he was then twenty-nine to her twenty-five. They became engaged in April, 1913, disengaged that July, reengaged in July, 1917, and finally parted that fall after Kafka had suffered a pulmonary hemorrhage on August 9, 1917, and been diagnosed as having tuberculosis in the apexes of both lungs.

While no letter from Felice to Franz survives, his enormous correspondence with her forms an epistolary novel in which the two are the sole major characters, as well as an autobiography which runs parallel to the entries in Kafka's diaries. His letters have been published as *Letters to Felice* (1967; ably edited by Erich Heller and Jurgen Born). They have been the subject of a brilliant commentary by Elias Canetti in his *Kafka's Other Trial* (1969; 1974 in English translation).

This is a lacerating, soul-searing text as Kafka pours out, sometimes three times a day, a monumental case history of his melancholic despair of self, his obsessive divination of life as his merciless enemy. A note of macabre angst, of nervous self-derision is present from the beginning. "To make it short: My health is only just good enough for myself alone, not good enough for marriage, let alone fatherhood." Karl succinctly sums up the polar differences separating Felice and Franz:

She was practical, commonsensical, self-confident about her qualities and abilities, and singularly lacking in the degree of sensitivity and imagination which made Kafka so miserable and so creative. There was absolutely nothing in their personalities, needs, or outlooks that would . . . make them suitable for each other.

Kafka's only magnificent obsession proved to be for his writing. During this infelicitous courtship, he and Felice met only half-a-dozen times, with Franz usually avoiding sex. Again, Karl's interpretation of the failed union is antipathetic to Kafka: "Felice was not his trial," he states, "but a creature in a kind of experimental laboratory—it was as if he had suddenly acquired a trusting animal he could put through his paces."

In the last, increasingly illness-racked years of his life, Kafka did experience true love and brief happiness with two other women, Milena Jesenska and Dora Dymant. Karl's treatment of these liaisons is more understanding. He recognizes that Milena, unhappily married to a philandering husband, was almost Kafka's intellectual equal, also suffered from bad lungs, and shared with him avant-garde ideas, a rebellious spirit, and even an autocratic father. Dora Dymant was nineteen to Kafka's forty when they met in 1923 on a Berlin beach. She was preparing to become a Hebrew scholar, was idealistic, passionate, and lonely, and immediately fell under his spell. In the last months of his life, Dora was his good companion, nurse, lover, and surrogate daughter.

Karl wonders what Kafka would have done, had he met Dora earlier and moved with her to Berlin, a hothouse center for the avant-garde in the 1920's, where he might have met Martin Buber, Rainer Maria Rilke, Thomas Mann, Hugo von Hofmannsthal, and Stefan George—Karl does not mention Bertolt Brecht. Such speculation seems irrelevant, since Kafka's genius was self-germinating and his creativity only flourished in the most reclusive solitude.

In analyzing Kafka's fiction, Karl usually stresses its cultural analogues to modernism. Thus, Kafka's first, great story, *The Judgment*, is modernist in having lightly sketched characters who exist only in the foreground, in featuring a landscape of desolation, in having an insufficiently motivated and explained narrative, in dramatizing sexual battles whose causes are ambiguous, and in its pervasive mood of reverie, blurring what belongs to the mind with what belongs to the surface of felt life.

The Metamorphosis is modernist in its sophisticated use of Freudian psychology with regard to the Oedipal conflict, and in its expressionist means of revealing inward truths. Karl's reading is also political. The novella deals with the Samsas as "a miniaturized nation, collapsing within, waiting for the death of a member, then recovering in the wake of his forgotten sacrifice." Moreover, the novella anticipates the impending World War I, as well as Kafka's own breakdown.

Karl also has a political interpretation of *The Trial* (1925): It, too, captures the sense of Europe as it passes through devastating war and postwar disasters, and its plot of a never-ending court case is reminiscent of Captain Alfred Dreyfus' trials in France in the 1890's, with an imploding legal system and disintegrating society.

As for *The Castle* (1926), it chronicles a journey into negation, into disillusioning nightmares, into murky mazes of artistic confusion. Karl believes that Kafka had not clearly defined the direction in which he sought to take this novel. Despite its reach toward seemingly infinite distances, the work emphasizes extreme inwardness, thus conducting a dialectic of liberation and imprisonment. Karl regards the hero-victim, K., as an artist who must journey into unknowns in order to understand the nature of his vocation, yet finds himself compromised by his association with people who misunderstand his art. K. fails, of course. Despite all of his movements, he never leaves the outskirts of the village, never finds the path leading to the Castle.

Karl's study has a number of virtues: He is immensely learned, and his book offers a comprehensive perspective of social, particularly intellectual history. He shows readers the Austro-Hungarian Empire's unwieldiness and disintegration, informs them of the precarious status of its Jews, and minutely traces both Kafka's literary career and private pains. Yet something crucial is lacking in this book. Karl's tone is too often coldly impersonal and occasionally even hostile toward his subject. Does he even care for Franz Kafka? One cannot be certain. What is certain, is that Karl does not even come close to explaining the magic whereby a writer of narrow range, pathological fears, and self-destructive personality used his literary genius to create texts that have become the universal language of this century and provided passports for all contemporary journeys.

Gerhard Brand

Sources for Further Study

Booklist. LXXXVIII, October 15, 1991, p. 398.
Boston Globe. November 24, 1991, p. 17.
Chicago Tribune. December 1, 1991, XIV, p. 6.
The Christian Science Monitor. November 12, 1991, p. 13.
Kirkus Reviews. LIX, September 1, 1991, p. 1138.
Library Journal. CXVI, October 1, 1991, p. 101.
Los Angeles Times Book Review. November 17, 1991, p. 1.
The New York Times. November 12, 1991, p. C17.
Publishers Weekly. CCXXXVIII, September 20, 1991, p. 118.

FREDERICK DOUGLASS

Author: William S. McFeely (1930-   )
Publisher: W. W. Norton (New York). Illustrated. 465 pp. $24.95
Type of work: Historical biography
Time: 1818-1895
Locale: The United States and Europe

An outstanding biography of the leading African-American orator and statesman of the nineteenth century, Frederick Douglass

> *Principal personages:*
> FREDERICK DOUGLASS, a former slave, an activist for African-American rights
> WILLIAM LLOYD GARRISON, a leading abolitionist
> SUSAN B. ANTHONY, a women's rights activist
> ELIZABETH CADY STANTON, a women's rights activist
> ABRAHAM LINCOLN, the sixteenth president of the United States
> OTTILLA ASSING, a radical German supporter and possible lover of Douglass
> JULIA GRIFFITHS, an English reformer and longtime friend and ally of Douglass
> JOHN BROWN, the radical fighter against slavery who led the attack at Harpers Ferry
> THOMAS AULD, Douglass' slave master, whom he both loved and hated

Frederick Douglass was the most eminent African American of the nineteenth century. Born in Talbot County, Eastern Shore, Maryland, in the year 1818 to a slave mother for whom he felt little attachment and a white father whom he never knew, young Frederick Bailey (his given name), after twenty years of slavery, fled to the North, where he became a leading orator and editor in the struggle for African-American freedom and civil rights. Biographers and historians have made him the subject of many articles and books that have attempted to understand the source of his genius and the meaning of his remarkable life. He himself told his story in three separate autobiographies: First in 1845 he published his fairly short *Narrative of the Life of Frederick Douglass* as an antislavery tract; in 1855 he expanded upon this in *My Bondage and My Freedom*; and finally in 1881 his mature memoirs, *Life and Times of Frederick Douglass* (revised in 1892), appeared as an expanded narrative of his life, describing his achievements and honors received while calling attention to those denied him because of his race.

In the twentieth century, African Americans have found in Douglass' life a model for a variety of political positions, from Black Nationalist to accommodationist. His 1845 autobiography and the 1948 biography *Frederick Douglass* by Benjamin Quarles (reprinted in 1968 amid the civil rights struggles) became standard reading in many history courses. In the 1980's, two major additional works gave new insights into an understanding of his life: Dickson J. Preston's *Young Frederick Douglass: The Maryland Years* (1980) examined in greater detail than ever before Douglass' life as a slave in Maryland, and Waldo E. Martin's *The Mind of Frederick Douglass* (1985) traced Douglass' intellectual development through his writings. Now there is a splendid, highly readable biography, William S. McFeely's *Frederick Douglass*, that promises to be the definitive work on his life.

As a slave, Douglass was shipped back and forth between masters in Talbot County, Maryland, and Baltimore, where he eventually worked in the shipyards. Against the laws and traditions of the time, he learned to read, and when he was twelve he somehow managed to purchase for fifty hard-earned cents a copy of *The Columbian Orator*, from which he recited great speeches and learned the art of oratory. His time in Baltimore provided him with hopes of freedom that were dashed when his master returned him to Talbot County in the years immediately following the Nat Turner revolt. Back in Talbot County, his master Thomas Auld found religion at a camp meeting, and when a neighbor manumitted his slaves, Douglass believed he too might be freed, but once again he was disappointed. Instead he was hired out to Edward Covey, whom Douglass described as a "nigger breaker," not because it was Covey's profession, but, as McFeely explains, because it was his reputation. Covey was a sadist whose savagery "strongly suggests a perversion of homosexual attraction," and when he beat Douglass, Douglass, out of desperation, fought back. It was the turning point of Frederick Bailey's life: "I was *nothing* before," he later wrote. "I WAS A MAN NOW," and one determined to be free.

Thomas Auld next hired him out to work for William Freeland, evidently a kindly master, but a master nonetheless. While working for Freeland, Douglass, by then a tall, strong seventeen-year-old, and five "revolutionary conspirators" decided upon a plan to run away to Pennsylvania. Deceived by an informant, Douglass was placed in jail, and only through the intervention of Thomas Auld was he saved from being shipped south. Instead, he was sent once more to Baltimore, where he returned to work in the shipyards. Finally in 1838 he escaped and became a great abolitionist orator and leader and a prominent spokesperson for women's rights. With the outbreak of the Civil War, he strongly supported Abraham Lincoln's wartime leadership and worked to recruit black troops to fight the war. His own sons joined the Union Army, and one, Sergeant Major Lewis Douglass, fought under Colonel Robert Gould Shaw at Fort Wagner, South Carolina.

After the war, Douglass became a leading spokesperson for radical reconstruction and the rights of the freed slaves. "Whether the tremendous war so heroically fought and so victoriously ended," he wrote, "shall pass into history a miserable failure, barren of permanent results . . . or whether . . . we shall . . . have a solid nation, entirely delivered from all contradictions and social antagonisms, based upon loyalty, liberty and equality," was the question he raised before the nation. His struggles for the Civil Rights Acts and the Fourteenth and Fifteenth Amendments frequently ended in frustration, but through it all he maintained a view of the Constitution as a document that extended liberties and rights to African Americans. It was in part this faith that accounted for his split with William Lloyd Garrison before the Civil War and with the women's suffrage movement afterward. His fight to obtain a Constitutional amendment that would grant suffrage to black men came at the expense of women, who were omitted from the rights granted under the Fifteenth Amendment. Douglass' position in this contest created a rift between him and his old allies, Susan B. Anthony and Elizabeth Cady Stanton, although both were to remain supportive of him for the rest of their lives.

That the Reconstruction produced such few positive results for black Americans was a great disappointment to Douglass. Granted minor offices by Republican presidents, he was continually slighted at official gatherings. Publicly, he would shrug off racial insults, but in his private correspondence he would frequently express his pain. After having served on a commission to investigate the annexation of the Dominican Republic, all the committee members except for Douglass were invited to the Ulysses Grant White House for dinner. Privately "cut . . . to the quick," he publicly remarked, "there is something so ridiculous about this dinner affair." Often cantankerous, and always concerned about his reputation and position in Washington society, he found himself more and more subject to bureaucratic rejection and condescension as his worldwide reputation grew. Through it all he maintained his regal bearing and worked to provide for his family, frequently in need, and to promote justice for black Americans. Perhaps misled by his own genius and talents, he maintained a belief in individual self-betterment, a theme he had often taken in the 1850's, particularly in a lecture entitled "Self-Made Men."

In the last years of his life he made a visit to Wye House, where he had once been a slave, and sat on the veranda of the plantation, sipping Madeira with the grandson of his old master. This seemingly gave him great pleasure. On another trip, he returned to England for a vacation and traveled throughout Europe in the grand manner with his second wife. In 1889, at the age of seventy-one, he accepted the position of United States minister to Haiti and served with some distinction until 1891. His last public service was a speech he gave at a women's rights rally in Washington, D.C., on February 20, 1895. Returning to his home, his beloved Cedar Hill, he collapsed and died.

What McFeely adds to the well-known outlines of Douglass' life is a psychological dimension that, while sometimes forced, does fill out the picture and make his complex character more understandable. Douglass' slave masters, especially Thomas Auld, with whom he had a love-hate relationship, quickly perceived in him a person of extraordinary talents. It was the women of his youth, however—Auld's wife, Lucretia, and Douglass' grandmother, who acted as surrogate mothers; his Baltimore slave mistress Sophie Auld, who taught him to read; and Aunt Katy, the cruel disciplinarian slave—who gave his life direction; they had a tremendous influence upon his later feminism and lasting affiliation with intelligent progressive women, most of whom were white, such as Susan B. Anthony, Elizabeth Cady Stanton, Amy Post, Anna Dickinson, and Lydia Child. In these relationships Douglass was always more at ease and secure than he was in the company of men.

McFeely implies that Douglass was most comfortable with his African-American wife Anna when he was away from her, traveling on his grueling speaking circuit.

With his second wife, Helen Pitts, an intelligent, literate traveling companion, and white, he felt completely at ease. Of Douglass' long association with Julia Griffiths, an avid English antislavery activist who assisted him in editing his journal the *North Star* and traveled with him on many of his speaking tours, McFeely gives no definitive judgment about accusations of sexual impropriety by "vicious gossips." He suggests that the anger leading to personal and physical attacks was more a question of "the breaching of racial lines, rather than the breaching of conventional marital ones." The criticism over their relationship, even within the abolitionist movement itself, became so great, however, that Julia Griffiths, unable to withstand the pressure, returned to England, where she married a clergyman, H. O. Crofts. For the rest of their lives, Julia and Frederick continued their relationship almost entirely through the mails, although in 1886 Douglass brought his new wife, Helen Pitts, to meet Julia in Saint Neots, Cambridgeshire, England.

Equally disturbing to nineteenth century moralists was Douglass' close affiliation with the fascinating German radical reformer Ottilla Assing. More than any other woman's, her influence upon him was great. Here McFeely implies with greater certainty that a sexual relationship did exist between Assing and Douglass. In a letter to her sister, Assing wrote that "if one stands in so intimate a relationship with a man as I do with Douglass, one comes to know facets of the whole world, of men and women, which would otherwise remain closed, especially if it is a man whom the entire world has seen and whom so many women have loved." McFeely concludes that, "given his charm . . . it is hard to imagine that they took very long to achieve such a relationship." Even after her death—she committed suicide shortly after receiving the news of Douglass' marriage to Pitts—Assing provided for Douglass by establishing a thirteen-thousand-dollar trust fund in his name, giving him its income for the remainder of his life "in recognition of his noble labors in the Anti-Slavery cause."

Douglass' relationships with whites, particularly white women, dominate McFeely's biography. McFeely gives insufficient attention to Douglass' interaction with other African Americans while measuring Douglass' successes in terms of the evaluations of his white contemporaries. It is unfortunate that Douglass' affiliation with such contemporaries as Martin Delany and Charles Lenox Remond, after whom Douglass named one of his sons, is not more fully explored. Moreover, of Douglass' loving and close friendship with Henry and John Harris, fellow slaves on the Freeland farm, McFeely hints at a homosexual attachment that only serves to distract from their youthful revolutionary camaraderie. Somehow, McFeely's restricted vision detracts from Douglass' own evaluation of his struggle with Covey, and he judges Douglass' famous "Open Letter" to his former master Thomas Auld as misguided and unfair. These important episodes can be understood only in terms of Douglass' total denunciation of everything and everyone connected to the institution of slavery. Like all humans, Douglass had his flaws, and like all biographers, McFeely has his faults, but both the example of Douglass' accomplishments and McFeely's writing of these accomplishments are worthy of note and could serve well as examples for historians and activists who continue Douglass' struggle against racial injustice in the United States.

Norman S. Cohen

Sources for Further Study

American Heritage. XLII, February, 1991, p. 14.
American History Illustrated. XXVI, July, 1991, p. 22.
Atlanta Journal Constitution. February 3, 1991, p. N10.
Chicago Tribune. January 20, 1991, XIV, p. 1.
Los Angeles Times Book Review. February 3, 1991, p. 1.
The New York Review of Books. XXXVIII, May 16, 1991, p. 12.
The New York Times Book Review. XCVI, February 17, 1991, p. 3.
Newsweek. CXVII, February 25, 1991, p. 61.
The Times Literary Supplement. May 31, 1991, p. 6.
The Washington Post Book World. XXI, January 20, 1991, p. 1.

FREEDOM
Volume I: Freedom in the Making of Western Culture

Author: Orlando Patterson (1940-   )
Publisher: Basic Books (New York). 487 pp. $29.95
Type of work: History
Time: The ancient and medieval world
Locale: The West

A brilliant history of freedom, which demonstrates that freedom has been a central value in Western civilization since the time of ancient Greece

> *Principal personages:*
> PERICLES, the ancient Athenian statesman
> PLATO, the ancient Greek philosopher
> AUGUSTUS, the first emperor of Rome
> JESUS OF NAZARETH, the founder of Christianity
> PAUL OF TARSUS, the apostle of Christianity

Orlando Patterson's *Freedom, Volume 1: Freedom in the Making of Western Culture* is the first installment of a profoundly ambitious history of freedom in the West. Patterson aims high. He dismisses the erudite, yet heavily circumscribed, intellectual histories of freedom that have dominated the field. These usually begin in the Enlightenment and treat freedom only as a disembodied idea. Arrogantly, they assume the immaculate conception of freedom at the dawn of the modern age. Patterson answers this literature with a rich analysis of the origins of Western freedom, the history of which, he declares, is at once more extensive and bound up with the hopes and fears of ordinary men and women. Patterson demonstrates that freedom has been integral to the growth of Western civilization. Yet Patterson's book is not a triumphal tale of the progress of Western virtue. He argues, to startling and disturbing effect, that freedom was born of slavery. Patterson believes that the experience of enforced servitude led people to value and institutionalize freedom. This insight gives Patterson's account a moral profundity lacking in previous histories of freedom. His study makes it clear that freedom has been a persistently longed-for and fought-for necessity, rather than a historically adventitious luxury.

Patterson's treatment of the concept of freedom is both sophisticated and nuanced. He does not attempt to define the term closely. He treats freedom as a historical and sociological reality rather than as a dictionary entry. Patterson does advance the view that freedom is best understood through time as having three distinct yet related elements. Patterson likens these elements to notes in a musical chord, which, though emphasized at different moments, form a harmonious whole. This chordal structure gives Patterson great analytical flexibility in tracing the contours of freedom's evolution in the West. The first and most obvious element of this chord is personal freedom. This refers to the individual's ability to pursue dreams without restraint, either by the state or by other individuals. Patterson observes that traditionally implicit in the notion of personal freedom is the understanding that one's actions are limited by the rights of others seeking comparable goals and desires. Thus, personal freedom is premised upon a degree of social equality. The second note of the chord is sovereignal freedom. This form of freedom allows some to behave as they please, regardless of the rights of others. Sovereignal freedom, a perquisite of elites, flourishes in a hierarchical social order in which the individual is assigned a particular role. Those dominant in such a society, because of the very subjection of the bulk of the population, are able to enjoy a high degree of liberty and equality among themselves. Though sovereignal freedom flies in the face of the contemporary understanding of freedom, Patterson notes that it was the preponderant conception of freedom for most of Western history. The final element of the chord is civic freedom. This refers to the capacity of people living in a state to participate in its governance. This sense of freedom comes from belonging to an established community and enjoying the privileges of membership. Civic freedom, unlike sovereignal freedom, assumes specific social obligations to a clearly defined political structure. Patterson hastens to point out that civic freedom does not necessarily require modern democracy. There have been many republics in the past, including that of the United States, that have limited political rights to a select group of citizens. All three elements of the chord, while more or less visible at particular periods in Western history, have been vital components of the Western intellectual tradition. The tensions between them explain the ongoing Western debate over freedom's meaning.

Though freedom is now an almost universally acclaimed value, there is nothing natural about this modern doctrine. The birth of the concept of freedom in the West resulted from particular historical circumstances. To underscore this point, Patterson briefly explores the failure of the non-Western world to cultivate freedom as a value. Most civilizations did not even possess a word to express the idea of freedom before they experienced contact with the West. Virtually every human society has, however, shared the institution of slavery, which for Patterson is the essential prerequisite for freedom. By its very nature, slavery created a class of people desperately yearning for a change in their situation, while their plight reminded nonslaves of the precariousness of their own position and the sweetness of their liberties. At the same time, the presence of a group of people in a community who were at once socially dead and completely at the mercy of their masters created problems for the nonslave population. In the most primitive slave societies, slaves served merely as adornments to the honor of their masters, and performed no significant function beyond this. Once slaves took on economic importance, however, the question arose of how to motivate them. Physical coercion alone usually proved inefficient, so masters held out to slaves the promise of release from their condition. Emancipation in non-Western societies did not lead to freedom in the Western sense, because that value held little appeal to cultures that emphasized social position as the individual's key to self-worth. In such societies, the individual was understood as a member of a class or clan, outside of which life had no meaning. Slaves emancipated in this social environment did not desire the modern conception of freedom, which would lead to a frightening social marginality, but rather a status enabling them to be integrated into the community. Thus, in the non-Western world, the ubiquity of slavery resulted only in the efflorescence of social stratification.

Freedom waited for the ancient Greeks to emerge into history. The Greeks, through a combination of lucky circumstance and hard effort, created an environment that nurtured freedom. Patterson describes a complex series of events that paved the way for the advent of freedom in the leading Greek city-state of Athens. Of crucial importance were economic developments that broke up the traditional structure of Athenian society during the sixth and fifth centuries B.C. Upper-class Athenians began cultivating labor and capital-intensive cash crops such as olives, figs, and grapes. Poorer farmers found themselves unable to compete with the larger estates and fell into economic bondage to the elite. The impoverished masses began to agitate in self-defense and threatened the aristocracy's traditional ascendancy. An influx of foreign-born slaves helped defuse the situation by providing the great landowners with the labor they needed. Simultaneously, the elite moved to protect its power by granting significant political concessions to the people and by inculcating an ethos of citizenship that emphasized the solidarity of all Athenians, regardless of class, against the slaves and freedmen in their midst. This political organization of ordinary Athenians accelerated the development of personal and civic freedom. The threat of Persian conquest during the Persian Wars of the early fifth century B.C. inspired the exaltation of sovereignal freedom. Greeks, in Athens and elsewhere, increasingly came to see themselves as free citizens, subject only to law, and as such different from, and superior to, the subjects of the monarchical despotisms beyond their borders. That their cherished independence came at the expense of a burgeoning population of unfree and disenfranchised laborers, and their own wives and daughters, troubled them not at all. The celebration of freedom in ancient Greece reached its apogee in Pericles' funeral oration, recorded in Thuscydides' history of the Peloponnesian War. Pericles, Athens' greatest statesman of the fifth century B.C., distinguished and honored all three elements of Patterson's chord of freedom. More than four hundred years before Christ, freedom as a fully articulated value, easily recognizable to a modern perception, had received widespread acceptance in Greece.

The decline of the traditional Greek city-state as a result of a series of debilitating wars in the fifth and fourth centuries B.C. led to the conquest of Greece by the kingdom of Macedonia. The Hellenistic Age that ensued was an age of despots, and the ideal of civic freedom necessarily suffered. A series of Greek philosophers responded to the changed political climate by shifting their speculative concerns from the demands of public life to the rewards of cultivating the inner being. Plato began this intellectual transformation by insisting that the external world of everyday events and objects merely reflected faintly the true realm of pure form. Wisdom lay in privately seeking virtue rather than pursuing the satisfactions of worldly success. The Stoics continued the quietist trend by identifying the good life with an inner adherence to the laws of nature. Freedom lay in achieving harmony with one's environment. The Stoic concern for individual enlightenment made it the ideal philosophy for the empire Rome forged from the wreckage of the Hellenistic kingdoms.

The Roman Empire preserved, if it did not equally implement, all the elements of the chord of freedom. Because of the enduring power of the aristocracy, the Roman Republic never achieved true democracy. The senatorial elite, exploiting the most extensive slave system of Western antiquity, enjoyed sovereignal freedom, and, as a consequence of their roles as legislators and administrators, evolved a political culture that exhibited a genuine sense of civic freedom. The lower orders of Roman society struggled against the oppression of the aristocracy and clung fiercely to the laws promulgated to protect their personal freedom. The advent of the Roman emperors saw a tacit public settlement in Rome. In exchange for imperial protection of their established liberties, the people agreed to sustain the new regime against its senatorial critics. This Imperial Roman model of freedom heavily influenced early Christianity. Though the movement begun by Jesus of Nazareth originated as a largely eschatological cult, it contained within it the seeds of a radically new view of freedom. Over time, Christianity developed into a religion the core value of which was freedom; the pivotal figure in this transformation was the apostle Paul. The genius of Paul lay in conceiving of Christianity as a religion of liberation. He accomplished this by elaborating the Christian doctrine of redemption. Christ's sacrifice on the cross made possible the spiritual rebirth of the individual and the establishment on earth of a community of believers, marked by a loving relationship of personal freedom. The chief hope of the believer, though, was identification with God in the afterlife, this willing surrender to the divine a recognition of the supreme sovereignal freedom of God. Paul's teachings brilliantly recapitulated in spiritual terms the secular experience of ordinary Romans. The liberating egalitarian impulses of the early Church tapped long-repressed aspirations among the people, while trusting submission to God came easily to people taught to revere the emperor. Pauline Christianity proved to have particular appeal to the extensive class of freedmen in Imperial Rome, who saw in it a reified reenactment of their own personal odysseys. Following the collapse of the Roman Empire, the Catholic church would nurture the value of freedom in the West. Even at the height of the Middle Ages, when the bulk of the population of Western Europe labored in various forms of servitude for their lords, the spirit of freedom showed itself to be remarkably tenacious. Villagers and townsmen worked incessantly to extract charters of liberties from the aristocracy. In the heart of what an earlier generation of historians foolishly termed a "dark age," men and women regarded freedom as a constitutive value in their lives.

Patterson's proof of the antiquity of freedom as a value in the West is a major achievement. As he notes himself, a subsequent volume continuing his history will only record the elaboration of patterns long established. Patterson's bold and brave book traverses many disciplinary boundaries as he tracks his multifaceted quarry. This leaves him vulnerable to occasional errors in detail or judgment, but these minor faults are overborne by the advantages of Patterson's synoptic method, which makes possible many fresh and fruitful insights. An important and attractive element of Patterson's analysis is his treatment of the role of women in the realization of Western freedom. Patterson believes that Greek women were instrumental in the articulation of personal freedom. Because of their peculiarly vulnerable situation, subject to the wills of fathers, husbands, and brothers, these women early spoke for moral autonomy and constructed an ethic centered on the necessary dictates of the human heart, as opposed to the legalistic norms of their masculine society. Patterson's sources for these speculations are somewhat questionable, being largely based on the female characters in tragic dramas written by men. Nevertheless, his argument is evocative and thought-provoking. Patterson is on much firmer historical ground in his discussion of the creative ways religious women in the Middle Ages carved out a sphere of freedom for themselves. These women, both in established orders and in lay movements, advocated an emotional, mystical union with God and a radical egalitarianism on earth. Patterson asserts, with good reason, that these women might have been the most free the world has seen.

Cogently written and encyclopedic in scope, Patterson's work breaks new intellectual ground. His linking of slavery and freedom is a sobering reminder of the darkness that coexists with the light in the human spirit. This is an important book that will spark debate for many years.

Daniel P. Murphy

Sources for Further Study

Boston Globe. December 3, 1991, p. 61.
Library Journal. CXVI, July, 1991, p. 112.
New Statesman and Society. IV, September 20, 1991, p. 43.
The New York Times Book Review. XCVI, November 17, 1991, p. 23.
The New Yorker. LXVII, September 23, 1991, p. 116.
Newsweek. CXIX, January 13, 1992, p. 60.
Publishers Weekly. CCXXXVIII, April 12, 1991, p. 47.
The Times Literary Supplement. October 25, 1991, p. 8.
U.S. News and World Report. CXI, December 16, 1991, p. 53.
The Washington Post. November 21, 1991, p. D1.

THE GENERAL OF THE DEAD ARMY

Author: Ismail Kadare (1936-   )
First published: Gjenerali i ushtrise se vdekur, 1963, in Albania
Translated from a French translation of the original Albanian by Derek Coltman
Publisher: New Amsterdam (New York). 256 pp. $18.95
Type of work: Novel
Time: 1962-1963
Locale: Albania

An Italian general and a priest are charged with supervising the recovery of the remains of their countrymen who fell in Albania during World War II and are confronted with the grim scars the war has left on the people of both nations

> Principal characters:
> THE GENERAL, an enthusiastic officer whose belief in the heroic nature of his mission rapidly erodes as the tragedy and the absurdity of his task sink in
> THE PRIEST, a remote, self-controlled clergyman; appointed as the spiritual comforter for the general, he attempts to understand the mentality of the Albanians, whose language he speaks fluently, by applying his knowledge of psychology
> COLONEL Z., the highest-ranking among the dead soldiers, who was the commander of the "Blue Battalion," a punitive unit responsible, like its leader, for many war crimes and atrocities
> THE OLD ROADMENDER, the foreman of the Albanian crew of workers, who is eventually killed through his contact with the still-infectious remains of the dead Italians
> THE ALBANIAN EXPERT, a young and elegant liaison person, translator, and obvious mouthpiece of the positions held by official Albania
> THE GERMAN TEAM, consisting of a one-armed lieutenant-general and a mayor who are embarked on a similar mission to that of their Italian colleagues and who behave with great insensitivity

Occasionally, history presents humanity with a bitter twist of events the intricacy of which seems to surpass the plotting of even the most skilled novelist or playwright; just such an occurrence appears to have happened in the case of the American reissue of Ismail Kadare's first novel *The General of the Dead Army* (1970). Kadare's novel, which celebrates the fierce fighting spirit and the nationalistic, independence-minded pride of Albania's Communist inhabitants, is offered to an English-speaking readership in the same year in which masses of desperate young Albanians fled to the shores of Italy, from which they were returned, sometimes at gunpoint, to a homeland still in the grip of hard-line Communism. Life has offered similarly drastic changes to the author himself, making him a political exile. As minister without portfolio under Albania's late Stalinist dictator Enver Hoxha, Kadare was among the privileged few Albanians permitted to travel to the West; in 1990, he fled the new Communist regime to settle in France.

Yet for an American reader, the irony of history that is so closely linked to *The General of the Dead Army* does not stop there. Instead, the mission of the Italian general and his priest, with its goal of repatriating the remains of soldiers resting in hostile soil, conjures up stark memories of the United States' plight in the aftermath of the Vietnam War—a parallel established at the end of Kadare's novel as early as 1963, when the general ponders the difficulties that his American North Atlantic Treaty Organization (NATO) colleagues "are facing in the jungles of Vietnam."

With its painfully curious place in contemporary history, Kadare's first novel derives its narrative strength and literary distinction from its structuring around the theme of the human price of war. Within this framework, the text gains special relevance by asking the challenging questions of how far guilt and shame for past actions, together with an inability to forgive, stand in the way of eventual reconciliation. Consequently, when the general and the priest land in Albania—the small Balkan country brutally invaded by Benito Mussolini's forces in 1939 and used as a launching stage for a disastrous campaign against Greece in 1940—and are greeted by a handful of officials, their governments have hammered out a careful agreement that permits the Italians to search for, exhume, and bring home their men. Yet the relationships among the individual people of both nations, who all grieve for their war dead and harbor old hatreds for one another, are even more difficult to put together than a diplomatic treaty and cannot be sorted out with the same bureaucratic efficiency with which each individual set of remains is packed, cataloged, and stored in an Albanian warehouse before being shipped back home as one big, silent cargo.

As their small team begins its sad operations, the general's sense of self-importance and his conception of his task in mythological rather than realistic terms is quickly washed away by the relentless rain of the November-gray Albanian countryside and the inherent ghoulishness of his more and more disquieting, monotonous, and frustrating task. Even though the general is aided by maps and lists that theoretically locate the wartime burial grounds and determine the identities of the men interred there, reality often throws up unexpected difficulties ranging from the cumbersome to the absurd, and the search becomes more and more drawn out as the weather deteriorates, in clear correspondence to the weakening of the general's morale.

Returning his characters to the capital city of Tirana after a first tour through the battlefields of the past, Kadare uses this brief rest to demonstrate how differently the general and the priest try to come to terms with their morbid experience and with the demise of the Italian army in Albania. In a clearly symbolic act that foreshadows the novel's climax, the general is barred by the silent command of the preternaturally self-controlled priest from rejoining life, which is allegorically represented through the young couples who meet to dance in the basement of the hotel where the two foreigners are staying. Seeking solace in alcohol instead, the general becomes irritated by the abstemious, aloof, and disciplined priest. The general in turn suspects the priest of having an immoral sexual affair with the attractive widow of Colonel Z., whose rich and aristocratic family had sought out the two men before their departure for Albania, as many relatives of the dead soldiers had done.

Thrown back on themselves in a difficult environment, the general and the priest act humanely and develop a close relationship, which their differences of character nevertheless keep extremely volatile and dynamic. Speaking as hostile, capitalist individuals, the two men paradoxically allow Kadare to deviate from the strict aesthetic prescriptions of "socialist realism" and to probe different literary approaches through their dialogue. Thus, while Kadare's descriptions of the joyful young couples and his seemingly casual yet highly functional insertion of such ideologically important details as the "two dishes piled high with oranges and apples" atop the hotel bar—to disprove Western notions of shortages—are clearly conformist, his narrative is certainly not so where the "deviant" characters of the general and the priest are concerned.

Even though this straying from the path of Communist orthodoxy obliged Kadare to rewrite parts of *The General of the Dead Army* before it could be published in Albania, his text still speaks with a remarkably independent voice, which often manifests itself through his examination of the two strangers—foreigners whose country has brought so much misery to their hosts. The artistic movement of the theater of the absurd, for example, is persistently and directly alluded to by the general, who confides in the priest that their conversations remind him of the "dialogues from some of the modern plays" he has seen (and his author must have read). Furthermore, the novel goes as far as to bestow great narrative attention on the priest's psychological, rather than Marxist-Leninist, thinking about the Albanian national character. Despite the fact that he starts his hostile analysis from such a "bourgeois," and thus "false," premise, his findings persuasively describe a people who are "so wild, so formidable" that "when they have once begun to fight there is no limit to how far they are prepared to go"; thus, they were able to shake off foreign subjugation and, it is implied, pose a serious threat to any future invader.

Against these prominently placed musings of the priest, the official, doctrinal explanation looks strangely isolated. It is, moreover, expressed only once—by the Albanian expert, as he responds directly to the priest and insists that to believe in a collective Albanian psyche is simply to be misled by what are in reality the remnants of "customs that were once imposed on us by our former oppressors and religion."

Having created for himself this degree of narrative freedom, Kadare continues to explore the full dimensions of the two Italians' confrontation with the slow-healing wounds made by the war. In accordance with this design, they soon meet an almost identical team of Germans, a lieutenant-general who lost one arm in the war and a fat mayor, who are engaged in a similar task made more difficult by their lack of clear maps. After their first encounter, the Italians learn that their more ruthless and more desperate doubles do not shy from stealing Italian dead and sending them back to Germany as their own men when their search does not turn up quickly enough a sufficient number of bodies; the mayor, moreover, is recalled when it is found out that he has accepted money for the speedy repatriation of specific soldiers who come from a well-off family.

Against this backdrop of grave robbery and disconsolate exhumation parties, the Albanian people are portrayed as possessing an inner strength and pride that make them bear the enterprise of the foreigners whose comrades once killed their own people. Their strength lets them accept even the death of the old roadmember, who, in another instance of the novel's many symbolic events, is killed by a virus from one of the dead soldiers. In a further dramatization of the Albanians' reaction to their plight, Kadare quotes from the Albanian partisans' appeal to feed the Italian deserters and not to kill their defeated enemies. He also introduces the story of the brothel that the Italians erect in his—and Enver Hoxha's—outraged hometown of Girokaster, a city that would figure centrally in his later novel *Kronikë në gur* (1971; *Chronicle in Stone*, 1987), which also contains this episode. There, in what is perhaps their single humane act, the fascist troops erect a marble monument, ironically the most splendidly adorned of all the graves the general and priest encounter, for a prostitute killed by an enraged city man whose son had fallen in love with her.

At the climax of the novel, the thoroughly disillusioned general finally overrides the objections of the priest, and together they attend a rural wedding party. History at last catches up with them, as they are confronted with both the presence of the war crimes of Colonel Z. and their own inability to evade the collective guilt of their nation. Old Nice, whose husband was hanged by Colonel Z. and whose fourteen-year old daughter was violated angrily throws at the general a sack that contains the bones of Colonel Z., whom she has murdered in revenge. Deeply troubled by his collective shame, the general ultimately tries to rid himself of his symbolic burden by throwing the sack in a raging river, thus preventing Colonel Z.'s family from going through with the charade of ceremonially interring him in a marble tomb erected for the purpose. During a desperate, drunken binge with his German counterpart, through which the general tries to escape the flood of telegrams sent by Colonel Z.'s family, the one-armed German offers to sell him one of his skeletons to satisfy the family and cash in on the promised honorific rewards. Yet the general has seen too much to agree, and on the Albanian day of liberation leaves the country together with the sullen priest, who has not forgiven him for his disposal of the sack.

With his final, liberating act, the general thus transcends the obvious limitations imposed on him by his rank and his mission and proves that an individual has the chance to act on an ethical decision, even if this act is only symbolic and can neither reanimate the dead nor right past wrongs. Because of similar independence of spirit, Kadare's *The General of the Dead Army* remains a powerful vision of national guilt and the individual's responsibility to live up to the challenges posed by a ferocious past. Unlike the regime under which it was written, Kadare's novel has stood the test of time well, and its message has a timeless clarity and relevance.

R. C. Lutz

Sources for Further Study

Boston Globe. March 20, 1991, p. 71.
National Catholic Reporter. November 22, 1991, p. 36.

The New York Times Book Review. XCVI, July 28, 1991, p. 18.
San Francisco Chronicle. May 5, 1991, p. REV9.
World and I. VI, April, 1991, p. 369.
World Literature Today. LXV, Autumn, 1991, p. 746.

GOETHE
The Poet and the Age, Volume I: The Poetry of Desire (1749-1790)

Author: Nicholas Boyle
Publisher: Oxford University Press (New York). Illustrated. 807 pp. $30.00
Type of work: Literary biography
Time: 1749-1790
Locale: Germany and Italy

The first volume of a projected three-volume biography of Johann Wolfgang Goethe, the greatest of all German writers

> *Principal personages:*
> JOHANN WOLFGANG GOETHE, the poet, dramatist, and sage
> FRIEDRICH SCHILLER, his friend, a distinguished poet and dramatist in his own right
> CHARLOTTE VON STEIN, Goethe's greatest woman friend

Havelock Ellis called George Henry Lewes's biography of Johann Wolfgang Goethe, originally published in 1863, "one of the most admirable biographies in the English Language." It is certainly the best biography of Goethe in English that we have had to this point, but Nicholas Boyle's superbly researched and brilliantly written study may finally give his Victorian predecessor strong competition for the honor of being the best Goethe biography in English. Lewes, George Eliot's lover and a fine journalist and critic, had met Goethe and had the advantage of living in the century that felt Goethe's presence and authority with the same awe and respect that the twentieth century felt for an Einstein or a Joyce. Nevertheless, Lewes did not permit his reverence to interfere with his journalistic objectivity. As a result, Lewes's biography is not only laudatory but also reliable.

Professor Boyle of Magdalen College, the University of Oxford, is also very much impressed with the genius of his subject, but instead of allowing the reputation of Goethe's genius to direct inquiry, Boyle simply follows the rich details to their inevitable flowering in strongly meditated reflections on Goethe's milieu, his times, and his works. For Boyle, Goethe is a poet of philosophical power; for Lewes, and indeed for most of Goethe's biographers, he is the sage who happens to be a poet. The centrality of Goethe's accomplishments as a poet, his intense lyricism, provides Boyle with the key to Goethe's historical importance. Petrarch, Friedrich Gottlieb Klopstock, Thomas Gray, and certainly Jean-Jacques Rousseau had stressed the legitimacy of the self as a subject suitable to lyrical expression, but it was Goethe, according to Boyle, who put in the shade all notions about the "devotional," "musical," or "transcendent" nature of the lyric poem and established as its reason for being the working out of identity in "poetic making." When Goethe published the eighth volume of his *Literary Works* in 1789 (he was forty years old) it contained a representative selection of his shorter poems. With no other connecting theme than his own personal history of poetic moments, this collection, together with the powerful dramatic poem *Faust* (which was not published until 1808), made Goethe "*the poet* . . . for the whole Romantic generation in Germany, England and even France."

William Wordsworth and Samuel Taylor Coleridge published their famous collection, *Lyrical Ballads*, in 1798, almost a decade after Goethe's eighth volume. The English poets are credited with initiating British Romanticism with this one collection. Certainly the influence of Goethe's fiercely independent subjectivity can be seen in many of their poems, but their hope that an essentially heterogeneous collection would answer to the transcendent theme of "how far the language of conversation in the middle and lower classes of society is adapted to the purposes of poetic pleasure" is precisely what has kept *Lyrical Ballads* an essentially English phenomenon in the history of Romantic and modern poetry. Goethe's lyrics, Boyle argues, although marvelously in tune with the German language and splendid linguistic achievements, are primarily breakthroughs in the depiction of how a highly sensitive and independent poet, responsible only to himself, can, "with complete personal integrity," fashion a poetry that is "pre-eminently the expression of his freedom."

Goethe's power to express his freedom in life and art provides the central theme of Boyle's biography. The book alternates between a meticulous review of important moments in Goethe's life and thoughtful and often highly insightful discussions of the major poetic works. Since Goethe was his own subject throughout his works— poems, novels, dramas—Boyle's moving from biography to practical criticism in an alternating pattern is not as destabilizing as it might seem.

Goethe was something of a child prodigy; in early adolescence he wrote a prose epic based on the biblical story of Joseph. At the age of twenty, after a less than satisfactory experience in law school, he went to Strasbourg, where he encountered the Gothic glories of the cathedral and the polymathic genius of the philosopher Johann Gottfried Herder. Herder introduced him to Homer and William Shakespeare, or rather succeeded in getting Goethe to personalize these literary giants so that they became organic to his own sensibility. The result was his first masterpiece, *Götz von Berlichingen* (1774), a historical drama redolent of Shakespeare, Homeric heroism, and Gothic exuberance, or, as John Ruskin, the Victorian sage, was to call it, "imperfection." Five years later, back in Frankfurt, restless and melancholy, Goethe produced his second major work, the short novel *The Sorrows of Young Werther*, which took the entire European reading public by storm. The secret of its power lies in its tragic admonition: Live too much by feeling, and you risk the fate of dying by it. "Freed from the control of any object, either natural or human, [Werther's] emotions swirl into hysteria."

So compelling was this story of a young man who commits suicide after his hopeless passion for a married woman leaves him bereft of any reason to go on living that a rash of suicides followed its publication. The plot seems melodramatic to modern tastes. The climax is a hysterical interview with Lotte, Werther's beloved, whom he fleetingly embraces before shooting himself with her husband Alfred's pistols. Werther dies at noon on Christmas Eve, after twelve hours of agony. Whatever today's readers might think, Goethe had touched the nerve of the age. Wordsworth, more than two decades later, affirmed the doctrine that Nature never deserted the heart that loved her. Not so with Werther. His most painful moment comes when he realizes that his tormented heart has lost him the solace of Nature's deep joys. Goethe had anticipated the tragic heart of the Romantic soul, and all of Europe shuddered at this proof of a new sublimity. Nature was all to the Romantics; to lose her represented a fall no less terrifying than the original fall of man.

Yet at the same time that Goethe could sound the depths of despair, he was already experimenting with heroic defiance in a lyrical ode such as "Prometheus," in which the Titan challenges Zeus with the realization that he, Prometheus, not only has imbibed at least some of Zeus's powers but is also closer to the very Nature that Zeus is hungry to experience.

As the author of these contrasting works, works that testify to his range and Olympian confidence, Goethe impressed the young Carl August, the seventeen-year-old heir to the duchy of Saxe-Weimar. The boy admired the bearing, genius, and authority of the twenty-five-year-old poet and celebrity. Goethe, in turn, was flattered by such aristocratic attention and slowly warmed to the idea of becoming the young Duke's companion and adviser. Within five years of his coming to Weimar in 1775, Goethe was already "Privy Councillor" of the realm. His duties went far beyond those of a mere factotum. He was in charge of public works and architectural planning, the inspector of forests and supervisor of mines, the drafter of the little duchy's foreign policy as well as master of protocol and domestic policy at the court in Weimar. He was playing the game of power on several fronts, and there is little doubt that these experiences later colored his imagination when he conceived his greatest work, the ultimate reflection by a European artist on the relations between knowledge and power—*Faust*.

The most important relationship of his life in these early years at Weimar was his friendship with Charlotte von Stein, an older woman of great charm who exercised an enormous influence on Goethe's growth. She was the wife of the Duke's chief equerry, and the two platonic friends had to take every precaution lest scandal distort the beauty of their relationship. They were drawn even closer together in the summer of 1777 when Goethe suddenly was informed of the death of his beloved sister, Cornelia. Brother and sister had been unusually close since childhood. It was the greatest bereavement of his life. Nevertheless, Goethe's creative energy did not flag. Although, on the whole, Goethe was dissatisfied with his literary progress in the Weimar decade, in the twenty months after Cornelia's death he "conceived and composed *Proserpina*, *The Triumph of Sensibility*, and *Iphigenia*, and started work on *The Birds*, wrote the grand and gnomic hymn 'Winter Journey in the Harz' and the poems 'To the Moon' and 'The Fisherman,' and completed the first book of *Wilhelm Meister*."

Boyle contends that Goethe sublimated his erotic attraction to Charlotte von Stein by paying excessive attention to her children; however frustrating this relationship was in certain ways, in others it continued to inspire Goethe's idealism and moved him to classical experiments in verse and drama. His main theme in these years was the struggle of the poet—with himself and his age. This is the theme that informs his drama *Torquato Tasso* (1790) and it underlies his work on the story of Wilhelm Meister, the novel that displaced Tasso as his principal project from 1782 to 1785. This novel, written in a plain style and rather prosaic in action, represents a curious taming of the picaresque tale. A young man joins a theatrical company, assumes responsibility for a lovely homeless waif, Mignon, and engages in endless discussions on literary matters. With this work Goethe invented the "Novel of Education," a genre that had an enormous influence on nineteenth century fiction, particularly the Victorian and early modern novel—from Charles Dickens' *Great Expectations* (1861) to Joyce's *A Portrait of the Artist as a Young Man* (1916).

This first volume of Boyle's biography closes with Goethe's flight from Weimar in 1786 for the rejuvenating art, landscape, and women of Italy. The responsibilities and personal tensions of Weimar had brought Goethe to the point where he needed desperately to recapture his Olympian individuality and to reaffirm his roots in the world of nature—the life of the senses in the fullest sense of the word. In Weimar he had gone through important intellectual and moral growth. Now, at thirty-seven years of age, he wanted to plunge into the river of life, to enter a world his imagination had lived in for years. It was time to walk its hills, join in its frolic and sensuality, bask in its great art; in short, eat and breathe the Mediterranean world. On his return to Weimar in 1788, he behaved as a truly liberated man. He exacted much more generous terms from the Duke; more money and greater freedom to write his poems and plays and to conduct his researches in art and natural science. Within a month of his return, he met his future wife—the direct, spirited, and pretty young woman of twenty-three years he would eventually marry, Christiana Vulpius. They had a son who was born on Christmas Day, 1789. The break with Charlotte von Stein was painful, but his friendship with Friedrich Schiller was blossoming. The French Revolution signaled irrevocable change throughout Europe. Goethe's greatest years lay ahead.

It will be Boyle's adventure to carry this story further. Judging from this first volume, one must conclude that Goethe's "life" is in good hands.

Peter Brier

Sources for Further Study

The Atlantic. CCLXVII, April, 1991, p. 102.
The Christian Science Monitor. June 12, 1991, p. 13.
London Review of Books. XIII, May 9, 1991, p. 9.
Los Angeles Times Book Review. June 9, 1991, p. 4.
The New York Review of Books. XXXVIII, October 24, 1991, p. 3.
The New York Times Book Review. XCVI, July 28, 1991, p. 3.

The New Yorker. LXVII, September 23, 1991, p. 109.
The Times Literary Supplement. May 10, 1991, p. 3.
The Wall Street Journal. May 16, 1991, p. A14.
The Washington Post Book World. XXI, May 5, 1991, p. 13.

THE GOLD BUG VARIATIONS

Author: Richard Powers (1957-   )
Publisher: William Morrow (New York). 639 pp. $25.00
Type of work: Novel
Time: The 1950's to 1970's
Locale: Champaign, Illinois, and Brooklyn, New York

The double love story in this novel provides a launchpad for the author's mental gymnastics that relate to genetics, the DNA molecule, intricate musical composition, information theory, computers, philosophy, and, finally, the overall meaning of life

Principal characters:
> JAN O'DEIGH, about 34, a reference librarian in the Brooklyn Branch of the New York Public Library
> FRANKLIN TODD, Jan's former lover, about 30, a graduate student in art history
> STUART RESSLER, now dead, a scientist who, at 25, helped to discover the mystery of the DNA molecule
> JEANETTE KOSS, a woman four years Ressler's senior who, although married, was his lover

The adventure Richard Powers has booked for his readers in *The Gold Bug Variations* begins on the title page and continues to the final aria, "Da Capo e Fine," on page 639. The title page reads thus:

The Gold Bug
VARIATIONS

At first glance, one gets the pun (or part of it), the first of thousands of high-level intellectual puns—if one can call a pun "high-level" without being oxymoronic—that appear in a steady procession throughout this tightly structured, masterfully controlled book. The title brings Johann Sebastian Bach's *The Goldberg Variations* immediately to mind.

One quickly realizes that Bach wrote thirty variations and that Powers' book has thirty chapters, that Bach's variations were based on four notes, four musical phrases, and that four is a controlling number in this book—and, by implication, in much of the order in the universe as Powers seems to interpret it. Pondering further, one realizes that the placement of the title on the title page—minimizing "The Gold Bug" and putting **"VARIATIONS"** in bold type—implies something. Can the title legitimately be read as *The Gold Bug: Variations*, which has quite a different impact from *The Gold Bug Variations*? Turning to the dedicatory page that follows, readers encounter Powers' first cryptogram: four rows of print, each containing eight sets of initials (4 + 4 × 4?) of people, some living, some dead, family, friends, and even some from whom the author has withdrawn his friendship, suggesting possibly his awareness of the overwhelming complexity of human relationships, a topic at the heart of this novel on one of its many levels.

To discuss the book from the standpoint of its basic story is perhaps to do it an injustice. The story is the pretext for the extremely complex philosophical treatise that constitutes the most important level of the book. Powers, a wordsmith of consummate skill, has brought all of his powers to bear upon producing a novel whose complexity of discrete parts is so tightly interwoven that the result reminds one of a magnificently decorated Navajo or Zuni straw basket so perfectly crafted that when it is filled with water nary a drop leaks out.

Unlike novels that start with characters from whom the ideas evolve, Powers' novels begin with ideas; the characters are mere instruments for their dissemination. This is true of Powers' earlier works, *Three Farmers on Their Way to a Dance* (1985) and *Prisoner's Dilemma* (1988), as well as of *The Gold Bug Variations.* This is not to say that the characterization in these three novels is weak, but merely that it is distinctly secondary to the ideological framework that appears to be in place before Powers begins writing.

Reading *The Gold Bug Variations* is hard work, just as reading *Three Farmers on Their Way to a Dance* is hard work. The aim of these novels is to educate, to stretch the mind. The author pours out his own superb education on every page, but in the process, he is also continuing his education. Readers who accompany him on the journey he has decided to take are expected to work hard, as he himself works. If they follow him, they stand a good chance of being rewarded much as he is rewarded by the intellectual discoveries, the exhilarating epiphanies he continually experiences.

Clearly, Powers wrote this book with neither a specific audience nor commercial success uppermost in his mind. He wrote it because it is part of his personal quest to unravel the mysteries that puzzle him. The scientific part of the book, the part that has to do with deoxyribonucleic acid (DNA) and the double helix, reflects his early premedical training. Having made his course correction into writing, however, he now uses scientific analogies and vocabulary in his literary search to find order in the universe.

Through Bach's inventions and the double helix of the DNA molecule, the author establishes the number four as quintessential in the universal order whose mystery he struggles to unlock—the four seasons, the four winds, the four corners of the earth, the four chambers of the heart. The romance that provides the story line for this novel involves four people—the two members of each pair four years different in age from each other. The course that it follows becomes intertwined in ways that suggest the double helix. The skill that it takes to reach this sort of outcome in any credible way is extremely rare.

Among the participants in the story are the narrator, Jan O'Deigh, a thirty-four-year-old reference librarian in the Brooklyn Branch of the New York City Public Library, and Franklin Todd, a graduate student in art history, who becomes Jan's lover. One member of the other pair in this romance is Stuart Ressler, a lifelong wrestler with ideas who had worked at the Urbana-Champaign campus of the University of Illinois a quarter of a century earlier. He had been a member of the group that had sought to discover the genetic code of the DNA molecule, and he had had an affair with Dr. Jeanette Koss, a married woman four years his senior, also a member of the research team.

Jan first meets Franklin, with whom she later falls in love, when he comes to her reference desk trying to unearth information about Ressler, with whom he works. Ressler threw over his career at some point in the past and now works the night shift in a computer billing operation. Jan unearths a few references to him in her search, including a picture in *Life* magazine with a beguiling caption.

Franklin takes Jan to meet Ressler, who is now in his early fifties. His unique characteristic is that, having turned from his scientific pursuits at the University of Illinois, he has embarked upon a minimalist existence in which it is unnecessary for him any longer to compete. He is, in a sense, a dropout—but for the best reasons. He wants to invite his soul, to cultivate his intellect in his own, private way.

When the story opens, Jan, home for a quick lunch, has plucked from her mailbox a typically laconic note from Franklin, who is no longer her lover. It tells her of Ressler's death, presumably from lung cancer, back in Illinois. The news unleashes a flood of reminiscence. Her mind goes back to a snowy weekend she and Franklin spent with Ressler in New Hampshire and to the long nights they spent talking while the computers went about the semisilent tasks Ressler and Franklin had programmed for them.

Returning from her lunch break an uncharacteristic two hours late, Jan goes about her work of answering the questions people bring to her desk. By the end of the day, however, she has submitted her two-week notice. She needs time to explore the mystery of Stuart Ressler and, more broadly, the mysteries of life to which her explorations of his life will lead her.

At times, Jan's quest becomes eerie and verges on the mystical. Ressler has grappled with the question of whether humans, as byproducts of the DNA process, can ever understand it. Paradoxically, Ressler fears that something that is capable of creating consciousness (life) may well be too complex for that consciousness to understand. This supposition explains in part why he has chosen to follow the course he has, why he has elected to settle for being—in the eyes of the world, at least—a failure. Powers seems to be asking whether, if a quest is futile, one is to be regarded a failure for having abandoned the quest.

Franklin has done almost the same thing. Tantalizingly close to owning a doctorate, he has settled for coming in second—and he apparently has done so without significant regret. Consistent with this line of thinking is the fact that both Jeanette Koss and Jan O'Deigh are unable to have children. They are barren women in a world that might be viewed quite nihilistically.

At the very end of the book, when Franklin seeks to renew his relationship with Jan, he suggests that they make a baby, knowing full well that Jan has had a tubal ligation and cannot conceive. The "baby" to which he refers may well be the publication of the notebooks she has been compiling in her effort to solve the Ressler puzzle, rather than a biological child. However one reads this portion of the book,

Jan denies Franklin, saying that eventually he will want the real thing, that anything between them will not last. The final words of this last full chapter ask, "Who said anything about lasting?"

Here, perhaps, is a clue to where Powers' search has led him. Perhaps life's only permanence is impermanence. Perhaps life does not have any meaning that those participating in it can discern. This is not to say that it has no ultimate meaning, but merely to suggest that those who quest after its meaning have embarked upon a fool's errand.

Is this Powers' comment on what he has done in this book? Is this the next major literary pronouncement after T. S. Eliot's *The Waste Land* (1922) on the place of humankind in the universal scheme? Powers has used his prodigious learning and monumental intellect to approach solutions to the questions life necessarily poses. Possibly, however, the only answer all this learning can deliver is that it cannot provide the answer.

Although Powers' writing is less accessible than the novels of John Steinbeck, Ernest Hemingway, Saul Bellow, and even of William Faulkner, Henry James, and Herman Melville, his intellect stands comparison with the intellects of even the most significant writers in United States literary history. Among contemporary novelists, he is most directly comparable to Thomas Pynchon and Don DeLillo. He has, however, already exceeded their accomplishments through his rare combination of bristling intellect and flawless, architectonic style.

If Powers does not attract a large contemporary readership—and the demands he puts on readers may result in this—it is safe to bet that years from now, people will still be reading and interpreting his books—and years from now, they will still be finding in them cryptic messages that no one has discovered before. Few of the canonical writers that large numbers of readers study have the combination of writing skill and intellectual acuity that Richard Powers consistently brings to his work.

R. Baird Shuman

Sources for Further Study

Chicago Tribune. August 4, 1991, XIV, p. 6.
Kirkus Reviews. LIX, June 1, 1991, p. 689.
Library Journal. CXVI, June 15, 1991, p. 106.
Los Angeles Times Book Review. September 29, 1991, p. 2.
The New York Times Book Review. XCVI, August 25, 1991, p. 9.
Publishers Weekly. CCXXXVIII, August 16, 1991, p. 37.
San Francisco Chronicle. September 1, 1991, p. REV9.
Time. CXXXVIII, September 2, 1991, p. 68.
The Wall Street Journal. September 3, 1991, p. A16.
The Washington Post Book World. XXI, August 25, 1991, p. 5.

GOOD BOYS AND DEAD GIRLS
And Other Essays

Author: Mary Gordon (1949-   )
Publisher: Viking (New York). 253 pp. $19.95
Type of work: Essays

*A collection of essays on men and women, the Catholic church, abortion, class, literature,
and the politics of reading by a wittily iconoclastic and morally alert novelist and critic*

Mary Gordon is best known as a novelist, and more particularly as a Catholic
novelist, a writer who has staked out a recognizable fictional territory for herself
and explored it with a subtle yet rigorous moral perceptiveness. In *Final Payments*
(1978), *The Company of Women* (1981), *Men and Angels* (1985), *The Other Side*
(1989), and the short stories in *Temporary Shelter* (1987), she has proved a sensitive
recorder of the dramas emerging from the problematic collisions of spirit and flesh,
of faith, love, sexuality, suffering, and salvation. With the knowing instinct of an insider, Gordon is able to make telling distinctions between Catholic and non-Catholic
sensibilities and impulses, to illuminate nuances of religious feeling that often go
unremarked. Though her shrewd and tough-minded yet flexible feminism clearly
places her outside the line of Catholic novelists extending through Evelyn Waugh and
Graham Greene, she nevertheless bears a family resemblance to these earlier writers
in the way she insists on foregrounding the inevitable relation of religious and secular experience and probing the nuggety moral dilemmas created by what can seem to
be conflicting realities.

Gordon is not only a writer of fiction, however; she is also a regular and accomplished essayist, having produced an impressive body of critical prose that has appeared over the years in *Commonweal, Atlantic Monthly, Salmagundi, The New York
Times Book Review,* and elsewhere. This present volume of collected essays demonstrates amply that she brings the same intelligence and unflinching sense of moral
engagement to bear in these essays that critics and readers have celebrated in her
novels. The same craftsmanship and linguistic flair mark this work, and the same
sense of values informs it. Divided into three sections on the basis of subject matter
("On Writers and Writing"; "The World, the Church, the Lives of Women"; "Parts
of a Journal"), the essays address topics as diverse as Edith Wharton's fiction, the
abortion rights controversy, the legacy of Andy Warhol, Archbishop Marcel Lefeb-
vre's militant traditionalist movement, and the relation of motherhood to author-
hood. Yet there is a shaping vision that connects all of Gordon's writing, and not
surprisingly, as the author herself suggests, this particular angle of vision is created
out of her early strict Catholic upbringing. Resistant and critical as she now is toward the contemporary church, she is also profoundly influenced by it, and aware of
the unexpungible centrality it retains in her intellectual and emotional life.

If the label "Catholic writer" means anything, it must at least mean a writer who
largely subscribes to a view of the world taken by the Catholic church, who develops
a particular habit of seeing and regarding the physical and nonphysical world. In her

autobiographical essay "Getting Here from There: A Writer's Reflections on a Religious Past," Gordon most directly speaks to this issue of growing up Catholic and its effect on her view of material reality, her way of perceiving and valuing the world. Expressing a healthy alarm at applying the phrase "spiritual quest" to her own religious history (finding it too otherworldly or too self-aggrandizingly male in its literary connotations), she nevertheless catalogs her progress. Beginning as an amusingly doctrinaire young girl striving to live a pure life and to correct the impurities so clearly visible around her (someone who would brandish a crucifix before her foulmouthed playmates and challenge them, in the manner of Saint Dominic, to "say it in front of Him"—which, to her chagrin, they would gleefully do), she moves into a more confused and rebellious adolescence, seeing herself as an outsider marked by her faith as different from others who seemed more truly American. Finally she reaches adulthood, a woman no longer in thrall to Catholic dogma or nursing the desire to be a nun, but carrying within her a distillation of values and views she cannot and will not shake off. While rejecting the dangers of Catholicism, its tendency toward abstraction (the refusal to admit that one has a physical body and inhabits a physical world) and dualism (the admission of a physical world coupled with the command to shun it as evil), she retrieves from the Catholic vision a valuable sense of life as a serious project, the sense that things do matter, that they do have consequences, and that one can never do enough. Pried loose from an orthodox faith, it is essentially a tragic vision of the human enterprise; and Gordon sees little to mitigate that tragedy, only, as she writes in an essay on German novelist Ingeborg Bachmann, a "brave, frail hope," some possibility of affirmation that comes from honestly, unsentimentally addressing the terms of existence and from making, in art, a new set of "saving" images. In her rebellion against the church, Gordon has not simply substituted art for religion, making new literary images instead of venerating old religious ones; rather, she has created in her art a point of view that insists on a similar moral scrutiny of implication and motive, the plumbing of the heart's depths for secrets that may provide the proper grounds for some redemptive act of love.

It should not be surprising, then, if Gordon responds most sympathetically to and writes most persuasively about other writers, Catholic or otherwise, who examine the "real" world uncompromisingly to discover and chart its moral dimensions. In fact, the literary essays of the collection are almost exclusively devoted to writers who turn an unblinking eye on the world, who cock a keen ear to catch the moral resonance of real events. It is a sign of Gordon's own depth of experience and her commitment to a literature that relates itself unashamedly to life that she understands this sort of writing to be demanding, to demand, above all, real courage. In fact, "courage" is the term most frequently used in the literary essays to signal approval. She recognizes that to look at life in a relentlessly truthful way, without the usual anesthetics of romance or melodrama, to occupy a moral position and express oneself in that position with assurance, power, and yet genuine humanity, certainly requires great strength, but even more a kind of bravery. If the writer is a woman, then the amount of courage needed is only compounded. So, again and again, Gordon will salute, for example, Flannery O'Connor for the admirable courage with which she confronts unbearable situations and the steadiness with which she habitually looks at the world, or Stevie Smith for the sheer courage that allows her, against tremendous odds, to go on loving life, seeing in the detritus of the ordinary the stuff of comedy, or J. F. Powers for his ability to see the comic possibilities of religion in the flawed and inept lives of priests while still honoring the toughness and integrity of the faith they so inadequately represent.

Here Gordon makes the critical distinction between seeing the horror of modern life and despairing over that horrific vision. Gazing into the abyss without blinking, turning from the edge and speaking with all the moral force imparted by that experience—this Gordon values and practices. It is the reason she celebrates Christa Wolf, a writer of intense seriousness who in her spare, urgent novels gives the sense of a "seer who has stared, with attention, mercy, and courage, into the world's heart." It is especially why she praises Mary McCarthy, a woman of letters who sums up all that Gordon most prizes in a writer: someone engaged, combative, discriminating (in love with excellence without being an elitist), and political in a way Gordon somewhat nostalgically sees as no longer open to one (that is, someone whose politics are grounded in ideas, in philosophy rather than sociology). McCarthy was a wide-ranging generalist who saw the world as full of interesting things—if one only looked—about which one could register interesting observations. It is easy to see why Gordon admires this older woman, and equally easy to see how she follows in her footsteps: There is the same assertive quality, the refusal to back away from a controversial topic, the same witty defiance of popular convention, the same sharp, questioning intelligence aimed at the big questions, the same marriage of logical argument and emotional resonance in her writing. The lively pessimism at the heart of McCarthy's view of life is detectable, Gordon suggests, even in the tone of voice, which she describes as the "stirring and disturbing tone of the born truth-teller." It is this particular truth-telling voice to which Gordon so deftly responds in these writers and that she so ably generates herself. Voice and vision: Gordon continually calls attention to the way an intensely candid voice, formal, without sentiment—one like Edith Wharton's, for example—can articulate the outlines of a tragic landscape and yet make that look like the only truly accommodating home for the human heart.

Although most of the essays on literature focus on women writers, Gordon turns her attention to several men also, in one or two cases to male writers like Ford Madox Ford, who make women feel welcome in their fiction, or to writers such as Theodore Dreiser, William Faulkner, and John Updike, who make fictions that a woman can scarcely penetrate and that, Gordon argues, an independent-minded woman should seriously question. Perhaps the most powerful, though probably not most controversial, piece in the collection is the title essay. There Gordon not only advances a view of the dominant myth of American literature created by the dominant line of male storytellers but also engages effectively in a feminist debate on the literary canon and the politics of reading. She identifies at the center of American literature the image of the moving boy, the innocent male in motion, on a quest for unfettered selfhood. Women, by contrast, are imaged as unmoving, as static lumps who serve merely to obstruct the heroic male struggle for self-fulfillment. They trap and corrupt men; they meet the male cry of the wilderness, the freedom of the frontier, with the restraints of civilization. They are death to the running boy. Since, in canonical American literature, readers are made to celebrate the freeing of the male from entrapment or to mourn his inability to move, they accept the death, even the murder, of the female. She is sacrificed so that the male may retain his purity or preserve his autonomy, and he escapes moral censure for disposing of this obstacle in his path.

The critic Leslie Fiedler noticed the same pattern when he observed that in American literature the only good woman is a dead woman, because the American dream is a dream of freedom and women are seen as enemies of freedom. Yet Gordon brings a cool feminist consciousness into play here, questioning the innocence of the celebrated boy-killers in Dreiser, Faulkner, and Updike, and exposing the fraudulent mythology that essentially legitimizes the elimination of women. She sees this myth, in its moral irresponsibility, as the stuff of adolescent male fantasy. She is saddened by its failure to account for the fact that the world we actually live in is one in which the questing self must encounter and live alongside other selves. She is also incensed and prompted to ask whether she should continue to read these works and, if so, how. By shifting her focus to the act of reading, which is a situated act, one undertaken out of the particulars of one's existence, she can raise the question of how a feminist reads a male text that claims to dramatize universal patterns of behavior but that in fact describes a singularly male experience, and an adolescent one at that.

As reading is a gendered act, Gordon must read as a woman, and as a woman she cannot share in the sexist fantasy of an Updike. She then must admit that he has a blind spot, that he cannot see the whole moral terrain in which his "good boys" are acting. It is his problem, not hers. Gordon's solution is, typically, a practical approach to reading the dominant male narratives, one that employs the notion of compensation: She will weigh the amount of pleasure derived from the author's aesthetic mastery against the displeasure caused by his distorted vision. Thus she is not giving up on male writers (except for a Joseph Conrad or a Herman Melville, whom she finds completely unavailable to women readers) but recognizing them as being unreliable guides, able to point out some remarkable feature of human life but missing others completely. It is a solution consistent both with her tough feminist critique of the male-dominated literary canon and with her broadly humane appreciation of aesthetic accomplishment wherever it appears, whether in the works of Edna O'Brien or Henry James.

If "Good Boys and Dead Girls" is a masterful essay in its withering indictment of the male stranglehold on American literature, her two essays on the abortion rights controversy are equally provocative, clear-eyed responses to a complex and divisive social issue. It is obvious that establishment figures and codes—in the academy, the church, or the society at large—hold no terrors for Gordon. Where she sees a morally dubious attitude or policy supported by institutional power, she will forthrightly question it. What is most impressive about her defense of abortion rights is the clarity of her reasoning (in "Abortion: How Do We Think About It?" and "Abortion: Do We Really Choose?"). She recognizes the obfuscating jargon surrounding the issue and the difficulty of putting moral and physical terms and realities together, but she insists that a woman's choice to abort is made in a context: It is connected to other choices made by a free and responsible moral agent. Her focus is on the acting female and on the acting sexual female. She responds, for example, to the accusation that the pro-choice position is self-indulgent and materialist by suggesting that the charge signals a discomfort on the part of antiabortionists with the idea of female sexuality, with female sexual pleasure and sexual autonomy. Throughout these two essays, Gordon is a powerful advocate of a woman's right to choose, but what is perhaps the most impressive rhetorical feature about the argument is the way she presents herself. She emerges as undogmatic, tolerant, and morally tenacious in coming to terms with an emotionally charged issue. She looks lucidly at the question and insists that it is, like most important questions presented in human life, complex and should be decided on the basis of how people really live, not on prejudices, fears, and anxieties about sex, society, life, and death.

In these two controversial essays—throughout the entire collection, in fact—Gordon enjoins her readers to look at life, and to look at it as fearlessly and independently as she herself does. More than anything, it is this sense of deep critical engagement, of genuine openness to the richly variegated world outside and the turbulent, richly complicated world inside, that marks Gordon's work. One of her journal excerpts is entitled "Some Things I Saw." Characteristically, it is more than a catalog of thoughtful or clever responses to a film, an exhibit, or a television series she has seen; it is a compendium of small *essais*, the real things, records of a lively mind engaging with an object, scrupulously observing it, moving back and forth between subject and object, and asking "What do I think?" "What do I feel?" "What, finally, do I know?" Reading these shrewd and elegantly pointed essays, being in the company of such a curious and alert mind, is a bracing intellectual adventure, an experience that readers of Gordon's fiction will not want to miss.

Thomas J. Campbell

Sources for Further Study

Booklist. LXXXVII, March 1, 1991, p. 1314.
Chicago Tribune. April 14, 1991, XIV, p. 3.
Commonweal. CXVIII, May 17, 1991, p. 327.
The Economist. CCCXIX, June 15, 1991, p. 87.
Kirkus Reviews. LIX, February 1, 1991, p. 153.
Library Journal. CXVI, February 15, 1991, p. 194.

The New York Times Book Review. XCVI, April 28, 1991, p. 9.
Publishers Weekly. CCXXXVIII, February 8, 1991, p. 46.
The Times Literary Supplement. July 26, 1991, p. 11.
The Wall Street Journal. April 18, 1991, p. A14.

GRINGOS

Author: Charles Portis (1933-   )
Publisher: Simon & Schuster (New York). 269 pp. $18.95
Type of work: Novel
Time: The 1980's
Locale: Mérida and other locales in Yucatán, Mexico

A comic novel about comradeship and conmanship in Yucatán

> *Principal characters:*
> JIMMY BURNS, the narrator, a former hunter of antiquities
> REFUGIO, his good friend, a fellow scavenger
> DOC FLANDIN, an eccentric archaeologist
> RUDY KURLE, an explorer and UFO fantasizer
> LOUISE KURLE, Rudy's sister, posing as his wife

In *Gringos*, Charles Portis' festive, comic eye and ear reach us from Yucatán via narrator Jimmy Burns, more or less resident of Mérida, where Americans have congregated to pursue art, novel-writing, archaeology, and leisure. Jimmy has sworn off foraging in Mayan ruins for treasure, but he is at heart a hunter, someone who enjoys going out and shining flashlights in people's faces to see if they match the descriptions of runaways and convicts from the States. This forager-protagonist has been a staple of Portis novels. Mattie Ross, in *True Grit* (1968), enlists Rooster Cogburn to help her find her father's killer. Ray Midge, in *The Dog of the South* (1979), looks for his runaway wife and the Ford Torino she and her lover are driving. Typical of Portis comedy, that Torino seems as valuable as the wife.

Jimmy Burns, who keeps a double-barreled shotgun handy, howitzer-like in length despite inches he has sawed off the barrels, appears in the first chapter wearing hand-me-down green polyester golf slacks. This attire emphasizes two facts about Jimmy—his semiclownishness and his scavenging. The pants were castoffs from an elderly man whose motor home Jimmy was paid to return to the States when the man and his wife, happy to have reached Mexico in it, could not imagine driving it home. Jimmy quickly changes, however, donning a pair of khakis pressed and starched according to his standards. Portis will have no bum as hero. Jimmy is fastidious after all; he has a code and, above all, practical experience and knowledge. This is Portis' identity as well. When constructing a comedy, the trick is to know enough about Mayan archaeology, artistic types in Mérida, and UFO believers to make fun of them while keeping them genuine.

The gringos and their habitation of an old Mexican town provide a seriocomic backdrop to the novel's action. "Gringos" means "gibberish" in Spanish. Jimmy numbers among his acquaintances Pleat (who has owned thirty cars in his lifetime), Minim (a member of the Bowling Hall of Fame), Coney (a painter who hums tunelessly and had an aluminum carburetor melt on the engine block in a car fire), and Mott (army-pensioned and "fifty percent psychologically disabled" according to army doctors, made vulnerable by "whatever the opposite of paranoia is called"). Set these and other expatriates in a place where centuries earlier the Mayans ruled and built their pyramids, and the result is a double-edged take on the subject: The nutty Americans are very nutty indeed, but if modern humans are nutty then how seriously should one regard their respect for the "ancient Mayans"?

Portis' gift is the deft creation and management of incongruity. "Christmas again in Yucatán," begins the story. Though Christmas is nothing new to Mexico, a Presbyterian American bounty hunter waking up and going to a Catholic church with the wife (actually sister) of a UFO enthusiast is a reader-catching opening for a book. Portis creates askewness and sees askewness. The Jimmy whom friends consider an opportunistic grave robber is actually a do-gooder with a Christian conscience and innocence. Portis lets Doc Flandin, a wacky but brilliant Mayanist, describe Jimmy: "Jimmy Burns is a pretty good sort of fellow with a mean streak. Hard worker. Solitary as a snake. Punctual. Mutters and mumbles. Trustworthy. Facetious." Jimmy reads this on a reference Doc wrote for him and ponders the combination of "trustworthy" and "facetious," which in the Portis cosmos mean pretty much the same. But can the reader trust Doc's assessment, given his habit of wearing a round cap which, he claims, keeps essential vapors in his skull?

That humans have a hard time talking without making nonsense (the "gibberish" of gringos) is Jimmy's unstated assumption. A corollary, confirmed by the behavior of archaeologists, UFO enthusiasts, and would-be revolutionaries, is that humans see things that are probably nonexistent. A wild array of seers in a country renowned for irrationality ("There was a catch-all provision in the Mexican constitution whereby any foreigner could be kicked out of the country at any time for any reason at all, or for no stated reason"): That is the recipe for the paradise of incongruity which is *Gringos*.

Jimmy's exchange of his polyesters for well-starched khakis suggests that the reader will have a responsible guide and other characters will have a responsible warder. They are certainly in need of one, in a world full of competing claims to possession of the secret of things. Doc Flandin's unfinished book will, he says, explain all the mysteries of the Indian civilization from Toltec to Inca. The complexities of Mayan glyphs he will decipher: "When I pressed him he was evasive. 'I can tell you this much and no more, for the present. These writings are not just calendric piffle.' Some other kind of piffle then. Thousand-year-old weather reports. *Champion Spark Plugs.*"

Jimmy's unofficial job is to keep people from being faked out, for, south of the border, "things had turned around, and now it was the palefaces who were being taken in with beads and trinkets." Still, salespeople are to be respected, forced as they are to produce without the guarantee of a weekly salary. Indeed, Portis allows the reader to infer, salespeople may be compared to creative writers, persuasive about illusion. A crowd gathers in the street. It is not the beginning of the long-planned revolution but a boy selling cake decorators, demonstrating ably while haranguing the crowd. "He was an artist with a sure hand, and a funny speaker too, a fine salesman." No more elegantly succinct description of Charles Portis, writer, exists.

Jimmy has himself been a salesman, and his friend Refugio is a natural master of the art. Presiding with patriarchal pride over his domain of oil drums, plastic pipe, and other industrial detritus, Refugio drives a hard bargain in cash-only transactions: "Refugio was going for the No. 3 close. This is where you feign indifference to the sale, while at the same time you put across your patience is at an end, that you are just about to withdraw your offer. On that point you mustn't bluff. You can't run a stupid amateur bluff."

Still, salesman Jimmy is the lone ironist amid self-proclaimed knowers of truth. Doc Flandin thinks he has cancer and prepares for his death, but he turns out to be fine. Everyone has a dodge, or is taken in by one. The arch-demon of flimflam is Dan, a fat ex-con who drives south with a carload of skinheads and kidnappees to find "the Holy City of Dawn," rumored to be the site for the appearance of *El Mago* and the end of the world. This slovenly false prophet believes his own concoction of gibberish, and Jimmy meets him for the second time in the Mayan ruins where Dan's crowd and a band of hippies wait for *El Mago*. Dan is preparing to sacrifice a freckled girl from the States and a Mexican boy with a bad complexion, and Jimmy's hand is forced. He blows off Dan's addled head with the goose gun. So much for pondering the darkness in the heart of men. When delusion—everywhere apparent—is unbridled, hard measures are required.

More typical and amusing, everyday flimflam is largely unintentional and constitutes the essence of human fellowship. Consider the bar conversation Burns overhears:

> "I have a stainless-steel plate in my head."
> "I am one-sixteenth Cherokee."
> "I have never voted in my life."
> "My mother ate speckled butterbeans every day of her life."
> "I don't even take aspirins."

Jimmy is right to beware attempted profundity. Perhaps it explains his distrust of the deepest commitment, romance with women. He does not fall in love but does end up married. His mate, Louise, is available after all, not the wife of Rudy Kurle but his sister, a neat Dickensian surprise revealed near the story's end. And what better basis than truth, rather than love, on which to found a relationship. "She had called me a bum and a vandal and an enemy of the human race. I thought she was slightly insane, and of a bone-deep lunacy not to be corrected by age. And yet we were comfortable enough with each other."

Gringos succors the reader. The world is full of light, not darkness, with Jimmy Burns at the narrative helm. The formidable real world, where monster types such as Dan carry on their crimes, is no match for Jimmy's goodness. He returns the kidnapped girl, LaJoye Mishell Teeter, to her family free of charge. Her father, candidate for mockery by any other comic novelist, receives Portis' endorsement. "The back of his neck, a web of cracks, was burnt to the color and texture of red brick from much honest labor in the sun. A badge of honor, you might think, but no, it was the mark of the beast. The thanks Dorsey and his people got for all their noon-day sweat was to be called a contemptuous name." Portis intimates that he would accept the badge of redneck novelist, but what redneck, after all, knows enough about Mayan artifacts and artists to write of them. What is redneck in Portis is the assumed possibility of goodness in a crazy world.

The artistry of *Gringos* is rare. There are no weak sentences, no cracks in the narrative veneer. Comic surprises and subtle commentary intermingle. The comic abyss yields one sweetly odd character after another, one shock of recognition after another. And, conservative that Portis is, his plot is satisfyingly tightly knit. After Dan's demise and the return of LaJoye Mishell, there are several other minor charac-ters who need attention since they helped create the City of Dawn illusion by their own longings for "something incommunicable." Jimmy, detective at heart, hangs round to hear it all spill out. Debunker, he remains standing in Mexico, where the very words need demythologizing. *Izquierda* means "left" as in "to the left." Jimmy thinks it "a truly sinister mouthful for so simple an idea as left." Listening to people talk, he absorbs and nods and notes and waits "for it, the point at which things go blurred." For the reader, the marvel is that so much can be communicated, articu-lated, devised, and arrayed with such comic clarity while giving such pleasure and comfort. There is light in the world. *Gringos* exists.

Bruce Wiebe

Sources for Further Study

The Antioch Review. XLIX, Spring, 1991, p. 309.
Booklist. LXXXVII, January 15, 1991, p. 1007.
Chicago Tribune. January 20, 1991, XIV, p. 8.
Kirkus Reviews. LVIII, November 1, 1990, p. 1490.
Library Journal. CXVI, January, 1991, p. 155.
Los Angeles Times Book Review. January 6, 1991, p. 3.
The New York Times Book Review. XCVI, January 20, 1991, p. 7.
Newsweek. CXVII, February 11, 1991, p. 60.
Publishers Weekly. CCXXXVII, October 26, 1990, p. 56.
The Washington Post Book World. XXI, February 10, 1991, p. 6.

THE HAPPIEST MAN ALIVE
A Biography of Henry Miller

Author: Mary Dearborn
Publisher: Simon & Schuster (New York). Illustrated. 368 pp. $24.95
Type of work: Literary biography
Time: 1891-1980
Locale: Brooklyn, New York; Paris, France; Big Sur, California; Pacific Palisades, California

A biography of Henry Miller published to coincide with the centennial of Miller's birth, using letters, reminiscences, manuscript notes, and memoirs to compile an account of the author's life and its relationship to his work

Principal personages:
HENRY V. MILLER, the controversial writer and social maverick
JUNE EDITH SMITH, his second wife
ANAÏS NIN, his friend, lover, and literary confidante
LAWRENCE DURRELL, his supportive friend, an accomplished novelist
MICHAEL FRAENKEL,
ALFRED PERLÈS, and
RICHARD OSBORN, Miller's friends in Paris
EMIL SCHNELLOCK, a longtime friend and correspondent of Miller
JAMES LAUGHLIN, a visionary publisher of Miller's work in America
BARNEY ROSSET, the publisher who introduced Miller's banned books in
the United States
JACK KAHANE, Miller's first publisher in Paris

Henry Miller's life seems to be made for biography, to almost call for a biographical examination: five marriages, numerous obstacles to artistic achievement, controversy that continues fifty years after his first book, fame combined with public calumny, origins in the last century and influence continuing into the next, and perhaps most of all an enduring appeal to an international reading public. Moreover, Miller himself, almost from the start, saw himself as an important figure long before he had accomplished anything as an artist, so he saved all sorts of notes, made carbons of early letters, kept an eye on posterity, and, in what is surely one of the greatest challenges to any biographer or critic, so intertwined the actual incidents of his life with an imaginative, fanciful adjustment of these events that the tangle he created may never be entirely cleared up.

For many years Miller's reputation as a sex-crazed satyr (according to his detractors) or a superhuman saint (according to his supporters) left no middle ground available for a relatively impartial investigator, but the passage of time, shifts in public perception of what is acceptable in literature and in life patterns, and the deaths of many of the people Miller knew have made it possible to write about him without the partisan furor that surrounded earlier efforts such as Bern Porter's *The Happy Rock* (1945)—which Mary Dearborn calls "a negligible collection of trivia"—or Jay Martin's *Always Merry and Bright* (1979). In addition, during the late 1980's, the appearance of a number of important books, especially the extremely candid, previously suppressed excerpt from Anaïs Nin's diary called *Henry and June* (1986), the correspondence between Miller and Nin published as *A Literate Passion* (1987), Miller's *Letters To Emil* (1989), and Miller's collected *Book of Friends* (1984), as well as the increasing availability of Miller's voluminous correspondence and the notes and manuscripts for early, unpublished efforts such as *Crazy Cook* and *Moloch*, which Miller labored over during the 1920's, have opened the field for a diligent researcher. In the centennial year of Miller's birth, the publication of biographies by Dearborn and Robert Ferguson (*Henry Miller: A Life*) has established a firmer foundation for both literary critics and historians and has provided the first relatively comprehensive, in-depth look at Miller's life for legions of readers who have seemed as fascinated with the man as with his work.

There are three major problems at the heart of Miller's life and work that a biographer must confront. The early stages of Miller's youth and his life before his first marriage are likely to remain clouded, since so little material is available, and the years after he began to achieve some recognition beyond a huge cult are moderately well covered by a variety of sources. What still must be organized, narrated, analyzed, and evaluated are the years in the 1920's when he grew into the man who could thrust *Tropic of Cancer* at the world in 1934; the years in the 1930's when he actually wrote *Tropic of Cancer, Black Spring* (1936), *Tropic of Capricorn* (1939), and many shorter pieces; and the entire question of how Miller used the materials of his life to fashion his major work. The formation of his artistic consciousness in the 1920's requires the biographer to blend many sources into a coherent narrative progression. The actual transmutation of the circumstances of his life in Paris into *Tropic of Cancer* requires a sensitivity to a complex of occasions—social, literary, psychological, and cultural. Additionally, the almost hopelessly confused interlinkage of life and art, myth and history, fact and meta-fact and proto-fact in a frequently surreal combination of genres requires not only a thorough knowledge of Miller's work but also a sufficient interest in it to be willing to consider its literary merits—its limitations and its persistent appeal in spite of almost total invisibility in university curricula.

Dearborn has taken her subject seriously enough to work her way through the daunting amount of material gathered in civic and academic libraries across the Continent and has chosen to confront the puzzling and almost inexplicable contradictions in Miller's behavior with an intelligent, informed strategy of speculation. Her psychoanalytic approach to Miller's family background may not be definitive in the absence of more evidence, but her ideas about the influences of a meek, bullied father drifting into the realm of homoerotic behavior and a termagant of a mother forever critical of the men in her house lead to some reasonable arguments concerning the roots of Miller's sexual attitudes. While not strictly a feminist in her perspective—she is much less sympathetic to June Smith, Miller's second wife and the focus of *The Rosy Crucifixion* trilogy (1949-1959) than is Ferguson—her extension of Kate Millett's attack on Miller as the exemplar of male sexual neurosis in the twentieth century is a plausible position for assessing Miller's novels, or "autobiographical romances" as he sometimes called them. She tends to be somewhat severe in her judgments of Miller's early attempts at work, family life, and self-education, and her depiction of the New York in which Miller lived until he was nearly forty lacks the scope and substance of Ferguson's skillful re-creation of milieu and mood, but she provides a substantial, informative, and intelligently arranged picture of Miller's growth as a man and his unsteady development as a writer. One of the limits of her approach, though, is that she tends to take Miller at his word both in his letters (where this trust is somewhat justified) and in his re-creations of his life during the crucial decade of the 1920's. Her dependence on *Plexus* (1953), the second volume of *The Rosy Crucifixion*, may have been determined by that book's documentary drabness, but the fact that the sexual energy that drove Miller's most compelling writing is missing does not mean that the volume is any more reliable as a strict guide to the author's life.

Similarly, Dearborn is very critical of Miller's apparent anti-Semitism, particularly as it is expressed in the unpublished manuscript of *Moloch*, but as Ferguson points out in a much more sophisticated (although still morally strict) interpretation, this is another area in which Miller's own uncertainty led him to rush into extremes of thoughtless vituperation, something that he himself recognized when his work reached the standard of achievement that began with the publication of *Tropic of Cancer* in 1934. As in other areas—especially his shifting attitudes toward religion, sex, and art—Miller often groped toward a position in public, trying out various approaches and eventually canceling most of what he had previously said, so that some of Miller's most critical statements are often balanced by complementary ones on the same subject.

If Dearborn is narrow in some of her judgments, the evidence she has assembled always indicates the basis for her conclusions, and even if the reader is inclined to doubt her verdicts, she has supplied sufficient evidence for further consideration. This is one of the most important criteria for a biography of any controversial figure, and on the crucial years in Paris, when Miller joined the impulses of his character with his discovery of a language and form for projecting it into literature, Dearborn combines thorough research with a strong explanation of how Smith, Nin, and others with whom Miller had important relationships were influential in the construction of his books. While Dearborn's presentation of Nin is not much more sympathetic than her depiction of Smith, the undertone of camouflaged disdain is not inappropriate, since, again, Dearborn offers enough material for other judgments to be made. A more serious defect, though, is her description of the ethos of the Miller-Nin relationship. The letters Miller and Nin exchanged convey a quality of feeling that Dearborn's account misses. This is a problem that occurs in Martin's biography as well, and it indicates the peril faced by a biographer—even one who writes competently—trying to re-create a situation that has been previously covered by subjects at their best. The excitement, the delight, the sensibility of the participants that is at the heart of the Miller-Nin relationship is suggested but not really evoked by Dearborn's account. This tends to unbalance it, so that her harsh opinion of the participants seems justified, but the importance of the romance is undermined and its place in Miller's life diminished. Ferguson avoids some of this difficulty by quoting more frequently and by providing a contextual frame that permits the words to coalesce into a guided self-portrait of the parties involved.

The question of how to handle incidents that the subject has already placed, sometimes more than once, into a literary form is one that Dearborn handles inconsistently, but in the case of Miller's life, the difficulties are so substantial that no solution is likely to be totally satisfying. The issue involves the entire attitude of the biographer to the work and to the subject, and it is on this crucial question that Dearborn's effort is most limited. One of the more interesting criteria proposed for a biography is Lord David Cecil's idea that it should enable the reader to recognize instantly its subject if that subject entered a room and began talking. On these grounds, Dearborn has succeeded moderately well. Yet if one were to accept John Clarke's much more demanding criteria that "the key to writing a good biography [is] *love*"—which Clarke glosses as "the love that is the advocacy of another standing before you at the portals"—then Dearborn has missed something vitally important. It may be too much to expect biographers to love their subjects, but in her general disregard for the merits of Miller's work, much of which she dismisses with brief summaries, Dearborn makes it clear that she does not rate Miller's work very highly. Her statement that Miller has received "almost no serious academic criticism" is hard to reconcile with such interesting and perceptive books as Bertrand Mathieu's *Orpheus in Brooklyn: Orphism, Rimbaud, and Henry Miller* (1976), Ihab Hassan's erratically brilliant study *The Literature of Silence: Henry Miller and Samuel Beckett* (1967), Jane Nelson's provocative Jungian study *Form and Image in the Fiction of Henry Miller* (1970), or J. D. Brown's compact and incisive *Henry Miller* (1986). The implication is that Dearborn is not really interested in the literary elements of Miller's work, and this means that the vital connection between the man and work is not firmly established.

The larger question that this raises is what motivated Dearborn to attempt the project in the first place. When Dearborn says in her preface that Miller in his books "constructed a facade of toughness" and that his story is about "twentieth-century male identity" and "one man who set himself in opposition to his culture and who, paradoxically, helped to define it," the cultural and social aspects of Miller's life and work are emphasized. In this area, her biography is quite satisfactory, and her substantial research presents a man who was often worried, fretful, anxious, and uncertain, his frustrations concerning his problems in getting his work into print compounded by public misunderstanding of his intentions and accomplishments. Miller's relationships with his five wives and various lovers are offered as examples of psychic dislocation, and his sexual exploits in his writing are interpreted as forms of psychic rejoinders and compensations. Yet in both his own books and in the writing about him, there is a different Miller present as well. The warmly humane, high-spirited, wildly enthusiastic and energetic artist of many other accounts and his own vibrant expression is rarely portrayed in Dearborn's volume. The mystery of how this man wrote all those books is only hinted at, and for this reason, while Dearborn's biography is a valuable addition to the growing body of Miller studies, it does not go much beyond the factual information it offers in explaining why Miller's writing caught the attention of so many people, and why his life and art continue to cause interesting trouble in the world of literature and beyond.

Leon Lewis

Sources for Further Study

Booklist. LXXXVII, March 1, 1991, p. 1281.
Detroit News. June 19, 1991, p. F3.
Kirkus Reviews. LXIX, March 15, 1991, p. 371.
Library Journal. CXVI, April 15, 1991, p. 93.
Los Angeles Times Book Review. July 7, 1991, p. 2.
The New York Times Book Review. XCVI, June 23, 1991, p. 1.
Publishers Weekly. CCXXXVIII, March 22, 1991, p. 68.
The Times Literary Supplement. August 30, 1991, p. 25.
The Wall Street Journal. May 30, 1991, p. A12.
The Washington Post Book World. XXI, May 5, 1991, p. 4.

HARD EVIDENCE

Author: Heather Ross Miller (1939-   )
Publisher: University of Missouri Press (Columbia). 64 pp. $14.95; paperback $7.95
Type of work: Poetry

These thirty-three poems penetrate with hard insistence the surfaces of experience in order to reach spirit and reveal myth in the ordinary

Until near the end of the twentieth poem ("Causing the Blind to See") in her carefully ordered collection of dramatic and interior monologues, Heather Ross Miller withholds the words of her title: *Hard Evidence.* In all three of the named sections of her book, the poet dares the reader to see, and what she would have the reader see is not the appearance that normally passes for reality. In the final section's title poem, the speaker says, "I command you: tell me,/ do waked-up eyes recognize anything? Does the hard evidence/ at first hand/ live up to your promising land?" By this point in Miller's book, that final question rings as much with social and political fervor as with spiritual intensity. The "promising land" brings to mind the "Promised Land," and it reminds also of the promises of the American Dream, so often unfulfilled.

Not since Flannery O'Connor has an American writer dealt so directly with the need for Christian vision. Miller's intensity, her comic gestures, colloquial diction, and reliance on myth (and, moreover, specifically Christian myth) oblige the reader to think of O'Connor, but Miller's work is not derivative. Like O'Connor, Miller is a fiction writer and a Southerner who writes about people and situations likely to strike the modern sensibility as grotesque.

"Causing the Blind to See," the title poem of the book's third section, opens with the words "At first sight." Then the speaker enumerates things such as hot-air balloons, firebrands, bursting barium, and "a lapis lazuli galaxy," all of which she says "crowd you." The woman says "Here's a picture of me. Look at it hard." To make her point stick, she amplifies in comic excess her injunction to the reader "to really see." She says "really take a look at, give the once-over,/ get a load of, ogle and glare and gape and gawk,/ wink-blink, contemplate and view." A glance is not sufficient for what Miller and her speaker would tell—or show.

The following poem, "Men Like Trees Walking," pushes further the poet's insistence upon "really seeing," which is to say achieving spiritual vision. The Gospel account of Christ's healing a blind man (Mark 8:24) provides the poem's title. After spitting upon the man's eyes and touching him, Jesus asks if he sees anything, and the man replies, "I see men as trees, walking." After Jesus again touches the man's eyes and makes him look up, "he was restored and saw everything clearly." Miller's witty poem involves a man addressing a blind woman, telling her "it's a blind alley, I mean stone blind,/ and we're flying blind,/ groping in the dark blindfolded,/ the blind leading the blind." He tells the woman "It's a big blind date./ I am your sighted friend," and looking through her "ruined eyes," he knows what she sees: "men like trees walking,/ and one man calling, Wait, look again." That "one man calling" is Christ, but the speaker himself, though he can tell the woman "This is seeing," is himself blind, glad that she does not see him "tap the curb,/ rap my tin cup." He is "walking like trees,/ trying to find white crumbs, stones,/ . . . walking like trees,/ then gone."

The urgency of Miller's meanings in the final fourteen poems of her collection does not prevent her retaining the quirkiness of the poems in her opening sections, but her poem "Magdalen" deals directly with what the Christian calls mystery. In simple but mythic ways, this poem makes explicit the book's specifically Christian import. Magdalen addresses the Christ: "You are the Rosetta stone." The allusion is open to anyone with a decent desk dictionary: The discovery of a basalt tablet of Ptolemy V (196 B.C.) multiply inscribed in Greek, Egyptian hieroglyph, and Demotic provided the key to deciphering hieroglyphics. The poem is wholly sensuous and identifies the Christ as a force which brings multiple images into one.

The final strophe of "Magdalen" returns the reader to the Rosetta stone, while also summoning up the stone which Mary Magdalen and her companions found rolled away from the sepulchre of Christ on the morning of the Resurrection (Mark 16). Magdalen says "the stone waits/ like my ear on your heart,/ my hand on your hand." The final mystery of the poem equates Christ with the Word and with the origin of spiritual sight. Magdalen tells Jesus, "And the word you speak/ translates morning into women who see angels,/ into one woman who, weeping,/ wakens you." The women not only witness a miracle but also participate in it with their weeping. Christ's "translation" makes the women one woman, thus removing distinctions among them, and they waken him.

"Presenting the Child in the Temple" updates the story of the Christ discoursing with the learned doctors when he was twelve. The speaker voices community sentiment about the shameless display of a fatherless boy in new clothes. This boy, younger than the twelve-year-old Christ (Luke 2:42-46), "colors in real blood,/ bears down hard, running out of line." He colors birds and "then kills them/ to show us he means business." The speaker admits that "these are hard words/ and like swords pierce our hearts," but "We just watch, hoping it's a phase." The poem may be an easier achievement than others in this section of Miller's book, but the ironies build from the speaker's failure to grasp that the Savior (of whom there are memories in fragments of hymns) is more than a momentary indiscretion to be suffered.

The next poem, "Instructions in the Faith," returns the focus to vision and, with its abruptly dramatic statement, rivals the best of the poems here. The poem is spoken to St. Paul by Christ, apparently at the very moment of Paul's conversion on the road to Damascus. The Bible account begins Acts 22:6 and ends several verses later with Ananias restoring Paul's sight and with the beginning of Paul's ministry to the Gentiles. "Before you came along breathing threats and murder,/ gathering evidence against me," Christ says, the Romans had already "pierced through me,/ rolled a big rock over the last of me." The allusion to the pierced side and the big rock recalls similar images in other poems in this volume. The words of Christ are starkly concrete: "In this blind breathless dark, Paul,/ I foraged three days/ still hunting anything, the faintest spark to get back." In a one-line strophe, the poet emphasizes the effort of the Resurrection: "It's important to get back." The final strophe makes clear that the fit which Paul is suffering will not end and things return to "normal."

"Leda Talks" reverts to classical mythology and the story of Leda's seduction by the king of the gods in the form of a swan. Miller's Leda is nothing like the woman in the Irish poet William Butler Yeats's celebrated "Leda and the Swan." This Leda is determined to get even for what was done to her when she was young and dumb. She plans to stuff the swan and exhibit him in a Tote-Em-In-Zoo. Confronted by Zeus's "duckfeet and your longhorns,/ your feathered glory, your shower of U.S. gold," the public will ask, "Where's the hole/ to put the nickel in nickel in nickel in?" Miller here conflates Leda's seduction with other seductions of mortals when Zeus took the form of a bull and of a shower of gold. Leda's resentment arises from crimes against other women by the irresponsible deity.

In Miller's updated version of the myth, Zeus has fixed it so Leda would "be well off,/ marrying money, living in a high rise," and he has given her model children. She, however, aims to "throw these kids away,/ and get new kids like the ones next door,/ plain ones, all my own,/ who do nothing." At the Tote-Em-In-Zoo, Leda, her "plain kids," and her "good husband" put the nickel in and watch Zeus, "old brute, move and mouth/ and transmute love." When detectives enter and demand to know "Where's Uncle God?" the new kids kick the machine. "He's a duck," they say, "a steer,/ the U.S. Mint!" Leda's final taunt is, "It's no accident,/ they are intelligent." "Leda Talks" derives from a classical myth, but the poem has relevance for a Christian society which would reduce God to a glorified "Sugar Daddy," a fictitious uncle, a mechanism motivated by nickels.

"Ambush" returns the reader to the Judaeo-Christian myth of Noah and the Flood, but the poem is spoken by a contemporary American woman. The relevant Scripture is Genesis 8, and the images, in part, are the familiar rainbow and the dove, "one of those croupy mourning doves,/ the kind that makes my throat hurt/ when I hear it." The woman describes an "old Jew" on a "cold American day"; he is "Packed in his boat, hoof to claw,/ the women quarreling." The speaker observes, "He had things on his mind"; then, in a startling departure, the woman opens her mail and pulls out "your last picture:/ dark moustache, a clear face,/ your boots, your gun." The ark and Noah apparently forgotten, she tells of a soldier appearing at her door; at first she thought the soldier was her son. The soldier tells her "plainly, politely,/ Your son: shot twice in the neck,/ and once in the gut."

The remainder of the poem addresses the son, and in doing so, it makes the reader see why the ark and Noah, the biblical setting are important. The woman wants her son's neck "wrinkled," his gut "spilled over a vulgar middle-age." She does not want him dead.

> I want you, not this blue clearing
> in the blind sky, this wild dove calling,
> promising it's all right and the rain's stopped.

The word "promising" takes the reader back to the question whether "the hard evidence at firsthand" lives up to "your promising land." Following in Genesis are accounts of the breakdown of the common language hitherto spoken on Earth and of the tensions and conflicts among the generations of the sons of Noah. The ambush has been set, and the woman tells her dead son, "I've got things on my mind// Tomorrow, son,/ I lace up the boots, I handle the gun."

The remaining few poems in *Hard Evidence* continue to reiterate the book's central themes, and they do so by returning to somewhat less explicitly Christian content. Miller's organization unifies through repeating situations and mythic allusions, but the poet's voice, her peculiar way of synthesizing her material, oblige the reader to recognize the book's continuity. "Antigone, Miss World!" in section 2 ("Dreamers") prepares the reader for "Antigone in Custody," in which the Greek heroine addresses "Old lover, broken brother," whom she has decently buried in defiance of King Creon's command. The speaker in "Antigone, Miss World!" is a drum majorette "strutting right past Jaycees, Civitans,/ and Lions twirling my baton." Like Leda, she is a "kewpie," but "the quick easy royalty/ of my crown, the prize of perfect teeth/ and sequined gown did not give presents to me." The problem is (as they say) all in the family: "my brother killed my brother,/ which is the same as killing baby sister,/ father, mother." The poem concludes with mention of a promise: "and with my promise, Jump! Kick the chair!/ I let loose Mama's dark hair,/ I noose Antigone."

"Antigone in Custody" includes among the bad things Antigone did, "her sins and transgressions," such trivial violations of convention as smoking cigarettes and cutting off "my hair, everybody looking." Antigone identifies what she has done wrong as sin; what her brother has done as pain. "I did it, brother, again and again/ and if for one, of course for two." The Greek original tells the reader that two brothers died in a civil war, and Creon arbitrarily selected one brother to honor as a hero, the other to be despised as a traitor. In Antigone's case, there is no doubt: She defied the State in the name of a higher law, and buried her brother. Perhaps the line "if for one, of course for two" means that Antigone acted for herself as well as for her brother. At any rate, the poem's final image is of "sands sift sifting/ sift sifting/ from my two deliberate hands." Antigone does not repent.

The ten poems in the opening section, "Bear Swamp State Park," establish the method, tone, and some of the book's chief themes. Meanwhile, they make curious connections with poems later in the book. The speaker in these first poems is the wife of a park worker, often absent, leaving her and their children alone. In "Bear Swamp, before the Children Go to Bed, We're Just Walking Around," one of the children says "I want the world pond still." The speaker later says that the children "mean/ things to stay still here in Bear Swamp,/ nothing to drag us off and kill us." In "Instructions in the Faith," Christ says that Paul is dancing around, slobbering, and hollering the name of God "as if you think fits might stop,/ as if you think things might stay/ where they are." This link between early and late poems helps the reader understand that the world of created things changes constantly, and is always a world of appearances.

In "Jungle Books and Just So," the narrator announces that gods and women blur "to one purring beast out in the yard." She applies a bestial word, "crouches," to herself, but says she is tamed by such simplicities as "a trip to town, a Pepsi, and my children." She recognizes that the "blurry part" of her husband (the you of the poem) is also the "god part/ . . . that presses four dark paddy-paws/ on top of your heart, dozes off, and purrs/ slant-eyed, watching you back." The commonplace Pepsi and the child language of "paddy-paws" bring to the notion of the blurred identities of humans, beasts, and gods a homely reality.

Nowhere predictable, *Hard Evidence* calls for reexamination of the bases of belief and action in a culture deluded by glitz, its sacraments debased and its gods trivialized. With her expanded image of desperation in "Entrance of Mary, Body and Soul," Miller concentrates the false dreams of a people: Barbie dolls trail "twelve-foot trains,/ their battery-powered bridal crowns/ twinkling like Vegas." These few lines capture the lack of meaningful myth through objective statement of some of American culture's tawdry substitutes. One thinks of Flannery O'Connor's Haze Motes and his theft of a shriveled mummy to serve as emblem of his "Church without Christ."

Miller provides her own apocalyptic vision in "Treasure City," the volume's penultimate poem, which imagines a time "after the bomb fell," leaving the shopping mall "like an old folks' home" and leaving reminders that "we did it." The words "we did it" recur: "We did it wrong./ And we feel sorry for ourselves." The speaker says, "it was easy getting started,/ easy as striking a match." The final strophe alludes to "our amusing blindness,/ our childish pity." All that remains is for the final poem, "Grandmother," to sum up as the speaker sweeps her hands and face "over four generations." She and an old man—"he could be God," she says—remain:

> The old man smiles and I sweep.
> We say by heart the babies to sleep.

Leon Driskell

Source for Further Study

The Charlotte Observer. November 11, 1990, p. D5.

HARLOT'S GHOST

Author: Norman Mailer (1923-　　)
Publisher: Random House (New York). 1310 pp. $30.00
Type of work: Novel
Time: 1955-1963; 1983-1984
Locale: Maine; Washington, D.C.; Berlin; Montevideo, Uruguay; Miami; Cuba

A mammoth and intermittently gripping novel of the Central Intelligence Agency, charting the career of Harry Hubbard, protégé of the legendary Hugh Tremont Montague ("Harlot"), and a key participant in CIA operations in Berlin, Uruguay, Cuba, Miami, and Washington, D.C.

> *Principal characters:*
> HARRY HUBBARD, the novel's narrator, a CIA agent
> BOARDMAN "CAL" HUBBARD, Harry's formidable father
> HUGH TREMONT MONTAGUE ("HARLOT"), a legendary CIA guru, Harry's mentor
> KITTREDGE, Montague's wife, Harry's cousin, and his beloved
> WILLIAM KING HARVEY, Harry's first boss in Berlin
> E. HOWARD HUNT, Harry's boss in Montevideo
> MODENE MURPHY, Harry's mistress, who is also involved with mobster Sam Giancana and President John F. Kennedy

Born into a family of wealth, prestige, and power, Harry Hubbard, the narrator of *Harlot's Ghost*, never imagines that he should do anything but follow in his father Cal's footsteps and join the Central Intelligence Agency (CIA). Still, Harry has never been sure of his manhood. Can he measure up to his father's record? Having hero-worshiped Cal throughout his childhood, Harry can remember only a few incidents in which he has captured his father's attention—a skiing accident, for example, when Harry broke a leg but steeled himself not to cry out during a long, jolting trip to the doctor. Cal, realizing his mistake in taking an unprepared Harry out to the slopes, calls himself a "fathead," and Harry endears himself to his father by his stoicism and his gallant refusal to accept his father's self-criticism.

Cal arranges for Harry's initiation into the world of male adventure by persuading Hugh Tremont Montague ("Harlot") to act as Harry's godfather and mentor. Montague takes the teenage Harry rock climbing, and while he admires Harry's courage, he advises him to give it up, for Harry will try to overcome his every weakness, and Montague suspects this could result in Harry's risking death.

By the time of his college years at Yale, Harry knows for certain that he is destined for the CIA. Receiving the call from Montague, he enthusiastically plunges into CIA training, simultaneously falling in love with Montague's wife, Kittredge, a brilliant psychologist—also working for the CIA—who has developed a theory she is anxious to explore: Every human being has two personalities, an Alpha and an Omega. She does not mean merely a split personality but two completely formed selves which may or may not be in sync with each other.

The novel works endless variations on the Alpha/Omega theme, interpreting both individual personalities and historical events in its terms. Kittredge herself, for example, is deeply in love with Montague and yet devotes an entire other self to Harry, confiding in him secrets and speculations that she never shares with her husband. This personal disloyalty and deception is also worked on a vaster scale in the CIA itself. Harry, for example, learns that he cannot survive in the agency without double-dealing—at one point serving both his first boss, William King Harvey, in Berlin while relaying information secretly to Montague. Later Harry will face much the same split with his own father—working for him on the Bay of Pigs invasion while doing side jobs for Montague, his second father.

Harry's first assignment, Berlin, is a melting pot of double agents. Everyone seems to be servicing at least two masters, and Harry quickly discovers that the politics of this ambiguous assignment have a sexual tenor as well. Dix Butler, the strapping former professional football player who befriends Harry, is not only running double agents but also apparently engaging in both homo- and heterosexual relationships, for he invites Harry to sodomize him, and he promises he will return the favor. Dix's point is that agents lead double lives; homosexuals lead double lives; consequently, agents are often homosexuals. Montague's own code name, Harlot, suggests what agents are: paid agents of pleasure, and it does not matter much whether that pleasure consists of sexual knowledge or political intelligence. Harlots and CIA agents are role-players who sell themselves.

Harry refuses Dix's invitation to have sex with him—apparently because Harry is afraid of the power Dix might hold over him as a result of their intercourse. There is a physical attraction between the men. Harry makes this clear when he kisses Dix on the lips in the very act of refusing Dix's plea for a more physically intimate relationship. There is no question that Harry covets the power that Dix commands, but to become his sexual partner would rob Harry of his slight claim to independence.

Harry's period in Berlin is inconclusive, and his departure is abrupt, for William King Harvey (renowned for building a tunnel underneath the Berlin Wall that has tapped into East German communications) discovers that Harry has been acting as Montague's agent. In Harry's next assignment, Montevideo, he learns how a CIA office is run, and he begins to recruit his own agents, one of whom, Chevi Fuertes, is able to penetrate the highest levels of the Uruguayan Communist Party. Working under E. Howard Hunt—arguably the most fascinating and best-realized character in the novel—Harry learns all the techniques of intelligence; he particularly admires the élan with which Hunt courts and stimulates his sources of intelligence.

During Harry's sojourn in Montevideo, Kittredge breaks off her long-running correspondence with him. They have never consummated their love for each other, but Montague has become suspicious and has cut off Harry's access to Kittredge. Driven by her love for her husband and her child, Christopher, Kittredge accedes to her husband's wishes and writes Harry that she is ceasing communication while hinting that they may resume contact at some future unspecified date.

Although Harry's feelings for Harlot become ambivalent, he continues to follow his mentor's instructions, keeping him fully informed on the ambitious Hunt's moves.

Hunt, no fool, is on to Harry, but knowing the ways of the agency prefers to use Harry precisely because of Harry's contacts with other powerful figures. Hunt is wary of Montague, and he does not dare to antagonize a rival for power, for Hunt's quest is for nothing less than the directorship of the CIA.

Norman Mailer does a superb job of creating a credible picture of the inner life of the agency. A reading of *Harlot's Ghost* provides convincing insight as to how an intelligence gathering agency becomes a self-absorbed "company"—the term often applied to it. Dominated by Anglo-Saxon Ivy League types, who take their opposition to Communism to be not merely politically right but virtually a religious principle, a Christian response to evil, the CIA becomes enmeshed in its own ethos, making it doubtful as to how much of an external threat to security actually exists.

Harry's personal failure comes with the Bay of Pigs invasion, in which he buys the CIA delusion that it can land a small expeditionary force on Cuba's shores, back it up with air support, and topple Castro. All the elements of failure are there to read: The Cuban exile groups are divided and infiltrated by double agents; administrations are changing and it is not clear that president-elect Kennedy will support even a covert use of American firepower; worst of all, the CIA is hopelessly deluded about the extent of the opposition to Castro in Cuba. There is also still much admiration for Castro outside Cuba—and even in the CIA, though no one will admit it. E. Howard Hunt runs himself ragged in trying to maintain his jerry-built coalition against Castro, involving Mafia elements that in retrospect seem a part of a ludicrous effort to embarrass and then to assassinate the Cuban leader.

In the very midst of the Bay of Pigs plot, Harry is involved in a torrid affair with Modene Murphy, mistress of Chicago mobster Sam Giancana and of President Kennedy. Montague has put Harry on Modene's case, but their affair takes on a life of its own as Harry jealously follows her shuttling between Giancana and Kennedy—yet another demonstration of Kittredge's Alpha and Omega theory, which is at its strongest in helping to explain how Kennedy, who is presented sympathetically, can simultaneously lead a country with considerable courage and acumen and yet feel the need to engage in the double-dealing of love affairs, even inviting Modene, in one instance, to share his bed with himself and another woman. Modene is offended, but she recognizes Kennedy's need not merely for sex but for various partners and confidants, for no one person can satisfy the dualism that is inherent in Kittredge's reading of human nature.

Kittredge herself resumes correspondence with Harry and promises a more intimate relationship (she will eventually betray Montague and marry Hubbard). She wants to know about every aspect of his work, and he obliges—only occasionally lying to her—thereby violating the CIA's rules of confidentiality. Harry's letters to Kittredge form the bulk of his Bay of Pigs narrative—as they do in his section on Montevideo. Indeed his correspondence is the way he can legitimately comment on the shaping of his own character, for ultimately this is what the novel is all about; Harry is the only character who is at once determined to make a success of himself in the CIA and yet who doubts his fortitude. In fact, the novel is framed at the

beginning and end by Harry's present (1983-1984), in which he is rereading his letters and diary-like accounts of the years between 1955 and 1963, and will presumably
go on (in the second volume of the novel) to recount more recent events in Saigon
and in the White House. *Harlot's Ghost* is an impressive evocation of one man's
experience in an incredibly complex organization that has been implicated in the
momentous events of the postwar world. The novel founders because everything has
to be filtered through Harry's sensibility, and no detail can be overlooked lest it distort the process by which Harry's character is formed. There is no plot, although the
novel opens with the hint of one: Montague is missing and presumed dead. Is he
really dead? Is he is the ultimate double agent? Has he gone over to the other side?
These are tantalizing questions which are never answered. Presumably, they will be
taken up in the second volume of the novel, although Mailer ends his first volume
with Harry's disturbing coda: "I might never finish the book of Harry Hubbard. . . ."

After 1,300 pages, it would not be surprising to learn that the sixty-eight-year-old
Mailer is exhausted. More than once, he has promised multivolume novels which
have never materialized. And *Harlot's Ghost* will have to stand by itself. As such, it
is an uneven work—one that reads like an eighteenth century epistolary novel, often
gripping because of the intimacy and directness letters can offer but also turgid and
sometimes improbable. For example, during the Cuban missile confrontation between the United States and the Soviet Union, Harry supposedly writes thousands of
words to Kittredge in the bathroom, hoping his colleagues will not notice his absence and call him incontinent in a crisis.

Kittredge is also a problem, or rather she is a convenience in the novel. Like many
of the characters, she sometimes sounds like herself and sometimes like Mailer,
especially when she is spouting his fondest ideas about dualism. She does not seem
to have much identity as a woman; she is there for Harry to adore. Even her Alpha/
Omega theorizing becomes tiresome, especially when it is repetitively used as a tag
line, a shorthand referent for explaining a character's behavior.

By making so much of the novel consist of letters, Mailer has convincingly captured the interior life of the CIA and shown how it has made incredible blunders
because of its self-absorption. As a novelistic strategy, however, the letters fail. Even
when they are fascinating, there are simply too many of them, and they are convulsed
with detail, which may strengthen verisimilitude while diluting narrative power. *Harlot's Ghost*, then, is a major work that fails, but it fails admirably. It cannot be
ignored, and its characters resonate—so much so that Mailer has nearly succeeded
in portraying a CIA that is commensurate with his imagination.

Carl Rollyson

Sources for Further Study

Chicago Tribune. September 29, 1991, XIV, p. 1.
The Christian Science Monitor. October 15, 1991, p. 13.

Los Angeles Times Book Review. September 29, 1991, p. 1.
National Review. XLIII, November 4, 1991, p. 54.
The New York Times Book Review. XCVI, September 29, 1991, p. 1.
The New Yorker. LXVII, November 4, 1991, p. 113.
Publishers Weekly. CCXXXVIII, August 16, 1991, p. 48.
Time. CXXXVIII, September 30, 1991, p. 48.
The Times Literary Supplement. October 18, 1991, p. 20.
The Washington Post Book World. XXI, September 29, 1991, p. 1.

HEAT AND OTHER STORIES

Author: Joyce Carol Oates (1938-   )
Publisher: E. P. Dutton (New York). 397 pp. $21.95
Type of work: Short stories
Time: The 1960's through the 1980's
Locale: The United States and Canada

In these twenty-five stories of violence and violation, Joyce Carol Oates explores brutal disruptions of daily life and heart-wrenching confrontations with ambiguity and evil

Since its beginnings with the gothic encounters of Edgar Allan Poe, the American short story has more often focused on borderline human experiences than on the center of everyday life. Short fiction has always zeroed in on disruptions of the everyday, when something happens that challenges the routine and thus upsets the comfortable value system derived from the ordinary. Whether the disruption is the result of an external force, such as the appearance of a mysterious stranger, or caused by an internal hallucination so vivid and powerful it seems external and real. In the twentieth century many of the best short-story writers who examine such disruptive and challenging experiences have been women.

Katherine Anne Porter, Eudora Welty, and Flannery O'Connor are three of the best such writers, well known for stories in which the ordinary is shattered by the intrusion of a mysterious and unfamiliar force. Joyce Carol Oates owes a powerful debt to these writers. One of Oates's best-known stories—"Where Are You Going, Where Have You Been?"—made even better known by the film adaptation *Smooth Talk* (1985) starring Laura Dern—is a classic example of the short story convention of the ominous and disruptive stranger who is ambiguous because one is never quite sure whether he is a realistic external figure or a hallucinatory internal force. In this new collection of twenty-five stories by Oates, her first since 1986, she pushes the convention of focusing on the breakup of the everyday by a powerful and ambiguous force to violent extremes, for the stories are filled with assault, rape, mutilation, and murder.

In spite of the violence, however, there is a curious bloodless feeling about this collection. It does not derive only from the obvious fact that Oates's intention is not to shock or to titillate; rather, it is that the stories seem to have been conceived in a literary test tube instead of having been created out of the gritty arenas of desire and physical reality.

Perhaps the most obvious statement one can make about Joyce Carol Oates, and it has been made many times, is that she is extraordinarily prolific. With twenty novels and sixteen collections of short stories to her credit, she has already exceeded the production of such giants of literary productivity as Charles Dickens and Thomas Hardy. In short, Oates writes a considerable amount and seemingly publishes everything she writes. It is a fact of her literary life that makes one suspicious that in spite of the serious surface of her work she is a one-woman industry. For all these misgivings, her novels win awards, and her stories frequently are included in award-winning short-story collections. There is no doubt that she knows the short-story form well and has studied it and practiced it more than most living writers.

As this collection amply shows, her work is often imitative and repetitive, and many of the stories seem to spring from a dispassionate artistic "what if" rather than from a passionate involvement in the lives of their characters. For example, in the story "Naked," a middle-aged woman, while hiking in a suburban wildlife preserve, is attacked by a gang of minority children who beat her, rob her, and leave her naked and alone. Although this is a potentially powerful situation suggesting both violation and vulnerability, the event is not so much probed as it is merely set up as a sort of test case of white, middle-class, middle-aged placidity. "The Knife" also centers on a middle-class woman who is attacked, this time in her home by two thieves. At issue here is the now-predictable convention in which the woman blames herself for the attack. She wonders if it is her fault for leaving the door unlocked or for not using the knife the rapist puts in her hands. At the end, she even questions if what happened to her was rape at all.

In "The Boyfriend," a thirty-six-year-old woman with a Ph.D. in economics finds herself not in love for the first time since she was a teenager and feels cut loose and free. She lets herself be victimized by a man who tries to rape her and who kicks her in the stomach—an attack that drives her to seek the protection of her last boyfriend. All three women in these stories think they are self-reliant and independent until male violence strikes; then they are not so sure. This sense of helplessness in the face of male brutality is a common theme in the collection.

"Leila Lee" is the story of a woman who marries a man with a twelve-year-old son who resents her and who hates his father for his abuse. The climax of Leila Lee's attempts to make the boy accept her is that the boy kills his abusive father with an ax. Leila Lee comforts the boy and plans to help him dispose of the body, but ultimately she can only hold him in a kind of grotesque pietà posture, knowing that her true love is for this "son" rather than for his father as a husband.

Three of the stories in the collection—"Craps," "Death Valley," and "White Trash"—form a kind of trilogy, for all focus on an uneducated and relatively inarticulate young woman, and all take place in the geographical and cultural desert in and around Las Vegas. In the first, the narrator tells her former husband the story of a crapshooter with whom she was once briefly involved whose treatment of her fluctuated between tenderness and cruelty as randomly as his luck fluctuated at the crap table. "Death Valley" focuses on a prostitute who goes into the desert with a man who alternates between roughing her up and quoting poetry to her. In a graphic scene, she slashes his throat with a razor blade that she carries in her purse. The slashing is only a fantasy, however; the most rebellion she can muster is to walk away from his car with clumsy dignity when he takes her back to her motel. In "White Trash," basically the same girl becomes involved with a jazz musician, hoping for a relationship with more feeling and emotion from him than she has had with other men. She soon realizes that all he wants is what every other man wants from her, however, and the story ends with her indifferently accepting this as the only relationship she can get. In many of these stories, women ultimately yield to their status as victims, helpless to do more than fantasize about their escape.

Several of the stories seem to derive from static situations with symbolic potential. The title story, for example, follows a familiar short-story convention of presenting grotesque characters involved in extreme situations. The focus is on twin girls, so much alike they are in effect the same girl, murdered by a simpleminded young boy. The story is told in a straightforward, laconic way, as if by someone who is an ordinary and uninvolved observer and yet who is simultaneously a very sensitive person fascinated by the killing, suspecting it means something. After all, the murdered girls are twins and the boy is mysteriously detached from ordinary reality; the narrator is not really sure what it all means, but tries to convince the reader that it must mean something.

Although the second story in the collection to focus on twins is more realistic than "Heat," still the purpose of the twins is to serve as an obvious metaphor of some mystical connection, a notion of the two being one in some way. In "Twins," the central event is the narrator's father's meeting with a mime whom he takes to be his long-lost twin. The dumb show confrontation is a metaphor of mirror reflection, which the mime pushes to extremes to mock the father in a grotesque way. After his father's death, the narrator says he continually sees him—or else his uncle, he is not sure which—in airports, in passing cars, in mirrors, concluding that although he is rarely alone, he is always lonely.

"The Buck" begins with the same convention; a narrator has observed a strange situation that sticks in the mind, and she must talk about it even though she is not sure exactly why. The story is about an old woman who tries to protect the wildlife on her six acres of farmland from hunters. When a local hunting enthusiast shoots a deer with a bow and arrow and it runs onto the woman's property, she drives the hunter off and tries to pull the arrow out of the deer's neck. The buck falls upon her, pinning her to the ground, and they die together. The narrator says that it is a story she cannot forget, for it is lodged deep in her like an arrow through the neck. It is a story she says she has told many times, thinking that maybe each time will make a difference by revealing a secret meaning and releasing her from her obsession. Yet the symbolic situation seems so obvious here—the old woman and the deer locked together in death so they have to be separated by force—that one wonders what is so secret and mystical about it.

Two of the stories in the collection focus on a bridge as a metaphor. "Sundays in Summer" zeroes in on a condemned bridge from which the narrator's cousin jumped as a young man and was killed. The real story, though, is the narrator's attempt to come to terms with her own childhood, when her parents spent too much time drinking in taverns. The bridge represents the forbidden, the dangerous, and the exciting, all of which presage her own life. The other bridge story, "Why Don't You Come Live With Me It's Time," is a sort of stylized fairy tale about a girl's efforts to attain independence. Her grandmother lives on the other side of a river spanned by a bridge that sways and rattles when crossed. When the narrator was about twelve years old and the bridge was closed for repairs, she climbed across on the steel girders to reach her grandmother's house, only to find her with a strange man and thus to realize that her grandmother's house was not a place to which she could escape any longer.

Another relatively simple symbolic story in the collection, "The Crying Baby," is about a middle-aged woman who hears the cries of a baby coming from the walls of her house. The cause of the sound, she finally realizes, was the miscarriage of her first pregnancy in the house thirty years previously. Although "it" was only six weeks old and more a discharge than a life, the woman knows that if she were to take a pickax and smash through the very foundation of the house, there would be no answer as to why she was being haunted. Whether this story is a pro-life parable or an exploration of the concept of the persistence of guilt is not clear, for it has no context to give it meaning.

Anyone familiar with the American short story in the last half century will find most of these new stories by Joyce Carol Oates familiar, for in many ways they are imitations of the stories of Porter, Welty, and O'Connor. Too many stories are derived from a purely intellectual motivation, and too few spring from the raw emotion they are meant to evoke. Joyce Carol Oates's stories, while seemingly violent and ragged, are actually quite prim and predictable. Ostensibly visceral, they are ultimately cerebral.

Charles E. May

Sources for Further Study

Booklist. LXXXVII, June 1, 1991, p. 1843.
Boston Globe. August 4, 1991, p. 15.
Chicago Tribune. August 4, 1991, XIV, p. 3.
The Christian Science Monitor. August 20, 1991, p. 14.
Houston Post. September 15, 1991, p. C4.
Library Journal. CXVI, July, 1991, p. 137.
Los Angeles Times. September 27, 1991, p. E4.
The New York Times Book Review. XCVI, August 4, 1991, p. 5.
Publishers Weekly. CCXXXVIII, July 5, 1991, p. 55.
The Washington Post Book World. XXI, August 25, 1991, p. 4.

HIS OTHER HALF
Men Looking at Women Through Art

Author: Wendy Lesser
Publisher: Harvard University Press (Cambridge, Massachusetts). Illustrated. 294 pp. $24.95
Type of work: Criticism (art, literature, film)

Lesser analyzes how a variety of male writers and visual artists represent women and attempt to understand their complex relationship to a female self with which they were once united

The essays contained in *His Other Half* are parts of a complicated series of dialogues Wendy Lesser carries on: with various "Men Looking at Women Through Art" (as the subtitle indicates); with the women in this art, often silent or imperfectly understood, whom she teases into conversation; and with feminist critics who tend to be suspicious of, if not hostile to, male representations of the female. Lesser seems equally unhappy with those critics (and artists) who ignore, denigrate, or otherwise restrict woman's central role in art and life and those who defend and praise women in part by using gender as an ineradicable badge, a wedge, and a weapon (a strategy traditionally used against women). Her book attempts to define woman as neither completely a part of nor apart from man and seeks to find a place for woman that is neither upon nor beneath a pedestal. To do this she frames her arguments very carefully. A few basic critical premises underlie and unify her comments on what might otherwise seem to be a wildly eclectic choice of subjects—including fiction by Charles Dickens, D. H. Lawrence, George Gissing, and Henry James, paintings by Edgar Degas, photographs by Cecil Deaton, poetry and criticism by Randall Jarrell, films by Alfred Hitchcock, and the screen images of Marilyn Monroe and Barbara Stanwyck—and these premises are both radical and conservative, revisionary and restorative.

Her opening statement is, like so much of her writing, straightforward and paradoxical: "Gender both does and does not matter." She certainly acknowledges that gender does matter: gender as not merely biological attributes but the whole ensemble of traits, roles, expectations, restrictions, and so on that define, in this case, "woman" in a particular culture as a formidable reality, one that cannot be wished away or easily changed or denied. Yet while gender distinctions separate, they do not necessarily isolate people into inaccessible compartments, and it is the traffic between compartments, so to speak, in which Lesser is particularly interested. Beneath and beyond gender distinctions, she suggests, there is a common, shared humanity, a notion perhaps best captured in Plato's fable in the *Symposium* (c. 384 B.C.) about androgyny. Originally, according to this story, there were unified human beings, composed of a man and a woman joined in a single body. Because these beings were so powerful, the gods split them into separate and individual men and women, who then spent their lives longing for their missing parts. For Lesser—and for many feminists as well, it should be noted—this myth pointedly summarizes much about the human condition: It suggests that the basic fact of life is separation into gender and that the basic motivating power of life is nostalgic desire, taking various forms, such as romantic love, erotic attachment, intellectual and artistic inquiry, expression, and communication. The quest to join another may restore a primal unity and heal a divided self, and many male artists, Lesser points out, offer valuable commentaries on this all-important quest.

The myth of androgynous origin is not simply a handy fable, uncritically accepted by Lesser as the basis of her analytic method. She argues that this myth has been not only restated but, in effect, tested and confirmed by modern psychological theorists. Sigmund Freud's theory of narcissism (broadly speaking, that when one loves someone else one is in a way loving oneself), R. D. Laing's concept of the "divided self" seeking wholeness, and Jacques Lacan's emphasis on a "mirror stage" that gives a child a simultaneous view of a self unified and continuous with one's surroundings and a self separate from one's surroundings echo Plato's myth in one way or another, and each of these theories has deeply influenced not only therapeutic techniques but also modern critical approaches to art. For Lesser, though, it is D. W. Winnicott who offers the most compelling statement of how individual wholeness and identity are forged by a process of looking and having one's look returned. One finds oneself by looking at another: child to mother, man to woman, artist to subject. Art has traditionally been described as a mirror held up to life, but Lesser revises this model: She investigates examples of art as a mirror "in which the portrait one gets back is not the self one expects, but the lost self for which one searches." Male artists are thus not outsiders looking in, but insiders looking out, and while their art is not necessarily always insightful or privileged—she gives examples of skilled artists such as Milan Kundera who nevertheless offer no sympathetic understanding of women— Lesser focuses on numerous examples of men for whom "the feminine represents a mode of access into the 'fictional' . . . [which provides] a way of commenting on, negotiating with, and possibly even altering that 'other' world . . . the world of our everyday reality."

Each of the chapters in *His Other Half* takes up a different aspect of how the artistic representation of women is often the core of a particular work, the point from which all basic themes, crises, and insights radiate. In stories and novels by Dickens, Lawrence, John Berger, Peter Handke, and Harold Brodkey, for example, the struggle to define one's self as a writer is intimately bound up with remembering and loving, but ultimately separating from, one's mother. These artists go beyond sentimentality—essentially a child's-eye view of the mother—to a revelation that may sound harsh to someone who has not worked through the dynamics of this relationship as completely as they have: that a man's story about a mother ends up being about "the extortion of sympathy." A man's relationship with his mother is the formative experience of his life—a reinterpretation of the Oedipal story, placing the mother, not the father, as the key figure—and all lessons about dependence, sympathy, and the limits of sympathy emerge from it. At least for these artists, wholeness and emotional growth come from the sad but liberating task of writing about the death of one's mother.

Other writers have different stories to tell and different images of women to relate or create and examine. Gissing's *The Odd Women* (1893) is, for Lesser, "one of the best portrayals of the women's movement," partially because of his deep sympathy for women who fall outside traditional social categories, especially those who for one reason or another end up unmarried, but also because it raises, intentionally or not, troubling questions about feminism, such as the tendency to let gender concerns override other important issues of class, economic oppression, and so on. In a much different way, the novels of Henry James are valuable not because of any particular positions they arrive at about women or their role in social and psychological life, but because of his insight—strikingly like Lesser's—that gender both does and does not matter, that it is both fixed and fluid, that the key difficulties of life—questions of making fine discriminations without becoming paralyzed, of being sympathetic without losing sight of values and limits—are shared, not divided, by the sexes. James's novels are an affront to feminism because they subject women characters who otherwise seem admirable and correct to intimate, withering, undermining analysis; and yet they are deeply feminist, at least in Lesser's redefined sense of the term, because of James's "congenial feminine sensibility," his sensitive and relentless focus on the complexities of women's thoughts, actions, feelings, and motives, and his unwillingness to accept easy generalizations or simplifications about what it is to be a man and what it is to be a woman. Randall Jarrell, the only poet that Lesser considers in detail in this book, shares with James an awareness that in some ways "we are all women together" (to quote a line from one of Jarrell's poems). Unlike James, Jarrell tends to divide men and women according to gender specific qualities (women are soft and sympathetic; men are hard, witty, detached), but these replicate divisions within his own self, and his examination of women is an integral part of the ongoing process of self-analysis that animates his poetry.

Lesser focuses not only on literature but also on visual arts, and her chapters on the latter are fascinating and instructive, particularly in an age that is increasingly visual rather than verbal but one which has by no means fully considered nor articulated the various codes of visual expression, communication, and representation. The pervasiveness and invasiveness of modern visual arts have heightened the awareness of the way women are defined by the quality of "to-be-looked-atness." Contemporary feminist critics emphasize that women are, in short, subjects of a gaze that is limiting or imprisoning even when it is respectful or adoring, which it often is not. Lesser chooses examples of artists who examine women as they are being looked at, but she broadens the notion of the "gaze" and rebuts the argument that it is always or even typically male, aggressive, hostile, and fixating. Degas' paintings of nude women, for example, portray not helpless, weak objects of voyeuristic male scrutiny but wonderfully private, graceful, secure women, observed but not disturbed. A male viewer of the nude woman in, say, *The Tub* (1886) can gain access to "the vanishing point toward which the best forms of erotic love strive to move: that imaginary place at which the other being is left alone in her self-contained privacy, even as one identifies with her body to the point of feeling it as one's own."

Lesser is not oblivious to the more sinister aspects of the male gaze that cannot be combatted by the lyrical absorption of Degas or the playful and resistant wit of Cecil Beaton, whose photographs present images of women who know they are being looked at but remain impenetrable: Their look back at the viewer is in some respects more profound and transfiguring than the viewer's look at them. Hitchcock is Lesser's prime example of an artist whose works seem to victimize women as they dramatize male fear of women and love. The risks in Hitchcock's films are great: As in William Shakespeare's *Antony and Cleopatra* (c. 1606), the glorious world constructed by love always hovers on the edge of betrayal, suspicion, doubt, frenzy, murder, and vertigo—a list that trails off into the literal titles as well as subjects of Hitchcock's films. Lesser, however, focuses not so much on the disturbing failure of such a work as *Vertigo* (1958) but on its heroic attempt to show a man's effort to overcome failure by "remaking" the woman he loved and lost, an attempt no less heroic and moving because it quickly degenerates from idolization to manipulation and brutal coercion. In contrast with *Vertigo*, a work of excess, Lesser interprets the 1956 version of *The Man Who Knew Too Much* as a successful feminist film, largely about the emergence of a woman from the clutches of a husband trying to subdue and remake her into someone more submissive. Still, Lesser admits, *The Man Who Knew Too Much* is the well-constructed set-piece, while *Vertigo* is the ambitious masterpiece, the work that provokes its audiences because it exposes even though it fails to resolve the linked and deadly problems of sexual desire and power.

The final chapters turn from directors looking at women to the women themselves, examining two actresses and the roles and images that were constructed for them, both with and without their collusion. The first subject is fairly predictable: Marilyn Monroe tops the list of Hollywood actresses whose main attributes are "to-be-looked-at" and "to-be-written-about." Much more than any other essay in the volume, this one is not only meditative and brooding but also rambling and overwrought, perhaps because the subject is so troubling and mysterious. Lesser examines Monroe not as a person but as an image, an image that in retrospect always seems about to crack or dissolve because of the tense contradictions it embodies: ingenuous sincerity and self-conscious artificiality, the promise of innocence and the ravages of experience, the surface beauty and deep despair of sexual desire. All of her roles, in film and in life, it seems, were ultimately sad ones, and her enduring significance is as "the perfect mirror for all of us," allowing viewers a glimpse of an absence, a void, an empty hole.

Lesser ends her book not with the "disembodied body" of Marilyn Monroe but with a much more bracing analysis of Barbara Stanwyck, whose screen image seems to be everything that Monroe's is not. Monroe falls, but Stanwyck floats; Monroe is looked at and sighs, but Stanwyck looks back and talks; Monroe inhabits a resistant and relentless world of absolutes, but Stanwyck, in most of her films with the key exception of *Double Indemnity* (1944), lives in a world that allows free play to her capacity to negotiate, instruct, and be instructed. Stanwyck's portrayal of Stella Dallas has been criticized by some modern feminist critics as a capitulation to outmoded and repressive notions of a woman's obligation to sacrifice herself for another. Lesser, however, suggests that Stanwyck's vulnerability, unlike Monroe's, is "fully conscious and intentional" and her selflessness is courageous and heroic, not obligatory and stifling.

Stanwyck also played characters who were more ruthless than selfless: violent, mean, duplicitous, manipulative, potentially terrifying women, especially to a male viewer. Yet the murderous ruthlessness of *Double Indemnity* is overridden by the instructive, humanizing ruthlessness of *The Lady Eve* (1941), where Stanwyck punishes the priggish Henry Fonda character "for his fear of worldly, sexy women." *The Lady Eve* provides Lesser with one of her best examples of the importance of art that recognizes that there can be life—productive, recuperative, joyous life—after the fall from Eden, from sexual unity. Her faith, demonstrated with admirable force and clarity throughout the book, is that male artists, such as Preston Sturges, the director of *The Lady Eve*, are capable of this kind of art. Male artists may have no unique insight into women, but they make valuable contributions to the study of "masculine" and "feminine," a study that Lesser hopes will one day allow humans to leave behind those troubling categories.

Sidney Gottlieb

Sources for Further Study

Boston Globe. March 7, 1991, p. 78.
Chicago Tribune. March 21, 1991, V, p. 3.
Library Journal. CXVI, February 15, 1991, p. 194.
Los Angeles Times Book Review. March 31, 1991, p. 6.
The Nation. CCLIII, October 14, 1991, p. 456.
New Statesman and Society. IV, May 31, 1991, p. 33.
The New York Times Book Review. XCVI, April 7, 1991, p. 15.
The Times Literary Supplement. June 7, 1991, p. 9.
The Wall Street Journal. March 27, 1991, p. A12.
The Washington Post Book World. XXI, March 10, 1991, p. 5.

A HISTORY OF MODERN CRITICISM, 1750-1950
Volume VII: German, Russian, and Eastern European Criticism, 1900-1950

Author: Rene Wellek (1903-   )
Publisher: Yale University Press (New Haven, Connecticut). 455 pp. $42.50
Type of work: Literary history
Time: 1900-1950
Locale: Germany, Russia, and Eastern Europe

A review of the major literary critics in Germany, Russia, and Eastern Europe from 1900 to 1950

Rene Wellek's latest volume in his monumental *A History of Modern Criticism: 1750-1950* is the next to last book in the project. It is also one of the most interesting volumes since it deals with such influential movements as Russian Formalism and with prominent figures such as Mikhail Bakhtin and Walter Benjamin in addition to critics and schools of criticism with which most American readers will be unfamiliar. Wellek is not only an expert on this material but he has also been a participant in and critic of some of the figures and movements he writes about. So it is a book that has a special claim to authority.

The first section of the book is devoted to German Symbolism. What these critics mean by "Symbolism" tends to be very different both from the connotations of the term associated with the French Symbolists and from the conventional generic meaning of the term in literary criticism. Wellek cites the view of symbolism of Friedrich Gundolf: "In symbolic art the I and the world coincide." These critics were preoccupied with the mystery behind the appearance that is revealed in the greatest art. The symbol was not, to them, a literary device—traditionally distinguished from allegory—but a mystical revelation. Wellek introduces this section by singling out Thomas Mann as a representative figure of this period. Mann did share the German Symbolists' nationalism and interest in a national literature but was not an important critic in his own right.

"Three Thinkers," a section on Sigmund Freud, Carl Gustav Jung, and Martin Heidegger, would seem at first glance one of the most significant parts of the book. Wellek, however, limits his discussion of these figures to the literary criticism they wrote; he does not discuss how their ideas influenced others. Reduced to this level, there is not much of continuing interest. Wellek discusses Freud's essay on *Hamlet* as an example of the Oedipus complex. Freud's idea of art as a continuation of play is also cited; this concept later became an important element of psychoanalytical criticism. Wellek concentrates on Jung's negative evaluation of Joyce's *Ulysses* (1922) and only briefly mentions at the end of this section Jung's concept of the archetype, which later became the theoretical basis of myth criticism. He also touches on Heidegger's existentialist views and on his desire for a national revival that led him to embrace National Socialism. Wellek also criticizes Heidegger for imposing his philosophy on his literary criticism. For Heidegger, literature was not "a linguistic or formal structure, but a mysterious pronouncement of Being."

Two sections on "Scholar Critics" follow; the first, dealing with Romance Philology, is fascinating. The first critic treated, Erich Auerbach, wrote an important book called *Mimesis* (1946; English translation, 1953). Wellek had reservations about the concept of "realism" underlying Auerbach's book when he reviewed it in 1953, and he still has some reservations. He finds problems in Auerbach's subjective and shifting concept of "realism." Even though Wellek admires Auerbach's learning, he is forced to question his methods in creating not literary history but instead one man's view of the nature of existence.

Wellek's discussion of Ernst Curtius and Karl Vossler is less sympathetic. The discussion of Leo Spitzer is much more interesting. Spitzer pioneered stylistics criticism. Wellek finds Spitzer's early criticism to be faulty since it relies on a subjective recognition of the "soul" of the writer. Spitzer tried to provide a justification for his method, but he could get no further than defining the moment of recognition as a "click." The later work of Spitzer was much more important. Wellek praises him for his ability to perceive and convey the sense of unity in a literary work; Spitzer's many studies of individual works stand as models of stylistics criticism.

The largest section of the book is devoted to the Marxist critics in Germany and Russia. The most important German Marxist critics are Walter Benjamin and George Lukács. Benjamin was not interested in aesthetic criticism—Wellek's major critical interest—but in the "truth content of a work of art." His later criticism after the rise of Adolf Hitler became more consciously Marxist as it emphasized the social conditions of the time as determinants of a work of art. Wellek dismisses some of this criticism as merely "ideology," but Benjamin's essay on Goethe for the *Soviet Encyclopedia* was rejected because it was not Marxist enough. Wellek claims that "Politics in a wide sense dominates the later writings of Benjamin as it dominated his life." Wellek, however, is not interested in discussing whether Benjamin's criticism met the test of orthodox Marxism. His concern is literary criticism and not ideological purity.

George Lukács was a more thoroughgoing Marxist critic, one who used the concept of social class in discussing genres and specific works. Wellek has great praise for Lukács' critical abilities, although he has doubts about Lukács' sociological reading of texts. One of Lukács' major critical principles is that of "realism." He used the concept of realism to discuss literature as a representation of social reality; this type of criticism can provide an insight into the workings of society and show how literature is ultimately derived from a social base. His later work, however, is marred, says Wellek, by a slavish devotion to the communist party line; Lukács' discussions of realism became a celebration of Socialist Realism.

The next section is on Russian criticism. The critics in the first part are poets. They, as a group, reject the social and utilitarian criticism that later was so dominant in Russia. Instead, they were connected with such literary movements as Futurism and Acmeism. The most important are Osip Mandelstam and Aleksandr Blok. Blok was a Symbolist and believed that artists created their own world through their art.

Nevertheless, he also supported the view of literature as valuable for its utility, the message it could send to the reader. Wellek praises his criticism as "lucid, sensible," although the criticism consists of only a few theoretical concepts and no close examination of specific literary works. Mandelstam was an important poet who shared the views of the Symbolists and the Acmeism group. His most interesting criticism, Wellek suggests, is found in his negative comments on contemporary poetry. The main use that Wellek sees in these critical works is the hope that they will illuminate the poetry of Mandelstam.

The next section deals with Russian Marxist critics. Nearly all of these critics stressed the social dimension over the formal element of literature. There was some debate about what the official position of the state should be toward the creative writer. Aleksandr Voronsky, for example, demanded a tolerant attitude since the censorship of art was absurd, but other groups wanted more restrictive rules. In 1925, the Central Committee formulated the policy that there was "no neutral art." The purpose of all art was to serve the Soviet state and the proletariat. In 1934, "Socialist Realism" was decreed to be the "only acceptable mode of Soviet literature."

The critics during this period took various positions on the nature and purpose of literature. Vladimir Lenin had seen art as a propaganda tool for the socialist movement, yet he was tolerant about deviations since he understood that literature did not easily lend itself to state control. Maxim Gorky saw art only as persuasion. Its purpose was not to provide delight but only instruction. Leo Trotsky went further; he saw society as the key shaping element. He also saw the possibility of reviving the genre of tragedy, but there would be no God in these plays, only social reality.

The section on Russian Formalism is one of the most interesting ones in the book. Wellek has sympathy with the aims and the accomplishments of this criticism since it asked—and partially answered—some basic questions about the nature of literature. Viktor Shklovsky is the most important theoretician of the movement in his concept of literature being constituted of devices; the presence of these devices distinguishes it from other types of writing by its "literariness." The function of the critic's analysis was to reveal the device that structures the work. Shklovsky also discovered another function for literature: "to restore the feeling for life." This was to be done by "defamiliarization," a sense of strangeness in the work that provoked a new response from the reader; it was not the mere reflection of social reality but defamiliarization was to make that "reality" strange and unfamiliar. Boris Eikhenbaum is best known for his essay on Gogol's *The Overcoat* (1842). He saw the work not as realistic but instead as absurd and grotesque. Like Shklovsky, he focused analysis on the artificial elements of the work.

The next section of the book is devoted not to a movement but to an individual critic, Mikhail Bakhtin. Bakhtin's views of the dialogical nature of the novel have generated a considerable amount great deal of recent criticism of novels and stories. Bakhtin contrasted the monological single voice of the epic to the multivoiced novel. Bakhtin also disagreed with the Formalists that literature is the sum of its devices;

his concept of the polyphonic and the Carnivalesque elements of literature contrasts directly with the analysis of the Formalists. Wellek has some reservations about Bakhtin's views on genre, but he praises him as an important and innovative critic.

The last part of the book deals with critics of Eastern Europe. He discusses one Polish critic, Roman Ingarden, who wrote an important book *Das literarische Kunstwerk* (1931; *The Literary Work of Art*, 1973). For Ingarden, a literary work possessed "an 'idea' or at least 'metaphysical qualities.'" He also saw four strata, or cognitive levels, in reader response to a literary work. These four levels of reading made up a complete and proper response by the reader. Wellek had some disagreements with Ingarden's discussion of the nature of a literary work in 1934, and he cites his own resolution of the problem in his essay on "The Mode of Existence of a Literary Work of Art" in his *Theory of Literature* (1949). Wellek recognizes the importance of Ingarden's work, even though he has chosen a very different solution to some of the same fundamental problems.

The last part of the section on Eastern European criticism deals primarily with the Czech critic, Jan Mukařovský. Mukařovský was a formalist who shared some positions with the American New Critics. He described the structure of a literary work as the "inner unification" of the various parts in the work. He also used a number of ideas of the Russian Formalists such as the device and "deformation," a version of the earlier "defamiliarization." Wellek points out, however, that Mukařovský had some difficulty including social values into his formalist criticism. Mukařovský tried to claim there were "extra-aesthetic" values but that the "artistic value" was dominant. His dilemma was finally resolved after World War II when he rejected his early aesthetic criticism in favor of Marxism.

Volume 7 of *A History of Modern Criticism, 1750-1950* is the best and fullest treatment of the criticism of Germany, Russia, and Eastern Europe from 1900 to 1950, although there are individual studies of many of these types of criticism that are much more detailed and authoritative. For example, there are books on Marxist criticism and Russian Formalism that go into far more depth than Wellek can in his survey. Wellek cites many of these works as his sources in the extensive bibliography at the end of the book. Wellek's book is very much a survey since he only summarizes the actual critical work of the specific critic and does not trace its influence or later development. The most interesting portions are on those critics with whom Wellek has had earlier exchanges, such as Erich Auerbach and Roman Ingarden. Wellek's own evaluations and judgments of individual critics are also very interesting and they give depth to the summaries.

James Sullivan

Sources for Further Study

Library Journal. CXVI, August, 1991, p. 102.
London Review of Books. XIV, February 13, 1992, p. 15.
The Washington Post Book News. XXI, December 8, 1991, p. 1.

A HISTORY OF PRIVATE LIFE
Volume V: Riddles of Identity in Modern Times

Editors: Antoine Prost (1933-   ) and Gérard Vincent
First published: Histoire de la vie privée: De la Première Guerre mondiale à nos jours, 1987
Translated from the French by Arthur Goldhammer; translated from the Italian by Raymond
    Rosenthal; translated from the German and edited by Mary Jo Maynes and Michele Mouton
Publisher: The Belknap Press of Harvard University Press (Cambridge, Massachusetts). Illus-
    trated. 630 pp. $39.95
Type of work: History
Time: The twentieth century
Locale: Primarily France; Sweden, Italy, Germany, and the United States

*This volume examines the effect of the twentieth century's sweeping cultural, social, and
political changes on private life and the institution of the family*

As its fifth volume, *A History of Private Life: Riddles of Identity in Modern Times*
represents the final installment and chronological climax of an acclaimed French
series. The book caps a broad historical inquiry—envisioned by two French senior
editors, the late Philippe Ariès, and Georges Duby—which began with a look at
private life in classical Greco-Roman times and pursued its topic through volumes
dealing with the Middle Ages, the Renaissance, and the period from the French
Revolution to the outbreak of World War I (for reviews of the first four volumes, see
Magill's Literary Annual, 1988, 1989, 1990, and 1991).

Originally published in France between 1985 and 1987, the volumes of *A History
of Private Life* gradually began to lose the broadness of scope promised by their title;
volume 4, for example, dealt almost exclusively with the French experience. For the
fifth volume, however, this widely criticized limitation has been corrected. This
American edition includes material not contained in the original French version; the
essays dealing with the development of private life in the United States, Italy, Germany, and Scandinavia (the latter appeared in the French original as well) bestow a
depth of inquiry that makes this volume attractive to a wider range of readers and
more closely fulfills the initial conception of the series.

Ironically, however, it is largely the material which deals with either a clearly
presented subgroup of French society, or with private life in another culture, that is
most accessible to an American reader. The first section of the book, "Public and
Private Spheres in France," written by one of the editors, Antoine Prost, often leaves
stumped a person who does not know the history of France in the twentieth century:
Figures such as Charles de Gaulle and groups such as the Popular Front are integrated into the narrative without a nod to readers unfamiliar with French history,
whereas the subsequent sections and essays do provide helpful maps of the historical
landscapes out of which the landmarks arise.

Nevertheless, for a reader willing to follow Prost through his ingenious discussion
of the often drastic and—for an American almost incomprehensible—relatively recent changes in French life, the first section proves rewarding. Here, Prost reveals
some of France's most private struggles, ideals, and obsessions. Themes such as the

increasing separation of workplace from living space, the weakening of traditional marriage, and massive urbanization and the emergence of an electronic mass culture are viewed from a distinctively French perspective.

With a good sense for the close relationship between physical space and environment on the one hand, and the possibilities for the individual to develop and maintain a sense of self on the other, Prost leads the reader into a land where living and working situations often pose specific challenges to a personal identity. In 1954, for example, French living quarters were still incredibly cramped. Additionally, scarcely more than half of the households had running water, and not more than one quarter provided residents with an indoor toilet; nine out of ten dwellings possessed neither shower, bathtub, nor central heating. Thus, as in premodern societies, much of life still revolved around communal sites such as public water pumps, neighborhood coal shops, and the streets into which people spilt. The role played by communal settings in French life waned as modern housing was erected. By 1973, 97 percent of all households had running water.

If there remains a sense that something is missing in this book, however, it results from a reader's longing for a more comparative approach to the startling facts of modernization. Often, Prost presents French conditions in relative isolation, and does not sufficiently develop connections to other cultures—an omission which one should not forgive the final volume of a series which won such praise for its comprehensive approach. Too rare are such moments of insight as this glimpse of the French reaction to American housing developments:

> When NATO forces withdrew from France in 1966 and housing developments abandoned by the U.S. Army were sold to French citizens, the new owners' first concern was to build fences. Within a few months a sort of suburban equivalent of the rural hedgerow had sprung up on what had been a continuous expanse of green.

More of this would have made for an even more valuable book.

The second section, entitled "A History of Secrets?" by coeditor Gérard Vincent, begins with a provocative quote from Jean-Paul Sartre: "We were never so free as under the German occupation." He points at the fact that because under the Nazis, the State was evil beyond doubt, all citizens gained personal freedom in that they could morally reject all public claims on their lives. In modern democracies, Vincent asserts, the situation is more difficult, since the individual must accept the moral validity of certain official limitations. For example, under a law that requires a truck driver to wear glasses if he or she fails a vision test, the "secret" of a trucker's insufficient sight has been ferreted out by the government, and the driver must morally consent to society's sanctions.

Vincent's overriding thematic concern with "secrets" leads him to discuss contemporary problems such as alcoholism, drug abuse, abortion, and "the eclipse of the male" under the rubric "Family Secrets." What was once suppressed is now flaunted. Similarly, Vincent's chapter on changing attitudes toward fitness and sexuality presents itself as a discussion of "the Enigma of Sex." Here, interestingly enough, Vincent's occasional inclusion of non-French material provides a startling involuntary demonstration of the cultural bias of the writer himself. His discussion of homosexuality, for example, suddenly quotes exclusively American and German studies; as illustration, he chooses a picture of American gays dressed in cowboy hats and leather pants, thus echoing perhaps the belief of France's first female prime minister, Edith Cresson, that the French male is the most heterosexual of them all.

The volume's third section, "Cultural Diversity in France," offers the American reader a portrait of a society far less homogenous than expected. There is Vincent's harsh treatment of the French Catholic Church, which he compares to French Communism; for Vincent, the latter constitutes an equally faith-based, hermetic system whose "moral asceticism" is "an extension of Judeo-Christian asceticism." Vincent's eventual rejection of Communism is based on the Party's Stalinist heritage and its Orwellian requirement that "with each new twist in the party line, party members had to change their tune—or quit the party."

This third section includes some of the best material in the book. In Perrine Simon-Nahum's perceptive and sympathetic depiction of French Judaism, the horrors which the Nazi occupation brought to France's often highly assimilated Jewish community are remembered in haunting detail. The emergence of a post-World War II sense of community among the survivors is presented as an example of individual people who perceive family, religion, and tradition not as burdensome relics but as an empowering presence in their modern lives.

Section 4 leaves the realm of France, introducing the reader to the private lives of other Europeans as well as Americans. As a rule, these individual sketches are well organized and offer the reader a rich, insightful, and generally balanced view of the situation in the cultures they highlight. Throughout, the authors clearly establish what is particular to the nations they discuss, and draw relatively few comparisons. This approach involves some duplication, but is rewarding in that the reader can discover emerging familiar patterns: There is evidence everywhere of the weakening of patriarchal control, and the experimentation with alternatives to traditional families; but there is also a strange resilience of the old institutions, among which the family appears most ineradicable.

It is left to the reader to discover these sweeping, general trends, and to observe the many variations on the overall themes and developments. No sustained attempt is made at ordering these individual experiences to form a universal Western pattern. Because of this, one may wonder on what basis the countries represented were selected; the omission of Great Britain seems puzzling.

Nevertheless, each individual essay provides the reader with a view of the challenges, pitfalls, and opportunities which the private self has encountered in various countries throughout the course of the twentieth century. Kristina Orfali's lovingly rendered portrait of Sweden courageously starts with a discussion of the factors which led to "the initial enthusiasm" and "the subsequent disillusionment" which the "Swedish model" has aroused in the West. Swedish society emerges as a system "governed by one collective morality" which can easily swing toward total bureaucratic control of the individual, who then finds refuge in the quintessential private space of the rural summer cabin.

Chiara Saraceno's portrait of the history of the Italian family is characterized by her audacious high-wire act between the two poles of personal (even autobiographical) memories and impersonal tables of statistics. She thus offers a full, varied documentation of her findings, which demonstrate that while Italian marriages remained more stable than most of their Western counterparts, there nevertheless exists a typical trend toward an increase in divorce cases, and the Italian man has become less patriarchal as the century has progressed.

The concise and methodical overview which Ingeborg Weber-Kellermann presents of the German family reaches back to the peasant and warrior tribes who peopled the forests of ancient Germany, and quickly moves to the modern era. The impact of historical events such as the foundation of the German Empire in 1871, the loss of World War I, and the rise of Nazism is closely related to the private reactions which changed the German family during these violent ruptures of recent history. Faced with the ruin and guilt of the postwar years, and living in a divided nation, Germans turned to the family as a place from which moral renewal could begin. Challenged by some critics as prolonging autocratic structures, the family came under pressure in the 1960's; from then on, Germany, too, has seen the emergence of alternatives to marriage.

Weber-Kellermann's intense interest in the status of women in both (formerly) West and East Germany provides a fortuitous link to Elaine Tyler May's concluding chapter on the American family. Here, some of the overriding ideas of other sections reappear in a familiar environment. For May, divorce cases constitute a narrative thread as she sketches the emergence of the "nuclear family" from its roots in the nineteenth century to its undisputed heyday during the 1950's, and its subsequent decline. At best, these special cases offer a snapshot of people caught in a personal storm during specific historic moments; at worst, they lead the author to speculate wildly about the private motives of individual people whose court records do not offer concrete evidence for her assumptions. Yet May's overall discussion of changes, possibilities, and the actual development of the American family is exciting to follow and full of interesting insights.

Overall, *A History of Private Life: Riddles of Identity in Modern Times* is a delight to read, and presents a fine variety of diverse cultures. But its authors often take specific positions, and try to persuade. This is not always done with any scholarly grace or political flexibility. When Prost, for example, asserts that in contemporary France, the "couple that lived together gained nothing by marrying" and that by doing so, "they often experienced a sense of loss" because "to marry was to make a commitment, to devote one's life to a purpose," some readers will be left with a sense of bewilderment at the logic of his argument.

The lavish illustrations again make this volume a pleasure to browse through. Perhaps nowhere else does the book so strongly convey a sense of the different cultures it presents. Ironically, however, the illustrations also point at the one fact which remains curiously marginalized, even unacknowledged, by the text: the global impact of American popular culture.

Probably unintentionally, the incredible, almost subliminal level at which things American have become part of every culture's fabric is illustrated most beautifully in a picture of a North African family in their French apartment. Here, dressed in traditional Arab clothes, the father sits on a blanket which bears the proud logo, "Battlestar Galactica." America, the picture shows, is at home everywhere in this century.

R. C. Lutz

Sources for Further Study

Los Angeles Times. November 6, 1991, p. E7.
St. Louis Post-Dispatch. December 22, 1991, p. C5.
Vogue. CLXXXII, January, 1992, p. 76.
The Washington Post Book World. XXI, November 17, 1991, p. 8.
Washington Times. November 10, 1991, p. B8.

A HISTORY OF THE ARAB PEOPLES

Author: Albert Hourani (1915-   )
Publisher: Harvard University Press (Cambridge, Massachusetts). Illustrated. 551 pp. $24.95
Type of work: History
Time: Seventh century to the 1990's
Locale: The Arab-speaking world (Spain, North Africa, the Middle East)

A noted Oxford scholar traces the political, cultural, and religious history of the Arab peoples from the emergence of Islam to the present

Albert Hourani's *A History of the Arab Peoples* is an ambitious and successful attempt to summarize fourteen centuries of political, cultural, and religious history of people who inhabited an area that encompassed Spain, North Africa, and the Middle East. The book, which also contains a thirty-page bibliography, several maps, and tables and lists of the Prophet's descendants, caliphs, dynasties, and prominent families, represents an important scholar's lifetime of research and is the fitting culmination of his earlier works: *Arabic Thought in the Liberal Age, 1798-1939* (1983), *Europe and the Middle East* (1980), and *The Emergence of the Modern Middle East* (1981).

Although he asserts that his book is intended for beginning students and general readers, Hourani includes such a wealth of information that most of his intended audience may be overwhelmed. When he discusses general subjects, such as Arab poetry and its relation to society, or when he includes short vignettes about representative Arab figures, the book is fascinating and most readable, but his accounts of political and religious dynasties read more like a densely packed textbook. For the benefit of his readers, there are helpful summaries introducing each of the five parts of the narrative, and the indexing is comprehensive enough to aid browsers and researchers looking for specific information.

Hourani divides his twenty-six-chapter book into five parts, each with a distinct focus or theme, though there are some recurrent themes that pervade the entire book: the essential unity of an Arab world tied to its religion, Islam; the failure to achieve the model "just" Islamic society; and a view of history influenced by the Arab historian Ibn Khaldun, the first figure mentioned in the book and a theoretician whose political ideas resonate throughout the book. In fact, Ibn Khaldun serves as a symbol of the continuity Hourani sees as characteristic of Arab culture.

Part 1, which spans the seventh to tenth centuries, concerns the emergence, development, and "articulation" of Islam, but Hourani devotes much attention to Arab poetry, another recurrent topic, and to the importance of the tribe. The focus is on the unity of faith and language and on how Islam is "articulated" through not only the Koran but also the "Pillars of Islam" and the *hadiths* (recorded traditions associated with Muhammad). The first part is particularly important, since it explains how the current Islamic sects originated and how schisms are themselves a tradition in Islam. Because of the scope of the book, Hourani does necessarily generalize, but some of the generalizations conceal fairly significant points. When he discusses the growth of Islam, Hourani states that "the momentum of action carried it into the frontier regions of the great empires and then, as resistance proved weak, into their hearts." "Momentum of action" implies that conquest was not sought, but only occurred, and "resistance proved weak" ignores the coercion employed by Islam. Such coercion involved several severe discriminatory laws against non-Muslims; Hourani makes the understatement that "the inducement to convert existed."

Part 2, which covers the eleventh to fifteenth centuries, delineates the way the Arab Muslim societies functioned as a unified order. Hourani focuses on the countryside, the cities, and the courts, as well as the continuing "articulation" of Islam, which is shown in its "divergent paths of thought," among them the development of Shī'ism. Hourani maintains his theme of unity by providing an interesting and illuminating account of the structure of the cities and the architecture of the buildings—cities and houses reflect the Islamic religion and culture. Another fascinating discussion concerns the position of women in Islam. Hourani states that the Koran asserts the "essential equality of men and women: 'Whoso doeth right, whether male or female, and is a believer, all such will enter the Garden.'" That quotation hardly asserts "essential equality," and Hourani does go on to list the many ways women's limits were defined by the *shari'a* (Muslim law derived from the Koran). While early Muslim women did, in fact, have more rights than many of their non-Muslim contemporaries, relatively little has changed for Muslim women, despite Hourani's repeated mention of attempts at improving their situation.

Part 3 discusses the Ottoman Age, the period from the sixteenth to the eighteenth centuries when the Arab people were under Turkish control. The best that can be said for the Ottoman Empire is that it was, for Hourani, "the last great expression of the universality of the world of Islam"; the least is that under Ottoman rule "there had been no advance in technology and a decline in the level of scientific knowledge and understanding." As the Ottoman Empire declined in the face of growing European power, Arab fortunes also declined. Thus, Hourani seems to imply that Arab scientific knowledge suffered under imperialism, first exercised by the Turks and then by the European powers. Another disturbing trend was the dramatic economic shift caused by the Arab world's becoming a supplier of raw materials and a consumer of finished products—this, too, contributed to technological stagnation. The blame for declining Arab technology may also be placed, however, on an educational system that, taking its cue from Islamic teaching methods, relied primarily on memorization, which has retained its importance even in modern Arab society.

The Ottoman imperialism was followed by the age of European empires, the subject of part 4 (1800-1939). In the introductory summary to this part of the book, Hourani identifies a topic that persists to the present: "A new kind of thought emerged, trying to explain the reasons for the strength of Europe and show that Muslim countries could adopt European ideas and methods without being untrue to their own beliefs." Unfortunately, this "new kind of thought" has produced in the Arab peoples emotions of envy and inferiority, on the one hand, and a defensive contempt for Western moral values, on the other. As Hourani observes, when Arab students study abroad, they are likely to suffer a "psychological displacement" as they are torn between two contradictory cultures. Americans who are confused about what appear to be intense and vacillating Arab positions can learn much from Hourani's discussion of this point, especially if they consider the number of Arabs who have relatives in the West, who have married Westerners, and who have studied abroad.

Despite "vested" interests in the Western world, Western imperialism rankled, not only politically but economically, as the Arab world increasingly became a supplier of raw materials and a consumer of finished products. Nationalism was inevitable and was expressed in two ways, through pride in the Arabic language and through efforts to "reform" Islam. Reforming Islam and reforming archaic institutions impeding progress were, however, often incompatible goals. One of the areas in need of reform was women's rights, which Hourani states were given impetus by nationalism, but he later admits that by 1939 the changes in women's status were relatively superficial, restricted as they were to advances that helped their societies prosper economically. One of the most significant nationalistic movements was the Muslim Brothers, an Egyptian movement originally created to promote individual and social morality through a return to the true Islam, a return that effectively repressed women.

In part 5, which concerns the period since 1939, Hourani discusses the "age of the nation-states," a time marked by increased nationalism. According to him, nationalism included a cluster of ideas: "the development of natural resources, popular education and the emancipation of women." While those Arab countries with oil and gas reserves did prosper, others (Jordan and Egypt) languished, beset by economic problems. (In fact, the hostility of the Arab have-not countries for the haves simmered until it later boiled over in the Persian Gulf War of 1991.) In terms of natural resources, nationalism became a divisive rather than unifying force for the Arabs. Despite Hourani's insistence that Saudi Arabia and the Gulf states "began giving aid on a large scale to the poorer states," that aid was not perceived as being adequate by the poorer nations, who later in 1990 were to express little sympathy for the plight of Kuwait and Saudi Arabia. The lack of Saudi investment in other Arab countries— the Saudis did invest heavily in the West—also hindered economic development and produced more hostility.

Readers of Hourani's book will have no illusions about the causes of the continuing Middle East crisis: Great Britain and France. The two powers were responsible for the Lebanese situation (the French protected Christian interests), the haves and have-nots (the British created the Gulf states to preserve their control of oil reserves), and the Palestinian problem (the British efforts to establish Israel). Hourani's analysis of the postwar boundary lines is interesting reading—he remarks in passing that Iran had claims on Bahrain that were not withdrawn until 1970. If Iraq had successfully annexed Kuwait in 1990, one wonders if a similar situation would have developed with Iran and Bahrain.

In light of Hourani's continuing discussion about the secular/sacred conflict regarding the degree to which Islam should be involved in political matters, developments in Egypt, Iraq and Syria, and Saudi Arabia are seen as examples of a longstanding Arabic tradition. Gamal Abdel Nasser's socialist movement in Egypt was very successful in the Arab world, especially when he defied the West over the Suez Canal, but the secular nature of the party ran counter to the fundamentalist Muslims (the Muslim Brothers) who urged the merger of church and state represented in Saudi Arabia and post-Shah Iran. Similarly, the Ba'th parties of Syria and Iraq have encountered, despite very repressive measures, opposition from the Shī'ites and the Muslim Brothers. During the Persian Gulf War, even the secular Saddam Hussein was photographed at prayer in an attempt to elicit support from fundamentalists as he attempted to convert a land-grab into a *jihad*, or religious war.

Readers of *A History of the Arab Peoples* will find the historical context against which current events—the Israeli-Palestinian conflict, the Sudanese war, the fundamentalist revolt in North Africa, and the ambitions of Syria (Greater Syria) and Iraq—are being played out. Like any historian, however, Hourani is selective in his coverage and has his own political stance, even if it is somewhat muted. He refers to the killings at the refugee camps of Sabra and Shatila as a "massacre of Palestinians on a large scale" and on the next page alludes to "attacks on U.S. Marines" without mentioning the suicide-bombing attack that killed more than two hundred Marines in Beirut. Nor are Syrian massacres of their own people (at Hama) at the same time given any mention. While Hourani notes the repressive measures of some Arab countries, there is no indication of the scope, magnitude, or means of repression (including chemical weapons) that Arab rulers have used against their own populations. Nor is there any indication of the extent of international terrorism being conducted by Libya and Syria.

Similarly, while Hourani keeps women's rights before the reader and acknowledges that fundamentalist Muslims are likely to "reinforce a traditional view of women's place in society," he suggests elsewhere that Muslim women were "often pillars of the system," that they in fact helped preserve it. This notion comes close to blaming the victim and overlooks the fundamentally inferior position, reinforced by the Koran, of women in Islamic society. Summarizing without comment from Fatima Mernissi's *Beyond the Veil: Male-Female Dynamics in Modern Muslim Society* (1985), a book that is critical of the Islamic view of women, does not reflect an accurate optimistic picture of women's rights in Arab-speaking countries.

Hourani's history is, nevertheless, an impressive achievement, one that incorporates many events, figures, and countries in an overall view of the Arab peoples. The strength of the book also resides in its organization, its structuring of themes, ideas, and motifs so that the Arab culture is seen as a constant, one that contains cycles or patterns that suggest a cultural religious unity, even if political unity or cohesion seems an unlikely prospect. Intended readers of the book will want to use Hourani's extensive bibliography—and other sources—to pursue some of the issues in more detail and to arrive at their own conclusions. *A History of the Arab Peoples* is essential reading for anyone interested in Islam and the Arab world.

Thomas L. Erskine

Sources for Further Study

Chicago Tribune. March 31, 1991, XIV, p. 1.
The Christian Science Monitor. April 19, 1991, p. 13.
Commentary. XCII, September, 1991, p. 56.
Foreign Affairs. LXX, Summer, 1991, p. 181.
Los Angeles Times Book Review. February 17, 1991, p. 1.
The New York Review of Books. XXXVIII, September 26, 1991, p. 50.
The New York Times Book Review. XCVI, March 31, 1991, p. 3.
The New Yorker. LXVII, May 13, 1991, p. 111.
The Times Literary Supplement. February 22, 1991, p. 5.
The Washington Post Book World. XXI, March 31, 1991, p. 1.

HOLOCAUST TESTIMONIES
The Ruins of Memory

Author: Lawrence L. Langer (1929-   )
Publisher: Yale University Press (New Haven, Connecticut). 216 pp. $25.00
Type of work: History
Time: The twentieth century, especially the period from 1933 to 1991
Locale: Europe and the United States

Utilizing the Fortunoff Video Archives for Holocaust Testimonies at Yale University, Langer explores the oral histories of former victims of the Holocaust and shows how their testimonies affect understanding of that disaster

Elie Wiesel survived Auschwitz, became a distinguished author, and won the 1986 Nobel Peace Prize. In April, 1977, he gave an address at Northwestern University. It was called "The Holocaust as Literary Inspiration." Although Wiesel and other noted writers have made that disaster a fundamental dimension of their work, he contended that his talk's title contained a contradiction. Wiesel's point was that the Holocaust, Nazi Germany's planned total destruction of the Jewish people and the actual murder of nearly six million of them, outstrips, overwhelms, and negates "literary inspiration." What happened then to the Jewish children, women, and men— and to millions of non-Jewish victims who also were caught in the Holocaust— eludes complete expression, to say nothing of full comprehension, now.

Such claims involve no mystification. Nor do they deny that the Holocaust is an explicable historical event that was unleashed by human beings for human reasons. Yet, as disclosed by the testimony of those who survived it, the Holocaust remains at the depths of personal experience a disaster that no description can equal. Tempting though silence may be, it provides no refuge from this condition. Words to cry out of those depths must be found. Therefore, Wiesel's address at Northwestern underscored how significant it was that there were writers in every ghetto, witnesses in every camp, who did their best to testify.

In particular, Wiesel called attention to the diaries of Zalman Gradowski, Leib Langfuss, and Yankiel Wiernik. Trapped by what Lawrence L. Langer calls "choiceless choices," those *Sonderkommando* members were condemned to burn the bodies of their Jewish brothers and sisters at Auschwitz-Birkenau and Treblinka. Listen, Wiesel urged, and then he read their words to his audience. Listen, listen—at one point, gripped by his own listening, Wiesel interrupted himself. "You must listen more," he insisted, "you must listen to more. I repeat, if Wiernik had the courage to write, you must listen." And then he read on.

No one has listened more or better than Lawrence Langer, a professor of English at Simmons College in Boston who had long been a leading interpreter of literature about the Holocaust. The proof is his *Holocaust Testimonies.* Profoundly, this book takes its readers into a region that Langer's subtitle aptly identifies as "the ruins of memory." Langer borrowed that phrase from another powerful writer, Ida Fink, whose personal Holocaust experiences led her to speak not about time "measured in months and years" but about time measured in scraps—separations, selections, silences—that forever fragment life and thwart its wholeness.

Langer's book results from years of painstaking excavation in the ruins of memory at the Fortunoff Video Archive for Holocaust Testimonies, established at Yale University in 1982. Its holdings—more than fourteen hundred testimonies that range in length from thirty minutes to more than four fours—are available for viewing. *Holocaust Testimonies* compels one to witness these moving accounts. The Fortunoff Archive is preparing a composite videotape to accompany Langer's book. That combination will provide potent ways to teach about the Holocaust.

Langer himself conducted many of the archive's interviews with Holocaust survivors or "former victims," as he prefers to call them. But Langer's exceptional accomplishment goes much further than that. Few people, if any, have witnessed more Holocaust testimonies. Nor has anyone observed so many of them so carefully. Definitely no one has written about these testimonies with more intensity, honesty, and telling impact.

A governing theme in Langer's findings comes from Maurice Blanchot, the author of *L'Écriture du désastre* (1980; *The Writing of the Disaster*, 1986), a study that helped to inform Langer's listening. "The disaster ruins everything," Blanchot's first sentence says, "all the while leaving everything intact." Like nature's changing seasons, the rising and setting of the sun, apparently life goes on for the Holocaust's former victims. Many testify, for example, how they married after liberation from the German camps, built homes in new surroundings, reared children, and advanced careers. Apparently their survival led to living lives that left everything intact.

Only apparently, however, because the disaster leaves everything intact in another, far more devastating sense. Leaving the survivors alone, it removes—takes the former victims away from—the stability and coherence that normal life assumes. Thus, for those who stayed alive after Auschwitz, life does anything but just go on. For the Holocaust's former victims, the disaster that came upon them so often pivoted around disorienting/orienting scraps of time, crucial moments involving what Blanchot calls the "sovereignty of the accidental," a tyranny that ruled and destroyed life with systematic capriciousness. Its disruptive impact makes the Holocaust a past ever present and always to be reencountered in the future.

Only one of the many testimonies that Langer sensitively weaves into his account, Philip K.'s epitomizes how "the disaster ruins everything." Resisting the reassurance of people "who pretend or seem to be marveling at the fact that I seem to be so normal, so unperturbed and so capable of functioning," Philip K. concludes *Holocaust Testimonies* by denying that "the Holocaust passed over and it's done with." No, he stresses, "it's my *skin*. This is not a coat. You can't take it off. And it's there, and it will be there until I die."

Ghettoized, starved, deported, tattooed, beaten, raped, gassed, burned, callously scattered to the winds, but some of it left permanently scarred to live—Holocaust skin both covers and recovers what Langer calls "an anatomy of melancholy." Physically rooted in the disaster, that anatomy is much more than skin-deep. Often buried deeply but incompletely by an impossible necessity to forget, the memory resurrected—but not triumphantly—by the anatomy of melancholy is laden with what another former victim, Charlotte Delbo, calls "useless knowledge." Dissenting from the conventional wisdom that knowledge is always useful, Delbo's phrase is another that echoes in Langer's listening, for *Holocaust Testimonies* shows how survival in Auschwitz did little to unify, edify, or dignify the lives of former victims. It divided, besieged, and diminished them instead.

Langer's account, it must be emphasized, protests against any impulse that would judge and find wanting what the former victims did in their conditions of Holocaust extremity. On the contrary, the entire book is an expression of esteem and admiration "to all the hundreds of men and women who told their stories before the camera." Judgment, to be sure, does speak in these pages—it seethes in quiet rage between the lines as one hears silently Langer's writing of the disaster—but that judgment is properly reserved for the German policies that systematized the Holocaust's choiceless choices and the perpetrators who administered them. The disaster that came upon the Holocaust's victims was designed to make evident what Nazi ideology proclaimed, namely, that Jews were sub- or even nonhuman, and its plan for doing so was to create conditions of domination so extreme that normal human life could not go on within them. That plan did not succeed entirely, but in the Nazi camps, as Leon H. puts it, "human life was like a fly." Hunger, to mention but one of the Holocaust's hells, was not only "devastating to the human body," as George S. testifies, but also "devastating to the human spirit, . . . and you didn't know how to function."

The victims of *l'univers concentrationnaire* did what they had to do—"This wasn't good and that wasn't good," remembers Hannah F., "so what choice did we have?" Sidney L. adds to that realization when his testimony begins with the fact that he was one of nine children. The Holocaust's desolation left him as his family's lone survivor. One glimpses how far life under German domination was removed from usual human expectations about choice and responsibility when, with disarming simplicity, he recalls, "I was never asked 'Do you want to do such and such?'" The glimpse, however, remains incomplete—"Well, how shall I describe to you how Auschwitz was?" puzzles Edith P. Her question, which is asked in one way or another by many of the Holocaust witnesses Langer heard, seems addressed to herself as much as to her audience.

Speaking from his own experience, Langer rightly insists that listening to these testimonies requires extraordinary effort. They can easily be distorted and falsified by the imposition of moral, philosophical, psychological, or religious categories—including what Langer calls "the grammar of heroism and martyrdom"—that are inappropriate because they belong to a universe of normal discourse that the Holocaust eclipsed. After Auschwitz, the human mind would naturally like to reduce the dissonance that Holocaust testimonies introduce, heal the heartbreak left intact in their wake. The yearning runs deep—especially as one reads *Holocaust Testimonies*—for justice to prevail, wholeness to be restored, moral expectation to be vindicated, and the human spirit to be triumphant. But that yearning collides with Langer's convincing insistence that the anatomy of melancholy does not forecast a high probability in favor of those hopes. The reader is split by Langer's book. In the ruins of memory expectation diminishes and yearning intensifies at once. As those feelings, conflicted and conflicting, resound in the testimony he has heard, Langer moves his reader to encounter them and to let the resulting tension remain as it must: unreconciled and unreconciling.

The stark bleakness of Langer's anatomy of melancholy calls for coming to terms, if one can, with a condition that recalls Blanchot once more. As though he had heard Helen K.'s lament ("I can't believe what my eyes have seen") and pondered the question posed by Edith P. and so many others ("Do you understand what I'm trying to tell you?"), Blanchot invites meditation on circumstances in which "there is a question and yet no doubt; there is a question, but no desire for an answer; there is a question, and nothing that can be said, but just this nothing, to say. This is a query, a probe that surpasses the very possibility of questions."

Optimism is scarce in the ruins of memory, but what Langer does find and carefully guard is "unshielded truth," an honesty that underscores what must be faced: "How overwhelming, and perhaps insurmountable," as he puts it, "is the task of reversing [the Holocaust's] legacy." That legacy dwells in memory that is deep, anguished, humiliated, tainted, and unheroic. Correspondingly, that memory disturbingly uncovers selves who are buried, divided, besieged, impromptu, and diminished. Such is the taxonomy that Langer's anatomy of melancholy requires.

Often with greater penetration than written narratives by former victims, Langer is convinced, their oral testimony divulges the disruptions within these dimensions of the Holocaust's legacy. Written words can be polished, edited, and revised; they can become art in ways that oral testimonies cannot. Langer wants both oral and written testimony to have the respect each kind deserves. So he stresses that written accounts by former victims typically have a narrative quality—beginning, middle, and end— that eludes their oral counterparts even when the latter move from pre-Holocaust events to those that occurred after liberation. Importantly, and thanks to the camera's eye, the oral testimonies that Langer heard are also visual. Spoken and unspoken, they communicate significantly through body language. In them hands and faces, especially eyes, have much to say. Such expressions, like the spoken thoughts they help to convey, are less controlled and controllable than written words.

Thus, even oral testimonies that start as chronological narratives are usually interrupted and disrupted by memories buried deep within—such as the one that constrains Edith P. to wonder, "Is there such a thing as love?" So harshly different from the world outside the ghettos and camps, such deep remembrances expose selves divided by the anguish they contain. "I talk to you," Isabella L. tells her interviewer, "and I am not only here, but I see Mengele [she lived in a barrack from which he chose women, including her sister, for his experiments] and I see the crematorium and I see all of that. . . . I am not like you. You have one vision of life and I have two. I—you know—I lived on two planets. . . . We have these . . . these double lives. We can't cancel out. It just won't go away. . . . It's very hard."

Within such anguish may be recollections of humiliation that besiege—"I left [my brother] there," laments Viktor C., "and I survived [prolonged weeping]. If I forget anything, this I will never forget." Even the present's recovered moral sensibility can taint memory by disapproving the impromptu acts one had to improvise— or failed to improvise—in the past: "How can you, how can you *enjoy* yourself?" Leo G. questions himself. The vulnerability that remains is intensified by recognition that Holocaust survival is less a heroic victory than a matter of chance. At times, Helen K. grieves, "I don't know if it was worth it."

These strains are not the only ones Langer heard. Some of the former victims tell about their determination to survive; they "knew" they would come out alive. Others accent their defiance against German brutality. There are also many who emphasize how important it has been for them to make their lives worthwhile and to retain some hope after Auschwitz. Philip K. speaks for many of his fellow survivors when he affirms, "We lost. . . . And yet we won, we're going on." Langer concludes that "several currents flow at differing depths in Holocaust testimonies." All of them, he adds, are "telling a version of the truth."

It would have been an immense contribution if Langer had only let those multiple truths be told. But the work he has done with such distinction—and it goes without saying how deeply he wishes history had not placed the task before him—required more. He met that demand by refusing the consolation that "a vocabulary of chronology and conjunction" could provide if it were permitted to transcend "a lexicon of disruption, absence, and irreversible loss." Declining that consolation, *Holocaust Testimonies* may make possible a greater sharing of the burden that goes with Langer's refusal. As this superb book helps its readers to understand, such sharing is awesome because it must contain all that Elie Wiesel meant when he testified that "the Holocaust demands interrogation and calls everything into question. Traditional ideas and acquired values, philosophical systems and social theories—all must be revised in the shadow of Birkenau."

John K. Roth

Sources for Further Study

Booklist. LXXXVII, February 1, 1991, p. 1112.
Choice. XXIX, September, 1991, p. 179.
Commentary. XCII, November, 1991, p. 57.
Commonweal. CXVIII, September 27, 1991, p. 552.
Foreign Affairs. LXX, Fall, 1991, p. 179.
Kirkus Reviews. LIX, February 15, 1991, p. 230.
Library Journal. CXVI, February 1, 1991, p. 87.
The New York Times Book Review. XCVI, April 21, 1991, p. 7.
Publishers Weekly. CCXXXVIII, February 8, 1991, p. 42.
The Virginia Quarterly Review. LXVII, Summer, 1991, p. 98.

HOW TO MAKE AN AMERICAN QUILT

Author: Whitney Otto (1955-   )
Publisher: Villard Books (New York). 179 pp. $18.00
Type of work: Novel
Time: The 1920's to the 1990's
Locale: A fictional small town in California

Using quiltmaking as a metaphor for women's lives, Whitney Otto interweaves the stories of the members of a quilting circle in a small California town

> *Principal characters:*
> FINN BENNETT-DODD, a young woman engaged to be married
> HY DODD, her grandmother, a widow
> GLADY JOE CLEARY, Hy's sister, also a widow and the owner of the house where the quilters meet
> ANNA NEALE, a black woman, Glady Joe's housekeeper and the unofficial leader of the quilting circle
> MARIANNA, a horticulturist, Anna's daughter by a white man
> SOPHIA DARLING, a woman who has sacrificed her own dreams for a husband and children
> EM REED, a woman whose marriage has been defined by her husband's frequent affairs
> CONSTANCE SAUNDERS, once happily married, now a widow, who is seeing Em's husband, Dean Reed
> CORRINA AMURRI, Hy's longtime friend, who lost a son in Vietnam

With *How to Make an American Quilt*, first-time novelist Whitney Otto has managed a difficult double feat, winning both critical and popular acclaim for her writing debut. Set in the fictional town of Grasse, California, the book chronicles the lives of the members of a weekly quilting circle, piecing together their stories in the way that a quilt is pieced together and forming a completed work that encompasses the themes and events that have shaped American women in the twentieth century. Marriages and children, love and betrayal, bigotry and disappointed hopes all mark the lives of Otto's characters as their stories and friendships unfold.

The event that serves as a springboard into the women's stories is the arrival in Grasse of Finn Bennett-Dodd, the granddaughter and great-niece, respectively, of Hy Dodd and Glady Joe Cleary, the two widowed sisters in whose home the quilting circle meets each week. Finn is engaged to be married and is spending the summer contemplating her future in an attempt to sort out her feelings about her upcoming wedding. A historian whose interest lies with the details of history rather than its sweeping themes, Finn is at a crossroads in her life and hopes that the lessons to be learned from the lives of the quilters will help her in her efforts to define herself.

After the prologue, which introduces Finn, the book itself is divided into seven chapters. Each chapter begins with a set of quilting instructions, and each set of instructions serves as an introduction to the woman whose story then follows. At times the women's lives overlap and intersect; more often they are private and unknown. What links them all, despite their differences, is their presence in the quilting circle and a sense that certain overriding influences—love, social mores, the time in which they have lived—have shaped each of their lives.

Finn Bennett-Dodd's story is presented first. She is young—twenty-six—and the pattern that will make up the balance of her life is only just beginning to reveal its design. She tells us "I have lost track of the sort of girl that I am. I used to be a young scholar; I am now an engaged woman. Not that you cannot be both—even I understand that—yet I cannot fathom who I think I am *at this time."* Her summer among her grandmother's quilting friends is an attempt to define her own place in the world, to come to grips with what marriage can be and the ways in which it may shape her life. Finn loves her fiancé, Sam, and her questions arise not from any doubts about her feelings for him but rather from a sense that she herself has lost her direction. Finn has a scholar's mind, however, and an abiding interest in the details that make up a human life, and she draws on both in her efforts to come to terms with the possibilities her future may hold. By listening to Hy, Glady Joe, and their friends, she hopes to find in their lives some key to what life as a woman may have to offer her.

Finn is closest to Hy and Glady Joe, and it is with their story that she begins. The two sisters, both widowed, share a house, friends, road trips to visit relatives, and an occasional marijuana cigarette—a secret indulgence supplied by Finn—and enjoy, to all outward appearances, a comfortable and companionable life together. Their past holds one secret, however; an event that is never mentioned but that neverthe-less colors the pair's relationship. Years earlier, when Hy's husband was dying, she sought comfort one afternoon in her brother-in-law's arms. Glady Joe and Arthur had long slept apart in a marriage founded more on friendship than passion, yet she guessed immediately what had occurred between her sister and her husband, and her hurt and resentment still color some aspects of her feelings for Hy. The experience taught Glady Joe one of life's most difficult lessons: Even those people you love will sometimes hurt you, and the pain of that hurt may last a lifetime.

Of all the women in the quilting circle, none serves as a better example of the repercussions of setting aside one's own dreams to follow social conventions than Sophia Darling. As a girl, Sophia's happiest moments were spent in the water, swim-ming and diving with such grace and skill that she catches the eye of her future husband when she is seventeen, poised on a diving board. Their affair results in a pregnancy and a hurried marriage that fails to become the lifetime of shared dreams she had envisioned. Her mistake, she finds, was that "she allowed him access to her body without revealing what was in her heart." Instead, she becomes a bored wife and mother, so secretly embittered by her lack of self-expression that she discour-ages her own daughter's hopes of attending college and responds to the girl's com-ment that there may be more to life than marriage and children with a curt, "There is nothing else." Her younger daughter's own unwed pregnancy begins to break the family apart, and Sophia finds herself facing the prospect of losing everything for which she gave up her girlhood dreams.

Constance Saunders represents a very different experience of marriage. A solitary woman who has little time or need for friendships with other women, she enjoys a happy relationship with her husband, Howell, contentedly moving wherever his job takes them until he at last retires to Grasse, where she indulges her passion for gardening and joins the quilting circle. Howell dies suddenly, however, and Constance, who has existed quite happily with very few other relationships in her life, is left alone and middle-aged, the center of her world gone. Dean Reed, the husband of one of the other quilters, begins dropping by to offer assistance with household chores, and although their relationship remains platonic, she finds herself on dangerous emotional ground both personally and with the other members of the circle.

For Em Reed, Dean's wife, their relationship brings about a turning point in a marriage that has been marked throughout by Dean's infidelities. Although she left him once early in their marriage, she returned and accepted a married life often filled with resentment over her husband's selfishness. Her reason for this acceptance is a common one: "In her heart, Em mistakenly thought that this man was meant to be her burden, the experience to strengthen her, make her so powerful nothing could touch her." Dean's relationship with Constance, which Em refuses to believe is platonic, so angers and humiliates her that she decides at last to leave him. While she is packing, however, she enters the studio where Dean, an art teacher and painter, keeps the many paintings he has done of Em over the years. Looking at them, she realizes that she is too close to Dean to leave him—he is too much a part of her life and knows her too deeply. Em's story is a lesson in many of the complexities of marriage; the ties that grow even when the union is a troubled one, the pattern of cyclical anger and forgiveness in which many couples live, and the hard truth that a husband can be capable of both love and betrayal.

Corrina Amurri serves as the novel's example of the pain and love that motherhood can bring. Corrina's son, Laury, enlists in the Army on his eighteenth birthday and is sent to Vietnam, where he is eventually listed as missing in action. The fears and pressures that haunt Corrina and her husband, Jack, draw Corrina closer to Laury's friend, Will Dodd—Hy's son—who has taken a very different road from that of his friend. Will's embrace of the 1960's counterculture—drugs, long hair, antiwar protests—has alienated him from his own parents. Corrina, however, is gradually developing her own doubts about the war, and it is to Will that she feels most comfortable expressing them. When they at last learn that Laury has been killed, Corrina and Jack must come to grips with the loss of a child to a cause neither of them truly understands. Corrina's experience is that of all mothers who have sent sons off to fight and have then had to bear the tension of waiting and later, for some, the pain of outliving one's own child.

The book's last two segments center on Anna Neale and her daughter, Marianna. For Anna, a longtime quilter and the unofficial leader of the Grasse quilters, quilting is much more than a hobby. It is a means of expression in a society that discourages or ignores self-expression by black women. As Anna herself explains, "I learned to speak with needle and thread long before society finally 'gave' me a voice—as if society can give anyone a voice; it can only take a voice away." The daughter of a black woman and a white man, Anna was reared by her great-aunt, Pauline, who worked as a maid in San Francisco and taught her niece the art of quilting. Part of Pauline's legacy to Anna was a quilt handed down through several generations, depicting life in Africa in the time before slavery. For both women, the quilt represents a heritage and a world of possibilities routinely denied to black women in American society.

It is a heritage that Anna will pass on to her only child, Marianna. A brief affair with a young white man while she is still a teenager leaves Anna pregnant, and it is while awaiting the birth of her daughter that she first meets Hy and Glady Joe, whose parents often employ "wayward" young women in need of a home until their children are born. Despite social conventions of the time, Glady Joe and Anna begin a tentative yet lasting friendship, often reading to each other as Glady Joe learns to quilt. After Glady Joe's marriage to Arthur Cleary, Anna supports her daughter by working as a maid for the couple.

Reared by her mother with a strong sense of self-confidence and an awareness of the world outside of Grasse, Marianna studies agriculture in college and eventually moves to France seeking work when it becomes clear that the jobs for which she is qualified are closed to black women in the America of the 1950's. In France, she grows flowers and has a series of lovers, although she refuses all offers of marriage and instinctively holds a part of herself in reserve, opting for an independence that sets her apart from many other women. When she at last returns to Grasse, she works for Glady Joe as a gardener, strikes up a friendship with Constance Saunders—a woman whose solitude and love of gardening strike a responsive chord in Marianna—and joins the quilting circle.

In the novel's final pages, the women of the quilting circle are planning a Crazy Quilt as a wedding present for Finn. Each woman will contribute a patch that she herself has designed—a square that embodies elements of her own life and that holds for her a special significance. Finn will take with her into her married life a gift that captures the essence of the quilters' lives, offering her a record of their experiences as she begins to discover the pattern of her own.

Janet Lorenz

Sources for Further Study

American Craft. LI, October, 1991, p. 24.
Booklist. LXXXVII, January 15, 1991, p. 979.
Chicago Tribune. April 28, 1991, XIV, p. 6.
The Christian Century. CVIII, July 10, 1991, p. 676.
Los Angeles Times Book Review. March 24, 1991, p. 3.
The New York Times Book Review. XCVI, March 24, 1991, p. 10.

Publishers Weekly. CCXXXVIII, February 8, 1991, p. 46.
St. Louis Post-Dispatch. June 9, 1991, p. C5.
The Times Literary Supplement. July 26, 1991, p. 19.
The Washington Post Book World. XXI, May 26, 1991, p. 12.

HUNTING MISTER HEARTBREAK
A Discovery of America

Author: Jonathan Raban (1942-   )
Publisher: HarperCollins (New York). 372 pp. $25.00
Type of work: Travel
Time: The late 1980's
Locale: New York City; Guntersville, Alabama; Seattle, Washington; Key West, Florida

The British writer Jonathan Raban experiences life in different American locales in an attempt to define the American temperament during the last years of the twentieth century

Principal personage:
JONATHAN RABAN, an English novelist, critic, and travel writer

Jonathan Raban is an Englishman with a fascination and sympathy for the American spirit as it exists in both fantasy and reality. At the beginning of the 1980's, in *Old Glory* (1981), he wrote of his experiences piloting a boat down the Mississippi River, tracing the journey of the archetypal American free spirit Huckleberry Finn. Starting in Minneapolis, Raban made his way down the continent to Louisiana, stopping along the shore to observe and record the characters he encountered. *Old Glory* captured America at the depressing end of the Carter tenure and the beginning of the so-called Reagan Revolution. Ten years later, Raban returned to the United States for another look. This time, rather than limit himself to one long swath of America, he chose to pick several geographically distant and distinct locales and to live in those places for an extended time, to become (as much as possible for a foreigner) a resident of each section. Thus, for a period of approximately two years (Raban's chronology in the book is vague at best, but he passes two Thanksgivings; in reality the time covered was from 1988 to 1990), the writer settles in, attempts to develop an acceptable identity for each community, and records his experiences as both observer and participant.

If in *Old Glory* Raban played at being Huck Finn, in *Hunting Mister Heartbreak* he takes as his model the French traveler and adventurer Michel-Guillaume Jean (Hector St. John) de Crevecœur (1735-1813), whose *Letters From an American Farmer* (1782) offered a largely optimistic, romantic view of the possibilities of the New World in America and helped to establish the European concept of the "American." Like de Crevecœur, Raban is predisposed toward the country, although he certainly recognizes its faults and foibles. Indeed, Raban approaches his material with a romantic's excitement and a modernist's eye. Despite his efforts at creating a certain drama on his journey (after leaving Liverpool, for example, his ship's near encounter with Tropical Storm Hélène occasions some very fine descriptive passages of an unruly ocean), Raban adopts a basically ironic, or perhaps whimsical, tone in chronicling his trip. Rather than amazed, Raban is more often surprised and bemused by what he sees.

The first section of the book describes Raban's voyage from Liverpool to New

York on the ship *Atlantic Conveyor*, an enormous container ship carrying European exports—cars, liquor, perfume, clothes—to America. Raban travels as a guest of the ship's owner and resides in a "roomy studio apartment furnished with bookcases, a refrigerator, a king-size bed, a comfortable sofa, a long desk of varnished pine, a cabinet for drinks and glasses, a coffee table and his own lavatory and shower." Having initially set up implied comparisons between himself and earlier travelers, Raban confronts humorously the fact that his journey is in most ways a privileged man's holiday. Indeed, throughout his wanderings, Raban associates mostly with the cultured and well-to-do. Even when he does choose to live in marginal areas, he recognizes that his stay is temporary, that he is not really of those people, that he is primarily an observer and an outsider. Thus, the American he sees is, with some exceptions, a selective one.

Raban's first stay is in New York City, where he sublets the apartment of a woman named Alice. She becomes the first of his several adopted identities (like de Creve-cœur himself, who changed his name after coming to America). "This deal was a technical breach of the regulations of the building, so I had been told to present myself to the doormen and the super as Alice's cousin, or at least her intimate friend. So far as the handicaps of sex and voice allowed, I had to be as nearly Alice herself as I could manage," Raban explains. As "Alice," Raban moves through the looking glass to explore the world beyond. He tries to see New York as Alice must see it. "If you were going to learn to live here, you'd have to go deaf to the sound of New York and set up house in the silent bubble of your own preoccupations. . . . For me the New York air was full of robbery and murder; for her, it would all be inaudible white noise."

Raban, of course, has been to New York before, remembers it from earlier visits, and records how the city— and, by extension, American society—has changed. What he witnesses is the last desperate splurge of American consumerism in the final years of Reagan. This conversion is best illustrated for him by Macy's Department Store, which he recalls as having been a haven for solid, inexpensive, everyday goods in the early 1970's. Now, however, Macy's "was platinum-card country; a twinkling gallery, as big as a battlefield, of gold, silk, scent and lizardskin. When I'd last been here, there had been a slogan painted over the entrance: IT'S SMART TO BE THRIFTY. Sometime between the age of Richard Nixon and the last days of Ronald Reagan, that homely touch of American puritanism had been whitewashed over. Only frumps were thrifty now." It is the world of Ralph Lauren, in Raban's view an artificial, pseudopastoral neverland of "besotted unrealism" garnered from repeated viewings of *Masterpiece Theatre*.

Raban recognizes that this absurd commercial rural fiction, with its "glorification of the cottage and country house, the wide open space, the hunting field, the horse and the yacht," is a reaction against the oppressive, growing poverty and violence of the city and society itself. Outside the dream world of the store he finds an army of the dispossessed, a "tribe," a "poor nation living on the leftovers of a rich one." The dichotomy he draws between the "Air People" (of which he is one)—the well-to-do who ride elevators to their high-rise apartments—and the street poor makes clear the extent the American self-image is built on a denial of truth, on the belief in the possibility of transcendence whatever the evidence to the contrary. "Success here didn't merely mean moving from position *A* to a more comfortable berth at *B*; it was, rather, a quality endemic to your personality and your national character—a peculiarly American state of being, in which you were continuously aspiring, striving, becoming. . . . It was an authenticating mark of the true-hearted American," he observes.

Tiring of New York, Raban next sets out for the Deep South, which he imagines as "some green and pleasant place where life felt more like life and less like guerrilla war." He chooses Guntersville, Alabama, near Huntsville, and drives there in his rented car. He moves into a small lake cabin in Polecat Hollow and sets about to become a Southerner. He is surprised at how easily he seems to gain acceptance by the community, although he is also aware of the limits of this acceptance. *"You want to find our town quaintly amusing?"* he imagines them saying. *"We know how to play along with that."* Because the woods spook him, and because he keeps getting angry, middle-of-the-night phone calls for someone named "Bri," apparently a former resident of the cabin, Raban "rents" a dog, an old black lab named Gypsy. Together they form a wonderfully funny partnership; Raban's description of their relationship displays his good humor and wit to best advantage. Away from the urban dangers of New York, he finds that the Alabama outdoors hold their own threats unknown to the typical rural Englishman. Yet he also finds that he quickly adapts to this way of life, and he soon takes on another persona, that of John Rayburn (the Guntersville approximation of his real name), gentleman writer.

As in New York, there is a violence underlying life in Guntersville. During his stay, two women are found murdered in the vicinity; there are rumors of devil worship; the specter of the mysterious "Bri" hangs in the air. Raban considers buying a gun and meditates on the essence of a natural American "savagery," even in such a small, apparently idyllic town; however, he finds much to admire in Guntersville as well. He recognizes that, in its low-key country life, it offers in reality what the Macy's Ralph Lauren displays project as fantasy. The faults are there, to be sure: There is ample evidence of racism, unyielding fundamentalist bigotry, uncomprehending blindness and cruelty. There is also, however, a kind of seductive allure that is finally more threatening to Raban. He knows he could easily be "assimilated" into this society, but he also knows that if he stays, he "would make that one mistake. Scratch John Rayburn, and he'd confess my own thoughts on politics, books, religion—thoughts that wouldn't wash in Guntersville."

The last third of the book describes Raban's air flight to Seattle, Washington, where he takes an old apartment in a run-down section of town, and then his final journey to the Florida Keys, where he returns to the sea, sailing a thirty-two-foot sloop up and down the coast. There is a loss of energy in these sections, although they are nevertheless entertaining. He continues his habit of trying new personas. In Seattle he becomes "Rainbird," an aspiring novelist. The city reveals itself as the inverse of New York, located across the continent, peopled by emigrant Asians rather than Europeans trying to create their own American identities in the New World, yet also beset by its own brand of violence and poverty (as Raban notes, the term "Skid Row" has its origins in Seattle). In Key West, at the tip of the country, he considers taking on the ultimate American persona, that of a nameless outlaw, a drug pirate smuggling dope under the very noses of the outmanned authorities. "If there was any place on the map of the United States where the elevated ideology of being an American finally unraveled, it was on the Keys. Morally and geographically, the Keys were *terminal*," Raban writes. In a sense, he returns to his initial disguise of Huck Finn appropriated ten years earlier in *Old Glory*, although Raban realizes that he now resembles Pap more than Huck. There the book ends, at the bottom of the country slipping out to sea.

Although *Hunting Mister Heartbreak* is presented as nonfiction, a thoughtful journal of Raban's excursion in America, the reader comes to recognize that the book is much more than an intriguing travelogue. It is, obviously, a meditation on the nature of identity, whether of a country or an individual. It is also less factually truthful than it appears to be. In a profile of Raban in *The New York Times Book Review*, significant omissions and changes in the book are noted. For example, the article states that Raban returned to London after his stays in New York and Guntersville to compose those sections of the book. While in Seattle he met another writer (not the one mentioned in the book) and she accompanied him to Key West, although he portrays himself as very much the loner during all of his travels. Raban, in fact, moved permanently to Seattle shortly after the time of the book's end. Thus, the Jonathan Raban character must finally be seen as a fiction. This is a point the book itself reiterates, not only in its insistence on disguise (which is what Raban does— he disguises himself within each community better to observe the workings of that community) but also in its manner of narration, which becomes more imaginary, governed more by the rules of fiction than of journalism, as the book continues. So it is that in Key West Raban finally stumbles on the mysterious "Bri" with whom he was confused in Guntersville. He imagines passersby labeling them as fellow bums, brothers under the skin, and thereby faces his own potential for sorriness and waste, which is the opposite and inevitable side of the ideal American character. Thematically, the event works, but it is the sort of episode that, even if true, gives the impression of being made up. Coming at the very end of the book, it seems almost clumsy. Perhaps it is a final demand that the reader recognize the scheme of Raban's work, acknowledge that it is the study of an idea rather than a reality.

The allure of the New World is that it offers individuals a chance to reinvent themselves, to take new names, to begin new lives. Jean de Crevecœur, Mister Heartbreak, is very much the guardian spirit of this idea and this work. The subtitle of the book is *A Discovery of America*. In reality, what Raban discovers is himself.

Edwin T. Arnold

Sources for Further Study

The Antioch Review. XLIX, Summer, 1991, p. 463.
Chicago Tribune. June 9, 1991, XIV, p. 4.
Library Journal. CXVI, April 15, 1991, p. 116.
London Review of Books. XIII, January 24, 1991, p. 17.
Los Angeles Times Book Review. June 9, 1991, p. 2.
The New York Times Book Review. XCVI, May 12, 1991, p. 7.
Publishers Weekly. CCXXXVIII, March 15, 1991, p. 49.
Time. CXXXVII, May 13, 1991, p. 76.
The Times Literary Supplement. November 23, 1990, p. 1263.
The Washington Post Book World. XXI, April 28, 1991, p. 3.

IF I HAD WHEELS OR LOVE
Collected Poems of Vassar Miller

Author: Vassar Miller (1924-   )
Introduction by George Garrett
Publisher: Southern Methodist University Press (Dallas, Texas). 358 pp. $28.95; paperback
    $14.95
Type of work: Poetry

This collection, spanning more than thirty years of American metaphysical poet Vassar Miller's work, explores the possibility of spiritual life in difficult and uncertain times

The villanelle that provides this collection with its title expresses the theme of the book. Under different circumstances, says the speaker, "If I had wheels or love," this would be world of delight and praise. "I could make prayers or poems on and on/ If I had wheels or love, I would be gone." These ideal conditions do not exist, however, and therefore the speaker is not gone but here, trying to make poems and praises in a flawed world.

This collection combines the previous eight books of American metaphysical poet Vassar Miller and adds a group of uncollected poems. The result is a solid volume with a graceful introduction by George Garrett, who notes that the "genuinely religious experience, dealt with directly by a living artist of the first rank, was as astonishing then [at the time of Miller's first book] as it is now or any time; shocking, really, in our secular and self-absorbed times." Indeed, Vassar Miller's melding of verbal dexterity with a tough-minded Christianity would win T. S. Eliot's approval. Other elements in her blend, Texas womanhood and physical handicap, give her poetry the unique flavor that has won it international praise. Miller's work was nominated for the Pulitzer Prize in 1961, and it has been widely anthologized both in America and in Europe.

Born in Houston in 1924, Miller has remained a lifelong Texas resident. Afflicted from birth with cerebral palsy and therefore limited in physical self-expression, she began writing as a child on a typewriter her father brought home from the office to amuse her. She went on to win early acclaim both for her craftsmanship and for the mixture of rebellion and resignation that characterizes her poems, and she has continued to write, publishing book after book over a period of almost forty years, refining her style and profiting from the literary currents that flowed about her.

Indeed, a reading of *If I Had Wheels or Love* is a trip through postwar American poetry, for while Miller's basic concerns remain the same and her voice is constant, her forms and styles reflect what was happening in each era of poetry and politics. Her 1950's poems have the formal exactness of the time. In the 1960's her poems loosen somewhat and become more personal, showing the influence of Anne Sexton, Sylvia Plath, and the other so-called "confessional" poets. Her 1970's poems are more socially conscious; the 1980's bring a renewal of interest in form. Miller has the distinction of having been both an Old and a New Formalist, with all the variations in between. Yet elements of pattern have always loomed large in Miller's work, and even her free verse might be more accurately described as idiosyncratically formal.

Paradox is a major element of Miller's work, especially in the early poems. Sonnets with Donne-like conclusions abound in the first collections, as do other paradoxical poems that explore the position of woman in the middle kingdom, between animal and angel, divided against herself. That Christianity makes heavy demands while offering gifts of solace is also a topic of her early verse, as is the ambiguity of the human impulse to speech. Many of these poems are addressed to God, demanding His intervention in her dark night of the soul; these poems bring to mind Donne's sonnet "Batter My Heart, Three Person'd God" (1633). An example from Miller's first book, *Adam's Footprint* (1956), is her sonnet "Paradox," which begins "Mild yoke of Christ, most harsh to me not bearing,/ You bruise the neck that balks, the hands that break you. . . ." The speaker piles paradox upon paradox until the conclusion, "Blind me to blindness, deafen me to deafness/ So will Your gifts of sight and hearing plunder/ My eyes with lightning and my ears with thunder."

If some of these poems play more to the mind than to the heart, the following collections become less mannered and more direct. Their burden remains the same— an energetic and muscular wrestling match with the angel—but the definition of womanhood within Christianity becomes more intrusive, the speaker more definitely feminine. "Spinster's Lullaby," from *My Bones Being Wiser* (1965), illustrates this change. The speaker, lulling the baby in her "scraggly lap," says

> I rejoice, no less a woman
>
> With my nipples pinched and dumb
> To your need whose one word's sucking.
> Never mind, though. To my rocking
> Nap a minute, find your thumb
>
> While I gnaw a dream and nod
> To the gracious sway that settles
> Both our hearts, imperiled petals
> Trembling on the pulse of God.

The woman recognizes that she will not ever have her own child, being a designated "spinster," but she resigns herself to a wider movement of consolation that includes both herself and the child she comforts by rocking.

Other poems include a painful awareness of the body, a heavy sense of self-rejection that Delmore Schwartz defined as "the withness of the body" in the epigraph to his poem "The Heavy Bear Who Goes With Me" (1938). As Schwartz's body is represented by the clumsy, gross bear that betrays his heart's intention, the body for Miller becomes a pig, birds, a dog, its own awkward self. "I lie with my body knotted into a fist," begins "Insomniac's Prayer." "Oh, who will unsnarl my body/ into gestures of love? Who will give my heart room/ to fly free in its

rickety cage?" Caring for the body with its constant demands and its few fulfill-
ments is a weight to the soul in these poems. Nevertheless, it is at least in part
through the body that the experience of the spiritual is made possible, as Miller
clarifies in such poems as "Pigself," which explains that the body

> needs to remember
> how its lush poverty
> provides its alphabet
>
> of grunts, groans, snuffles, and snorts
> so that spirit can spell
> even the word for God.

Miller's middle period includes a number of poems describing and characterizing
women of individuality and courage. Two such poems from *Onions and Roses* (1968)
give gentle blank-verse sketches of Miller's Aunt Helen and of Elizabeth Barrett
Browning. The Browning poem never names the woman it describes, but from the
perspective indicated in the title, "The Protestant Cemetery in Florence," gives a
brief life of the heroine whose escape from a tyrannical father was romanticized in
the popular 1930's drama *The Barretts of Wimpole Street.* Miller reminds us that
Browning's life was not so glowing as the play. "For I remember how you in a letter/
Wrote, 'Father could have kept me had he loved me/ More openly,'—dark secrets
future doctors/ Would probe for offered on your outspread palm./ And you took
morphine till the day you died. . . ." Miller's Elizabeth Barrett Browning does not
get away. "You looked behind you always, back toward death/ Wherein alone you
could have borne to hear/ Your brother's name, love never having borne/ The heavy
past away." The implication that no one escapes, that one cannot get away from
oneself, is characteristic of Miller's message.

The poem "Remembering Aunt Helen" gives a concrete portrait of an admired
woman, with a meditation on the nature of goodness and its particular, individual
manifestations. The speaker ruminates, "Remembering how you told a little boy/
who asked to buy your cat, 'Honey, we don't/ sell what we love,' I think how most
old maids'/ affection for their pets is loneliness,/ while yours was charity." The
speaker wishes to share in the goodness of this woman but realizes that a style of
goodness is not to be copied. Saints are as individual as snowflakes.

Miller's 1974 collection, *If I Could Sleep Deeply Enough*, is perhaps her most
formally relaxed. It and her subsequent book, *Small Change* (1976), are brief and
consist mostly of short poems with a personal or social edge. These poems reflect a
desire for a true peace both in the personal realm and in the public. They are often
short free-verse poems with a suggestion of music in a minor key. "Tired," the text
of which provides the title of the earlier collection, is an example:

> If I could
> sleep deeply enough,
> I might touch the eye
> of dark, life.

The falling rhythms and flat emphasis on last words underscore the impression of an unfulfillable yearning that is depicted as thirst: "Yet the way I sleep,/ men drink salt. . . ."

The livelier music of "Homecoming Blues" (from *Small Change*) is appropriate too. The poem describes how the house fails to greet the returning speaker and refuses to communicate with her, and how she responds to its lack of greeting: "And 0 0 0 0/ I wish I could call my mother/ Or eat death like candy."

The next long collection, *Struggling to Swim on Concrete* (1984), is much more formal and contains Miller's only long poem. "Love's Bitten Tongue" is a sequence of twenty-two interlocking sonnets detailing the challenges and contradictions of Christianity and celebrating the Resurrection as their solution. Like many of Miller's poems, this sequence is in a sense a prayer for the gift of prayer. Its well-crafted discipline is balanced by the sincerity of its religious thought. The reader may wish Miller had undertaken other such extended projects.

The last two sections of Miller's book, *The Sun Has No History* (1981) and "If I Had Wheels or Love" (uncollected poems), even more than the preceding one bring her work full circle, returning to the formal and the metaphysical, especially in the uncollected poems. (These may, of course, date from the earlier eras of her work.) Yet the concluding sections do not lose the immediacy and casual tone of her intermediate collections, even when the poems are formal. Some of them have a wry twist that gives a bitter-lemon tone to these reflections, as in "Every Damn Time," which begins, "If I left home to see my lover/ I do not have,/ my eyes would still turn back/ to my lonesome bed." Such lines might seem self-indulgent until the reader gets to the third unrhymed quatrain: "For I resemble my father/ who longed to get away,/ and started cursing as a gyp-joint/ the first town he came to." The common quirks and inconsistencies of human nature are so clearly described that the reader cannot help but smile and identify.

Slightly more allusive, less immediately accessible, these poems express again the crises and the contradictions of the spiritual life. Human possibility and destiny are contrasted with nature's inarticulate presentness in the compelling poem "The Sun Has No History," which concludes:

> The sun has no history.
> Only I, bearing
> my Adam and Eve on my back,
> dragged under, dragged down, may leap
> up to the saddle of hope.

For Miller, Christianity is the weight that lifts, and our humanity is both our prison and our escape. Ingenuity welded to belief make the poems in *If I Had Wheels or Love* convincing.

Janet McCann

Sources for Further Study

Choice. XXIX, September, 1991, p. 99.
The Houston Post. May 12, 1991, p. C5.
National Catholic Reporter. May 10, 1991, p. 26.
Publishers Weekly. CCXXXVIII, January 25, 1991, p. 51.
University Press Book News. III, June, 1991, p. 37.
World and I. VI, June, 1991, p. 392.

IMAGINARY HOMELANDS
Essays and Criticism, 1981-1991

Author: Salman Rushdie (1947-   )
Publisher: Granta Books/Viking (London). 432 pp. $24.95
Type of work: Essays and literary criticism

A collection of essays and reviews on literature, politics, and culture published between 1981 and 1991 by the author of The Satanic Verses

Even before *The Satanic Verses* (1988) appeared and became an international episode—with riots and book-burnings in Great Britain, India, and Pakistan; bomb threats and bombings at bookstores and Rushdie's publisher's offices in England and America; a death sentence and a bounty of $5.2 million placed on Rushdie's head by Iran's Ayatollah Khomeini; and the author driven underground, guarded at an undisclosed location by the Special Branch of Scotland Yard—Salman Rushdie had already established himself as one of the most important writers in contemporary Britain.

His second novel, *Midnight's Children* (1981), was awarded the prestigious Booker-McConnell Prize; his third, *Shame* (1983), was also highly praised. Throughout the 1980's, Rushdie also wrote essays, eloquently and often: about the politics of religion and race in Margaret Thatcher's Britain, Indira Gandhi's India, and Mohammad Zia-ul-Haq's Pakistan; about writers and books from India and Pakistan, Africa, Britain, Europe, South America, and the United States; about the vocation of the writer and the powers of literature, the potential of the imagination and the dangers of censorship; and, repeatedly, about migration as the archetypal experience of the twentieth century. *Imaginary Homelands* brings most of these essays together with the several major statements Rushdie has written in the wake of *The Satanic Verses* controversy to form what amounts to an extraordinary intellectual autobiography.

Born in Bombay, Rushdie was sent to be educated in England at fourteen and made that country his home. Although his parents were members of the Muslim minority in India, neither they nor he was religious. At fifteen, he reports in "In God We Trust," he lost his faith and found himself "drawn towards the great traditions of secular radicalism—in politics, socialism; in the arts, modernism and its offspring." He attended Rugby, where he experienced British racism at first hand, and Cambridge, where he discovered the writers who shaped his own aspirations, and then spent several years as an advertising copywriter. Gradually, the experience that he would make his own—the experience that had made him—pressed itself upon him as an inevitable subject. Migration—losing one's country, language, and culture and finding oneself forced to come to terms with another place, another way of speaking and thinking, another view of reality—is Salman Rushdie's great theme; metamorphosis is its metaphor, and reflections on migration and metamorphosis permeate these essays as thoroughly as embodiments of them populate his novels.

"Writers in my position, exiles or emigrants or expatriates," Rushdie says in this collection's title essay, "are haunted by some sense of loss, some urge to reclaim, to look back, even at the risk of being mutated into pillars of salt." Such a writer comes to understand, however, that "we will not be capable of reclaiming precisely the thing that was lost; that we will, in short, create fictions, not actual cities or villages, but invisible ones, imaginary homelands, Indias of the mind." In his own fictions, Salman Rushdie has created just such imaginary homelands: an India of the mind in *Midnight's Children*, a Pakistan of the mind in *Shame*, an Islam, Bombay, and London of the mind in *The Satanic Verses*. While they are not precisely real, these imaginary homelands capture the essence of reality as seen through the eyes of characters who, like their author, face the challenge of straddling two cultures.

The word "translation," he points out, comes from the Latin for "bearing across," and "having been borne across the world, we are translated men. It is normally supposed that something always gets lost in the translation; I cling, obstinately, to the notion that something can also be gained." As he writes in an essay on John Berger, "the migrant is not simply transformed by his act; he also transforms his new world." As Rushdie has amply demonstrated in his own writing, the gains from this transformation are real and many.

One such gain is a tremendous potential for reinvigorating both the language and the form of the novel. Rushdie's works overflow with a mélange of voices, images, and inventions: digressions and disquisitions, anecdotes and myths, mundane details and philosophical meditations, puns, jingles, song lyrics, catchphrases, names, and ideas that only he could have brought together. Drawn from both the world he left behind and the world into which he has been thrust, they expand one's sense of what is while enriching one's sense of what the novel can be and do.

"Description is itself a political act. . . . [R]edescribing a world is the necessary first step towards changing it," Rushdie writes, and this suggests another contribution that the migrant can make to world culture. By describing the world as he does in his fiction and nonfiction, Rushdie can help to change those aspects of society that he so often laments and protests against in these essays: the institutional racism and nostalgia for past glories of Thatcher's England, where immigrants are daily victims of discrimination and a stubborn adherence to a self-image drawn from the nineteenth century ignores the millions of people whose arrival in Britain has changed it from an island of homogeneity to a polyglot crossroads of cultures; the religious sectarianism that has led to the assassination of three Gandhis and threatens to tear the very idea of a united India apart at the seams; and the politicization of Islam into a nationalistic "revolt against history" by leaders such as General Zia and Ayatollah Khomeini.

Another contribution the migrant can make, Rushdie argues in a landmark 1984 essay on one of his intellectual heroes, Günter Grass, is a commitment to tolerance: "To experience any form of migration is to get a lesson in the importance of tolerating others' points of view. One might almost say that migration ought to be essential training for all would-be democrats." It is difficult to read such a statement without thinking of how much Salman Rushdie has suffered at the hands of people who have not learned this lesson. Although he has attempted to conduct his professional life as normally as possible since being forced underground in 1989, although he has avoided inserting his personal situation into most of his essays and reviews, many of the comments Rushdie makes in essays written both before and after his ordeal began cannot help but have a deeper and more immediate authority in the light of what has happened to him.

Rushdie's comments on the role of the writer in confronting the powers-that-be in "Outside the Whale" (1984), for example, seem almost prophetic. Attacking George Orwell's essay "Inside the Whale" (1940) for counseling the writer to choose quietism rather than political activism, Rushdie insists "that works of art, even works of entertainment, do not come into being in a social and political vacuum; and that the way they operate in a society cannot be separated from politics, from history. For every text, a context. . . ." Consequently, he argues, "there is no whale. We live in a world without hiding places." In "Imaginary Homelands," he argues that "the real risks of any artist are taken in the work, in pushing the work to the limits of what is possible, in the attempt to increase the sum of what it is possible to think." Unfortunately, his experience has demonstrated how true the former statement was, and how incomplete the latter—has shown just how dangerous it can be to try to increase the sum of what it is possible to think in a world where many wish to diminish the freedom of thought and expression.

Occasionally, Rushdie does refer explicitly to his predicament in reviews written after 1989. Reading Philip Roth's description of the conflict that arose between him and the Jewish community with the publication of *Goodbye, Columbus* (1959), he cannot help but find Roth's responses to being villified "very moving, even helpful, to this similarly beleaguered writer." Noting in his review of Gabriel García Márquez' *Clandestine in Chile: The Adventures of Miguel Littín* (1987), which was impounded and burned by the Pinochet government, that the book continues to exist while Pinochet is falling, he consoles himself with the thought that "to burn a book is not to destroy it." He praises Christoph Ransmayr's novel *The Last World* (1990) as "a parable of the ability of art to survive the breaking of the artist," but he cannot help but qualify his praise of Ransmayr's vision of art conquering all. "Art can look after itself," he wryly observes. "Artists . . . can be crushed effortlessly at any old tyrant's whim."

Rushdie has also used his situation for comic effect. He admits to envying Isaac Bashevis Singer's freedom to be irreverent about God and the Devil: "no fundamentalists are after *him*, no government has banned *his* book for blasphemy. Look at what the fellow gets away with!" His response to Thomas Pynchon's fabled desire for privacy is the funniest sentence in memory to have appeared on the front page of *The New York Times Book Review*. "So he wants a private life and no photographs and nobody to know his home address," Rushdie writes in the argot of one of Pynchon's zonked-out space cadets. "I can dig it, I can relate to that (but, like, he should try it when it's compulsory instead of a free-choice option)."

Imaginary Homelands is full of similarly witty and apt observations on other subjects. The message of Richard Attenborough's film *Gandhi* (1982), he says, "is that

the best way to gain your freedom is to line up, unarmed, and march towards your oppressors and permit them to club you to the ground; if you do this for long enough,
you will embarrass them into going away." Edgar Allan Poe is "among the myriad
references" in Umberto Eco's *Il Pendolo di Foucalt* (1988; *Foucault's Pendulum*,
1989), "but it doesn't help. This Pendulum is the pits." The collection is also full of
careful, insightful, and provocative readings of several dozen writers, ranging from
Saul Bellow and Italo Calvino to Julian Barnes and Kazuo Ishiguro. Nadine Gordimer, Rushdie writes in a typically sensitive and perfectly phrased observation,
"has been radicalized by her time—or, rather, by her attempt to *write* her time—
and it's fascinating to watch history happening to her prose." "The real plot of *Moby
Dick* [1851] takes place inside Ahab; the rest is a fishing trip," he states. "Magic
realism," he argues in a comment on the fiction of García Márquez that explains
much about his own work, "is a development out of Surrealism that expresses a
genuinely 'Third World' consciousness."

Günter Grass's *Die Blechtrommel* (1959; *The Tin Drum*, 1962) was one of the
primary inspirations of Rushdie's own desire to be a writer, and his summary of the
lessons he learned from Grass is a fair description of the aesthetic that has made his
own novels so extraordinary. "This is what Grass's great novel said to me in its
drumbeats: Go for broke. Always try and do too much. Dispense with safety nets.
Take a deep breath before you begin talking. Aim for the stars. Keep grinning. Be
bloody-minded. Argue with the world." He has tried to learn those lessons, he says.
"And one more, which I got from that other, immense work, *Dog Years*: when
you've done it once, start all over and do it again and do it better."

The last section of *Imaginary Homelands* includes three statements of self-defense—
of himself and of art—that are alone worth the price of admission. The book concludes with Rushdie's December, 1990, statement "Why I Have Embraced Islam,"
which is best passed over in silence. The two books he published in the year after the
statement was issued—*Haroun and the Sea of Stories* and this collection—make it
abundantly clear that Rushdie continues to remember Grass's lessons and that he
learned a few from James Joyce, too.

"I will try to express myself in some mode of life or art as freely as I can and as
wholly as I can," Joyce's Stephen Dedalus declared, "using for my defence the only
arms I allow myself to use—silence, exile, and cunning." Like Joyce's migrant artificer, Salman Rushdie continues to find ways to express himself from his exile,
steadfastly refusing to be turned into a pillar of salt.

Bernard F. Rodgers, Jr.

Sources for Further Study

The Atlantic. CCLXVII, June, 1991, p. 120.
Booklist. LXXXVII, March 15, 1991, p. 1434.

Chicago Tribune. June 16, 1991, XIV, p. 8.
Kirkus Reviews. LIX, March 1, 1991, p. 309.
Library Journal. CXVI, April 15, 1991, p. 94.
London Review of Books. XIII, April 4, 1991, p. 18.
New Statesman and Society. IV, March 29, 1991, p. 32.
The New York Times Book Review. XCVI, June 2, 1991, p. 15.
Publishers Weekly. CCXXXVIII, March 8, 1991, p. 61.
The Times Literary Supplement. March 29, 1991, p. 61.

IMMORTALITY

Author: Milan Kundera (1929-   )
Translated from the Czech by Peter Kussi
Publisher: Grove Weidenfeld (New York). 345 pp. $21.95
Type of work: Novel
Time: The 1980's and the early nineteenth century
Locale: Chiefly Paris and Germany

In the post-ideological age of "imagology," Immortality *is essential reading: an object of active wonder in a world of passive consumption and consensus "truth"*

> *Principal characters:*
> AGNES, a woman born of a gesture who makes herself in her father's image
> PAUL, her husband
> LAURA, her sister
> JOHANN WOLFGANG VON GOETHE, the nineteenth century German writer
> BETTINA VON ARNIM, Goethe's self-appointed confidante
> RUBENS, one of Agnes' lovers
> PROFESSOR AVENARIUS, a friend of the narrator and foe of "Diabolum"
> MILAN KUNDERA, the narrator and "author"

Since the publication of his first novel, *The Joke* (1967), in Czechoslovakia in the heady and short-lived days of the Prague Spring, when it seemed that Eastern European socialism could wear not only a human face but a humorous one as well, Milan Kundera has repeatedly surpassed himself as one of the twentieth century's most interesting novelists, outstripping his critics' efforts to keep his fiction within carefully defined aesthetic and political boundaries. Like *The Joke*, even the relatively circumscribed novels *Life Is Elsewhere* (1973) and *The Farewell Party* (1976) clearly point to the richly virtuoso style of *The Book of Laughter and Forgetting* (1979) and the dizzying brilliance of *The Unbearable Lightness of Being* (1984), a seemingly unfilmable fiction by a former professor of film made into a motion picture whose commercial and critical success may have contributed to Kundera's writing of his sixth and amazingly best novel as a paradoxical collection of intensely visual but nonetheless entirely unfilmable images.

Immortality is (to borrow one of the novel's own phrases) "a harmonious collection of uniformity and freedom." The description seems at once apt and inadequate, for nothing and no one in Kundera's novel exists in isolation; no utterance, as Mikhail Bakhtin said of Fyodor Dostoevski's fiction, is without its "intense sideward glance" at someone else's word. In its context, the above-quoted phrase is ambivalent, a potential joke at the reader's expense: "I'm glad that we have so many radio stations in France and that at precisely the same time they all say the same thing about the same things. A harmonious combination of uniformity and freedom— what more could mankind ask?" For more, certainly, than the advertising jingles, announcements for fur-coat sales, and news of the latest derogatory biography of Ernest Hemingway that the novel's first-person narrator, "Milan Kundera," hears as he turns the dial. It is this profusion of words indiscriminately heard and passively consumed that Kundera, both as novelist and as narrator, seeks to expose and over-come in a novel that is speculative in nature and polyphonic in form, an exploration rather than a representation, a field of play in which themes are inquiries and the characters are experimental selves (or "possible selves," as Kundera calls them in *The Unbearable Lightness of Being*). Kundera's characters are always enigmas (that is their freedom), as irreducible to any one role as the novels themselves are irreduc-ible to either idea or ideology.

As Kundera points out in *The Art of the Novel* (1986), the novel's *raison d'être* is to discover what only a novel can by exploring its own formal possibilities and by examining existence rather than representing an agreed-upon reality. Opposing total-itarianism in all its guises, capitalist as well as communist, aesthetic as well as sociopolitical, Kundera creates a novelistic form at once meditative and postmodern in order to counter "the termites of reduction" and "the nonthought of received ideas" that characterize the twentieth century. Neither nostalgic nor utopian, he ac-cepts the Heideggerean view that "the essence of man has the form of a question." In shaping his novels, he turns away from the nonthought of received forms and toward principles of structure arbitrarily and self-consciously drawn from nonnarra-tive fields: "an architecture based on the number of seven" and the "tone row" of certain fundamental words.

One can attempt to read *Immortality* along more conventional lines (in much the same way that the film version of *The Unbearable Lightness of Being* chose to "read" Kundera's novel), in terms of linear plot and mimetic characterizations. Unfortu-nately for the reader in search of plot and character, *Immortality* begins prior to the point at which a conventional novel would: not with its (ostensible) main character but with its narrator, "Milan Kundera," seeing a woman in her early sixties leaving the pool at the health club where he is waiting for his friend, Professor Avenarius, and waving to the lifeguard who has just given her a swimming lesson. Charming and elegant, the gesture belongs to a twenty-year-old, not a sixty- or sixty-five-year-old woman, yet Kundera finds it as captivating as he does comical, making the woman ageless. "And then the word Agnes entered my mind. Agnes. I had never known a woman by that name." Thus in the space of a page Kundera has introduced three of the novel's main characters: Agnes, Avenarius, and himself; the old woman will not figure except as a looming absence. He has called attention to the relation between world and word, and he has developed a line of thinking more associational and coincidental than causal. Born of a gesture, Agnes will in turn give birth to an image in Kundera's mind of a half-empty bed and then to a husband, Paul (a law professor and radio columnist), a daughter (Brigitte), a job (cybernetics expert), a background (Swiss), parents (both dead—it is, Kundera decides, exactly five years since the death of her beloved father, who left her his money, his love of solitude, his ironic faith in God the Computer, and his way of dying); and a sister (Laura, in some ways her opposite, in others her mirror: Both are gifted—one scientifically, the other musically—but neither pursues greatness). Although born of an image and therefore linked to the similarly engendered Tomas in *The Unbearable Lightness of*

Being, Agnes seems even more like the earlier book's Sabina and Tereza; it is as if, having explored their two very different possibilities separately, Kundera now chose to follow where they might lead when combined in a single self (a situation similar to the one in which Tomas finds himself as he pursues two very different desires in pursuing Sabina and Tereza). "What is unbearable," Agnes believes, "is not *being* but *being one's self*." Seeking to put an end to "carrying [her] painful self through the world," she will die when her narrative, but not her car, collides with an anonymous suicidal girl (like Agnes another solitary self) who enters the novel via a brief radio news report.

To present Agnes in this way is to misrepresent not her but Kundera's novel, for important as she is, she represents only one line of character development and thematic interest. The historically verifiable Bettina von Arnim represents another. Whereas Agnes chooses anonymity, solitude, and effacement—in a word, mortality—Bettina used her love affairs with famous men as "a trampoline upon which she threw her entire body in order to be tossed upward to the heights where the God incarnate in history dwells." Sitting on Goethe's knee and later recording his conversation, she drew on the Romantic cult of genius and sentimentality while carefully engineering her own entry into immortality as beloved confidante, or, less charitably, as hanger-on. If immortality is, as Goethe claimed, being remembered, then Bettina was the one who would determine how Goethe (and others) would be remembered: via her skewed writings and doctored correspondence.

Immortality develops along three other character fronts—on three other levels—as well. There is the character known only by his nickname, Rubens, the (anti) hero of the sixth of the novel's seven parts, who conducts an on-again, off-again affair with Agnes. There is also Professor Avenarius, friend of Kundera and foe of Diabolum, the spirit of an age that is no longer able to distinguish the important from the unimportant, the humorous from the horrific. The Mercedes-driving professor battles Diabolum by slashing automobile tires while jogging through the streets of Paris at night. His aim, however, is not ecological protest but egotistical pleasure—a pleasure that, strangely, depends upon his remaining anonymous to all but Kundera. Finally, there is Kundera himself as a character in his novel, friend of Avenarius and creator of Laura, with whom the professor will have an affair.

The novel's characters provide one way of reading *Immortality*—a rather hazardous one, given the various and often overlapping ontological spheres they occupy. Because that way is partial at best, *Immortality* requires that the reader consider alternate reading strategies, such as concentrating on the "tone row" of recurring fundamental words and images: mirrors, highways versus roads (the one linear and important only as a space to cross, the other meandering, digressive, and important in and for itself), the "dial" of passing time versus the metaphorical horoscope whose meaning is that life "does not resemble a picaresque novel in which . . . the hero is continually being surprised by new events that have no common denominator" but resembles instead the "composition that musicians call *a theme with variations*." To overthrow the tyranny of the dial is not to surrender to the utopia of timelessness (the "lives" of Agnes, Paul, Laura, and Rubens will proceed through time toward death, and the novel "Kundera" writes will take two years to reach its end). It is rather an attempt to open up an alternative space for the play of mind and imagination less constrained by the "intelligible continuity" of causal-sequential plotting, downplaying (but not dismissing) the diachronic plane in favor of sheer synchronicity and the anti-Aristotelian aesthetic of the episode.

The two most frequently recurring words in the novel's tone row are "image" and "immortality." The latter, the novel suggests, is not a spiritual state but instead the very human desire to control one's future, to devise what is ominously called the "final solution" to the question of the self. It is an effort in large part motivated by man's inability to accept his mortality. Against Bettina's image of Goethe as romantic lover and Romantic genius, Kundera offers the "ridiculous" immortality of Goethe, dressed like a scarecrow and joking with a Hemingway noticeably touchy about the latest unflattering biography. Similarly ridiculous are novelist Robert Musil's dying while lifting weights and Jimmy Carter's suffering a mild heart attack while jogging—an image "immortalized" by television cameras. One might add the image of Kundera in the aftermath of the Prague Spring, with Soviet troops occupying his country and the author himself in exile, suddenly transformed into a Czech émigré protest writer, his novel *The Joke* in its editorially rewritten English translation reduced to a mere anti-Communist tract. Fighting image with image, Kundera proclaimed the novel not a satire but a love story.

Like Christ's poor, images are always with us, more or less monolithically in Communist countries, more insidiously present in capitalist ones. Images present, project, protect, offering the self what it most desires, identity and the illusion of individuality, but only at considerable risk, for the self can never be its image. Agnes borrows a kind of image, a gesture from her father's secretary, claiming it as her own (and all she believes it implies, including her father's love for this woman). When she sees her sister using the same gesture, the same one Kundera saw the elderly woman make, Agnes feels betrayed, deprived of her very being. The novel traffics in images, opening them to the semiotic inquiry that "imagology" attempts to deny. Imagology begins where history, ideology, and more especially inquiry end. This new totalitarianism proclaims that only the image is real, "our image in the eye of others," an image that "will always live in truth," because truth has been redefined in terms of public opinion polls. The "parliament of truth" ushers in a form of spiritual impoverishment not much different from the ideology that afflicts and constrains the characters in Kundera's earlier writings.

Asked by his friend Professor Avenarius what he is writing, Kundera replies that it is "impossible to recount." *Immortality*'s readers would certainly agree, and some, perhaps many, would also agree that this impossibility is not, as the professor says, "a pity" but, as Kundera contends,

An advantage. The present era grabs everything that was ever written in order to transform it into films, TV programs, or cartoons. What is essential in a novel is precisely what can only be expressed in a novel, and so every adaptation contains nothing but the nonessential. If a person is still crazy enough to want to write novels nowadays and wants to protect them, he has to write them in such a way that they cannot be adapted, in other words, in such a way that they cannot be retold.

Reading these particular words by this particular Kundera, one is reminded of the film version of *The Unbearable Lightness of Being* (a title that, incidentally, the narrator claims was wrong for that novel but right for this one). Philip Kaufman's 1988 film version reduces the polyphonic complexity of Kundera's fifth novel to the uniformity and passive accessibility of linear plot. It thus succumbs, as films and criticism often do, to the synechdochic fallacy, substituting a part for the whole. The ostensible inadequacy of the novel's title and the inexact duplication of names (*Immortality* and the one chapter entitled "Immortality") point to the novel's speculative nature and advantageous and adventitious form: something beyond the garden of forking paths of Jorge Luis Borges' *ficciones* and Milorad Pavic's novels in the form of dictionaries and crossword puzzles—the novel as a network of signifiers spreading meditatively and endlessly in every direction.

Robert A. Morace

Sources for Further Study

America. CLXV, September 28, 1991, p. 198.
Chicago Tribune. May 12, 1991, XIV, p. 1.
Los Angeles Times Book Review. May 19, 1991, p. 3.
The Nation. CCLII, June 10, 1991, p. 770.
The New York Review of Books. XXXVIII, May 30, 1991, p. 3.
The New York Times Book Review. XCVI, April 28, 1991, p. 7.
Publishers Weekly. CCXXXVIII, March 29, 1991, p. 77.
Time. CXXXVII, May 13, 1991, p. 75.
The Times Literary Supplement. May 17, 1991, p. 17.
The Washington Post Book World. XXI, May 5, 1991, p. 3.

IMPATIENT ARMIES OF THE POOR
The Story of Collective Action of the Unemployed

Author: Franklin Folsom (1907-   )
Publisher: University Press of Colorado (Niwot). Illustrated. 558 pp. $35.00
Type of work: History
Time: 1808-1942
Locale: The United States

A history of unemployed Americans from the days of the early republic through the Great Depression of the 1930's, focusing on what they did to alleviate their condition

> *Principal personages:*
> JACOB S. COXEY, an Ohio businessman and the head of an army of unemployed during the 1890's
> HERBERT BENJAMIN, an activist for the unemployed during the 1930's and a member of the Communist Party
> HERBERT HOOVER, the president of the United States at the outbreak of the Great Depression
> HUEY LONG, a Louisiana governor and United States senator, head of the Share Our Wealth movement in the 1930's
> FRANKLIN D. ROOSEVELT, the president of the United States whose New Deal during the 1930's helped alleviate unemployment distress
> UPTON SINCLAIR, the author and socialist, who campaigned for the California governorship with the promise to end poverty in California
> CHARLES F. TOWNSEND, a Long Beach, California, dentist whose "Townsend Plan" attracted wide support during the 1930's

The crisis of being unemployed in the United States goes back to the earliest decades of the republic. In 1807, President Thomas Jefferson urged the establishment of an embargo on all American exports in an attempt to free United States shippers from interference by Great Britain and France, then locked in the struggle of the Napoleonic Wars. Whatever its impact upon the nations of Europe, Jefferson's embargo soon created casualties in the United States. In New York City and elsewhere, American sailors lost their employment and demanded of the local authorities bread and jobs, not private charity or the poorhouse. Other workers soon joined the sailors in their plight. A few jobs were created, some food was provided, and some jobless went to debtors' prison; others were encouraged to find better days on the western frontier. In time, the embargo was canceled, the economy improved, and many of the formerly unemployed again found work. As America continued to industrialize and urbanize, however, the problem of unemployment remained, reaching crisis proportions during the years of economic panic and depression: 1837, 1857, 1873, 1893, 1907, and most tragically during the years of the Great Depression that began in 1929. It is the story of the unemployed that Franklin Folsom tells in *Impatient Armies of the Poor*.

Folsom has had an extraordinarily full literary life. A native of Colorado, he was a Rhodes Scholar at the University of Oxford in the 1920's. He has worked as a college instructor and as a director of adult education, and he served in the merchant marine during World War II, but throughout his long life he has been primarily a free-lance writer. Folsom has written numerous books, sometimes in collaboration with his wife, Mary Elting, on such varied topics as archaeology, the West, baseball, geography, language, children's stories, Christopher Columbus, and the Soviet Union. The problem of the unemployed, however, is among Folsom's greatest interests and concerns. During the 1930's, he was personally involved in various unemployment organizations, and he states in the epilogue to *Impatient Armies of the Poor* that he began the manuscript in 1936 and pursued the topic during his own periods of unemployment during the next half century. Few literary works have had such a long gestational period.

Although a work of history, *Impatient Armies of the Poor* is also partly a personal memoir of the author's involvement in some of the events of the 1930's. Folsom tells the story of the unemployed from the early nineteenth century, but half the volume concentrates upon the years of the Great Depression. The book is organized chronologically, and Folsom's literary approach is primarily narrative rather than analytical. His focus is on the unemployed, and he tells of their struggles and difficulties in the face of economic disasters brought about by conditions beyond their personal control: industrialization, the swings of the business cycle from boom to bust and back again, the economic system of capitalism, and the prevailing ideologies of American society, which have extolled individualism and permitted government aid to business and industry but denied it to workers and the unemployed.

This is history written from the bottom. Although many individuals, from presidents to hobos, have played parts in the story of America's unemployed, Folsom's study concentrates upon what the great anonymous body of the unemployed have done to help themselves. In his opinion, to concentrate upon the achievements of individuals is to miss the story of how unemployment has affected vast numbers of Americans. Written without resort to academic phraseology and lacking the analytical frames of reference now common in the writing of social history, *Impatient Armies of the Poor* is a passionate portrayal of persons, groups, and classes often left out of traditional history, which usually focuses on the elite and the powerful.

Folsom's approach is different. He argues that the initiative that might eventually have led to government action on local or national levels has come not from the top, even among those in power sympathetic to the problems of the unemployed, but from the unemployed themselves. Throughout American history, the jobless have been the catalysts for change and not merely the recipients of it. Without their demands, relief and reform—no matter how imperfectly achieved—would likely not have come about at all. From the demonstrations of the naval Jack Tars in 1808 to the speeches and petitions of the unemployed in the 1830's and the 1850's to the armies of the jobless descending on the nation's capital in the 1890's, the actions of the unemployed have forced authorities to act, even if only halfheartedly. Folsom strongly criticizes some of the icons of twentieth century progressivism and liberalism. The author claims that Theodore Roosevelt was more concerned with putting down potential anarchy than with providing for public works projects for the jobless and that Mayor Fiorello La Guardia of New York City acted cowardly in refusing to receive a delegation of the unemployed during the Great Depression. Even Franklin D. Roosevelt becomes something of a cipher in the story of the development of the relief and public works programs of his New Deal.

Folsom points out that the jobless have not merely wanted relief or assistance. What they have demanded from the earliest days has been work. Jobs, not charity—and particularly not charity from private sources—has been the cure needed, Folsom argues. The unemployed have demanded government action, government response, government jobs if the private sector refused or was unable to employ all those wishing to work. Private charity often has not only been inadequate but also personally demeaning for those receiving such assistance, inasmuch as it creates a power relationship between haves and have-nots, even if that relationship has been hidden by the religious and moral considerations inculcated early in American society. To many of the unemployed, the right to a job has been seen as a part of the necessary social order, not something to be left to the chance workings of the economy or to be alleviated by the good works of individuals.

The author does not explicitly advance a particular ideological position, but the roots of *Impatient Armies of the Poor* lie in the radicalism of the political left of the 1930's, and that radicalism consistently colors Folsom's interpretation of events. The first half of the book, on the unemployed in the nineteenth century, is the least satisfactory portion. There is much of interest, such as the stories of the various unemployment armies of the 1890's, of which that led by Ohio's Jack Coxey was the best-known, though not necessarily the most significant. Yet the work comes most alive when it reaches the year 1929 and the onset of the Great Depression, the point at which Folsom's personal involvement in the problems of the jobless began.

As factories closed and businesses went bankrupt, workers by the millions lost their jobs. In 1931, numerous local hunger marches took place throughout the United States, and under the leadership of Herbert Benjamin, a member of the Communist Party, there was a national hunger march on Washington in December, 1931. The marchers' demands were for unemployment insurance and relief for the jobless. Another hunger march was directed against Henry Ford's Dearborn, Michigan, facilities. Violence resulted, and several people were killed. In the summer of 1932, thousands of World War I servicemen descended upon Washington demanding early payment of their adjusted compensation bonuses, which were not due until 1945. Alleging Communist influence and violence, President Herbert Hoover ordered the Army, under General Douglas MacArthur, to act. Using force, MacArthur drove the veterans and their families from their temporary camps. The bonus was not paid until 1936, but Hoover was defeated in his attempt for reelection in 1932.

In the interval between the November, 1932, presidential election and the inauguration of Franklin D. Roosevelt in March, 1933, there was a second National Hunger March. Delegations from forty-six states took part. Again, the Communist Party was active in organizing the march, but other political and labor organizations also gave it their support. Again, fear of Communist influence led the Washington authorities to resort to methods that, according to the author, were unnecessary and inhumane, even to the extent of depriving the demonstrators of toilet facilities. Folsom also discusses organizations such as the Unemployment Leagues and other movements to the left of the major political parties. Some were led by Communists, some by socialists, and some by maverick individuals such as Huey Long, senator from Louisiana, with his Share Our Wealth plan, which he claimed would end the Depression. In California, Charles F. Townsend, a dentist, advocated giving a pension of two hundred dollars to every American over the age of sixty. This, he argued, would revitalize the entire economy. Also in California, Upton Sinclair, the muckraking author of *The Jungle* (1906) and a socialist, ran for the governorship promising to end poverty in California by creating a state system of production to employ the jobless. Sinclair was defeated, Townsend's plan was not adopted, and Huey Long was assassinated, but Folsom argues that they and the various demonstrations, protests, marches, and organizations did move Roosevelt and his administration toward providing greater relief, employment on public works projects, and social security. Without pressure from the bottom the plight of the poor would have been much, much worse.

Although not entirely uncritical of America's Communist Party, Folsom obviously admires the lead that the Party and its individual members took during the Great Depression in organizing the poor and unemployed in demanding jobs and relief. Thus, it is ironic that *Impatient Armies of the Poor* was finally published in 1991, after the apparent failure of Marxism and the fall of Communism in Eastern Europe and the Soviet Union and after capitalism and the free-enterprise system seemed supreme and secure. Yet the author argues that without the demands of the organized poor and unemployed, the capitalist system will never adequately take notice of or care for those at the bottom of society. In a passionate warning against overconfidence, Folsom has written a most timely and relevant volume.

Eugene S. Larson

Sources for Further Study

Bloomsbury Review. XI, June, 1991, p. 5.
Bookwatch. XII, April, 1991, p. 2.
Choice. XXVIII, June, 1991, p. 1698.
The Nation. CCLIII, July 29, 1991, p. 166.
University Press Book News. III, June, 1991, p. 17.
The Village Voice. December 10, 1991, p. S13.

IN SEARCH OF HUMAN NATURE
The Decline and Revival of Darwinism
in American Social Thought

Author: Carl N. Degler (1921-   )
Publisher: Oxford University Press (New York). 400 pp. $24.95
Type of work: Social science and history of science
Time: The 1880's to the 1980's
Locale: The United States

A study of the efforts of American social scientists to explain the source of differences in human nature and behavior

> *Principal personages:*
> CHARLES DARWIN, the evolutionary theorist
> FRANZ BOAS, an anthropologist who attacked the notion that race explained
>   differences in human mental activities
> MARGARET MEAD, the anthropologist and cultural determinist

Are differences in group human behavior the result of biology or culture? Can these differences be eliminated through education or changes in the social environment, or are behavioral variations forever bound up in our genes? Does the level of sophistication of an ethnic group at a given time provide any insight into its potential to achieve a higher level of technological or cultural sophistication? This book is a study of the shifting attitudes of American social scientists—anthropologists, psychologists, political scientists, sociologists—toward these questions. These are questions that in the past have been cast in terms of nature versus nurture, the existence of innate racial characteristics or gender distinctions, or racial superiority.

Degler begins with Darwin's own publications and the theories of the Social Darwinists of the late nineteenth century and ends with the work of the sociobiologists of the 1980's. In a generally chronological discussion, he documents the widespread acceptance of biological explanations at the beginning of the twentieth century, the triumph of the cultural explanations prior to World War II, and the subsequent rising interest in biological explanations. He concludes with a brief discussion of the state of research in the mid-1980's and the rise of theories that have lessened or eliminated the distinctions between humans and animals. His focus is primarily on issues of race—especially black-white—and gender. Chapters are organized around themes rather than time periods.

Degler relies primarily on the published scientific literature, although he occasionally cites popular literature written by scientists. Only rarely does he use an unpublished letter for information. He is presenting the public debate. If his social scientists held private beliefs different from their public pronouncements, Degler is unconcerned.

"Darwinism" is Degler's catchphrase for any theory that argued that all of human nature, including morality and emotions, evolved in the same manner as did physical characteristics. Such theories saw human culture as the result of innate or (once genes were discovered) genetic influences. Changes could occur only slowly, on a Darwinian time scale. As in evolutionary biology in general, Darwin serves as a symbol or shorthand for a general type of orientation, whatever the nature of the connection—or lack of one—between a specific theory and the details of Darwin's thought. The "revival" in the book's subtitle is of evolutionary biological explanations, not of Darwin's nineteenth century theory of human evolution.

Central to Degler's examination is the work of Franz Boas. He presents Boas as a radical thinker who worked tirelessly to eliminate the perception that social differences were the result of, or linked to, physical differences. Boas argued that social or cultural dissimilarities were the result of the different histories of human groups, not of dissimilar biologies. Savages were not intellectually inferior to those living in civilizations with advanced technology; they had simply not utilized their potential to its fullest. In making such arguments, Boas flew in the face of accepted scientific and social doctrine in the United States in the late nineteenth century. A German Jew who immigrated to the United States because of the anti-Semitism of his homeland, Boas brought to his anthropological research a belief in equal opportunity. He challenged the racism of his profession and his adopted country. In doing so, he was not arguing for cultural relativism. He accepted a hierarchy of cultures, with white, Euroamerican culture as the highest. He saw no reason, however, why African Americans and other groups could not become fully integrated into that culture over time.

Degler credits Boas' ultimate victory in the scientific community to the widespread acceptance of the ideology of equal opportunity among social scientists. Degler claims that in the 1920's, at a time when the United States as a whole was plagued by racism and prejudice, the social science community was committed to securing opportunity for the socially disadvantaged. The subsequent linkage of biological determinism with the ultimate horrors of Nazi Germany reinforced the commitment of scientists to cultural explanations and their rejection of race as an important distinction among humans.

Yet the commitment to cultural explanations was relatively short-lived. Research on animal behavior after World War II conducted by European ethologists and sociobiologists raised questions about the relationship between animal and human social behavior. These researchers were obtaining data, both from controlled laboratory experiments and from observations of animals in the wild, indicating similarities between animal and human behavior. Social scientists saw the possibility of applying the insights of ethology to questions that had resisted cultural answers throughout the twentieth century. One of these was the incest taboo.

The taboo against incest is a universal human cultural characteristic. Although the specific details vary, every culture prohibits marriage or sexual relations between certain close relatives. Degler dedicates an entire chapter to the failure of anthropologists to explain the taboo in cultural terms, the discovery by ethologists that animals, too, practice incest avoidance, and the introduction by sociobiologists of a biological explanation of the human incest taboo. He offers this as a striking example of the many uses of biological knowledge by social scientists in the 1960's and 1970's.

Although Degler is examining debates carried out for the most part at professional meetings and in the technical journals and monographs of the scientific community, he is aware (as were the social scientists) that the issues raised were very significant for the larger American society. Scientific theories and experiments had implications for concrete political, economic, and social concerns that were central to late nineteenth and twentieth century America. Examples include both race relations and laws concerning gender distinctions. Could segregation be justified on the grounds that African Americans were innately intellectually inferior to whites? Were women unqualified for certain jobs because of their biological differences from men? The policy and legal implications of these scholarly debates are clear.

It is in this context that Degler performs some revisionism in the course of the book. He criticizes a number of conclusions of Stephen J. Gould, among them the widely accepted inference that the passage of the Immigration Act of 1924 was influenced by the findings and conclusions of social scientists experimenting on racial differences in human intelligence. The Immigration Act of 1924 greatly restricted immigration from Southern and Eastern Europe. Some scholars, including Gould, have held this law responsible indirectly for the deaths of millions during the Holocaust. If the law had not been in effect, Gould contends, millions more might have left Europe for the United States in the 1920's and 1930's, escaping death in the concentration camps. The Immigration Act of 1924 is frequently presented as an example of the life-and-death implications of what on the surface appear to be theoretical scientific discussions. Degler categorically rejects this interpretation, citing work by other historians on the issue that shows no direct correlation between the intelligence research and the passage of the bill; this finding agrees with his own conclusion that, in the early 1920's, social scientists were increasingly turning from biological explanations of differential intelligence.

As an example of the best of intellectual history, Degler clearly and precisely recapitulates and analyzes the ideas of important thinkers. He also explains the intellectual, social, and cultural influences on at least some of those thinkers that led them to accept or reject certain ideas. He makes it clear that ideas are the products of human beings, who frequently have agendas that influence their thinking and their reactions to the ideas of others. Scientists do not always evaluate ideas according to some abstract, objective scale. Frequently, their evaluations reflect how well such ideas fit into previously held ideological positions. Ideas are created by human beings who themselves are influenced by their environment and experiences. Degler's discussion of Boas is an excellent example of how taking this approach illuminates the history of ideas.

The weakness of Degler's approach is that American social scientists have never uniformly accepted or rejected theories. Perhaps more important, the individual disciplines never moved in lockstep. Psychology, for example, as Degler himself admits, resisted cultural explanations much more than did anthropology. Because Degler uses no quantitative measures, the reader is never sure how representative or significant particular scientists were. The views of individuals are used to provide evidence for transformations within a heterogeneous group. He also intermingles discussion of social scientists from different disciplines, despite the acknowledged disciplinary differences on this issue. What on the surface appear as dialogues or debates may in fact have been scientists writing for different audiences who were unaware of one another's research. The social science community is more complex than Degler's book indicates.

As a study of early twentieth century American scientific views of race, especially of the influence of Boas, this work is excellent. For the more recent period, Degler has not yet sorted out the story.

Marc Rothenberg

Sources for Further Study

Choice XXIX, September, 1991, p. 207.
Kirkus Reviews. LXIX, March 1, 1991, p. 295.
Library Journal. CXVI, June 1, 1991, p. 172.
Los Angeles Times. April 16, 1991, p. E5.
The New Leader. LXXIV, August 12, 1991, p. 15.
The New York Times Book Review. XCVI, March 17, 1991, p. 1.
Publishers Weekly. CCXXXVIII, March 8, 1991, p. 60.
Science News. CXXXIX, June 1, 1991, p. 350.
The Washington Post Book World. XXI, July 7, 1991, p. 12.
The Wilson Quarterly. XV, Summer, 1991, p. 98.

IN THE PALACES OF MEMORY
How We Build the Worlds Inside Our Heads

Author: George Johnson
Publisher: Alfred A. Knopf (New York). 255 pp. $22.95
Type of work: Science and psychology

The exact mechanism by which the brain both learns and remembers remains a mystery; Johnson details the investigations of a neuroscientist, a physicist, and a philosopher who are converging to close this knowledge gap

> *Principal personages:*
> GARY LYNCH, a neurobiologist investigating how memory causes new circuits to form in the brain
> LEON COOPER, a physicist exploring how memories are recorded and arranged inside the brain
> PATRICIA CHURCHLAND, a philosopher with a medical degree who is trying to bridge the disciplines of philosophy and biology in their study of the mind

It is astonishing, and perhaps even pleasing, to be reminded that, for all of humankind's scientific advances, something so simple and basic as human memory remains a mystery. Despite intensive research, no one is able to say precisely how and where memories are stored in the brain. The mechanism that allows one to remember that George Washington was the first president of the United States, that one's best friend from fifth grade had a dog named Susie, or that the local coffee shop serves a blue-plate special on Thursdays is still one of nature's best-kept secrets.

In *In the Palaces of Memory*, the scientific race to uncover this secret is documented in exquisite detail. George Johnson, a *New York Times* journalist, gives a rich (and, for the nonscientifically inclined, sometimes dizzying) account of the latest theories and experiments. His book is not an encyclopedia of all that is current in the field of brain and memory research, nor is it an argument for one particular theory over another; rather, *In the Palaces of Memory* is an action-adventure story. It is the heat of the race to uncover the workings of memory that makes Johnson's book so fascinating. *In the Palaces of Memory* is as much about the way scientists actually discover things as it is about the knowledge produced by science itself.

For the uninitiated, Johnson's book is an eye-opener. One meets scientists with egos, blind spots, petty jealousies—and the same kind of idiosyncratic genius and creative flair one usually expects only from bohemians and artists. One observes the course of scientific research flowing not, as one might have presumed, relentlessly and logically forward, building upon good ideas while discarding bad, but tracing a winding path, up, down, and around the politics of funding, almost as arbitrarily as the vicissitudes of fashion. One theory may fall into disrepute only to be revived again thirty years later, or a new and quite plausible theory might pop up but be virtually ignored because it does not incorporate the currently fashionable synapse or the chemical compound of the day. This is not to say that Johnson debunks science or scientists; rather, he humanizes them.

Johnson focuses on three researchers in particular: Gary Lynch, a biochemist at the University of California, Irvine, who studies synapses (the gaps neurotransmitters cross when transferring nerve impulses from one cell to another); Leon Cooper, a physicist at Brown University, who shared the 1972 Nobel Prize for the theory of superconductivity and who now works with artificial intelligence, simulating the operation of nerve nets in large computing systems; and Patricia Churchland, a professor of philosophy at the University of California, San Diego, who, having studied the mind for years in the abstract, took classes at medical school to get a closer look at the physical brain and now attempts to provide the neuroscience movement with philosophical underpinnings.

With each of his protagonists, Johnson drops the reader into the center of a scientific controversy. Among neuroscientists such as Gary Lynch, for example, there is agreement that learning affects the synaptic connections between nerve cells—but whether the change occurs at the sending neuron or the receiving neuron is in hot debate. Johnson details the warring hypotheses, experiments, and conclusions of the postsynapticists and the presynapticists, then introduces a physicist, Leon Cooper, who thinks such slavish attention to the neuron is beside the point.

Cooper believes that it is not so much what goes on inside a neuron that matters as how each neuron interacts with others, the web of neural connections that yields the full thinking and remembering capacity of the brain. He has little interest in the passive biochemical act of recording information. Rather, Cooper wonders how the brain generates its information, how it codes, stores, categorizes, and how it perceives and retrieves patterns. A theorist who believes that theorizing is as much a fine art as music or painting, Cooper is most enthralled with how the brain performs this function, its actual physical mechanism for theorizing. Cooper's approach to solving this problem is also no doubt annoying to the biologists. He is trying to construct a workable model of a neural network on computer in an attempt to simulate the mapping procedure of the brain. It is the "software," the very program the brain runs, that Cooper endeavors to duplicate; the "hardware" (whether biochemical neurons or a machine) assumes less significance.

The philosopher, Patricia Churchland, for the most part agrees with the direction in which Cooper has been moving. Unlike most of her colleagues in the field of philosophy, she takes a materialist and reductionist view of the mind, believing that everything is made of matter and energy, so that brain states and mental states must be one and the same. She is convinced that the answers to philosophical questions about the mind lie within the architecture of the brain itself, and that those who have principally studied this mechanism, the neuroscientists, would benefit by opening themselves to philosophical thinking.

As the resident philosopher of the neuroscience movement, Churchland bridges the gap between the disparate fields, trying to strike a balance, for example, between neuroscience and the extremes of the artificial intelligence movement, which can be so enamored with the mind as a logical system that the physiology of the brain gets neglected. Given her understanding of biological processes, where nature's procedures often work far differently from what one might have presumed, she proposes that the brain is probably not a neatly designed and logically laid-out machine but rather an accumulation of evolutionary strategies and tricks that have developed over time to meet the needs of survival.

Throughout Johnson's journey alongside these three pioneers at memory's gates, one nagging issue arises again and again: One of the biggest problems in studying the mind is that one must use the mind to do it. The concepts and perceptions of the very instrument one is using may be functioning as a kind of filter or blindfold to the results. Certainly, there is the knotty human problem of growing too attached to one's methodology or theory. Consider one of the current leaders in neurophysiological research, Eric Kandel, who studies the biochemical effects of learning on the nervous system of a sea snail called *Aplysia*. Kandel has enjoyed king-of-the-hill status in the neurosciences, attracting grants and disciples as honey draws bees. Yet for all his achievements, his results stand on a possibly shaky premise, which is that nature employs the same biochemical procedures for the human brain as for the sea snail. It may not. Lynch, on the other hand, has been studying synaptic changes in rats, whose brains are a little more like human brains. Yet Lynch does not escape the problem of attachment to hypothesis either. When test tube results fail to produce the glutamate binding he expects, rather than abandon his theory, Lynch simply makes some adjustments. The problem is not just that a researcher might be unwilling to discard his theory when his experiment fails to confirm it, or that his theory might stand on a shaky assumption, but that the research itself might be flawed by any number of biases stemming from the mind that conceived it. This has been the philosophers' long-standing objection to science. The design, implementation, and interpretation of any scientific experiment is as limited as the mind that has produced it.

Physicist Cooper describes the problem with the following analogy: Imagine that you have dropped down to Earth from another planet. You notice that every morning an object is thrown onto your porch. You do not have any concept for "newspaper" in your brain, so you perform various physical and chemical analyses of the object. You notice it is heaviest on the seventh day and lightest on the sixth, you analyze the ratio of white to black and find it is fairly constant, you discover that sometimes the chemical composition changes—but, because you don't have any understanding of what a newspaper is or what it is for, most of your observations are irrelevant. Your experiments have missed the point, which might also be true of much neuroscientific research.

That is why Cooper believes the neuroscientist must have something of a poet's or a dreamer's mind-set, a capacity to leap outside of the mind's own limiting framework to a new understanding. Says Cooper:

> To understand how we learn and remember or where thinking, consciousness, and self-awareness come from may require a leap as great as that taken by Galileo when he ignored air resistance, or Newton when he extended gravity from the earth's surface to the moon, or Einstein when he redefined time. It may be that various deep properties will arise in a relatively straightforward

manner as collective properties of simple systems—or it may be that some very profound change of point of view will be required.

Given that the quality of the mind that studies the mind is so important, Johnson's profiles of these three researchers take on extra significance. Certainly, Lynch, Cooper, and Churchland are all prominent in their respective fields, but so are a number of others (many of whom make brief or even extended appearances in Johnson's book). Yet why does Johnson choose to focus on Lynch, Cooper, and Churchland? It may be because they exemplify the kind of scientist best suited for the frontiers of mind exploration. Perhaps, by virtue of his selection, Johnson is redefining some of the key qualities necessary for breakthrough scientific thinking. Lynch, Cooper, and Churchland are all highly creative thinkers; moreover, each is a maverick in his or her own specialized field, having spent a number of years outside the mainstream. Perhaps most important, each is also quite comfortable with crossing disciplines. The days when scientists, philosophers, and psychologists all studied the mind in the isolation of their respective fields, like the proverbial blind men studying the elephant, are over. To make the kind of leap in point of view that Cooper is talking about, narrow scientific specialists will have to start speaking one another's languages. The traditional boundaries between disciplines may have been simply illusions of convenience that must be breached in order to uncover the remaining secrets of the mind.

No doubt many of the scientific controversies in *In the Palaces of Memory* will at some point be resolved, though as a document of their unfolding, Johnson's book will still make excellent reading. He has a novelist's skill for bringing the tension and drama of this race, as well as its primary characters, to life. Johnson's summaries of the relevant scientific methods and principles are clearly and carefully drawn, but given the complexity of the subject one wonders how many readers are as capable of juggling the concepts and language of neurobiology, physics, and philosophy as he is.

Dana Gerhardt

Sources for Further Study

The Antioch Review. XLIX, Spring, 1991, p. 299.
Booklist. LXXXVII, February 15, 1991, p. 1164.
Chicago Tribune. January 25, 1991, V, p. 3.
Kirkus Reviews. LVIII, December 1, 1990, p. 1655.
Library Journal. CXVI, February 1, 1991, p. 90.
Los Angeles Times Book Review. February 10, 1991, p. 2.
Nature. CCCLI, May 16, 1991, p. 200.
The New York Times Book Review. XCVI, February 24, 1991, p. 11.
Publishers Weekly. CCXXXVII, December 21, 1990, p. 37.
The Washington Post Book World. XXI, February 17, 1991, p. 1.

INDIA
A Million Mutinies Now

Author: V. S. Naipaul (1932-   )
Publisher: Viking (New York). 521 pp. $24.95
Type of work: Travel and current affairs
Time: 1962-1989
Locale: India

V. S. Naipaul's third travel book dealing with the Indian subcontinent assesses the current situation—political, economic, and cultural—in his ancestral homeland a quarter century after his first visit there

Since the publication of *A Passage to India* in 1924, British writing about India has in many cases replicated the basic structures and themes of E. M. Forster's novel. One thinks of Paul Scott's Raj Quartet, in particular the first volume, *The Jewel in the Crown* (1966), where the plot turns on the rape of an Englishwoman by rioting natives; or of Ruth Prawer Jhabvala's *Heat and Dust* (1975), in which miscegenation and an Englishwoman's rebellious curiosity motivate the novel's major events. The hold of what Edward Said has called "orientalism" over the British imagination of the subcontinent—even for those who are not British by birth but whose cultural formation reflects the persistence of late imperial fantasies—remains strong indeed.

The marks of British imperial ideology are everywhere apparent in *India: A Million Mutinies Now*, but what is perhaps most striking to someone whose training is in British literary tradition is how the book—self-consciously, one presumes—reproduces features from Forster's novel. The latter opens with a description of the mud and general squalor in the mythical North Indian town of Chandrapore that is echoed in Naipaul's brief evocation of Bombay upon his arrival there:

> Bombay continued to define itself: Bombay flats on either side of the road now, concrete buildings mildewed at their upper levels by Bombay weather, excessive sun, excessive rain, excessive heat; grimy at the lower levels, as if from the crowds at pavement level, and as if that human grime was working its way up, tide-mark by tide-mark, to meet the mildew.

It is not that Naipaul's portrait is in some gross sense false—Bombay surely *is* hot and damp—but that placed here, in the opening paragraphs of a book that will, purportedly, tell the story of contemporary India, it reassures a literate Western readership that they are on familiar ground. The India they will see is one they are already prepared to understand, one that has been, as it were, prefabricated for them by countless previous narratives from Rudyard Kipling and Forster to the film *Gandhi* (1982).

Nor do the parallels with *A Passage to India* end here. It is quite striking that the final chapter, "The House on the Lake: A Return to India," takes place in Kashmir. While Forster's novel ends in an unnamed princely state, where Dr. Aziz has moved to escape the oppression of British India, David Lean's film indelibly fixed its imaginative location by shooting the final episode in Kashmir's stunning landscape. Moreover, the whole apparatus of corrupt locals (a boatman extorts an exorbitant fee from Naipaul for his services), the proximity of the lake to the dwellings and hotel, the tensions between Hindus and Muslims (a theme that recurs throughout the narrative), not to mention the appearance of a man named Aziz—all these obviously staged details are intended to recall the final section of *A Passage to India*, as Naipaul assumes the role of Forster's omniscient narrator, commenting on the futility of the independence movement. Naipaul, as it happens, is not so pessimistic about what independence has brought, but it remains clear that he is far from cheerful about the nation's current prospects.

Naipaul's subtitle refers to the famous sepoy rebellion of 1857, in which native troops rose up against their British commanders and seized control of large sections of Northern India from the Punjab to Uttar Pradesh (then part of the United Provinces). He writes of this historic event some two-thirds of the way through the book, speaking contemptuously of the nationalist interpretation that took the Mutiny to be the first blow in the struggle against the British Raj:

> The British annexation of Onde was one of the things that led to the Indian Mutiny of 1857. In colonial times, and for a period afterwards, this was called by some the First War of Indian Independence. But this was a 20th-century view, 20th-century language, and a kind of mimicry, seeking to give to old India something of the socialist dynamism the Russians found in their own history. The Mutiny was the last flare-up of Muslim energy in India until the agitation, 80 years or so later, for a separate Muslim state of Pakistan.

Naipaul symptomatically adopts the British spelling for Awadh, the Mughal province that was still ruled by the Nawab until 1856, when Lord Dalhousie, the governor-general, annexed it on the slender pretext of corrupt administration. Naipaul's account omits mention that this annexation was part of a systematic policy pursued by Dalhousie and the British East India Company to acquire "legally" large blocks of Indian-ruled territory that it had not previously conquered by force of arms. The overthrow of Wajid Ali Shah, Awadh's last independent ruler, was merely the last in a series of rationalized territorial thefts—the culmination, one might say, of a century's plundering of India by the British. In addition, Naipaul's claim that the 1857 Rebellion was essentially a Muslim affair runs up against virtually all the best historiography, both British and Indian, which makes it plain that large sections of the indigenous populace, Hindus and Muslims alike, either took up arms directly or supported the sepoys. As is his wont, Naipaul here adopts the self-serving views of the colonialists, who ever since independence have been nostalgic for the good old days of the British Raj and bitter about the lack of gratitude their former subjects have shown for all the improvements and benefits British rule provided them.

The passage just cited also betrays one of Naipaul's favorite themes: the way in which the formerly colonized "mimic" the customs and practices of their former rulers. Of course, there is a *tu quoque* to be recognized here, as the dust-jacket portrait, displaying the author in tweed jacket, Oxford cloth shirt, and carefully knotted tie, emphasizes. Naipaul cannot be unaware that he has made himself over into the perfect British gentleman, or that he has become one of the premier spokespersons for the anti-Third World prejudice that dominates cultivated opinion in the metropolitan West. Unlike his British masters, however, Naipaul's praise for the achievements of the Raj cannot but be tinged with unease and bitterness, perhaps even, on occasion, with a certain sympathy for the plight of those who have suffered all the contradictions bequeathed to the subcontinent by colonial rule.

These two conflicting ideological strands are most visible in Naipaul's contrasting portraits of leftist politics in Bombay and in Calcutta. The latter, on Naipaul's account, once the seat of British rule (though he misdates the capital's removal to Delhi, which occurred in 1912, not in 1930), "began to die when the British went away." His disdain for the Communist government—originally the Left Front, which included more groups than the dominant Communist Party of India-Marxist (CPI-M)—that has ruled West Bengal for most of the past quarter century is plain throughout chapter 5, as he chronicles the many ills of urban life in Calcutta. But this familiar anti-communism takes a back seat to Naipaul's real target: the Naxalite movement, which erupted in the late 1960's in part out of a split within the CPI-M itself. Naipaul's portrait of the Naxalite leader Charu Mazumdar drips with irony and obvious contempt, particularly when it comes to the Naxalites' adoption of terrorism. Barely mentioned is the long history of Bengali terrorism, dating back to the decline of the *swadeshi* movement after 1907, and the role, not altogether negative, that it played in dislodging British rule. Indeed, the 1857 Rebellion itself played a not insignificant part in creating a viable revolutionary mythology that has successfully mobilized masses of ordinary people to resist injustice and oppression at the risk of their own lives. One need not be an advocate of terrorism to understand how it can function to sustain revolutionary social movements—and not only in India.

Earlier, in the opening chapter entitled "Bombay Theatre," Naipaul tells the story of his encounter with Namdeo Dhasal, founder of the Dalit Panthers, the militant political movement of what in the metropolitan West are typically known as "untouchables." The movement's name was adopted on the model of the American Black Panthers, a gesture Naipaul characterizes as "a romantic borrowing; it encouraged the—too simple—belief that the Dalits . . . were in India what black people were in the United States." Despite the inappropriateness of the comparison, however, Naipaul pursues it himself, attributing the decline of both to the fragmentation that set in after their success. Later on, he says of Namdeo that "his career seemed to be like the careers of a number of Black Power people in the United States." And yet, there are differences, which Naipaul is quick to observe:

> talking to him in this little room of the Bombay house, I felt that he was the prisoner of an Indian past no one outside could truly understand. It had been harder for him to break out, to reject the past, than it had been for black people in the United States. And now Namdeo was again, if in a different way, a prisoner of India, with its multiplicity of movements and desperate needs; he could easily sink again. It wasn't really possible for him, as it might have been possible for a black activist in the United States, to withdraw, to settle for ease.

Ignoring for the moment the questionable interpretation of black activists' relative freedom, one can affirm the underlying intuition that this passage asserts: to wit, that Indian society's historical density differentiates it sharply from societies like our own that are, by comparison, much less tradition-bound.

Nor is this powerful presence of the past altogether destructive, as Naipaul recognizes in the demeanor of "the long, patient line of dark men and women on one side of the road" whom he sees on his arrival in Bombay: "people at the bottom, full of emotion, with no politics at that moment, just rejecting rejection." It is a great pity that Naipaul cannot more often muster the obvious sympathy he evinces here, or that he is incapable of recognizing how such "rejecting rejection" is often made possible by political movements that have failed to realize their immediate goals. But it is a greater pity still that a writer with such obvious blindnesses, powerful prejudices (particularly against Muslims), and willed ignorance (even an amateur of Indian history would not make the elementary errors sprinkled throughout this book) has been taken (along with some few others) to be the authentic voice of Indian civilization today. Naipaul understands all too well, one surmises, the extent to which he is a creation of the West, the mystery is that his Western audience—virtually the only one he has—cannot recognize this as well and maintain a healthy skepticism towards his elegant, seductive trashing of the non-Western world he despises so heartily.

Michael Sprinker

Sources for Further Study

Chicago Tribune. January 6, 1991, XIV, p. 5.
The Christian Science Monitor. February 28, 1991, p. 11.
Foreign Affairs. LXX, Summer, 1991, p. 182.
Los Angeles Times Book Review. January 13, 1991, p. 9.
The New Republic. CCIV, June 10, 1991, p. 23.
The New York Review of Books. XXXVIII, February 14, 1991, p. 3.
The New York Times Book Review. XCV, December 30, 1990, p. 1.
ORBIS. XXXVI, Winter, 1992, p. 156.
Publishers Weekly. CCXXXVII, November 9, 1990, p. 48.
Time. CXXXVII, January 14, 1991, p. 61.
The Times Literary Supplement. October 5, 1990, p. 1059.

INDIA

Author: Stanley Wolpert (1927-   )
Publisher: University of California Press (Berkeley). Illustrated. 273 pp. $27.50
Type of work: History
Time: Prehistoric to the twentieth century
Locale: India

A wide-ranging introduction to the geography, history, politics, art history, and current problems of India

Stanley Wolpert, the author of *A New History of India* (1977) and of a previous book also entitled *India* (1965), has written a readable, solid introduction to the land and people of one of the world's most complex countries and civilizations. Evidently conceived for the nonspecialist for whom India may be only a name on a map, the new *India* addresses the subcontinent under the successive rubrics of geography, history, religion, society, arts and sciences, and politics. The result is both balanced and a bit bland, nourishing and yet at the same time slightly predigested. Ideally, perhaps, this book should be read as an hors d'oeuvre that will pique the reader's curiosity to continue to more specialized, more detailed, and theoretically more self-aware views of this complex country.

Wolpert professes to a "lifelong romance with India" in his preface, but there is little hint of the wild or passionate in his treatment of the subcontinent. In fact, there is something more than slightly academic about the thorough coverage of the subject under his progressive rubrics, as if one were reading a high-school textbook rewritten for adults. Only rarely does the reader have the sense from Wolpert's account of what it is like to live in or even visit India, a sense of the colors and sounds and texture of life. Indeed, this lack of "feel" the prose gives a reader is mirrored and presaged by the rather dull-looking and not very striking black-and-white photographs that serve as the book's illustrations.

Appropriately enough, Wolpert comes closest to offering this kind of interesting detail in his chapter devoted to a consideration of Indian society. Yet at these moments he seems almost apologetic, as if this were not relevant to his real purpose. For example, he writes: "The rich deep green of rice fields before harvest or the gold of mustard surrounding the lime-washed white huts and well-swept lanes of a prosperous village appear so peacefully integrated into the natural environment of many regions of India's countryside that it is almost too easy to wax romantic about the pastoral beauty of village life." Yet the reader almost wishes he had given in to this "easy" enterprise, thereby perhaps infusing a touch of the poetic into what is otherwise so sober a recitation of facts. The closest Wolpert comes to this in the remainder of the text tends unfortunately to the cliché-ridden, as in the statement that "India and the River mirror each other, bubbling with life, always changing, ever the same."

The value for the uninitiated of the introductions to Indian topography and history that open the book is self-evident. In addition, Wolpert points to some of India's looming problems: its ever-increasing population, leading to deforestation and hence to erosion of the land, and the overload on urban services originally conceived for far fewer people. Yet though it is useful to have overviews of these relatively straightforward subjects united in a single volume, they are of a kind widely available in other reference works.

The chapters that follow are both more complex and more problematic, in that some tensions between the position of the narrator/author and that of his subject begin to surface. To a certain extent, the dominant tone is that of the professor telling stay-at-homes all they need to know and may well sound patronizing. "Most Indians," Wolpert tells the reader, "are gentle, nonviolent people, in part perhaps because they view all life as interrelated, and believe in the potential cosmic significance of individual deeds or actions and their implications, extending over a hundred or more lifetimes." Whether or not this is true, it is clearly the opinion of an avowed outsider to the civilization regarding which the generalizations are offered—and Wolpert offers neither evidence for his assertion nor acknowledgement of its presumption.

Instead, as is often the case when he permits himself generalizations of this sort, Wolpert prefers to submerge the subjectivity of his perception in a tone of gentle irony. Here he switches immediately from a statement about outsiders to one that seems to include himself and his potential audience as well: "One must thus be careful where one treads, for the very earthworm beneath one's foot shares cosmic connections. We never know where the ripple-current we set in motion could lead." Of course, he does not mean "we," but "they," as the first sentence of the passage has made clear. Those to whom this statement is addressed end in a position of bemused distance masquerading as the attempt to put themselves in the place of others. Wolpert seems insufficiently clear about his own position on the matter, having buried a clear delineation of approval or disapproval in the urbane pretense of identification.

The problem with this is not that such a viewpoint is untenable; indeed, it is clear that few Westerners will be able to justify fully the customs of non-Western societies. Certainly, Wolpert is making clear his fundamental forgiveness, rather than condemnation, of such foibles as he delineates, but the problem is that Indian society may not want such forgiveness. Wolpert's viewpoint is at all times that of the slightly distanced professor, unflappable, interested, and above all not about to be drawn out to the point where his own presuppositions can be questioned. The pretensions of this work, that is, are to objectivity; it is, however, clear that finally it is quite subjective indeed. Nevertheless, so circumspect is the expression of this fundamental subjectivity that it may pass as all but invisible. Yet what else can a book of fewer than three hundred pages entitled—with no visible attempt at irony—simply *India* be, save subjective? How to summarize such a vast amount of material save under subjective rubrics?

Wolpert's tack of all but submerging judgment under a sheen of bemused tolerance colors as well his treatment of those aspects of Indian life that seem least attractive to outsiders, including Muslim-Hindu violence, the treatment of women, and the lack of privacy in Indian society. In all cases, he makes as strong a case as he can for not condemning the Indian reality outright and then seems to throw up his hands and side with the more generally held Western point of view, which thus remains unquestioned. The result is that the reader may come to see Wolpert's careful presentation as something of an evasion and long for a clearer delineation of opinion on the part of the author, a more honest consideration of the implications of a Westerner writing a Western-oriented introduction for Western readers.

Ultimately, for example, Wolpert does his best to relativize Hindu-Moslem religious violence by pointing out, accurately enough, that "India has not been the only country in the world to be plagued by religious conflicts. More Protestants and Catholics have murdered one another in religious wars than have Hindus and Muslims." Yet finally (and perhaps unsurprisingly), he is unable to justify such violence, referring to the postindependence murders as "homicidal savagery" and writing, with a tone of sorrowful head-shaking, of the way contemporary riots between Muslims and Hindus are started.

In the same vein, his consideration of the traditionally subservient role of women in Indian society (each of whom was taught to consider her husband as her god) is clearly informed by sympathy to their plight. He is especially in favor of Indira Gandhi's outlawing of the dowry, whose nonpayment sometimes leads to the "accidental" burning to death of the wife. Yet he seems willing to let his position all but trail off in the suggestion of nonjudgmental relativism, writing that "communities as a whole usually close ranks to defend what we view as barbaric behavior meriting the most severe punishment, but what is often judged through traditional Indian eyes as appropriate 'self-help' and as exemplary or a 'good lesson' to others."

For all this attempt to avoid having to take a stand regarding local perceptions of Indian customs, Wolpert does in fact possess firm opinions about Indians and their social institutions. He speaks categorically, for example, of "the fragmentation of Hindu society that has always been its greatest weakness." In addition, he allows himself generalizations about the Indian character: "There is, indeed, more 'passivity' in Indian personalities than we generally find among Americans of comparable age and status." To be sure, he hastens to de-essentialize such qualities, ascribing them to nurture rather than nature: This "passivity" (the word itself, the reader should note, used only within scare quotes) is "a product in great measure of lifelong accommodation to the many competing voices, needs, demands, and aspirations of the large extended family. If all clamored at once, none could be heard."

This is a theory, and a plausible one. Yet so concerned is Wolpert to preserve the fiction of the objective or at least judiciously uninvolved spectator that it is neither properly laid out nor justified. So too for his statement that "Indians for the most part are an obedient, deferential people, accepting of 'higher' authority." Once again he offers an explanation through environment—"such obedience is family-inculcated"—as if the gesture on his part to offer any explanation at all makes unnecessary a justification either of the initial assertion or of the status of this particular explanation as the correct one.

Wolpert's brief consideration of contemporary politics at the end of the book, perhaps because it deals with slightly more tangible subjects, seems more satisfying, explaining the deep fissures within Indian democracy that led to the 1991 assassination of Rajiv Gandhi. This act, of course, occurred after the book was published, yet Wolpert's thumbnail sketch of the status of Indian Tamils in the southeast (who claimed responsibility for the suicide bombing) goes a long way to making it plausible in retrospect.

Bruce E. Fleming

Sources for Further Study

Booklist. LXXXVII, April 1, 1991, p. 1540.
Far Eastern Economic Review. CLIII, August 22, 1991, p. 30.
The Guardian Weekly. CXLIV, April 7, 1991, p. 18.
Library Journal. CXVI, March 1, 1991, p. 102.
San Francisco Review of Books. XVI, Number 1, 1991, p. 53.
The Washington Post Book World. XXI, March 3, 1991, p. 5.

THE INFECTION OF THOMAS DE QUINCEY
A Psychopathology of Imperialism

Author: John Barrell
Publisher: Yale University Press (New Haven, Connecticut). Illustrated. 235 pp. $30.00
Type of work: Literary and cultural criticism

Barrell isolates recurring images of death and "Oriental" evil in De Quincey's literary works that he relates to biographical incidents from De Quincey's childhood and an imperial mindset prevalent during the Romantic and Victorian eras

The Infection of Thomas De Quincey: A Psychopathology of Imperialism moves from personal history to cultural psychology, richly fulfilling the promise of a "cultural studies" approach to interpreting literary texts and an individual writer's place in literary history. This is neither a standard biography nor a linear analysis of Thomas De Quincey's lifework. Rather, John Barrell focuses on patterns of images in De Quincey's fiction and nonfiction, carefully isolating the recurring fears that these images indicate in order to trace the links between one man's psychology and the mindset of his era. While occasionally repetitious, Barrell's analysis is usually eye-opening and always courageous in its attempt to place De Quincey's prejudices and anxieties in a complex cultural context.

Thomas De Quincey (1785-1859) is best known for his infamous *Confessions of an English Opium-Eater* (1821), in which he explored with shocking frankness his addiction to the drug and vividly detailed his drug-induced visions, but De Quincey also authored hundreds of other essays and fictional pieces over the course of his long and stormy life, one that stretched through the Romantic era and well into the reign of Queen Victoria. Full of colorful descriptions of imaginary landscapes and gruesome acts of violence, De Quincey's autobiographical, critical, and fictional works seem perfectly suited for a psychologically based interpretation. But Barrell resists the tendency of many critics deploying this methodology who simply pick out scenes that "represent" the various crises and conflicts of some "universal" psychological development process. Barrell notes that many of De Quincey's works share a common setting and atmosphere; their action takes place against an "Oriental" backdrop and contain Asian characters and images. These intersecting elements allow Barrell to explore the connections between literary representation and social policy, for De Quincey wrote during the years of British colonial expansion in India and the Opium Wars in China.

Before Barrell turns his critical eye to British social history, he examines in detail De Quincey's own personal history. Barrell focuses first on the 1792 death from hydrocephalus (water on the brain) of De Quincey's beloved sister Elizabeth. De Quincey, just seven years old at that time, was plagued by guilt throughout his life for not having saved her, even though her illness was then neither preventable nor curable. His guilt was exacerbated by an incident that occurred on the day after Elizabeth's death. Secretly making his way to the room in which his sister's body was lying, De Quincey kissed Elizabeth for the last time, an innocent enough act, but one that for him was forever associated with feelings of pollution and sinfulness. Perhaps it was the secrecy of the kiss, its occurrence in a bedroom behind closed doors, or its connection to hidden incestuous desires, but for some compelling reason that even Barrell admits no one will ever fully understand, this incident and De Quincey's profound guilt were replayed time and again in various forms throughout his writings.

Inseparable from the above were other key familial relationships that played roles in De Quincey's psychological formation. His father was a merchant whose business often took him away from home. His mother had pretensions to aristocracy and decorated the original family name "Quincey" with the aristocratic "De." She later dropped the addition, but Thomas retained the new, elongated name throughout his life and passed it on to his own family. From his childhood relationship with his parents, De Quincey seemed to have developed a lifelong need for approval and recognition. While his mother and father remain shadowy figures in Barrell's study and in De Quincey's own work, their absence in fact tells us as much as their presence would.

De Quincey was an alienated, lonely child, which meant that certain isolated interactions with siblings inevitably and indelibly colored his personal memories and perceptions of himself and the world. Besides his guilt over the death of Elizabeth, his violent hatred for his older brother William is a key to understanding aspects of his adult representations. William's bullying tendencies and status as a favorite son led to both jealousy and rage in De Quincey, feelings that did not die after William's own death at age fifteen from typhoid fever. And as in the case of Elizabeth, the manner of this death is noteworthy, for it helps explain De Quincey's lifelong references to similarly afflicted and peculiarly described individuals. De Quincey believed that Elizabeth's hydrocephalus was a result of a long walk in a lush landscape, one that became inextricably tied to the landscapes of the Orient in his works. Similarly, William's typhoid fever was a disease that even the medical community of the nineteenth century commonly associated with the East. Thus both the hated brother and the beloved sister become linked in death to differing cultural conceptions of Asia, ones that included both a fascination with and fear of Eastern mystery and danger, and perceptions of the Orient as a source of both potential pleasure and pollution.

Barrell argues that these complex elements find their way into De Quincey's work in the form of "involutes"—De Quincey's own term for inextricably interwoven sets of images and ideas. Involutes are personal archetypes that, for Barrell, suggest both psychological and social interpretations. Images of disease, a motionless woman, a closed door, and moist, threatening landscapes weave in and out of De Quincey's writings, suggesting myriad personal and political fears. William is explicitly associated with tigers in De Quincey's autobiographical essays, suggesting ways of interpreting the numerous other tigers in his fictional and political works. Similarly, turbans and other head coverings evoke memories of Elizabeth's shrouded body. The personal and the political become inseparable as De Quincey's family history becomes the lens through which he perceives his society and vice versa.

In many of De Quincey's representations, Barrell also notices a pattern that he describes as "this/that/the other," in which the observer ("this") is caught between unknowns, the "that" and "the other," the former more domestic and acceptable, the latter more foreign and intrinsically evil. Again, Elizabeth and William play roles in such a dynamic. Elizabeth and images associated with her are frequently perceived as "that," the "female," which unnerves and mystifies De Quincey, whose shaky masculine self-image needs constant reaffirmation. William and his images, however, are often cast as "the other," the potent and potentially murderous opponent. De Quincey's perception of the international landscape becomes populated with figures and groups designated similarly, some simply unknown, others more actively threatening.

A particularly interesting example of Barrell's analysis comes in chapter 3, "Nympholepsy," which carefully examines De Quincey's fascination with Elizabeth-like young women and his culture's erotic interest in childlike female bodies. In his reading of the novella "The Household Wreck" (1838), Barrell explores images of feminine innocence that exemplify nineteenth century culture's desire to protect women from traditionally male pursuits and from foreign men and influences. Like De Quincey's descriptions of Elizabeth, the heroine of the tale, Agnes, is young, beautiful, and essentially passive. She is also in need of a strong male protector; even so, the narrator is self-consciously powerless to render aid to her. She is wrongfully arrested for petty theft and imprisoned by a man described as a "bloody tiger." Here the biographical meets the social and psychological, for in Barrell's schema, the narrator participates in a stereotypical designation of women as "that"—different from men, in need of protection, childlike but seductive. But the tigerish man who causes her death is truly "the other," a menacing, William-like figure who is the transmitter of an "Oriental" death, for Agnes dies in jail from typhoid fever that she contracts while incarcerated.

Chapter 7, "Diplopia," elaborates on the "double vision" that Barrell indicates is characteristic of De Quincey's division of threats into "that" and "the other" and his tendency to move in and out of identification with various characters. In his examination of De Quincey's "On Murder considered as one of the Fine Arts" (1854), an essay detailing the gruesome Williams murders of 1811, Barrell also links this "diplopia" to the reading public's fascination with lurid tales of mass murder. With whom does the reader actually identify in such works? On the personal level, De Quincey's essay portrays many of the recurring anxieties and patterns of images that characterize his texts, ones clearly heightened by the coincidence of name between the murderer and De Quincey's own brother. The reader finds an intrusion into a locked room, a guilty lingering over a bed, and a focus on a corpse, as the murderer Williams breaks into a shop and massacres an entire family. But as Barrell notes, this essay implicitly shifts the guilt that De Quincey habitually felt over the Elizabeth "incident" onto the shoulders of a figure representing his brother. Barrell deepens such analysis as he examines De Quincey's reportage of another set of murders from 1826, perpetrated by the two McKean brothers. In these passages, De Quincey again uses the "this/that/the other" distinction to comment upon the roles of the obviously innocent victims of the crime (this), the criminally complicit but not actually murderous younger of the two brothers, whose observation of the actual slaughter De Quincey portrays with a considerable self-identification and guilt (that), and the older brother-murderer (the other), whose quasi-sexual violation of his female victim and surreptitiousness help brand him as a menacing "Oriental" figure. In Barrell's reading, the fluidity with which De Quincey and the reader move in and out of identification here leads to a heightened denigration of the menacing "other" figure whose actions rivet the reader and narrator but whose difference from them is continually reinforced. De Quincey thereby provides entertainment to a voyeuristic audience and works through his own guilt by making a William-like individual the culprit in an Elizabeth-like person's death.

The international and specifically imperial implications of such representations are carefully developed as Barrell turns from De Quincey's personal writings and descriptions of British crimes to his later essays on the British empire. In chapter 9, "Leontiasis," Barrell examines how socially reinforced masculine desires to protect women helped fuel Britain's predatory imperial designs. De Quincey's essay "Ceylon" (1843) portrays the Sinhalese people of the island as "feminine," as immobile women, much like De Quincey's sister Elizabeth, who are threatened with violation by a violent male force, the Kandyans of the island, who are represented as "tiger-like." De Quincey justifies British imperial control of the island as "this" (the British) saves "that" (the Sinhalese) from "the other" (the Kandyans). In such writings, personal psychology, a society's gender politics, and a nation's imperial fantasies effectively become one cultural project and product. Barrell argues that the three were so thoroughly interconnected that to analyze one is necessarily to evoke the other two.

This, however, does lead to one possible objection to Barrell's study. Unfortunately, he makes few references to any works other than those written by De Quincey. While the connections between De Quincey's personal psychology and the ways in which he represented numerous scenes are clear, it would only deepen Barrell's analysis to examine carefully how other writers worked similarly to "feminize" colonial spaces and participated in the same "this/that/the other" structure when discussing British projects in Asia. Barrell produces consistently fine analysis of individual psychology, but simply through omission, is weaker in his interpretation of the "cultural" psychology that produced and reinforced imperial projects. As critics Sandra Gilbert and Susan Gubar explored in *Sexchanges* (1989), volume 2 of *No Man's Land: The Place of the Woman Writer in the Twentieth Century*, numerous essayists and authors of adventure stories used similar paradigms and characterizations to engage an explicitly male audience in stories of domination and control of an "other." Barrell focuses so exclusively on De Quincey that he loses some of the force of his argument concerning the culture that produced the writer and many others during the era.

One reason that such omissions become obvious is that often Barrell's analysis appears repetitious. He discusses the Williams murders several times in different chapters and returns to the same images repeatedly, long after his reader has accepted that the pattern is pronounced in De Quincey's work. In chapter after chapter, he isolates the Elizabeth figure, the William figure, the tiger, and the guilty observer. More than two hundred pages of such basic charting of involutes could benefit from considerable condensing and rearranging. This would open up space for a discussion of related authors and a wider variety of literary representations. Barrell's interpretations are always fascinating, but could be widened in scope and organized more effectively.

To isolate such problems is not to imply that Barrell's study is seriously compromised. The reader simply must remain patient and expect some circularity rather than a consistent linearity in the progression of the book. Indeed, the rewards for such a recasting of expectations are considerable. Barrell provides a persuasive reevaluation of an era and an individual writer's psychology. In his conclusion, Barrell questions the numerous scholars who imagine De Quincey happily reunited with his sister after his death in 1859; instead, asks Barrell, would not the prospect of such a reunion be particularly frightening for a man whose life was so thoroughly guilt-ridden after their last encounter? According to Barrell, no scholar should simply gloss over the unpleasant details of De Quincey's strange life and literary imaginings, for it is precisely such unpleasant traits and bizarre characterizations that are the most revealing about his personal worldview and that of his culture. After considering the strong evidence that Barrell submits, the reader cannot help but agree.

Donald E. Hall

Sources for Further Study

Choice. XXIX, November, 1991, p. 437.
The Guardian. May 9, 1991, p. 24.
The Literary Review. Number 157, July, 1991, p. 46.
London Review of Books. XIII, May 9, 1991, p. 11.
New Statesman and Society. IV, May 24, 1991, p. 44.
The New York Times Book Review. XCVI, June 2, 1991, p. 27.
The Observer. May 12, 1991, p. 54.
The Times Literary Supplement. July 5, 1991, p. 7.
The Washington Post Book World. XXI, May 26, 1991, p. 13.

ISAAC AND HIS DEVILS

Author: Fernanda Eberstadt (1960   )
Publisher: Alfred A. Knopf (New York). 338 pp. $22.00
Type of work: Novel
Time: The 1960's to the 1980's
Locale: Gilboa, New Hampshire

A novel that follows a brilliant protagonist through the first twenty-two years of his life to his ultimate triumph over the demons of madness and despair that threaten his self-realization

> *Principal characters:*
> ISAAC HOOKER, the protagonist, a gifted young man
> SAM HOOKER, his father, a high school teacher
> MATTIE DOUCETTE HOOKER, his mother, the owner of a taxi company
> TURNER HOOKER, Isaac's younger brother
> AGNES URQUHART, Isaac's teacher and best friend, eventually also his lover

In her first novel, *Low Tide* (1985), Fernanda Eberstadt established herself as a talented young writer. Critics, however, suggested that her characters seemed to stagnate in their obsessions, while her baroque, highly allusive style impeded the narrative. In her second novel, *Isaac and His Devils*, it is clear that Eberstadt has profited from the reviews of her first work. In the first chapter, she establishes her newborn protagonist as a sympathetic character, with much to overcome but with an admirable mind and will. From that point on, the story proceeds at a steady pace. Although still complex, Eberstadt's poetic and philosophical passages show evidence of careful pruning; they amplify the narrative, rather than halting it. As for the major characters, while they are as grotesque as those in *Low Tide*, they are more represen tative of the universal human condition than those in the earlier novel. If some of their habits are unique, their struggles against apathy and acquiescence are not. Therefore, the major characters in *Isaac and His Devils* compel a sympathy that those in *Low Tide* could not.

Late in the novel, the protagonist muses that even if God is absent from the world, the devils are still present. These devils attempt to defeat the human will, to overcome energy with apathy, to transform hope into despair, and if possible to drive their victims to madness. From the time of his birth, Isaac Hooker, the central character in this coming-of-age story, seems like easy prey for these demons. He has poor vision and is partially deaf. Soon it becomes clear that he will always be a large, clumsy, physically unattractive person with sloppy ways and irritating habits.

In Isaac, one is reminded of the eighteenth century man of letters Dr. Samuel Johnson, who had similar physical problems and unappealing habits along with intellectual gifts that were evident from his earliest years. This reaction is no accident, for Eberstadt was inspired to write Isaac's story after she had read a biography of Johnson. Throughout his life, Johnson struggled against a paralyzing melancholy, which he defeated through his deep religious faith, as well as through some desperate measures such as working mathematical problems.

While his character is similar to that of Johnson, Isaac's solutions are different, as is evident in the fourth and final section of the book, when he goes through his dark night of the soul. Having left Harvard, where he had been little more than a target of cruel jokes, in order to return to the only security he had known, the love of his mistress, Isaac has taken a menial job and settled for a life without challenges. When his father dies, Isaac seems to be shocked into an appraisal of his own situation, and he, too, dies a kind of death, retreating to his bed, even rejecting the attentions of his devoted mistress. Evidently Isaac must battle his demons totally alone. At the end of the book, the strong-willed Isaac has won, and with confidence in his own powers he leaves the small New Hampshire town of his birth for the larger battlefield of New York City.

Eberstadt's vision of life as a struggle with apathy and despair is reiterated in the life story of Sam Hooker, Isaac's father, which is related in snatches and flashbacks while Isaac's own account is proceeding in chronological fashion.

In his own youth, Sam, too, had been intellectually curious and therefore unlike his schoolmates. Although he was not particularly interested in teaching or in a lifetime of disciplined research, Sam knew that he loved books and ideas above all else, and it was natural that he should drift into graduate school, intending to obtain a master's degree and then a doctorate. Although a professor friend warned him about the dangers of husband-hunting women, Sam began to date a young, fun-loving girl, Mattie Doucette, on a casual basis. Part of Mattie's appeal was the fact that she did not read or think, except about fun and money, and thus she was a diversion from Sam's mental exertions. The professor's dire predictions came true. Before long, Sam was trapped; worse, his wife despised his academic ambitions and used her pregnancy as an excuse to get him out of school and into a job. Sam became a high school teacher in Gilboa, New Hampshire.

Thus by the time Isaac is born, Sam is already defeated. Despised and bullied by his wife, deadened by his daily contacts with bored and backward students, he becomes so paralyzed by despair that he even stops reading. There is only one person who can inspire him; ironically, it is the very baby who was the cause of his departure from graduate school. Although he loathes teaching the ignorant boors at his high school, Sam finds his true vocation in presiding over the intellectual development of a child who is so exceptional. While Isaac's other teachers, who feel threatened by him, consistently punish him for his very creativity, Sam patiently answers his questions and systematically provides him with stimuli for his highly original mind. Thus Sam lives vicariously through his brilliant son.

One way in which Sam stimulates Isaac's imagination is by taking him exploring the hilly countryside around Gilboa. As the two ride, they observe and speculate. On one occasion, Isaac notices not only that the people he sees are poor, but that they are simply lounging about without any purpose. Isaac's first impulse is to be judgmental; however, Sam points out that what the boy is seeing is not laziness but defeat. The struggle in life, he explains, is between endeavor and lassitude, hope and despair; without a strong will, one can fall into a "slump" and never emerge. Sam knows only too well how the devils of apathy can destroy the most promising life.

When Sam and Isaac return home from that car trip, Isaac tells his mother about what he has seen. Interestingly, her reaction is completely different from Sam's compassionate comments. Mattie has nothing but contempt for people who do not bestir themselves to do something, anything; she makes it clear that she includes Sam in that category. This episode points out Mattie's only admirable quality, her strength of will; fortunately, this is the quality that Isaac has inherited from his mother, and the quality that enables him to win when the devils besiege him after his father's death.

Certainly, Mattie recognizes that life involves struggle. Unlike Sam and Isaac, however, Mattie does not question herself or her goals. All of her struggles are external ones, and because she embodies the principle of energy, she enjoys conflict. Even though she does not show much interest in Isaac, she ventures forth to do battle when she learns that a group of thugs have beaten him up. It is the battle itself that she loves, and even though she does not win so much as an admission of guilt from the mothers of the boys, she glories in repeating her verbal attacks, which in her eyes have brought her a great victory.

Although Mattie has the strong will that Sam lacks, she herself lacks his appreciation of books and ideas. In this distinction between Mattie and Sam, Eberstadt dramatizes the second major conflict of the novel. Sam values culture, intellect, the things of the mind and the spirit; Mattie values only money.

At first, Sam did not see this quality in Mattie. As a girl, Mattie seemed to care only for having fun; it was that quality that attracted the serious Sam. Soon after their marriage, however, it becomes clear that her goal in life is to accumulate money. For the sake of money, she sees Sam sentenced to a job he hates; for the sake of money, she spends every waking minute at her cab company, letting her children go dirty, ill-fed, and ill-clothed. She does not want to waste either time or money on her family. Indeed, as a thoroughgoing materialist, she is the natural enemy of people like Sam and Isaac; as intellectuals, they must be considered parasites in her world, which sees their interests not as culturally significant but as personal self-indulgence. Mattie's attitude is evident throughout the novel. When as a child Isaac tries to ask her questions that go beyond the immediate, Mattie refuses to listen. Later, when he wins an important award, it is Sam who goes to the school; Mattie is busy making an extra run for the cab company. Such incidents are not mere chance; at least subconsciously, they reflect Mattie's hostility toward everything that Sam and Isaac hold dear.

The conflict between those dedicated to the material world and those who dwell in the world of ideas is underlined by Mattie's relationship with her two sons. She finds Isaac repulsive; in contrast, she can see no flaws in her younger son, Turner Hooker, who spends most of his time in "masculine" activities. Turner hunts animals as feverishly as Mattie pursues wealth. Interestingly, Turner spends most of his time hunting animals, not women, and after Sam's death he completes the identification with his mother by moving into her bed, in a peculiar though probably chaste relationship.

Eberstadt dramatizes this conflict between the two worlds through three episodes involving Sam's *Columbia Encyclopedia*. When Sam is still in graduate school, shortly after his marriage, he brings home the encyclopedia, which he has just purchased. To him, it is a treasure. To the furious Mattie, it is a waste of money. From that time on, the battle lines are drawn. Sam's perception of the encyclopedia as somehow a compendium of everything that is valuable in human life is emphasized after Isaac has had his prize book destroyed by the thugs. In a touching expression of profound love, Sam offers the encyclopedia, which he has now stopped reading, to Isaac, who will cherish it. Isaac is too upset, however, to understand the significance of his father's gesture, and he refuses. In the final pages of the novel, after Isaac has defeated his demons and risen from his bed, the encyclopedia appears again. Isaac goes to his mother's house to get the encyclopedia, which he says his father had always intended for him. Even though Mattie has no use for it, she is too greedy to give the book to Isaac, and threatens him with a pistol. Where Sam would have backed down, Isaac stands firm, and although his mother shoots him, wounding him slightly, he escapes with the book that represented all of his father's values.

After that important drive in the New Hampshire hills, Isaac believes that he has a method to defeat the devils of apathy that seem to threaten everyone except energetic, unthinking people like his mother. There are three elements in his formula: luck, over which one has little control; will, which one may inherit but must exert; and, finally, love. In love, where Sam was unlucky, Isaac has good fortune. There are two people who love Isaac selflessly and totally, his father and his teacher, Agnes Urquhart, who first becomes his best friend and later his mistress. Because Agnes shares Isaac's values, her love is supportive and constructive; combined, the love of Sam and of Agnes for Isaac can forestall the damage that his destructive mother was driven to do to him.

While reviewers have praised the prose, the characterization, and the structure of *Isaac and His Devils*, it is perhaps the assertion of such positive values as thought, spirit, and love against the pervasive materialism of our time that makes Eberstadt's novel so impressive. It is comforting to know that a Samuel Johnson can survive and triumph at the end of the twentieth century.

Rosemary M. Canfield Reisman

Sources for Further Study

Booklist. LXXXVII, April 1, 1991, p. 1544.
Chicago Tribune. May 10, 1991, V, p. 3.
Kirkus Reviews. LIX, February 1, 1991, p. 123.
Library Journal. CXVI, March 15, 1991, p. 114.
Los Angeles Times Book Review. May 19, 1991, p. 12.
The New York Times Book Review. XCVI, June 30, 1991, p. 20.

The New Yorker. LXVII, August 26, 1991, p. 79.
Publishers Weekly. CCXXXVIII, February 15, 1991, p. 74.
The Times Literary Supplement. July 5, 1991, p. 20.
The Wall Street Journal. July 9, 1991, p. A14.

ISLANDS, THE UNIVERSE, HOME

Author: Gretel Ehrlich (1946-   )
Publisher: Viking Press (New York). 196 pp. $19.95
Type of work: Essays

Islands, the Universe, Home, *Gretel Ehrlich's second collection of natural history essays, combines lyrical explorations of place with thoughtful meditations on the relation of the human to the natural world and on the patterns that connect all life*

"We live not only on the earth, but in the earth; we are part of the dynamic process of every inter-living element and system," writes essayist Gretel Ehrlich. "I search for the ways in which landscape, plants, animals mirror our psyches and spirits, and similarities between, for example, the chemical workings of the human brain and the workings of the cosmos. All patterns connect; in natural fact there is human meaning." For Ehrlich, the microcosm is reflected in the macrocosm, the atom in the universe, and each natural fact is a potential metaphor or spiritual insight into the nature of things.

A talented natural history writer with a concise and distinctive style, Gretel Ehrlich published a first collection of essays, *The Solace of Open Spaces* (1985), that won her wide critical acclaim. "Wyoming has found its Whitman," wrote Annie Dillard. Ehrlich has published a novel, *Heart Mountain* (1988), and a short-story collection, *Drinking Dry Clouds* (1991), and her essays have appeared in *Harper's Magazine* and *The Atlantic Monthly*. She received a Guggenheim fellowship to complete her newest essay collection, *Islands, the Universe, Home*.

The ten essays in *Islands, the Universe, Home* were written over a period of three years on Ehrlich's ranch in Shell, Wyoming, and from her travels in California, Hawaii, and Japan. Her essays, though personal and reflective in nature, taken together trace the cycle of the seasons against the raw but beautiful Wyoming landscape. She captures the grandeur of the American West, but with an artistic sensibility attuned to Japanese aesthetics. Each of her essays is shaped by a distinctive landscape—a place and a season—but each setting then becomes for Ehrlich the occasion for a rich personal discourse on a variety of scientific, philosophical, and cultural topics. Each of her essays is prefaced by a Japanese brush painting that serves as a visual outline for her thought. Her style is concise, pithy, and direct, like Western speech, but her material is wide-ranging and discursive, filled with quotes, anecdotes, reflections, and meditations shared in the manner of good conversation. She draws upon her ranching experiences for outdoor descriptions of winter calving, searching for a lost dog, and hiking through the fire-devastated Yellowstone Park, but she moves easily from these direct experiences to discussions of topics ranging from physics, astronomy, and botany to anthropology and neurology. She moves nimbly back and forth between fact and metaphor, between description and allusion.

The wide-ranging intelligence that Ehrlich brings to her essays reflects her diverse education. Reared in California, she studied at Bennington College, the University of California at Los Angeles Film School, and the New School for Social Research.

Well-read and widely traveled, she brings a rich fund of personal experience and literary and scientific allusions to her essays. She finds a personal affinity between the new cosmology of astrophysics and the ascetic purity of Japanese Zen Buddhism and Shintoism. As with any good journal writer or personal essayist, it is finally her personality, as revealed through her essays, that engages the reader, who appreciates the attentiveness of a lively, engaging mind always alert to the mysterious interconnectedness of things. "*Nothing in this world is plain,*" she asserts.

In her essay "Island," an excursion to a small island in the middle of a lake on Ehrlich's Wyoming ranch stimulates a series of meditations on the nature of islands. "Islands are places where exchanges occur," Ehrlich asserts. "Because the boundaries are so sharp, islands remind us of beginnings and endings, of birth and the arousal of consciousness of the evolutionary movement from water to land and air." Her title metaphor is an analogy drawn from astronomy, from the curious ways that matter mirrors itself from the very large to the very small. The vast, floating spiral galaxies in the universe resemble in a curious way the tiniest patterns of microscopic life or even the neurological patterns of the brain. Islands are also the spaces that help to define the shape of living forms. Even the brain thinks in islands, Ehrlich claims, in the way in which it works to "string events into temporal arrangements like pearls or archipelagos." Islands, then, are not monuments to isolation but ways of understanding our relatedness: "Islands beget islands: a terrestrial island is surrounded by an island of water, which is surrounded by an island of air, all of which makes up our island universe."

In "This Autumn Morning," Ehrlich describes the end of the hot, dry summer season and the beauty of death at the end of a season. Life and death are everywhere interconnected, she discovers, as she and her husband drive through the fire-blackened Yellowstone Park a year after the great forest fires of 1988 and find new buffalo calves and their mothers grazing in park meadows among the carcasses of winter-starved bison and vigorous new stands of grasses where wildfires had raged the summer before. She describes the natural ecological system of Yellowstone, of which fire is an integral part, as cycling from mature lodgepole pine, to fire, to black ash, to buffalo grass, to wildflowers, and to new lodgepole pine seedlings the next summer. Life, to death, to life, the cycle continues, bringing life out of death. She writes of the hardships of late winter calving for both livestock and ranchers on the high plains, where the temperature may be sixty above one day and twenty below the next, with the calves arriving during a spring blizzard. "On a ranch," she writes, "death is as much a constant as birth."

At times, her prose is as evocative as poetry, as when she describes being taken to a moon-viewing room in an ancient temple in Kyoto, Japan. There she sat and watched the phases of the moon reflected through rice paper cutouts. The exquisite delicacy of the moment is reflected in the quiet reverie of paddling a canoe across her Wyoming lake on a September night, admiring the reflection of the moon on the still surface of the water. Life teaches her the hard lessons of letting go, as when she had to face the loss from cancer of her friend and mentor, "Mike." "You have to mix death into everything," a painter friend once told her. "Then you have to mix life into that."

Perhaps the finest essay in this collection is "The Bridge to Heaven," an account of Ehrlich's travel experiences in Japan with her friend and fellow writer Leila Philip. In her quest of remote Shinto mountain shrines in northern Japan, she pauses to explain how the austere landscape of steep, alpine mountains, rocky coastline, and sea has shaped the Japanese sensibility. Native Shinto beliefs helped to shape the deep Japanese reverence for nature, and Buddhism, which arrived later from mainland China, deepened and enriched the religious spirit of the Japanese people. "When Buddhism, with its philosophy of transience, fused with Shinto," observes Ehrlich, "religious pilgrimage through the mountains expanded a sense of sacredness from specific temple sites to the entire geography—wherever the pilgrim's feet happened to land."

Ehrlich and her companion traveled north to the sacred snowy mountains of Northern Honshu. They intended to visit the remote, rugged, mountainous region in which Zen master Matsuo Bashō wrote his famous *Oku no hosomichi* (1694; *The Narrow Road to the Deep North*, 1933). "Path is goal, goal is path" is what Buddhists say, meaning that life is a journey, and the journey is life. Ehrlich's immediate goal was to retrace Bashō's ascent of Mount Haguro on June 3, 1689, and to visit the famous Shinto shrine on the top of the mountain. She was also eager to learn about the ascetic *yamabushi* practices of the priests and monks associated with the Shugendo sect—a blend of Shinto and Tendai Buddhism—whose practices are particularly severe. Walking for her was spiritual exercise, the physical exertion a way of stripping away the personal barriers of comfort and inattentiveness. While she was in Northern Japan, Ehrlich also hoped to meet one of the few remaining *itako*, elderly women mediums who go into a trance and communicate between the living and the dead. Ehrlich gave a medium the name of a friend who had died fourteen years earlier, but the *itako* could not make contact with him because his "spirit world" was so far away and his Welsh dialect was so strange to her. Ehrlich's interest in traditional Japanese culture, she recalls, amused her sophisticated, Westernized Japanese hosts.

Ehrlich's last three essays focus on the related ideas of home and a sense of place. As a displaced Californian, she is particularly sensitive about the human need for permanent roots and a sense of place. She admires how the mythology of the Chumash Indians of California contributes to their sense of their native environment along the Pacific coast and the Santa Barbara Channel Islands. A visit to those islands on a diesel-powered excursion boat becomes the occasion for her meditations on the history and anthropology of the Chumash people, who were vanquished and all but destroyed by the early Spanish settlers after living peacefully for almost eight thousand years. "Islands are evolutionary laboratories," Gretel Ehrlich observes, and their fate may anticipate the fate of the rest of Earth's life, as the planet rapidly becomes, in biologist Paul Ehrlich's words, "a system of habitat islands surrounded by a sea of human disturbance."

Homes ought to blend into their environment, Ehrlich observes in her essay "Architecture." She regrets that Wyoming has no indigenous architecture, that no architectural legacy has taken hold, so that housing there has a temporary look. Like Frank Lloyd Wright, she believes that homes should be extensions of their immediate environment; instead of being barriers, they should allow interchange between the inside and outside. "A house is a platform on which the transaction between nature and culture, internal and external, form and formlessness occurs," she writes. Design must come from within, reflecting the unruliness of nature. "A house is bent into shape by space, topography, and prevailing winds," she continues, and "in turn, its captured space reshapes what is beyond its walls." She describes her ideal house as set among rocky granite walls, with a stream flowing within, walls and rooms made with local materials, and its floor levels shaped by topography, function, and view.

Her last essay, "The Fasting Heart," brings her back to her Wyoming home in the landscape of winter. With the land stripped of life, winter is the season to concentrate the will. Ehrlich quotes from the ancient Chinese philosopher Lao Tzu about the need to "hear not with your ears but with your mind; not with your mind but with your spirit. Let your hearing stop with the ears, and let your mind stop with its images. Let your spirit, however, be like a blank, passively responsive to externals." With the advent of spring, she returns to her seasonal ritual of staying up through the night to serve as a midwife to heifers and to doctor sick calves. Enlightenment, she recalls, is trackless, and "the path of knowledge and the path of ignorance are the same."

Gretel Ehrlich's essays are difficult to categorize precisely because they are so thoughtful and wide ranging. Through her use of the journal form, Ehrlich's ten essays offer the thoughts and reflections of a talented new natural history writer. They mark the point where science and religion meet in the reflective personal essay. In her essays, she employs Eastern spiritual insights to create a genuine Western aesthetic, shaped by the land, climate, and terrain of her adopted Wyoming home. In her lyrical descriptions of the landscape of the American West, she is a worthy successor to Joseph Wood Krutch and Edward Abbey.

Andrew J. Angyal

Sources for Further Study

Booklist. LXXXVIII, September 1, 1991, p. 21.
Boston Globe. November 6, 1991, p. 51.
Chicago Tribune. November 3, 1991, XIV, p. 7.
The Christian Science Monitor. November 14, 1991, p. 11.
Kirkus Reviews. LIX, September 1, 1991, p. 1131.
Library Journal. CXVI, August, 1991, p. 99.

New Woman. XXI, November, 1991, p. 26.
Publishers Weekly. CCXXXVIII, July 25, 1991, p. 46.
San Francisco Chronicle. September 15, 1991, p. REV1.
The Washington Post Book World. XXI, September 29, 1991, p. 6.

J. EDGAR HOOVER
The Man and the Secrets

Author: Curt Gentry (1931-   )
Publisher: W. W. Norton (New York). 846 pp. $29.95
Type of work: Biography
Time: The 1920's to 1972
Locale: The United States

The self-righteous, paranoid J. Edgar Hoover reorganized a government agency in disarray and ran it despotically for the next forty-seven years, successfully resisting the efforts of four United States presidents to dismiss him

> *Principal personages:*
> J. EDGAR HOOVER, the director of the Federal Bureau of Investigation (FBI) for forty-seven years
> CLYDE A. TOLSON, Hoover's associate director, close friend, and sole heir
> FRANKLIN DELANO ROOSEVELT, the thirty-second president of the United States, about whose wife, Eleanor, Hoover spread unsavory rumors
> JOHN FITZGERALD KENNEDY, the thirty-fifth president of the United States
> ROBERT FRANCIS KENNEDY, the attorney general of the United States from 1961 until 1964
> RICHARD M. NIXON, the thirty-seventh president of the United States; in office when Hoover died

John Edgar Hoover began to use the name J. Edgar Hoover in the early 1920's to avoid confusion with a petty hood who shared his full name. Hoover did not want to be mistaken for this miscreant. The son of a government bureaucrat, Hoover was born in Washington, D.C., to middle-class parents and he remained a Washington resident all of his life.

The young Hoover considered becoming a minister in the Presbyterian church, of which he became a member in his teens. Serving in the U.S. Army's Reserve Officer Training Corps (ROTC) as commander of his high school's company altered his ambitions.

Hoover imposed his personal code of behavior on the ROTC company, demanding that officers under his command attend its formerly optional weekly meetings, have a fighting spirit, and be outstandingly decorous. When he became director, he applied to the FBI the same standards he had imposed upon his ROTC company.

Although Hoover was offered a scholarship to the University of Virginia upon his graduation from high school, he preferred to remain in Washington. He wanted to study law at George Washington University, which then had a special late afternoon and early evening program limited to government employees. In 1913, Hoover, to make himself eligible, took a job as a messenger at the Library of Congress, just four blocks from his home.

He rose successively to the positions of cataloger and clerk, gaining in the process considerable expertise in how to gather and organize information efficiently. Later, it was the Library of Congress's method of classification upon which he based the classification of records in the FBI.

By 1916, Hoover had earned a bachelor of law degree, and the following year he earned a master's degree in law. By that time, the United States had entered World War I. Hoover qualified for a commission. In July of 1917, however, having been admitted to the District of Columbia bar, he took a job as a clerk at the U.S. Department of Justice at a salary just short of a thousand dollars a year.

One of the attractions of the new job was that it carried with it exemption from the draft. He was not, presumably, a draft dodger, but his father, who had suffered from emotional problems, had had to resign pensionless from forty-two years of government employment. Hoover and his brother, Dickerson, had to support the family.

A compulsively hard worker who achieved results regardless of what methods he had to use, including outright deceit and lying, Hoover rose quickly in the Justice Department, whose top men had as much disregard for the niceties of constitutional law as Hoover did. He was promoted several times in his first year there. Because he worked on his own at odd hours and on weekends, he quickly came to the attention of his superiors, who came increasingly to depend upon him.

The war with Germany had caused the passage of a series of repressive acts, including the Espionage Act (1917), the Alien Deportation Act (1918), and the Sedition Act (1918). These produced exactly the climate of hysteria and distrust in which Hoover, flag-wavingly patriotic and unfailingly self-righteous, could flourish best. The times were exactly right for one of his ilk to advance at the Justice Department.

Working under Attorney General A. Mitchell Palmer, who, citing wartime exigencies, violated the civil rights of many citizens, Hoover learned that ruthlessness paid and that it could become a sure road to rapid advancement. He also learned that if one could create an illusion of threats to national security, practically any repressive actions could be justified.

Within a year, Hoover had progressed sufficiently to have his own secretary. After endless interviewing, he hired Helen Gandy, who remained with him until his death and who, as soon as he was dead, systematically destroyed the secret files that had been the terror of Washington politicians, including more than half of the eight presidents under whom Hoover had served.

When Palmer left the Department of Justice after Warren G. Harding's election, Hoover's job was threatened. Understanding fully, however, the inner workings of bureaucracies, Hoover allied himself to the new attorney general, Harry M. Daugherty, making himself indispensable to Daugherty by his diligence and by sharing with him some of the secret files on radicals he had been squirreling away. On August 22, 1921, Daugherty appointed Hoover, then twenty-six, assistant chief of the Bureau of Investigation, as the FBI was called until 1935.

As a citizen of the District of Columbia, Hoover could not vote, so no record existed of any political affiliation for him. Functioning apolitically, he was acceptable to members of both political parties. Working with the bureau convinced Hoover that it had to be divorced from politics, and on May 10, 1924, when Attorney General Harlan Fiske Stone appointed him acting director, he accepted the appointment on the condition that such must be the case.

Stone made it clear that Hoover's appointment was temporary and would be terminated when Stone found the right person for the job. At the time Hoover became acting director, the bureau was a dumping ground for all sorts of political appointees, many of them incompetent hacks. Its operation was inefficient and expensive.

Hoover soon changed that. He approached his new job like a whirling dervish. When Stone sent him a list of things he wanted done, Hoover acted immediately, doing Stone's bidding within days. On December 10, 1924, Stone called Hoover to his office and told him that he could drop the word "acting" from his title. Thus began a career that was to end only with Hoover's death forty-seven years later.

In 1928, Hoover hired Clyde A. Tolson, who became his closest and constant companion, as a special agent. Tolson, who had a bachelor of arts degree and a bachelor of law degree from George Washington University, had been confidential secretary to Secretary of War Newton D. Baker and was four years Hoover's junior. It was rumored that the two were homosexual lovers, although such rumors have not been substantiated. Neither Hoover nor Tolson ever married, and Hoover, on his death, named Tolson as his sole beneficiary.

Years before, Hoover had begun his famed enemies list and had begun to accumulate secret files on large numbers of people. Through these files, which came to include dossiers on hundreds of thousands of citizens, Hoover blackmailed people in the highest positions in government and other highly visible positions. Having accumulated them, he was virtually unable to resign as director of the bureau, despite the efforts of nearly every president after Franklin Roosevelt to oust him. He could not risk having anyone gain control of the secret files.

Frequent presidential efforts to remove Hoover were thwarted by Hoover's threat to release from his files information that would virtually destroy each of the presidents under whom he served or members of their immediate families. He had a particular vendetta against the Kennedy family, and his files on John Fitzgerald Kennedy were extremely threatening to the president. Hoover received information about Lee Harvey Oswald's threats against the president three weeks before Kennedy's assassination in Dallas on November 22, 1963, but he did not act on this intelligence, nor did he cooperate fully with the Warren Commission when it investigated the Kennedy assassination.

The Hoover vendetta against the Kennedy family continued after the president's death. Hoover's ostensible boss, Attorney General Robert Kennedy, was his particular enemy. His assassination in Los Angeles in 1968 removed the threat of his becoming president, a reality with which Hoover would have found it very difficult to live.

J. Edgar Hoover: The Man and the Secrets makes one realize the need for a thorough psychoanalytical biographical study of J. Edgar Hoover, a man so obsessed with his own sense of righteousness that he could not tolerate human diversity. His moral rigidity threatened the fabric of the very society he was charged to protect.

His sexual repression resulted in an unhealthy voyeurism that he indulged by collecting information about the private sexual lives of hundreds of thousands of people.

His voyeurism was exemplified by the fact that his own bedroom windows were covered with both venetian blinds and draperies that usually remained drawn, and a screen was placed in front of the windows. He feared that people would spy on him, because spying on other people in intimate situations had become a way of life for him.

Hoover had a screening room at the FBI in which he viewed pornographic films and films that his agents took while spying on subjects. All these activities were for the best of reasons: assuring national security as defined by a psychologically disturbed despot who worked hard to convince himself that he was taking the morally high road.

Curt Gentry, whose book, at 846 pages, maintains a high interest level that propels readers through it with remarkable speed, makes an extremely interesting point when he touches on Hoover's provincialism. Here was a man who lived and died in Washington, D.C. He knew little about life outside that unrealistic microcosm, in which politicians came and went with every midterm and presidential election.

Washington's wheels are oiled by rumors that often lead to overstated, sometimes hysterical reactions. Gentry speculates that Hoover, who would not leave Washington even to attend the University of Virginia, some hundred miles away, viewed his actions often as a means of protecting his hometown rather than his nation. In his mind he could justify his actions, including the blackmail he perpetrated against countless people, some of whose lives were ruined as a result.

Hoover ran the FBI as his own personal operation, allowing its makeup to reflect his racial prejudices. Gentry shows how he also charged taxpayers for an incredible number of personal expenditures on his home. He siphoned off for his personal use as much money as he could, and no one made him accountable for his graft because he had too much on any would-be whistle-blowers to permit them the freedom to act.

Illustrative of his methods were his actions against Congressman Martin Dies, chair of the House Committee on Un-American Activities, who wanted to depose Hoover. Dies, who considered himself the nation's chief agent for controlling subversives, had his own ambitions, most of them no more honorable than Hoover's. The ambitions of these two self-righteous men caused them to clash.

Hoover sent FBI agents to spy on the Dies Committee and spread rumors that Dies planned to leave the Democratic Party and make a run for the vice presidency as a Republican. The attorney general charged Dies with interfering with the FBI's investigations. Dies went to President Roosevelt to complain vehemently about this charge and about Hoover.

A compromise was struck through the intervention of Robert Jackson, Roosevelt's attorney general at the time, and the situation seemed under control. Meanwhile, however, Hoover uncovered information that in December, 1941, Dies had accepted a two-thousand-dollar bribe to sponsor a piece of legislation. Hoover's evidence of this malfeasance was incontrovertible. When confronted with it, Dies had no choice but to throw himself on Hoover's mercy or risk ruin. In return, Dies never attacked Hoover or the FBI publicly or officially again.

R. Baird Shuman

Sources for Further Study

Chicago Tribune. September 8, 1991, XIV, p. 1.
Library Journal. CXVI, August, 1991, p. 110.
Los Angeles Times Book Review. September 8, 1991, p. 1.
The New York Times Book Review. XCVI, September 15, 1991, p. 3.
The New Yorker. LXVII, September 9, 1991, p. 96.
Newsweek. CXVIII, September 23, 1991, p. 50.
Publishers Weekly. CCXXXVIII, July 19, 1991, p. 43.
Time. CXXXVIII, October 14, 1991, p. 87.
The Wall Street Journal. August 29, 1991, p. A10.
The Washington Post Book World. XXI, November 3, 1991, p. 13.

THE JAMESES
A Family Narrative

Author: R. W. B. Lewis (1917-   )
Publisher: Farrar, Straus & Giroux (New York). Illustrated. 696 pp. $35.00
Type of work: Biography
Time: 1789-1916
Locale: The United States and Europe

A masterful collective biography of three generations of an eminent American family

> *Principal personages:*
> WILLIAM JAMES, SR., an Irish immigrant and merchant
> HENRY JAMES, SR., his son, a mystical theologian
> MARY WALSH JAMES, Henry's wife
> WILLIAM JAMES, their son, a psychologist and philosopher
> HENRY JAMES, their second son, a novelist
> GARTH WILKINSON JAMES, their third son
> ROBERTSON JAMES, their fourth son
> ALICE JAMES, their daughter and youngest child
> ALICE GIBBENS JAMES, wife of the younger William James

Accomplishment sometimes displaying an inclination to run in families, biographers from time to time attempt biographies of such families. Both the organization and the proportions of such works pose considerable problems. The less-accomplished family members must be given their due. Unlike the failures and mediocre achievements of the great mass of people, theirs must be more or less sympathetically and interestingly explained, although the biographer knows full well that they would not be written or read about at all but for their bloodlines. A considerable cast of family members complicates the usual author's dilemma as to the adjustment between thematic and chronological requirements. The wisps and strands of diverging lives and vital relationships must be woven together with the same sort of skill necessary in a well-populated novel, though with fewer permissible liberties, less poetic license. Only the brave and patient life-writer need apply.

Madelon Bedell's *The Alcotts: Biography of a Family* (1980) and Milton Rugoff's *The Beechers: An American Family in the Nineteenth Century* (1981) represent such American family biographies, and F. O. Matthiessen even did *The James Family* (1947) on a limited scale, but R. W. B. Lewis' *The Jameses: A Family Narrative* is in a number of ways the most satisfactory—the most composed, as Henry James might have noted with an artist's appreciation and perhaps a set of quotation marks— American family biography yet to appear. Lewis has chosen a rare family. Henry James, Sr., could speak and write well enough to earn the respect of Ralph Waldo Emerson, his sons William and Henry are towering figures in their fields of endeavor, and his daughter Alice is a fascinating and poignant personality who has already drawn the attention of a biographer. As a consequence of the volubility of these four Jameses, the vast labors of earlier Jamesians, and the resources of libraries such as those at Harvard University (to name just one locus of Lewis' research), there is a plethora of information.

Of course, such advantages impose their own burdens, and to the problems of organization and emphasis that of selectivity adds its considerable weight. Lewis' book is nearly seven hundred pages long, but Leon Edel's five-volume life of Henry James contains more than three times as many pages, and Lewis could not allow Henry to dominate *The Jameses*. He allots substantial chapters to Henry's and William's Irish immigrant grandfather, to Henry, Sr., to their younger brothers Garth Wilkinson and Robertson ("Wilky" and "Bob," respectively), and to their sister Alice (drawing upon Jean Strouse's biography). Attention is given to the women who married Jameses, especially Alice Gibbens, who became the psychologist William's wife, and, in an appendix, to "The Later Jameses." There is less about other relations; even Minnie Temple, a cousin to the younger Henry James of whom previous Jamesians have made much, plays a decidedly minor role here. Lewis keeps firmly to those bearing the James surname.

The book has four sections, the first, "Generations," devoted to the earlier William and Henry James, father and son. The second, "Family Stories," discusses the Henry James, Sr., family up to the time of the children's young adulthood, about 1875. "Joinings and Departures" takes the family members up to 1892, by which time the parents and two of the children were dead. "Parts of a Unity" focuses on the apex of William's and Henry's careers, with glances at their surviving brother Bob, until William's and Bob's deaths in 1910. Henry's final years receive only the most cursory attention. While it is apparent that Henry's final illness and death, to which Edel devoted much attention, constituted no part of Lewis' scheme, one might have expected more about the composition of Henry's three autobiographical works of these years.

Because the William James who emigrated from Ireland in 1789 proved to be a shrewd commercial man, later generations of Jameses, who inherited little of his business acumen and none of his bourgeois interests, were able to devote themselves to a decent quota of gentlemanly leisure and to literary and educational endeavors that did not demand any immediate financial return. Thus William, who settled in Albany and prudently bought most of the village of Syracuse, deserves recognition as the man who enabled Henry, Sr., to shepherd his family back and forth from Europe and to write theological books of interest only to a coterie of intellectuals. In turn, Henry's son William could deliberately pursue a medical degree he never intended to turn to a medical practice, and Henry, Jr., could cultivate a long intimacy with leisured Americans and Europeans of the sort who populate his intricate fiction.

The elder Henry James's theological unorthodoxy, which played a part in attracting the friendship of Ralph Waldo Emerson, reflected a restless nature that took the form, after his marriage to Mary Robertson Walsh in 1840, of moving from Albany to New York to London to Paris, and, after returning to New York, of migrating as far as Geneva and Bonn before settling with Mary and their five children in Newport, Rhode Island, in 1860. The children, born between 1843 and 1850, thus endured a bewildering variety of uprootings and educational experiments that seemed to incline them to replicating in their own adult years their father's restlessness, the younger Henry becoming the citizen of the world that his father attempted fitfully to be.

Wilky and Bob James were rather ordinary people who happened into an otherwise gifted family; however, they were not totally devoid of Jamesian ability. For example, Lewis quotes a letter from Bob to his friend William Dean Howells, the editor and novelist, in which he converts his longstanding aversion to his father-in-law into a "fantasy-ridden" narrative at least potentially "reminiscent of some early story by his brother Henry." Yet the Civil War, in which both younger James brothers served, victimized them. The severely wounded Wilky never recovered his full vigor and died in his thirties, and it appears that the war contributed also to the alcoholism that dogged Bob throughout his later life.

Alice exercised her considerable wit and verbal facility primarily in letters and in her diary but lacked the mental and physical stability necessary to be much more than one of the valetudinarian spinsters that substantial nineteenth century families so readily produced. Lewis implicitly poses, but leaves the reader to ponder, the difficult question of whether, in another time and other circumstances, her abilities might have flowered.

Inevitably, Lewis focuses most intently on the brothers William and Henry, and the contrast between the development of these two geniuses is one of the author's strongest and most original accomplishments. Much of his account of their relationship resembles Leon Edel's, but Lewis' purpose obliges him to avoid Edel's emphasis on Henry's difficulties as the second son, only fifteen months younger than a brilliant brother who may have seemed to be the favored one. William is seen here as another groping soul—groping toward an intellectual career and toward a satisfactory marital relationship; both came into being only slowly and painfully. Henry, on the other hand, seems always to have acknowledged the inevitability of a literary career and to have recognized the prudence of a single but fruitfully social life. As a result, although William's condescending attitude toward Henry as a mere writer of fiction emerges clearly, Lewis generates more sympathy than Edel for the struggling elder brother.

He also provides enough detail about William's family life to elicit sympathy for his wife Alice, who for weeks and months at a time had to superintend their children (there were eventually four) while he escaped on vacations and professional speaking tours. The couple's relationship—intense, loving, but frequently stormy—like most of William's experiences, provided this introspective thinker with fodder for his psychological and philosophical speculations. Lewis goes so far as to call his influential *The Principles of Psychology* (1890) "a replaying of William James's private life" of the two decades leading up to its publication.

The relationship of relationships in this book, however, is that of William and Henry, whose careers, Lewis shows, were in many ways parallel. While William investigated extrasensory perception in the 1890's, for example, Henry turned out numerous ghost stories, of which *The Turn of the Screw* (1898) is the most famous. While William devised the psychological term "stream of consciousness," Henry was writing the psychological novels that, if not precisely stream-of-consciousness fiction, pointed in a direction later taken by writers such as James Joyce and Virginia Woolf (who can properly be described as having been influenced by both James the psychologist and James the novelist). William, however, failed to recognize that the characters in his brother's narratives were exhibiting the vaguely discontinuous mental processes that he was describing with some precision for the first time in the history of psychology.

Both men crowded impressive endeavors into their last full decade, the first of the twentieth century. William's *The Varieties of Religious Experience*, based on his celebrated Gifford lectures in Edinburgh, Scotland, appeared in 1902; Henry's *The Wings of the Dove*, the first of a triad of novels that capped his career, appeared just a few weeks later. For the next few years, William, who had previously taught physiology and psychology, turned to philosophy at Harvard, while Henry published two more major novels, *The Ambassadors* (1903) and *The Golden Bowl* (1904), in astonishingly swift succession. Finally, in 1907 both brothers brought out final master pieces, *Pragmatism* and *The American Scene*.

Pragmatism is the final fruit of William's philosophical pondering and, though short, constitutes in Lewis' judgment a summa, containing the fruit of William's medical training as well as his psychological, religious, and literary expertise. Again based on a series of lectures, *Pragmatism*, beginning with its subtitle, *A New Name for Some Old Ways of Thinking*, exemplifies his artful and engaging style. The word was not new, but it was James who gave it its application of interpreting the concept of truth according to its practical effects.

Henry's *The American Scene* described his native land as he saw it in 1904-1905, after an absence of more than twenty years. Then sixty-one years old, Henry would later turn to autobiographical writing and the preparation of a new and revised edition of all the works on which he wanted his reputation to stand. His return to once-familiar sights begins the process of looking back at his earlier life, but the book nonetheless observes the contemporary scene, as its title suggests. If Henry's book of 1907 views the United States through a veteran novelist's eye, William's represents, in Lewis' words, "the text that more than any other established a definitive American mode of philosophic thought."

Though never of one mind, William and Henry grew closer as they aged, especially after the death of their sister Alice in 1892, even though most of the time an ocean separated them. Henry's writing fascinated William, although he seemed to think of it as more of an inspired accident than anything else. As far as William was concerned, Henry was a writer who broke all the rules but somehow succeeded— very much the way William's scientific colleagues regarded him. Neither saw his own chosen vocation in the conventional way, and both felt free to be innovative. They had before them the example of their father, who, with little sympathetic intellectual companionship or readership, kept steadfastly writing theological works for decades. Lewis suggests that the influence of their unorthodox father persisted in their refusal to reject, in the interests of science or realism, the intuitive and shadowy aspects of human nature. Yet they gained credit as scientist and realist, respectively.

While Lewis' book will doubtless appeal most to inveterate Jamesians, it can certainly be read profitably by those with little previous knowledge of this remarkable family. Its style is both graceful and lively, and it keeps coherently to its purpose as the record of "a remarkable American family." Some readers may find its documentation both sparse and intractable, but its index is copious and thorough. More than sixty photographs, particularly well chosen and arranged, complement the text.

Robert P. Ellis

Sources for Further Study

Chicago Tribune. August 18, 1991, XIV, p. 3.
The Christian Science Monitor. August 13, 1991, p. 13.
Library Journal. CXVI, August, 1991, p. 101.
Los Angeles Times Book Review. August 11, 1991, p. 3.
The New York Review of Books. XXXVIII, October 10, 1991, p. 3.
The New York Times Book Review. XCVI, August 4, 1991, p. 1.
Newsweek. CXVIII, August 26, 1991, p. 55.
Publishers Weekly. CCXXXVIII, June 21, 1991, p. 48.
The Times Literary Supplement. October 11, 1991, p. 6.
The Washington Post Book World. XXI, September 1, 1991, p. 5.

JEAN RHYS
Life and Work

Author: Carole Angier
Publisher: Little, Brown (Boston). Illustrated. 762 pp. $35.00
Type of work: Literary biography
Time: 1890-1979
Locale: Dominica, England, and France

A detailed biography of one of the saddest writers who ever lived, with critical assessments of her novels interspersed

> *Principal personages:*
> JEAN RHYS, a novelist
> LANCELOT HUGH SMITH, her first great love
> JEAN LENGLET, her first husband
> FORD MADOX FORD, her literary mentor and lover
> LESLIE TILDEN SMITH, her second husband
> GEORGE VICTOR MAX HAMER, her third husband

Jean Rhys occupies a unique position in the history of the twentieth century novel. Scottish and Welsh by heritage, she grew up in Dominica, a West Indian island that colored her perceptions deeply. Nurtured by the modernist writer Ford Madox Ford, she began publishing in the 1920's, the heyday of James Joyce and Virginia Woolf. Yet her most famous novel, *Wide Sargasso Sea*, came out in 1966, and she continued writing well into the following decade. Ostensibly, her novels all plead the case of women's causes, yet she refused to be labeled "feminist" and enjoyed provoking interviewers who attempted to label her so. Jean Rhys was an anomaly, a misfit, and appropriately enough that is the subject of all of her fiction—what it feels like to be an outcast, someone doomed forever to exist on the fringes of society.

For virtually all of her eighty-nine years, Jean Rhys lived on the fringes. She never intended to be a writer; she originally wanted to act. She received a small amount of recognition for her first published novel, *Postures* (1928)—published in the United States as *Quartet* (1929)—and for the three that followed it: *After Leaving Mr. Mackenzie* (1931), *Voyage in the Dark* (1934), and *Good Morning, Midnight* (1939). Then, with the onset of World War II, she disappeared into obscurity. For decades, people who knew of her work thought of her as dead. Eventually, an actress interested in the dramatic possibilities of her novels not only tracked her down but also inspired her to get back to writing. The result was Jean's finishing *Wide Sargasso Sea* in the mid-1960's and finally receiving the acclaim she had deserved for so many years.

With the publication of *Jean Rhys: Life and Work*, the Canadian writer Carole Angier is attempting to drag Jean further into the public spotlight. Angier met Rhys in the 1970's, on the heels of public rediscovery. In 1985, she published a short critical and biographical study of the writer. Now she has written a full-blown opus, again combining biography and criticism—a 750-page expansion of the earlier work's 120 pages. It is an exhaustive and exhausting meditation on the life of one of the saddest writers who ever lived.

Jean was born Ella Gwendolen Rees Williams to a colonial doctor and his wife living in Roseau, Dominica. The most significant event of Jean Rhys's early years may be something that took place before her actual birth. An infant sister died, presumably of dysentery. Angier hypothesizes that the Williamses had Jean in an attempt to assuage their grief over this tragedy. Perhaps her parents' mood of mourning—especially her mother's—explains the sense of emptiness and rejection that Jean felt even as a child.

The girl who came to England in 1907 to live with her Aunt Clarice was already a sort of outsider whose cultural differences only served to marginalize her further. Jean attended the Perse School in Cambridge and decided to take up acting. Her voice proved to be a fatal liability, for the English thought she sounded like a black. Eventually, Jean learned to whisper rather than risk further embarrassment. She also chose to become a chorus girl, an improper career for a girl from a middle-class family. It implied that she was on display, looking for a wealthy man to keep her, and indeed, Jean's long adult life did come to revolve around her relationships with men.

The first of these men was Lancelot Hugh Smith, a conventional stockbroker who was forty years old to Jean's twenty. The two were lovers for about two years, during which time Jean was desperately reliant on Hugh, both financially and emotionally. Eventually, at his cousin Julian's urging, Hugh extricated himself from the affair. Jean was devastated; the psychic wound she suffered over Hugh's abandonment would mark her for life. She continued to keep in contact with her former lover over many years; he even paid for an abortion she had in 1913. Always, the thought of him hurt her unimaginably.

In 1917, Jean began a romance with Jean—or "John"—Lenglet, a half-French, half-Dutch man residing at Jean's boarding house. The two ran off to Europe together and were married in 1919. In fact, Lenglet had not bothered to annul a previous marriage, but his bigamy never seemed to affect Jean, and in 1925 the earlier marriage was legally terminated. This sloppiness on John's part was characteristic. He was plagued all through their marriage by difficulties with immigration papers. Eventually, he took to embezzling. An additional problem was the death of the Lenglets' infant son. While the child lay suffering in a hospital, Jean and John drank champagne at home, trying to deny the tragedy.

They had a second, healthy child in 1922, a girl named Maryvonne. Yet Jean was not suited to motherhood. Financial pressure offers a partial explanation of why, over the years, Jean spent so little time with her daughter, but only a partial one. On some level, Jean must have been rejecting her daughter, just as she herself had been rejected. Almost from birth, Maryvonne was boarded out. She lived with her mother only at short intervals and later chose to stay with her father, not Jean.

John considered himself a journalist, and Jean began keeping a kind of literary diary herself. Eventually, an acquaintance introduced Jean to Ford Madox Ford, the novelist, encouraging her to show him her "diary novel." Ford marveled over Jean's talent and published a short story of hers in the *Transatlantic Review*. He also sug-

gested that she change her name from Gwen Williams to Jean Rhys. Inevitably, the
thirty-four-year-old Jean became sexually involved with the fifty-year-old Ford. Meanwhile, John was arrested for embezzlement. Destitute and confused, Jean moved in
with Ford and his lover Stella Bowen. It was an explosive situation that ended in
misery for all involved.

By the mid-1920's, Jean was publishing *The Left Bank* (1927), her first book of
short stories, and bouncing from Lenglet to Ford and back again. Eventually, Jean
left Ford on ugly, acrimonious terms. The whole affair inspired four different books:
one each by Ford, Stella, and John, and Jean's first novel, *Quartet*, much the finest
of the batch. In it, Jean marked out the territory that would continue to be hers for
the rest of her writing career: the solitary struggle of a beautiful woman without
resources, facing daily life with a self-defeating sense of her own futility.

These two early books inspired grudging admiration in most critics who read
them, especially for Jean's spare, poetic sense of language. One fan of hers was
Leslie Tilden Smith, the mild-mannered English agent who began to represent Jean.
By 1928, the two were living together in England. It was not until 1932 that Jean and
John bothered to get divorced. Then, in 1934, Jean married Smith.

The marriage lasted until Smith's death in 1945. It was hardly a happy one, yet it
seems to have been a productive partnership for Jean as a writer. During the 1930's,
she published three novels, all basically autobiographical, and all, to Carole Angier's
mind, showing increasing self-awareness. Yet in life, Jean's bitterness and confusion
only mounted. Leslie Smith appears to have been a mild-mannered, faithful husband, but his very mildness antagonized Jean. She began to drink more, and drink
brought out intense anger in her. She fought with Leslie, sometimes physically. She
resented his relatives, who resented her, and rarely was there enough money for the
couple.

In 1936, Jean went back to Dominica for the only time in her adult life. It was a
mixed experience for her, for she found the island much changed. She began to be
paranoid about other people's reactions to her. On returning to England, Jean began
to plot not one but two novels about Dominica. Yet the work progressed badly.
Once, during a fight with Leslie, she burned the typescript of a novel.

World War II was misery for Jean as well as Leslie. While he served his commission, she moved from town to town, drinking and worrying about her daughter in
Holland. This is where her life becomes hard to follow. Angier speculates that Jean
may have attempted suicide and may also have been committed to an institution.
Eventually, Leslie was forced to resign his commission. His health became more and
more fragile. The couple moved to a remote cottage in Dartmoor, where Leslie died
of a heart attack in 1945. Jean, in the next room, delayed phoning for help an uncon-
scionable time—the effect of alcohol, perhaps, or of her characteristic sense of
paralysis.

Though Jean rarely spoke of her love of Leslie, his death seemed to disturb her
enormously. Nevertheless, by 1946, a cousin of Leslie named George Victor Max
Hamer was romancing Jean. Two years to the day after Leslie's death, they were

married. They moved to suburban London, where Jean's mental deterioration continued. She drank, fought with neighbors, and was arrested for assault. She even spent time in the hospital section of Holloway Prison. Several psychologists found Jean sane, yet her pathetic, self-defeating behavior continued for years. Meanwhile, her third husband followed the path of her first. He was arrested and convicted of larceny.

By this point, Jean was hardly writing at all. Those who remembered her work thought she had died during the war. Then an actress named Selma Vaz Dias decided to create a radio monologue out of *Good Morning, Midnight*. She tracked Jean down via a notice in the *New Statesman*. Though nothing initially came of the contact, Jean was amazed to find that anyone cared about her. In 1956, the British Broadcasting Corporation (BBC) decided to give the green light to Selma's program. With it came a renewal of interest in Jean's writing and impetus for her to get back to work on her Caribbean novel.

That novel, *Wide Sargasso Sea*, would not be published for almost ten years. It was torture for Jean to write, for a variety of reasons. One was her husband's ill health. Max Hamer suffered stroke after stroke, and Jean was determined to care for him. Her old resentment often flared up, however, for men in general and for the fact that Max was keeping her from writing. Once, she actually hit the sickly man.

Jean always experienced difficulty writing, and *Wide Sargasso Sea* was the most challenging thing she ever wrote. A kind of prequel to *Jane Eyre*, the novel offers a portrait of Antoinette's childhood and of her marriage to Rochester. Although Antoinette is clearly akin to Jean Rhys's earlier heroines, she is also a woman of another century and the creation of another writer. The first section of the novel, told from Antoinette's perspective, proved very trying for Jean, for it offers a first-hand account of descent into madness. More difficult was the second section of the novel, which is told from Rochester's point of view. It was the only time Jean Rhys placed herself inside a man's head. As such, it represents a triumph over the novelist's solipsistic tendencies.

Even given these difficulties, Jean managed to finish the novel substantially several years before it was released. Everyone who read the manuscript adored it. Yet Jean's obsessive perfectionism kept her from allowing her editors to publish it. Finally, Max died. Soon after, Jean dreamt of giving birth. She took this as an omen and finally let her book go out into the world.

One would expect the acclaim—and the money—that the author received on the release of *Wide Sargasso Sea* to have mitigated the unhappiness of her life. Perhaps it did somewhat, but only a little. Jean's misery had become chronic. Not even the rerelease of her other novels or an award of the Commander of the British Empire (CBE) could ease her condition for long. The amazing thing, though, is how long Jean continued to live and how well she went on writing. A collection of short stories, *Sleep It Off Lady* (1976), and an autobiography, *Smile Please* (1979), are works that she authored in her mid-eighties. Jean once wrote that she had to earn her death by writing. She went on earning it almost into her eighty-ninth year.

As a biographer, Carole Angier's chief virtue is her unflappable objectivity. It would be easy to imagine another writer adopting Jean's point of view too faithfully or condemning Jean heavily for her often appalling behavior. Angier has no ax to grind. She does not wish to make Jean Rhys into a feminist heroine or to twist her achievement into an unlikely shape. One feels almost always that Angier is weighing the evidence dispassionately and arriving at highly reasonable conclusions about this difficult writer's life.

Nevertheless, one cannot help feeling that Jean Rhys deserves a better biography than this prosaic and prosy book. It is not content merely to narrate Jean's life story. Larded into the biography are critical chapters on Jean's five published novels, chapters that are not only inappropriate but decidedly unstartling as criticism. These chapters also turn out to be thoroughly redundant. Given how shadowy much of Jean's life was and given the autobiographical nature of her writing, Angier finds herself turning repeatedly to the fiction for insights into Jean's existence. Time and again, one finds Jean's novels analyzed in the biographical sections and reanalyzed in the critical sections. Angier also has problems organizing her chronologies. Often, she will look ahead from a specific point in time to chart the arc of a particular relationship, then she will retell the same story later, when the time scheme of the biography has caught up with her. Granted, Jean Rhys's life provides a challenge to a writer in its long duration and its redundancy. Still, a determined and resourceful editor could have probably shortened Angier's book by half.

As a writer, Jean Rhys believed in distillation. She took the facts of her sordid existence and selected her details carefully. Then she honed the work, chiseling away at her words to balance all the misery with a formal beauty. The magic of her fiction comes as much from what is unsaid as what is said. In *Jean Rhys: Life and Work*, things are said and said again. The lines are all etched in, but the vividness is gone, and so is the shapeliness.

Richard Glatzer

Sources for Further Study

Chicago Tribune. June 16, 1991, XIV, p. 3.
The Christian Science Monitor. July 16, 1991, p. 13.
London Review of Books. XII, November 22, 1990, p. 22.
Los Angeles Times. September 13, 1991, p. E10.
The New York Review of Books. XXXVIII, October 10, 1991, p. 40.
The New York Times Book Review. XCVI, June 30, 1991, p. 20.
Publishers Weekly. CCXXXVIII, April 19, 1991, p. 54.
The Spectator. CCLXV, December 1, 1990, p. 53.
The Times Literary Supplement. November 23, 1990, p. 1257.
The Washington Post Book World. XXI, June 23, 1991, p. 1.

JOE

Author: Larry Brown (1951-   )
Publisher: Algonquin Books (Chapel Hill, North Carolina). 345 pp. $19.95
Type of work: Novel
Time: The late 1980's
Locale: Northern Mississippi

An essentially Southern tale, Joe *is a forceful novel about personal standards of honor and decency; in its characterization of the protagonist and in its ambiguous resolution of conflict, it bears a universal theme*

> Principal characters:
> JOE RANSOM, a hard-drinking, truck-driving, thoroughly independent man's man
> WADE JONES, an evil, lazy drunkard
> GARY JONES, an illiterate, half-starved fifteen-year-old boy remarkable for his ambition and intuitive integrity

After one other fine novel, *Dirty Work* (1989), and two collections of gritty, tough-to-the-bone short stories, *Facing the Music* (1988) and *Big Bad Love* (1990), Larry Brown has written a breakthrough book simply entitled *Joe*. Literary critics' approval has turned into well-deserved general acclaim with the publication of this seamless tale of the redemptive power of personal honor. *Joe* is that good, that well written, that profound, all in all the novel that fulfills the promise of Brown's earlier efforts.

This book, however, requires no antecedents, not even those of William Faulkner, to whom the author is often compared. *Joe* creates its own world, one perhaps more familiar to connoisseurs of Southern literature, but one from which only the most squeamish or fastidious will turn away in horror. Rural Mississippi has an abundance of white columns and magnolias, long-necked women and courtly gentlemen, but that is not the milieu to which Larry Brown delivers his reader. This Mississippi is verdant, half-wild still, a place where a shotgun shack is a palace indeed for the poor whites and blacks who live off its county roads and in its pine forests. Peopled not by the bluebloods of romance but by the rednecks of reality, Brown's Mississippi is a land of great beauty and great violence. There, men ride around in trucks stocked with shotgun racks and beer-laden coolers, and sometimes a good buddy along for company. There, Tammy Wynette is a goddess, Hank Williams a hero, and Elvis Presley a saint.

Brown re-creates this land in prose so apt that the reader sees its wild beauty, feels its social and economic tensions, and hears its distinctive voice. With "the shade deep and strong like a darker world within the outer," Brown describes a "place of cane thickets and coon dens and the lairs of bobcats, where the sun at its highest cast no light over the rotted stumps and stagnant sloughs." It is, then, a deceptive world, one where quiet beauty hides a noisome stench.

A product of this place, Joe Ransom is a man who literally draws his strength from prowling its back roads. He knows its forests; he is hired to defoliate them by a lumber company. He knows its people; he hires them for the crew that poisons the trees to make them harvestable. He is at home with its drunkards, its unemployables, its criminals and wastrels; of them, he is not one of them. Middle-aged, an ex-con himself, a hard drinker and a fighter, Joe makes enough money to go his own way, is thick-necked enough to get away with it, and lives by his own rules even when threatened with a return to the penitentiary. Divorced, he still loves his wife but realizes that she is probably right to leave him. Not even for love would he change his hard-fisted, thirsty ways.

His wife, lonely in her freedom, his daughter, pregnant with an illegitimate child, and his son who stays away from him, all seem unable to direct him to any act he does not want to perform. They are characters, meaningful and important in his life, but people for whom he cannot be other than he is: "They were like dreams, real but not real. He closed his eyes and it all passed away."

No more real to Joe is the woman his daughter's age with whom he shacks up, the rich widows to whom he gives his time when he has it, or the whores whom he visits when he has the need. More real, perhaps, is the vicious dog he alone can control with cuffs and kicks. Not entirely agreeable or tractable, Joe is his own man, strong enough to dig buckshot from his own bicep, generous enough to share his cigarettes and beer with anyone who asks, mean enough to unleash his crazed pit bull in a bordello.

Brown builds this character as effectively through dialogue as through narrative. Most telling is his friendship with the storekeeper John Coleman, another independent sort with whom he goes for a long, drunken ride. They speak as much in silences as in words. "They rode and drank. Joe sucked a cut knuckle and wished for his dog to lick it. John Coleman agreed that it would help." Joe does not need to answer when John explains a point of personal pride, "God knows I've done plenty of drinking and stuff in my time, but I be damn if I ever tried to cheat anybody out of any money." Just so, John does not need to caution Joe when they are stopped by a callow deputy. With redneck empathy, John understands that Joe "wouldn't let anybody mess with him, he didn't care who. And he was drinking."

Even in the narrative itself, Brown establishes a cadence of down-home dialect and colloquial descriptions so true that they are understood universally. His characters speak the language of their region, use its colorful, often profane, figures of speech, and reveal their fondness for belligerent terseness in the omitted words or phrases: "A sumbitch slaps me better look out"; or, "They ain't a goddam thing at home"; and, "you lookin good today." Joe tells a dog who refuses to yield right of way "That's a good way to get run over," and the incident is pure and true to the character—a half-drunk good old boy who leans out of his cab to admonish a yard cur.

Brown's language is direct, honest, and unencumbered. Descriptions arise naturally from the object; the author requires no extra flourish in this lean, tailored prose. From a fire, "sparks rose fragile and dying, orange as coon eyes in the gloom." The reader knows the fatigue of working the land in summertime when Brown describes hay balers, "their wavering figures struggling relentlessly over the parched ground, their toiling shapes remorseless and wasted and indentured to the heat that rose from the earth and descended from the sky in a vapor hot as fire."

Into this world, Joe's world, comes unbidden and unwanted a family so wretched that its members would have been evicted from Tobacco Road. Wade Jones is a monster, a man so desperate for drink that he has allowed one son to be run over and another to be sold to a childless couple. He terrorizes his older daughter into running away and makes life around him so miserable that the younger one elects an animal-like mutism. His wife, addled by the sale of her child, lives in bovine misery, and his son, Gary, is so illiterate and innocent to civilized life that he does not know what a stop sign is for or how to use a toothbrush. Wade stoops to fail, and no act is so low, no vice so heinous, that he will not try it, if it results in a pack of cigarettes, a few dollars, or a six-pack of beer. Almost comic in his cadging, he is not content with petty thievery if murder or pimping his own twelve-year-old daughter profit him more. Malodorous, so poor that he "squats" in a squalid shack rather than work, stupid in manner and speech, Wade Jones is all the same wise to sin, rich in corruption, and dangerous in spirit. He makes of *Joe* a novel of morals: He is evil, nemesis to the innocent Gary and anathema to the world-weary protagonist.

Gary, who reckons himself to be about fifteen years old, knows enough to realize that he, his mother, and his little sister suffer for the old man's mania for drink. The boy has an innate sweetness that makes him recoil from the memories of his hard life, and he wants to join some part of the human race, even if only by buying Joe's used truck and by having, and keeping, a job. He signs on with Joe, and his sad resignation to his father's loutish behavior, his raging ambition for an old truck, and his wild-child innocence touch the older man. Redemption for Joe will come in saving Gary from his fate.

Such salvation is possible only because Joe is at heart a good man, an honorable man whose laws, although not those of polite society, are no less rigid for being bound to a code of behavior that winks at gambling and prostitution, that allows him even to murder another man if the cause is right, but that brooks no indecent act, no cowardice, no offense to friendship, no undue malice to any man or woman. Most important, he demands, from the sheriffs, from his wife, from his friends, the freedom to be himself, to find his own errant way to truth. This good, flawed man finds it in the face of a corrupting evil so vile that it sullies the innocent and offends the most compromised.

The novel's resolution is all the more chilling for having been foretold in symbol-rich language. Soaring hawks, snarling dogs, angry wasps: These are not only colorful plot devices but also portents. Early in the story, Gary has a run-in with Russell, a man with whom Joe has been feuding for years. Appropriately, the altercation is caused by Gary's intuitive response to a snake: "He saw the moccasin, immobile on the bank among the dried sticks and shriveled roots, a phantom appearing out of nothing. Without thinking he reached for the largest rock he saw and heaved it over.

It made a great splash." Later, in a strange, unexplained incident, Joe goes to a friend's house only to find a horrible, premonitory scene. A woman lies dead at the feet of a blind man, "his hair . . . white, shaggy, disordered. . . . He said one word: 'Joe?' " He drives away "through the black night, into oak hollows, past standing deer with eyes like bright green jewels, who raise their ears and stared as he passed by them and beyond." In the morning, he remembers most from what he had witnessed "the milky blue opaque eyes dead and lifeless and unblinking and the woman undeniably dead, too, so still, so quick."

Brown redeems his sordid tale in the very telling of it. It is a fine story, and Joe is an unforgettable character, able finally to set aside his self-hatred and apathy in order to achieve a sort of nobility. His attempts to help Gary are fumbling, misguided even when he teaches him to drink, but the boy could do a lot worse than learn from Joe. He takes the boy to a whorehouse, and the rough, good-natured woman who initiates Gary into the mysteries of sex is an image of Joe himself, the redneck with a heart of gold. What Larry Brown created in this remarkable fiction is a fully realized gem of a story, certainly no ordinary *Joe.*

William U. Eiland

Sources for Further Study

Atlanta Journal Constitution. October 6, 1991, p. N11.
Chicago Tribune. September 29, 1991, XIV, p. 4.
Kirkus Reviews. LIX, July 15, 1991, p. 872.
Library Journal. CXVI, August, 1991, p. 141.
Los Angeles Times. October 24, 1991, p. E8.
The New York Times Book Review. XCVI, November 10, 1991, p. 25.
Publishers Weekly. CCXXXVIII, July 19, 1991, p. 46.
Southern Living. XXVI, September, 1991, p. 142.
Time. CXXXVIII, October 28, 1991, p. 96.
The Washington Post Book World. XXI, October 20, 1991, p. 9.

JOHN DEWEY AND AMERICAN DEMOCRACY

Author: Robert B. Westbrook
Publisher: Cornell University Press (Ithaca, New York). 570 pp. $29.95
Type of work: Biography
Time: 1859-1952
Locale: Primarily the United States

Emphasizing the social thought of John Dewey, who is arguably the twentieth century's most important American philosopher, Westbrook's intellectual biography documents Dewey's profound faith in participatory democracy

> *Principal personages:*
> JOHN DEWEY, the philosopher, social theorist, and educator
> CHARLES SANDERS PEIRCE, a philosopher and mathematician
> William James, a psychologist and philosopher
> RANDOLPH BOURNE, a social critic and pacifist
> WALTER LIPPMANN, a journalist and essayist
> REINHOLD NIEBUHR, a theologian and social theorist

Along with Charles Peirce and William James, John Dewey (1859-1952) advanced the philosophical movement known as American pragmatism. To distinguish his version from those of Peirce and James, Dewey called his philosophy "instrumentalism." The name appealed to him because he liked to think of human intelligence as a probing instrument people must use to solve life's personal and social problems. Frequently, habitual responses are sufficient, but Dewey was especially impressed by the ways in which life challenges custom and tradition. Fresh inquiry is often called for, he stressed, and his philosophy sought to organize human intelligence to meet such challenges, particularly as they appeared in public life. These concerns made Dewey a staunch advocate of democracy, which he regarded as a moral ideal.

Born in Burlington, Vermont, Dewey taught in high schools before completing his doctoral studies at Johns Hopkins University. Peirce was one of his teachers, but Dewey's dissertation focused on a critique of the famous German philosopher Immanuel Kant. After ten years of teaching at the University of Michigan, Dewey went to the University of Chicago in 1894. There, he helped to found a famous laboratory school and also became much involved in social issues provoked by urbanization, technological advances, and the arrival of increasing numbers of immigrants to the United States. In 1904, Dewey left Chicago for New York City and Columbia University, where he taught until his retirement. A prolific author, in works such as *Democracy and Education* (1916), *Human Nature and Conduct* (1922), *Individualism Old and New* (1929-1930), and *A Common Faith* (1934), he argued that human existence is fundamentally an ongoing social process that enjoins people to use critical methods of inquiry that are essential for and conducive to democracy.

In this worthwhile intellectual biography, Robert B. Westbrook, a professor of history at the University of Rochester, shows that few American minds have been as penetrating and brilliant as John Dewey's. It is even possible that none has taken democracy with greater seriousness. Thus, Westbrook's book begins aptly with an epigraph by Charles Frankel. "To know where we stand toward Dewey's ideas," Frankel once contended, "is to find out, at least in part, where we stand with ourselves."

Frankel's point, which Westbrook's book explains and elaborates, rings true, for John Dewey was a philosopher whose thought covered virtually every major philosophical issue. His work on those questions, moreover, was not done in cultural isolation. On the contrary, Dewey's thought repeatedly stressed the importance of social and historical context. Thus, he took his American setting, including the relation of the United States to the rest of the world, very seriously.

Westbrook acknowledges that his book is not the complete biographical treatment that Dewey's life deserves. Yet the author has little need for modesty, to say nothing of apology. For one thing, Westbrook himself points out that Dewey, unfortunately, left little behind in the way of a record of his own interior life. There is abundant correspondence, but much about the man, he concludes, "remains opaque" nevertheless. At least from a psychological point of view, Westbrook is less than entirely confident that he can explain why Dewey's thought developed as it did. As for what Dewey thought, however, Westbrook believes that he does understand Dewey—indeed, he believes, and with considerable justification, that he understands him far better than interpreters who, in Westbrook's ironic judgment, have explored "the origins and impact of ideas that never existed" in Dewey's mind. Westbrook's success in this regard, and the insight that his readers gain, is exacted at a price. For even though he finds Dewey's prose no more difficult than that of many modern philosophers, he cites sympathetically Justice Oliver Wendell Holmes's quip that Dewey wrote as "God would have spoken had He been inarticulate but keenly desirous to tell you how it was."

Nevertheless, Westbrook's study, which concentrates on Dewey's social thought and on his understanding of democracy as "a way of life," is full of insights that corroborate the claim made by Frankel in the book's epigraph. For American readers especially, to meet Dewey is to encounter a thinker who can help them know who they are and where they stand. That said, it must be underscored that the epigraph to Westbrook's book does not imply that readers—then or now, American or not—will or even should necessarily agree with Dewey. This American philosopher, arguably the most important one in the twentieth century, was criticized as well as esteemed by people worldwide. These diverse reactions had much to do with Dewey's distinctive dedication to democracy. His work covered three generations of American experience, and it contributed to the key debates in the nation's intellectual and political life from the 1890's until his death at the age of ninety-two. By explicitly exploring "Dewey's career as an advocate of democracy," Westbrook shows how Dewey and his thought were controversial and suggests why the man and his philosophy remain so.

In sum, central to Westbrook's thesis is the view that Dewey has received many misplaced accolades. For example, if Dewey became, as historian Henry Steele

Commager once said, "the guide, the mentor, and the conscience of the American people," or if he would have been the leading candidate for "national philosopher," assuming such an office existed, those tributes cannot have been based on the actual practice of Dewey's philosophy in the United States. Dewey's democratic theory, contends Westbrook, has always been a long way from full implementation in American society. Thus, he argues, "it is more accurate to see Dewey as a minority, not a majority, spokesman within the liberal community, a social philosopher whose democratic vision failed to find a secure place in liberal ideology—in short, a more radical voice than has been generally assumed."

Westbrook locates the radical quality of Dewey's vision in its emphasis on participatory democracy. Dewey held the belief, perhaps partly nurtured by his New England upbringing and advanced by his concerns about education, that men and women were not only capable of self-government but also that they could maximize their growth and fulfillment—individually and communally—only if they participated actively, intelligently, and critically in political, social, and cultural life. Dewey took this belief to be one profoundly embedded in democratic ideals, and for him democracy was real only to the extent that such participation was respected, encouraged, and expanded. Ideals of this kind were what Dewey had in mind when his 1939 essay "Creative Democracy: The Task Before Us" observed that "the task of democracy is forever that of the creation of a freer and more humane experience in which all share and to which all contribute."

Westbrook is correct: A democracy that thoroughly embodied the democracy Dewey defended would be much more open and egalitarian, less savaged by the divisions of class, race, and gender, than the democracy of the United States forty years after Dewey's death. In many quarters, including those that have embraced democratic "realism" or democratic "elitism"—government for the people but advisedly not by the people—Dewey's vision would even be derided as utopian foolishness. Yet Dewey was not undone by such criticism. As the debates went on, he refused to take a path that led liberalism to water down democratic ideals. He rejected "realism" that substituted the mitigation of conflict between competing selves and factions for the hope of advancement toward a nobler sense of community. Dewey persisted in affirming that a more participatory democracy could accommodate pluralism and diversity by shared enterprises within what Dewey called "a common faith."

Westbrook's interpretation does make Dewey a minority voice. In that role, however, Dewey provides an important critical corrective by emphasizing what he took to be both the logic of democracy and its fundamental optimism about human nature and conduct. Westbrook rightly argues that Dewey's understanding of democracy was not purely a matter of political reflection. This philosopher's reckoning with questions about ethics, education, psychology, natural science, even about logic and inquiry themselves, had implications that supported democratic institutions and relationships. Similarly, those institutions and relationships could flourish only where people were trained to value and enact open inquiry, judgment grounded in the actual human experience, and a willingness to revise their views in the light of shared criticism. Authoritarian methods, dogmatic convictions, untested beliefs—these were Dewey's enemies. Because power and privilege are so often bound up with them, his unmasking of their ways was not welcomed by everyone.

One of Westbrook's best contributions is that he does not treat Dewey's thought abstractly. True to Dewey's own understanding of how inquiry happens, Westbrook shows how Dewey's involvement in the concrete social issues of his own time and place provoked his reflection. That reflection aimed at providing a framework for sound interpretation and critical understanding that went beyond particular cases. Yet philosophy, Dewey urged, ought not to go too far beyond particular cases. Its task is to help people live well within them. If that is so, then philosophy must keep close contact with lived experience.

"Philosophy," Dewey wrote in 1917, "recovers itself when it ceases to be a device for dealing with the problems of philosophers and becomes a method, cultivated by philosophers, for dealing with the problems of men." Whether he was considering education or religion, politics or social justice, he made that point again and again in one way or another. By the time pneumonia ended his long life on June 1, 1952, philosophy had become dominated by the technical interests of language analysis and the esoteric perspectives of symbolic logic. Thereby it largely lost sight of the social, cultural, and political problems that Dewey thought philosophers so much needed to probe. Westbrook's epilogue, "The Wilderness and the Promised Land," not only traces some of those developments but also suggests that post World War II political theory in the United States reflected more of "realism" than of Dewey's idealistic, participatory emphases.

If those tides have turned in the 1990's, and it is better recognized again that critically inquiring communities of participation are essential for the health of democracy, Westbrook laments that the nation lacks "public intellectuals" who can match John Dewey. Westbrook hopes that shortcoming can be overcome, although he makes clear that he is not nostalgically recommending "an uncritical or whole-sale recovery of Dewey's philosophy." That objective, he underscores, would not be compatible with Dewey's thought anyway. What is needed, he argues, is recognition that Dewey's philosophy of democracy "merits another, closer look." Through his carefully written book, which shows how Dewey did indeed craft "a democratic philosophy of a depth and scope unparalleled in modern American thought," Westbrook has improved the odds that such steps will be taken.

John K. Roth

Sources for Further Study

The Atlantic. CCLXVIII, November, 1991, p. 152.
Journal of the History of Ideas. LII, July, 1991, p. 532.
Library Journal. CXVI, April 15, 1991, p. 96.

London Review of Books. XIII, July 25, 1991, p. 3.
The Nation. CCLIII, October 14, 1991, p. 450.
National Review. XLIII, September 23, 1991, p. 46.
The New Leader. LXXIV, May 20, 1991, p. 13.
The New York Times Book Review. XCVI, September 22, 1991, p. 48.
Publishers Weekly. CCXXXVIII, April 19, 1991, p. 50.
The Washington Post Book World. XXI, July 7, 1991, p. 1.

THE JOURNALS OF JOHN CHEEVER

Author: John Cheever (1912-1982)
Edited by Robert Gottlieb
Publisher: Alfred A. Knopf (New York). 399 pp. $25.00
Type of work: Journal
Time: The 1940's to the 1980's
Locale: Primarily the United States

These selections from John Cheever's voluminous journals reveal the wellsprings of his art in drafts of his work and more important in the obsessions and experiences he transformed into fiction

Culled from twenty-nine looseleaf notebooks filled over some thirty-five years and representing just one-twentieth of the estimated total of three to four million words, *The Journals of John Cheever* is an amazing, at times literally astonishing, work. Part confession and part workbook, it often seems less a record of observations and experiences than a labyrinth of obsessions real and imagined. The publication of daughter Susan Cheever's two memoirs, *Home Before Dark: A Biographical Memoir of John Cheever* (1984) and *Treetops: A Family Memoir* (1991), son Benjamin Cheever's selection of his father's letters, and Scott Donaldson's magisterial 1988 biography made abundantly clear the various horrors at Cheever's personal heart of darkness: the emotional insecurity that began during adolescence with the breakup of his parents' marriage; his ensuing and certainly ambiguous relationship with his older brother Fred, the first of his many surrogate fathers; his love for and bitterness toward his wife of forty years; his wayward sexuality (both homo- and hetero-); his financial and professional worries. (As early as 1979—two years after a *Newsweek* cover story hailing 1977's *Falconer* as "Cheever's Triumph"—none of the libraries to which Cheever had offered his journals expressed any interest; clearly Cheever's fears about the value of his work and his importance as a writer were not entirely unfounded.) Although Cheever's journals do not startle the reader with new revelations, they do reveal much about their author, layering the horrors as it were, fleshing out the obsessions.

For a writer who had chosen to make a life of letters, who from the time he was seventeen knew that writing was the only thing he wanted to do and the only thing he would do—unlike almost all other "serious" writers, Cheever taught little, did not start out writing advertising copy, and published hardly any essays or reviews— the effect of the various blows (real and imagined) to his ever-fragile sense of self-esteem must have been (to use one of Cheever's favorite words) inestimable. The honors received late in life—and there were many of them—mattered, of course, but they could not, one suspects, entirely dispel the feelings of insecurity, unworthiness, and "otherness" that haunted him throughout his career. Reading Alwyn Lee's *Time* cover story upon publication of *The Wapshot Scandal* (1964), Cheever characteristically remarked that the essay "in its discretion, its cunning, rendered me as a serious and likable person when I could, on the strength of the evidence, be described as a fat slob enjoying an extraordinary run of luck." Slight in stature though for a time bloated—"fat"—with alcohol, lacking even a high school diploma (though he would receive an honorary degree from Harvard in 1981), driven by guilt and hypersensitivity, Cheever seems a rather special case of Edward Everett Hale's man without a country. For all his WASPishness and New England genealogy (again, real and imagined), Cheever was, or believed himself to be, a man without an identity, a socially and psychologically displaced person. Place in Cheever's fiction is always important but is not so much realistically described as acutely felt, whether New York, suburban Shady Hill, St. Botolphs, Italy, or Eastern Europe. In a remarkably revealing and yet ultimately circular and even self-canceling passage written in 1957, Cheever ponders "the mystery of a gratifying sense of identity that I don't recall experiencing in Europe. In an upper-class gathering I suddenly think of myself as a pariah—a small and dirty fraud, a deserved outcast, a spiritual and sexual importer, a loathsome thing. Then I take a deep breath, stand up straight, and the loathsome image falls away. I am no better and no worse than the other members of the gathering. Indeed, I am myself. It is like a pleasant taste on the tongue. Perhaps I had less time for self-consciousness abroad." Similar transformations occur in many Cheever fictions, most notably and triumphantly in *Falconer*. The energy that drives Cheever's stories, novels, and journals, and his life, however, derives less, if at all, from self-assurance than from a self-doubt born of and manifesting itself in the deep division within Cheever himself, between aspiration and desperation, lewdness and decorum, creativity and self-destruction, the sexual and the spiritual, between what he believed were the "constants" in his nature and what he hoped were mere (although frequent) aberrations. "I am tired of this thread of love and whiskey, of courage and memory that is the only thing to hold my world together," Cheever wrote in 1955. "I am tired of threads and other frail things." His weariness aside, twenty years later he finds himself in precisely the same situation: "That bridge of language, metaphor, anecdote, and imagination that I build each morning to cross the incongruities in my life seems very frail indeed."

The various threads Cheever fashioned, the bridges he constructed in his writing and in his life, held no better than William Butler Yeats's famous center. In Cheever's case, however, the rough beasts were not slouching towards Bethlehem from without but towards his eighteenth century farmhouse on the idyllically named Cedar Lane in Ossining, New York, from within. Cheever wrote for much the same reason that he skied, skated, swam, biked, scythed the fields, fertilized the lawn, painted the shutters, ran errands: to celebrate and connect his world, to make the constants more visible, the aberrations less possible, and to keep the beasts at bay. "The splendid thing about working happily is that it leaves me with very little energy for bitterness, anger, impatience, and long indictments." As his fiction and these journals demonstrate, Cheever had energy to spare and often used it to burn the very same bridges he had spent his mornings building so painstakingly on paper. His relationships with those he loved—his brother Fred and wife Mary in particular—were generally combative and competitive. Cheever sought from them the love, understanding, and forgiveness he was unwilling himself to give (to others and to himself). He was prone to a cloying, childish self-pity: Sitting at Mary's feet, trying once again to win back her affection, he suddenly sees "that I am in exactly the position of a doormat." Yet in Cheever self-pity is never far from self-reproach: "When we say 'Christ, have mercy upon us,' we don't ask for a literal blessing, I think. We express how merciless we are to ourselves."

Cheever seems to have been forever poised between worlds, between states of perpetual expectancy and perpetual dissatisfaction, in search of spiritual wholeness but fearing that this longing was nothing more than a desire to escape from the intolerableness of his own past, his own self. Lamenting the narrowness of his life and the anxieties he so often felt, he posited a nearly Emersonian nature, spacious and eternal. In a parallel way, he lamented the smallness and constricted scope of his fiction—short stories chiefly, set in carefully zoned, homogeneous communities like Shady Hill. Yet in (again) an almost Emersonian way, Cheever understood that the relationship between self and other, each and all is one of correspondence rather than scale. That understanding provided little lasting comfort to a writer who—his many protestations to interviewers notwithstanding—did think of writing as a competitive sport, one in which he believed himself destined to play the part of designated loser: less successful, less productive, less weighty (in pages and in profundity) than Saul Bellow, Norman Mailer, Philip Roth, John Updike, and others (including Vladimir Nabokov, whose work, so different from his own, Cheever especially liked). Cheever's dreams in which his face appears on a postage stamp and President Dwight Eisenhower is seen reading *The Wapshot Chronicle* (1957) offer the same strange mixture of legitimate longing for recognition on the one hand and blackly humorous self-mockery on the other that characterizes so many of his stories and novels.

The journals fascinate page-by-page but are perhaps most fascinating when suggesting in certain cases and detailing in others the ways in which Cheever's fiction is—again, remarks to interviewers notwithstanding—crypto-autobiography, in however special and decidedly angled a way, in terms of both recurrent themes and individual scenes. In the journals, the reader discovers not only Cheever drafting and perfecting the bits and pieces of stories and novels but also the very wellsprings of his art in the events of his daily life (or rather in his perception of those events). In *Falconer*, for example, Farragut's brother, Eben, tries to get his wife's attention, which she directs toward the television set, by appearing on the humiliating *Truth or Consequences*-like show he has seen her watching. Eben takes his fall, gets laughed at, picks himself up, dries himself off, and returns home:

> "Hey, hey, did you see me on television?" She was lying on a sofa in the living room by the big set. She was crying. So then I thought I'd done the wrong thing, that she was crying because I looked like such a fool, falling into the tank. She went on crying and sobbing and I said, "What's the matter, dear?" and she said, "They shot the mother polar bear, they shot the mother polar bear!" Wrong show. I got the wrong show, but you can't say that I didn't try.

Six years before *Falconer* appeared, Cheever wrote in his journal of an evening with his wife:

> Later, on TV, a polar bear is murdered. "They've shot the mother polar bear!" she cries; and she cries, she sobs, "They've shot the mother polar bear!" And I think that perhaps I should go on TV, that if I approached her through the tube on the shelf above the sink I might win her interest and her affection, but I would have to be disguised as a mother polar bear, or some other wild, innocent, and wronged animal.

The line dividing life from literature, fact from fiction, the autobiographical from the autotelic, blurs, as at times does the line separating one story or novel from another: A passage originally written for *Bullet Park* (1969) appears, slightly revised, in *Falconer*, despite the very considerable differences between those two works. Cheever writes that "I have dreams of a density I would like to bring to fiction." In retrospect, it is precisely this dreamlike quality that most characterizes Cheever's fiction—perhaps even his manner of perceiving himself and his world. The everyday is often rendered in an almost surreal manner; conversely, the most absurd events are rendered matter-of-factly. "Absolute candor does not suit me," he writes, a point Mary chose to understand in her own way: "You're just making up one of your little stories," she tells him at one point, her dismissal as full of truth as it is of malice.

"I have been a storyteller since the beginning of my life, rearranging facts in order to make them more interesting and sometimes more significant," Cheever states, and, candid in their own way, the journals do not explain either Cheever or his fiction in terms of direct statements and simple equations. Rather, they deepen and extend both in terms of an unstable set of relationships arranged, like Cheever's numerous dreams, on the basis of metonymic displacements and metaphoric condensations. Moments of lucid vision and lyrical affirmation aside, Cheever was never Ralph Waldo Emerson's "transparent eyeball," one with his world. Self-absorbed rather than self-reliant, he was more a polyphonic voice never quite coinciding with his world or himself. For making more of that voice available, Cheever's family and especially his longtime editor, Robert Gottlieb, deserve both thanks and praise. Some will, of course, second-guess editorial choices: passages selected (as well as those omitted), absence of annotations, citing of full names for family members and public figures only (whose privacy is being protected here, given the openness of both the collection of Cheever's letters and Donaldson's fair and forthright biography?). Yet the very abstractness that certain of these editorial choices help to create is oddly appropriate. Cheever may have kept his journals on a more or less daily basis, but the rhythm is seasonal and liturgical, not diurnal, the movement circular, not progressive, a matter of recurrent obsessions rather than specific topical references (of which the journals have remarkably few). "Cheever's triumph" came, then, not in *Falconer*, for all its self-exorcising brilliance, but in his struggle with the self-begotten demons that had beset him all of his life, and in his more than candid record of that struggle.

Robert A. Morace

Sources for Further Study

Boston Globe. September 29, 1991, p. 15.
Chicago Tribune. September 22, 1991, XIV, p. 1.
Kirkus Reviews. LIX, August 15, 1991, p. 1055.
Library Journal. CXVI, September 15, 1991, p. 76.
Los Angeles Times Book Review. October 13, 1991, p. 3.
The New York Times Book Review. XCVI, October 6, 1991, p. 1.
Newsweek. CXVIII, October 14, 1991, p. 66.
Publishers Weekly. CCXXXVIII, August 23, 1991, p. 51.
Time. CXXXVII, March 18, 1991, p. 80.
The Washington Post Book World. XXI, September 22, 1991, p. 3.

JUMP
And Other Stories

Author: Nadine Gordimer (1923-   )
Publisher: Farrar, Straus & Giroux (New York). 257 pp. $20.00
Type of work: Short stories

Sixteen new stories by South Africa's Nobel Prize-winning author

As the first woman to be awarded the Nobel Prize for literature in twenty-five years, Nadine Gordimer rocketed to universal fame. Such is the power of the prize that in the weeks immediately following its announcement, her books were nearly unattainable, even wholesalers being sold out. In awarding the prize at a time when South Africa was losing its status as international pariah (purportedly Gordimer had been on the "short list" for several years), the Nobel committee may have been hoping to spare South Africa the embarrassment of seeing one of its previously banned authors honored by the world's most prestigious prize. If that is so, the decision may backfire, for Gordimer has lost none of her moral indignation, and the South Africa depicted in these stories is no different from the one anatomized in her last collection, *Something Out There* (1984; See *Magill's Literary Annual*, 1985).

In interviews given before and after the Nobel Prize was awarded, Gordimer claims that the political dimensions of her work arise because apartheid is an inescapable fact of the life around her, not because she is by nature politically inclined. The stories in this collection support this claim about herself, for politics is more often the leaven of the loaf than the bread itself; politics informs and shapes her plots and characters, and only occasionally does it seem an end in itself. The underlying themes of Gordimer's short fiction remain what they have been: fear, betrayal, and the distortions of personal relations caused by racial tension and misunderstanding.

The title story, "Jump," is one of the most overtly political in the collection. Its unnamed protagonist lives alone in a dreary hotel under protective custody. The son of colonial parents, he was arrested by his country's black government for unwittingly taking photographs of a military installation. Thus radicalized, he joined the disloyal white opposition as a white-collar soldier, a purveyor of arms and intelligence, a pampered bureaucrat coolly supplying the means by which atrocities were perpetrated. He does not himself understand why one day he walked out of the whites' headquarters and into the enemy's office, bringing with him a headful of important information. Perhaps it was learning that the planeloads of children brought over the border were not refugees but prisoners supplied to satisfy the lusts of weary soldiers. Whatever the cause, this jump has landed him in cushioned isolation, estranged from his parents, too fearful of reprisals to leave, comforted only by the young girl he found in his room when he arrived. Even in this story, however, the random horror of revolution and counterrevolution is depicted not as a deficiency of ideology but as a failure of morality. One is reminded of T. S. Eliot's *The Waste Land* (1922) or of Graham Greene's sordid and soiled moral atmosphere. The only way out for this victim seems to be one final jump—from the top story of his decaying hotel.

As the short story is related to the fable, it is not surprising that Gordimer relies occasionally on this form, as she does in "Once Upon a Time." A writer, badgered by her publisher for a children's story, composes a lurid cautionary tale one sleepless night: A family living "happily ever after" slowly but inevitably increases its security system against blacks until finally it is living behind a brick wall topped with razor wire. To this point, the tale has moved with almost dull predictability, but the ending is horrible in its swift and matter-of-fact description of the boy's mutilation by the very wire that was to protect him. Like most fables, the moral is too overt and the events are too contrived, but the story illustrates if nothing else the effectiveness of the surprise ending.

While "Jump" and "Once Upon a Time" emphasize the punishment oppression inflicts on the oppressors, "The Ultimate Safari" shows graphically its effects on those forced to flee in order to survive. Through the eyes of the eleven-year-old girl who narrates, the reader sees the sufferings of one refugee family. Perhaps the most remarkable feature of this story is its lack of melodrama. When troops burn the family's home and kill the mother, when the grandparents and grandchildren trudge through a game preserve eating less than the protected animals, when the grandfather must be left behind to die if the others are to survive, there is no straining after effect, no piling on of horrific description. The bare facts and stark contrasts are allowed to speak for themselves, as is the narrator's touchingly desperate optimism that someday all will be restored.

A similar effect is achieved in "Amnesty," only here the subject is the courtship and marriage of a young black couple. Theirs would be ordinary lives were it not for his increasingly active role in a labor union. Inevitably, he is jailed, leaving his pregnant girlfriend to struggle on her own. Perhaps the most horrific part of the story is the simple bureaucratic callousness that prevents the man's family members from visiting, even though they have traveled far and spent all their available money, because they neglected to obtain a permit. After five years in prison, he is released, but there can be no "normal" life for them now, as his first commitment is to politics. Her solace, apart from the child, is to contemplate the land that once was hers and to wait for that day when she can "come back home."

"Home" examines a different level of society, the white professional class, but politics affect it in much the same way, transforming a loving couple into strangers, a trusting husband into a suspicious one, because his wife becomes absorbed in the problems of releasing her jailed mother, brother, and sister-in-law.

Gordimer's skill at narrative construction shines in "My Father Leaves Home," a quasiautobiographical story of universal and disturbing implications. The narrator (presumably female) is part of a pheasant-hunting expedition in Eastern Europe, in the unnamed country of her father's birth. While waiting at a train station, her mind drifts back to the time when her thirteen-year-old father left his village for South Africa, carrying little more than his watchmaking tools and the rudiments of his craft. As he makes a living repairing and selling watches, he gradually loses his Jewish heritage; he marries a local woman, joins the Masons, begets children, adopts the racial attitudes of the whites around him. These and other pieces of the story seem like unrelated fragments until the hunt itself, the horror of which strikes the narrator as she watches the beaters flush helpless birds from their cover and is reminded of the fate of the powerless everywhere:

> Death advancing and nowhere to go. Blindness coming by fire or shot and no way out to see, shelling peas by feel. Cracks of detonation and wild agony of flutter all around me, I crouch away from the sound and sight, only a spectator, only a spectator, please, but the cossack's hooves rode those pleading wretches down. A bird thuds dead, striking my shoulder before it hits the soft bed of leaves beside me.

To her everlasting credit, however, Gordimer has no sentimental illusions that the oppressed are automatically morally superior to their oppressors. That is brought home in the deceptively conventional "Some Are Born to Sweet Delight," which seems until the very end an almost formulaic love story. The vacuously pretty daughter of a lower-middle-class family gradually falls in love with the lodger her family has taken in, a quiet and polite young man from somewhere in the Middle East. Since this is South Africa, where racial issues are never moot, the reader may easily be lulled into thinking that this is a story in which love conquers all. Even the parents gradually come to like their daughter's choice, particularly as the young man is so proud of his wife-to-be that he sends her home to meet his parents. In a turn of events worthy of O. Henry, however, her plane explodes in midair, destroyed by a bomb he disguised as a last-minute gift. Unfortunately, the shock value of the ending is diluted by an anticlimactic concluding paragraph, a fault that also mars the otherwise effective "A Moment Before the Gun Went Off." In both stories, the temptation to make a telling political point gives rise to artistically weak endings.

"Teraloyna" picks up the hunting motif of "My Father Leaves Home" and the fable quality of "Once Upon a Time" and combines them into a curious illustrative history of an insignificant island and its people, the Teraloyna. They are of mixed race, and so they assimilate easily into the new countries of the world—the United States, South Africa, Australia—but their tiny island is less fortunate. Overrun first by goats brought by settlers or salvaged from shipwreck, the island becomes an eroded wasteland, fit by its location only to become a weather station. Again man intervenes, this time bringing a pair of kittens that beget a devastating overpopulation that again destroys the island's ecological balance. Presumably, these man-induced environmental disasters are paralleled by the fate of the Teraloyna people themselves, who in their diaspora become oppressors and oppressed, killers and victims. The ironic ending in which descendants of the Teraloyna are brought in to shoot the marauding cats is rather too pat, and overall the fable is marred by the unassimilated comparison between human and animal predation.

These themes are much more subtly and effectively handled in "Spoils," the best story of the collection. Presented by multiple points of view—a technique that Gordimer has mastered and uses to great advantage—the story also works on multiple levels. Part anatomy of the trivial irritations of marriage, part description of the social dynamics of a weekend party, part contrast between white wealth and black poverty, the story unites and transcends these ideas by using metaphors from nature. This is achieved by an incident that arises plausibly from an evening cookout on a private game preserve: A strange noise fills the intervals between conversations, and the guests speculate as to what it could be. The native cook identifies it for them and offers to lead an expedition to see the lionesses and their zebra prey. In the eerie light of a car's headlights, the lionesses appear "unreal" to a woman who prefers to deny what her husband sees—the essential reality of this timeless scene. The next day, the native cook leads them on a return expedition to the carcasses, where nature's essential economy is demonstrated in the "spoils" taken from the dead zebras by various species of beetles, each of which performs its own function. Man takes his own spoils as well, for the native cook expertly carves from a zebra's haunch a choice piece of steak—just enough so that the lions will not retaliate by taking one of his children.

Short-story writers since Anton Chekhov have known the trick of ending a story with a significant, unifying gesture, and in "Spoils" this technique is masterfully demonstrated. The various themes and incidents of the story fall neatly (but not too neatly) into place. The conflicts and imbalances of human society, suggested by the quarreling couple, the ex-political prisoner, and the poverty of the native cook and his family, are suddenly revealed in a new perspective. Yet there is no romantic idealization of nature, for the ferocity of the lions, the repulsiveness of vultures, and the curious efficiency of the opportunistic beetles are clearly faced. The irony of nature's balance is emphasized at man's expense, but this is not all, for the uses of language—to equivocate, to lacerate, to cover up, and to euphemize—are revealed throughout as the source of much that is wrong with humans. The unique gift that makes fiction possible is also that which makes it necessary.

A story like "Spoils" stands out in part because it is less overtly political than the others. As fine as Gordimer's political writing is, the fact that racial politics provides most of these stories with their impetus gives them a certain similarity. "Comrades," for example, illustrates the impossibility of communication between wealthy whites and poor blacks, however honorable their intentions, however similar their political philosophies. Likewise, the subtleties of South Africa's "peculiar institutions" cannot be conveyed to outsiders in "What Were You Dreaming?" There may also be an essential similarity between the couple in "Safe Houses" and illicit lovers everywhere, but this cannot outweigh the effect of politics on driving the story's female protagonist into emotional isolation and her lover into involuntary exile.

In short, the political dimension of these stories is a mixed blessing, on the one hand conferring thematic importance and contemporary relevance to everything Gordimer writes while on the other hand distorting to some degree the human relationships that are more important than politics. Perhaps that is why the suggestiveness of story line is so important to the success of her stories. In the most memorable of these tales, as in "Keeping Fit," the power of the story is directly related to the ability of the central incident to transcend the particularities of South Africa. In "Keeping Fit," a complacent broker goes out for his Sunday morning jog only to be swept up in the chaos of his country's intertribal violence. He is saved by the "butterscotch-coloured upper arm" of a woman who pulls him to the safety of her pathetic little shack. Intense as his experience is, however, there is no way for him to assimilate it into his character or communicate it to his family or friends. He will be a different man from this time forward, but isolated. Some of Gordimer's best writing in this volume describes his terror and isolation, and such is the power of the experience that it transcends its peculiarities of time and place.

The quality of Gordimer's writing is never in question. She has a painter's eye for telling detail and the stylistic resources to make these details suggest something far beyond themselves. Her characters are occasionally representative types (the bored and lonely wife, the angry husband, the well-meaning white liberal), but in the successful stories she takes the reader beyond surface similarities to individual personalities. Through these characters, the reader glimpses the realities of daily life in South Africa, and by extension wherever racial or ethnic hatred corrodes the lives of all it touches, rich and poor, oppressed and oppressors, young and old. Perhaps the most haunting image of the book is that of the beaters in "My Father Leaves Home" flushing the hapless pheasants from their cover, for this is an image of the politics of hatred everywhere. Nadine Gordimer takes the reader to the heart of such politics, and so doing richly deserves the prize she has won and the readership that prize has brought with it.

Dean Baldwin

Sources for Further Study

Booklist. LXXXVII, July, 1991, p. 2011.
Chicago Tribune. September 8, 1991, XIV, p. 8.
The Christian Science Monitor. October 9, 1991, p. 13.
Library Journal. CXVI, August, 1991, p. 149.
Los Angeles Times Book Review. October 6, 1991, p. 2.
New Statesman and Society. IV, October 18, 1991, p. 38.
The New York Times Book Review. XCVI, September 29, 1991, p. 7.
Newsweek. CXVIII, October 14, 1991, p. 40.
Publishers Weekly. CCXXXVIII, July 12, 1991, p. 51.
The Times Literary Supplement. October 11, 1991, p. 14.
The Washington Post Book World. XXI, September 8, 1991, p. 9.

KING EDWARD VIII
A Biography

Author: Philip Ziegler (1929-   )
Publisher: Alfred A. Knopf (New York). Illustrated. 552 pp. $24.95
Type of work: Biography
Time: 1894-1972
Locale: Principally Great Britain; also France, Bermuda, and the United States

This well-balanced biography of the man who left the throne of England for the woman he loved draws on new archival evidence and many interviews to give the most intimate and personal portrait yet of the unfortunate Edward VIII

> *Principal personages:*
> EDWARD ALBERT CHRISTIAN GEORGE ANDREW PATRICK DAVID, the Prince of Wales, eventually King Edward VIII of Great Britain, later Duke of Windsor
> KING GEORGE V, his father
> QUEEN MARY, his mother
> GEORGE VI, his younger brother
> WALLIS WARFIELD SIMPSON, Edward's wife after he became Duke of Windsor

Of the making of books about Edward VIII and the Abdication Crisis of 1936 there would seem to be no end. In the popular romantic memory, he will always be the man who gave up the throne of England for the woman he loved. In the minds of many, the romance of Edward VIII and Wallis Warfield Simpson ranks with those of Romeo and Juliet, Antony and Cleopatra, and Tristan and Iseult. The truth, as it usually is, is more mundane. Ziegler's book is essentially a sad tale of misdirection, waste, and loneliness. No doubt if the archives, letters, and interviews of friends and family still existed from the days of those other famous lovers, we would have entirely different, more prosaic versions of their stories as well.

There is little romance in this story, which Ziegler tells with great fairness, with style, and even with elegance. This is an "official" biography; indeed, the British edition is subtitled "The Official Biography." Ziegler, the author also of well-regarded books on Mountbatten and others, was given unrestricted access to the royal archives as well as privileged access to various groups of restricted papers elsewhere. The book under review, however, does not suffer from the stodginess and careful restraint that are the usual qualities of official biographies. While he is eminently fair to Edward VIII, Ziegler does not ignore or gloss over the facts of the life of his subject; he does not hide the weakness of character and judgment that the documents available all too clearly expose.

The book falls naturally into three convenient parts. The first and third parts, of about two hundred pages each, serve as introduction and coda to the central section of about one hundred pages, which covers Edward VIII's brief reign and the Abdication. After the setting out of Edward's years before he became king, and after the detailed and even intimate record that establishes clearly his character, opinions, and qualities, the second and third parts have some of the inevitability of a Greek tragedy; given a knowledge of the first forty years of Edward VIII's life, no one should have been much surprised at what the final thirty-six were to bring.

The future Edward VIII, always known as "David" to his family and friends (his brother, the future George VI, was known as "Bertie," and his brother's wife, Elizabeth, as "Cookie"), was unfortunate in his parents, his education, his tutor, and his friends. He could well be said to have had no real friends, only hangers-on and a few acquaintances—a condition that lasted through his life. He was trained for the navy, as his father had been, but he could not be said to have been educated. His tutor was a notably unimaginative and philistine former schoolmaster. His father, whom Ziegler insists had a good heart and really loved his eldest son, had little ability to communicate, was inclined to sententiousness, frequently found fault, and worried greatly about proper clothes and small points of royal or social etiquette. His mother, Queen Mary, was closer to him, but she too was addicted to good advice, and her rigid views were to cause the young prince much pain in later years. All in all, he grew up as a shallow and conventional thinker who read little; he had the usual biases of his age and class, and he much preferred to be doing rather than thinking.

He was independent minded, disliking the trappings of royalty and frequently wishing to be treated as "one of the boys," but it was not to be. He was generally coddled and his way made smooth. During World War I, he wished with all his heart to serve in a useful capacity, but he was restricted to ceremonial occasions and duties in France. He felt acutely his place as a protected member of an age group that was shedding its blood; he sought, when possible, danger, even though he frankly admitted his fears.

It was during the war that several of his staff arranged for his first sexual experiences with an experienced prostitute. During the years before he became king, he was to have at least two serious affairs and a number of casual liaisons. After he became involved with Mrs. Simpson, however, he remained true to her for the rest of his life.

A key word that recurs throughout the book and that is especially common in the first part is "charm"; everyone—family, friends, political leaders, and casual acquaintances, in diaries, memoirs, interviews, and reminiscences—remarks at length on the effect of the charm of the young boy and later of the man. The same sources make many references to Edward's boyishness and his rather wistful smile. He retained these traits well into maturity; it is not hard to conclude that Edward VIII was a rather pleasant child who never grew up. He was addicted to physical exercise and a spare diet that allowed him to keep his trim and slender figure throughout his lifetime. There were some who saw him as emaciated.

During his more than twenty-five years as Prince of Wales, Edward was subject to the direction of many. His family, his secretaries, the Cabinet, and the Prime Minister all had some say about what he was to do, especially his many visits, trips, and tours. Edward was often inclined to rebel against the arrangements made for him, but the important point is that he almost always ended up doing what was required of him. When more serious decisions needed to be made at the time of the Abdication, he wished to have his own way but in the end submitted again.

The Prince of Wales met Wallis Simpson first in 1931; by 1934, she had firmly established her authority over him. He was in fact besotted with her, and he remained so for the rest of his life. The Prince's private life was a matter of concern to the Royal Family and the government, but the matter came to a head only with Edward's accession to the throne upon the death of George V. The story of the progression of the maneuverings, the pressures, the advice given on all sides, the role of the press, has been often told, and Ziegler has no new evidence to add to the now-familiar story. The question of interest, which Ziegler only briefly touches upon, is what else could—or should—Edward have done. He could, of course, have cut himself off from Wallis, but this he was emotionally and psychologically incapable of doing. He could have kept this throne and kept his lover as a discreet mistress, a solution a number of his predecessors had found, but Wallis wished marriage and he was unable to deny her. It is a moot point whether Wallis seriously expected to be queen, but she was a most determined and dominating woman. Edward VIII probably never really appreciated his true position, and he was ultimately to give up the throne because of the incompatibility of his private wishes and public duty.

It is in the aftermath of the Abdication that Ziegler finds reason for his harshest criticism of Edward; as might be expected, the problem was money. Ziegler makes clear that Edward lied to his brother and others about his income and financial state in negotiating with his brother for arrangements after the Abdication. Whether Edward acted on his own or whether he was influenced by Wallis, who had a reputation for acquisitiveness, is not known.

Edward's years following the Abdication were sad and lonely ones. The central concern of the last part of the book is the Duke of Windsor's rumored involvement with German diplomats or agents. Ziegler makes clear that the Duke was never any sort of traitor, and that there is no evidence that he treated in any way with Germany or its agents—though he did at times speak carelessly and deliver himself of half-baked political opinions. The Duke's principal concern through his years of exile was to have Wallis officially recognized by the Royal Family; this never happened, though in 1967 the Duchess did meet Queen Elizabeth II, and in 1972, at Edward's funeral, she stayed at Buckingham Palace. Edward never seemed to have regretted his abdication except for what it denied to Wallis. The Windsors did what Wallis wanted. Ziegler's conclusion is that while the Duke deeply loved Wallis, she did not love him.

Apart from several years which Edward spent as Governor of Bermuda during World War II, and in spite of continued requests from the Duke to be given some sort of useful job, the Windsors did little. The Duke became more and more conservative in his views while living well. The Windsors lived mainly in France, taking frequent vacations (from what, one wonders), entertaining and being entertained. British officialdom seems to have been small-minded in its refusal to find any meaningful job for the Duke, but there was always the question of just what he could do. He was probably best fitted for a job supplying a glossy front to some enterprise. Indeed, given his talents and traits, he might have made a successful used-car salesman.

There are two points that emerge from the book, though Ziegler does not stress them. The first is that, wherever one's sympathies lie in regard to Edward VIII and the Abdication, no one involved comes off very well. There are no true heroes or villains in the affair. Edward did what he did partly out of weakness; politicians did what they did out of motives that ultimately had nothing to do either with Edward himself or with the glory and honor of the British Empire; and the members of the Royal Family did what they did often out of pique and a strict adherence to arcane principles.

A second point that must strike the reader is how petty so much of what happened really was. Even the Abdication, presented by politicians, the Royal Family, and the press as of earthshaking importance, was a rather small matter; British life would have continued in its natural course—as it did—regardless of who sat on an essentially powerless throne. The lengthy arguments about whether Wallis was entitled to be styled "her Royal Highness," the flutterings in the dovecotes of Whitehall when certain people from England called upon the Windsors in France, the refusal of the Royal Family to acknowledge Wallis, and the concern of George V for absolutely correct attire are simply a few examples of the small-mindedness and triviality of much associated with the life of Edward VIII. Seen from a distance, much seems silly, and Edward himself seems a small-minded and trivial man despite his charm.

Philip Ziegler has written a very fair book that gives a more personal and intimate view of Edward VIII than has been available before. Ziegler eschews condemnation and lets the facts speak for themselves. He is rarely harsh, but he does not compromise his presentation. This is essentially a character study of Edward VIII, presented in the context of history. Edward was a weak man subjected to strains, both public and private, that were beyond his capacity to handle. Some would have him a bumbling fool, a tragic hero, or a fairy prince. He was none of these. The real questions raised by this biography concern the Duchess of Windsor—her motives, her attraction, and her dominance—but *Edward VIII* does not answer them. One may hope that Philip Ziegler will devote his many talents in the future to her biography.

Gordon N. Bergquist

Sources for Further Study

Chicago Tribune. February 17, 1991, XIV, p. 5.
The Economist. CCCXVI, September 29, 1990, p. 100.

Library Journal. CXVI, January, 1991, p. 114.
London Review of Books. XII, November 8, 1990, p. 12.
Los Angeles Times Book Review. February 3, 1991, p. 2.
New Statesman and Society. III, September 28, 1990, p. 32.
The New York Times Book Review. XCVI, February 10, 1991, p. 14.
The New Yorker. LXVII, March 4, 1991, p. 95.
Publishers Weekly. CCXXXVII, November 30, 1990, p. 62.
The Times Literary Supplement. September 28, 1990, p. 1021.

THE KITCHEN GOD'S WIFE

Author: Amy Tan (1952-   )
Publisher: G. P. Putnam's Sons (New York). 415 pp. $22.95
Type of work: Novel
Time: 1920-1990
Locale: China and California

Although the book focuses initially on the problems of communication between an immigrant Chinese mother and her American-born daughter, its bulk traces the painfully tragic circumstances of the mother's life as an abused wife in China during the 1930's and 1940's

> *Principal characters:*
> WEILI "WINNIE" JIANG, the main protagonist and narrator, Chinese immigrant to the United States, married first to Wen Fu, then to Jimmy Louie, mother of Pearl
> PEARL LOUIE BRANDT, the secondary protagonist and narrator, Weili's daughter
> WEN FU, Weili's abusive first husband in China
> JIMMY LOUIE, Weili's loving Chinese-American second husband
> HULAN "HELEN" KWONG, longtime friend of Weili
> JIAGUO, Hulan's first husband in China
> HUAZHENG "PEANUT," Weili's cousin and childhood companion
> PHIL BRANDT, Pearl's Caucasian husband, a pathologist

Amy Tan's *The Kitchen God's Wife* is a readily recognizable successor to her first book, the 1989 bestseller *The Joy Luck Club* (see *Magill's Literary Annual,* 1990). It is cast in the same thematic, substantive, and stylistic mold. Unlike *The Joy Luck Club,* however, which assumed the form of a cycle of related short stories revolving around four mothers and their four daughters, *The Kitchen God's Wife* is a full-fledged novel. Like its predecessor, *The Kitchen God's Wife* is Asian-American and generational in subject and feminist in perspective: Its point of departure is the lack of communication between mother and daughter, a mother who is a Chinese-American immigrant and a daughter who is American born, but its scene quickly shifts from California to China, and the orbit of its pathos broadens to include the ugly husband-wife relationship that the mother had with her first husband. Both mother and daughter are first-person narrators of the novel, with mother clearly dominating in length as well as in interest; both narratives, addressed directly to the reader, have a performative quality to them, especially that of the mother, who is telling the reader what she has told the daughter. The mother's narrative is also couched in a tangy patois of Tan's concoction that manages to capture vividly and credibly the rhythms and turns of immigrant Chinese speech and allows the narrator to tell her tale with a winning individuality, humor, and irony. As the narratives unfold, the novel takes on elements of confession, *Bildungsroman,* and even epic.

The confessions come as catharsis and solution to the mother-daughter problem of communication. This problem exists on several levels. On the fairly simple level of linguistic miscommunication, it highlights the generational difference between the immigrant and the native-born and is tragicomic in effect: When the daughter, Pearl, says "beach," the mother, Weili, hears "bitch"; when Weili says that she has chosen the clothes and casket at a funeral, Pearl understands her to say that it will be a closed casket ceremony. During their lifetime (Weili is seventy, Pearl forty), such miscommunications have condensed around major paranoid secrets that mother and daughter are hiding from each other and that gnaw at their relationship like tumors or cancers (images of such potentially malignant growths appear noticeably in the book). Pearl's secret, about which everybody but her mother knows, is that she suffers from multiple sclerosis. Weili's secret is her fear that Pearl is not the child of her loving second husband Jimmy Louie but of her heinous first husband Wen Fu, who had raped her the week before she left China to marry Jimmy. The overarching form of the novel is the mutual confession of these fearful secrets, which leads to the reconciliation of mother and daughter.

Beneath this formal canopy of confession, one finds a vital and fully fleshed-out *Bildungsroman*; although Pearl's confession is brief, Weili's is in fact a gripping three-hundred-page account of her life, the pain of which she has kept hidden from her daughter. It is this life story that may be read as the *Bildungsroman* of a girl with a very fragile sense of self-worth who grows into a woman capable of asserting her choice of a husband at gunpoint—a heartwarming variant of the shotgun wedding.

For this purpose, Tan places her protagonist Weili in a bourgeois family in the male-dominated society of China from the 1920's to 1949. The traumatic childhood event that sends Weili's self-esteem plummeting is the (to her) inexplicable way in which she is abandoned by her mother, a replacement secondary wife of a wealthy Shanghai merchant with a ménage of five concubines. Instead of being the apple of her mother's eye, Weili grows up fostered and tolerated by unloving aunts, marginalized in an island village away from her father's hearth in the city. Weili never sees her mother again; for them, there is no chance to break the silence that stifles their mother-daughter relationship.

As a tolerated relative, Weili is brought up with no great expectations for herself. She plays second fiddle to her girl cousin Peanut; and, as is common in a Confucian society, both girls are treated as inferior to Peanut's brother. Weili thus gratefully accepts Wen Fu as husband, though he had initially come to court Peanut but had been rejected by her family as too déclassé.

Weili's unhappy childhood is only the prologue to the tragedy of her marriage. She quickly discovers that she has married an entirely selfish man and an abusive sexual pervert. From the other women of the family, however, Weili can expect no solidarity. On the contrary, Weili's mother-in-law believes that it is necessary "to be dutiful to a terrible person," and that "a woman always had to feel pain . . . before she could feel love." Wen Fu is a cheat who passes himself off as his deceased brother so that he can qualify academically for the air force (General Claire Chennault's "Flying Tigers") and who carelessly squanders away Weili's dowry. He gambles recklessly, rapes a servant who later dies in a botched abortion, beds a mistress in Weili's room, and beats his infant daughter into retardation and death. A cowardly pilot who turns tail at the glimpse of an enemy fighter, he is a swaggerer and bully, good only for molesting nurses and shooting a poor farmer's pig that is blocking his road. In crashing a jeep (bought with Weili's money), Wen Fu loses an eye and metaphorically takes on his true aspect, a cannibalistic cyclops. In the character of Wen Fu, Amy Tan successfully epitomizes all the heinous traits of the male. Almost as vile as Fyodor Dostoevski's father Karamazov, Wen Fu is more hateful than Alice Walker's Mr. Albert because he is irredeemable.

During her marriage to this brute, Weili endures the sufferings of a Griselda, but Weili is no unquestioning saint and consequently grows in awareness, independent judgment, and, finally, rebelliousness. When Wen Fu humiliates her undeservedly before their guests, Weili wonders about the male-is-right ethos that impels her guests to conspire to keep silent about such patent indignity and unfairness. After she realizes what a brutal and abusive father Wen Fu is, Weili exercises the choice of aborting the fetuses they conceive. She also discovers that men find her attractive, and she even dares to think of happiness with another worshipful pilot who is unfortunately killed. Eventually she meets and falls in love with Jimmy Louie, a considerate and loving Chinese-American interpreter attached to the American forces in China. Before she can exercise her choice of a husband, however, an act unthinkable to her in her youth, she must wrest a divorce from Wen Fu. To do this, she empowers herself by cunning and force, coopting the very two instruments that Wen Fu has so often employed against her: She tricks him into signing their divorce papers and then uses his own revolver to extricate her airplane ticket to the United States from him. Thus Weili grows from a marginalized girl with no self-esteem and few options into a woman who chooses which child to bear, which man to marry, and who empowers herself by guile and gun to realize her choice.

Other women characters in the book show a corollary development either in empowerment or in solidarity. For example, Peanut, Weili's cousin, who had been married to a homosexual by her unwitting family, empowers herself by deserting him and joining a group of women revolutionaries. Weili's somewhat obtuse confidante Hulan ("Helen"), who is initially convinced of the supreme value of marriage and thus betrays Weili's first attempt to run away from Wen Fu, later shows her solidarity with Weili by helping her hold up Wen Fu and effect her final escape.

It ought to be said that *The Kitchen God's Wife* is not simply a male-bashing book. Not all men are ogres like Wen Fu, though the male-dominated structure of Chinese society is unambiguously shown to be in crying need of reform. One example of a male chauvinist who undergoes a radical change is Jiaguo, Hulan's husband and a fellow pilot of Wen Fu. Jiaguo had originally seduced, impregnated, and abandoned Hulan's sister; when that wretched woman dies in childbirth after a beating from Jiaguo, she curses him. To propitiate her spirit, Jiaguo turns over a new leaf, marries Hulan, treats her with consideration, and even mortifies his sensuality by remaining celibate with her (somewhat to Hulan's chagrin). Then there is the model of the Chinese-American male in the character of Jimmy Louie, Weili's second husband: He is charming, adoring, and compassionate, attractive to many women but devoted only to one, and he makes a loving home for Weili and their children in Fresno, California: Indeed, as Wen Fu represents the pits of male viciousness, so does Jimmy Louie mirror the peak of male virtue.

Into this account of Weili's sorrows, Amy Tan seems to have infused several tantalizing epic archetypes. For example, Weili's narrative, like that of Homer's Odysseus, is one about suffering borne during a lengthy journey undertaken during times of war. Odysseus' arena is the Mediterranean during the Trojan War. Weili's odyssey occurs during the Japanese invasion of China, and she flees the breadth of that country from Shanghai through Hangchow, Nanking, and Wuchang to Kunming and back. In an interesting allusion to Homeric archetype, the one-eyed Wen Fu can be regarded as Tan's equivalent of the Hellenic cyclops. (Is it entirely accidental that Weili's oldest friend is nicknamed "Helen"?) Odysseus journeys to Hades during his voyage; Weili also experiences a metaphorical death and rebirth on her way to Kunming when she traverses a dangerous fog-bound mountain road, at the end of which she comments: "We were like people who had truly died and come back." Living in a polytheistic culture, the protagonists of both Tan's and Homer's works experience their adventures under the auspices of female deities: Pallas Athena in Homer's case, the kitchen god's wife in Tan's. The beginning of Tan's novel also resembles the beginning of Homer's epic; both authors initiate their action through the rather slow-moving narrative of a child searching for an exciting parent. In Pearl's instance it is a search to understand her much-traveled mother, in Telemachus' a search to ascertain the fate of his long-voyaging father. Both works also conclude on their protagonists' reestablishment of hearth and home—one in his original kingdom of Ithaca, the other in her new world of California. Such parallels, fortuitous or not, point up the universal qualities and broad appeal of the experiences about which Tan writes.

Tan's novel will be especially engaging for readers with an interest in feminist, ethnic, or immigrant issues, yet it also raises larger human concerns about fundamental decencies and repressive societal structures. In sum, *The Kitchen God's Wife* serves up good reading; it entertains with empathetic characters, lively incidents, and a labyrinthine plot, and it elevates with unambiguous moral indignation against villains, unreserved admiration for heroines.

C. L. Chua

Sources for Further Study

Chicago Tribune. June 9, 1991, XIV, p. 1.
Library Journal. CXVI, June 1, 1991, p. 198.
Los Angeles Times Book Review. June 16, 1991, p. 2.
The New York Times Book Review. XCVI, June 16, 1991, p. 9.
Newsweek. CXVII, June 24, 1991, p. 63.
Publishers Weekly. CCXXXVIII, April 12, 1991, p. 45.

Time. CXXXVII, June 3, 1991, p. 67.
The Times Literary Supplement. July 5, 1991, p. 20.
The Wall Street Journal. June 17, 1991, p. A8.
The Washington Post Book World. XXI, June 16, 1991, p. 1.

THE LAST LEOPARD
A Life of Giuseppe di Lampedusa

Author: David Gilmour (1952-   )
Publisher: Pantheon Books (New York). Illustrated. 223 pp. $22.00
Type of work: Literary biography
Time: 1896-1957
Locale: Sicily

This study of Sicily's most famous twentieth century author presents the life of Giuseppe di Lampedusa against the background of his partly autobiographical masterpiece and only novel, Il Gattopardo

> *Principal personages:*
> GIUSEPPE TOMASI DI LAMPEDUSA, the subject of the biography and the last of a Sicilian family
> BEATRICE MASTROGIOVANNI TASCA E FILANGERI DI CUTÒ, his mother, Duchess of Palma, later Princess of Lampedusa
> ALESSANDRA ("LICY") WOLFF TOMASI DI LAMPEDUSA, his Latvian wife and literary executrix
> LUCIO PICCOLO, his cousin, a Sicilian poet
> GIOACCHINO ("GIÒ") LANZA TOMASI, Giuseppe di Lampedusa's adopted son and heir

Imagine a childhood of fading privilege, an adulthood of shattered glory, and final years of almost-realized fame; this, in essence, was the tragedy of Sicily's most brilliant author, Giuseppe Tomasi di Lampedusa, Prince of Lampedusa, Duke of Palma. He died in 1957, impoverished and almost unknown, immediately before publication of *Il Gattopardo* (*The Leopard*, 1957), which made him, posthumously, Sicily's most famous twentieth century author. David Gilmour's study *The Last Leopard: A Life of Giuseppe di Lampedusa* is a rich evocation of this brilliant man against the backdrop of Don Fabrizio, the fictive protagonist of *The Leopard*, who combines the glory, brilliance, and ultimate tragedy of the whole Lampedusa line.

Giuseppe was born amid the palaces that provide the scenes of his novel. As a nobleman he was trained to do nothing, and like Don Fabrizio he watched as history, war, and probate eroded and ultimately took his family's wealth, lands, and titles. Like Don Fabrizio, Giuseppe watched with detached interest, realizing like the hero of his novel that he was caught between the demise of feudal aristocracy and the emergence of popular politics. Appropriately, his wife, Alessandra ("Licy") Wolff Tomasi di Lampedusa, was herself of Latvian nobility. She, too, felt historically displaced when her country was absorbed by the Soviet Union and Stormsee, the Latvian estate in which she literally reigned, became a Russian agricultural school. What their marriage lacked in passion it more than supplied in mutual sympathy.

Licy found some consolation in her work; she was a Freudian psychologist who was able to practice her profession more easily after World War II, when she moved permanently to Palermo and lived with Giuseppe on the Via Buttera. Giuseppe, on the other hand, was a brilliant but uncredentialed student of literature and history.

He knew more about British, French, Italian, and Russian literature than many professors; he spoke these languages fluently, and added Spanish a decade before his death. He knew European history intimately and knew the history of Sicily as one might know childhood nursery rhymes. Even so, an uncredentialed expert is no expert in the modern world, and so Giuseppe's brilliance served his family and close friends alone. Had Giuseppe finished one of the abortive attempts he made at acquiring a university degree, it probably would have made little difference in his life. Though he would give private lessons in the years after the war, it would never have suited his station to have taught under the aegis of an institution—or for pay.

Gilmour's subject is thus a difficult one; unlike most lives, that of Lampedusa contracts rather than expands as it proceeds. Just as Lampedusa is about to achieve the recognition he should have had much earlier in life, he dies. The reader is left with a life of diminishing returns and no triumphs. Lampedusa was an undistinguished soldier in World War I, was discharged after a few months of service in World War II, and seldom traveled farther than the outskirts of Palermo after 1946. A reader of Gilmour's study might thus ask how one can make a life, in which essentially nothing has happened, interesting. Even so, Gilmour does this, for Lampedusa's life was wedded to Sicily as firmly as that of Don Fabrizio was, and the actual as well as the fictive life contain the greatness of tragedy.

Extinction of the Lampedusas proceeded irreversibly from the abolition of feudalism in 1812. Changes in the system of primogeniture resulted in subdivision of their estates, and the Lampedusa family's penchant for indifference to the rapidly changing social atmosphere hastened its fall. When Giuseppe's great-grandfather died intestate in 1885, a lengthy court battle ensued for the Lampedusa properties. These houses and lands, which dotted Sicily and Tuscany and included an island off the Sicilian coast, were the prizes in a struggle that would not end until after World War II. By that time, the war had accomplished what even the enormous legal costs of nearly seventy-five years had not managed: Bombed-out shells of once-grand houses complemented the long-unworked fields amid which they stood.

Having salvaged some furniture and the majority of his library, Lampedusa retired to an unfashionable section of Palermo and began to contemplate his youth and its unfulfilled promise. He read Marcel Proust and Stendhal, appreciating the subtlety of both and decrying what he came to consider the melodramatic obviousness of twentieth century Italian literature. Lampedusa developed a thesis, primarily as a result of reading French literature, that its delicacy and inferential character were preferable to Italian "heaviness," by which he meant everything from the allegory of Dante Alighieri to the *verismo* of Giovanni Verga. Lampedusa would contend that the emergence of Italian opera, from that of Claudio Monteverdi to that of Giuseppe Verdi, marked out a downward course that all Italian art would follow. For this reason Lampedusa disliked opera, particularly Italian opera; consequently, many who knew him before publication of his single masterpiece thought him un-Italian. It is paradoxical, then, that *The Leopard* is itself the most singularly Italian and specifically Sicilian evocation of life published since the works of Verga.

The two most important women in Lampedusa's life were his mother, Beatrice, and his wife. In many ways they were alike, though one was Palermettan, the other Latvian. Both were aristocrats to the bone and aristocrats in the old style. They expected much of the world and were confident that their class was essential to it. When, for example, her son was assigned artillery duty on a particularly dangerous part of the front, Beatrice managed to have him reassigned behind the lines. This happened in World War I, though it is a measure of Lampedusa family influence that Giuseppe managed to satisfy most of his World War II military obligation as a Red Cross liaison and on the island of Sicily.

Just as Beatrice watched over Lampedusa in the first half of his life, so Licy did in the second. Theirs was a marriage in most ways based on mutual need and intellectual sympathy rather than passionate love. Lampedusa interested Licy with his talk of literature and knowledge of history; they had first met in Italy, though Lampedusa had visited her at her Latvian estate several times in the years before their marriage. Licy was more than a decade older than Lampedusa, but she was at the time trapped in a loveless marriage to a man who proved to be homosexual. All this happened in the years immediately preceding World War II, and after several urgent appeals to his mother, the forty-two-year-old Lampedusa received her permission to marry.

Licy's wealth might have saved the Palermo Lampedusas, but the German invasion of Latvia followed by the Russian counterinvasion and seizure of Stormsee sealed Licy's fate. The couple had lived apart for the first years of the war, Licy in Riga, Latvia, and Lampedusa in Palermo, but with her wealth gone Licy had no alternative but to join her husband on Sicily. Beatrice, who had retired to a barely habitable wing of her bombed-out home, died soon after her daughter-in-law's arrival, and Licy became the primary influence on Lampedusa's life.

Fortunately, Licy was a psychologist, and she was able to practice her profession much more easily in urban Palermo than in rural Stormsee. She treated her patients in the couple's home on the Via Buttera and encouraged Lampedusa to give private tutorials to younger cousins on virtually the entire corpus of European literature. Lampedusa wrote thousands of pages of notes for these tutorials, and the close reading he had to do coupled with the relative ease with which he wrote convinced him in the final years of his life that creative writing was his missed vocation. He thus began, in the early 1950's, to gather material for what would in 1957 be published as *The Leopard*, a novel whose English title derives from the Lampedusa family crest but whose Italian title, *Il Gattopardo* (the panther), symbolizes the exotic nature of the once-powerful Sicilian aristocracy.

Another influence on the aspiring but aging author was his cousin Lucio Piccolo. Well into his own middle age, Piccolo successfully published a small book of verse, reflections on modern Sicily, but in a style that more closely resembled that of French Symbolists such as Stéphane Mallarmé or Charles Baudelaire than that of any Italian contemporary. Lampedusa was convinced that his own perceptions were as valid as those of his younger cousin, and he came to consider that writing *The Leopard* was the only means of preserving ideas that, as the very last of the Sicilian Lampedusas and one of the last Sicilian nobles, would otherwise die with him.

The folkloric nature of *The Leopard* might account for what its first reviewers saw as its disconnectedness; yet this apparent incoherence is actually its most distinctive feature. The parts of the novel come together as the perceptions of Don Fabrizio. Though Lampedusa was hardly a James Joyce, it is Don Fabrizio's ability to discern a pattern in the apparently unrelated, seemingly insignificant experiences of life that a reader of *The Leopard* most admires. What might have been merely a work of regionalist fiction becomes a novel of transcendent human experience. In his ability to achieve this, Lampedusa approaches Fyodor Dostoevski.

Gioacchino ("Gio") Lanza, Lampedusa's great-nephew, recognized this ability to synthesize the disparate elements of history, life, and literature. He was a faithful student of Lampedusa's tutorials and encouraged him to write. Gio was the son Lampedusa had never had and the heir he wished to have. Thus, despite the fact that Gio was well into his twenties and that his parents were quite alive, Lampedusa legally adopted him as his son. Gio's natural parents were nonplussed, as one might imagine, but the adoption took place in the year before Lampedusa's death, when he was severely ill with the cancer that would ultimately take his life. No monetary wealth of any significance and no property of any value were involved; what was important was the Lampedusa name and a suitable heir.

Ironically, though not surprisingly when one considers the pattern that informed Lampedusa's life, Licy signed a publication agreement for *The Leopard* that yielded only meager royalties for this international bestseller. Even though Lampedusa did not survive to enjoy his success, he left the world a legacy, and that, after all, was what he most desired.

Robert J. Forman

Sources for Further Study

Kirkus Reviews. LIX, June 15, 1991, p. 768.
Library Journal. CXVI, August, 1991, p. 100.
Los Angeles Times Book Review. August 18, 1991, p. 1.
The New Republic. CCV, December 9, 1991, p. 36.
New Statesman and Society. I, November 18, 1988, p. 41.
The New York Review of Books. XXXVIII, December 5, 1991, p. 3.
The New York Times. August 21, 1991, p. C16.
Publishers Weekly. CCXXXVIII, June 21, 1991, p. 46.
The Spectator. CCLXI, November 26, 1988, p. 42.
The Washington Post Book World. XXI, August 18, 1991, p. 8.

THE LETTERS OF D. H. LAWRENCE
Volume VI: March 1927-November 1928

Author: D. H. Lawrence (1885-1930)
Edited, with an introduction, by James T. Boulton and Margaret H. Boulton, with Gerald M. Lacy
Publisher: Cambridge University Press (New York). Illustrated. 645 pp. $79.50
Type of work: Letters
Time: March 22, 1927-November 14, 1928
Locale: Villa Mirenda, near Florence, Italy; Austria; Germany; Switzerland; and Ile de Port-Cros, near Toulon, France

The sixth volume of a new scholarly edition of D. H. Lawrence's letters, covering a period of reduced travel caused by the author's illness and the private publication of his most notorious novel, Lady Chatterley's Lover

The 768 letters in this volume bring to 4,749 the total published in the new Cambridge University Press edition of D. H. Lawrence's correspondence. When the seventh and final volume appears, more than 5,600 letters will be available, almost half of which were previously unpublished. Like its predecessors, volume 6 is handsomely produced and graced by such useful editorial aids as a detailed chronology, maps, period photographs, notes on obscure references and foreign phrases, an excellent introduction, and a carefully prepared index. Indispensable to scholars, this edition will only enhance Lawrence's reputation as one of the premier letter writers in English literature.

A persistent theme in Lawrence's life since about 1915, when he and his wife Frieda were subjected to rabid xenophobia and censorship during World War 1 in England, was his ceaseless search for a true home. Preceding volumes followed the Lawrences around the globe after their bitter severance from England in 1919, with significant stays in Sicily, Australia, Old and New Mexico, and various spots in Italy. A sort of recurrent rhythm was apparent in these earlier letters, beginning with Lawrence's disappointment in and rejection of the familiar locale, his longing for a vitalist paradise in a place remote from the world's urban centers, the initial impressions of the actual place upon arrival, inevitable disillusionment, an attempt to adjust to and accommodate the anomalous elements, renewed enthusiasm, disappointment and frustration, and the repetition of the cycle as the next locale emerged as the new source of yearning. This restless, open-ended search was the unifying force not only of the letters but also of Lawrence's postwar fiction in such works as *Kangaroo* (1923), *St. Mawr: Together with the Princess* (1925), and *The Plumed Serpent* (1926).

A change is evident in the period covered by this volume. Although Lawrence still restlessly yearned for a spiritual home and periodically proposed trips to such far-flung spots as India, China, Egypt, and Ireland, as well as return visits to his beloved mountain ranch in New Mexico, he was in fact no longer able to pursue his dream through his travels. In the twenty-one months covered in volume 6, he never left Europe; nor did he even visit his homeland. More than half of the time was spent in the Villa Mirenda, outside Florence, where the Lawrences rented a home for slightly more than two years. Such travels as there were—visits to Germany, Austria, and Switzerland—were comparatively brief and uneventful.

Lawrence's declining health was largely responsible for this reduced orbit of movement. From childhood on, he suffered from a variety of respiratory ailments, and after a pulmonary hemorrhage nearly killed him in Mexico in 1925, he was diagnosed as tubercular and given a year or two to live. (He would live, it turned out, for another five years, dying of tuberculosis in March, 1930.) A second hemorrhage confined him to bed at the Villa Mirenda for most of July, 1927. His fragile condition clearly ruled out strenuous activities. Still, Lawrence sought a salubrious climate and tried, whenever possible, to pass the winters in sunny locales and summers in the mountains. Preoccupied with his health, yet desperately refusing to admit the severity of his disease, he was prone to extreme mood swings. He was inclined to blame his volatile temperament on the "money-grubbing" values of the day, or the puritanism of the censors, or the rigors of the climate, or a malevolent "spirit of place," or even male menopause. "I think men have perhaps a greater 'change of life' in the psyche, even than women. . . . It's often unpleasant, but the only thing is to let it go on and accept the differences and let go the old." These letters make clear the extent to which Lawrence's quest itself was conditioned by the precariousness of his health: "I feel a bit like Noah's dove who has lost the ark and doesn't see any sign of an olive bough—and is getting a bit weary on the wing."

Notwithstanding his weariness, Lawrence managed to rally his energies sufficiently to produce a considerable amount of writing. This brief period saw the publication of *Mornings in Mexico* (1927), *The Woman Who Rode Away and Other Stories* (1928), *Lady Chatterley's Lover* (1928), dozens of journalistic pieces, and a fine short story, "The Man Who Loved Islands." He also wrote the travel sketches published posthumously as *Etruscan Places* (1932) and produced a number of paintings later exhibited at the Warren Gallery in London (until they were seized by censorious authorities). The letters offer much useful information about the creation and the sale of these works.

The most important of these creative efforts is the "case" of *Lady Chatterley's Lover*, clearly the centerpiece of this volume. Lawrence wrote three different versions of the novel at the Villa Mirenda between October, 1926, and March, 1928. One reason he rewrote rather than merely revised for publication was his fear, which proved well founded, that the novel would be seen as pornographic. He insisted that it was "not really improper—I always labour at the same thing, to make the sex relation valid and precious, instead of shameful. And the novel is the furthest I've gone. To me it is beautiful and tender and frail as the naked self is. . . ." That he realized the contemporary readership was unprepared for his "frankly phallic" novel is amusingly apparent in the pains he took to keep his own sisters and his mother-in-law from being aware of the book. That he nevertheless believed that the work should be available to the open-minded is equally apparent in the ambitious campaign he waged to get it published despite heavy odds. First, he tried to prepare expurgated versions for his English and American publishers, Martin Secker and Alfred A.

Knopf, respectively. When this attempt failed (understandably, he found himself unable to cut what he saw as "valid and precious"), he arranged for a private printing of one thousand copies to be made available for sale by subscriptions through the mail. Typesetting and proofreading were complicated by the fact that the Florentine printers knew little or no English; progress was delayed when it was discovered that there was enough type for only half the novel to be set at a time. Meanwhile, Lawrence personally engaged in promoting sales by writing potential customers around the world and, in England and America, by seeking proxies among friends willing to search for more subscribers. The intrigue involved in all of this makes for entertaining reading, and the results in terms of subscriptions sold (particularly in England) were impressive. In America the postal service was more vigilant and began to confiscate most copies at the port of entry. Not for another three decades could the novel be legally obtained in the United States and Great Britain.

Lawrence was at first excited by the sensation caused by his daring "campaign" and by the appearance of the novel itself, which "exploded like a bomb amongst most of [his] English friends, and they're still suffering from shell-shock." His good friend and fellow writer Richard Aldington deemed the novel "a feather in the cap of the 20th Century." One early reviewer wrote that Lawrence "has carried realism to a pitch seldom aspired to in the whole history of literature. And the result is a fine novel, bold and stark." More typical, unfortunately, was the reviewer who found the novel "one of the most filthy and abominable ever written . . . an outrage on decency," and the one who went so far as to conclude that *Lady Chatterley's Lover* was "the most evil outpouring that has ever besmirched the literature of our country." Such a reception, of course, only confirmed Lawrence's expectations, a sad recurrence of the sort of reaction he had experienced in 1915 after the publication of *The Rainbow*. Yet his determination remained unwavering: "I believe in the living extending consciousness of man. I believe the consciousness of man has now to embrace the emotions and passions of sex, and the deep effects of human physical contact. This is the glimmering edge of our awareness and our field of understanding, in the endless business of knowing ourselves. And no censor must or shall or even can really interfere."

As this passage suggests, Lawrence's ill health and inability to travel far from the Villa Mirenda did not appreciably diminish his capacity for independent thought and striking expression. His letters, like his fiction, persistently champion what he called "the phallic consciousness, as against the irritable cerebral consciousness we're afflicted with." By responding to "our real animal nature, which we still bear within us," he believed that "we must battle and fight against the world of the 'pure idea' . . . and of the machine." To the psychoanalyst Trigant Burrow, he wrote that the fundamental modern spiritual ailment derives from the frustration of the "societal instinct," the need for meaningful and lasting human relations; the sense of being essentially cut off, homeless, persona non grata, was after all a primary strain in Lawrence's own life and career. During a period in which the alienated masses of Italy, Germany, Spain, and elsewhere were susceptible to coercion by charismatic leaders who preyed on their feelings of victimization, it is tonic to find Lawrence recognizing, as early as March, 1928, that Fascism represented a "false power forced against life." Leadership, he wrote to Rolf Gardiner, must be "based on the reciprocity of tenderness," for the "reciprocity of power is obsolete." In letters to Charles Wilson, known as the "pitman poet," he argued that the solution to the problems of disenfranchised workers was not to be found in ideologies of the right or left or in material improvements but in "the deepening and widening consciousness." This is what he was after in his art, even as his illness made it increasingly difficult for him to pursue otherwise: "the new relationship [which] will be some sort of tenderness, sensitive, between men and men and men and women, and not the one up one down, lead on I follow . . . sort of business."

The difficulties inherent in this quest for a new kind of relationship—societal as well as personal and marital—are abundantly present in these letters. Lawrence's disagreements with old friends and disciples such as Dorothy Brett, Mabel Dodge Luhan, and John Middleton Murry are much in evidence, as are his difficult dealings with publishers, agents, and critics. There are scores of vivid and revealing references to other writers such as Norman Douglas ("still thinking of Jerusalem and preferring Chianti"); Edward Compton Mackenzie ("vain, shallow, theatrical, and somewhat ridiculous"); Aldous Huxley ("so serious and professorial . . . [with] dry-mindedness and underneath social morality"); and James Joyce (*Finnegans Wake* was "just stewed-up fragments of quotation in the sauce of a would-be dirty mind. Such effort! Such exertion!"). Lawrence is often irritating but seldom dull or trivial. These letters allow one to see, as it were in action, the many sides of the complex and compelling character of a man often considered the most significant English novelist of the twentieth century.

Ronald G. Walker

Sources for Further Study

The Guardian. August 29, 1991, p. 21.
Guardian Weekly. CXLV, September 15, 1991, p. 28.
London Review of Books. XIII, December 5, 1991, p. 14.
The New York Review of Books. February 13, 1992, p. 27.
The Times Literary Supplement. September 13, 1991, p. 12.

THE LETTERS OF RUDYARD KIPLING
Volume I: 1872-89
Volume II: 1890-99

Author: Rudyard Kipling (1865-1936)
Edited, with an introduction, by Thomas Pinney
Publisher: University of Iowa Press (Iowa City). Illustrated. 2 volumes. Volume I: 386 pp. $42.50; Volume II: 390 pp. $42.50
Type of work: Letters
Time: December, 1872-December, 1889; January, 1890-December, 1899
Locale: London and other locations in England; Lahore, Allahabad, Simla, and other locations in the Punjab, India; San Francisco and other locations in the United States; Toronto, Canada

Issued as a two-volume set initiating an ongoing series, the early letters of Kipling reveal a young writer of rare energy, exuberance, and curiosity emerging from relative obscurity to fame on two continents

Thomas Pinney's meticulous edition of the Kipling letters is a welcome addition to previously published and ongoing collections of letters by other eminent Edwardians, among them Joseph Conrad, E. M. Forster, George Bernard Shaw, and William Butler Yeats. In fact, the Kipling collection has appeared after the publication of notable Georgian letters, such as editions for James Joyce, D. H. Lawrence, C. S. Lewis, Katherine Mansfield, and Virginia Woolf.

One reason for the tardy publication of Kipling's letters is that his correspondents were widely scattered across at least three continents. To assemble the collection from libraries and private holdings throughout the Indian subcontinent, Great Britain, and North America must have been a formidable task, even in the age of photocopies and fax machines. Another reason is that Kipling himself acted to impede future publication of many sensitive epistles. Although most of the writer's correspondents, according to Pinney, kept his letters—at least after he became a prominent figure in the early 1890's—Kipling destroyed numerous personal letters. After his father died in 1911, Kipling "indulged in an orgy of burning" half a century of the family papers. His sister once testified to what she called "the frenzy of burning any letters or papers connected with his youth." Later, Kipling destroyed his letters to his uncle, Sir Edward Burne-Jones, at least the "saucy ones," according to Sir Sidney Cockerell; and he regularly burned most of the letters sent to him. We have no way of knowing whether letters by such notables as Mark Twain, Thomas Hardy, Robert Louis Stevenson, Henry James, or Theodore Roosevelt were consigned to the flames; but we know for certain that Kipling refused requests from biographers for letters and, according to Pinney, "each such request must have reminded him that the only real protection against such curiosity was to destroy the material desired." Finally, Pinney notes with regret that Mrs. Kipling was, "if anything, an even more dedicated destroyer than her husband." As a result, Kipling's output of letters so far reveals little intimate information. Biographers of Kipling will have to read between guarded lines of his correspondence—or seek elsewhere, in the revelations of contemporaries—for a persuasive psychological portrait of his very private character.

Nevertheless, Pinney has had a vast store of surviving letters from which to draw his edition. He has had "in hand the texts of about 6300 letters in manuscript, copy, or printed form, drawing from 138 collections, public and private, and from 135 printed sources." Immense though this collection is, it still is dwarfed by Shaw's lifetime production of 250,000 letters and postcards. Of course, Shaw rarely if ever burned his letters, either for reasons of misguided shame or reticence. Moreover, to give Kipling his due, his India letters might well have smacked of the little indecencies of the barracks-room or newspaper office. Fortunately, his "saucy" production escaped the fate of another adventurer in the Punjab, Sir Richard Francis Burton, whose wife probably destroyed a far more substantial posthumous legacy. (Curiously, Kipling was acquainted with Isabella Burton, and in his letter of October 26, 1887, he describes her as "the wittiest woman in India" and proposes to dedicate his 1888 volume *Plain Tales from the Hills* to her.)

Allowing for Kipling's reticence—perhaps hypersensitivity—in the direction of self-portraiture, his letters reveal him in an extraordinarily vivid light. On the positive side, the collection so far will certainly elevate Kipling's literary standing among critics, who tend to view him from an anticolonialist stance as reactionary, sentimental, or simplistic. As his letters prove, Kipling was by no means a one-dimensional figure. Witty, inventive, curious, exuberant, he is nearly always an entertaining writer. Readers might have expected as much. What they are also likely to discover from the letters is a quality of shrewdness, playfulness, sharpness of satirical insight, and generally a fund of good common sense. The total impression of Kipling that one receives in that of a serious, not merely clever, writer, an artist continually experimenting with words as tools of his craft, whether in jotting down extemporaneous (often doggerel) verse or sharpening his vision to render concrete his descriptions of persons, places, and events.

On the other hand, Kipling's letters will support the negative judgments made by some of the writer's detractors. Few letters indicate the kind of anguished introspection typical of his contemporary Conrad, who reviewed colonialism in its worst aspect. Prior to the 1890's, Kipling seemed indifferent to the cause of British imperialism, even to the point of satirizing the ineptitude of administrators. As his fame spread following the publication of the complete English edition of "Indian Railway Library" stories (1890), *The Light That Failed* (1890), and *Barrack-Room Ballads* (1892), he could write with amusement (or irony) how he himself had become in the public mind the image of imperialism: "What the deuce is an 'Imperial' photograph? The committee informs me I've got to be photoed that way and—I don't know how" (letter to Robert Underwood Johnson, November 4, 1895). Kipling then sketched a caricature of himself wearing a papal tiara, and concluded: "Something like this?"

Kipling's detractors will also find in the letters evidence that reveals his limited emotional range. To be sure, many letters are affectionate, frank, and outgoing, especially those to Edmonia Hill and later to Louisa Baldwin. Yet taken as a whole,

Kipling's letters so far lack a core of anger, romantic passion, or eroticism. There are no letters—perhaps none escaped destruction—to Florence Violet Garrard, to whom he became engaged in the summer of 1880, and only six addressed to Caroline Taylor, to whom he became engaged in 1889. Surprisingly, there are no letters at all to Caroline Balestier (whom he married January 18, 1892), from the time he met her, perhaps in November, 1890, until the completion of volume 2, 1899. A sample of Kipling's tepid ardor is his letter to Caroline Taylor (December 9, 1889), in which he lectures her soberly on his religious credo: "I believe after having seen and studied eight or nine creeds in Justification by work rather than faith, and most assuredly do I believe in retribution both here and hereafter for wrong doing as I believe in a reward, here and hereafter for obedience to the Law." He continues his letter to his fiancée: "There! You have got from me what no living soul has ever done before," and later concludes his letter, "Never mind what I was going to say you shall hear it next week. But I love you—I love you and again I love you. Good night dear one and bless your dear heart."

Awkward using the prose of romantic confession, Kipling otherwise delights in less passionate but frank and openhearted discourse. In the same letter he remarks: "In the first place I am not a poet and never shall be—but only a writer who varies fiction with verse." In many letters Kipling playfully deprecates his prospects or his talents. To Walter Besant, whose *All in a Garden Fair* (1883) he much admired as an inspiration for his own life, he writes: "Mr. Lang was wrong. I am not young—only 'an old man spotted with decaying youth' for I have seven years of Indian journalism behind me and they leave one neither happy nor hopeful" (November 20, 1889). To John Addington Symonds he denigrates his drawing skills: "It is good to think that you liked some of the stories. Would that I could show you the line and sepia illustrations for *In Black and White* drawn by my father who being an artist knows how to draw the natives he has lived among for a quarter of a century and having bred me knows exactly what my pen's driving at better than all the world" (December 9, 1889). Finally, to William Ernest Henley he writes: "Yes, men tell me I am young in this country but I have put seven years of India behind me and they do not make a man younger or more cheerful" (January 31, 1890). To this bluff, unsentimental writer he concludes his letter with masculine bravado: "At present I am divided between the broken top-joint of my rod, and a reel that won't croon properly. Literature is a weariness of the flesh—all books are wicked and the only real thing in the world is a four pound bass coming up with the tide at the mouth of the Torridge, my hook in the right hand top angle of his mouth."

Yet most of Kipling's letters develop quite a different, more deeply respectful attitude toward literature. Often he writes with admiration about books and writers. After he has exchanged enough letters with Henley to appreciate his correspondent's sturdy moral nature, he writes unaffectedly: "In good seriousness I am doing better than writing with my good right hand. I am throwing away what I have written with both as it used to be in the old days and it's grateful and comforting. Chiefly—and this I would impress upon you—I am sitting still and quiet, for the good of my soul"

(December 3-4, 1893). After an unidentified woman has written sentiments in his praise at the expense of reproving Henry James, Kipling responds: "But why object so fiercely to Henry James? He's by way of being a personal friend of mine and I fancy that he has given me a very pretty send off in the collected edition which I gather you have been reading" (April 30, 1891). As further evidence of his serious concern for writing as an art form, he condemns vulgarians who have requested his views on an American laureateship: "Somehow they can, by merely writing about it, knock all the beauty, honour, wit, wisdom and reverence out of anything in the world and leave behind only the smell of an overheated hotel ante-room, or of a hollow tooth" (to Henley, January 18-19, 1893). And to Charles Eliot Norton he writes: "I have the Arnold letters. Folks say they are dull but that's absurd. It's the fine quality of that expert razor never losing its edge as it goes through the board school grindstone that makes me take off my hat to it" (January 8, 1896).

Always generous in his praise of writers, including then-aspiring writers (see his letter to Sarah Orne Jewett, January 1897), Kipling turns a considerate ear as well to a host of lesser people, including cranks, who fuss over illnesses and petty grievances. To Mrs. Thomas Hardy he writes: "I am glad to hear your ankle is better. One can get such very unpleasant accidents from and off and under a bicycle—as I have found out to my cost" (November 4, 1897). Courteously, he offers Irving Bacheller his regrets over a requested interview: "I can only regret that it is impossible for me to see my way to any sort of interview. Of course anything that Mr. Parker would do would be, I know, entirely dignified and inoffensive but the fact of my being once interviewed would lead to all sorts of complications from other quarters; and I could not in reason refuse after I had once broken the rule which I find secures my time to myself" (January 5, 1896). Pinney is right in seeing Kipling's forbearance toward bores as a sign of his people-pleasing disposition. Yet beyond a desire to please, the writer usually shows a kindly, sensitive, humane core sometimes obscured by his bluff-hearty manner. Readers will come to like Kipling the man, in spite of his emotional reticence and occasional pomposity, in spite of his conventional late-Victorian morality and his political conservatism, even in spite of his fatuities. Kipling loved his life, and his exuberance is contagious.

Leslie B. Mittleman

Sources for Further Study

The Atlantic. CCLXVII, May, 1991, p. 123.
Choice. XXVIII, June, 1991, p. 1639.
London Review of Books. XIII, March 21, 1991, p. 13.
Los Angeles Times Book Review. March 31, 1991, p. 4.
The Observer. December 2, 1990, p. 65.
The Spectator. CCLXVI, February 16, 1991, p. 29.

The Times Literary Supplement. December 21, 1990, p. 1367.
University Press Book News. III, June, 1991, p. 34.
The Virginia Quarterly Review. LXVII, Summer, 1991, p. 559.
Washington Times. February 25, 1991, p. D5.

A LIFE OF KENNETH REXROTH

Author: Linda Hamalian (1950-   )
Publisher: W. W. Norton (New York). Illustrated. 444 pp. $25.00
Type of work: Literary biography
Time: 1905-1982
Locale: Chicago, San Francisco, Santa Barbara

An authoritative and judicious life of an important American poet, noteworthy for his pivotal role in the San Francisco literary renaissance, for his expert blending of Eastern and Western elements in his poetry (including translations), and the author, in Hamalian's opinion, of some of the best poems in the twentieth century

Principal personages:
KENNETH REXROTH, an influential poet, translator, and critic
DELIA REXROTH, Kenneth's mother, who imbued him with a love of literature and a desire to improve himself
CHARLES REXROTH, Kenneth's father, handsome, romantic, and a ladies' man
ANDREE SCHAFER REXROTH, Kenneth's first wife, a painter of great intensity, subject to severe epileptic fits which shortened her life
MARIE KASS REXROTH, Kenneth's second wife, a trained nurse and administrator, who supported and catered to Rexroth's whims
MARTHE LARSEN REXROTH, Kenneth's third wife, a graduate student who tried to cope with Rexroth's desires as secretary, lover, and childbearer
MARY REXROTH, the daughter on whom Rexroth doted
KATHERINE REXROTH, the second daughter Rexroth tended to neglect
CAROL TINKER, Rexroth's "live-in secretary" and fourth wife who eased his final years
JAMES LAUGHLIN, Kenneth's lifelong friend and founder of New Directions, which published much of Rexroth's work

In the preface to her biography, Linda Hamalian admits that, meeting Kenneth Rexroth late in his career, she fell under his spell. She was attracted to his seasoned good looks, his charm, and his erudition, and she could imagine the thrill of having him address poems to her as he so often did to the women in his life. She also admits, however, that the Kenneth Rexroth she discovered in her research for the biography was far different from the one she imagined. Indeed, her biography is a compelling work precisely because she captures both the lure of his poetic persona and the reality of his everyday life.

Rexroth spent most of his early years in Chicago, struggling to cope with the early death of his mother. He was eleven years old when she died, and she had already (knowing she would die) instilled in her son a code of independence and a love of literature. On the one hand, Rexroth was a tough kid, the model for one of James T. Farrell's characters in his great trilogy, *Studs Lonigan* (1932-1935), an epic of Chicago's rough Irish immigrant neighborhoods. On the other hand, Rexroth kept seeking a replacement for his mother, an image of woman as nurturer of the male ego. So needy was Rexroth in this respect that his early relationships with women often fizzled quickly as they backed away from a young man who demanded so much of them in the way of psychic support.

Charles Rexroth, Kenneth's father, was an alluring, romantic figure, but he was rarely up to the task of supporting his family or of providing his son with an image of a man who could stand without the props of female succor. While still a teenager, Kenneth became a socialist, harshly critical of what he saw as a capitalistic, exploitative, and violent system; however, he never seems to have seriously questioned his own sexism or realized just how much his prolific career depended upon the sacrifices of his women.

In the first half of the biography, Hamalian allows this aspect of Rexroth's character to tell itself, narrating incidents in which both his love of and exploitation of women is apparent without judging him in her own words. Gradually, as Rexroth's ill treatment of women comes to form a pattern and to be explicitly raised by the women he abuses, Hamalian allows herself to evaluate his conduct, using such phrases as "double standard" to convey Rexroth's hypocrisy. The evidence against him is so overwhelming at this point that the biographer's analysis seems overdue. Indeed, Hamalian should be commended for her restraint, for she exposes the worst in Rexroth without ever losing sight of the fine points in his character or of the value of his work.

There may be several reasons for Hamalian's tactful handling of Rexroth's sexism. His attitudes were typical of his time: Many men presumed that women should relinquish or at least scale back their own careers to further their husbands'. Then, too, in his first marriage to the artist Andree Schafer, Rexroth seems (momentarily) to have risen above his prejudices—not only respecting her talent as a painter but also trying to live the dream of equality fostered by the international socialist movement. Whereas many men might have fled the temperamental Andree and perhaps would have been undone by her severe epileptic seizures, Rexroth ministered to her in moments of crisis, learning how to massage her forehead and sometimes ward off her worst fits. The dissolution of their marriage seems to have had more to do with their powerful ambitions and conflicting characters than with Rexroth's attitudes toward women.

Although Rexroth remained a lifelong socialist, he soon became wary of the Communist Party and of Stalinists, in particular, for he clearly saw that they were manipulated by Moscow and had little interest in developing an indigenous socialism. Rexroth was as fearless in attacking them as he was in opposing the worst excesses of capitalism. Similarly, he did not hesitate to attack poets such as T. S. Eliot and Ezra Pound both for their politics and for their poetics, favoring the down-to-earth, concrete verse forms of William Carlos Williams and Carl Sandburg.

As Hamalian charts the development of Rexroth's poetic career, she quotes short passages from his best work conveying the charm of both the poet and the man. These gems embedded in the narrative give the biography and its quiet prose a kind of glitter, embellishing Hamalian's sober estimates with Rexroth's own lyrical style. The only difficulty with such an approach is that the biographer cannot demonstrate just how great a poet Rexroth was. Instead, flashes of brilliance are provided, inviting the reader to turn to Rexroth's work in extenso. There is really no remedy for this problem; quoting at length from the poet's work in the narrative would be disruptive—unless the biographer provides (perhaps in a separate chapter) a set piece that explores in detail the poet's accomplishments.

Rexroth rarely held a full-time job. During the war, however, he worked a full-time shift in a mental ward, fulfilling his obligations as a conscientious objector. Here, Rexroth was able to practice his principles, dealing gently with the most violent inmates, caring tenderly for them with rubdowns and hot baths and opposing those who would use violence to calm aggressive patients.

In his own life, Rexroth could not achieve a similar peace. His second wife, Marie, a trained nurse and successful hospital administrator, seems to have been the first woman Rexroth actually struck. It happened in the course of an argument, one of the many in which Rexroth accused Marie of not appreciating his poetry and of pursuing her own selfish interests. Marie's "selfish interests," as Hamalian documents, were precisely what allowed Rexroth to write poetry. He could not support himself and would not look for full-time jobs. What is more, there is ample evidence in Marie's letters and from her friends that she did value her husband's writing and that his complaints were often the peevish ravings of a spoiled, immature man.

By his middle forties, Rexroth had settled into a comfortable pattern of womanizing, which Marie disliked but tried to tolerate. With Rexroth issuing ultimatums to her that would have meant forsaking her career and having a child, Marie divorced him, but continued to associate with him—at times helping him and his third wife, Marthe, who bore Rexroth a child in opposition to his repeated requests that she have an abortion.

As a father, Rexroth proved to be attentive—particularly to his first child, Mary, whom he took on hikes in the mountains and taught to be independent. He spent less time on Katherine but sorely missed his children during his separations from Marthe. Manners and grooming were important to him, and his children always saw him at the table dressed in a jacket. He was finicky about his food and lent his home a formal, even ceremonial quality—at one point lighting a menorah on Friday nights even though he was not religious in any formal sense.

The marriage to Marthe was no more peaceful than the one to Marie. Indeed, both Rexroth's violence and his philandering seem to have increased. Yet Rexroth could not forgive Marthe or the poet she eventually fell in love with and seemed to think that he was the one who had been wronged and deceived. Like Marie, Marthe put up with enormous abuse from Rexroth, leaving him several times before making her final break with him.

Throughout his stormy marriages, Rexroth's reputation as a poet, critic, and promoter of the California literary scene grew. He became a public personality with a newspaper column and radio program. He developed as a performer, often reading his poetry to the accompaniment of jazz. Although neglected by the East Coast literary establishment, by his fifties he was the recipient of prestigious awards, including a Guggenheim fellowship that allowed him to travel in Europe and to write some of his best poetry and produce his acclaimed translations. A new generation of poets—including Lawrence Ferlinghetti, Allen Ginsberg, and Gary Snyder—came to Rexroth, seeking his advice and paying tribute. Rexroth often responded generously, though in later years he came to resent certain poets who had eclipsed him by winning a greater share of public attention and literary awards.

Always a vigorous sportsman—skier and mountain climber—Rexroth remained robust until the last five years of his life, when he was fortunate to attract Carol Tinker, one of the many young women who clustered around him. At this point, Rexroth's life had been made comfortable also by a teaching position in Santa Barbara and by various commissions. Indeed, throughout his career he had been singularly fortunate in having the support of James Laughlin, publisher of New Directions, who often lent the poet money and kept his work in print.

As he grew older, Rexroth's attitudes hardened. Used to being lionized, he found it difficult not to dominate every literary gathering. Always sensitive about his physical appearance (he would not wash dishes for fear of spoiling his carefully manicured hands), aging proved a trial for him, eased considerably by the indefatigable ministrations of Tinker, who became his fourth wife.

There is evidence (somewhat conflicting) that in his last ten years Rexroth did confront his complex attitudes toward women, for he produced a significant body of verse in women's voices, even perpetrating a hoax that he had translated a Japanese woman's poetry when in fact the poems were his own. Was Rexroth, for once, really trying to see things from the woman's point of view? Hamalian is not certain. He could just as easily have enjoyed the joke or thought of the poetry as a challenge to his imaginative powers as a poet. Yet there is no denying the amount of energy he put into researching and translating women poets in his last years—even if he perversely annoyed women in one audience by claiming he was reading a woman's poetry to them because she had been one of his lovers.

Hamalian wisely does not try to resolve the contradictions in Rexroth's life. On the contrary, she makes him live precisely by showing the complexity of his character and circumstances. She is compassionate without indulging in special pleading, fair but not evasive. She evokes the feeling of what it was like to live day-to-day with Rexroth, but she does not lose sight of the poems which transcend the daily occasions of their creation. It is hard to see how she could have produced a more balanced, informed, and moving biography.

Carl Rollyson

Sources for Further Study

Bloomsbury Review. XI, June, 1991, p. 7.
Booklist. LXXXVII, February 15, 1991, p. 1173.

Chicago Tribune. April 28, 1991, XIV, p. 6.
Choice. XXIX, October, 1991, p. 280.
Kirkus Reviews. LIX, February 1, 1991, p. 153.
Library Journal. CXVI, April 1, 1991, p. 121.
Los Angeles Times Book Review. May 5, 1991, p. 1.
Publishers Weekly. CCXXXVIII, January 25, 1991, p. 42.
The Washington Post Book World. XXI, April 14, 1991, p. 4.

A LIFE OF PICASSO
Volume I: 1881-1906

Author: John Richardson (1924-   )
Publisher: Random House (New York). Illustrated. 548 pp. $39.95
Type of work: Biography
Time: 1881-1906
Locale: Malaga, Barcelona, Madrid, Spain; Paris, France

A superb, painstaking reenactment of Picasso's life and art, carefully correcting earlier erroneous accounts, and setting the artist in the context of his age, shrewdly assessing the artist's own myth, and providing a rich evocation of his origins

> *Principal personages:*
> JOSE RUIZ BLASCO, Picasso's father, a mediocre artist who supported but became estranged from his son's great talent
> MARIA PICASSO LOPEZ, Picasso's cheerful, supportive mother
> SALVADOR RUIZ BLASCO, Picasso's uncle, an early patron of his art
> MANUEL PALLARÈS, Picasso's friend and fellow artist, the first of several father figures and mentors
> CARLES CASAGEMAS, Picasso's self-destructive friend, an artist who figures in several of Picasso's early works
> MAX JACOB, a poet and artist, one of Picasso's confidants instrumental in shaping his view of literature and art
> JAIME SABARTÈS, Picasso's lifelong friend and secretary
> FERNANDE OLIVIER, Picasso's first great love
> GUILLAUME APOLLINAIRE, a poet who greatly influenced Picasso's painting
> ALFRED JARRY, a flamboyant artist who never met Picasso and yet profoundly influenced his art
> GERTRUDE STEIN, one of Picasso's important patrons in Paris
> HENRI MATISSE, Picasso's great rival

In the first of a projected four volumes, John Richardson provides a fascinating, in-depth portrayal of Picasso's life and art. In chapters that usually cover a year or less, the biographer re-creates the young artist's explosive development, the family tensions that arose from Picasso's iconoclastic canvases and boisterous behavior, his three journeys to Paris before permanently settling there, the brief periods of doubt and timidity when he seemed to pull back from his original insights, and his triumphant breakthrough at the age of twenty-five, producing not only several masterpieces but a body of work already the equal of the greatest long-lived artists.

In his father's eye, Picasso was destined to be an artist; accordingly, he was given an education that would equip him for a distinguished academic career. Soon, however, Picasso rejected his father's conventional, second-rate style of painting and sought out the most innovative and colorful personalities—first in Malaga, and then in Barcelona, Madrid, and Paris. In later life, Picasso would present himself as a self-made artist, claiming that he had never drawn or painted as a child but had somehow sprung fully formed and capable of creating mature works before his teenage years.

Richardson never doubts Picasso's genius, but the biographer wisely threads his way through the artist's self-aggrandizing reminiscences, ratifying, on the one hand, Picasso's faith in his precocity, and on the other hand, rejecting his more outrageous claims. The artist did develop quickly—by sixteen he was capable of producing mature work—but there is no evidence that as a very young child Picasso ranked as a prodigy. Similarly, stories told by Jaime Sabartès and other Picasso intimates are subject to the biographer's careful checking of time and place and are often corrected in the light of other evidence. Richardson often has to consider conflicting accounts, which leads him to conclude: "No wonder so much of what has been said about Picasso turns out to be equally true in reverse."

One of the powerful unifying themes of Richardson's biography is what he calls the *mirada fuerte*, the powerful gaze or stare that Picasso could turn on the people who became the subjects of his art. Viewing Picasso as essentially a Spanish artist—in spite of his many years in France and the undoubted influence of French art on his work—Richardson shows how this personal characteristic was also a cultural characteristic that pervaded Picasso's life and work, manifesting itself in his stunningly original portraits and in his affairs with several women. He had a way of taking total possession of his subjects, virtually violating them, and Richardson does not excuse Picasso's misogyny, recognizing that it is an indispensable part of the artist's energy and motivation. Consequently, he presents (without using the word) a powerfully sinister view of Picasso's genius.

At almost all periods of his life Picasso had "devoted dogsbodies," often older men, artists, who supported his art, gave him places to stay and money, and who generally sacrificed themselves to his talent—just as Picasso's father and Uncle Salvador had done. In at least one case, that of Carles Casagemas, who committed suicide in 1901, the attachment to Picasso proved disastrous. To remain strong within Picasso's overwhelming artistic orbit required considerable personal strength and talent. The poet Guillaume Apollinaire successfully abetted and withstood Picasso's genius, which had a ruthless, self-involved side apparently interested in others only as avenues to the creation of art or to the satisfaction of his appetite. Usually life and work were combined: Thus Fernande Olivier became not only the artist's "first great love" but also his model, whom he would lock in his studio, forbidding the promiscuous Olivier to have friendships with other men, even though she was married to another man at the time of their liaison.

"Picasso lacked moral courage," Richardson notes in making a distinction between the bravery of the artist's work and his far from exemplary life: "In art Picasso was a hero, less so in life." An artist with a growing "drama and style," Picasso named himself, so to speak, taking his mother's name (to the chagrin of his father's family) and refusing (after his first pliant years) to follow his father's advice.

Paris, Richardson shows, was an indispensable element in Picasso's rapid mastery of art; it replaced the provinciality of Barcelona and Madrid and appealed to the artist's open sensuality. In Paris, Picasso surrounded himself with poets—in later life, he wrote poetry himself, which Richardson suggests was of very high quality—and absorbed ideas that were quickly translated into paintings. In Max Jacob, "an encyclopedia of erudition," Picasso found a guide who could cleverly guide him through the "maze of French culture." Through Jacob, the artist assimilated the heterodox ideas of Alfred Jarry, whom Richardson credits with inspiring (in part) the conception of Picasso's *Les Demoiselles d'Avignon* (1907), the grotesque masterpiece that ends Richardson's first volume but will also be the beginning of his second. The distorted faces of that painting are linked to Jarry's campaign to disorder the senses and to "detonate all traditional canons of beauty, good taste and propriety." In Apollinaire, Picasso found his "ideal counterpart," looking for ways to "destroy old canons," and not afraid to exploit the darkest sides of himself to further his art.

Picasso realized that Henri Matisse was his chief rival as a great twentieth century painter, and Richardson demonstrates how carefully Picasso groomed himself to compete with Matisse's greatest compositions, holding back the public exhibition of certain works until he was sure they were equal to or surpassed Matisse's. Although the painters knew and respected each other, their relationship cooled—perhaps inevitably so, since Picasso's art usually aimed to shock while Matisse's sought to soothe.

Richardson is diverting on the subject of Gertrude Stein, confirming her importance as an early patron and publicizer of Picasso's work who often missed its significance because of her self-preoccupation. In Richardson's view, she was an engine of egotism who baffled Picasso (he had great trouble in creating his famous portrait of her) and yet continued to attract him, even after his work ceased to attract her.

Throughout his biography, Richardson is careful to balance a sense of Picasso's life experience, his relationships with other artists, his affairs with women, and Picasso's awareness of his predecessors. Not only would Picasso sometimes copy the work of other masters, he even imitated their signatures, engaging in what amounted to a magical rite that presumed he could imbibe the essence of great art. On his return home from one of his trips to Paris, he was angered to learn that his mother had brushed away the dust from his clothes because Parisian dust was dear to him, as though it contained some distillation of what he had absorbed.

One of the pleasures of reading this biography is its profuse illustrations, which can immediately verify Richardson's observations of Picasso's borrowings from old masters. Thus his *Woman with a Fan* (1905) is juxtaposed against *Woman with a Fan* (1638-1639) by Diego Velázquez and *The Marcellus Eris* (1819) by Jean-Auguste-Dominque Ingres, both of whom Richardson can prove Picasso studied. In characteristic fashion, Picasso reversed the downward gesture of Velázquez while borrowing the upward gesture, profile, and even the somber mood, although not the subject matter, of Ingres. Chapter 27 of Richardson's biography is titled "Plundering the Past," and the epigraph from T. S. Eliot—"The bad poet imitates: the good poet steals"—precisely captures the biographer's point about Picasso's strong eye, the *mirada fuerte*, that told him exactly what to plunder. Without Richardson's equally keen eye, these influences on Picasso's art could easily go unnoticed.

Similarly, the biographer points out the impact of Paul Gaugin and other French antecedents on Picasso's great painting, *The Saltimbanques* (1905). In perhaps the finest passage in the biography, Richardson shows how through various studies in watercolor, gouache and charcoal, pen, and oil on canvas, the artist evolved his portrayal of these wandering performers, so individualized, looking off in different directions, not quite making eye contact, and yet so clearly a unit, a family, a coherent group expressive of a particular way of life but also of the estrangement and togetherness of human beings. What is most remarkable—and comprehensible only because Richardson is able to reproduce Picasso's study in pen for the painting—is that Picasso based the composition of *The Saltimbanques* on his own hand (it appears in the drawing), placing the figures in the positions of his fingers and suggesting how the figures are, in effect, the digits of human experience, separate yet bound to one another.

Richardson writes with a deep awareness of Picasso scholarship and biography. Sometimes his eagerness to correct earlier accounts may seem excessive—as when he spends several paragraphs discussing exactly when and how Picasso and Apollinaire met. Yet he is aware that these previous reports do not merely distort the record, they tend to establish a mythology about the artist, obscuring the real conditions in which he developed and often simplifying and obscuring the more interesting and more complex ways in which Picasso achieved greatness.

At the same time, Richardson is not afraid to admit there are gaps in his knowledge, areas that elude even the most exhaustive research, so that he is forced to say "we can only guess" or "would that we knew." And sometimes Richardson does guess and does speculate, briefly wondering, for example, at how Picasso reacted to his shortness, his want of a few inches that might have made him a perfect physical specimen.

Because Richardson is writing a four-volume biography, he occasionally has the need to adumbrate the future, to allude to events beyond the scope of the first volume. Sometimes this technique can disrupt the narrative flow of a biography and make for irritating digressions. But Richardson's command of his subject is so clear and so subtle that his rounding out of stories, explaining how certain relationships ended many years later in Picasso's life, is not distracting. On the contrary, it sharpens a sense of Picasso then measured against what he was to become and enhances expectations for the subsequent volumes of this finely gauged biography.

Richardson begins *A Life of Picasso* explaining his own friendship with the artist, begun in the 1950's and ending only with the artist's death in 1973. Richardson had the good fortune to realize early that he would someday write Picasso's biography, so he took notes of conversations and had the opportunity to ask the artist many questions and to observe his reactions. Throughout his narrative Richardson makes sparing but insightful use of this personal connection to his subject, supplying his biography with an added dimension, an abiding sense of the meeting of minds between the biographer and his subject.

Carl Rollyson

Sources for Further Study

ARTnews. XC, May, 1991, p. 99.
Los Angeles Times Book Review. February 24, 1991, p. 1.
The New Republic. CCIV, April 22, 1991, p. 38.
New York. XXIV, February 25, 1991, p. 113.
The New York Review of Books. XXXVIII, March 28, 1991, p. 3.
The New York Times Book Review. XCVI, March 3, 1991, p. 1.
People Weekly. XXXV, April 8, 1991, p. 34.
Publishers Weekly. CCXXXVIII, January 11, 1991, p. 84.
Time. CXXXVII, February 18, 1991, p. 65.
The Times Literary Supplement. September 13, 1991, p. 16.
Vogue. CLXXXI, March, 1991, p. 243.
The Wall Street Journal. May 3, 1991, p. A9.
The Washington Post Book World. XXI, February 10, 1991, p. 1.

THE LIGHT THE DEAD SEE
The Selected Poems of Frank Stanford

Author: Frank Stanford (1948-1978)
Edited, with an introduction, by Leon Stokesbury
Publisher: University of Arkansas Press (Fayetteville). 111 pp. $22.00
Type of work: Poetry

These poems offer convincing proof that when Frank Stanford died by his own hand at age twenty-nine, the world lost a major poet-in-the-making

The Light the Dead See offers readers Arkansas poet Frank Stanford's best work: those sometimes dreamlike, many times nightmarish excursions into a mythic Southland, a cruel and rapacious Southern United States where personae maim and kill out of an unnamed obsession in hopes of reclaiming their youth and their lost paradise.

This volume is not for the squeamish. There is madness here and terror: thievery, malice, and murder alongside a strange kind of redemption brought by the blacks who populate most of the poems, people with such names as Born in the Camp with Six Toes, Ray Baby, Baby Gauge, Chinaman, Rollie Pollie Man. This world is based in part on a real one—namely the Memphis, Tennessee, Stanford knew in childhood—but it is a place of fabulous things, where Baby Gauge rides a gar fish, Mose Jackson throws dice for snake-eyes, and the Midget flees the knife blade.

Frank Stanford was himself a mystery. He spent his formative years in Memphis, where he lived with his mother, Dorothy Gildart, and his father, A. F. Stanford. In later life, he was shocked to learn that Gildart had adopted him, and this revelation no doubt had a sizable impact upon his art. Another shock came when Stanford's father moved him and his mother to a virtually all-white area in Arkansas, from his beloved black friends in Memphis.

The selections in this book of verse include not only some of Stanford's best published poetry but also some unpublished work written between 1968 and 1974. The poems begin with those taken from *The Singing Knives* (1971) and include works from *Ladies from Hell* (1974), *Field Talk* (1975), *Shade* (1975), *Arkansas Bench Stone* (1975), *Constant Stranger* (1976), *The Battlefield Where the Moon Says I Love You* (1977), *You* (1979), and *Crib Death* (1979).

In his poems, Stanford allows readers into his inner world but does not tell them what they are apprehending. This realm is a dangerous place where visions of mutilation and death prevail. Here, then, is a journey into a surreal black South, violent and hate-filled:

> Jimmy ran down the road
> With the knife in his mouth
> He was naked
> And the moon
> Was a dead man floating down the river.

It is, as editor Leon Stokesbury points out, the South of Mark Twain's Huckleberry Finn one hundred years after Huck lit out for the Territory. Here, mutilation comes in many forms: Arms are cut to cement a friendship, throats are slashed, people are blinded. Yet a reader encountering these causal mutilations finds it difficult to decipher their meaning; Stanford apparently intends it so, wanting to hold the keys to the coded messages himself. Yet, as in a surrealistic painting by Giorgio De Chirico or Salvador Dalí, even if the meaning is not readily accessible, one senses things that the symbols mean. In these works, a steady stream of images assault the reader: birds, fish, boats, snakes, knives, hooks, coffins. Their meanings may be obscure, but their juxtapositions make them powerful in the way a shaman's words are powerful.

Stanford's poems, populated with references to cut-off hands and buckets of blood, take one into a torture chamber that he envisions to be life itself, sadistic and vital. The poet's world is also a kind of closed system: No one escapes; all are caught in and contribute to this hell. There is a frenzied desire for meaning, but also a knowledge that meaningfulness is a fantasy, or that it exists but is unattainable, except perhaps in shards and fragments:

> I am holding my hands together
> like a gloveless hunter
> drinking water in the morning
> or calling up owls in the forest,
> I am holding my hands together
> like a hunter in winter
> with his hands in the water
> washing away the blood.

What is real to Stanford is pain and death, death looming larger the farther one goes into the volume. Death comes many ways, but mostly violently and suddenly, by shotguns and sharp knives. In "The Snake Doctors," a hog, its life threatened, attempts an escape. After being tortured by knife-wielding assailants, the hog, in a fury of spurting blood, is at last dispatched, leaving the boat where it is killed full of blood.

As in so much of the poetry written by Stanford, a man who had a Catholic education, there is a religious sensibility—or at least remnants of one. The hog in "The Snake Doctors" could almost be a Christ symbol, an innocent hounded to a terrible death by sadistic men. Often in his work, Stanford makes evident the religious quality of this pursuit, couching it in the language and form of a dream: "I dreamed I saw Holy Ghost walking around the campfire/ He was a wild hog with blood on his tushes." This sacramental language hints at some kind of sacred investiture in the commonplaces of life, but Stanford's meaning remains elusive and forever his secret.

His characters, black and white, are often suspicious, and sometimes fearful, isolated beings joined by violence. Basically, their talk is of killings, bad fates, threats, and fights. They cavort in an opaque dream scene where nothing seems connected and where one dream vision passes into another: "I dreamed the Chinaman's peg leg/ I dreamed I was fishing in heaven with Sho Nuff/ and Jesus cleaned the fish." Each character has real vitality, though little corporality. This vitality seems unfocused and frustrated, without an outlet. Passionate claims and threats seem stillborn; they have no effect, no context, and little inherent meaning, for they are disconnected images, the floating stuff of dreams and nightmares.

Sexual frustrations, always present in the poems, though veiled, are less veiled in the poem "The Picture Show Next Door to the Stamp Store in Downtown Memphis." Here, an onlooker watches a parade of girls led into the "picture show" by a nun. In his fury, he turns a soft-drink dispenser into a guillotine (but why?—to punish the girls, the nun, or himself?). A feeling of suffocation and impotence runs through this work, a stifled fury that may trigger violence. In other works, impotence and thwarted love figure largely; in still others, one finds oblique references to castration.

Stanford's poems are claustrophobic: Everything that occurs seems to be under death's all-encompassing influence. In fact, it is easy to see Stanford's verse as illustrating humanity's attempted flight from death and its promise of annihilation, his characters hoping somehow to keep their own deaths at bay by substituting other creatures and human beings as scapegoats.

Yet at the end of the volume is the poem giving it its title, "The Light the Dead See," a paen to death and the life beyond it. This poem, written just prior to Stanford's suicide, has a quiet acceptance of death most of the other poems seem to lack. It is as if, at long last, the poet has found that death is a friend, not the enemy he used to think it was—a force that leads to life eternal. From the claustrophobia of this life, Stanford finds a release and an ultimate freedom. He pictures the "wise and honest" dead having seen a light that "grows, a white flower." After dying, they have seen a "signalman swinging a lantern"; then they have beheld the faces of those whom they loved who died before them.

At last, in the next-to-the-last stanza, the poet stops talking about others and starts talking about himself as if he had died. He beholds the wonder of a dead father sitting motionless in a field ("The harvest is over and his cane chair is mended") who, while the wind blows, has his hair cut by his wife. It is an evocative, powerful poem bespeaking the poet's acceptance of death and his belief in another life in another realm.

Had Stanford lived, editor Stokesbury maintains, he would have joined the ranks of great American poets, so much potential had he. Even a cursory reading of *The Light the Dead See* demonstrates that here was a writer of real imaginative power creating a world unlike that of any other poet: unnerving in its casual cruelty and monstrous presences and marvelous in its evocation of a primal South, magical and distant.

Uncontestably, there are fine poems here. One need only read "The Singing Knives," "The Gospel Bird," "The Snake Doctors," or "Island Funeral" to detect genius.

There is a pungency here coupled with an incantatory, hallucinogenic quality that makes these poems alive and memorable.

In short, the volume is one poetry lovers should spend time with, since, as with any important poetry, there is about it a magic that defies easy categorization or explanation. To read it is to lose one's bearings and enter a timeless region populated by nightriders, midgets, and swamp fishermen; by killers intent on murder and mayhem; by men who clean their fingernails by moonlight; by a man who cuts off his hand at dawn; by a man in a store looking for a "good knife." Violent though this world is, somehow it is not a wearying one, perhaps because the images are surreal and therefore alluring and mysterious. Here is a lost world of a despairing poet: the ruined paradise with traces left of its vanished glory, where Cain's descendants kill new Abels, indeed a place of nightmare and dream.

John D. Raymer

Sources for Further Study

Bloomsbury Review. XI, July, 1991, p. 21.
Ploughshares. XVII, Fall, 1991, p. 281.
University Press Book News. III, September, 1991, p. 33.

LILA
An Inquiry into Morals

Author: Robert M. Pirsig (1928-   )
Publisher: Bantam Books (New York). 409 pp. $22.50
Type of work: Philosophical novel
Time: The 1980's
Locale: The Hudson River Valley and New York City

Robert Pirsig sails down the Hudson River with an emotionally disturbed woman named Lila, an encounter that forces him to define what he means by sanity, science, truth, and morality

> *Principal characters:*
> LILA BLEWITT, an unemployed waitress
> PHAEDRUS, the alter ego of Robert Pirsig
> RICHARD RIGEL, an acquaintance of Lila and Pirsig
> VERNE DUSENBERRY, a former colleague of Pirsig

One of the most familiar and powerful patterns in world literature is that of the journey. Typically, the journey features the complicated wanderings of a hero who undergoes some sort of spiritual or psychological transformation in the process of wandering. The journey always proceeds simultaneously on the physical and the spiritual levels, because the hero inevitably discovers a new reality, one that necessitates a change in personal values. This archetypal pattern would include such familiar figures as Gilgamesh, Jonah, Odysseus, Robinson Crusoe, Captain Ahab, and Huckleberry Finn.

In his first book, *Zen and the Art of Motorcycle Maintenance: An Inquiry into Values* (1974), Robert Pirsig made extensive use of the journey pattern as he recounted a dramatic motorcycle trip that he and his son, Chris, took across the western United States. The story of that journey formed the core of one of the most influential and oft-quoted books in twentieth century America, catapulting its author to celebrity status and making the book a kind of instant classic. The book deals with repairing motorcycles and other broken objects as a metaphor for taking control of one's life. Pirsig relied heavily on the ideas of Plato and on the meditative and aesthetic techniques of Zen Buddhism. He also introduced the reader to his alter ego, a philosophical character named Phaedrus. It was as Phaedrus that Robert Pirsig spent time in a mental hospital. His recovery and the subsequent writing of *Zen and the Art of Motorcycle Maintenance* all depended upon his discovery of the crucial importance of quality in day-to-day living. That preoccupation with quality, and all of its moral and social implications, inspired him to write *Lila: An Inquiry into Morals.*

But *Lila* does not take up where *Zen and the Art of Motorcycle Maintenance* left off. It is not intended to be a sequel, and the reader can pick up *Lila* and read it profitably without having been immersed in the previous book. Pirsig makes no attempt to fill in the gaps between the two works, but he does make use of Phaedrus again, letting him tell the story. The celebrity status Pirsig achieved from *Zen and the Art of Motorcycle Maintenance* is important, however, because it explains Pirsig's desire to escape from the limelight, buy a large sailboat, and begin a voyage that would take him from the Great Lakes, down the Hudson River, around Manhattan, and down the Eastern Seaboard. Again, the voyage itself is a critical part of the learning process, and Pirsig emphasizes that the solitude and relative invisibility of life on a boat is precisely what he needs to carry on his philosophical inquiries. Richard Rigel, one of his sailing acquaintances, frequently needles Pirsig because of that celebrity status. When Pirsig meets his publisher during a brief stopover in New York City, he picks up two large canvas sacks of fan mail, proof positive that the world outside is still waiting for him.

For Pirsig—or Phaedrus, as he styles himself—the journey is a learning device, and the boat becomes a kind of floating study. Phaedrus explains that he had become impatient with most ways of taking notes or making journal entries. He wanted a nonlinear, infinitely expandable tool that could include all of his ongoing thoughts and revisions. So he hit upon the simple expedient of using slips of paper each of which contained a note about some important idea. When slips began to cohere logically under some heading or topic, he would group them together under a plastic tab attached to an index card. The advantage of this system was that it guaranteed random access and flexibility. Phaedrus could add, subtract, or rearrange slips or topics as his thinking progressed.

His ultimate goal was to arrive at a metaphysics of quality, the one megatopic that implied or subsumed all the subordinate ones. Eventually, Phaedrus accumulated some eleven thousand slips of paper with scores of topic headings or categories. These slips were collected in library card-catalog trays and stored in the pilot berth of the sailboat, always within easy reach of Phaedrus.

In addition, Phaedrus designed five special categories to make the system as personal and flexible as possible: "Unassimilated," a category for spur-of-the-moment thoughts and ideas; "Program," a category that contained instructions for processing the other slips, a kind of software package for the computer of his mind; "Crit," a category that listed all the slips that could be destroyed (the category also provided a mandatory waiting period to guarantee that no slips were destroyed in a moment of extreme anger or frustration); "Tough," a category for ideas that were unique or just didn't belong in any other grouping; and "Junk," a category for duplicates of previous slips or ideas that needed more refinement.

Phaedrus spends a considerable amount of time describing this methodology to the reader because he expects close attention and participation in the process of creating the resultant book. *Lila* is an unusually interactive work: The reader will have to create a system of mental slips and card trays to process the immense amount of thought that occurs on the boat journey from Kingston, New York, on the Hudson River, down to Nyack, thence to New York City, and, finally, to Sandy Hook, just beyond Manhattan.

Into the philosophical and nautical voyaging of Phaedrus intrudes Lila Blewitt, sometime waitress and prostitute, who picks him up in a bar in Kingston and who literally upsets the neat trays of ideas that had been accumulating in the pilot's berth—and in Phaedrus' mind. She and Phaedrus become wildly intoxicated in the bar, performing a dance of Dionysian excess, finally collapsing in a drunken stupor on Phaedrus' boat. Like Phaedrus, Lila is unnervingly direct and terrifyingly candid. Her very presence becomes a catalyst, especially since another sailor named Richard Rigel, a boyhood acquaintance of Lila, has challenged Phaedrus to prove how Lila could be considered a person of quality. In spite of her unpredictable behavior, vulgar jewelry, and utter lack of sexual restraint, Phaedrus finds her fascinating. He immediately recognizes that in solving the puzzle of Lila he will simultaneously solve the riddle of quality, the idea that has been hounding him during his entire voyage.

Phaedrus and Lila do experience some precious moments together. The boat provides a lulling and beautiful ambience, and she seems to adapt to this small, compartmentalized world of berths, buoys, sails, and hatches with an unconscious grace and natural delight. Phaedrus describes one memorable evening when Lila prepares a dinner of steak, fried potatoes, and salad. They are both famished, and the prospect of eating is almost as pleasurable as the food itself. Lila experiences moments of Zen-like intensity as she directs her total concentration on simple acts such as slicing and frying each sliver of potato as if it were a perfect little work of art. Later that evening, she visits his bed and makes love to him in a way that is at once tenderly erotic and painfully vulnerable.

Lila forces Phaedrus to focus on society and the great social codes that seem to govern even the smallest details of day-to-day life. Although his thinking about quality, morality, and society will eventually result in a fairly coherent system of ideas, Phaedrus wants the reader to think along with him and to share the various steps that lead to his personal metaphysics of quality. This personal philosophy is really an attempt to explain why people change and why society is always lagging behind those changes. Phaedrus expresses this idea again and again, with different examples, by using the antipodal words "static" and "dynamic." Lila is dynamic, but Richard Rigel (her critic) is clearly static, passing judgment on her with a set of antiquated moral ideas that do not apply to her situation or to the twentieth century as a whole.

Lila is one of many misfits whom Phaedrus admires profoundly. The first is a child prodigy named William James Sidis, who read classical Greek and other languages by the age of five, entered Harvard at eleven years of age, and then led a life of apparent obscurity. Phaedrus discovered through his reading, however, that Sidis had left many manuscripts and had published widely under a pen name. Among other ideas, Sidis had successfully predicted the existence of black holes at a time when no one had dreamed of such things and had shown how white American social values of independence and freedom depended heavily on the values of the American Indians who had just been conquered.

This focus on Native American Indians is critical because one of Phaedrus' mentors, Verne Dusenberry, had introduced him to the peyote rituals of the Northern Cheyenne at the same time that he had pointed out the inconsistencies in standard anthropological practice, which tended to treat Indians as objects. A more human-centered anthropology was what Phaedrus found in the work of Ruth Benedict, who told the anecdote of a Zuni Indian who was banished and punished for violating tribal customs but who, nevertheless, returned to save the tribe from extinction. Social codes, Phaedrus concluded, are always in need of reformation; there is an important dynamic quality in people that facilitates these changes. Phaedrus wanted a theory that would describe such changes accurately, hence the need for his metaphysics of quality. "Quality" was only a name for the activity of seeking improvements in society. For that reason, Phaedrus also admired the philosopher William James, who had grown mightily impatient of the subject-object distinction in science and whose work, Phaedrus believed, tended toward more advanced notions such as relativity.

All these sublime philosophical speculations are rudely interrupted when Lila and Phaedrus dock the boat in New York City. She tries to recruit a former friend to serve as a deckhand on the boat, an undertaking that manages to enrage all the participants. Phaedrus leaves to keep an appointment with Robert Redford, and while they are discussing a possible film deal, Lila wanders around the city without her much needed tranquilizers—or her wallet. Ultimately, Phaedrus finds her waiting on the boat, rain-soaked and catatonic, holding a rubber doll that she mistakes for Dawn, her long-dead daughter and the cause of the collapse of her marriage.

Lila's condition prompts Phaedrus to recall his own experience in the mental hospital and to philosophize about sanity and insanity. At this point, he shocks the reader with the admission that he was never actually cured but simply played the part of the sane man in order to escape the horrors of the asylum. In his metaphysics, the insane are simply playing by a different set of rules. He offers many examples of alternate realties that are routinely ignored by supposedly rational people. This meditation on sanity concludes a whole series of internal dialogues in which Phaedrus condemns various aspects of society. The Victorians, in his view, operated entirely by social convention without any regard for intellectual honesty. Their culture was replaced by the Modernists of the 1920's, who emphasized intellect and reason to such an extent that a counterrevolution occurred in the excesses of the Hippies during the 1960's. The emotional excesses of those turbulent days persisted into the 1970's and 1980's as drugs, street violence, gangs, and urban problems increased on a year-to-year basis. A metaphysics of quality, which Phaedrus finally equates with a search for the good, might very well be a panacea for all these tragic social ills.

In the end, Phaedrus determines that all life can be divided into four systems of value: the inorganic, the biological, the social, and the intellectual. Quality is the engine that drives existence, the dynamic force that strains to improve and revolutionize the four systems (as in the process of evolution) toward something that resembles Plato's idea of the good. Quality, Phaedrus says, is the true meaning of the Greek word for goodness or virtue, *arete*, and the Sanskrit root *Rta*, which produced such modern English words as "right" and "ritual."

Sadly, when Phaedrus comes to these profound conclusions, Lila has seemingly lost all touch with any kind of reality. Richard Rigel anchors beside them at Sandy Hook, and Lila insists on leaving with him. Like Lila, the reader has come to the end of the voyage, an experience that has somehow been palpably physical and utterly metaphysical, strangely beautiful and painfully tragic. Pirsig succeeds in writing a brilliant novel of ideas, uniting in one voice the inner and outer realities of experience. It is almost impossible to forget Phaedrus. His haunting and enchanting voice, with all its questions and observations, becomes a lasting touchstone for the quality of life itself.

Daniel L. Guillory

Sources for Further Study

Chicago Tribune. October 13, 1991, XIV, p. 3.
The Christian Science Monitor. November 5, 1991, p. 15.
Los Angeles Times Book Review. October 27, 1991, p. 2.
The New York Review of Books. XXXVIII, December 19, 1991, p. 59.
The New York Times Book Review. XCVI, October 13, 1991, p. 15.
Publishers Weekly. CCXXXVIII, August 16, 1991, p. 44.
The Spectator. CCLXVII, October 19, 1991, p. 39.
Time. CXXXVIII, October 28, 1991, p. 93.
The Times Literary Supplement. October 18, 1991, p. 21.
The Washington Post Book World. XXI, October 13, 1991, p. 3.

THE LIVES OF NORMAN MAILER
A Biography

Author: Carl Rollyson (1948-   )
Publisher: Paragon House (New York). Illustrated. 425 pp. $26.95
Type of work: Biography
Time: 1923-1991
Locale: Principally New York City

An alert and sensitive literary biography of one of the most controversial and talented of contemporary American authors

Principal personages:
NORMAN MAILER, an author, filmmaker, politician, and celebrity
BEA SILVERMAN MAILER, his first wife
ADELE MORALES MAILER, his second wife, whom he stabbed
JEANNE CAMPBELL MAILER, his third wife
BEVERLY BENTLEY MAILER, his fourth wife
CAROL STEVENS MAILER, his fifth wife
NORRIS CHURCH MAILER, his sixth wife

Brave is the biographer who writes the story of a still-living subject, and braver still the biographer who tackles an individual who has surprised the public and confounded his critics in the past and may yet surprise and confound again. When the subject of the biography is an artist, whose life extends beyond his personality to his work—for neglected novels rediscovered, forgotten paintings found, and dismissed films revived are the constant, if unacknowledged, possibilities and hope of every artist—then the biographer has set out on a course hedged about with more than the usual share of dangers. Add to this already dangerous path a subject who has a volatile personality, a propensity, even compulsion, to shock, and an outrageous talent and intelligence often put to complex and infuriating projects; that is the challenge Carl Rollyson faced when he set himself to writing *The Lives of Norman Mailer.*

Seldom has a book been so aptly entitled, for the subject has crashed and stormed—no less forceful verbs will do—his way through the American literary, intellectual, political, and cultural scene since his brilliant debut, *The Naked and the Dead* (1948), with an aggressive, pugilistic energy that has both fascinated and appalled onlookers. There is Mailer the novelist, Mailer the journalist, Mailer the filmmaker, Mailer the mystic biographer of Marilyn Monroe, Mailer the political activist and candidate, Mailer the wife-stabber, Mailer the brawler, Mailer the thinker, Mailer the . . . well, the blanks are there for the biographer to complete, and Rollyson has not shirked the challenge.

Carl Rollyson has undertaken the task of putting a modern Proteus between two covers, and he has succeeded brilliantly. There are many Mailers, and Rollyson has rendered them in clear, unvarnished view, the shadows of defeat and failure mixed with the lights of triumph and success. Norman the Pulitzer Prize winner is here, and so is Norman the Barbarian and all the other Normans in between.

Mailer's life and literature are connected to a degree unusual even for American authors, who tend to have their personalities and their books melded together in popular and, to large extent, scholarly minds. Particularly in the twentieth century, American authors have been celebrities whose antics beyond the typewriter and outside the study have influenced their public recognition. F. Scott Fitzgerald carousing in Paris; Ernest Hemingway bothering large, dangerous animals in Cuba and Africa; J. D. Salinger reclusing in rural New Hampshire; Jack Kerouac road- and mind-tripping across America—these are more than writers; they are characters in an external fiction observed with greater interest than anything in their books.

To this crew comes Norman Mailer, who, as Rollyson amply demonstrates, seems to have the greatest need and greatest ability to create and re-create his own persona, a multiply guised figure who fashions himself anew with each book, each television appearance, each interview. He is like Heracleitus' river; one never encounters the same Mailer twice. Why this should be is a mystery that Rollyson does not fully penetrate; no fault to him, for such a task would be impossible. What Rollyson does accomplish, however, is to chart the passage of Norman Mailer through his career, tracing the changes, the shifts, and the new characters that the man constructs for himself, usually as a concurrent effort with his latest literary project.

Perhaps, Rollyson suggests, Mailer has been in flight from his upbringing as a bright Jewish boy whose mother always believed him destined for greatness and whose evident intelligence and talents made that maternal dream more than a fantasy. Perhaps, Rollyson also acknowledges, a creative artist such as Mailer has little choice but to fashion himself anew, using those changes as his method of growth and development. Or perhaps, Rollyson admits, there are other reasons, richer or darker than can be comprehended. Much of the value in this biography is its flexibility, which accommodates such an elusive figure.

That the changes are there, however, is beyond question, and Rollyson has produced a biography that lucidly and briskly follows them, tying them as is appropriate to Mailer's development as a writer. This book is a literary biography in the best sense, because it takes the reader through Mailer's career as an author, a career that manages to be both impressive and disturbing.

Here is Mailer the young lion, bounding into the arena with *The Naked and the Dead*, one of the most impressive debuts in American literature. That debut was both an achievement and an agony for Mailer, for there is no greater burden than promise, and Mailer surely has pondered Fitzgerald's wise, sad observation that "there are no second acts in American lives."

What then is a brilliant young war novelist to do but destroy that particular character and set out to create a new one, a rebel suitable for turbulent times as the century nears midpoint. Creation is painful, and not always successful. The two novels that follow, *Barbary Shore* (1951) and *The Deer Park* (1955), are ambitious in conception, flawed in execution, and attacked on reception. Unable or unwilling to retreat to the safety of his early accomplishment—a flight no honest artist would allow—Mailer commits himself more firmly to opposition, becoming, in his own phrase, a "psychic outlaw" and finding unexpected kin among other outcasts: the beats, the blacks, the hipsters. Mailer senses a tide flowing there, and there he goes.

It is not an easy journey, and Mailer, for all his talent, energy, and fierce desire, does not make it gracefully. His short stories for the period show a writer struggling against internal and external currents, trying to find a place that is uniquely his but—and this is key to its paradoxical truth—a place that is not too secure. Security is death, while danger is life.

During this time, Mailer writes about many things, but especially about sex, and the image of Norman the enemy of women is born, not totally untruthfully. In stories such as "The Time of Her Time," sexual pleasure is equated with violence, and women seem portrayed not as partners or equals but literally as vessels to be used and discarded. Beyond this coarse view there is more complex and ambivalent consideration of human relations and sexuality; Rollyson's careful and perceptive analysis of these stories brings out their unexpected depths. Indeed, throughout this work, the literary critiques are those rarest of things, sharp enough to please the professional scholar, yet accessible enough for the casual reader.

During Mailer's time, however, both the professional and casual reader have often misperceived him. This danger of public misperception is courted, even encouraged, by Mailer in his eclectic collection, *Advertisements for Myself* (1959), in which he not only presents his writings but also comments upon them, illuminating why and how they came to be written. In this sense, the book is a "biography of a style," but it is also style as biography, the writer and the writing merging so that the public and presumably private aspects become one. In many ways, after this point there is no private Mailer, and he takes the most daring step possible for a writer: He will invent himself anew with each book, in full view of the audience. Some writers work without a net; Norman Mailer works without a net over a pool full of sharks.

It is a dangerous move and in many ways a political one, and Mailer is drawn, inevitably, inexorably, to politics itself: not doctrinaire politics filled with the mundane realities of issues and records, the tedium of platforms and campaigns; instead, the politics of personality, a combination of inspired (and misinspired) innovation, antiestablishment posturing, and some genuine insight. Gathering these shards together, Mailer occasionally falters, claims more than his realistic due, as when he announces that his designation of John Kennedy as a "hipster" was decisive in the close 1960 presidential election. (In some smoke-filled political Elysium, Chicago ward bosses roll their eyes and grin.) Still, Mailer has his moments, his clear vision and fresh voice, and they are finally combined in the work they merit, *The Armies of the Night* (1968). In this book, he is without peer and almost beyond category, greater than a journalist and yet more than a participant.

The Armies of the Night is the central book of Mailer's career, and Rollyson is correct to place it in its true context. The Norman Mailer who has been bent upon re-creating himself in public view needed something akin to T. S. Eliot's concept of "objective correlative," some outside object he could play against and use to define himself. Mailer's foray into politics had begun the process, but the march on the

Pentagon to protest the escalating war in Vietnam reveals and confirms Mailer's true goal: It is not politics, but myth, which Mailer will use as both backdrop and role, environment and substance.

The essential quality of myth, as Mailer perhaps intuitively realizes, is that it resides in gritty particulars, specific individuals. Raptured by myth, nobodies become somebodies, then become everybodies, transformed from their quotidian selves into archetypes but retaining the quirks and tics that make them individuals. Indeed, little personal faults are magnified to encompassing passions, and individual traits mirror universal ones. So a drab country girl becomes a golden film star, and, somehow, something more. So a barely articulate Midwestern brooder becomes a murderer, then becomes Nemesis. Both are understood and revealed by Norman Mailer in this new, mythic perception.

Marilyn (1972) and *The Executioner's Song* (1979) are mythic biographies, faithful to the truths that lurk, hidden but telling, in their facts. The first book is savaged by many critics, unappreciated by many more; the second is hailed as a masterpiece, wins Mailer his second Pulitzer Prize, and largely restores his faltering literary reputation. Yet the central point that connects the two works, which Rollyson rightly recognizes even if most critics do not, is their essential similarity. In truly mythic fashion, Mailer has become Marilyn Monroe, has become Gary Gilmore. He has, once again, re-created himself, but so thoroughly and persuasively that Norman Mailer seems to have vanished, subsumed beneath speculation and intuition in *Marilyn*, masked behind the telling clutter of crucial detail in *The Executioner's Song*. The path from the Pentagon steps to Hollywood and the Utah state prison may seem a curiously indirect and unconnected journey, but Rollyson's excellent travel guide reveals the inherent rightness, the seeming inevitability, of Mailer's course.

So now, re-created again, Mailer pauses. He has found his method but he distrusts his medium. There is about it the suspicion of journalism—mere journalism, some will sneer, perhaps even Mailer himself in some dark, midnight moments. The old novelist's ambition still burns, that impulse to do something on the grand scale. Mailer produces *Ancient Evenings* (1983), a tour of ancient Egypt with reincarnation via sex as its central theme and guiding motif. Sex and re-creation: The reader is back in familiar Mailer territory, although the pyramids look a little odd.

Ancient Evenings is very long, densely packed, and, by most critical accounts, a mess. Still, it is Mailer's return to serious fiction, and so it brings his first love together with his belief in mythic re-creation. There is no enduring personality, the novel proclaims (and Mailer's career demonstrates), there is only the personality that continually creates and re-creates itself.

The same theme occupies *Harlot's Ghost* (1991), another enormous novel, this time about the United States Central Intelligence Agency and an agent whose various personalities, although not as mystic as an antique Egyptian's, are equally elusive. Once again, the critics and the reviewers wobble; do they have a handle on this writer, or do they not? Mailer has become too important to be ignored, but is he any good?

The question remains to be answered. Those who want to make a start of it should begin with Carl Rollyson's biography. "This is not a good time to be publishing a biography of Norman Mailer," Rollyson begins his introduction. On the contrary, when the biography is as well written, thoughtful, and intelligent as this one, then it is indeed a very good time to publish a biography of this most difficult, provocative, and, just perhaps, truly original writer.

Michael Witkoski

Sources for Further Study

Booklist. LXXXVIII, October 1, 1991, p. 235.
Kirkus Reviews. LIX, August 1, 1991, p. 996.
Library Journal. CXVI, September, 1991, p. 192.
Publishers Weekly. CCXXXVIII, September 6, 1991, p. 86.
The Washington Post. October 29, 1991, p. C3

LONE STAR RISING
Lyndon Johnson and His Times, 1908-1960

Author: Robert Dallek (1934-   )
Publisher: Oxford University Press (New York). Illustrated. 699 pp. $30.00
Type of work: Biography
Time: 1908-1960
Locale: The United States

Dallek offers a balanced assessment of Lyndon Johnson from his birth until his election as vice president of the United States

> *Principal personages:*
> LYNDON B. JOHNSON, a Texas politician, the thirty-sixth president of the United States
> LADY BIRD JOHNSON, his wife
> SAM EALY JOHNSON, his father
> REBEKAH BAINES JOHNSON, his mother
> JOHN CONNALLY, an aide to Johnson, later governor of Texas
> THOMAS G. CORCORAN, an aide to President Franklin D. Roosevelt
> DWIGHT D. EISENHOWER, the thirty-fourth president of the United States
> FRANKLIN D. ROOSEVELT, the thirty-second president of the United States
> HUBERT H. HUMPHREY, a United States senator from Minnesota
> WALTER JENKINS, an aide to Johnson
> RICHARD B. RUSSELL, a United States senator from Georgia
> SAM RAYBURN, a Texas congressman
> ALVIN J. WIRTZ, an Austin, Texas, lawyer, and early supporter of Johnson

In his autobiographical memoir *The Good Times* (1990), Russell Baker recalls his days as White House correspondent for *The New York Times* during the mid-1950's. At that time, Baker observes, the Senate was remarkably well supplied with talented leaders, but one, Majority Leader Lyndon Johnson of Texas, stood alone: "Johnson was a flesh-and-blood, three-volume biography, and if you ever got it written you'd discover after publication that you'd missed the key point and got the interpretation completely wrong and needed a fourth to set things right." Multifaceted and complex, Johnson reminded him of a character from a Russian novel. The challenge inherent in the subject's complexity and the overwhelming amount of biographical material in existence—millions of pages of documents and thousands of taped interviews—have not deterred a number of biographers from attempting to unravel the riddles inherent in Johnson's life and career. During his lifetime, he was the subject of several campaign biographies, usually hagiographic, but at least one scathing attack appeared during his tenure in public office.

Following Johnson's death in 1973, a series of single-volume biographies appeared, each shedding considerable light on his life. Among these, the works of Doris Kearns Goodwin, Merle Miller, and Ronnie Dugger—all relying heavily on the oral testimony of Johnson intimates and contemporaries—are particularly valuable. The challenge of the full-length three-volume study was first assumed by Robert Caro, whose first volume, *The Years of Lyndon Johnson: Means of Ascent*, appeared in 1982.

Following the publication of his second and more controversial volume, *The Path to Power* (1990), a book that probes the darker sides of Johnson's personality and career, Caro announced that his task might require four volumes instead of three.

Dallek, who has previously published books on Franklin D. Roosevelt and Ronald Reagan, has assumed the challenge of the full-length scholarly biography, though he expects to complete his work in two lengthy volumes. One major objective is a better-balanced, fairer view of Johnson than other biographies have accorded the subject. Lightly documented and accessible to the general reader, Dallek's book draws heavily upon the mine of materials found in the Johnson Presidential Library and on taped interviews housed there and elsewhere. The title *Lone Star Rising* is remarkably well chosen, for it directs attention to the Texas background that served as a backdrop to Johnson's ambition and explains much about his character.

The biography chronicles Johnson's life from its beginning in the Texas Hill country to his election as vice president in the 1960 national election. During that time, Johnson served twenty-eight years in public life, beginning as a secretary to Con grooman Richard Kleberg. All the significant American political events, conflicts, and movements of the mid twentieth century swirl about Johnson: the Depression, the New Deal, World War II, the Cold War, the arms race, space exploration, the Civil Rights movement, and the social and economic entitlement legislation Johnson championed during his term as president. Thus, the biography recapitulates those significant times.

During the Depression, Johnson was appointed director of the National Youth Organization in Texas by President Roosevelt in 1935 and held the position until 1937, when he won a special election as congressman from the tenth district of Texas. After losing a special senatorial election in 1941, he remained in the House of Representatives until he won a Senate seat in 1948. There he served successively as minority whip, minority leader, and majority leader. He is generally regarded as the most effective majority leader ever to serve in the Senate, a judgment Dallek supports.

Exploring a life of glaring inconsistencies and contradictions creates uneasiness among readers, for it reminds them that real people, unlike those of literary works, are not all of a piece, a realization that arises from a deeper examination of character and motives than most undertake willingly. The complexity of Johnson's life can hardly be exaggerated, although a biographer can provide plausible explanations for many of his personal traits and his actions. Like his daunting physical presence, the conflicting qualities within the man existed on the grand scale. The pragmatist and idealist, the populist and the tycoon, the mixture of virtues and vices, exaggerated admiration of riches and power and identification and sympathy for the poor, the crude frontiersman and the social charmer—these and more contradictions combined to form Johnson as the most complex political figure of his time. As Dallek observes, Johnson's extremes were in part a way of manipulating others and molding them to his will.

A second quality that made Johnson daunting, one that supports the view that he was larger than life, was his almost unbelievable energy. As a boy he was often indolent, showing no particular interest, direction, or promise; but from the time he began college at Southwest Texas State Teachers College in San Marcos, he threw himself into his work with a level of energy that made it impossible for others not to notice him. In every position he held, from secretary to Congressman Kleberg to Senate majority leader, he directed all of his energies to the task, achieving results that most observers thought impossible. His week consisted of seven days, not five, and his working hours were fifteen and sixteen daily, not eight. A driven man, his only genuine interest in life was politics. He drove his staff unmercifully, but he did not demand of them as much as he demanded of himself. As Dallek's narrative shows, he possessed a genius for understanding—and manipulating—others along with an ability to master the workings of institutions. Perhaps because of his father's reputation as a state legislator and the initial benefits Johnson reaped from it, he learned to attach himself to experienced mentors, who aided him in mastering the organization and workings of institutions such as the Senate.

Dallek's title implies the importance of Johnson's Texas political background, a very different one from that of other states, which molded his career and his political goals. From his family background in the Texas Hill Country, Johnson gained both the desire to excel and the personal psychological conflicts that Goodwin explored in her early biography. Once he had entered public life, he encountered the realities of the prevailing Texas one-party politics that Dallek admirably describes. To characterize political life as rough-and-tumble is an understatement. Despite his clearly positive view of Johnson, Dallek demonstrates that, far from rising above the chicanery, skulduggery, ballot-stuffing, and corner-cutting that were the rules of the game, Johnson excelled at them. In political campaigns, no one paid attention to legal limits on political spending; instead, the objective was to spend whatever was required to win. Johnson attracted enough wealthy supporters that he could usually win against heavy odds. Dallek sheds as much light as one reasonably can on the contested 1948 senatorial election, in which Johnson's supporters were accused by his opponent of stealing the election by stuffing ballot boxes. A fair assessment does not exonerate anyone; it demonstrates rather the difficulty of ascertaining which side stole the greater number of votes.

As Dallek explains, the generally low level of political contests in Texas was exacerbated by the split between liberals and conservatives that developed within the Texas Democratic Party. It originated in 1940 with the break between President Franklin D. Roosevelt and his Texan vice president, John Nance Garner, over Roosevelt's decision to run for a third term. Texas politicians who had supported the New Deal remained liberal Roosevelt loyalists, whereas Garner's supporters constituted a conservative core of opposition in the state. Johnson, a firm New Dealer, remained a supporter of the president; yet following Roosevelt's death, after the political climate in Texas had changed dramatically and he had been elected to the Senate, he made so many concessions to conservatives that liberals felt betrayed. As senator, he mastered the art of compromise and generally was effective in putting together unholy alliances to pass bills in the national interest. In foreign affairs,

Johnson strongly advocated bipartisanship and unity and gave solid support to most initiatives of the Republican administration. This led him to expect a similar bipartisan spirit after he became president and to experience bitter disappointment when it was not forthcoming.

Yet despite his strong inclinations toward concession and compromise, Johnson remained, as Dallek explains, a New Dealer. An important and carefully developed thesis of Dallek's book is that Johnson's political goal from his beginning in politics was the integration of the South into the American economy. This could be accomplished, he believed, only through federally directed programs and through federal intervention in the regional economy. For all his sympathy with Southern colleagues in the Senate, Johnson was not one of them. He believed that the South wasted its potential for progress fighting for such lost causes as segregation and that the result was a stagnant economy that harmed all Southerners. The New Deal held out hope for progress to the region, and Johnson as congressman and senator made sure that those he represented benefitted from the programs it spawned.

By explaining Johnson's motives and clarifying the contexts of his words and deeds, Dallek achieves a fair and sometimes sympathetic analysis. As an example of his method, one might cite a comment made by Lady Bird Johnson's father, Harold Taylor. When she was deliberating whether to accept Lyndon's hasty proposal following a whirlwind courtship, her father remarked that some of the best deals were made in a hurry. On the surface, this appears the crude response of a cattle trader perhaps eager to rid himself of the burden of a grown daughter. Yet Dallek points out that he made the comment in order to balance contrary advice from her favorite unmarried aunt to the effect that if Lyndon loved her he would be willing to wait for her.

A second example concerns Johnson's role as director of the National Youth Organization in Texas. In this position, he took a keen interest in helping blacks but did little to help the equally large minority of Hispanics in Texas. This preference has been seen as cynical political maneuvering, since Washington was pressing for aid to blacks and ignoring Hispanics. As Dallek explains, Johnson understood the realities of life in Texas: Hispanics, while they lived under a poverty as severe as that of blacks, were not so devastated by the Depression. Because of their concentration in rural South Texas, they were not plagued by hunger and unemployment to the degree that Texas blacks were. In supporting blacks, Johnson was not being cynically expedient but pragmatically realistic, applying his principle that politics is the art of the possible—an art he mastered early in life.

Dallek's study achieves in large measure the balanced view he attempts. His Johnson demonstrates all the qualities of ambition, craving for power, and willingness to compromise that one finds in other portraits, yet he is capable of acts requiring political courage, as when he refuses to sign the Southern Manifesto supporting segregation in the South. Dallek's thesis is that Johnson never abandoned his liberal New Deal position, motivated as he was by the effort to bring the South into the economic mainstream through federalism. He accepted compromises and delays but never abandoned his original stance. Dallek's thesis helps explain Johnson's success with domestic programs when he later became the thirty-sixth president.

Stanley Archer

Sources for Further Study

The Atlantic. CCLXVIII, September, 1991, p. 114.
Chicago Tribune. August 18, 1991, XIV, p. 1.
The Christian Science Monitor. August 30, 1991, p. 12.
Houston Post. August 18, 1991, p. C8.
Los Angeles Times Book Review. August 11, 1991, p. 2.
National Review. XLIII, September 23, 1991, p. 45.
The New York Times Book Review. XCVI, July 21, 1991, p. 1.
Newsweek. CXVIII, July 22, 1991, p. 52.
Publishers Weekly. CCXXXVIII, June 14, 1991, p. 49.
Time. CXXXVIII, July 29, 1991, p. 6.
The Washington Post Book World. XXI, July 21, 1991, p. 1.

THE LOSER

Author: Thomas Bernhard (1931-1989)
First published: Der Untergeher, 1984, in Germany
Translated from the German by Jack Dawson
Afterword by Mark M. Anderson
Publisher: Alfred A. Knopf (New York). 190 pp. $19.00
Type of work: Novel
Time: The 1950's to the 1980's
Locale: Austria

The surviving member of a trio of friends recalls the events and circumstances that had shaped their relationship since they participated together in a summer course at the Mozarteum in Salzburg twenty-eight years earlier

> *Principal characters:*
> GLENN GOULD, a fictionalized reflection of the late Canadian pianist
> WERTHEIMER, a pianist destroyed by Gould's genius
> AN UNNAMED NARRATOR, an aspiring essayist on Gould's genius

Thomas Bernhard, the gadfly of the Austrian cultural establishment for years, died in February, 1989. By his own definition a troublemaker, Bernhard repeatedly attacked the leading figures, institutions, and cherished illusions of a country which, however, he never chose to leave. He quarreled publicly, in print and in court, with prominent critics, stage and musical directors, and national politicians. During the ceremony at which he was awarded the Austrian national prize for literature in 1968, Bernhard drove the minister of culture from the auditorium with a response marked by inflammatory criticism rather than the expected gratitude.

Both in his fiction and in the five volumes of his autobiography, published from 1975 to 1982, Bernhard repeatedly targets facets of Austrian society and culture with his invective. He recalls with spiteful pleasure, for example, the ease with which the Austrian educational system shed the symbol of political tyranny after World War II while maintaining its authoritarian spirit. When Bernhard was a schoolboy, the swastika hanging on the front wall of his classroom had been replaced overnight by a cross, but the outline of the Nazi symbol long remained visible in the background. Many years later, the remnants of fascism and anti-Semitism in Austrian society became the thematic center of a play that Kurt Waldheim called "an insult to the nation." *Heldenplatz* (1988, Heroes' Square), performed in Vienna's prestigious Burgtheater a few months before Bernhard's death, brought the final round of the longstanding feud surrounding his writing to a controversial climax.

The Loser, one of Bernhard's first novels to appear after the series of autobiographical studies, is also full of anti-Austrian sentiment. The narrator takes particular aim at Salzburg and its claim to be a haven for the creative spirit. It is permeated instead, he writes, by provincialism and antipathy toward artists. Austria's educational system, its family structure, even its trains and inns come under heavy fire in the thoughts of Bernhard's narrator. Both the academy of music in Vienna and the celebrated Mozarteum in Salzburg suffer severe criticism in *The Loser*, a novel set against the larger backdrop of the Austro-Germanic classical musical tradition with a narrative focus on the intertwined fates of three piano students.

As he did in several other works of fiction written at the time, Bernhard drew heavily from his own experience for *The Loser* and began to borrow selectively from the biographies of other public figures as well. In the early 1950's, he had himself been a music student both in Vienna and at the Mozarteum in Salzburg. The death of the Canadian musical genius Glenn Gould in October, 1982, however, was doubtless the immediate impetus for the novel in which a fictionalized Gould plays a major role. Unlike Bernhard, the narrator of the work has abandoned his homeland for Madrid, where he hopes to complete his essay on Gould, a task that consumes him but one that seems destined to remain incomplete. Although he probably never met the pianist in person, Bernhard must have been fascinated by his single-minded devotion paradoxically expressed by his sudden retirement from the concert stage at the age of thirty-two. Both the real Gould and Bernhard's fictional reflection discarded the public life of the virtuoso and the human vanities connected with it, not in order to abandon their art, but to perfect it. At this point, however, literary imagination and biographical fact part ways. Following his early retirement from the public eye, the real Gould increasingly turned to recording technology to minimize the chance of human fallibility entering into musical reproduction. Bernhard's figure, on the other hand, continued to depend on an inhuman conception of his own genius. He fantasizes about becoming one with his Steinway, merging with the piano to eliminate the human element in the process of transforming the music on the page into the sensory realm.

Bernhard had no illusions about the faithful re-creation of even his own life's story in written form, an attitude that allowed him to appropriate and alter Gould's biography without artistic compunction. Early in the novel, the narrator recalls the circumstances of his death at a point prior to the onset of the narration. In this novelistic version, he had succumbed at the age of fifty-one to a fatal stroke while playing the *Goldberg Variations*, a fabricated, even though fitting, end for this century's foremost interpreter of Johann Sebastian Bach. Although not at the keyboard, the real Gould did die from a stroke just days before a new recording of the *Goldberg Variations* was released. Bernhard further embellished Gould's biography with a large dose of his own Austrophobia. In the memory of the narrator, the fictional figure supports and substantiates his cynical disdain for the cultural pretensions of Salzburg, the city where the novel's characters first met and studied twenty-eight years previously.

Most of the events to which the novel refers took place during these twenty-eight years and are filtered through the perspective of the narrator's recollections. Gould shares his central role in these recollections with a figure named Wertheimer, the third member of the trio that had studied piano together for a summer at the Mozarteum. The meeting of the two Austrians with the Canadian had been a fateful one in determining the further courses of their lives. As the narrator describes it, Gould's innate genius had undermined the confidence of the other two in their talent so suddenly and to such a degree that both gave up their hopes for musical careers of their own. The narrator wasted little time in regretting his fate and almost immediately gave away his Steinway to the young daughter of a local teacher. For Wertheimer, on the other hand, who eventually followed the narrator's example and got rid of his piano, the meeting with Gould had thrown his life into a downward spiral that ended with his suicide soon after Gould's death. By giving Wertheimer the nickname the "loser" during the summer they spent together in Salzburg, Gould seems to have played a part in prescribing this trajectory.

At the point when the narration begins, the narrator has been to Wertheimer's funeral and is on his way back to Vienna, from where he plans to return to Spain. This objective action in the narrative present becomes clear to the reader, however, only after many pages filled with a stream-of-consciousness narration of the past, a flood of memories that has risen to the surface of the narrator's consciousness in the wake of his friend's suicide and funeral. With the narrator's facility for recall in a state of apparent overstimulation, various themes in these memories return again and again, often linked to other memories in the process. The narration does not proceed from beginning to end, but as these associative linkages become increasingly inclusive, a picture of the past twenty-eight years emerges. Allusions to Bach's *Goldberg Variations*, for example, provide associations to several key events in this emerging picture. Gould first displayed his overpowering genius to the vulnerable Wertheimer while playing this piece at the Mozarteum. After hearing only a few bars and before they had even met, Wertheimer had given up on his own talent— a major talent, as the narrator repeatedly affirms, but incomparably weaker than Gould's. When Gould returned to the Salzburg Festival two years later, he came to play the *Goldberg Variations*. Much later in their lives, he would send the narrator his recording of the work for his fiftieth birthday. One year after this and only days prior to the narrative present, just before he leaves Vienna for Wertheimer's funeral in Switzerland, the narrator plays this recording. At the very end of the novel, during his return trip to Vienna after the funeral, he repeats this gesture one last time, symbolically closing a relationship with the same musical notes with which it had begun.

The narrator fills in the past for the reader not by remembering one event after another but by gradually adding information to key themes and allusions that are repeated throughout the narration. Events occur in the text as they happen to occur in the narrator's consciousness, not according to the historical order of the events themselves. As this order of the past becomes apparent through the accretion of information, the outer frame of the narrative present also becomes evident. In stylistic imitation of Glenn Gould's mastery of musical counterpoint, Bernhard plays off the linearity of events as a kind of literary counterpoint to the swirling memories of his narrator.

From the first sentence of the novel, the reader is aware that the narrator is entering an inn, but its location and the reason that he has stopped there emerge only very slowly. He repeatedly alludes to this location, but his absorption in his memories seems to block out any narration of the present moment. Gradually, however, the present connects with the past as the inn gains a specific location and significance. It is well into the second half of the novel before the innkeeper arrives on the scene to greet the guest and the focus of the narration turns to the present. The narrator has stopped over on his return to Vienna at this particular inn because it is in convenient proximity to Wertheimer's country house in Traich. Before he returns to Madrid, he wants to inspect the papers and notes that his friend has left behind. He hopes to find clues and materials for that obstinate essay on Gould that he has been writing and rewriting for years. When he finally arrives at Traich, Wertheimer's housekeeper tells him the strange story of the revelry that had taken place there during Wertheimer's last days. The normally reclusive Wertheimer had invited a number of musicians and artists for an extended stay but had regularly forced them out of the house and into the woods with his incessant piano playing, attempting, the housekeeper surmises, to drive his guests crazy. Asked by the narrator about his employer's papers, the housekeeper relates how he had helped Wertheimer burn notes by the thousands during the final days before his suicide.

Again and again over the years, Bernhard has exemplified in his works the Baroque wisdom about the futility of human efforts and aspirations in any endeavor. Wertheimer is simply the most obvious "loser" in the trio of characters in this novel. For the narrator as well, even though he still clings to his ambition, there is little hope for success in his writing projects. He has not published anything he has written in twenty-eight years and plans to destroy his ninth attempted essay on Gould when he returns to Madrid. Yet even for the born artist such as Gould, who played without effort and without apparent ambition, there is no lasting triumph, since death overtakes him before either of the others. He too is a loser to this final reality, ironically staged by Bernhard to occur while Gould is playing the work that displayed his artistry better than any other.

Yet Bernhard's achievement as a writer does not lie in the originality of his moral message but rather in the linguistic mastery of his breathlessly long sentences. Rhythmically constructed and unchecked by conventional paragraph or episodic markings, they seem to propel the reading process forward with their own energy and thrust. The emotional fury, the bitterness and anger often directed by his frustrated characters in long tirades at specifically Austrian circumstances are always superbly controlled. The question is not whether but how soon Austria will forgive the impertinence of its brilliant son and absorb his rebellion into a cultural legacy that includes other genial spirits such as Wolfgang Amadeus Mozart, Sigmund Freud, and Georg Trakl who suffered—and profited creatively—from a painful ambivalence toward their native land. Even in death, Bernhard has not made it easy for his maligned fatherland. He stipulated in his will that, for the duration of the legal copyright, none of his works were to be published or performed posthumously in Austria.

Francis Michael Sharp

Sources for Further Study

Booklist. LXXXVIII, September 1, 1991, p. 27.
Chicago Tribune. September 15, 1991, XIV, p. 6.
Kirkus Reviews. LIX, July 1, 1991, p. 803.
Library Journal. CXVI, August, 1991, p. 140.
The New York Times Book Review. XCVI, September 8, 1991, p. 15.
Publishers Weekly. CCXXXVIII, July 5, 1991, p. 58.
Quill and Quire. LVII, July, 1991, p. 50.
The Village Voice. October 8, 1991, p. S7.
The Wall Street Journal. October 8, 1991, p. A20.
The Washington Post Book World. XXI, September 15, 1991, p. 4.

LOW LIFE
Lures and Snares of Old New York

Author: Luc Sante
Publisher: Farrar, Straus & Giroux (New York). 414 pp. $27.50
Type of work: History
Time: 1840-1919
Locale: New York City

A history of New York City from about 1840 until the beginning of Prohibition in 1919, focusing on the crime, corruption, disease, poverty, and dissipation afflicting the ignorant masses packed into the tenements of Manhattan

> *Principal personages:*
> PHINEAS T. BARNUM, a famous New York showman, con artist, preacher, speculator, and politician
> STEVE BRODIE, a flamboyant New York saloonkeeper who became a legend by purportedly jumping off the Brooklyn Bridge
> ANTHONY COMSTOCK, a prominent reformer of the period who became a symbol of moral fanaticism
> GEORGE WASHINGTON "CHUCK" CONNORS, a famous Bowery character whose speech, manners, and dress came to epitomize the spirit of the Gay Nineties Bowery
> STEPHEN CRANE, a famous American author who wrote fiction and articles about New York City's lower classes
> TIMOTHY D. "BIG TIM" SULLIVAN, a prominent politician notorious for rigging elections and embezzling public funds
> WILLIAM MARCY "BOSS" TWEED, the ruthless head of a powerful political organization known as the Tweed Ring
> WALT WHITMAN, the famous poet and journalist who helped to romanticize the New York lower classes

Luc Sante, who was thirty-seven when *Low Life* was published, was born in Verviers, Belgium. After moving to New York toward the end of the 1960's social revolution, he lived in a dilapidated Lower-East-Side tenement building for more than ten years while struggling to survive as a free-lance writer. During this period, he became curious about the city's past and began to delve into it by reading books, examining old photographs, and visiting the many old landmarks that had miraculously managed to survive all the demolition and construction of the twentieth century. His story is confined to what he calls Manhattan's "realms of attraction and concealment, the bazaars and the underworld: the Bowery, Satan's Circus, Hell's Hundred Acres, Hell's Kitchen, the slums, the waterfront." He stops short at 1919, the year of the Volstead Act and the Red Scare, evidently believing that subsequent events, including the influx of nonwhite minorities, would require a whole volume in themselves.

Sante divides his book into four sections. The first is entitled "The Landscape" and deals with the growth of Manhattan from a peaceful farming area into the maze of buildings dominated by fantastic skyscrapers that exists today. It is hard to realize that in the 1820's land could be bought in the vicinity of Seventy-second Street and Fifth Avenue for as little as a thousand dollars an acre. Sante's description of the gridiron layout and rapid development of the city is so detailed that it could be appreciated only by residents of New York; others may want to skip it and get on to the lures and snares that are promised in the book's subtitle.

Part 2, entitled "Sporting Life," deals with entertainment, saloon life, dope, gambling, and prostitution. The book's subtitle, "Lures and Snares of Old New York," is rather misleading, because there is nothing salacious or even titillating about any of its description. Like the grim old black-and-white photographs liberally distributed throughout the book, the prose conveys a feeling of almost unmitigated despair.

Prostitutes, then as now, were physically abused and financially exploited. Call houses were far more common in the nineteenth century. Although they offered their inmates protection from predatory males, the management customarily took the lion's share of the earnings. Many prostitutes became addicted to drugs and alcohol, and the madams who ran the houses made it a practice to get their employees hooked. At one time it was estimated that one-fortieth of the total population of the city was engaged in prostitution. Syphilis and gonorrhea were rampant.

The entertainment of the period seems pathetic, a desperate attempt to escape, if only for a few hours, from the squalor, toil, and gnawing insecurity of lower-class life. The clang of the cash register drowned out the music and laughter; real gaiety and good fellowship were rare commodities. As in Victorian England, intoxication was a means of escape from the unbearable reality of daily existence.

Along with contemporary photographs, mostly obtained from various New York museums and the New York Historical Society, Sante includes a few still shots from Hollywood films to illustrate the difference between the reality of lower-class life and the romanticized and sanitized version that popular films such as *The Bowery* (1933) and *Dead End* (1937) implanted in the popular imagination. The old photographs of freezing men standing in lines to get a loaf of stale bread or a ticket handed out by an enterprising politician entitling the holder to a free bed in a flophouse bring to mind Theodore Dreiser's harrowing chapters describing George Hurstwood's moral deterioration and eventual suicide in *Sister Carrie* (1900). Real life for many poor people of the period was nearly as grueling and precarious as life in the German concentration camps during World War II.

The third section of *Low Life* is entitled "The Arm" and describes the forces of order, repression, and profit. The first chapter in this section deals with "Gangland" and discusses some of the famous New York gangs such as the Bowery Boys, the Dead Rabbits, the Plug Uglies, and the Swamp Angels, as well as some of the more prominent individuals of the period. Violence was just as rampant then as now, but the ethnic makeup was different: Blacks and Hispanics were small minorities and carried little weight until after World War II.

The second chapter in "The Arm" deals with the corrupt and ineffectual "Coppers" and the third chapter with "The Tiger," the infamous Tammany Hall, which controlled the city through violence and bribery. Other chapters in this section deal with reformers and other outsiders who were either horrified or enchanted by the immorality of the mushrooming city. Sante quotes extensively from famous writers, including Nathaniel Hawthorne, William Dean Howells, Charles Dickens, Walt Whitman, Stephen Crane, Theodore Dreiser, and Mark Twain, whose observations help to establish the flavor of life in old New York.

Because of the ineffectuality of the police and the justice system, especially with regard to the poor, the gangs represented a law unto themselves. There were some areas in the city into which the police would venture only in forces of a half-dozen officers. Young slum-dwellers graduated from youth gangs to adult gangs that robbed and murdered with impunity. One of the most notorious gangs of the period, the Whyos, offered the following menu of services:

Punching	$2
Both eyes blacked	$4
Nose and jaw broke	$10
Jacked out	$15
Ear chawed off	$15
Leg or arm broke	$19
Shot in leg	$25
Stab	$25
Doing the big job	$100 and up

Part 4 of *Low Life* is entitled "The Invisible City." Here Sante discusses orphans, derelicts, struggling artists, and various anonymous street people. The plight of children was the worst of all. They were often neglected, abused, or put to work in sweatshops or peddling such items as flowers, cigars, and neckties. One of the most widespread occupations for small boys was selling newspapers, and Sante states that the great majority of the newsboys were homeless. Another common occupation for young boys was as free-lance bootblacks. Many children lived on the streets, as children still do in South America, India, and other parts of the Third World. Sante states that in the prevailing conditions of extreme poverty, many families could provide for their children only through the nursing stage, and most lower-class children were expected to be self-supporting by the age of twelve. Many children became involved in petty crime such as shoplifting and picking pockets because it was their only means of survival. There were numerous enterprising Fagins who organized children and taught them how to steal. Child prostitution involving both boys and girls was not only common but also openly conducted.

In the chapter entitled "Carnival," Sante describes some of the major riots of the period, including the famous Draft Riots of 1863 in which an estimated two thousand people were killed and about eight thousand wounded. There was never any real organization to these outbreaks; they were not politically inspired but were spontaneous expressions of the general resentment of the exploitative conditions that were felt, if not clearly understood, by the masses. Sante ostensibly maintains an objective attitude toward his subject, but he makes it clear enough that he blames the wealthy class, along with the crooked politicians, for much of the crime and moral laxity exhibited by the poor.

Sante's book is a strange mixture of straight reportage and colorful metaphor. His prose sometimes sounds like French translated into English, and at times it can be almost as difficult to understand his meaning as it is to understand some modern poetry. For example, in discussing the organization of his book he writes:

> The categories can be seen as corresponding to the cards in a Tarot deck of New York City, or . . . to the archetypal figures in a gambler's dream book. They are the constituents of New York's vocabulary of symbols, the objects and creatures in its zodiac. . . .

At other times he sounds objective and dispassionate, like a reporter intent on getting down the facts, although his selection of details finally comes to seem haphazard, if not whimsical. He states that he did not intend to write a literal history of the period but rather intended to follow his own fancy in studying his subject. "This is by no means a work of academic history," he writes.

> In researching it, I was guided more by chance and intuition than by method. I was more interested in legends than in statistics, in rumors than in official reports.

Sante relied heavily on books about the period but evidently did not spend any time consulting original sources such as newspaper files or correspondence. He states in several places that the newspaper reporting of the day was vague and inaccurate, but it seems surprising that this should have bothered him, in view of the fact that he was interested in legends and rumors. Since he does not pretend to have written a comprehensive history of New York City or to have contributed anything in the way of original scholarship, the book must be judged as a specimen of that unique contribution to world literature, the school of New Journalism. His history is personal and impressionistic. Although the book is neatly divided into sections and chapters, some topics are covered in detail while others of equal importance are treated sketchily.

In recent years, Sante has been moderately successful as a journalist. He has been published by the prestigious *The New York Review of Books* as well as by *The New Republic* and *Harper's Magazine*. As a foreign-born writer and a relative newcomer to New York City, he has an original perspective. He is in the tradition of the many foreign writers such as Charles Dickens, Oscar Wilde, and Alexis de Tocqueville who have been able to see aspects of American life that Americans themselves tend to overlook because they take them for granted. Sante makes the reader aware of the really strange phenomenon represented by the growth of New York into the world's most important city in a remarkably short time. London, Paris, and Rome took many centuries to evolve into cities of dominant international status, whereas because of the wealth of the land and the frantic desire of immigrants for freedom and opportunity, New York seemed to sprout its skyscrapers overnight.

Although Sante paints many thumbnail portraits, including ones of such flamboyant personalities as Steve Brodie and Boss Tweed, the overall impression of his book is that of a great city almost creating itself, like some sort of monstrous robot using human beings as mere implements in the process. Because of its spectacular buildings and intricate underground infrastructure, New York, more than any other city in the world, gives the impression of being a living thing that feeds on the hapless people who are magnetized to it from all over the globe. Sante was both horrified and fascinated by this incredible American city, and he has managed to get much of his feelings into his book.

Bill Delaney

Sources for Further Study

Booklist. LXXXVII, August, 1991, p. 2096.
Chicago Tribune. September 27, 1991, V, p. 3.
Fortune. CXXIV, December 30, 1991, p. 136.
Library Journal. CXVI, June 1, 1991, p. 163.
Los Angeles Times Book Review. September 29, 1991, p. 4.
The New York Times Book Review. XCVI, September 29, 1991, p. 14.
Publishers Weekly. CCXXXVIII, July 12, 1991, p. 59.
The Village Voice. October 15, 1991, p. 79.
The Wall Street Journal. September 4, 1991, p. A10.
The Washington Post Book World. XXI, September 1, 1991, p. 3.

THE MacGUFFIN

Author: Stanley Elkin (1930-   )
Publisher: Linden Press/Simon & Schuster (New York). 283 pp. $19.95
Type of work: Novel
Time: The 1990's
Locale: An unnamed mid-sized city near St. Louis

The MacGuffin *is Elkin at his best: compassionate, bitter, wildly inventive, and wonderfully funny*

> *Principal characters:*
> ROBERT (BOB, BOBBO) DRUFF, a fifty-eight-year-old streets commissioner
> ROSE HELEN, his wife
> MIKEY, their son
> DICK and DOUG, Druff's drivers
> MARGARET GLORIO, a buyer for a local department store
> SU'AD AL NAJH, a Lebanese student killed by a hit and run driver
> THE MACGUFFIN, Druff's narrative muse

Arthur Miller's archetypal twentieth century American tragic hero, Willy Loman, leads as if inevitably to the inarticulate working-class characters of Raymond Carver's minimalist short stories. By a more circuitous route, Willy also leads to the sprawling, maximalist novels of one of contemporary American fiction's most undeservedly under-read writers, Stanley Elkin. Brilliant as Carver's highly regarded fiction is, it comes to the reader in the recognizable and readily assimilated form of Hemingway-like reticence. Elkin's fiction is altogether different—demanding not because it is difficult (in the erudite style of James Joyce or the opaque manner of Henry James) but because it requires an adjustment of expectations (and as a result a change of reading strategies) on the reader's part. Elkin's fiction shows among other things that humor—even black humor—can be just as appropriate a medium for the thwarted aspirations of a Willy Loman as the mode of domestic tragedy, however tempered it may be by contemporary irony, in the stories and novels of Carver and other like-minded, writer-workshop-trained minimalists. In addition, Elkin's fiction is, as theirs rarely is, interesting page by page, sentence by sentence (rather than merely plot by plot, character by character). In Elkin there is never just the page; there is always page after page. Carver's characters can only occasionally bring themselves to speak; Elkin's characters cannot not talk. Drawing on a carnivalesque range of American pop culture, they do not so much speak as spiel, not so much argue as harangue, obsessively, compulsively, endlessly, never letting one word suffice when twenty will do.

Elkin's linguistic manic depressives are an outraged and outrageous lot: a modern James Boswell; a department-store owner sent to jail for being "a bad man"; a late-night radio talk-show host; a Cincinnati bail bondsman; a kindhearted liquor-store owner murdered during a holdup and sent to hell ("the ultimate inner city") for taking God's name in vain; an Englishman organizing a transatlantic outing to Disney World for a group of children suffering from grotesquely funny but altogether fatal diseases; the rabbi of Lud, which is not a town but a collection of cemeteries; and above all Ben Flesh, a franchiser extraordinaire crisscrossing the country by car just as the early-1970's energy crisis strikes and just as multiple sclerosis (Elkin's own disease) begins to unravel Flesh's nervous system (and as the members of his ersatz family begin dying of their own blackly humorous maladies). "'Be hard, Mr. Softee,'" a stiff-upper-lip child (bleeding from all pores as he slowly dies of something called "Lassa fever") tells the franchiser, whose too too flaccid flesh will resolve itself into not a dew but a parking-lot-size sea of thawing frozen custard. Following typically Elkin logic, Flesh will of course fail as surely as will the electricity that once kept the custard frozen, suffering his cruel disease as Ellerbee, the liquor store owner, must suffer his fate, learning that God created hell only in order to have an audience for his stand-up comedy routines. Elkin's characters might well sympathize as they endure all God's bad jokes, for even as they suffer their various defeats and injustices they share this borscht-belt God's need to tell stories—and the need to have them heard.

Created in the dual image of his two makers—the afflicting God and the postmodern author—Robert/Bob/Bobbo Druff of *The MacGuffin* may well be Elkin's most masterful creation. First appointed to his job as the once-inexhaustible federal highway funds began to dry up, kept on not on the basis of merit or even loyalty but merely to fulfill a campaign pledge, this commissioner of streets in an anonymous mid-sized city located somewhere near Elkin's own St. Louis finds himself, at fifty-eight, "on the downhill side of destiny." His ungainly physique and declining health (bad heart, collapsed lung, poor circulation, medication-induced sexual impotence) contribute to the general loss of force that, paradoxically, fuels Druff through his forty-hour-long odyssey. A kind of Rodney Dangerfield, Druff cannot quite earn or even buy anyone's respect. Full of fears about losing his job, his drivers, his mind, and (ironically) even his way over the very streets he nominally rules, Druff feels and is ridiculous. Thinking of himself as the butt of a joke he does not understand, he finds some consolation in chewing coca leaves and, in the typically and brilliantly Elkinish language of his fantasies, "the If-I-Were-King subjunctivication of his life."

Druff does more than chew coca leaves and fantasize to while away the hours and soothe his battered ego. Druff narrates, turning simple lies, insignificant excuses, and brief daydreams into full-blown narratives replete with interesting characters, developed plots, and a warehouse full of material drawn from the quotidian reality he otherwise finds so unfulfilling. Narrators, however, need narratees. Druff's wife, Rose Helen, whose simmering "savage resentment" nearly matches Druff's, refuses to listen to him, even in her sleep. Druff's drivers are pressed into service, as is Margaret Glorio, with whom Druff has a brief and comical affair. On their first date, Druff tries to cover his nervousness by talking nonstop about his wife and son and, until he is caught, popping coca leaves.

"If nothing happened to you," Druff thinks, "you had to fall back on your character, spinning your life out of whole cloth, disaffiliate from the world." What happens to Druff is both insignificant and absurd—a joke life—but the character on which Druff has to fall back proves not simply inadequate but virtually nonexistent. Running for public office earlier in his career, Druff had no platform and no record; he had only the generic but oddly sincere slogan, "Vote for Bob Druff," something not even his wife was willing to do. Lacking both audience and constituency (except as witness to his painfully self-conscious pratfalls), Druff is forced to play all the roles himself.

Enter the MacGuffin. For Alfred Hitchcock, the "MacGuffin" was whatever was required to make the plot of one of his films proceed (a message slipped in someone's pocket, for example, or switched suitcases). For Druff it is something more (and for Elkin's reader, unlike Hitchcock's filmgoer, something more self-referential). It is nothing less than "the Muse of his plot line," which he invokes "with fervid, almost hot Hail-Mary hope." The MacGuffin is what gives Druff and his "bozo itinerary," his "pointless odyssey," shape and significance, and not incidentally relief from his own self-conscious inconsequentiality. Yet even as he turns to the story of another, Druff soon comes to imagine himself at the very center of his MacGuffin-inspired, double-stranded plot. One strand focuses on the hit-and-run death of his son Mikey's Lebanese girlfriend, Su'ad al-Najif, four months earlier (in which Druff, as Mikey's father and as streets commissioner, feels doubly involved). The other strand focuses on the plot Druff believes is afoot to oust him from his job—perhaps because of what others think he knows or might learn about Su'ad's death: "What terrified him now was that whatever it was it turned out they were trying to pin on him, so many were in on it. Not a ring, no conspiracy or compact, plot, scheme, plan, deal or design, but a cabal, out and out." What saves Druff from becoming the butt of his self-engendered paranoid joke is his role as self-aware artificer. Thus when the MacGuffin, itself a specialist in the improbable, accuses Druff of straining the plot, Druff replies, "The MacGuffin. MacGimicks Are Us."

Other than Robert Coover, no one writing today packs a sentence quite as full as Elkin, and no one packs a plot quite the way Elkin does either. *The MacGuffin* begins with a Friday-morning tour of the city streets, with Druff ostensibly in search of potholes, and proceeds by introducing MacGuffins aplenty as a way of filling the narrative holes by creating a temporary patch of plot. The novel proceeds primarily in terms of Druff's verbal "riffs" and more especially in slightly longer narrative flights of Druff's imagination (his first meeting with Su'ad, his picking up an ill-fitting suit at Brooks Brothers, his picking up Margaret Glorio at a restaurant bar, his courtship of Rose Helen thirty-six years before). Despite his fear "of again blurting out the hideous non sequitur perched on [his tongue] like irresistible candy," Druff's narrative is almost entirely in the form of non sequiturs that soon take on a zany logic of their own. Druff's efforts to fashion an entirely unified causal plot prove hilariously illogical. Once again, however, Druff's awareness of the absurdity of his MacGuffin-inspired story saves him from the ultimate non sequitur, the final irrationality—believing that his world and his individual existence are based on continuity rather than contiguity.

Drawing on Hitchcock's films, William Shakespeare's *Macbeth* (1605), William Faulkner's novels, James Joyce's *Ulysses* (1922), and Samuel Taylor Coleridge's *Rime of the Ancient Mariner* (1798), Elkin creates a field of verbal and intertextual play. Yet he never allows the reader to forget that it is fear, frustration, and anger that drive Druff to his MacGuffin-inspired flights of outrageous imagination and narrative pyrotechnics and away from his thirty-year-old son with his "rigorous, repetitious lockstep ways." Mikey, however, is more than a comic case of arrested development and object of Druff's wrath. He is made in his maker's image, with his lack of any real skills, his absurd but wholehearted commitments, his manic weightlifting, and above all his insecurity and ludicrous fears (which he also shares with his mother, who worries she will burn to death because she will not hear her smoke alarm, because the batteries in her hearing aid will have run down). A combination of "raw, bleeding need and nutty fatuity," Mikey is a chip off the old parental block. "I need you because," Druff says to his wife. The same indefinite need compelled Druff to deliver his self-pitying and strangely funny deathbed speech to Mikey twenty years before, on the occasion of Druff's first heart attack. It is this same need that continues to lead Druff, in Meg Glorio's words, "to put too much stock" and "set too much store," not in anything in particular but rather in the putting stock, the setting store. Ultimately, Druff is not interested in answers and ends, not even in finding out what really happened to his Lebanese MacGuffin, Su'ad. "The fact was . . . solutions were boring, never as interesting as the trouble they were brought in to put an end to." Thus *The MacGuffin* ends with Druff going to bed, "hoping not to sleep, daring not to dream," aware of what he is: the raw material for his MacGuffin-inspired but self-engendered tales of the Faulknerian heart in conflict with itself, aware that not only will it not prevail, it will not even endure.

Robert A. Morace

Sources for Further Study

Chicago Tribune. March 17, 1991, XIV, p. 5.
Choice. XXVIII, July, 1991, p. 1778.
Los Angeles Times Book Review. March 10, 1991, p. 3.
The New Republic. CCIV, May 20, 1991, p. 44.
The New York Times Book Review. XCVI, March 10, 1991, p. 5.
The New Yorker. LXVII, April 22, 1991, p. 115.
Partisan Review. LVIII, Summer, 1991, p. 478.
Publishers Weekly. CCXXXVIII, January 18, 1991, p. 46.
Time. CXXXVII, March 25, 1991, p. 70.
The Wall Street Journal. CCXVII, February 22, 1991, p. A9.
The Washington Post Book World. XXI, March 10, 1991, p. 7.

MADOC
A Mystery

Author: Paul Muldoon (1951-   )
Publisher: Farrar, Straus & Giroux (New York). 261 pp. $19.95
Type of work: Poetry

A book-length poem, which fully lives up to its subtitle, being part philosophical romp, part cultural quest, part epistemological conundrum, and total imaginative celebration

While most readers' attention will be drawn to the book-length title poem of Paul Muldoon's sixth and most ambitious volume, it should be noted at the outset that this title poem is prefaced by seven pieces which are much more representative of the poet's method prior to "Madoc" and which serve as a telling and testing prologue to the strange epic which comprises the bulk of the book. At first glance, these seven items seem somewhat out of place, and the difficulty in referring to them straightforwardly as poems underlines that sense of dislocation. They have little relation to one another. Formally, they are eclectic ("The Key" being in prose, "Asra" consisting of two lines). Tonally, they may seem somewhat wayward—the moving "Cauliflowers," an oblique elegy for Muldoon's father, and one of the poet's most evocative and moving works (its depth of feeling all the more noteworthy in a poet as notoriously tight-lipped as Muldoon), opens with an epigraph from *The National Enquirer.* Moreover, they have no apparent bearing on their extended companion piece, except that they provide a basis for Muldoon to perpetuate extravagantly the formal whimsy of all of his books since *Mules* (1977) by closing with a long poem.

With Muldoon, however, the reality of the case is not what lies, reconciled and compensatory, beyond dislocation and difference. On the contrary, the fact that the opening septet of poems have nothing to do with each other or with the larger project to which they are attached is one of their common features. This paradoxical reality—that entities resemble each other by sharing the aspect of difference—is a guide to these individual poems, to their constituting part 1 of *Madoc*, and to the nature of "Madoc" itself. Muldoon has earned an international reputation, which the verve and originality of "Madoc" will undoubtedly enhance and consolidate, for the elliptical, poker-faced, riddling, and somewhat surreal perspectives of his verse.

Evidence of his technical facility, his formal and tonal informality, the rapidity and quirkiness of thought's movement in Muldoon's poetry (aspects of his art which are sometimes referred to as cinematic), is abundantly to the fore in the seven prefacing poems of *Madoc*. In addition, however, such features have the effect of being present not merely for their own sake. They serve as an overture to the title poem, or rather, the title poem becomes a means of working out their implications. The purely imaginative project which constitutes "Madoc" is the end product of the challenging, light, witty, fastidious artistic sensibility which has been at play in all Muldoon's work prior to the publication of *Madoc*. Or perhaps it would be more in keeping with the spirit of "Madoc" to suggest that it constitutes a parallel universe to that of the somewhat more intimate concerns of Muldoon's lyrics. As such,

"Madoc" articulates with the calmness and idiosyncracy of genius the looking-glass world that all writing inevitably and ultimately denotes, existing, as it concludes about another's writing, "parallel to the parallel/ realm to which it is itself the only clue."

Although his work has been available in the United States since the publication of *Mules* (1977), some sense of Paul Muldoon's background may be useful in locating some of the energies and purposes which inform "Madoc." A native of Northern Ireland, he completed his secondary education there at roughly the same time as the present civil strife reached the stage at which British troops were introduced. This development, in turn, was followed by a notable escalation in violence of various kinds in the community. Despite the inescapable cultural and psychological effects of coming of age socially and educationally in such an environment, and despite the example of older poets from Northern Ireland, such as Seamus Heaney, John Montague, and Michael Longley addressing the sociocultural realities of their native province under such radically altered circumstances, Muldoon has not devoted much imaginative energy directly to the matter of Ulster. His response has been typically oblique, understated, more transformative than documentary. Yet it may be that this response is ultimately at least as eloquent as those of his elders by virtue of its characteristic aesthetic.

Muldoon's uses of uncertainty, his keen sense of the fragmentary, his apparently deadpan attitude to the reader's interrogation, his quiet amusement at how difficult it is to pin anything down, the transparent craftsmanship with which these elements are brought into coexistence, articulating the potential of relationship without ever necessarily attaining it, may be taken as a gloss on the discontinuous but enduring realities of Northern Ireland. This gloss, however, is also a repertoire of strategies which facilitate formal comprehension of Northern Ireland's paradoxical continuum of disruption. By the use of these strategies Muldoon places within the realm of formal discourse and, thereby, within the realm of cultural admissibility conditions for which no other text exists. The sustained critique of narrative which forms a fundamental formal and philosophical element in such earlier longer poems as "The More a Man Has the More a Man Wants," in *Why Brownlee Left* (1980), and "7 Middagh Street," in *Meeting the British* (1987), as well as in "Madoc," may be thought of as a reproach to the linearity of his native province's historicism. At the same time, Muldoon's commitment to such a critique enacts alternatives to traditional modes of telling, and therefore of comprehending what is told. Ultimately, the claim that the distinctiveness of Muldoon's sensibility is entirely indebted to the conditions under which it initially came to the fore is much too simplistic. Nevertheless, neither should these conditions be considered irrelevant to the ethos of containable transformation with which Muldoon's verse is suffused.

This ethos receives an impressively sustained, challenging, and invigorating airing in "Madoc." The poem's ostensible subject matter, its subtextual narrative, owes something to the original poem of the same name. This *Madoc* was written by the minor English Romantic poet, Robert Southey, and published in 1805. It too tells a tale of adventure in the New World. Its eponymous hero is an ancient Welsh warrior who journeys across the Atlantic, defeats the "Aztecas," and participates in numerous dangerous escapades, many of them bloody and all of them typical, and typically unacknowledged, representations of imperialist exploits. Muldoon, however, does not take the subject matter of Southey's *Madoc* as the focus of his poem. With a sly sleight-of-hand which is representative of Muldoon's usual relationship to his material, he concentrates instead on the set of circumstances to which the first *Madoc* may be considered a compensatory response.

Ten years before publishing his *Madoc*, Southey and his more illustrious poetic contemporary, Samuel Taylor Coleridge, concocted a scheme to travel the Atlantic and set up an ideal community there. The actual location of this utopia was to be north-central Pennsylvania, on the banks of the Susquehanna, and it was envisaged that it would be run along "pantisocratic" lines, an idealistic manifestation of communism. In the event, however, the project was never realized.

Muldoon takes this generalized background to Southey's *Madoc* and follows it through. In other words, he envisages the two Romantic idealists having set up their community, and views the achievement—again, typically—through the less than reliable eyes of one of their descendants, a certain South. In addition to ostensibly continuing an actual plot abandoned by the historical personages Southey and Coleridge, and to approaching this continuation from back to front through the problematic personage of South, Muldoon also adds a number of other filtering and mirroring devices.

These devices are of two basic kinds, conceptual and formal. From a formal standpoint, Muldoon's "Madoc" resists classification as an epic, or at least resists the epic as exemplified by Southey's *Madoc*. Instead of being a prolix, leaden continuum, Muldoon's poem is a sprightly sequence of episodes, aperçus, asides, anecdotes, riddles, and whimsicalities. Some of these are in prose. Some consist of a single line. Two rely almost exclusively on drawings, one of which is a map denoting the general whereabouts of two towns relevant to the pantisocratic site. One of these towns is named Athens, the other Ulster. Most of the pieces, however, are brief, elliptical lyrics in the familiar Muldoon vein, though tending to greater concentration and opacity than their predecessors. The poems are linked together by a network of historical, narratological, and literary repetitions too elaborate—or, like a net, too full of holes—to grasp fully on a single reading. Among these repetitions, however, is that of "de-dum," an economical reminder of the limits and inadequacies of language—or at least of vocabulary—and at the same time of the persistent rhythm of cerebration, that song without words.

Even more diverting is the poem's conceptual apparatus, particularly since it is not clear if Muldoon intends it in the spirit in which T.S. Eliot supplied the notes to *The Waste Land* (1922)—as much an intellectual joke as a source of enlightenment. All the poems in "Madoc" are untitled, but each comes surmounted with the name of a philosopher, in square brackets—though even here Muldoon is not consistent, providing now and then the name of a literary figure—that of Lord Byron, for one, of whose work Muldoon has edited a selection. Most of the major, and a good number of the minor, names in Western philosophy are represented, from Anaxagoras to Zeno and including such well-known late twentieth century intellectuals as Jacques Derrida, Michel Foucault, Han-Georg Gadamer, Paul Ricoeur, and Julia Kristeva. The last-named heads a poem which in its entirety goes "Signifump. Signifump. Signifump."

The point of quoting these lines is not merely to show Muldoon's "Madoc" at its most mysterious but to suggest something of its method. Any suggestion must be tentative, not only because of the poem's overall difficulty, but also out of respect for that difficulty. The imaginative freedom which Muldoon arrogates to himself in the name of "mystery" is a freedom to which his reader aspires, as does, perhaps, each individual item of which "Madoc" is constituted. Clearly, "[Kristeva]" is only notionally a poem. Its significance is hardly in what it says, but rather in the formal and aesthetic questions it asks. These include questions as to origin, inspiration, language, text. To operate at the literal level which readers of Muldoon overlook at their peril, this one-line inscription asks, What's the idea?

In a much more persistent and acute manner, this is the very question being asked by bracketing each of the pieces of "Madoc" with the name of a celebrated philosopher, or question-poser. There is no obvious, or perhaps necessary, correlation between poem and philosopher, thus bracketed. The invitation extended by the association is not to guess the answer to a question which is latent in the given textual alliance, but to wonder what the question might be—to wonder in various senses of the word, to align oneself with the open-endedness of mystery, rather than with the closure of system, which is what philosophers historically have tended to do. The game of philosophical name-association, which is one of the ones Muldoon encourages the reader to play, is both a self-contained dimension of "Madoc" and a model of its more problematic concerns. In the same way, any verbal construct is merely an analogue of a world which it cannot finally embrace or sublimate. The poem also gives hints of South's speculations on his origins, and on the possibility of naming his world as origin and heritage. And, as if that weren't enough, these speculations lead in turn to the initial fiction of Muldoon taking up where Southey and Coleridge's idea left off, an idea which has a certain sense of irrational quest about it.

There is a sense in which the extravagance of Muldoon's imaginative conceit and the transparent style and strict tempi of the pieces of "Madoc" make it seem a collaboration between Rube Goldberg and Ludwig Wittgenstein. And it is useless to deny that many first-time readers will experience some of the frustration of having to deal with a product of two such idiosyncratic conceptualists. One predictable source of frustration is the poem's seemingly exhaustively reflexive character. Yet, whatever frustrations lie in store, and however many critical exegeses appear to decode this dazzling performance, one of the most immediate and undeniable pleasures of "Madoc" which await the reader is a sense that the spirit of Ariel, the beneficent sprite from William Shakespeare's *The Tempest* (1611), presides over it. This is the spirit which reorders the world in order to renew a fresh sense of its possibilities, and who does so in full consciousness of the forces which repress the inspiration of renewal. The simple injunction which concludes one of the volume's introductory poems, "Tea," is perhaps the most sensible one to abide by in reading "Madoc." In "Tea," the poet finds himself with nothing in the house but "some left-over squid cooked in its own ink and this unfortunate cup of tea. Take it. Drink." By taking the poet at his word, the well-disposed reader will be refreshed.

George O'Brien

Sources for Further Study

Chicago Tribune. September 8, 1991, XIV, p. 8.
Library Journal. CXVI, April 1, 1991, p. 123.
Listener. CXXIV, November 1, 1990, p. 35.
London Review of Books. XII, December 20, 1990, p. 18.
Los Angeles Times. May 9, 1991, p. E12.
The New York Review of Books. XXXVIII, May 30, 1991, p. 37.
The New York Times Book Review. XCVI, July 28, 1991, p. 14.
The Observer. April 28, 1991, p. 58.
Publishers Weekly. CCXXXVIII, February 22, 1991, p. 206.
The Times Literary Supplement. October 12, 1990, p. 1105.

MALCOLM
The Life of a Man Who Changed Black America

Author: Bruce Perry
Publisher: Station Hill (Barrytown, New York). Illustrated. 542 pp. $24.95
Type of work: Historical biography
Time: 1925-1965
Locale: The United States

This critical study of Malcolm X revises earlier images of his life and public career, presenting a man whose childhood was burdened with hardship and violence and who was driven by the need for acceptance by the society he condemned as racist and self-destructive

> *Principal personages:*
> MALCOLM X, Black Muslim leader and cogent spokesman for black nationalism who was born Malcolm Little and adopted the Muslim name Al Hajj Malik Al-Shabazz
> BETTY SANDERS SHABAZZ, his wife
> EARL LITTLE, his father
> LOUISA LITTLE, his mother
> ELLA LITTLE, his oldest half-sister, with whom he lived in Boston and who was one of his major sources of strength
> MARTIN LUTHER KING, JR., the highly influential civil rights leader who epitomized the nonviolent approach to racial liberation

A twenty-year search by Bruce Perry for the historical Malcolm X has resulted in a more detailed and more intimate analysis of the famous black leader's life than *The Autobiography of Malcolm X* (1965) by *Roots* author Alex Haley. In key respects, Perry's book departs from and corrects the earlier work, which Haley wrote from Malcolm's own memories. From the quotidian details of Malcolm's life to the larger issues of his father's death and Malcolm's self-image, Perry provides a quite different picture. Yet, the two works complement each other by providing varying insights into the complex character of the man hailed by many as the quintessential spokesman for black nationalism and racial pride.

Malcolm X, Perry argues, was shaped by his troubled childhood and youth. The son of a self-ordained Garveyite Baptist preacher who abused his family, young Malcolm knew little of the security which a happy childhood requires. His father, Earl Little, failed to tell his second wife, Louisa, about an earlier marriage and three children he had left without notice or financial provision. The daughter of a Scottish father and a Grenadan mother, Louisa followed Earl Little from place to place and job to job in the early days of their marriage. Montreal, Philadelphia, Omaha, and Lansing, Michigan were temporary homes for the Littles as Earl drifted without any apparent plan. Malcolm was born in 1925 in Omaha, where Louisa gave birth also to Philbert and Hilda. Attracted to the ideas of black nationalist Marcus Garvey, Earl Little became involved with the Omaha branch of the Universal Negro Improvement Association (UNIA), which Garvey had founded in his native Jamaica in 1914 and transplanted in the United States by the end of World War I. This was the closest thing to a sense of belonging that Malcolm found during his childhood.

Resistance by the Ku Klux Klan in Omaha was, according to *The Autobiography of Malcolm X*, one of the factors that prompted Earl to take his family to Milwaukee shortly after Malcolm's birth. This was not true, Perry notes, although Earl did move his family from Omaha, and eventually to Lansing, Michigan. This migratory pattern was not the only problem that undermined young Malcolm Little's sense of security. There was also tension related to his light skin color. His mother, whose parentage bequeathed her a fair complexion, emphasized that she was West Indian, not African American, and at times vigorously scrubbed Malcolm's face and confessed to a white friend that if she bathed him enough she could "make him look almost white. . . ." Yet, she encouraged Malcolm to play in the sun to darken his skin lest he think he was superior because of his fair color. According to Perry, this ambivalence left a mark on the boy's psyche. Neither parent consistently approved of him. Malcolm believed that his mother saw her own light skin as evidence of her illegitimacy and his as a constant reminder of that.

Many other painful experiences dogged the steps of Malcolm. When he was only five years old his father died in Lansing. According to the autobiography prepared by Haley, Earl Little was killed by racists in the Black Legion, white men wearing black robes and hoods, who left him on a streetcar track to be crushed. Perry's research indicates that Earl's death was accidental, that he fell under the wheels of a streetcar. He suffered a partially severed leg and other injuries and died despite medical efforts to save him. Earl had frequently beaten his wife and otherwise abused her and the children, but his death became, somewhat ironically, further reason for Malcolm to be sensitized to problems of racial identity and the seeming hopelessness of his young life.

The young boy with such inauspicious beginnings experienced little relief. His mother Louisa suffered mental illness and was institutionalized when Malcolm was fourteen. Other disappointments, including failure in his effort to become a prize-fighter, caused him to withdraw into an isolated world of his own. Rebellion against authority symbols, argues Perry, caused further difficulties that eventually drew him into a life of street crime and even prostitution.

His dreams of becoming a boxer, then an attorney, or a writer, all eluded him. In foster homes and often on the streets, he had little sense of direction, but he retained a strong desire to be somebody important. By the end of World War II, he had been involved in break-ins and other crimes, including homosexual prostitution. In Boston in 1946, where he lived with his half-sister Ella, he was arrested during a break-in attempt. By his own admission, which Perry takes seriously, Malcolm wanted to be stopped and courted arrest.

Malcolm was sentenced to a ten-year prison term but was paroled in 1952, two years before the landmark *Brown v. Board of Education* case that triggered the Civil Rights movement. During the postwar period when black leaders were beginning to articulate their demands for reform, Malcolm was educating himself in prison. There he came into contact with the Lost-Found Nation of Islam movement led by Elijah

Muhammad. In it Malcolm found a means to express himself, to identify with a cause that would allow him to be persuasive and influential. The Nation of Islam (NOI) condemned white people, emphasized black separatism, and, in a sense, did provide a forum for young Malcolm X. Ironically, however, it was not truly engaged in social reform and kept Malcolm isolated from the early stages of the Civil Rights movement. Eventually Malcolm found it restrictive. He had conflicting feelings about the Black Muslims as he did about other entities in his life: "A similar ambivalence pervaded his feelings about the Nation of Islam, whose refusal to engage in political activity during the zenith of the civil rights struggle was apparently very difficult for him to bear." Malcolm played an "errand boy" role for Elijah Muhammad and referred to himself as Elijah's "slave."

It was not a simple matter, however, to leave the Nation of Islam. The catalyst in bringing about his break with Elijah Muhammad's organization was a remark Malcolm made about the assassination of President John F. Kennedy in late 1963. "Chickens coming home to roost never did make me sad," he said; "they've always made me glad." Angered by the damage he believed had been done to the Nation of Islam by Malcolm's remark, Elijah Muhammad officially silenced him, closing to him the rostrums of Temple Seven in New York and other facilities of the NOI. Although humiliated, Malcolm controlled his feelings as well as he could, but it was obvious to Alex Haley during his interviews for the autobiography as well as to many others, that irreparable damage had been done to the relationship. Soon, boxer Muhammad Ali (Cassius Clay) of Louisville, Kentucky, replaced Malcolm in NOI circles as the public symbol of black masculinity. The Black Muslims had given Malcolm a forum and a public image of the articulate, manly African American. Called a sissy in his younger days, but always aspiring to be a cogent, influential man, he had devoted himself to Elijah Muhammad's organization. He had become Malcolm X under its aegis, dropping his "slave name," Malcolm Little. As early as 1952, upon his release from prison, he had begun to speak out forcefully against the ubiquitous racism he saw in white culture. He edited a paper called *Muhammad Speaks*; by 1954, he had gone to Harlem to lead the mosque there. Popular, dynamic, albeit troubled by strong internal conflicts, Malcolm X became the Nation of Islam's most influential preacher. But with the 1963 rift, he was forced to try it on his own.

The split affected Malcolm X deeply. Suffering from severe headaches and a sense of emotional trauma, he feared that he had a brain tumor. His physician, Dr. Leona A. Turner, assured him that he did not and that he did not need Elijah Muhammad. He could be successful in his own right. Further encouragement came from his wife, Betty. Malcolm had met Betty Sanders within NOI circles. She typed for him on occasion and was impressed by his air of authority. Despite his ambivalence toward marriage, Malcolm was strongly attracted to the tall, dark-skinned nursing student. She had college training and a strength that Malcolm admired. Their marriage in 1958 endured despite his domineering role. He did not beat Betty as his father had done to his own mother, but he did impose restrictions, and she played the role of the nontraveling Muslim wife. Malcolm apparently loved her, though he was less than unequivocal on that; Perry links his coolness toward her to the "male chauvinism [that was] the predictable result of past tyranny."

In this, as in virtually all respects, Perry's account is psychohistorical. His extensive coverage of Malcolm's wandering, painful childhood and crime-laden young adulthood are pivotal to his approach. Half of his study analyzes the last two years of Malcolm's life, from his break with the Nation of Islam to his assassination in New York in February 1965. During that period Malcolm founded his separate Muslim Mosque, Inc. and had a meteoric career as a tough-talking militant who, according to Perry, was masking his continuing insecurity: He attacked the establishment within which he actually wanted to excel. Malcolm X spoke of "revolution by any means necessary" during the period when Martin Luther King, Jr., was articulating a nonviolent philosophy in which Malcolm had little faith. Despite a new name, Al Hajj Malik Al-Shabazz, he was known among friends and in the press as Malcolm X.

The strengths of Perry's book include its extensive probing of Malcolm's childhood, the rather full account of Malcolm's rise to prominence within the Black Muslim movement, and the focus on the inner conflicts and dreams of an important figure in recent American history. That Perry is unflaggingly committed to revealing the real man is apparent. But there are problems with both the methodology and the outcome of this biography. Lacking adequate written sources, of which there are comparatively few, Perry relied on Malcolm's prison records and hundreds of interviews with family members, friends, associates, and people who have studied Malcolm's career. There is a strongly subjective quality to such sources, and while Perry has used them critically and analytically, the reader is left wondering whether the real Malcolm X has yet been discovered.

The pervasive emphasis is upon the inner man, burdened by his past and unable fully to be what he professed. Malcolm X appears in Perry's account as an articulate, even charming and charismatic figure who is gifted in speech and intellect. His subtitle suggests that Malcolm was a major figure in changing black Americans. But he also influenced people of other races and American society's self-perception. That dimension is not treated adequately by Perry to bring a complete picture of Malcolm X's historical role. The author's corrections of details of earlier work, to the extent that he has firmly accomplished that, are valuable, but also lack sufficient documentation to obviate the need for further study. One thing is clear. Perry confirms Malcolm's difficulty in accepting nonviolent social change as the compelling method of the Civil Rights movement. Malcolm admired Dr. Martin Luther King, Jr., and indeed visited the famous Southern Christian Leadership Conference leader in Selma, Alabama only days before Malcolm was gunned down by disillusioned extremists. Perry denies FBI complicity in Malcolm's assassination. The coverage of Malcolm's final days is rich and interesting. One senses in it the drama of his untimely death.

Perry acknowledges Malcolm's importance. Although he had brought about no major legal victories for the Civil Rights movement and won no public office, he did change America: "because of the way he articulated his followers' grievances and anger, the impact he had upon the body politic was enormous. He mobilized black America's dormant rage and put it to work politically." With that Perry encapsulates the central implication of his study and perhaps hints at the need to look beyond the psychohistorical method to complete the task of revealing the real Malcolm X.

Thomas R. Peake

Sources for Further Study

Booklist. LXXXVII, June 15, 1991, p. 1912.
Chicago Defender. November 12, 1991, p. 15.
Detroit News and Free Press. September 15, 1991, p. G8.
Ebony. XLVI, October, 1991, p. 18.
Kirkus Reviews. LIX, May 15, 1991, p. 656.
Library Journal. CXVI, June 15, 1991, p. 86.
Los Angeles Times Book Review. September 8, 1991, p. 3.
The New York Times Book Review. XCVI, November 24, 1991, p. 11.
Publishers Weekly. CCXXXVIII, May 24, 1991, p. 41.
The Washington Post Book World. XXI, August 4, 1991, p. 4.

MAO II

Author: Don DeLillo (1936-   )
Publisher: Viking (New York). 241 pp. $19.95
Type of work: Novel
Time: 1989
Locale: An unidentified rural area in the Northeast United States, New York City, London, Athens, and Beirut

Writing, terrorism, power, media images, and "unexpended faith" are compellingly and compulsively combined to form one of DeLillo's most grimly humorous and deeply disturbing works

> *Principal characters:*
> BILL GRAY, a reclusive novelist
> SCOTT MARTINEAU, his devoted assistant
> KAREN JANNEY, a Moonie bride who comes to live with Scott
> BRITA NILSON, a photographer
> ABU RASHID, the leader of a Maoist terrorist group
> CHARLES EVERSON, Bill Gray's editor
> JEAN-CLAUDE JULIEN, a hostage

Don DeLillo is American fiction's master of menace, inscriber of ominous surfaces in which the only direction to go is "deeper into the mystery." It is, however, a mystery that is postmodern to its hollow core, a mystery undercut by DeLillo's distinctive brand of edgy humor, as in *Ratner's Star* (1976) and especially *White Noise* (1985), his breakthrough book. Even *Libra* (1988) is funny—oddly, inappropriately so given its ostensible subject, the Kennedy assassination. If at times DeLillo runs the risk of being too ponderous and portentous for his own good, the risk is worth it, for no one writing today—no American writer in particular—comes as close as he does to exposing the nature of the postindustrial, postmodern malaise, or mania, from disaster to celebrity to conspiracy theories and now, the appeal as well as the terror of terrorism to that strange new beast, Media Man.

Mao II, DeLillo's tenth novel, begins with a pretext: the mass wedding of sixty-five hundred couples at Yankee Stadium, presided over by the Reverend Sun Myung Moon. As Rodge, father of one of the brides, Karen, explains, this "is what happens to all the unexpended faith" after God has exited the world. "This" is also what Rodge had thought his middle-classness would protect him from: "He's got a degree and a business and a tax attorney and a cardiologist and a mutual fund and whole life and major medical. But do the assurances always apply?" Searching in vain for his daughter in the "undifferentiated mass," Rodge begins to understand that the assurances do not apply. Neither do the narrative assurances, as *Mao II* jump-cuts from one pretext to another. After thirty years, a famous but reclusive novelist, Bill Gray, is about to have his photograph taken. Like so much in this novel, the two pretexts are strangely connected. Bill's reclusiveness is linked—and not just comically—to "God's famous reluctance to appear," and his deciding to make an appearance (even a photographic one) is tied to his "loss of faith" in the novel he has been writing and revising over the past twenty-three years. Like the ordinary but nonetheless messianic Reverend Moon, Bill has become a cult figure who attracts some more of that "unexpended faith." Bill's biggest fan (as in fanatic) is Scott Martineau, whose dedication borders on the pathological: a loner in the Lee Harvey Oswald tradition who goes not to Russia but, after considering Tibet, to Bill. "He had a life now and that's what mattered." Devotion here is mixed with dependency and tinged with a strong dose of Nietzschean *ressentiment*; protecting Bill from the outside world becomes Scott's full-time obsession—an act of proprietorship, with Bill serving as Scott's work-in-progress. Scott is more than merely obsessive-possessive; he is self-reflexive in a terrifyingly (yet again comically) childlike, credulous way: "Bill needs Scott," Scott says to himself.

Two women also appear at Bill's, one briefly, the other not so much permanently as less temporarily. Brita Nilson has her own work-in-progress—a collection of writer's photographs (chiefly reclusive writers, such as Bill), a "basic reference work," she explains, "just for storing" (in much the same way Scott compulsively catalogs and stores all of Bill's papers). Karen is the Moonie bride whom Scott, on one of his infrequent trips away from the house, inadvertently rescued from her deprogrammers. "All spin and drift," she gravitates to whatever center of force is nearest—Scott, Bill, Brita, Moon—avatars all of the "total vision" she desires (though desire may be too strong a word to use in Karen's case). Awash in the "waves and radiation" of her times, she watches television, or watches rather the pure image itself stripped not just of sound but, more important, of all historical context. Not surprisingly, Karen desires to become an image: Who would have thought, she thinks to herself during the mass wedding, that she would be in Yankee Stadium surrounded by thousands of people taking her picture. From devotion such as hers delusions necessarily spring.

Mao II is in large part a novelist's meditation on the relation between makers of images and consumers of images, between writers and readers, artists and audience, and as such evokes the very context of which Karen remains ignorant: J. D. Salinger, Thomas Pynchon (whose blurb appears on the book's dust jacket), and the slightly less reclusive DeLillo himself. Readers of *Libra* will also see in Bill Gray some resemblance to Nicholas Branch, who sits in his study, surrounded by Central Intelligence Agency (CIA)-supplied material on the Kennedy assassination about which he is to write the official report that no one outside the CIA, and perhaps no one inside the CIA either, will ever read. Bill's relation to his book proves no less strange than his relation to his readers (one sent him a severed finger; Scott sent himself; Karen offers her body; and even Brita believes she "knows" Bill because she has read his books; he is the word made flesh, possessor of some special power). Bill on the other hand claims that he writes not to exert power but to find his way back to the innocence of childhood (a dangerous place, if the novel's two most childlike characters—Scott and Karen—are any indication); or failing that to use his writing to discover himself, or failing that just to survive: his situation for the past two years spent revising and perhaps for the entire twenty-three he has spent writing the novel that now seems "all forced and wrong," the book that has become "his hated adversary."

Bill sees an escape route when his former editor, Charles Everson, involves him in helping to free a hostage, a young Swiss United Nations worker who is at least nominally a writer (fifteen published poems to his name). In DeLillo nothing is ever simple and straightforward. Helping free this hostage will also publicize the terrorist group (Maoist rather than fundamentalist) that is holding him: "The hostage is the only proof they exist." It will also publicize the existence of the new human rights group to which Everson belongs and which he may be using as a front for securing the book Bill hates, Scott says should not be published, and Everson, as editor, needs to consolidate his own waning powers in the world of corporate publishing. (Everson incidentally sends his message about wanting to see Bill through Brita, who thus becomes implicated, in the reader's mind at least, in a larger, perhaps paranoid plot worthy of Pynchon—or the CIA.) And then there is Bill, who wants not only to put the book and the past twenty-three years behind him but also to become the kind of politically engaged writer he longs to be (echoes of Jean-Paul Sartre, Albert Camus, Andre Malraux, and, strangely, Aleksandr Solzhenitsyn, who managed to be both engaged and, in his fortress-like retreat in the United States, reclusive). Moreover, becoming involved with a hostage's release will provide Bill with fresh material—or perhaps not so fresh, given the parallels between Bill's situation and the hostage's. Although it is claimed that Bill is not an autobiographical writer, it is clear that he uses his writing not only as a mode of thinking about large issues but also as a means for understanding himself. It proves a rather ambiguous self, for as Scott learns while rummaging through Bill's personal effects like some celebrity's unauthorized biographer, Bill Gray was born Willard Skansey, Jr. It is a secret Scott promises never to divulge (promises himself, of course), and it is a secret which links Bill Gray to F. Scott Fitzgerald's Great Gatsby: self-made men in more than one sense. Writing about the hostage becomes Bill's way of writing about himself. "He wanted to know what it was like to know the extremes of isolation." The reader, however, will never know whether the passages dealing with the hostage's experiences "represent" the hostage's views or are mediated by Bill (and thus form pages in Bill's newest work-in-progress). Reading *Mao II* entails dropping through levels of fiction-making, texts within texts, yet DeLillo's novel is the very opposite of claustrophobically self-referential. Writing about the writer Bill Gray is DeLillo's way of writing about contemporary culture.

Especially intriguing is the connection DeLillo makes based on, or at least anticipated by, the title of Diane Johnson's 1982 collection of reviews, *Terrorists and Novelists*. According to Bill, the two are involved in a zero-sum game. The situation is similar to the one Philip Roth described in 1960: "the American writer in the middle of the twentieth century has his hands full in trying to understand, describe, and then make credible much of American reality. It stupefies, it sickens, it infuriates, and finally it is even a kind of embarrassment to one's meager imagination." The situation Bill describes is worse still: The novelist has been supplanted by the terror-

ist. Bill longs for the power to shape readers' lives—the way they think and see—
that after Samuel Beckett Bill believes only terrorists now seem to possess. As novelist, Bill wants his work to serve as Mao's "Little Red Book" did: as a force binding a people together, less a text written on paper than history itself inscribed on the
masses. Bill also fears becoming what Mao became and what Scott wants him to be,
a myth rather than a man: remote, inaccessible, the source of awe and tabloid speculation. Yet Scott is right in one respect, that the rumors that have circulated about
Bill since he went into seclusion thirty years before are linked to "the world's oldest
stories" and are in fact "not about Bill so much as people's need to make mysteries
and legends." Paradoxically, in trying to free himself from the cult of the author by
going into hiding, Bill only fuels the fire, turning himself into a pure, disembodied
sign open to what Umberto Eco calls "endless semiosis."

For all its brevity, *Mao II* proves a surprisingly "excessive" work, proliferating its
own interpretive possibilities and ending not once but three times. In the first, Bill
wends his way toward Beirut, is hit by a passing car in Athens (accident or assassination?), and takes a ferry to Lebanon, where upon arrival his body is found by
one of the cleaning crew. "He said a prayer and went through the man's belongings,
leaving the insignificant cash, the good shoes, the things in the bag, the bag itself,
but feeling it not a crime against the dead to take the man's passport and other forms
of identification, anything with a name and a number, which he could sell to some
militia in Beirut." Thus the end, or non-end, of "Bill Gray." In the second ending,
Karen returns to Bill's hideaway where she and Scott will live happily ever (?) after,
awaiting Bill's return, his second coming, while refueling the mass cult's millennial
speculations about Bill. Ending number three does not so much conclude the novel
as close its narrative frame, turning the novel back on itself, a narrative Ouroboros, a
postmodern *Finnegans Wake*. Brita, who had earlier compared being driven to Bill's
hideaway to "see[ing] some terrorist chief at his secret retreat in the mountains,"
now travels to Beirut to photograph Abu Rashid, leader of the terrorist group that
had been holding the Swiss hostage whom they had hoped to trade (up) for the
better-known Bill Gray. As part of her routine for a "shoot" Brita likes to talk with
her subjects—a fairly easy matter with Bill, once Scott is gotten out of the way, but
much more problematic with Abu Rashid, as the two must speak through a translator
whose words do not literally represent Abu Rashid's; the translations seem more like
editorializings: deleting here, adding there, altering everywhere—a point lost on all
present but the reader, and perhaps the translator. The chief is not entirely in charge
despite the fact that his hooded followers wear T-shirts emblazoned with his like-
ness; they maintain silence to signify (the translator says) that, as his "children,"
they have all adopted his identity.

As a Maoist, Abu Rashid is the Mao II of *Mao II*: a cloned image in the ideological serigraph called history. Like Andy Warhol's famous soup cans, Marilyn Mon-
roes, and Chairman Maos, DeLillo's extraordinary novel extends Walter Benjamin's
well-known analysis of "The Work of Art in the Age of Mechanical Reproduction"
to include history, or rather, those images which pass for history in the popular

culture and, more specifically, those images witnessed by Karen during her sound-less television trances: people being crushed to death at a soccer match, Khomeini's funeral, Tiananmen Square (where Karen sees the army's routing of the students in generic terms: "One crowd replaced another"). The progression of televised images becomes the ultimate serigraph, out-Warholing Warhol. Reading *Mao II*, one thinks of the quaintness of Shakespeare's "All the world's a stage" and thinks too of Karl Marx's comment at the beginning of *The Eighteenth Brumaire of Louis Bonaparte*: "Hegel remarks somewhere that all facts and personages of great importance in world history occur, as it were, twice. He forgot to add, the first time as tragedy, the second as farce." In *Mao II*, the farce is not at all broad but instead almost Beckett-like in its grim attenuation. The novel as a whole and each of its four sections are preceded by a "historical" photograph: Tiananmen Square, the Moonie mass mar-riage, a huge portrait of Khomeini with a horde of seemingly tiny Iranians massed under his chin, children in bombed-out Beirut. *Mao II* is not "about" these scenes; it is rather about a world in which the serious novel has become marginalized and/or commodified; where images have replaced ideas, where "access" has replaced aware-ness, and where, most disturbingly, "the future belongs to crowds."

Robert A. Morace

Sources for Further Study

American Book Review. XIII, October-November, 1991, p. 18.
Booklist. LXXXVII, February 15, 1991, p. 1162.
Chicago Tribune. June 23, 1991, XIV, p. 1.
Commonweal. CXVIII, August 9, 1991, p. 490.
The Economist. CCCXIX, June 15, 1991, p. 86.
Kirkus Reviews. LIX, March 1, 1991, p. 266.
Library Journal. CXVI, April 15, 1991, p. 124.
London Review of Books. XIII, September 12, 1991, p. 13.
Los Angeles Times Book Review. June 9, 1991, p. 3.
Maclean's. August 12, 1991, p. 43.
New York Magazine. XXIV, June 17, 1991, p. 84.
The New York Review of Books. XXXVIII, June 27, 1991, p. 17.
The New York Times. CXL, May 28, 1991, p. C15.
The New York Times Book Review. XCVI, June 9, 1991, p. 7.
The New Yorker. LXVII, June 24, 1991, p. 81.
The Observer. September 1, 1991, p. 54.
Publishers Weekly. CCXXXVIII, April 12, 1991, p. 44.
Quill & Quire. LVII, July, 1991, p. 50.
The Spectator. CCLXVII, September 7, 1991, p. 34.

The Times Literary Supplement. August 30, 1991, p. 20.
The Village Voice. XXXVI, June 18, 1991, p. 65.
The Wall Street Journal. June 13, 1991, p. A14.
The Washington Post Book World. XXI, May 26, 1991, p. 1.